THE OXFORD ENCYCLOPAEDIA OF

EUROPEAN COMMUNITY LAW

VOLUME I

INSTITUTIONAL LAW

A. G. TOTH
Dr.Jur., Ph.D.

Professor of Law in the University of Strathclyde

CLARENDON PRESS · OXFORD

1990

Oxford University Press, Walton Street, Oxford OX2 6DP
Oxford New York Toronto
Delhi Bombay Calcutta Madras Karachi
Petaling Jaya Singapore Hong Kong Tokyo
Nairobi Dar es Salaam Cape Town
Melbourne Auckland
and associated companies in
Berlin Ibadan

Oxford is a trade mark of Oxford University Press

Published in the United States
by Oxford University Press, New York

British Library Cataloguing in Publication Data
Toth, Akos G.
The Oxford Encyclopaedia of European Community law.
Vol. 1, Institutional law
1. European Economic Community, Law
I. Title
341.24'22
ISBN 0–19–825589–6

Library of Congress Cataloging in Publication Data
Toth, A. G.
The Oxford Encyclopaedia of European Community law / A.G. Toth.
Contents: v. 1. Institutional law.
1. Law—European Economic Community countries—Dictionaries—
English. I. Title.
KHE926.T67   1990   349.4'03—dc20   [344.003]   89–23024
ISBN 0–19–825589–6

Typeset by Hope Services (Abingdon) Ltd
Printed in Great Britain by
the Alden Press, Oxford.

PREFACE

The creation of the European Communities and their new legal system has produced a host of legal terms and concepts which either have no equivalent in national law or have acquired an entirely new and independent meaning in the context of a supranational Community law. It is a fundamental principle of this law that its terms and concepts must be interpreted uniformly in all the Member States, in the light of its own peculiar features and objectives. This is a necessary prerequisite for ensuring the unity and coherence of Community law in the face of its simultaneous application in twelve (or thirteen) different national jurisdictions.

The above considerations underline the need for a set of clear and concise definitions and explanations which may be consulted by those who are called upon in their day-to-day activities to interpret or apply Community law, whether they be Community institutions or Government agencies, tribunals or private organizations, practising or academic lawyers, researchers or students, and whether or not they are specialists in this branch of the law.

This book has been written with the aim of meeting that need. My primary intention has been to present the whole body of European Community Law in the form of a work which contains legal definitions of its terms and concepts as they are used in the Treaties and acts of the institutions and, above all, as they have been interpreted in the extensive case-law of the European Court of Justice. I have felt, however, that a simple dictionary-type presentation would not do justice to the richness and complexity of the subject and that it would probably be of only limited practical usefulness. The entries have therefore been drafted in such a way that a short and concise definition is normally followed by a longer and more detailed explanation, analysis, or description, putting the term or concept in the wider context of Community law as a whole. This has resulted in a work which is, in essence, an Encyclopaedia as well as a Dictionary of Community law.

It is hoped that such a book might usefully fill a gap in the existing literature on Community law. While there are many excellent legal dictionaries and encyclopaedias in use, covering various national legal systems as well as International and Comparative Law, so far as I am aware it has never been attempted in any language to produce an encyclopaedia in the field of European Community Law of a kind similar to the present work. Yet, during the course of writing I have become more and more convinced that an encyclopaedic form of presentation is eminently suited to the nature of Community law which, dealing with a wide range of diverse and only loosely connected topics, does not easily lend itself to systematic treatment within the framework of a traditional treatise or textbook.

The book is divided into three volumes. Volume I covers *Institutional Law*; Volumes II and III, to be published later, will cover *Substantive Law* and *Community Policies*, respectively. The term 'Institutional Law' is used here in the broadest possible sense: it includes the constitutional, administrative, and external relations law of the Communities, the law of remedies and of procedure, and the sources and general principles of Community law. Each Volume is designed to form a complete, self-contained unit. Therefore, the first volume, covering a distinct area of Community law, may be used on its own pending the publication of the second and the third. The relatively few cross-references to entries to be included in Volumes II and III are indicated with an asterisk for the convenience of the reader.

Within each volume, the entries are arranged in alphabetical order. All terms and concepts of some importance occurring in the book but not given a separate entry are included (and cross-referenced as appropriate) in the List of Entries, which thus also serves as an Index. All relevant sources and authorities are fully cited with the main emphasis being placed upon definitions and interpretations given by the European Court of Justice. In line with other legal dictionaries and encyclopaedias, case and other references have been incorporated in the main text in order not to distract the reader's attention by constantly referring him to the foot of the page. This also makes the case-law relevant to a particular entry more easily ascertainable. Preliminary rulings are cited by the name of one party, direct actions by the names of both parties. Beside saving space, this method of citation at once indicates the nature of the proceedings involved. Cases are normally cited by their short titles as printed in the European Court Reports. Cases not yet reported in the ECR at the time of proof-reading are cited in the text by volume and paragraph only (e.g. [1988] ECR para. 12); the page numbers at which these cases will appear in the ECR, where available, or the date of the judgment, may be found in the Table of Cases. Where a definition appears in, or a proposition is supported by, a long line of cases, usually only the earliest and the most recent of those cases are cited. In the case of several similar (or identical) judgments, normally only that printed first in the ECR is cited.

In addition to the Court's decisions, frequent references are made to the opinions of the Advocates-General, mainly in the following three situations. First, where they raise a point of law which is not, or only briefly, dealt with by the Court. Secondly, where they contain an extensive analysis or a detailed historical or comparative survey of a rule or principle. Thirdly, where they present a view or a solution different from that adopted by the Court.

The entries are concluded by extensive cross-references (which sometimes also occur within the text to indicate that a particular point is further discussed elsewhere) and, where appropriate, by a list of further reading. Since these lists are also cross-referenced, as a general rule a book or article is only cited once, under the entry to which it is most closely relevant, unless it deals with two or more subject-areas in more or less equal proportion. In that case, it appears under both (all) entries. As there is no separate Bibliography as such, the more general works covering wide subject-areas such as Community law, the European Communities, the Institutions or the European Court of Justice, are included in the list of further reading after the entry to which they relate.

The book is intended to serve two different purposes. First, it is envisaged that as a work of reference it can be used on its own for obtaining instant information on a point of Community law. Secondly, since it contains full references to the sources, authorities and academic writings, it is hoped that it may serve as a basic research tool into any area of Community law.

The manuscript was completed in March 1989, and the law is generally stated as I understood it at that time. Nevertheless, it has subsequently been possible to incorporate the most important developments that have taken place during the course of 1989 and the first half of 1990.

In conclusion, I wish to express my grateful thanks to Sir Gordon Slynn, Judge of the European Court of Justice, to Lord Mackenzie Stuart, a former President of the Court, and to the Court itself, for a generous grant which made it possible for me to visit the Court in Luxembourg during the final stages of the preparation of the manuscript. Using the Court's facilities enabled me to fill the many gaps in the text and to catch up with the latest developments in the case-law. In this context, I would also like to thank the staff of the Court's Information Office, Library, Registry, and Translation Service for the readiness with which they fulfilled my every request. I feel that I should particularly thank Mr Paul Farmer, at the time acting as Information Officer, for his efficient and friendly assistance during the whole time of my visit. I am also grateful to the Society of Public Teachers of Law for a grant with which they assisted me in the preparation of the book. I am particularly grateful to Professor Henry G. Schermers and to Professor John W. Bridge for their valuable comments on early drafts of selected entries and for the encouragement which they gave me in connection with the project. For any errors and omissions the responsibility is mine alone. My thanks are also due to the successive secretaries, too many to mention individually, who typed the manuscript over the years, and to the staff of Oxford University Press for the care and efficiency with which they have produced the book.

As before, my greatest debt is to my wife without whose unfailing support and encouragement this book could never have been written.

Glasgow
August 1990   A. G. TOTH

CONTENTS

LIST OF ENTRIES

x

ABBREVIATIONS

AA	Act of Accession
ACP	African, Caribbean, and Pacific (States)
A.-G.	Advocate-General
AJCL	*American Journal of Comparative Law*
AJIL	*American Journal of International Law*
Art.	Article
Bull. EC	*Bulletin of the European Communities*
BYIL	*British Yearbook of International Law*
CA	Court of Auditors
CARP	Court of Auditors' Rules of Procedure
CE	Compulsory expenditure
CFI	Court of First Instance
CMLR	*Common Market Law Reports*
CML Rev.	*Common Market Law Review*
Comm.	Commission
Comp. Rep. EC	Report on Competition Policy
COREPER	Committee of Permanent Representatives
CRP	Council's Rules of Procedure
Dec.	Decision
Dir.	Directive
Doc.	Document
EAEC	European Atomic Energy Community
EC	European Communities
ECJ	European Court of Justice
ECR	*European Court Reports*
ECSC	European Coal and Steel Community; Treaty establishing the ECSC
ECSC Statute	Statute of the Court of Justice of the ECSC
ECU	European Currency Unit
EEC	European Economic Community; Treaty establishing the EEC
EEC Statute	Statute of the Court of Justice of the EEC
EIB	European Investment Bank
EIB Statute	Statute of the EIB
EL Rev.	*European Law Review*
EMS	European Monetary System
EP	European Parliament
EPC	European Political Co-operation
EPRP	European Parliament's Rules of Procedure
ESC	Economic and Social Committee
Euratom	European Atomic Energy Community; Treaty establishing the Euratom
Euratom Statute	Statute of the Court of Justice of the Euratom
FIDE	Fédération Internationale pour le droit Européen

TABLE OF CASES

European Court of Justice

Preliminary rulings are cited by the name of one party, direct actions by the names of both parties.

Alphabetical

Numerical

TABLE OF COMMUNITY TREATIES

TABLE OF COMMUNITY ACTS

TABLE OF
COMMUNITY
ACTS

TABLE OF INTERNATIONAL
AGREEMENTS

TABLE OF UNITED KINGDOM STATUTES

▶ **ABANDONMENT OF CLAIMS** Termination of proceedings, other than annulment, default, and reference proceedings, pending before the ECJ by the parties mutually renouncing their claims against each other before the Court has given its decision. A simple notification thereof to the Court will result in the removal of the case from the register (Art. 77 RP; see also Case 62/72 *Bollmann* [1973] ECR 269 at p. 279 *per* A.-G. Roemer).

See also Discontinuance of proceedings, Settlement.

▶ **ABSOLUTE BAR TO PROCEEDINGS** Incurable defect in an application or in a reference for a preliminary ruling of such a fundamental nature as mandatorily to prevent the ECJ from proceeding with the case, for example where the Court manifestly has no jurisdiction or where the case constitutes a *lis pendens*. The ECJ may at any time of its own motion consider whether there exists such a bar and, if so, may declare the application or reference inadmissible (Art. 92(2) RP; Cases 31 and 33/62 *Wöhrmann* v. *Commission* [1962] ECR 501 at p. 512; Case 68/80 *Hayange* [1980] ECR 771; Case 138/80 *Borker* [1980] ECR 1975 at p. 1977. See also Art. 92(1) RP and Case 46/81 *Benvenuto* [1981] ECR 809 at pp. 810–11).

See also Absolute inadmissibility, Admissibility of action, Jurisdiction, *Lis pendens.*

▶ **ABSOLUTE INADMISSIBILITY** Automatic, independent, and mandatory bar to proceedings of such a nature as to prevent any examination of an application, even from a purely formal point of view. This concept, which is known in some national legal systems (see, for example, the concept of *improponibilita* in Italian law), is not recognized in Community law, where any question as to the admissibility or inadmissibility of an application or reference must be examined and decided upon by the ECJ in accordance with the relevant formal and procedural requirements, even where there is an absolute bar to proceeding with the case (Case 3/54 *ASSIDER* v. *HA* [1955] ECR 63 at pp. 73–4 *per* A.-G. Lagrange).

See also Absolute bar to proceedings, Admissibility of action.

▶ **ABSOLUTE NULLITY** Automatic and complete invalidity (as opposed to mere voidability) of an act, entailing its legal non-existence *ab initio* even without its being declared null and void by a competent court. Such an act cannot produce any legal effects. Owing to the operation of a presumption of validity and for reasons of legal certainty, Community law does not as a rule recognize the concept of absolute nullity. Thus the substantive illegality of an act, however serious it may be, does not as a rule render the act void but voidable, i.e. liable to annulment by the ECJ subject to the conditions of an action for annulment (Cases 7/56 etc. *Algera* v. *Common Assembly* [1957] ECR 39 at pp. 60–1; Cases 15 to 33/73 etc. *Schots-Kortner* v. *Council, Commission and Parliament* [1974] ECR 177 at p. 191 *per Curiam*, p. 197

per A.-G. Trabucchi; see also Cases 60 and 190/81R *IBM* v. *Commission*
[1981] ECR 1857 at p. 1863). Generally, similar considerations apply to formal
defects also. Nevertheless, absolute nullity is conceivable, within strictly
defined limits, in really extreme cases involving particularly serious and
manifest defects of competence (e.g. an obvious lack of power or its usurpation
by the institutions), of procedure (e.g. lack of deliberation), or of form (e.g.
lack of signature or publication) (Cases 19/60 etc. *Fives Lille Cail* v. *HA*
[1961] ECR 281 at p. 307 *per* A.-G. Roemer; Cases 15 to 33/73 etc. *Schots-
Kortner* v. *Council, Commission and Parliament*, above, *per* A.-G. Trabucchi;
Case 15/85 *Consorzio Cooperative d'Abruzzo* v. *Commission* [1987] ECR
1005 at p. 1036). Thus a measure taken by the institutions in a field which
falls within the exclusive competence of the Member States would lack all
legal basis in Community law and could probably be regarded as an absolute
nullity (Cases 6 and 11/69 *Commission* v. *France* [1969] ECR 523 at p. 539
per Curiam, p. 550 *per* A.-G. Roemer). However, the only case so far in
which the ECJ has actually considered an act to be non-existent in law (for
lack of a statement of reasons) seems to represent an extreme view of the
importance of reasoning as a formal requirement, and has not been followed
in subsequent case-law (Cases 1 and 14/57 *Usines à Tubes de la Sarre* v. *HA*
[1957] ECR 105 at pp. 112–13).

See also **Presumption of validity.**

▶ **ACCELERATION DECISIONS** 1. Decisions of the Representatives of the
Governments of the Member States meeting in Council of 12 May 1960 (*JO*
1960, p. 1217) and of 15 May 1962 (*JO* 1962, p. 1284) providing for
additional reductions in customs duties over and above those required by Art.
14 EEC, with effect from 1 January 1961 and 1 July 1962, respectively,
thereby accelerating the pace of the establishment of the Customs Union. As a
result, the achievement of the Customs Union was in 1965, two years ahead
of the timetable laid down in Art. 14 EEC.

2. Council Decision 66/532 of 26 July 1966 (*JO* 1966, p. 2971) providing
for the complete abolition of customs duties and quantitative restrictions as
between the Member States, and for the application of the Common Customs
Tariff to trade with third countries in respect of industrial products, as from 1
July 1968, i.e. eighteen months earlier than required by the Treaty. This
Decision is based on the concept of a selective acceleration of actions which as
a whole were to be completed by the end of the transitional period at the
latest, i.e. 31 December 1969, and it applies only to measures to which
it specifically refers. Consequently, it does not apply to charges having
equivalent effect to customs duties or to measures having equivalent effect to
quantitative restrictions (Case 94/74 *IGAV* [1975] ECR 699 at p. 711); nor
did it bring forward the date of expiry of the transitional period within the
meaning of Art. 8 EEC (Case 27/78 *Rasham* [1978] ECR 1761 at p. 1767).
Taken under Art. 235 EEC, the Decision is not in the nature of an international
agreement between the Member States (as perhaps the 1960 and 1962
Decisions might be described), but it is a genuine Community measure.

Intended to have repercussions on the Common Market as a whole, it is capable of producing direct effects within the Member States in conjunction with Arts. 9 and 13(2) EEC and any measures taken in their implementation (Case 38/69 *Commission* v. *Italy* [1970] ECR 47 at pp. 56–7; Case 33/70 *SACE* [1970] ECR 1213 at pp. 1221–3).

See also Transitional period.

▶ **ACCESSION TREATIES** Treaties whereby European States may become Members of the EEC and Euratom and parties to the Treaties establishing those Communities (Arts. 237 EEC, 205 Euratom); accession to the ECSC and the ECSC Treaty takes place by means of a Decision of the Council and by the deposit of the instrument of accession with the French Government (Art. 98 ECSC).

Any European State may apply to become a Member of the Communities (ibid.), and although there is no express provision on this point and although each Community forms a separate legal entity, it is generally accepted that a new State may only join all three Communities at the same time, but not one or two of them separately. The application for accession must be addressed to the Council. Under the ECSC Treaty, the Council decides unanimously on the application after obtaining the opinion of the Commission. It is also for the Council to determine the terms of accession, likewise acting unanimously (Art. 98 ECSC). Under the EEC Treaty, the Council takes a unanimous decision on the application after consulting the Commission and after receiving the assent of the European Parliament, which is required to act by an absolute majority of its component members. However, the conditions of admission and the adjustments to the Treaty necessitated thereby are the subject of an agreement between the Member States and the applicant State. This agreement must be ratified by all the contracting States in accordance with their respective constitutional requirements (Art. 237 EEC; the provision requiring the assent of the European Parliament was inserted by Art. 8 of the Single European Act of 1986, which amended Art. 237). The procedure is basically the same under the Euratom Treaty, except that here the assent of the EP need not be obtained (Art. 205 Euratom, which was not amended by the SEA). The conditions of accession and the adjustments to the Treaties are usually set out in a single *Act of Accession* (AA) which is annexed to the Treaty of Accession and to the Council Decision taken under the ECSC Treaty, of which both it forms an integral part.

So far, the following three Accession Treaties have been signed, each accompanied by a Commission Opinion, a Council Decision concerning accession to the ECSC, a Council Decision on admission to the EEC and Euratom, an Act of Accession, and a number of Annexes, Protocols, and Declarations listed in a Final Act, the Annexes and Protocols forming an integral part of the Act of Accession:

- *Treaty of Accession of 22 January 1972*, signed in Brussels, concerning the accession of Denmark, Ireland, and the United Kingdom; the Treaty entered into force on 1 January 1973 (*OJ* 1972 L73. The Treaty was

3

also signed by Norway but, in view of the adverse result of a referendum, Norway failed to ratify it);

- *Treaty of Accession of 28 May 1979*, signed in Athens, concerning the accession of Greece; the Treaty entered into force on 1 January 1981 (*OJ* 1979 L291);
- *Treaty of Accession of 12 June 1985*, signed in Madrid and Lisbon, concerning the accession of Spain and Portugal; the Treaty entered into force on 1 January 1986 (*OJ* 1985 L302).

It may be noted that since the third enlargement the following States have submitted formal applications for accession to the Communities: Turkey (on 14 April 1987, see *Bull. EC* 4–1987, p. 11); Austria, subject to the condition that her neutrality status would be maintained (on 17 July 1989, see 23rd *Gen. Rep. EC* (1989), p. 329); Cyprus and Malta (on 4 and 17 July 1990, respectively, see 'The Week in Europe', 19 July 1990), while on 18 July 1990 Hungary anounced her aim to become a full EC member by 1995 (ibid.). The Commission does not intend to negotiate on new membership until 1992 (ibid.).

The three Treaties and Acts of Accession are based on the same basic principles, follow the same structure, and contain many identical or similar provisions (these will not be cited separately below). There are, of course, variations in the detailed provisions setting out the adjustments to the Treaties and the transitional measures.

The basic principle of accession to the Communities is that 'the provisions of Community law apply *ab initio* and *in toto* to new Member States, derogations being allowed only in so far as they are expressly laid down by transitional provisions' (Case 258/81 *Metallurgiki Halyps* v. *Commission* [1982] ECR 4261 at p. 4279). Thus, the effect of accession is to extend the whole body of Community law in force at the time of accession to all undertakings and natural and legal persons in the new Member States, who/which are, from the moment of accession, subject to the application of that law on an equal basis with other undertakings and persons in the Community (ibid. at p. 4280, rejecting claims by Greek undertakings seeking exemption from the steel production quota system. See also Cases 31 and 35/86 *LAISA* v. *Council* [1988] ECR 2285 at p. 2317).

In its opinions given on the three applications for accession, the Commission stated the above principle in much broader terms, saying that 'in joining the Communities the applicant States accept without reserve the Treaties and their political objectives, all decisions taken since their entry into force, and the action that has been agreed in respect of the development and reinforce-ment of the Communities'. Moreover, accession to the Communities entails recognition of the binding force of certain basic rules and principles of Community law, such as the doctrines of the direct effect and supremacy of Community law and the procedures for ensuring its uniform interpretation. Finally, observance of the principles of pluralist democracy and respect for human rights, forming part of the common heritage of the Member States, is also an essential element of membership of the Communities (this last statement only appears in the opinions given on the Greek, Spanish, and Portuguese applications).

The above principles have been transformed into binding legal obligations by the Accession Treaties (including the Council Decisions on accession to the ECSC) and by Part One of the Acts of Accession. Thus, Art. 1(3) of the Accession Treaties lays down the basic rule that the provisions concerning the rights and obligations of the Member States and the powers and jurisdiction of the institutions of the Communities as set out in the ECSC, EEC, and Euratom Treaties shall apply in respect of the Accession Treaties and the Acts of Accession which form an integral part of those Treaties. Since the powers and jurisdiction referred to include those of the ECJ, the Court has jurisdiction, amongst other things, to give a preliminary ruling under Arts. 177 EEC/150 Euratom on the interpretation of the Treaties and Acts of Accession (Case 44/84 *Hurd* [1986] ECR 29 at p. 75; but see also at p. 77).

According to Art. 2 AA, from the date of accession the provisions of the original Treaties and the acts adopted by the institutions become binding on the new Member States and are to appy in those States under the conditions laid down in those Treaties and in the AA. The ECJ has held that to avoid discontinuity ('legislative vacuum') in the Community legal system in its application to the new Member States, all the acts of the institutions which had been adopted prior to the date of the accession became binding on and applicable within those States, including acts adopted during the interim period between the signing of the documents concerning accession and the time when accession in fact took effect. During that period, the interests of the new Member States were protected by the information and consultation procedure laid down in an agreement annexed to the Final Act (Cases 39/81 etc. *Halyvourgiki* v. *Commission* [1982] ECR 593 at pp. 613–14).

In addition to the original Treaties and the acts of the institutions (secondary legislation), the new Member States are under an obligation to accept the whole *acquis communautaire* in existence at the date of accession, that is to say, (1) the decisions and agreements adopted by the Representatives of the Governments of the Member States meeting in Council; (2) all other agreements concluded by the existing Member States relating to the functioning of the Communities or connected with their activities (Art. 3(1) AA); (3) the conventions provided for in Art. 220 EEC and related protocols (Art. 3(2) AA); (4) the international agreements concluded by the Communities (Art. 4(1) AA); (5) the international agreements concluded by the Communities and the Member States, acting jointly ('mixed agreements') and related agreements concluded by the Member States (Art. 4(2) AA); and (6) the internal agreements concluded by the Member States for the purpose of implementing them (Art. 4(3) AA). Moreover, the new Member States are 'in the same situation' as the existing Member States in respect of (7) declarations or resolutions of, or other positions taken up by, the Council, and in respect of (8) those concerning the European Communities adopted by common agreement of the Member States; they must accordingly observe the 'principles and guidelines deriving from those declarations, resolutions or other positions' and must take such measures as may be necessary to ensure their implementation (Art. 3(3) AA). However, the ECJ has pointed out that this last provision does not attach any additional legal effect to the measures to which it applies. It is merely intended to ensure that the new Member States are subject to the same obligations as the original Member States by virtue of the measures in question. They may not therefore rely on the fact that such measures were adopted in their absence (Case 44/84 *Hurd*, above, at p. 79).

The provisions of the AA may not as a rule be suspended, amended, or repealed other than by means of the procedure laid down in the original Treaties for their own amendment (Art. 6 AA). However, those provisions of the AA the purpose or effect of which is to repeal or amend acts adopted by the institutions, otherwise than as a transitional measure, have the same status in law as the provisions which they repeal or amend and are subject to the same rules as those provisions (Art. 8 AA). The ECJ has interpreted Art. 8 AA as allowing the institutions, acting in accordance with the procedure normally applicable to the amendment of secondary legislation, to introduce subsequent amendments to the acts which had been amended by the AA (Case 203/86 *Spain* v. *Council* [1988] ECR paras. 5–6). On the other hand, Art. 8 AA does not have the effect of subjecting to judicial review the legality of the provisions to which it refers. The Court has held that the adaptations to the acts of the institutions set out in the AA itself (i.e. in Annex I) are the subject of an international agreement between the old and the new Member States. Therefore, they do not constitute 'acts' of the Council within the meaning of Arts. 173 EEC/146 Euratom but provisions of primary law which may only be suspended, amended, or repealed by means of Treaty amendment. The Court itself has no jurisdiction to consider their legality. By contrast, the adaptations to the acts of the institutions listed in Annex II were to be adopted by the institutions (Council and Commission) themselves, in accordance with the guidelines and the procedure laid down in the AA. These adaptations are therefore 'acts of the institutions', which are subject as such to the general rules on the review of legality by the Court provided for in the Treaties (Cases 31 and 35/86 *LAISA* v. *Council*, above, at pp. 2317–19).

In order to facilitate the adjustment of the new Member States to Community law, all three Acts of Accession have made the application of the original Treaties and of the acts of the institutions subject to certain clearly specified transitional measures ('derogations'). These measures terminated, as a general rule, at the end of 1977 (first accession) or of 1985 (second accession), respectively. The Act of Accession 1985 does not lay down any similar final date (Art. 9 AA). The ECJ has held that the provisions of the various Acts of Accession must be interpreted by reference to the underlying principles of the Communities as laid down in the Treaties. Therefore, the derogations allowed by the AA must be interpreted restrictively and with a view to facilitating the attainment of the aims of the Treaties and to applying their rules in their entirety (Case 231/78 *Commission* v. *United Kingdom* [1979] ECR 1447 at pp. 1459–62, interpreting the first AA; Cases 194 and 241/85 *Commission* v. *Greece* [1988] ECR 1037 at p. 1060, interpreting the second AA. *See also under* **Transitional period**).

Finally, it may be mentioned that there are no provisions in the Treaties enabling a Member State to withdraw from the Treaties and thereby terminate its membership of the Communites. This problem may therefore be approached from two different angles. First, it may be argued that in the absence of a provision of Community law, this question is governed by the general rules of public international law relating to the termination of treaties. According to these rules, as codified in Arts. 54 *et seq.* of the Vienna Convention on the Law of Treaties of 1969, a treaty which contains no provision regarding its termination and which does not provide for denunciation or withdrawal is in principle not subject to denunciation or withdrawal unless: (1) it is established that the parties intended to admit the possibility of denunciation or with-drawal; or (2) a right of denunciation or withdrawal may be implied by the nature of the treaty (Art. 56(1)). Since the EEC and Euratom Treaties were concluded for an 'unlimited period' (Arts. 240 EEC, 208 Euratom; the ECSC Treaty was concluded for a period of fifty years, Art. 97), and since their aim is to achieve the full economic and social integration of the Member States eventually leading to a European Union, it is clear that it cannot be established that the parties intended to admit the possibility of withdrawal from member-ship or that a right of (unilateral) withdrawal may be implied by the nature of the Treaties. Therefore, the withdrawal of a party may take place 'at any time by consent of all the parties' (Art. 54(b)). In the absence of unanimous consent, it seems that the only relevant ground listed in the Vienna Convention which might allow a Member State to withdraw from the Communities would be a 'fundamental change of circumstances' as defined in Art. 62. Moreover, in accordance with the law of State succession, a change in the legal personality of a Member State may affect its continued membership of the Communities (e.g. secession of part of a State, merger of two States). It must be stated, however, that even although the substantive rules and principles of international law might be applicable to these questions, the Member States would be bound not to submit any possible dispute that might arise in connection with an intended withdrawal to any method of settlement other than those provided for in the Treaties (Arts. 87 ECSC, 219 EEC, 193 Euratom, assuming that such a dispute would concern 'the interpretation or application' of the Treaties).

A second line of argument could be to say that since withdrawal from the Communities would inevitably entail amendment of the Treaties (e.g., amongst other things, amendment of their territorial scope of application, of the composition of the institutions), it could be dealt with under the provisions relating to Treaty amendment (Arts. 96 ECSC, 236 EEC, 204 Euratom). Since under these provisions the Treaties may only be amended by 'common accord' of the Member States, the end result would be the same as under the rules of general international law.

The method of Treaty amendment was used when, as a result of the introduction of home rule on 1 May 1979 and of a consultative referendum held on 23 February 1982, the Danish Government announced the intention of Greenland to withdraw from the Communities (for background and the Commission's opinion on the status of Greenland, see *Bull. EC* 1–1983, p. 13 and Suppl. 1/83—*Bull. EC*). The withdrawal was legally achieved by the conclusion of a Treaty amending, with regard to Greenland, the Treaties establishing the European Communities. The Treaty was based on the provisions relating to the amendment of the original Treaties (see above), it was signed by all the Member States on 13 March 1984, and, following ratification by all of them, entered into force on 1 February 1985 (*OJ* 1985 L29/1). Since Greenland was not a Member State of the Communities but only part of a Member State, its withdrawal did not raise fundamental legal issues concerning the possibility of withdrawal from membership as such. The Treaty of 13 March 1984 amended the territorial scope of application of the original Treaties and established Greenland's status as an overseas territory which remains associated with the EEC under Part Four of the EEC Treaty relating to Overseas Countries and Territories (OCTs). In addition to the Treaty of 1984, Greenland's relationship with the Community is now governed by a member of different instruments: a Protocol on special arrangements for Greenland annexed to the Treaty; a ten-year Agreement on fisheries together with a five-year Protocol on the conditions relating to fishing; and a Regulation laying down certain specific measures in connection with the special arrangements on fisheries (all published in *OJ* 1985 L29; see also *Bull. EC* 2–1984, p. 37; *Bull. EC* 2–1985, pp. 17, 28).

See also *Acquis communautaire*, Adaptation decision, European Communities.

Further reading 1. BOOKS: Bathurst *et al.* (eds.), *Legal Problems of an Enlarged European Community* (1972); Puissochet, *The Enlargement of the European Communities: A Commentary on the Accession of Denmark, Ireland and the United Kingdom* (1975); Schneider, *From Nine to Twelve: Europe's Destiny?* (1980); Seers and Vaitsos (eds.), *The Second Enlargement of the EEC. The Integration of Unequal Partners* (1982).

2. ARTICLES: Aurrecoechea, 'Some Problems Concerning the Constitutional Basis for Spain's Accession to the European Community' (1987) 36 *ICLQ* 14; Brinkhorst and Kuiper, 'The Integration of the New Member States in the Community Legal Order' (1972) 9 *CML Rev.* 364; Dagtoglou, 'The Southern Enlargement of the European Community' (1984) 21 *CML Rev.* 149; de Blois and Crisham, Conference Report, 'A Community of Twelve?' (1979) 16 *CML Rev.* 509; Due and Gulmann, 'Constitutional Implications of the Danish Accession to the European Communities' (1972) 9 *CML Rev.* 256; Editorial, 'The Greek Accession Treaty' (1979) 16 *CML Rev.* 342; id., 'The Second Enlargement' (1982) 19 *CML Rev.* 213; Evrigenis, 'Legal and Constitutional Implications of Greek Accession to the European Communities' (1980) 17 *CML Rev.* 157; Foighel, 'Home Rule in Greenland: A Framework for Local Autonomy' (1980) 17 *CML Rev.* 91; Harhoff, 'Greenland's Withdrawal from the European Communities' (1983) 20 *CML Rev.* 13; Mitchell, Kuipers, and Gall, 'Constitutional Aspects of the Treaty and Legislation Relating to British Membership' (1972) 9 *CML Rev.* 134; Santaolalla Gadea and Martinez Lage, 'Spanish Accession to the European Communities: Legal and Constitutional Implications' (1986) 23 *CML Rev.* 11; Temple Lang, 'Legal and Constitutional Implications for Ireland of Adhesion to the EEC Treaty' (1972) 9 *CML Rev.* 167; Weiss, 'Greenland's Withdrawal from the European Communities' (1985) 10 *EL Rev.* 173.

3. OFFICIAL PUBLICATIONS: (*a*) *First enlargement*: Suppl. 1/72—*Bull. EC*; *Bull. EC* 9–1973, p. 24; (*b*) *Second enlargement*: *Bull. EC* 1–1976, p. 6; Suppl. 2/76—*Bull. EC*; *Bull. EC* 5–1979, p. 7; 1–1981, p. 9; (*c*) *Third enlargement*: *Bull. EC*

3–1977, p. 8; 5–1978, p. 7; 10–1978, p. 7; 11–1978, p. 7; Suppls. 5/78 and 9/78—
Bull. EC; *Bull. EC* 2–1979, p. 20; Suppl. 8/82—*Bull. EC*; *Bull. EC* 10–1984, p. 9;
3–1985, p. 7; 6–1985, p. 7; 1–1986, p. 7; (*d*) *In general*: *Bull. EC* 4–1978, p. 7;
Suppls. 1/78, 2/78, 3/78—*Bull. EC*.

▶ *ACQUIS COMMUNAUTAIRE* The Community patrimony: the whole
body of rules, principles, agreements, declarations, resolutions, positions,
opinions, objectives, and practices concerning the European Communities,
whether or not binding in law, which has developed since their establishment
and which has been accepted by the Community institutions and the Member
States as governing their activities. Thus, the concept of *acquis communautaire*
is much broader than the concept of Community law which generally denotes
the corpus of binding rules laid down in the Treaties and in acts of the
institutions and binding legal principles recognized as such by the Court of
Justice.

The notion of *acquis* plays an important part in many different contexts,
but its most important function has been in relation to the successive
enlargements of the Communities. In that context, it expressed the idea that
by acceding to the Communities, the new Member States accepted without
reservation 'the Treaties and their political objectives, all decisions taken
since their entry into force, and the action that has been agreed in respect of
the development and reinforcement of the Communities' (Final Communiqué of
the Hague Summit Conference of 1–2 Dec. 1969, point 13, 3rd *Gen. Rep. EC*
(1969), p. 486; see also the opinions of the Commission given on the
applications of the new Member States in connection with the 1973, 1981,
and 1986 enlargements). This principle has been transformed into legally
binding obligations by Arts. 2–4 of the Acts of Accession of 1972, 1979, and
1985. In particular, Art. 3(3) ensures that, in addition to the original Treaties
and the acts adopted by the institutions, the new Member States are 'in the
same situation as the original Member States in respect of declarations or
resolutions of, or other positions taken up by, the Council and in respect of
those concerning the European Communities adopted by common agreement
of the Member States' (for an interpretation and application of this provision,
see Case 44/84 *Hurd* [1986] ECR 29 at p. 79; see also Cases 31 and 35/86
LAISA v. *Council* [1988] ECR 2285 at p. 2317. *See further under* **Accession
Treaties**).

In addition to enlargement, the concept of *acquis* has played a prominent
part in the various documents prepared in connection with institutional
reform and the establishment of a European Union. Thus, the Report of the
Three Wise Men on the European Institutions, submitted in November 1979,
emphasizes that 'the first and greatest task is the maintenance and consolidation
of the *acquis*, with any adjustments that modern conditions may demand'
(*Bull. EC* 11–1979, p. 25 at p. 28). Art. 7(1) of the Draft Treaty establishing
the European Union, adopted by the European Parliament on 14 February
1984, expressly states that 'The Union shall take over the Community
patrimony' (*OJ* 1984 C77/33; *Bull. EC* 2–1984, p. 7). Likewise, when the
Committee on Institutional Affairs (Dooge Committee) proposed that a

9

conference be convened to negotiate a draft European Union Treaty, it indicated that such a Treaty should be based, amongst other things, on the *acquis communautaire* (Report of 29–30 Mar. 1985, Part IV, *Bull. EC* 3–1985, p. 102).

Finally, the concept of *acquis* is also relevant to the external relations of the Communities. Thus, Art. 2 of the Third ACP–EEC Convention (Lomé III) states that one of the fundamental principles of ACP–EEC co-operation is that the security of their relations is based 'on the "*acquis*" of their system of co-operation'.

See also **Accession Treaties, Community law.**

▶ *ACTE CLAIR* (**DOCTRINE OF**) Doctrine according to which a legal provision whose meaning is clear and unequivocal does not require any interpretation.

As a general principle of interpretation, the doctrine is recognized in most legal systems under the maxim: *in claris non fit interpretatio*. In a special sense, however, the doctrine of the *acte clair* has been developed in French law to restrict the situations in which a court has to refer preliminary questions (*questions prejudicielles*) to another court or to the executive for decision, to cases raising genuine difficulties of interpretation. Accordingly, the referring court is deemed to have a broad margin of discretion to determine whether or not an 'act' is 'clear' and whether or not a reference is necessary. This doctrine has subsequently been applied by the French *Conseil d'État*, and to a lesser extent by the *Cour de Cassation*, in the context of references to the ECJ for preliminary rulings under Art. 177 EEC (for cases in which the *Conseil d'État* has so applied the doctrine, see the opinion of A.-G. Capotorti in Case 283/81 *CILFIT* [1982] ECR 3415 at p. 3437 and the articles cited below).

Reliance on the doctrine by the supreme courts of the Member States in the context of Art. 177 EEC has been severely criticized on two main grounds. First, it has been said that the doctrine is based on a logical fallacy known as *petitio principii*. It is illogical to reject the need for interpretation on the ground that the meaning of a provision is clear, since in order to establish whether that is the case, the court must first interpret the text. Secondly, it has been pointed out that the effect of the doctrine is to render nugatory the obligation imposed by Art. 177(3) EEC on national courts of last resort. By claiming that a provision is 'clear' and therefore not referring it to the ECJ, those courts can upset the whole system of preliminary rulings, whose main purpose is to ensure that the ECJ is the final authority in the matter of interpreting Community law (see Case 283/81 *CILFIT*, above, at pp. 3435–7 *per* A.-G. Capotorti, and the papers by Pescatore and Questiaux cited below. For a qualified acceptance of the doctrine in the context of Art. 177 EEC, see Cases 28 to 30/62 *Da Costa* [1963] ECR 31 at pp. 44–5 *per* A.-G. Lagrange, and his article cited below).

The ECJ itself seems to have accepted the doctrine of the *acte clair*, albeit subject to certain strict conditions. In determining the circumstances in which courts and tribunals of Member States, against whose decisions there is no judicial remedy under national law, may be exempted from the obligation to refer preliminary questions to the ECJ under Art. 177(3) EEC, the Court has stated: 'Finally, the correct application of Community law may be so obvious as to leave no scope for any reasonable doubt as to the manner in which the question raised is to be resolved. Before it comes to the conclusion that such is the case, the national court or tribunal must be convinced that the matter is equally obvious to the courts of the other Member States and to the Court of Justice. Only if those conditions are satisfied, may the national court or tribunal refrain from submitting the question to the Court of Justice and take upon itself the responsibility for resolving it. However, the existence of such a possibility must be assessed on the basis of the characteristic features of Community law and the particular difficulties to which its interpretation gives rise' (Case 283/81 *CILFIT*, above, at p. 3430).

See also **Interpretation of Community law, Preliminary ruling, Reference proceedings.**

Further reading: Bebr, 'The Rambling Ghost of "Cohn-Bendit": Acte Clair and the Court of Justice' (1983) 20 *CML Rev.* 439; Editorial, 'The Cohn Bendit Decision of the Conseil d'État' (1979) 4 *EL Rev.* 65: id., 'Article 177 EEC and the Obligation to Refer' (1983) 8 *EL Rev.* 81: Lagrange, 'The European Court of Justice and National Courts. The Theory of the Acte Clair: A Bone of Contention or a Source of Unity?' (1971) 8 *CML Rev.* 313; Pescatore, 'Interpretation of Community Law and the Doctrine of "Acte Clair" ', in Bathurst *et al.* (eds.), *Legal Problems of an Enlarged European Community* (1972), p. 27; Questiaux, 'Interpretation of Community Law', ibid. p. 47; Rasmussen, 'The European Court's Acte Clair Strategy in CILFIT' (1984) 9 *EL Rev.* 242.

▶ **ACTION AGAINST MEMBER STATES** 1. Direct action brought by the Commission before the ECJ 'for the purpose of obtaining a declaration that the conduct of a Member State infringes Community law and of terminating that conduct' (Cases 15 and 16/76 *France* v. *Commission* [1979] ECR 321 at p. 339). It is an enforcement procedure which provides 'means of implementation and is the *ultima ratio* enabling the Community interests enshrined in the Treaty to prevail over the inertia and resistance of Member States. It is a procedure far exceeding the rules heretofore recognised in classical international law to ensure that obligations of States are fulfilled' (Case 20/59 *Italy* v. *HA* [1960] ECR 325 at p. 339).

The duty of the Member States to comply with Community obligations arises both from the general rule of customary international law *pacta sunt servanda* and from specific provisions of Community law itself. Thus, Art. 5 EEC provides that 'Member States shall take all appropriate measures, whether general or particular, to ensure fulfilment of the obligations arising out of this Treaty or resulting from action taken by the institutions of the Community. They shall facilitate the achievement of the Community's tasks. They shall abstain from any measure which could jeopardize the attainment of the objectives of this Treaty.' (See also Arts. 86 ECSC and 192 Euratom.) In the interpretation of the ECJ, this provision is the expression of the more general rule imposing on Member States and the Community institutions mutual duties of genuine co-operation and assistance within the framework of Community law (Case 44/84 *Hurd* [1986] ECR 29 at pp. 81, 82–3. On the duties of Member States arising from Art. 5, see also Case 804/79 *Commission* v. *United Kingdom* [1981] ECR 1045 at pp. 1075–6 and Case 325/85 *Ireland* v. *Commission* [1987] ECR 5041 at p. 5087).

The importance of the fulfilment of Community obligations has been summed up by the ECJ thus:

In permitting Member States to profit from the advantages of the Community, the Treaty imposes on them also the obligation to respect its rules. For a State unilaterally to break, according to its own conception of national interest, the equilibrium between advantages and obligations flowing from its adherence to the Community brings into question the equality of Member States before Community law and creates discriminations at the expense of their nationals, and above all of the nationals of the State itself which places itself outside the Community rules. This failure in the duty of solidarity accepted by Member States by the fact of their adherence to the Community strikes at the fundamental basis of the Community legal order. (Case 39/72 *Commission* v. *Italy* [1973] ECR 101 at p. 116; Case 128/78 *Commission* v. *United Kingdom* [1979] ECR 419 at p. 429—'Tachographs' case.)

It follows from the absolute nature of the duty to fulfil Community obligations that Member States may not justify their failure to do so by invoking:

- a similar failure on the part of other Member States or the Community institutions, since they may not take the law into their own hands (see e.g. Cases 90 and 91/63 *Commission* v. *Luxembourg and Belgium* [1964] ECR 625 at p. 631; Case 52/75 *Commission* v. *Italy* [1976] ECR 277 at p. 284);
- any conditions, reservations, and objections expressed by them in the course of the Community law-making process (see e.g. Case 38/69 *Commission* v. *Italy* [1970] ECR 47 at pp. 56–7; Case 39/72 *Commission* v. *Italy*, above, at p. 115);
- the principles of direct effect and the supremacy of Community law, since those principles do not absolve Member States from the obligation of removing from their internal legal order provisions which are incompatible with Community law (see e.g. Case 104/86 *Commission* v. *Italy* [1988] ECR 1799 at p. 1817);
- the provisions, procedures, and practices of the national legal or constitutional order (see e.g. Case 30/72 *Commission* v. *Italy* [1973] ECR 161 at p. 172);
- the fact that the failure was due to the action or inaction of a constitutionally independent institution, such as Parliament, since the duty to carry out Community obligations falls upon the Member States as such (see e.g. Case 77/69 *Commission* v. *Belgium* [1970] ECR 237 at p. 243);
- unforeseeable political circumstances and difficulties, such as governmental crises, dissolution of Parliament, etc. (ibid.);

- practical difficulties arising at the stage of national implementation (see e.g. Case 39/72 *Commission* v. *Italy*, above, at p. 115; Case 128/78 *Commission* v. *United Kingdom*, above, at p. 429).

The enforcement procedure may be divided into two distinct stages. The first (administrative) stage consists of a compulsory preliminary procedure initiated by the Commission. The second (judicial) stage consists of the action itself before the ECJ. Since there are important differences, as regards both stages, between the ECSC and EEC/Euratom Treaties, these will be considered separately below.

(*a*) **Under the ECSC Treaty** (Art. 88), if the Commission considers that a Member State has failed to fulfil an obligation, it must record this failure in a 'reasoned decision' after giving the State concerned the opportunity to submit its comments. The Commission must set the State a time-limit for the fulfilment of its obligation. The opportunity to present observations is an essential guarantee of the right to be heard and must therefore be afforded in substance and not merely in form. A failure to grant it will entail annulment of the 'reasoned decision' on the ground of infringement of an essential procedural requirement (Case 20/59 *Italy* v. *HA*, above, at pp. 341–2). As regards its legal nature, the 'reasoned decision' differs fundamentally from an ordinary 'decision' which the Commission may take under Art. 14 ECSC in exercise of its legislative and executive competences. Unlike the latter, the 'reasoned decision' may simply record a breach of a pre-existing obligation but may not have a legislative content itself (ibid. at p. 338; Cases 6 and 11/69 *Commission* v. *France* [1969] ECR 523 at p. 543). The reasons supporting the decision must be such as to justify the recording of the breach. They must specify not merely the provisions of Community law infringed, but also the nature and extent of the infringement (Case 20/59 *Italy* v. *HA*, above, at p. 339).

Against the 'reasoned decision' the State concerned may institute proceedings before the ECJ within two months of its notification. The Court has unlimited jurisdiction in the matter. Unlike the position under the EEC/Euratom Treaties, the action is thus brought against the Commission and is aimed at the annulment of the decision by showing that the State has in fact complied with the obligation in question. Nevertheless a State may not, within the framework of such an action, challenge the validity of the original measure itself which laid down the obligation, nor may it bring into issue *ex post facto* the substantive questions dealt with by it. This could have been done only in an action for annulment under Art. 33 within the proper time-limit and subject to the Court's limited jurisdiction (Case 3/59 *Germany* v. *HA* [1960] ECR 53 at pp. 59–61; Cases 6 and 11/69 *Commission* v. *France*, above, at pp. 543–4).

If the action is well founded, the ECJ will annul the 'reasoned decision'. The legal consequences of the Court's judgment may vary according to the grounds on which it is based. Thus, an annulment on purely formal or procedural grounds (e.g. the Commission's failure to observe the rules relating to the preliminary procedure) will clearly not amount to a finding

13

that the Member State has not committed a breach of its obligations. It seems that in such a case the Commission may, after rectifying the formal defect, record the same default in a further 'reasoned decision'. Annulment on substantive grounds may mean any or all of the following: (i) the Commission has incorrectly interpreted the nature and scope of the Member State's obligation; (ii) it has incorrectly specified the State's conduct required to comply with the obligation; (iii) the State has not committed a breach. If the action is dismissed, the Commission may, with the assent of the Council, impose the following sanctions: (i) suspend the payment of any sums owed to the State; (ii) take measures to correct the effects of the infringement. Against these sanctions further proceedings may be instituted before the ECJ within two months.

(*b*) **Under the EEC and Euratom Treaties** (Arts. 169 EEC, 141 Euratom), if the Commission considers that a Member State has failed to fulfil an obligation, it must deliver a 'reasoned opinion' on the matter after giving the State concerned—by a formal notice—the opportunity to submit its observations. The ECJ has stated that 'such an opportunity constitutes an essential guarantee required by the Treaty and amounts to an essential procedural requirement' (Case 31/69 *Commission* v. *Italy* [1970] ECR 25 at p. 33). Respect for this guarantee means that an alleged failure to fulfil an obligation in relation to which the State has not been given the opportunity to present its observations cannot be considered by the Court in the ensuing action (ibid.). Consequently, where the Commission changes the subject-matter of its complaint at the judicial stage, it must set in motion the preliminary procedure again (Case 7/69 *Commission* v. *Italy* [1970] ECR 111 at p. 117). The Commission is required to give the Member State concerned a 'reasonable period' for the submission of its observations and for compliance with the reasoned opinion or, if appropriate, for the preparation of its defence (see Case 293/85 *Commission* v. *Belgium* [1988] ECR 305 at pp. 351–3, where the Court dismissed an action as inadmissible on the grounds that the periods fixed by the Commission—eight days for the submission of observations and fifteen days for compliance with the reasoned opinion—were unjustifiably short considering the complexity of the matter). The preliminary procedure may be derogated from only in special cases expressly provided for by the Treaties (see Arts. 93(2), 100A(4), 225(2) EEC; 38(3), 82(4) Euratom).

The significance of the preliminary procedure has been summed up by the ECJ thus: 'The purpose of that preliminary procedure which comes within the general scope of the supervisory task entrusted to the Commission under the first indent of Article 155 is, in the first place, to give the Member State an opportunity to justify its position and, as the case may be, to enable the Commission to persuade the Member State to comply of its own accord with the requirements of the Treaty. If this attempt to reach a settlement is unsuccessful, the function of the reasoned opinion is to define the subject-matter of the dispute. On the other hand, the Commission is not empowered to determine conclusively, by opinions formulated pursuant to Article 169 or by other statements of its attitude under that procedure, the rights and duties of a Member State or to afford that State guarantees concerning the compatibility of a given line of conduct with the Treaty. According to the system embodied in Articles 169 to 171 of the Treaty, the rights and duties of Member States may be determined and their conduct appraised only by a judgment of the Court. *A fortiori*, the Commission cannot, in the attitudes which it adopts and in the opinions which it is obliged to deliver under Article 169, exempt a Member State from compliance with its obligations under the Treaty. Such assurances cannot have the effect, in particular, of precluding individuals from relying in legal proceedings, on the rights conferred upon them by the Treaty in order to contest any legislative or administrative measures of a Member State which may be incompatible with Community law' (Cases 142 and 143/80 *Essevi and Salengo* [1981] ECR 1413 at pp. 1432–3).

By setting out the failure of the Member State and specifying the measures deemed to be necessary to put an end to the infringement, the 'reasoned opinion' determines the precise limits within which the Commission may later bring the matter before the ECJ (see below). As regards its legal nature and form, however, the 'reasoned opinion' is not a binding act. It cannot therefore lay down new obligations for the Member State, i.e. obligations which had not yet existed when the preliminary procedure was commenced. Neither the 'reasoned opinion' itself nor the refusal or failure of the Commission to deliver one (and thus to initiate the enforcement procedure against a Member State) may be challenged before the Court (Case 48/65 *Lütticke* v. *Commission* [1966] ECR 19 at p. 27; Cases 6 and 11/69 *Commission* v. *France*, above, at p. 542). Although it must contain 'a coherent statement of the reasons which led the Commission to believe that the State in question has failed to fulfil an obligation under the Treaty' (Case 7/61 *Commission* v. *Italy* [1961] ECR 317 at p. 327), it may not be attacked on the ground of inadequate reasoning (ibid. at p. 336 *per* A.-G. Lagrange).

If the Member State concerned does not comply with the 'reasoned opinion' within the period laid down by the Commission, the latter may (but is not obliged to) institute proceedings against the State before the ECJ. The application made by the Commission must be based on the same facts, grounds, and issues on which the 'reasoned opinion' has been based and in respect of which the Member State has been given an opportunity to present its observations. In other words, there must exist an identity of subject-matter between the administrative and the judicial stages; the Commission is not permitted to widen the scope of the latter (Case 45/64 *Commission* v. *Italy* [1965] ECR 857 at pp. 864–5; Case 193/80 *Commission* v. *Italy* [1981] ECR 3019 at p. 3032). Acting in the general interest of the Community, the Commission is not required to show the existence of any particular legal interest in the bringing of the action (Case 167/73 *Commission* v. *France* [1974] ECR 359 at pp. 368–9). Nor is the Commission prevented from bringing the case before the ECJ by the existence of adequate remedies available to individuals through the national courts, since the two procedures have different objectives and effects (Case 85/85 *Commission* v. *Belgium* [1986] ECR 1149 at pp. 1168–9).

The onus to prove non-fulfilment of a Community obligation is upon the Commission (see e.g. Case 298/86 *Commission* v. *Belgium* [1988] ECR para. 15), but the Member State concerned is required to co-operate bona fide by supplying clear and precise information indicating the measures taken in performance of its obligations (Case 96/81 *Commission* v. *Netherlands* [1982] ECR 1791 at p. 1803; Case 192/84 *Commission* v. *Greece* [1985] ECR 3967 at p. 3979). These measures must be adopted within the time-limit laid down in the 'reasoned opinion'; subsequent compliance with the opinion cannot prevent an action (Case 7/61 *Commission* v. *Italy*, above, at p. 326; Case 39/72 *Commission* v. *Italy*, above, at p. 112). Refusal to co-operate with the Commission by not communicating to it the information requested constitutes a breach of Art. 5 EEC. That breach is even more serious where the failure to co-operate continues before the Court itself, preventing it from accomplishing its task under Art. 164 EEC (Case 240/86 *Commission* v. *Greece* [1988] ECR 1835 at p. 1858; Case 272/86 *Commission* v. *Greece* [1988] ECR paras. 30–2). As under the ECSC Treaty (see above), the Member State may not challenge the legality of the original Community act laying down its obligations; this could have been done only in an action for annulment brought under Art. 173 EEC or Art. 146 Euratom within the proper time-limit (Cases 6 and 11/69 *Commission* v. *France*, above, at p. 539). The bringing of the action before the ECJ is not subject to any limitation period; the Commission has a wide discretionary power to select the most appropriate time for that purpose (Case 7/68 *Commission* v. *Italy* [1968] ECR 423 at p. 428; Case 7/71 *Commission* v. *France* [1971] ECR 1003 at p. 1016).

If the ECJ finds that a Member State has failed to fulfil an obligation under the Treaties, the State is required to take the necessary measures to comply with the judgment of the Court (Arts. 171 EEC, 143 Euratom). While these provisions lay down no time-limit within which the judgment must be complied with, the ECJ has held that the implementation of a judgment must be commenced immediately and must be completed as soon as possible. Any unreasonable delay will constitute a new infringement (Case 131/84 *Commission* v. *Italy* [1985] ECR 3531 at p. 3536). The judgment of the Court amounts to 'a prohibition having the full force of law on the competent national authorities against applying a national rule recognised as incompatible with the Treaty and, if the circumstances so require, an obligation on them to take all appropriate measures to enable Community law to be fully applied' (Case 48/71 *Commission* v. *Italy* [1972] ECR 527 at p. 532; Cases 24 and 97/80R *Commission* v. *France* [1980] ECR 1319 at p. 1333). In particular, 'all the institutions of the Member States concerned must . . . ensure within the fields covered by their respective powers, that judgments of the Court [under Art. 171 EEC] are complied with. If the judgment declares that certain legislative provisions of a Member State are contrary to the Treaty the authorities exercising legislative power are then under the duty to amend the provisions in question so as to make them conform with the requirements of Community law. For their part the courts of the Member State concerned have an obligation to ensure, when performing their duties, that the Court's judgment is complied with' (Cases 314 to 316/81 and 83/82 *Waterkeyn* [1982] ECR 4337 at pp. 4360–1).

Since, however, the purpose of a judgment delivered under Arts. 169 to 171 EEC is primarily to lay down the duties of Member States, rights for the benefit of individuals derive, not from such a judgment, but from the actual provisions of Community law having direct effect in the internal legal order. Where the Court finds that a Member State has failed to fulfil its obligations under directly effective provisions, 'it is the duty of the national court, by virtue of the authority attaching to the judgment of the Court, to take account, if need be, of the elements of law established by that judgment in order to determine the scope of the provisions of Community law which it has the task of applying' (ibid. at p. 4361).

Generally speaking, the defaulting Member State is obliged to eliminate the consequences of the infringement with retroactive effect (i.e. with an effect going back to the commencement of the infringement). Thus, the State is obliged to re-establish the complete status quo ante (*restitutio in integrum*). This may involve the obligation to make payment or restitution of sums illegally withheld or collected and, where necessary, to pay compensation for any injury suffered (Case 6/60 *Humblet* v. *Belgium* [1960] ECR 559 at p. 569). While the Court has no power to prescribe for the Member State what specific measures to take, this will follow from the 'reasoned opinion' of the Commission defining the nature and the extent of the State's default. As the ECJ has stated, 'since the aim of the Treaty is to achieve the practical elimination of infringements and the consequences thereof, past and future, it is a matter for the Community authorities whose task it is to ensure that the requirements of the Treaty are observed to determine the extent to which the obligation of the Member State concerned may be specified in the reasoned opinions . . . delivered under Article 169 . . . and in applications addressed to the Court' (Case 70/72 *Commission* v. *Germany* [1973] ECR 813 at p. 829). The judgment of the Court necessarily has an *erga omnes* effect in so far as it establishes 'the basis of a responsibility that a Member State can incur as a result of its default, as regards other Member States, the Community or private parties' (Case 39/72 *Commission* v. *Italy*, above, at p. 112). It is the duty of the Commission to ensure that the Member State complies with the Court's judgment, if necessary by instituting a second enforcement procedure (Case 48/71 *Commission* v. *Italy*, above, at p. 531; Cases 24 and 97/80R *Commission* v. *France*, above, at pp. 1330–1).

2. In addition to the enforcement procedures under Arts. 88 ECSC, 169 EEC, and 141 Euratom (see (1) above), the ECJ has both compulsory (Arts. 89(1) ECSC, 170 EEC, 142 Euratom) and optional (Arts. 89(2) ECSC, 182 EEC, 154 Euratom) jurisdiction to entertain actions against Member States which are brought by other Member States. Action against a Member State may also be brought under an 'arbitration clause' (Arts. 42 ECSC, 181 EEC, 153 Euratom). In respect of non-fulfilment by Member States of obligations under the Statute of the European Investment Bank, the Board of Directors of the Bank enjoys the powers conferred upon the Commission by Art. 169 EEC (Art. 180(a) EEC). Under the Euratom Treaty, the Commission may institute

17

Action against sanctions

proceedings against a Member State in the matter of granting licences (Art. 21(3) Euratom) and for the purpose of establishing certain infringements of the Treaty by a person or undertaking (Art. 145(2) Euratom). Individuals have no standing under any of the Treaties to bring direct action against a Member State before the ECJ on any ground whatsoever (see Case 1/82 *D.* v. *Luxembourg* [1982] ECR 3709 at p. 3716; Case 276/86 *Belkacem* v. *Germany* [1986] ECR 3975 at p. 3977). Formerly it was possible for a Community official to sue his own State before the ECJ for an alleged infringement of his privileges and immunities granted by Community law, but such a possibility no longer exists (Case 1/82 *D.* v. *Luxembourg*, above; see also Case 6/60 *Humblet* v. *Belgium*, above, at pp. 567 *et seq.*).

See also **Arbitration clause, Compulsory jurisdiction, Jurisdiction, Optional jurisdiction,** *Restitutio in integrum.*

Further reading 1. BOOKS: Audretsch, *Supervision in European Community Law*, 2nd edn. (1986); Bebr, *Development of Judicial Control of the European Communities* (1981), ch. 6; Hartley, *The Foundations of European Community Law*, 2nd edn. (1988), ch. 10; Schermers, *Judicial Protection in the European Communities*, 4th edn. (1987), ch. 2, part III; Toth, *Legal Protection of Individuals in the European Communities* (1978), vol. ii, ch. 9.

2. ARTICLES: Audretsch, 'Supervision in the EEC, OECD, and Benelux: A Difference in Degree, but also in Kind?' (1987) 36 *ICLQ* 838; Barav, 'Failure of Member States to Fulfil their Obligations under Community Law' (1975) 12 *CML Rev.* 369; Dashwood and White, 'Enforcement Actions under Articles 169 and 170 EEC' (1989) 14 *EL Rev.* 388; Evans, 'The Enforcement Procedure of Article 169 EEC: Commission Discretion' (1979) 4 *EL Rev.* 442; Everling, 'The Member States of the European Community before their Court of Justice' (1984) 9 *EL Rev.* 215; Gilmour, 'The Enforcement of Community Law by the Commission in the Context of State Aids: The Relationship between Articles 93 and 169 and the Choice of Remedies' (1981) 18 *CML Rev.* 63; Mertens de Wilmars and Verougstraete, 'Proceedings against Member States for Failure to Fulfil their Obligations' (1970) 7 *CML Rev.* 385; Schermers, 'The Law as it Stands against Treaty Violations by States' (1974/2) *LIEI* 111.

▶ **ACTION AGAINST SANCTIONS** Direct action brought before the ECJ, aimed at the review by the Court of a decision of the Commission imposing a sanction. The relevant provisions of the ECSC Treaty (Art. 36) refer to 'pecuniary sanctions' and 'periodic penalty payments'. 'Pecuniary sanctions' may be of two (and only two) kinds, i.e. fines and surcharges for delay. The EEC Treaty (Art. 172) refers to 'penalties' which comprise fines, penalties, and periodic penalty payments. The Euratom Treaty (Art. 144) simply refers to 'sanctions' which may be of both a financial and a non-financial nature. Since the Member States have not conferred upon the Communities criminal jurisdiction proper, the various sanctions at the Commission's disposal are strictly of an administrative, and not a penal, character.

Under all three Treaties, the ECJ has been given unlimited jurisdiction in actions against sanctions (see the provisions referred to above). Owing to such jurisdiction, these actions cannot, strictly speaking, be classified as actions for annulment (where the Court's jurisdiction is limited), even though they are usually primarily aimed at the annulment of the decision imposing the sanction. At the same time, they cannot properly be regarded as an entirely different and independent, *sui generis* type of recourse either, in the sense in which, for example, an action for damages is treated as a *sui generis* type of remedy. The correct position seems to be to regard them as a special case, a subcategory, of the broader concept of action for annulment. It follows that they are governed by the general rules relating to annulment proceedings except to the extent to which they are subject to their own special rules, to be discussed below, arising from the Court's unlimited jurisdiction.

The close connection between actions for annulment and actions against sanctions becomes apparent in cases (mainly occurring in the field of the competition law of the Economic Community) in which the challenged decision of the Commission is not confined to the imposition of a sanction but contains additional substantive measures as well. These may consist in the establishment of an infringement of Community law, in a refusal to grant an exemption under Art. 85(3) EEC, or in an order requiring the applicant to terminate the infringement in respect of which the sanction has been imposed. The latter may require performance of certain acts or, more frequently, abstention from the continuation of certain actions, practices, or situations which have been found to be contrary to Community law (see e.g. Cases 6 and 7/73 *Commercial Solvents* v. *Commission* [1974] ECR 223 at p. 255; Cases 40 to 48/73 etc. *Suiker Unie* v. *Commission* [1975] ECR 1663 at p. 1913; Case 73/74 *Papiers Peints* v. *Commission* [1975] ECR 1491 at p. 1510). In such cases the applicant may request, and the Court may order, any one of the following three measures:

1. annulment of the decision *in toto*, i.e. both the clauses relating to the imposition of the sanction and those containing or ordering additional substantive measures (see the first and second cases cited above);
2. annulment of the decision in part, i.e. only in so far as it imposes the sanction, while leaving the rest in force (see the third case cited above);
3. reduction of the amount of the fine or penalty imposed, while leaving the decision as a whole in force (this is usually presented only as a subsidiary or alternative claim, see the third case cited above).

In case (1), the action will take on a mixed form. It will be an action for annulment proper, subject to the ECJ's ordinary (limited) jurisdiction, as regards the additional measure; while it will be an action against sanctions, falling within the Court's unlimited jurisdiction, as regards the sanction itself. In cases (2) and (3), the action will fall in its entirety within the Court's unlimited jurisdiction.

From the unlimited jurisdiction of the Court two main consequences follow. First, the Court is not confined to an examination of the objective legality of the decision imposing the sanction in the light of the four grounds of action. Rather, the Court is free to deal with the case in all its aspects, factual and legal. In competition cases, for example, the Court has unfettered discretion to reassess the relevant market conditions which have led the

Commission to impose the fine or penalty. It may annul the fine if it finds that the Commission's intervention was 'unjustified in the actual temporal and factual circumstances in which it took place' (Case 26/75 *General Motors* v. *Commission* [1975] ECR 1367 at p. 1380; see also Case 41/69 *Chemiefarma* v. *Commission* [1970] ECR 661 at p. 704 *per* A.-G. Gand; Case 7/72 *Boehringer* v. *Commission* [1972] ECR 1281 at p. 1292 *per* A.-G. Mayras).

Secondly, the Court has power not only to annul, but also to vary the challenged decision by reducing or even increasing the fine or penalty (Art. 17 of Reg. 17, *OJ Sp. Edn.* 1959–62, p. 87; Art. 24 of Reg. 1017/68, *OJ Sp. Edn.* 1968(I), p. 302; Art. 14 of Reg. 3975/87, *OJ* 1987 L374/1; Case 8/56 *ALMA* v. *HA* [1957] ECR 95 at pp. 99–100). Generally, the Court will determine the question whether the fine or penalty is excessive in the light of the following factors: gravity, duration (or frequency), and consequences of the infringement; whether it was committed intentionally or negligently; importance of the rule violated in the system of Community law; economic capacity and financial position of the applicant; the amount of the fine or penalty in relation to the maximum laid down by the relevant provision of Community law; etc. Moreover, the Court may take into account both extenuating and aggravating circumstances, to the extent to which these have not already been considered by the Commission when assessing the sanction (see e.g. Case 8/56 *ALMA* v. *HA*, above, at p. 100; Case 1/59 *Macchiorlati Dalmas* v. *HA* [1959] ECR 199 at p. 205; Case 41/69 *Chemiefarma* v. *Commission*, above, at pp. 701–3; Case 48/69 *ICI* v. *Commission* [1972] ECR 619 at p. 663; Cases 6 and 7/73 *Commercial Solvents* v. *Commission*, above, at p. 257; Cases 40 to 48/73 etc. *Suiker Unie* v. *Commission*, above, at pp. 2021–3).

See also **Action for annulment, Administrative procedure*, Fine*, Limited jurisdiction, Pecuniary sanction*, Penalty*, Periodic penalty payment*, Sanction*, Surcharges for delay*, Unlimited jurisdiction.**

Further reading: Bebr, *Development of Judicial Control of the European Communities* (1981), ch. 7; Schermers, *Judicial Protection in the European Communities*, 4th edn. (1987), ch. 3/I/D; Toth, *Legal Protection of Individuals in the European Communities* (1978), vol. ii, ch. 8.

▶ **ACTION FOR ANNULMENT** Direct action brought before the ECJ for a declaration that an act of a Community institution is void. Since judicial review of the legality of acts of the institutions is exercised by the Court mainly in annulment proceedings, these proceedings occupy a central position in the system of remedies created by the Treaties.

1. **Under the ECSC Treaty,** an action for annulment may be brought under one of two main provisions: Art. 33 or Art. 38. In addition, an action may be instituted under the following special provisions, which have however been invoked very rarely or not at all so far: Arts. 37 (see Cases 2 and 3/60 *Niederrheinische Bergwerks* v. *HA* [1961] ECR 133 at pp. 144 *et seq.*), 63(2)(2), 65(4)(2) (see Case 1/58 *Stork* v. *HA* [1959] ECR 17 at pp. 25 *et seq.*; Case 12/63 *Schlieker* v. *HA* [1963] ECR 85 at p. 89), and 66(5)(2) (see ibid.).

Under Art. 38, an action for annulment may be brought, on grounds of lack of competence or infringement of an essential procedural requirement, against the European Parliament or the Council. The action may be instituted only by a Member State or the Commission but not by private individuals or organizations (see Case 66/76 *CFDT* v. *Council* [1977] ECR 305 at p. 310). The right of action is available to each Member State individually, and its exercise by a Member State or the Commission is not subject to any additional condition such as proof of an interest or capacity to bring proceedings (Case 230/81 *Luxembourg* v. *Parliament* [1983] ECR 255 at p. 284). Art. 38 has no counterpart in the EEC and Euratom Treaties in that those Treaties contain no express provision enabling the European Parliament to participate in annulment proceedings before the Court, either as an applicant or as a defendant (see below). Nevertheless, the ECJ has held that since the single Parliament is an institution common to the three Communities it necessarily acts in the field of all three Treaties when it adopts a resolution relating to its own organization or operation. Therefore, the jurisdiction of the Court and the proceedings under Art. 38 ECSC are applicable to acts of the Parliament which relate 'simultaneously and indivisibly' to the spheres of all three Treaties. Thus, Luxembourg was able to challenge a resolution of Parliament dealing with the question of its own seat and purporting to transfer officials from Luxembourg to Strasbourg and Brussels, under Art. 38 ECSC alone and without the need to resort to Arts. 173 EEC and 146 Euratom (ibid. at pp. 282–3). Nevertheless, for a resolution of the Parliament to be challengeable for annulment, it must be 'of a specific and precise decision-making character, producing legal effects' (Case 108/83 *Luxembourg* v. *Parliament* [1984] ECR 1945 at p. 1958, dealing with the same issues as the previous case). Since under the ECSC Treaty neither the Parliament nor the Council possesses wide-ranging decision-making powers, the scope of application of Art. 38 remains necessarily limited.

Under Art. 33 ECSC, an action for annulment may be brought against the Commission only (see Case 66/76 *CFDT* v. *Council*, above, at p. 310). Since under that Treaty the Commission is the chief decision-making body, it is Art. 33 which provides the most important means for judicial review. Proceedings may be instituted by a Member State, the Council, undertakings, and associations of undertakings. The right of action of the Member States and the Council is unqualified in that they may challenge any decision or recommendation of the Commission, whether general (normative) or individual, whether addressed to them or to others, and whether having any specific legal effect upon them or not. The mere fact of an objective violation of the law establishes their interest in the matter. By contrast, the right of action of other parties (hereinafter: private parties) is limited in two important respects. First, a private party must qualify as an undertaking or an association within the technical meaning of these terms as laid down in Arts. 48 and 80 ECSC. Persons other than undertakings or associations, such as private individuals (Case 12/63 *Schlieker* v. *HA*, above, at p. 89), Community officials (Case 10/55 *Mirossevich* v. *HA* [1956] ECR 333 at p. 340), or local authorities such as municipalities (Case 222/83 *Municipality of Differdange* v. *Commission*

21

[1984] ECR 2889 at p. 2896), cannot institute proceedings under Art. 33. Secondly, private parties may challenge only decisions or recommendations concerning them which are individual in character and general decisions or recommendations which they consider to involve a misuse of powers affecting them. Thus, in order for an action brought by a private party against an act of the Commission to be admissible under Art. 33, it is necessary, first, that the act in question should constitute a decision or recommendation and, secondly, if the act is individual in nature, that it should concern the applicant or, if it is general in nature, that it should involve a misuse of powers affecting the applicant.

Whether an act of the Commission is a 'decision' (or a 'recommendation') must be decided in the light of Art. 14 ECSC, which lists and defines the various binding (i.e. decisions and recommendations) and non-binding (i.e. opinions) measures. Owing to the essential unity of Arts. 14 and 33, only the binding measures within the meaning of Art. 14 may be the subject of an action for annulment under Art. 33. The only exception is an opinion delivered by the Commission under Art. 54(5) ECSC, which has the force of a decision (Cases 1 and 14/57 *Usines à Tubes de la Sarre* v. *HA* [1957] ECR 105 at p. 114 *per Curiam*, p. 117 *per* A.-G. Lagrange). Nevertheless, in considering whether an act of the Commission is challengeable for annulment, it is the object and the contents, rather than the form, of the act which are decisive (*see further under* **Decision, General decision, Individual decision**).

The distinction made by Art. 33 between individual and general decisions/ recommendations has significance only where the applicant is an undertaking or an association. In that case, where an act is individual (i.e. administrative or executive) in character, it is also necessary that it should 'concern' the applicant. The ECJ has interpreted this requirement quite liberally. Thus, apart from the obvious case where a decision is addressed to it, an undertaking is 'concerned' not only by a decision—whoever is the addressee— which directly affects its position (Case 18/57 *Nold* v. *HA* [1959] ECR 41 at p. 51), but also by a decision which permits advantages to be granted to its competitors (Cases 24 and 34/58 *Chambre Syndicale de la Sidérurgie* v. *HA* [1960] ECR 281 at p. 292; Cases 172 and 226/83 *Hoogovens Groep* v. *Commission* [1985] ECR 2831 at pp. 2846–7; Case 236/86 *Dillinger Hüttenwerke* v. *Commission* [1988] ECR para. 8). Moreover, it is not necessary that the applicant should be the only, or almost the only, undertaking concerned by the decision, nor that it should prove conclusively, for the purposes of admissibility, that it is so concerned. A prima-facie case is quite sufficient at that stage (Case 30/59 *Steenkolenmijnen* v. *HA* [1961] ECR 1 at pp. 16–17).

Where an act is individual and concerns the applicant, a private party may invoke any or all of the four .grounds of action, i.e. lack of competence, infringement of an essential procedural requirement, infringement of the Treaty or of any rule of law relating to its application, and misuse of powers (Case 18/57 *Nold* v. *HA*, above, at p. 51). However, where an act is of a general (i.e. legislative) nature, a private party may challenge it on the ground of misuse of powers only, which includes the concept of misuse of procedure

(Case 250/83 *Finsider* v. *Commission* [1985] ECR 131 at pp. 151, 154; Cases 32, 52, and 57/87 *ISA* v. *Commission* [1988] ECR 3305 at p. 3327). Moreover, the applicant must also be able to show, at least prima facie for the purposes of admissibility (ibid.), that it is 'affected' by, i.e. that it is the direct subject or the victim of, the misuse of powers alleged. This is a clear restriction imposed by the Treaty on the right of action of private parties as opposed to that of the Member States and of the Council. The latter may rely on any or all of the four grounds of action, irrespective of whether the challenged measure is individual or general in character. Clearly, the Treaty did not intend to grant private parties the right to initiate the review of the 'constitutionality' of general decisions, that is, their conformity with the Treaty, since they are in fact quasi-legislative acts (Case 8/55 *Fédération Charbonnière de Belgique* v. *HA* [1956] ECR 245 at pp. 257–9; Cases 55 to 59/63 etc. *Modena* v. *HA* [1964] ECR 211 at p. 228).

An action for annulment must be instituted by all parties within a period of one month. Where the Treaty provides for the publication of the challenged measure, as in the case of general decisions/recommendations, this period runs from the fifteenth day after publication thereof in the *Official Journal*. Where the Treaty provides for the notification of the measure, as in the case of individual decisions/recommendations, the period runs from the day following the receipt by the person concerned of the notification thereof. These time-limits are extended by various degrees on account of the applicant's distance from the seat of the ECJ (Art. 33(3) ECSC in conjunction with Art. 81 RP and Annex II to RP).

If an action is well founded, the ECJ will declare the challenged decision or recommendation to be void. Such a declaration (annulment) will have *erga omnes* (general) and *ex tunc* (retroactive) effects (Case 3/54 *ASSIDER* v. *HA* [1955] ECR 63 at p. 70; Case 5/55 *ASSIDER* v. *HA* [1955] ECR 135 at p. 146 *per* A.-G. Lagrange, interpreting the previous judgment. In both cases, the French original uses the term *erga omnes* which is rendered in the English translation as 'for all purposes'. For the meaning of this term, see below under the EEC Treaty). Where a particular provision is severable from the rest of the measure, partial annulment is possible (see e.g. Case 66/63 *Netherlands* v. *HA* [1964] ECR 533 at p. 546). Owing to the limited jurisdiction of the Court in annulment proceedings, the Court can neither replace nor amend (vary) the measure but must refer it back to the Commission, which is then required to take the necessary steps to comply with the judgment (Art. 34(1) ECSC). The Court may not indicate, still less prescribe, what particular measure the Commission should take (Case 30/59 *Steenkolenmijnen* v. *HA*, above, at p. 17). However, the Commission must, in appropriate circumstances, ensure equitable redress for any harm resulting directly from the measure declared void including, where necessary, the payment of appropriate damages (Art. 34(1) ECSC). If the Commission fails to take within a reasonable time the necessary steps to comply with the judgment, proceedings for damages may be instituted before the Court (Art. 34(2) ECSC).

2. **Under the EEC Treaty,** the general rules relating to the action for annulment are contained in Arts. 173, 174, and 176, to which Arts. 146, 147,

and 149 correspond verbatim in the **Euratom Treaty.** The following discussion is limited to the EEC provisions although everything said is, in principle, applicable to the Euratom Treaty also. It may be noted that, subject to the general conditions laid down in Art. 173 EEC, action for annulment may also be brought under Art. 180(b) and (c) EEC. Under Art. 180(b), any Member State, the Commission, or the Board of Directors of the European Investment Bank (EIB) may institute proceedings against 'measures adopted by the Board of Governors of the Bank'. It seems that only measures which are capable of producing legal effects *vis-à-vis* third parties and are susceptible of affecting the rights of the Commission may be challenged by the latter (Case 85/86 *Commission* v. *Board of Governors of the EIB* [1988] ECR 1281 at pp. 1316–17). The action must be brought against the Board of Governors as an organ of the Bank, and not against the Bank itself (ibid. at [1986] ECR 2215 at p. 2218). Under Art. 180(c), Member States and the Commission may, under certain specified conditions, institute proceedings against 'measures adopted by the Board of Directors of the Bank'.

Under the express provisions of Art. 173 EEC, an action for annulment may be brought by a Member State, the Council, the Commission, and by any natural or legal person; it may be brought against the Council or the Commission only (but not, for example, against the Court of Justice, see Case 91/76 *De Lacroix* v. *Court of Justice* [1977] ECR 225 at p. 229). The action must be directed against the particular institution which adopted the contested measure (see e.g. Case 100/74 *CAM* v. *Commission* [1975] ECR 1393 at p. 1418; Case 256/84 *Koyo Seiko* v. *Council and Commission* [1985] ECR 1351 at p. 1353).

Art. 173 does not expressly mention the European Parliament among the institutions whose measures may be challenged. The reason is that, in its original version, the EEC Treaty merely endowed the Parliament with powers of consultation and political control rather than with the power to adopt legally binding measures. The position has, however, changed as a result of the successive amendments of the Treaty whereby Parliament has acquired increased powers in areas such as the Community budget and the holding of direct elections. In these fields, it now has the power to adopt binding measures. In the light of these developments, in Case 294/83 *Les Verts* v. *Parliament* [1986] ECR 1339 at pp. 1365–6 the ECJ has held that an interpretation of Art. 173 which excluded the acts of Parliament from those which can be contested would lead to a result contrary to both the spirit and the system of the Treaty. In particular, the Court has pointed out that the EEC is a 'Community based on the rule of law, inasmuch as neither its Member States nor its institutions can avoid a review of the question whether the measures adopted by them are in conformity with the basic constitutional charter, the Treaty'. The general scheme of the Treaty is such as to make a direct action available against 'all measures adopted by the institutions . . . which are intended to have legal effects'. This must necessarily apply to the Parliament also, otherwise its measures could encroach on the powers of the Member States or of the other institutions, or exceed the limits of Parliament's powers, without the possibility of referring them to the Court for review. On the basis of these considerations, the Court has concluded that, in spite of the silence of Art. 173, 'an action for annulment may lie against measures adopted by the European Parliament intended to have legal effects vis-à-vis third parties', provided that the other conditions laid down in that Article are satisfied. As a result, political groupings have been able to challenge—and ultimately have annulled—decisions of various organs of Parliament concerning the reimbursement of election campaign expenses incurred in connection with the 1984 European elections (ibid. at pp. 1366–7), while the Council could contest and obtain the annulment of the general budget of the Communities for 1986 (Case 34/86 *Council* v. *Parliament* [1986] ECR 2155 at pp. 2201–3).

The question whether the European Parliament may appear not only as a defendant but also as an applicant before the Court under Art. 173 (*legitimation active*), i.e. whether it has *locus standi* to challenge acts of the Council and the Commission, was raised for the first time in Case 302/87 *Parliament* v. *Council* [1988] ECR. In that case, Parliament sought the annulment of Council Dec. 87/373 laying down the procedures for the exercise of implementing powers conferred on the Commission. In essence, Parliament argued that a right of action under Art. 173 was necessary (*a*) to maintain the institutional balance; (*b*) to enable it effectively to control the other institutions; (*c*) to enable it to defend its prerogatives against them; and (*d*) to complement its rights to challenge their inaction and to intervene in annulment proceedings instituted by others (which rights had already been recognized by the Court in previous cases). However, the ECJ did not accept these arguments. The Court held that (*a*) the scheme of the Treaties indicated that the Treaties did not intend to create a parallelism between the capacity to appear as a defendant and the right to appear as an applicant in annulment proceedings; the latter did not follow from the former; (*b*) Parliament's control over the other institutions was ensured by means other than the right to bring legal proceedings against them: Parliament exercised political control over the Commission under Arts. 143 and 144 EEC, and it was able to exert influence upon the Council in the legislative field through the consultation and co-operation procedures; (*c*) it was in the first place the Commission's responsibility under Art. 155 EEC to ensure that Parliament's prerogatives were respected; and (*d*) there were no necessary links between the action for annulment and the action for failure to act or the right to bring an action and the right to intervene. Moreover, the Court pointed out that when the Member States amended the EEC Treaty through the Single European Act of 1986, they deliberately made no change to Art. 173. Therefore, the Court concluded that the actual wording of Art. 173 did not enable the Court to recognize the *locus standi* of Parliament to bring an action for annulment under that provision (ibid. paras. 12–28).

As under the ECSC Treaty, the Member States, the Council, and the Commission are regarded as privileged applicants in that they enjoy an unqualified right of action, to be discussed further below. In contrast to the ECSC Treaty, however, the concept of the other parties ('natural or legal persons', hereinafter: private parties) is nowhere defined in the EEC Treaty.

25

The reference to 'any' such person justifies the broadest possible interpretation. Thus, in order to possess a right of action, it is not necessary for a natural person to be a national of, and/or resident in, a Member State; nor for a legal person to have been formed in accordance with the law of a Member State and/or to have its registered office, central administration, or principal place of business within the Community. Any natural or legal person who/which can satisfy the conditions of admissibility laid down in Art. 173(2), to be discussed further below, has *locus standi* to bring an action for annulment. The right of action of Community officials in staff cases is, however, subject to the special provisions of Arts. 90 and 91 of the Staff Regulations (Art. 179 EEC. *See further under* **Staff cases**).

Unlike the ECSC Treaty, the EEC Treaty does not specify by name the Community measures that can be the subject of an action for annulment (at least where the applicant is a Member State or an institution). Art. 173 only provides that 'The Court of Justice shall review the legality of acts of the Council and the Commission other than recommendations or opinions' (which are non-binding measures under Art. 189 EEC). In interpreting this provision, the ECJ has held that 'that remedy is available in order to ensure, as required by Article 164, that in the interpretation and application of the Treaty the law is observed, and it would be inconsistent with that objective to interpret restrictively the conditions under which the action is admissible by limiting its scope merely to the categories of measures referred to in Article 189 [i.e. regulations, directives, decisions]. In order to ascertain whether the measures in question are acts within the meaning of Article 173 it is necessary, therefore, to look to their substance. According to the consistent case-law of the Court any measure the legal effects of which are binding on, and capable of affecting the interests of, the applicant by bringing about a distinct change in his legal position is an act or decision which may be the subject of an action under Article 173 for a declaration that it is void. However, the form in which such acts or decisions are cast is, in principle, immaterial as regards the question whether they are open to challenge under that article. In the case of acts or decisions adopted by a procedure involving several stages, in particular where they are the culmination of an internal procedure, it is clear from the case-law that in principle an act is open to review only if it is a measure definitively laying down the position of the Commission or the Council on the conclusion of that procedure, and not a provisional measure intended to pave the way for the final decision' (Case 60/81 *IBM* v. *Commission* [1981] ECR 2639 at pp. 2651–2; see also Case 22/70 *Commission* v. *Council* [1971] ECR 263 at pp. 276–8—'ERTA' case). The fact that an act or decision is oral does not in principle preclude the possibility of its being the subject of an action for annulment (Cases 316/82 and 40/83 *Kohler* v. *Court of Auditors* [1984] ECR 641 at p. 656).

Apart from regulations, directives, and decisions proper within the meaning of Art. 189, the ECJ has so far declared the following measures to be challengeable acts or decisions under Art. 173:

(*a*) A 'notice' or 'communication' issued by the Commission rejecting a complaint made under Art. 3 of Reg. 17 seeking the establishment of an infringement of Art. 85 or 86 EEC, or discontinuing the procedure relating to such complaint, as being a 'final' or 'definitive' decision on the matter (Case 210/81 *Demo-Studio Schmidt* v. *Commission* [1983] ECR 3045 at pp. 3063–4; Case 298/83 *CICCE* v. *Commission* [1985] ECR 1105 at pp. 1122–3; etc. See also Case 26/76 *Metro* v. *Commission*, below).

(*b*) A 'communication' by which the Commission informs the applicant under Art. 5 of Reg. 3017/79 that an anti-subsidy proceeding would not be initiated against a non-Member State, as undertakings and associations injured by subsidization practices have a legitimate interest under that regulation in the initiation of protective action by the Community (Case 191/82 *FEDIOL* v. *Commission* [1983] ECR 2913 at pp. 2931–6).

(*c*) Communication by the Commission of confidential documents belonging to an undertaking to a third party who has made a complaint against that undertaking under Art. 3 of Reg. 17 (Case 53/85 *AKZO Chemie* v. *Commission* [1986] ECR 1965 at pp. 1989–90).

(*d*) A 'notice' sent by the Commission under Art. 15(6) of Reg. 17, bringing a provisional exemption from fines to an end, as being a measure constituting the culmination of a special procedure (Cases 8 to 11/66 *Cimenteries* v. *Commission* [1967] ECR 75 at pp. 91–3).

(*e*) 'Proceedings' of the Council regarding the negotiation and conclusion by the Member States of the European Road Transport Agreement, as being a measure designed to lay down a course of action binding on both the institutions and the Member States (Case 22/70 *Commission* v. *Council*, above).

(*f*) Refusal by the Commission to make a payment to which it had unilaterally committed itself previously, although an 'action for payment' as such is inadmissible (Case 44/81 *Germany* v. *Commission* [1982] ECR 1855 at pp. 1874–6).

(*g*) Measures adopted by organs of the European Parliament (which must be regarded as measures adopted by the Parliament itself) intended to have legal effects *vis-à-vis* third parties, such as decisions concerning the reimbursement of election campaign expenses incurred in connection with the European elections (Case 294/83 *Les Verts* v. *Parliament*, above, at pp. 1366–7), or the act of the President of the Parliament declaring that the Community budget has been finally adopted (Case 34/86 *Council* v. *Parliament*, above, at pp. 2201–2).

(*h*) A decision of the Commission which is based both on the EEC Treaty and on the ECSC Treaty since 'if the contested measure relates simultaneously and indivisibly to the spheres of more than one Treaty, an action is admissible to the extent to which the jurisdiction of the Court and the remedies provided for by the relevant provisions of one of the Treaties are applicable to the measure in question' (Case 222/83 *Municipality of Differdange* v. *Commission*, above, at p. 2895).

By contrast, the ECJ has found the following measures not to be open to review under Art. 173:

(*a*) Refusal by the Commission of a request by a private individual to

27

initiate an enforcement procedure against a Member State under Art. 169 EEC (Case 48/65 *Lütticke* v. *Commission* [1966] ECR 19 at p. 27).

(*b*) Refusal by the Commission to give 'advice' amounting to no more than a mere opinion within the meaning of Art. 189 (Case 15/70 *Chevalley* v. *Commission* [1970] ECR 975 at p. 980).

(*c*) A telex message sent by the Commission to a national intervention agency expressing a non-binding opinion (Case 133/79 *Sucrimex* v. *Commission* [1980] ECR 1299 at p. 1310).

(*d*) National laws and measures adopted by the authorities of the Member States (Case 46/81 *Benvenuto* [1981] ECR 809 at p. 810; Case 142/83 *Nevas* v. *Social Welfare Fund for Lawyers, Athens* [1983] ECR 2969 at pp. 2970–1).

(*e*) The initiation of a procedure by the Commission under Art. 3 of Reg. 17 and a statement of objections under Art. 2 of Reg. 99/63, concerning infringements of Art. 85 or 86 EEC by the applicant, as being purely interim procedural measures adopted preparatory to the decision representing the culmination of the procedure (Case 60/81 *IBM* v. *Commission*, above, at p. 2654).

(*f*) A letter sent by the Commission informing the applicant that it is not eligible to participate in invitations to tender under Art. 25 of Protocol No. 2 to the Lomé Convention of 1975 on financial and technical co-operation (Case 182/80 *Gauff* v. *Commission* [1982] ECR 799 at p. 817).

(*g*) A measure adopted by the Commission's representative approving or refusing to approve the award of public works contracts under Title VII of the Lomé Convention of 1979 (Case 126/83 *STS* v. *Commission* [1984] ECR 2769 at p. 2779; Case 118/83 *CMC* v. *Commission* [1985] ECR 2325 at pp. 2344–6).

(*h*) The adaptations to acts of the institutions set out in Annex I to the Act of Accession 1985, since they do not constitute acts of the Council but provisions of primary law, i.e. of the Act of Accession itself. By contrast, the adaptations adopted by the institutions in accordance with Art. 27 of the Act of Accession are subject to the general rules on the review of legality provided for in the Treaty (Cases 31 and 35/86 *LAISA* v. *Council* [1988] ECR 2285 at pp. 2317–19).

(*i*) Measures of the European Parliament and, generally speaking, measures of any institution which produce legal effects solely within that institution and create no rights and obligations for third parties (i.e. measures of internal organization) (Case 78/85 *Group of the European Right* v. *Parliament* [1986] ECR 1753 at p. 1757; Case 190/84 *Les Verts* v. *Parliament* [1988] ECR 1017 at p. 1035; Case 230/81 *Luxembourg* v. *Parliament*, above, at p. 302 *per* A.-G. Mancini).

The Member States (as well as the Council and the Commission) enjoy an unqualified right of action in that they may challenge any 'binding act' as defined by the Court above, including regulations, directives, and decisions within the meaning of Art. 189 (even where they unqualifiedly voted for their adoption in the Council, see Case 166/78 *Italy* v. *Council* [1979] ECR 2575 at p. 2596), whether addressed to them or to others and whether having any specific legal effect upon them or not. Their right of action is not conditional upon proof of an interest since the mere fact of an objective violation of the law establishes their interest in the matter (see e.g. Case 41/83 *Italy* v. *Commission* [1985] ECR 873 at p. 888; Case 45/86 *Commission* v. *Council* [1987] ECR 1493 at p. 1518).

By contrast, the *locus standi* of natural and legal persons is restricted in two ways. First, they may challenge only such acts of the Council and the Commission as fall within one of the following three categories:

(*a*) decision addressed to the applicant;
(*b*) decision addressed to another person;
(*c*) decision in the form of a regulation.

Secondly, if the act falls within the second or third category it is further necessary that it should be of 'direct and individual concern' to the applicant (Art. 173(2) EEC). As the ECJ has stated, the purpose of this requirement is to ensure that legal protection is also available to a person who, while not the person to whom the contested measure is addressed, is in fact affected by it in the same way as is the addressee (Case 222/83 *Municipality of Differdange* v. *Commission*, above, at p. 2896). It follows from the case-law of the ECJ discussed above that the term 'decision' must be taken to include not only measures having the title of 'decision' within the meaning of Art. 189, but also any other 'act' capable of producing legal effects upon the applicant, including acts of the European Parliament. The ECJ examines in the context of admissibility whether the above-mentioned requirements have been fulfilled.

The admissibility of actions for the annulment of decisions addressed to the applicant normally raises no problem. By contrast, in actions challenging decisions addressed to another person, who may be either another natural or legal person or a Member State (see Case 25/62 *Plaumann* v. *Commission* [1963] ECR 95 at pp. 106–7), the requirement that the applicant must prove that he is 'directly and individually' concerned by such a decision presents a difficult, often insurmountable, obstacle. Owing to a restrictive interpretation by the ECJ of the concept of 'direct and individual concern', only a minority of such actions has been found admissible so far (see below).

However, in its more recent case-law the Court has considerably relaxed the strict requirements of admissibility in respect of at least the following categories of cases involving decisions addressed to others: competition, State aid, anti-subsidy, and anti-dumping proceedings (the latter involve regulations rather than decisions addressed to others and are further considered below). Thus, in a series of cases, listed individually under (*c*), (*e*) and (*h*) below, the Court has held that 'where a regulation accords applicant undertakings procedural guarantees entitling them to request the Commission to find an infringement of Community rules, those undertakings should be able to institute proceedings [before the Court] in order to protect their legitimate interests' (Case 169/84 *COFAZ* v. *Commission* [1986] ECR 391 at p. 414; see also the opinion of A.-G. Verloren van Themaat at pp. 395 *et seq.*). In particular, the Court has stressed the importance of the part played by the applicant in these cases in the administrative procedure before the Commission preceding the adoption of the final decision. Thus, the Court has accepted the

29

following as evidence of direct and individual concern: the fact that the applicant was at the origin of the complaint which led to the opening of the investigation procedure; the fact that its views were heard during that procedure; and the fact that the conduct of the procedure was largely determined by its observations (ibid. at p. 415). Therefore, while the Court still continues to apply a strict interpretation of the concept of direct and individual concern in general (*see under* **Direct concern, Individual concern**), in these four types of proceedings, at least, its overriding consideration seems to be to afford effective procedural guarantees and legal protection to all applicants who can establish a sufficiently important legitimate interest in the matter deserving such protection.

The following is a chronological list of cases or categories of cases in which the Court has so far admitted applications for the annulment of decisions addressed to others:

(*a*) Cases 106 and 107/63 *Toepfer* v. *Commission* [1965] ECR 405 at pp. 410–12, where German importers successfully challenged a Commission decision addressed to Germany and retroactively authorizing it, under the relevant agricultural regulations, to retain certain protective measures imposed on the importation of maize and other cereals from France.

(*b*) Case 62/70 *Bock* v. *Commission* [1971] ECR 897 at pp. 907–8 and Case 29/75 *Kaufhof* v. *Commission* [1976] ECR 431 at pp. 41 *et seq.*, where German importers successfully challenged Commission decisions addressed to Germany under Art. 115 EEC and authorizing it, as a protective measure, to exclude from Community treatment certain products originating in a third country and put into free circulation in the other Member States (see also Case 59/84 *Tezi* v. *Commission* [1986] ECR 887 and Case 11/82 *Piraiki-Patraiki* v. *Commission* [1985] ECR 207 at pp. 241–6, where the protective measures were authorized by the Commission under Art. 130 of the Act of Accession 1979).

(*c*) Case 26/76 *Metro* v. *Commission* [1977] ECR 1875 at pp. 1898–901, where the Court found admissible, although not well founded, an application for the annulment of a Commission decision addressed to another undertaking and granting it exemption under Art. 85(3) EEC in respect of a selective distribution system. The contested decision was adopted as the result of a complaint submitted by the applicant, and the Court held at p. 1901 that 'it is in the interests of a satisfactory administration of justice and of the proper application of Articles 85 and 86 that natural or legal persons who are entitled, pursuant to Article 3(2)(b) of Regulation No. 17, to request the Commission to find an infringement of Articles 85 and 86 should be able, if their request is not complied with either wholly or in part, to institute proceedings in order to protect their legitimate interests'. (See also Case 210/81 *Demo-Studio Schmidt* v. *Commission*, above, and Case 75/84 *Metro* v. *Commission* [1986] ECR 3021 at pp. 3079–80.)

(d) Case 92/78 *Simmenthal* v. *Commission* [1979] ECR 777 at pp. 797–8, where an Italian producer of corned beef successfully challenged a Commission decision addressed to the Member States, fixing the minimum selling prices for frozen beef put up for sale by the intervention agencies.

(e) Case 730/79 *Philip Morris* v. *Commission* [1980] ECR 2671 at p. 2687, where the Court found admissible, although not well founded, an application for the annulment of a Commission decision addressed to the Netherlands, declaring a proposed investment aid to be incompatible with the Common Market under Arts. 92 to 94 EEC. The applicant, a tobacco manufacturer in the Netherlands, would have been the recipient of the aid. Subsequently, the Court accepted that Commission decisions addressed to Member States under Arts. 92–3 EEC concerning State aid were challengeable (i) by the recipients of the aid (Case 323/82 *Intermills* v. *Commission* [1984] ECR 3809 at p. 3824; Cases 296 and 318/82 *Netherlands and Leeuwarder Papierwarenfabriek* v. *Commission* [1985] ECR 809 at p. 821, etc.); (ii) by their competitors, provided that they played a part in the procedure and that their position on the market was significantly affected by the aid (Case 169/84 *COFAZ* v. *Commission*, above, at p. 415) and (iii) by their representative organization which played a part in the procedure under Art. 93 (Cases 67, 68, and 70/85 *Van der Kooy* v. *Commission* [1988] ECR 219 at pp. 268–9).

(f) Case 135/81 *Groupement des Agences de Voyages* v. *Commission* [1982] ECR 3799 at p. 3809, where the Court held that a Commission decision to accept a tender submitted by a company in competition with one of the applicants 'may . . . be regarded as having caused "direct and individual" injury to the [applicant] association . . . since if the association could submit a tender . . . it obviously had an interest in having its tender accepted'. However, the action was dismissed as being out of time.

(g) Case 294/81 *Control Data* v. *Commission* [1983] ECR 911 at p. 927, where the applicant successfully challenged a Commission decision addressed to the Member States establishing that computers of certain types may not be imported into the EEC free of CCT duties. The decision was adopted as a result of an application for import submitted by the applicant.

(h) Case 191/82 *FEDIOL* v. *Commission*, above, at pp. 2935–6, where the Court recognized that undertakings which lodged a complaint with the Commission under Art. 5 of Reg. 3017/79 asking it to initiate an anti-subsidy proceeding against a non-Member State have the right to bring an action before the Court for a review as to whether the Commission had observed the procedural guarantees granted to complainants by the regulation. (See also Case 187/85 *FEDIOL* v. *Commission* [1988] ECR para. 6 and Case 188/85 *FEDIOL* v. *Commission* [1988] ECR para. 6, both concerning complaints lodged under Art. 5 of Reg. 2176/84.)

(i) Case 283/82 *Schoellershammer* v. *Commission* [1983] ECR 4219 at p. 4226, where the Court, without at all considering the question of admissibility, declared void a Commission decision addressed to Germany and establishing that the repayment of import duties in the applicant's case was not justified. On the question of admissibility, see the opinion of A.-G. Mancini at p. 4228. (See also Cases 98 and 230/83 *Van Gend & Loos* v. *Commission* [1984] ECR 3763, especially the opinion of A.-G. Mancini at p. 3783; Case 160/84 *Oryzomyli Kavallas* v. *Commission* [1986] ECR 1633; and Case 148/87 *Pedersen* v. *Commission* [1988] ECR.)

31

(*j*) Cases 228 and 229/82 *Ford* v. *Commission* [1984] ECR 1129 at p. 1159, where the Court held that a Commission decision relating to a proceeding under Art. 85 EEC and addressed solely to Ford AG was of direct and individual concern to Ford of Europe, both companies being the subsidiaries of Ford Motor Company. The Court annulled the decision.

(*k*) Case 294/83 *Les Verts* v. *Parliament*, above, at pp. 1367–9, where the Court accepted that certain decisions of organs of the European Parliament granting aid to rival political groupings in connection with the 1984 European elections were of direct and individual concern to the applicant, itself a political grouping. The Court annulled the decisions.

(*l*) Case 297/86 *CIDA* v. *Council* [1988] ECR 3531 at p. 3553, where the Court ruled that a decision of the Council appointing the members of the Economic and Social Committee could be challenged by candidates who were nominated by a Member State but not appointed by the Council.

While an act which qualifies as a decision is open to challenge by private parties, one which constitutes a genuine regulation is not. Thus, the line drawn between decisions and regulations basically determines the extent to which natural and legal persons enjoy judicial protection under Art. 173 EEC. The narrower the scope of the concept of a decision the more restrictive that protection. Nevertheless, Art. 173(2) entitles private individuals to contest a decision which is 'in the form of a regulation'. The ECJ has held that 'the objective of that provision is in particular to prevent the Community institutions from being in a position, merely by choosing the form of a regulation, to exclude an application by an individual against a decision which concerns him directly and individually; it therefore stipulates that the choice of form cannot change the nature of the measure' (Cases 789 and 790/79 *Calpak* v. *Commission* [1980] ECR 1949 at p. 1961; Case 162/78 *Wagner* v. *Commission* [1979] ECR 3467 at pp. 3486–7; etc.). However, the Court has rejected attempts by private parties to interpret that provision so that the term 'decision' could also cover genuine 'regulations'. The Court has said that 'such a wide interpretation conflicts with the fact that Article 189 makes a clear distinction between the concept of a "decision" and that of a "regulation". It is inconceivable that the term "decision" would be used in Article 173 in a different sense from the technical sense as defined in Article 189' (Cases 16 and 17/62 *Producteurs de Fruits* v. *Council* [1962] ECR 471 at p. 478).

In considering whether an act is a decision or a regulation the Court uses one or both of two tests. The first is to uncover the true *legal nature* of the act in question in the light of the abstract definitions given in Art. 189 of decisions and regulations and by taking into account its object and content, not merely its official title. The main criterion for the distinction lies in the individual or general application of the act. Broadly speaking, an act will be a decision (and thus open to challenge) if it is essentially of an administrative (individual) nature, i.e. governs an individual legal relationship and applies to a limited number of defined or identifiable persons. On the other hand, an act will be a regulation (and thus excluded from challenge) if it is essentially of a legislative (normative) nature, i.e. applies to 'categories of persons viewed abstractly and in their entirety' (ibid.). Thus, the Court has defined a regulation as 'a measure which is applicable to objectively determined situations and which involves immediate legal consequences in all Member States for categories of persons viewed in a general and abstract manner' (ibid. at p. 479). 'Moreover, a measure does not lose its character as a regulation simply because it may be possible to ascertain with a greater or lesser degree of accuracy the number or even the identity of the persons to which it applies at any given time as long as there is no doubt that the measure is applicable as the result of an objective situation of law or of fact which it specifies and which is in harmony with its ultimate objective. Furthermore, the fact that a legal provision may have different practical effects on the different persons to whom it applies in no way contradicts its nature as a regulation provided that the situation to which it refers is objectively determined' (Case 6/68 *Zuckerfabrik Watenstedt* v. *Council* [1968] ECR 409 at p. 415. The Court has repeated these definitions in a number of subsequent cases, may of which are cited below. *See also under* **Decision, Regulation**).

The second test is to examine the *legal effects* of the act in order to ascertain whether it concerns the applicant directly and individually. Where it so concerns him, it will be regarded as an actionable decision as in the Court's opinion the aim of Art. 173(2) is 'to ensure the legal protection of individuals in all cases in which they are directly and individually concerned by a Community measure—in whatever form it appears—which is not addressed to them' (Case 69/69 *Alcan* v. *Commission* [1970] ECR 385 at p. 393; Case 160/88R *FEDESA* v. *Council* [1988] ECR para. 25). Thus, 'if a measure entitled by its author a regulation contains provisions which are capable of being not only of direct but also of individual concern to certain natural or legal persons, it must be admitted, without prejudice to the question whether that measure considered in its entirety can be correctly called a regulation, that in any case those provisions do not have the character of a regulation and may therefore be impugned by those persons under the terms of the second paragraph of Article 173' (Cases 16 and 17/62 *Producteurs de Fruits* v. *Council*, above, at p. 479. See also the cases listed below).

In principle, it woud appear necessary to use both tests simultaneously or, more precisely, to use the second test only after the first has been satisfied and the provision in question found to be a decision by its nature. However, the ECJ has not been entirely consistent in this matter. It has not always examined whether an act is, *by its legal nature*, a regulation or a decision. In practice, the Court has often determined the nature of an act in the light of its *legal effects*, i.e. whether it concerns the applicant directly and individually, rather than by using the abstract definition of a regulation as a measure of general application (see e.g. Case 40/64 *Sgarlata* v. *Commission* [1965] ECR 215 at p. 226; Cases 41 to 44/70 *International Fruit Company* v. *Commission* [1971] ECR 411 at pp. 421–2; Case 72/74 *Union Syndicale* v. *Council* [1975] ECR 401 at p. 409). In its more recent case-law, however, the Court usually applies the formula that 'it is . . . necessary to appraise the nature of the contested measure and in particular the legal effects which it is intended to produce or in fact produces' (see e.g. Case 147/83 *Binderer* v. *Commission*

33

[1985] ECR 257 at pp. 270–1; Case 26/86 *Deutz und Geldermann* v. *Council* [1987] ECR 941 at p. 951).

In the light of these two tests, a binding Community act or an individual provision of it should in theory always be capable of being classified either as a decision or as a regulation. The same measure cannot, in principle, be both a decision and a regulation (Cases 16 and 17/62 *Producteurs de Fruits* v. *Council*, above, at p. 484 *per* A.-G. Lagrange; Case 45/81 *Moksel* v. *Commission* [1982] ECR 1129 at p. 1144). Nevertheless, there are instances in the case-law which seem to contradict this principle. Thus, in Case 264/82 *Timex* v. *Council and Commission* [1985] ECR 849 at pp. 865–6 the Court held that a regulation imposing a definitive anti-dumping duty was 'legislative in nature and scope', inasmuch as it applied to 'traders in general', yet at the same time it constituted a decision which was of direct and individual concern to the applicant who was 'one of those traders' (see further below under point (*d*)).

In practice, moreover, difficulties often arise on account of the existence of certain intermediate or mixed forms, borderline cases between individual and general acts, which do not easily admit of classification. (See e.g. Case 6/68 *Zuckerfabrik Watenstedt* v. *Council*, above, where A.-G. Roemer expressed the opinion at pp. 417 *et seq.* that the contested act was a challengeable decision in the form of a regulation, while the Court held at pp. 414–15 that it was in fact a regulation and dismissed the action as inadmissible. Compare this with Case 100/74 *CAM* v. *Commission*, above, where, conversely, A.-G. Warner was of the opinion at pp. 1406 *et seq.* that the challenged measure was a regulation and that accordingly the action should be held inadmissible, while the Court recognized at pp. 1401–3 that it was a decision and held the application admissible. See under point (*b*) below.) In the absence of a third category, such intermediate acts often fall to be classified as regulations although they may be in the nature of a 'general decision' or a 'regulation for a particular case', i.e. may have effects analogous to those of a decision rather than possessing a normative character. The reason why they are likely to be classified as regulations is that the Court ultimately uses one basic criterion only to distinguish a decision from a regulation (and this follows from the Court's restrictive interpretation of the concepts of 'direct' and, particularly, 'individual' concern): i.e. the class of persons affected. Thus, the Court classifies as individual decisions only those measures for which the number of addressees is objectively and unalterably fixed at the time when the measure is adopted and, conversely, classifies as regulations or normative acts all those measures for which the number of persons affected cannot be determined at that moment because it may vary during the period of validity of the measure (*see further under* **Individual concern**).

Such a narrow interpretation of the concept of a decision has been criticized on the ground that it does not pay heed to the basic constitutional principle of a comprehensive judicial protection. While the Court has recognized that the system established by the EEC Treaty lays down more restrictive conditions than the ECSC Treaty for the admissibility of applications for annulment by private individuals, it has not been prepared to admit that its own interpretation of the respective concepts of a decision and of a regulation is more restrictive of individual rights than warranted by the text of the Treaty. It has been unwilling to widen that interpretation lest the concept of a decision be enlarged to such an extent as to endanger the system of remedies created by the Treaty which, in the Court's opinion, permits individuals to apply for the annulment only of specific decisions addressed to them or of measures which affect them in an analogous manner (see e.g. Cases 16 and 17/62 *Producteurs de Fruits* v. *Council*, above, at pp. 478–80; Case 40/64 *Sgarlata* v. *Commission*, above, at p. 227; Case 6/68 *Zuckerfabrik Watenstedt* v. *Council*, above, at p. 415; Case 101/76 *Koninklijke Scholten-Honig* v. *Council and Commission* [1977] ECR 797 at p. 808). In general, the Court still adheres to the above principles (from the more recent case-law, see e.g. Case 147/83 *Binderer* v. *Commission*, above; Case 26/86 *Deutz und Geldermann* v. *Council*, above, at pp. 951–2), and has been willing to relax the strict conditions of admissibility only in respect of regulations imposing anti-dumping duties (see below under point (*d*)). As a result, the Court has so far declared admissible applications by private parties for the annulment of regulations in a relatively small number of cases. These are listed below in chronological order:

(*a*) Cases 41 to 44/70 *International Fruit Company* v. *Commission*, above, at pp. 420–3, where the Court found admissible, although unfounded, applications for the annulment of a Commission regulation refusing to issue import licences for dessert apples coming from third countries. The Court held that the contested measure was not a provision of general application but a 'conglomeration of individual decisions' taken under the guise of a regulation since when it was adopted the number of applications for import licences which could be affected by it was unalterably fixed. Similarly, in Cases 87/77 etc. *Salerno* v. *Commission and Council* [1985] ECR 2523 at pp. 2534–5 the Court found that the contested regulation, which provided for the recruitment of 56 officials mentioned by name, was not a measure of general application but a series of decisions concerning each official individually, and declared the action admissible.

(*b*) Case 100/74 *CAM* v. *Commission*, above, at pp. 1401–3, where the Court found admissible, although unfounded, an application for the annulment of a Commission regulation providing that exports of cereals in respect of which the advance-fixing certificate was dated prior to 7 October 1974 should not benefit from an exceptional increase in the threshold price. The Court held that the contested regulation applied to a fixed and known number of cereal exporters, of whom the applicant was one, identified by the fact that they had applied for advance fixing during a particular period prior to the adoption of the regulation. They were therefore directly and individually concerned by it.

(*c*) Case 88/76 *Exportation des Sucres* v. *Commission* [1977] ECR 709 at pp. 725–6 and Case 112/77 *Töpfer* v. *Commission* [1978] ECR 1019 at p. 1030, where the Court held that provisions of agricultural regulations referring to a clearly defined category of export licences, namely those issued before a certain date and still valid on a certain date, both being prior to the

35

adoption of the provisions, amounted in substance to a decision in respect of the holders of such export licences.

(*d*) Case 113/77 *Toyo Bearing* v. *Council* [1979] ECR 1185 at pp. 1203–5 and four other cases, ibid. at pp. 1277, 1303, 1337, 1363 ('Japanese Ball Bearing' cases), where certain Japanese companies and their European subsidiaries successfully challenged a Council regulation concerning the imposition of anti-dumping duties on ball bearings originating in Japan. The Court held that the regulation in fact constituted a decision adopted in the form of a regulation as it applied only to the four major Japanese producers named in it, to their subsidiaries, and exclusive importers. In Cases 239 and 275/82 *Allied Corporation* v. *Commission* [1984] ECR 1005 at pp. 1030–1 the Court stated in general terms that regulations 'imposing anti-dumping duties are liable to be of direct and individual concern to those producers and exporters who are able to establish that they were identified in the measures adopted by the Commission or the Council or were concerned by the preliminary investigations'. On the other hand, the position is different in the case of independent importers established in the Member States who, in contrast to exporters, are not expressly named in the regulations and are consequently not concerned directly and individually by them. Such importers may not challenge the regulations before the ECJ directly, although they may contest before the national courts individual measures taken by the national authorities in application of the regulations, requiring them to pay anti-dumping duties. In the context of these proceedings, they may indirectly contest the regulations by means of a reference for a preliminary ruling (see also Case 307/81 *Alusuisse* v. *Council and Commission* [1982] ECR 3463 at pp. 3472–3, rejecting an application brought by an importer. The Court followed its ruling given in the first *Allied Corporation* case in Case 53/83 *Allied Corporation* v. *Council* [1985] ECR 1621 at p. 1656 and in five cases beginning with Case 240/84 *Toyo Bearing* v. *Council* [1987] ECR 1809 at p. 1851). In Case 264/82 *Timex* v. *Council and Commission*, above, at pp. 864–6 the Court went further by recognizing that regulations imposing anti-dumping duties may be of direct and individual concern not only to producers and exporters but also to manufacturers and traders within the Community, even if they are not mentioned by name in the regulations, provided that they played a part in the anti-dumping proceedings (e.g. by lodging the complaint which gave rise to the proceedings and by expressing a view during the proceedings) and that their position on the market was taken into account in fixing the duty. Finally, referring to the first *Allied Corporation* case, above, the Court established that importers associated with exporters may also challenge a regulation imposing an anti-dumping duty, particularly where the export price has been calculated on the basis of their selling prices on the Community market (Cases 277 and 300/85 *Canon* v. *Council* [1988] ECR para. 8; this was one of six sets of anti-dumping cases decided on the same day; in the others the question of admissibility was not raised).

(*e*) Case 138/79 *Roquette* v. *Council* [1980] ECR 3333 at pp. 3355–6; Case 139/79 *Maizena* v. *Council* [1980] ECR 3393 at pp. 3418–19, where a French and a German company manufacturing *inter alia* isoglucose successfully challenged a Council regulation fixing production quotas for isoglucose in respect of the applicants, who were therefore both directly and individually concerned by it.

(*f*) Case 232/81 *Agricola Commerciale Olio* v. *Commission* [1984] ECR 3881 at pp. 3895–6; Case 264/81 *Savma* v. *Commission* [1984] ECR 3915 at p. 3932, where the Court declared void Commission regulations repealing, with retroactive effect, an earlier regulation on the sale by tender of olive oil held by the Italian intervention agency, and reopening the sale.

Although Art. 173(2) makes no reference to directives, it does not necessarily follow from this that directives may never be challenged by natural or legal persons. Thus, in Case 160/88R *FEDESA* v. *Council*, above, paras. 25–30, where an association and two companies sought the suspension of the operation of a Council directive, the Court, referring to its earlier case-law, found it necessary to examine whether the directive in question was, by its nature, a measure of general application. In so doing, the Court used exactly the same test as in the case of regulations. Only when the Court was satisfied that the directive produced, through the national legislation adopted for its implementation, genuine legislative effects, did it dismiss the application for interim measures. It would seem to follow from this that where a directive is, in reality, a 'decision in the form of a directive', it may be challenged by private parties who can prove that they are directly and individually concerned by it.

An action for annulment brought by any applicant, whether Member State, institution, or private party, must be based on one or more of the four grounds of action which are the same as under the ECSC Treaty, i.e. lack of competence, infringement of an essential procedural requirement, infringement of the Treaty or of any rule of law relating to its application, and misuse of powers (*see further under* **Grounds of action**).

The action must be instituted by all parties within a period of two months. Where the Treaty provides for the publication of the challenged measure, as in the case of regulations, this period runs from the fifteenth day after publication thereof in the *Official Journal*. Where the Treaty provides for the notification of the measure, as in the case of directives and decisions, the period runs from the day following the receipt by the applicant of the notification thereof. In the absence of notification to the applicant, the time-limit runs from the day on which the measure came to the knowledge of the latter (see e.g. Case 59/84 *Tezi* v. *Commission*, above, at p. 919; Case 236/86 *Dillinger Hüttenwerke* v. *Commission*, above, paras. 14–15). These time-limits are extended by various degrees on account of the applicant's distance from the seat of the ECJ (Art. 173(3) EEC in conjunction with Art. 81 RP and Annex II to RP).

If an action is well founded, the ECJ will declare the act concerned to be void (Art. 174(1) EEC). Such a declaration (annulment) will have *erga omnes* (general) and *ex tunc* (retroactive) effects (see e.g. Case 50/69R *Germany* v. *Commission* [1969] ECR 449 at p. 455 *per* A.-G. Gand; Cases 9 and 11/71 *Compagnie d'Approvisionnement* v. *Commission* [1972] ECR 391 at p. 411 *per* A.-G. Dutheillet de Lamothe). By virtue of the *erga omnes* effect, everyone, i.e. the Member States, the institutions, and private individuals,

37

must regard the act concerned as null and void, definitively and for all purposes. The question of validity may not be raised again in any legal proceedings. By virtue of the *ex tunc* effect, the act is annulled, not from the date of the judgment, but from the date on which it entered into force, i.e. *ab initio* (see e.g. Cases 97/86 etc. *Asteris* v. *Commission* [1988] ECR 2181 at p. 2209). It must, accordingly, be regarded as if it had never existed in law and the parties to the dispute must be restored to their original legal position (*restitutio in integrum*) (see Case 22/70 *Commission* v. *Council*, above, at pp. 278–9). Moreover, if the act is of the law-making type, all further implementing measures adopted under it, whether general or individual, must also be regarded as being null and void, since they are rendered without legal basis by the judgment.

In order to mitigate the far-reaching and sometimes unpredictable consequences of annulment, in the case of a regulation the ECJ has been authorized to state, if it considers this necessary, which of the effects of the regulation which it has declared void shall be considered as definitive (Art. 174(2) EEC). This provision enables the Court: (*a*) to restrict the retroactive effect of annulment 'in the interest of the uniform application of Community law throughout the Community' and for 'important reasons of legal certainty' (see Case 112/83 *Produits de Maïs* [1985] ECR 719 at p. 747; Case 34/86 *Council* v. *Parliament*, above, at p. 2212); (*b*) to restrict the *erga omnes* effect of annulment for reasons of legal certainty and to protect acquired rights, even where the annulled act is not a regulation but a decision affecting persons other than the applicant as well (Case 92/78 *Simmenthal* v. *Commission* [1979] ECR 777 at pp. 811–12, where the Court annulled a decision 'in so far as the decision affects the applicant'); and (*c*) to maintain the effects of the annulled regulation until such time as the relevant institution has replaced it by a new one so as to avoid discontinuity of its operation during the interim period (see Case 81/72 *Commission* v. *Council* [1973] ECR 575 at p. 586; Case 264/82 *Timex* v. *Council and Commission*, above, at pp. 870–1). Where a particular provision is severable from the rest of the measure, partial annulment is possible and is particularly justified where the measure, taken as a whole, is favourable to the interests of the applicant (Case 17/74 *Transocean Marine Paint Association* v. *Commission* [1974] ECR 1063 at p. 1081).

Owing to the limited jurisdiction of the ECJ in annulment proceedings, the Court can neither replace nor amend (vary) the annulled act but must refer it back to the relevant institution, which is then required to take the necessary measures to comply with the judgment of the Court (Art. 176(1) EEC). The Court may not indicate, still less prescribe, what particular measure the institution should take (see e.g. Case 53/85 *AKZO Chemie* v. *Commission*, above, at p. 1990). Although the Council or the Commission thus retains a certain margin of discretion, it must reconsider the situation in the light of the judgment, and adopt a new measure with due regard not only to the operative part but also to the relevant decisive grounds of the judgment (Case 92/78 *Simmenthal* v. *Commission*, above, at pp. 811–12; Cases 97/86 etc. *Asteris* v. *Commission*, above, at p. 2208). Where the ground for annulment is a formal or procedural defect (e.g. lack of reasoning, failure to consult the consultative bodies or to hear interested parties) the institution may reinstate—in certain circumstances even with retroactive effect—the annulled measure after having rectified the defect (Case 114/81 *Tunnel Refineries* v. *Council* [1982] ECR 3189 at pp. 3208–10; Case 347/82 *Alvarez* v. *Parliament* [1984] ECR 1847 at pp. 1854–5). The measures taken by the institution are subject to renewed judicial review in the framework of a possible further action for annulment (see e.g. Case 30/76 *Küster* v. *Parliament* [1976] ECR 1719 at p. 1725). A failure of the institution to take the necessary steps within a reasonable time may be brought before the Court, in appropriate cases, by means of an action for failure to act. Under the EEC Treaty, the obligation to comply with the Court's judgment implies full *restitutio in integrum* (Case 4/69 *Lütticke* v. *Commission* [1971] ECR 325 at p. 343 *per* A.-G. Dutheillet de Lamothe), but does not include an obligation to make good any damage caused by the annulled act. Such damage may be recovered by means of a separate action under Arts. 178 and 215(2) EEC (Art. 176(2) EEC). Although the duty to give effect to the Court's judgment is imposed only on the institution whose act has been declared void, the *erga omnes* effect of annulment may require also third parties to take appropriate actions. Thus, the annulment of a regulation, directive, or decision may entail for the Member States the obligation no longer to apply any measures adopted by them in implementation thereof, and even to repeal such measures formally in the interests of legal certainty. These implementing measures, having lost their legal foundation, must be regarded as illegal.

See also Association*, Decision, Direct concern, Directive, *Erga omnes* effect, *Ex tunc* effect, General decision, Grounds of action, Individual concern, Individual decision, Interest to sue, Judicial review, Limited jurisdiction, Notification, Opinion, Plea of illegality, Publication, Reasoned decision, Reasoned opinion, Recommendation, Regulation, *Restitutio in integrum*, Retroactive effect, Right of action, Staff cases, Undertaking*.

Further reading 1. BOOKS: Bebr, *Development of Judicial Control of the European Communities* (1981), ch. 2; Hartley, *The Foundations of European Community Law*, 2nd edn. (1988), part IV; Schermers, *Judicial Protection in the European Communities*, 4th edn. (1987), ch. 2; Toth, *Legal Protection of Individuals in the European Communities* (1978), vol. ii, ch. 5.

2. ARTICLES AND PAPERS: Dinnage, 'Locus Standi and Article 173 EEC' (1979) 4 *EL Rev.* 15; Editorial, 'The Greens Scale the Barrier of Article 173 EEC' (1986) 11 *EL Rev.* 189; id., 'The AKZO Case: A Boost to Due Process' (1986) 11 *EL Rev.* 245; Greaves, 'Locus Standi under Article 173 EEC when Seeking Annulment of a Regulation' (1986) 11 *EL Rev.* 119; Harding, 'Decisions Addressed to Member States and Article 173 of the Treaty of Rome' (1976) 25 *ICLQ* 15; id., 'The Private Interest in Challenging Community Action' (1980) 5 *EL Rev.* 354; id., 'The Review of EEC Regulations and Decisions' (1982) 19 *CML Rev.* 311; Lauwaars, 'The Admissibility of the Action for Annulment: The IBM Case', in O'Keeffe and Schermers (eds.), *Essays in European Law and Integration* (1982), p. 29; Rasmussen, 'Why is Article 173 Interpreted against Private Plaintiffs?' (1980) 5 *EL Rev.* 122; Schermers, 'The Law as it Stands on the Appeal for Annulment' (1975/2) *LIEI* 95; Stein and Vining, 'Citizen Access to Judicial Review of Administrative Action in a Transnational and

Federal Context' (1976) 70 *AJIL* 219; also in Jacobs (ed.), *European Law and the Individual* (1976), p. 113; Toth, 'The Individual and European Law' (1975) 24 *ICLQ* 659; van Gerven, 'The Legal Protection of Private Parties in the Law of the European Economic Community', in Jacobs (ed.), *European Law and the Individual* (1976), p. 1.

▶ **ACTION FOR DAMAGES** Direct action brought before the ECJ for the purpose of obtaining compensation for damage caused by the institutions or by the servants of the Communities in the performance of their duties, other than damage arising from a breach of contract. The legal basis for the action is the non-contractual liability of the Communities for wrongful acts or omissions, as laid down in the Treaties.

Although the actual texts of the relevant provisions of the ECSC Treaty (Art. 40) and of the EEC/Euratom Treaties (Arts. 178 and 215(2) EEC; 151 and 188(2) Euratom) differ, the action for damages is subject to broadly similar conditions under all three Treaties. In distinguishing between this form of action and proceedings concerning judicial review of the legality of the institutions' conduct (i.e. actions for annulment and actions for failure to act), in a consistent line of decisions the ECJ has held that the action for damages constitutes an independent (autonomous) form of action which has its own special function in the system of remedies created by the Treaties and is subject to conditions designed to suit its own particular purpose. It is based on a type of jurisdiction which is clearly different from that which the Court exercises in actions for judicial review. It is distinguished from annulment and default proceedings by reason of its aim, grounds, and effects. Its aim is not to contest the objective legality of the institutions' conduct and to bring about the annulment of an illegal act or the adoption of a particular measure, but to establish subjective rights to financial compensation for actual losses sustained. Its grounds are not the four grounds of action on which the annulment of a measure may be sought, but the existence of a wrongful act or omission, i.e. an official fault, on the part of the institutions or their servants committed in the performance of their duties. Its effects do not extend so far as to allow a direct control of the activities of the institutions through the annulment, with *erga omnes* and retroactive effect, of a measure or through the establishment of an obligation to take a measure, but are restricted to the payment of specified damages, i.e. an act affecting the applicant alone. The jurisdiction of the Court in actions for judicial review is strictly limited; in actions for damages it is plenary or unlimited (see in particular Cases 9 and 12/60 *Vloeberghs* v. *HA* [1961] ECR 197 at pp. 213–14 *per Curiam*, p. 226 *per* A.-G. Roemer; Case 4/69 *Lütticke* v. *Commission* [1971] ECR 325 at p. 336; Case 5/71 *Zuckerfabrik Schöppenstedt* v. *Council* [1971] ECR 975 at p. 983; Case 153/73 *Holtz & Willemsen* v. *Council and Commission* [1974] ECR 675 at p. 692; Cases 197 to 200/80 etc. *Ludwigshafener Walzmühle* v. *Council and Commission* [1981] ECR 3211 at p. 3243; etc.).

It follows from its autonomous nature that the action for damages is not in principle subsidiary to the two actions involving judicial review. Consequently, the various restrictions as to admissibility imposed by the Treaties upon private individuals in the context of the latter are not applicable to it. This has the important consequence that even though an action for damages is usually founded on the illegality of a formal, binding act or of a failure to act, this does not in itself require the prior establishment of such illegality by means of separate proceedings, available under much stricter conditions, such as an action for annulment or for failure to act or a reference for a preliminary ruling. Rather, the ECJ has the necessary power to examine as an incidental matter within the framework of an action for damages the legality of the conduct alleged to have caused the damage. Even the fact that in certain special circumstances an action for damages could bring about a financial result identical or similar to that which a successful action for annulment or for failure to act could produce (e.g. fixing of new prices for agricultural products, payment of refunds), and thus enable private persons to achieve an aim which they could not have achieved under the much stricter conditions of the latter, is also not of such a nature as to prevent the admissibility of the action. Even if determination of liability may in substance be linked with a review of legality, the conditions for the admissibility of an action for damages are established separately from those governing actions for annulment and for failure to act. It is precisely these factors that underline the importance of the action for damages in the overall system of remedies as a form of recourse which can, at least in part, make up for the rather limited rights that private individuals enjoy in respect of the other forms of action (see the cases cited above and also Case 238/78 *Ireks-Arkady* v. *Council and Commission* [1979] ECR 2955 at p. 2972—'Quellmehl' case; Case 175/84 *Krohn* v. *Commission* [1986] ECR 753 at p. 770).

Nevertheless, an action for damages may not be used instead of an action for annulment (or failure to act) for a purpose for which the latter is the proper remedy (e.g. *restitutio in integrum*). As the ECJ has held on a number of occasions, mainly in staff cases, 'although a party may take action by means of a claim for compensation without being obliged by any provision of law to seek the annulment of the illegal measure which causes him damage, he may not by this means circumvent the inadmissibility of an application which concerns the same illegality and has the same financial end in view' (Case 59/65 *Schreckenberg* v. *Commission* [1966] ECR 543 at p. 550; Case 799/79 *Bruckner* v. *Commission and Council* [1981] ECR 2697 at p. 2714). In other words, it is not possible to remove, out of time, by means of an action for damages, the adverse financial consequences of a measure which could have been, but was not, challenged in time by an action for annulment.

Nor may an action for damages be used as a vehicle for bringing before the ECJ disputes arising between individuals and national authorities in connection with alleged damages caused by the latter in the course of the domestic implementation of Community provisions. As the ECJ has stated,

even though an action for damages under Articles 178 and 215 of the [EEC] Treaty constitutes an independent action, it must nevertheless be assessed having regard to the whole of the system of legal protection of individuals set up by the Treaty. If an individual takes the view that he is injured by a Community legislative measure which he regards as illegal he has the opportunity, when the implementation of the measure is entrusted to national authorities, to contest the validity of the measure, at the time of its implementation, before a national court in an action against the national authority. Such a court may, or even must, in pursuance of Article 177, refer to the Court of Justice a question on the validity of the Community measure in question. The existence of such an action is by itself of such a nature as to ensure the efficient protection of the individuals concerned. (Cases 116 and 124/77 *Amylum* v. *Council and Commission* [1979] ECR 3497 at p. 3560—'Isoglucose' cases.)

Basing itself in part upon such considerations, in a long line of cases the ECJ has held that where the damage consists solely of the undue payment to the national authorities of certain sums (e.g. import or export levies and duties, monetary compensatory amounts, countervailing charges) alleged to have been improperly levied by them in application of a Community provision, a claim directed exclusively at the refund of such sums will involve a dispute which is purely internal to the relationship between the applicant and the national authority and not one which can in principle engage the non-contractual liability of the Communities. An action for the repayment of such sums is in reality aimed at *restitutio in integrum* by means of the annulment of the national measure imposing them and must therefore be brought in the competent national courts. These must settle the dispute by applying Community law as to substance and national law as to competence, procedure, and form. Such an action must be directed exclusively against the national authority which adopted the measure imposing the charge. It may not, in the disguise of an action for damages, be brought before the ECJ against the Community institutions (see e.g. Case 96/71 *Haegeman* v. *Commission* [1972] ECR 1005 at pp. 1014–15; Case 46/75 *IBC* v. *Commission* [1976] ECR 65 at pp. 79–80; Case 12/79 *Wagner* v. *Commission* [1979] ECR 3657 at pp. 3671–2; Case 133/79 *Sucrimex* v. *Commission* [1980] ECR 1299 at pp. 1310–11). The position is not in principle different where the claim is directed not at the refund of sums incorrectly paid but, on the contrary, at the payment of sums (e.g. export refunds, carryover payments) withheld by the national authorities which may be due to the applicant under Community law (Case 99/74 *Grands Moulins* v. *Commission* [1975] ECR 1531 at pp. 1538–40).

Where, however, a charge was wrongly imposed because the underlying Community provision itself was illegal and invalid, the Community may have to bear subsidiary liability for any amounts which cannot be recovered from the national authorities in the national proceedings. In such a case an action for damages will lie before the ECJ provided that the applicant has previously exhausted all available domestic administrative and judicial remedies, and the Community will also be liable for any consequential damage that the person concerned may have suffered over and above the undue payment of the charge (Cases 5, 7, and 13 to 24/66 *Kampffmeyer* v. *Commission* [1967] ECR 245 at pp. 263 *et seq.*). A direct action for damages is moreover also always available before the ECJ where a prior exhaustion of the national remedies could not, in the circumstances of the individual case, lead to the compensation sought. This may be the case, for example, where the applicant is simply not in a position to bring the necessary action before the national courts (see e.g. Cases 67 to 85/75 *Lesieur* v. *Commission* [1976] ECR 391 at pp. 405–6; Cases 197 to 200/80 etc. *Ludwigshafener Walzmühle* v. *Council and Commission*, above, at pp. 3243–4) or where the damage complained of was caused not by a positive Community act but by an omission or refusal to act, i.e. an omission to provide for the payment of the amounts sought or refusal to issue the licences requested. In these situations the national authorities are clearly unable to provide a remedy since they have no power to adopt, amend, or supplement the Community measures in question (Case 43/72 *Merkur* v. *Commission* [1973] ECR 1055 at p. 1069 *per Curiam*, pp. 1079–84 *per* A.-G. Mayras; Case 126/76 *Dietz* v. *Commission* [1977] ECR 2431 at p. 2441; Case 238/78 *Ireks-Arkady* v. *Council and Commission*, above, at p. 2971). As the ECJ has pointed out, 'it is true that . . . the admissibility of . . . an action [for damages] may in certain cases be dependent on the exhaustion of national rights of action available to obtain the annulment of a national authority's decision. In order for that to be the case, however, it is necessary that those national rights of action should provide an effective means of protection for the individual concerned and be capable of resulting in compensation for the damage alleged' (Case 175/84 *Krohn* v. *Commission*, above, at p. 769; Case 81/86 *De Boer Buizen* v. *Council and Commission* [1987] ECR 3677 at p. 3692).

It follows from the foregoing that the non-contractual liability of the Communities and that of the Member States, as well as the jurisdiction of the ECJ and that of the national courts to deal with such liability, are carefully separated. As the ECJ has stated,

the combined provisions of Articles 178 and 215 of the Treaty only give jurisdiction to the Court to award compensation for damage caused by the Community institutions or by their servants in the performance of their duties, or in other words for damage capable of giving rise to non-contractual liability on the part of the Community. Damage caused by national institutions, on the other hand, can only give rise to liability on the part of those institutions, and the national courts retain sole jurisdiction to order compensation for such damage. Where . . . the decision adversely affecting the applicant was adopted by a national body acting in order to ensure the implementation of Community rules, it is necessary, in order to establish the jurisdiction of the Court, to determine whether the unlawful conduct alleged in support of the application for compensation is in fact the responsibility of a Community institution and cannot be attributed to the national body. (Case 175/84 *Krohn* v. *Commission*, above, at pp. 767–8; Cases 89 and 91/86 *L'Étoile Commerciale* v. *Commission* [1987] ECR 3005 at p. 3026. See also Case 101/78 *Granaria* [1979] ECR 623 at pp. 638–9.)

Where, however, an injury is caused by a conduct which is illegal and wrongful under both Community law and national law (i.e. the damage is contributed to by both the Community and the national institutions), it will create joint liability in the Community and the Member State and the matter will fall within the concurrent jurisdiction of the ECJ and the national courts. Because of the careful separation of those jurisdictions, however, there is at present no forum in which, and no legal system under which, proceedings could be instituted against both defendants jointly. Separate actions may have the disadvantage of either inadequate or excessive damages being awarded by the two different courts applying different rules or of the injured party being driven from pillar to post without being able to find satisfaction in either forum (see Cases 5, 7, and 13 to 24/66 *Kampffmeyer* v. *Commission*, above, at pp. 266–7 *per Curiam*, p. 279 *per* A.-G. Gand, where the ECJ, while establishing the liability of the Community in principle, postponed giving a final judgment on the actual amount of damages until the competent national courts have decided upon the question of the concurrent liability of Germany). Whether, in the event of full compensation being awarded by one of the forums against one of the defendants, there is any legal means for it to obtain reimbursement from the other defendant is doubtful.

Under all three Treaties, the Communities alone are liable, each within its own field of competence, to make good any damage caused by their institutions or by their servants 'in the performance of their duties'. An action for damages must, therefore, always be brought before the ECJ, which has exclusive jurisdiction in the matter (Cases 9 and 12/60 *Vloeberghs* v. *HA*, above, at p. 214; Case 9/69 *Sayag* [1969] ECR 329 at p. 335 *per Curiam*, pp. 339, 345–6 *per* A.-G. Gand), and against the relevant Community. As the personal liability of Community servants towards third parties is absorbed by the liability of the Communities, it is neither necessary nor possible to institute separate proceedings against servants themselves for the recovery of damage caused by them in the performance of their duties. However, the ECJ has held that 'the Community is only liable for those acts of its servants which, by virtue of an internal and direct relationship, are the necessary extension of the tasks entrusted to the institutions' (Case 9/69 *Sayag*, above, at p. 336, where the ECJ has held that the driving of a private car by a servant in the course of his employment cannot in principle constitute the performance of his duties, save under very exceptional circumstances). The personal liability of the servants towards the Communities is governed by the Staff Regulations and the Conditions of Employment and is subject to the jurisdiction of the ECJ (Arts. 40(2) ECSC, 215(3) EEC, 188(3) Euratom). The non-contractual liability of the Communities for damage caused by their institutions or by their servants outside the performance of their duties is not governed by Community law but by the *lex loci delicti* in accordance with the rules of private international law. Any action involving such liability falls within the jurisdiction of the competent national courts (Arts. 40(3) ECSC, 183 EEC, 155 Euratom).

Although, as stated above, an action for damages should in theory be brought against the particular Community whose liability is involved, in practice it may be directed against the institution or institutions (representing the Community) whose conduct gave rise to the matter. Where the alleged damage arises not from the conduct of an institution but from agreements concluded by the Member States, such as the Treaties and Acts of Accession, the matter falls outside the scope of the non-contractual liability of the Communities and hence outside the jurisdiction of the Court (Case 169/73 *Compagnie Continentale* v. *Council* [1975] ECR 117 at p. 134; Cases 31 and 35/86 *LAISA* v. *Council* [1988] ECR 2285 at p. 2320). Since under the ECSC Treaty only the Commission has powers the exercise of which is capable of causing 'damage' forming the basis of non-contractual liability, this Community is always represented by the Commission alone. On the other hand, the EEC and Euratom may be represented either by the Commission or by the Council or by both institutions jointly, i.e. where the matter has its origin both with the Commission and with the Council, the first for having made a proposal, the second for having legislated (Cases 63 to 69/72 *Werhahn* v. *Council* [1973] ECR 1229 at pp. 1247–8; Case 44/76 *Milch-, Fett- und Eier-Kontor* v. *Council and Commission* [1977] ECR 393 at p. 405). Whether the European Parliament and the ECJ are capable of causing damage 'in the performance of their duties', and whether they may appear as defendants in actions for damages other than those brought by their own officials, is doubtful.

Under all three Treaties, an action may be instituted by any natural or legal person, without restriction as to nationality, residence, place of establishment, registered office, or central administration, who/which has suffered an injury as a result of an act or omission of the Communities (for the right of action under Art. 40 ECSC, see Cases 9 and 12/60 *Vloeberghs* v. *HA*, above, at p. 214). It is, however, doubtful whether Member States as 'legal persons' have a right of action, while it seems certain that non-Member States have no such right. Any dispute between a non-Member State and the Communities concerning the non-contractual liability of the latter raises issues of international responsibility which must be decided in accordance with the rules of public international law and not in accordance with the 'general principles common to the laws of the Member States' which alone the ECJ has jurisdiction to apply (*see further under* **External relations**, section V).

Normally, an action for damages may be instituted only after damage has actually occurred. In several cases, the ECJ dismissed as inadmissible premature applications for compensation submitted at a time when the damage complained of had neither arisen, nor was certain, i.e. when it was only 'a future damage, which can neither be assessed at this point nor even regarded as certain to occur' (Cases 9 and 25/64 *FERAM* v. *HA* [1965] ECR 311 at pp. 320–1; see also Cases 55 to 59/63 etc. *Modena* v. HA [1964] ECR 211 at p. 229). However, in its subsequent case-law the Court recognized that the Treaties did not prevent it from being asked to declare the Community liable for 'imminent damage foreseeable with sufficient certainty even if the damage cannot yet be precisely assessed'. To prevent even greater damage, the Court pointed out, it might prove necessary to bring the matter before the Court as soon as the cause of damage was certain (Cases 56 to 60/74 *Kampffmeyer* v. *Commission and Council* [1976] ECR 711 at p. 741; Case 44/76 *Milch-, Fett- und Eier-Kontor* v. *Council and Commission*, above, at p. 407). Nevertheless, the Court will still dismiss applications in respect of future damage which is both doubtful and imprecisely defined (Case 147/83 *Binderer* v. *Commission* [1985] ECR 257 at p. 272).

An action for damages is barred after a period of five years from the occurrence of the event giving rise thereto (Arts. 40 ECSC Statute, 43 EEC Statute, 44 Euratom Statute). The ECJ has held that this period of limitation 'cannot begin before all the requirements governing an obligation to provide

45

compensation for damage are satisfied and in particular before the damage to be made good has materialised. Accordingly . . . [where] the liability of the Community has its origin in a legislative measure, the period of limitation cannot begin before the injurious effects of that measure have been produced, and consequently . . . before the time at which the applicants . . . were found to incur damage which was certain in character . . . It follows from this, moreover, that the commencement of the period of limitation cannot be the date on which the unlawful measures adopted by the Community entered into force or, *a fortiori*, the date of their publication' (Cases 256/80 etc. *Birra Wührer* v. *Council and Commission* [1982] ECR 85 at pp. 106–7; for the actual computation of the limitation period, see the second judgment in the same cases, [1984] ECR 3693 at pp. 3727–9). The ECJ has also stated that 'the expiry of the limitation period cannot constitute a valid defence to a claim by a person who has suffered damage where that person only belatedly became aware of the event giving rise to it and thus could not have had a reasonable time in which to submit his application to the Court or to the relevant institution before the expiry of the limitation period' (Case 145/83 *Adams* v. *Commission* [1985] ECR 3539 at p. 3591. In that case the action for damages was brought in July 1983, while the 'event giving rise thereto' occurred towards the end of 1974. The Court held the action not to be time-barred since the applicant could not have become aware of that event until the preparatory inquiry in the proceedings). The period of limitation is interrupted if proceedings are instituted before the Court or if prior to such proceedings an application is made by the aggrieved party to the relevant institution which is then followed by an action before the Court (see Cases 5, 7, and 13 to 24/66 *Kampffmeyer* v. *Commission*, above, at p. 260; Case 11/72 *Giordano* v. *Commission* [1973] ECR 417 at pp. 424–5).

See also **Action for annulment, Action for failure to act, Causal connection, Damage, Limited jurisdiction, Non-contractual liability,** *Restitutio in integrum*, **Unlimited jurisdiction.**

Further reading 1. BOOKS: Bebr, *Development of Judicial Control of the European Communities* (1981), ch. 5; Hartley, *The Foundations of European Community Law*, 2nd edn. (1988), ch. 17; Schermers, *Judicial Protection in the European Communities*, 4th edn. (1987), ch. 3/I/B; Toth, *Legal Protection of Individuals in the European Communities* (1978), vol. ii, ch. 7.

2. ARTICLES: Bronkhorst, 'Action for Compensation of Damages under Articles 178 and 215, para. 2, of the EEC Treaty: Stabilisation and Development' (1983/1) *LIEI* 99; Durand, 'Restitution or Damages: National Court or European Court?' (1975–6) 1 *EL Rev.* 431; Green and Barav, 'Damages in the National Courts for Breach of Community Law' (1986) 6 *YEL* 55; Harding, 'The Choice of Court Problem in Cases of Non-contractual Liability under E.E.C. Law' (1979) 16 *CML Rev.* 389; Hartley, 'Concurrent Liability in EEC Law: A Critical Review of the Cases' (1977) 2 *EL Rev.* 249; Rudden and Bishop, 'Gritz and Quellmehl: Pass it on' (1981) 6 *EL Rev.* 243; Schermers, 'The Law as it Stands on the Appeal for Damages' (1975/1) *LIEI* 113.

See also under **Non-contractual liability.**

▶ ACTION FOR FAILURE TO ACT Direct action brought before the ECJ for the purpose of compelling a Community institution (the Council or the Commission) to adopt an act where a failure to do so constitutes an infringement of Community law. In enabling the Court to review the legality of the institutions' inaction, this form of action is designed to provide a remedy which is complementary to that afforded by an action for annulment, with which it has a number of features in common.

1. **Under the ECSC Treaty**, the general rules relating to the action for failure to act are laid down in Art. 35, to which the discussion below is limited. Apart from Art. 35, the ECSC Treaty contains a number of provisions affording specific remedies for the Commission's failure to act in specified situations, such as Arts. 37, 58(1), 59(1), 59(5), 59(6), and 61(3). These provisions are only available to Member States and, with the exception of Art. 37, provide for non-judicial remedies.

Under Art. 35 ECSC, an action for failure to act may be brought against the Commission only. The preliminary administrative procedure (to be discussed below), which is a necessary prerequisite for instituting legal action before the ECJ, may be set in motion by the Member States, the Council, undertakings, and associations (as defined in Arts. 48 and 80 ECSC), 'as the case may be', i.e. whichever of these persons has an interest in the matter (Cases 7 and 9/54 *Industries Sidérurgiques Luxembourgeoises* v. *HA* [1956] ECR 175 at p. 189). Persons other than undertakings and associations, such as private individuals, cannot institute proceedings under Art. 35 (Case 12/63 *Schlieker* v. *HA* [1963] ECR 85 at p. 89; see also Cases 9 and 12/60 *Vloebergbs* v. *HA* [1961] ECR 197 at pp. 211–12). Although Art. 35 does not expressly state so, it seems evident that only the persons entitled to initiate the compulsory preliminary procedure have the right to bring the case before the ECJ (Case 12/63 *Schlieker* v. *HA*, above, at p. 92 *per* A.-G. Roemer).

The Commission's failure to act may arise in two different situations. First, where the Commission is required by the Treaty, or by rules laid down for its implementation, to take a decision or make a recommendation and fails to fulfil that obligation. Here the Commission is under an obligation to act and the outcome of such action is either a decision or a recommendation. As Art. 88 ECSC imposes a duty on the Commission to call upon Member States by means of a decision to fulfil their Community obligations whenever the Commission considers that they have failed to do so, an omission to use this power of control gives rise to a right to bring an action for failure to act (Cases 7 and 9/54 *Industries Sidérurgiques Luxembourgeoises* v. *HA*, above, at p. 190; see also Case 30/59 *Steenkolenmijnen* v. *HA* [1961] ECR 1 at pp. 15–17). By means of this action it is thus possible to compel the Commission to open Art. 88 proceedings against a Member State. Secondly, the Commission's failure to act may also arise in a situation where the Commission is not obliged but merely empowered by or under the Treaty to take a decision or make a recommendation and abstains from doing so. However, in that case an action lies only if such abstention constitutes a misuse of powers. Consequently, the action must be based on the sole ground of misuse of powers

47

(see Cases 42 and 49/59 *SNUPAT* v. *HA* [1961] ECR 53 at pp. 77–8; Cases 19/60 etc. *Fives Lille Cail* v. *HA* [1961] ECR 281 at p. 294).

Before an action for failure to act may be instituted before the ECJ, the prospective applicant must comply with a compulsory preliminary administrative procedure. Non-compliance with this requirement will entail the inadmissibility of the action (Case 17/57 *Steenkolenmijnen* v. *HA* [1959] ECR 1 at p. 8; Cases 24 and 34/58 *Chambre Syndicale de la Sidérurgie* v. *HA* [1960] ECR 281 at p. 299). As a first step, the prospective applicant must 'raise the matter' with the Commission, i.e. it must, by a formal communication addressed to the Commission, specifically and unequivocally request the adoption of a particular measure which can only be a decision or a recommendation (see Cases 22 and 23/60 *Elz* v. *HA* [1961] ECR 181 at pp. 187–8; Case 75/69 *Hake* v. *Commission* [1970] ECR 535 at pp. 542–3). This must be done within a reasonable time once it becomes clear that the Commission intends to remain inactive (Case 59/70 *Netherlands* v. *Commission* [1971] ECR 639 at pp. 652–4. For a criticism of this judgment, see Case 7/71 *Commission* v. *France* [1971] ECR 1003 at pp. 1026–7 *per* A.-G. Roemer). The request made to the Commission is important in three respects. First, it provides the starting-point for the various time-limits granted to the parties concerned (see below). Secondly, it gives the Commission an opportunity to reconsider its position. Thirdly, and most importantly, it determines the limits within which the subsequent action may be brought before the ECJ. This action must be based on essentially the same legal grounds on which the request had been based. The applicant may not demand, at the judicial stage, the performance of an act which it had not specifically requested during the course of the administrative procedure (Cases 41 and 50/59 *Hamborner Bergbau* v. *HA* [1960] ECR 493 at p. 505; Cases 24 and 34/58 *Chambre Syndicale de la Sidérurgie* v. *HA*, above; Case 75/69 *Hake* v. *Commission*, above).

Following the request, the Commission has two months within which to act. If at the end of two months it has not taken any decision or made any recommendation, proceedings may be instituted before the ECJ within a further period of one month against 'the implied decision of refusal which is to be inferred from the silence of the Commission on the matter' (Art. 35(3) ECSC). The application must be accompanied by documentary evidence of the date on which the request was lodged with the Commission (Art. 22(2) ECSC Statute). At this point the Treaty thus adopts a fiction, i.e. that the Commission's silence constitutes an 'implied decision of refusal'. The action is to be brought, therefore, not against the Commission's inaction but against its (implied) refusal to take the requested measure (Cases 7 and 9/54 *Industries Sidérurgiques Luxembourgeoises* v. *HA*, above, at pp. 193–4). This has the important consequence that, technically, the action will be one for the annulment of the implied negative decision and, as such, will be governed in all respects by the rules relating to actions for annulment as laid down in Art. 33 ECSC (ibid. at p. 191). That is why it is often said that under the ECSC Treaty an action for failure to act is just a variation, a special case, of an action for annulment (ibid. at pp. 208 *et seq. per* A.-G. Roemer). If the Commission adopts the measure requested after the institution of proceedings, the action becomes 'purposeless' and the Court will not give a ruling on the matter (ibid. at p. 193; Case 75/69 *Hake* v. *Commission*, above, at p. 541).

2. **Under the EEC and Euratom Treaties,** an action for failure to act differs on many important points from its counterpart under the ECSC Treaty. These differences have their reasons in, and broadly correspond to, the differences between the actions for annulment under the two systems. The general rules relating to the action for failure to act are contained in Arts. 175 and 176 EEC to which Arts. 148 and 149 Euratom correspond verbatim. The following discussion is limited to the EEC provisions although everything said is, in principle, applicable to the Euratom Treaty also.

While under Art. 175(1) EEC an action for failure to act may be brought against the Council and the Commission only, Art. 175(3) enables natural and legal persons to complain to the Court of Justice that 'an institution of the Community' has failed to act. Although the European Parliament is not expressly mentioned among the institutions whose inaction may be challenged, it would seem that the same reasons which led the Court to recognize that an action for annulment may lie against binding measures of the European Parliament also support a similar right of action against Parliament's failure to act (see Case 294/83 *Les Verts* v. *Parliament* [1986] ECR 1339 at pp. 1365–6; *see further under* **Action for annulment**). Proceedings may be instituted by the Member States, the 'other institutions of the Community', and natural or legal persons. In confirming that the European Parliament is included amongst the 'other institutions of the Community' entitled to bring proceedings, the ECJ has stated that Art. 175 'gives the same right of action to all the Community institutions. It is not possible to restrict the exercise of that right by one of them without adversely affecting its status as an institution under the Treaty, in particular Article 4(1)' (Case 13/83 *Parliament* v. *Council* [1985] ECR 1513 at p. 1588). Although the Court refers to 'all the Community institutions', it is questionable whether it would be possible—or proper—for the Court itself to bring an action under Art. 175 and thus to act as both party and judge in the same cause contrary to the *nemo judex in re sua* principle. As in an action for annulment, the Member States and the institutions enjoy a privileged position to be discussed further below. The concept of 'natural or legal persons' (hereinafter: private parties) must be given the same wide interpretation as for the purposes of annulment proceedings.

Inaction by the Council or the Commission is subject to judicial review only in so far as it constitutes an 'infringement of the Treaty' or, it is submitted, of any rules laid down for its implementation. The institution must be under a legal obligation to take a certain action so that its failure amounts to a breach of a duty. Unlike the position under the ECSC Treaty, a failure to exercise a discretionary power is not actionable (see Case 13/83 *Parliament* v. *Council*, above, at p. 1596, where the Court accepted the Council's argument that the failure of the latter institution to introduce a Common Transport Policy was not a 'failure to act' within the meaning of Art. 175 as the Treaty gave the Council a discretion to determine the substance of the measures required to implement such a policy. See further below). Moreover, in order for an action to succeed, it is not sufficient to refer in general terms to a 'violation of the Treaty'. The applicant must specify the exact provisions of Community law which in his opinion require the Council or the Commission to take the measure sought (see Cases 10 and 18/68 *Eridania* v. *Commission* [1969] ECR 459 at p. 483 *per Curiam*, p. 494 *per* A.-G. Roemer). Thus, the general duty of the Commission under Art. 155 EEC to ensure that Community law is observed by all those subject to it is too general an obligation to serve as a basis for an action (Case 6/70 *Borromeo* v. *Commission* [1970] ECR 815 at p. 822 *per* A.-G. Gand).

The categories of measures which it is possible to elicit by means of an action for failure to act differ according to whether the applicant is a Member State/institution or a private party. In the absence of any limitation in Art. 175, the Member States/institutions as privileged applicants may request the adoption of any binding (i.e. regulation, directive, decision, etc.) or non-binding (i.e. recommendation, opinion, legislative proposal, etc.) measure, addressed to anyone, including general law-making measures as well as individual decisions. Moreover, they do not have to show any particular legal interest in the measure concerned as they are assumed to have a general interest in seeing that the institutions duly carry out their obligations. Nevertheless, in Case 13/83 *Parliament* v. *Council*, above, at pp. 1592–3 the ECJ held that even an institution may only request the adoption of measures which can be defined with a sufficient degree of precision 'to allow the Court to determine whether their adoption, or the failure to adopt them, is lawful' and to enable the defendant institution to identify them individually and to adopt them in compliance with the judgment of the Court. The Court held that since the Parliament did not state which measures the Council ought to have adopted to introduce a Common Transport Policy, the failure of the Council to implement such a policy did not constitute 'a failure to act sufficiently specific in nature to form the subject of an action under Article 175' (ibid. at p. 1597). On the other hand, the failure of the Council to extend freedom to provide services to the transport sector involved failure to adopt measures 'whose subject-matter and nature may be determined with a sufficient degree of precision' and was, therefore, a 'failure to act' within the meaning of Art. 175 (ibid. at p. 1600).

By contrast, the right of action of natural or legal persons is restricted in that they may only bring an action if an institution 'has failed to address [to them] any act other than a recommendation or an opinion' (Art. 175(3) EEC). As the ECJ has stated, a private party must be 'in the precise legal position . . . of the potential addressee of a legal measure which the [institution] has a duty to adopt with regard to him' (Case 246/81 *Lord Bethell* v. *Commission* [1982] ECR 2277 at p. 2291). It would seem to follow from this that the only measure that a private party may seek under Art. 175 is a binding act to be addressed to him personally, although the act does not necessarily have to be in the form of a 'decision' within the meaning of Art. 189. This follows from the reference in Art. 175 to 'any act' and from the wide interpretation that the ECJ has given to the concept of an 'act'. Accordingly, the term 'act' includes, irrespective of form and designation, 'any measure the legal effects of which are binding on, and capable of affecting the interests of, the applicant by bringing about a distinct change in his legal position' (Case 60/81 *IBM* v. *Commission* [1981] ECR 2639 at p. 2651). Although the Court has given this definition for the purposes of an action for annulment under Art. 173, it would seem that the same definition applies equally in the context of an action for failure to act under Art. 175. This is because the Court itself had stated in an earlier case that 'the concept of a measure capable of giving rise to an action is identical in Articles 173 and 175, as both provisions merely prescribe one and the same method of recourse' (Case 15/70 *Chevalley* v. *Commission* [1970] ECR 975 at p. 979; see also Case 13/83 *Parliament* v. *Council*, above, at p. 1592. For the view that an 'act' under Art. 175 is not necessarily identical with a 'decision', see also Case 8/71 *Komponistenverband* v. *Commission* [1971] ECR 705 at p. 715 *per* A.-G. Roemer; Case 125/78 *GEMA* v. *Commission* [1979] ECR 3173 at p. 3198 *per* A.-G. Capotorti.) Nevertheless, this statement must now be interpreted in the light of Case 302/87 *Parliament* v. *Council* [1988] ECR para. 16, where the Court pointed out that there is not always a necessary link between an action for failure to act and an action for annulment. This is because there are certain acts, such as the draft budget, the failure to adopt which may be challenged under Art. 175 but which, when adopted, may not be challenged for annulment, being of a purely preparatory nature.

It follows from the foregoing that private parties have no *locus standi* under Art. 175 to enforce the adoption of general law-making measures (since these can never be 'addressed to' particular private persons), measures addressed to others (even if, it would seem, such measures concern them 'directly and individually', see Case 125/78 *GEMA* v. *Commission*, above, at p. 3199 *per* A.-G. Capotorti), and non-binding measures. In particular, the ECJ has so far declared that the following measures cannot be elicited by natural or legal persons through Art. 175:

(*a*) Regulations and other general measures having law-making character (Case 15/71 *Mackprang* v. *Commission* [1971] ECR 797 at p. 804; Case 134/73 *Holtz & Willemsen* v. *Council and Commission* [1974] ECR 1 at p. 11; Case 90/78 *Granaria* v. *Council and Commission* [1979] ECR 1081 at pp. 1092–3).

(*b*) Legislative proposals to be submitted by the Commission to the Council (Case 134/73 *Holtz & Willemsen* v. *Council and Commission*, above).

(*c*) Initiation of proceedings by the Commission against a Member State under Art. 169 EEC for a failure to fulfil a Community obligation (Case 48/65 *Lütticke* v. *Commission* [1966] ECR 19 at p. 27 *per Curiam*, pp. 29 *et seq*. *per* A.-G. Gand; see also Case 103/63 *Rhenania* v. *Commission* [1964] ECR 425 at p. 433 *per* A.-G. Roemer). In this respect the EEC Treaty is clearly more restrictive than the ECSC Treaty, where it is possible for private parties to compel the Commission by means of Art. 35 to open the corresponding proceedings against a Member State under Art. 88 (see above).

(*d*) Opening of investigations by the Commission into the activities of

51

third parties with a view to a possible application to them of EEC competition rules (Case 246/81 *Lord Bethell* v. *Commission*, above, at p. 2291).

(*e*) A final decision by the Commission upon a complaint made under Art. 3(2)(b) of Reg. 17 regarding the existence of an infringement of EEC competition rules by third parties (Case 125/78 *GEMA* v. *Commission*, above, at pp. 3189–90).

(*f*) A mere 'advice', 'opinion', 'declaration', or 'information' not having binding legal effects (Case 6/70 *Borromeo* v. *Commission*, above, at p. 819; Case 15/70 *Chevalley* v. *Commission*, above, at p. 980; Case 182/80 *Gauff* v. *Commission* [1982] ECR 799 at p. 817; Cases 83 and 84/84 *N.M.* v. *Commission and Council* [1984] ECR 3571 at p. 3575).

Before an action for failure to act may be instituted before the ECJ, the prospective applicant must comply with the requirement for a compulsory preliminary administrative procedure which is essentially similar to that under the ECSC Treaty. As a first step, the institution concerned must be 'called upon to act', i.e. informed with unequivocal clarity of the precise measures which it is required to take (Case 8/71 *Komponistenverband* v. *Commission*, above, at p. 716 *per* A.-G. Roemer; see also Case 13/83 *Parliament* v. *Council*, above, at p. 1589). In the absence of this, the subsequent action will be inadmissible (see e.g. Case 84/82 *Germany* v. *Commission* [1984] ECR 1451 at p. 1491). If within two months of being so called upon the institution has not 'defined its position', the action may be brought within a further period of two months (Art. 175(2)).

On this point a major difference exists between the ECSC and the EEC Treaties. Under the former, the institution can only avoid an action by adopting, within the two months, a formal decision or recommendation which is, in turn, subject to an action for annulment. Under the latter, all that is needed to achieve the same result is a 'definition of its position'. The term 'definition of position' has been interpreted by the ECJ extremely widely so as to include practically any statement of the view taken by the institution of the subject-matter of the request quite irrespective of the form in which it is made. Thus, the institution concerned may remedy its failure to act and thus prevent an action not only by a formal (i.e. binding) measure granting or refusing the request (which can in turn be challenged for annulment), but also by an informal (i.e. non-binding and non-reasoned) reply expressing a willingness or unwillingness to act or containing a measure other than the one requested (see e.g. Case 48/65 *Lütticke* v. *Commission*, above, at p. 27; Case 8/71 *Komponistenverband* v. *Commission*, above, at pp. 710–11; Case 42/71 *Nordgetreide* v. *Commission* [1972] ECR 105 at p. 110). Since such a reply may never be challenged before the ECJ, a situation may arise where a party may be left without any judicial remedy against the institution's conduct, neither the action for failure to act nor the action for annulment being available (as in Cases 48/65 and 42/71 mentioned immediately above). This could be avoided by simply construing the term 'definition of position' as meaning 'definition of position by a formal (i.e. binding) act', as under the ECSC Treaty, which act would then be subject to annulment in the usual way.

Nevertheless, a reply which neither denies nor confirms the alleged failure to act nor gives any indication of the institution's views as to the measures requested by the applicant, will not be regarded as a 'definition of position' within the meaning of Art. 175 (Case 13/83 *Parliament* v. *Council*, above, at p. 1590). It should be mentioned, however, that in Case 302/87 *Parliament* v. *Council*, above, para. 17 the Court stated rather surprisingly that an express refusal to act (which is clearly a 'definition of position') may still be challenged under Art. 175 since 'it does not put an end to the failure to act'.

As under the ECSC Treaty, the application made to the ECJ must be accompanied by documentary evidence of the date on which the institution was requested to act (Art. 19(2) EEC Statute). The application must be based on essentially the same legal grounds on which the request was based. Since the EEC Treaty does not employ the fiction of an 'implied negative decision', all that the Court is required to do is to establish the dilatoriness of the institution and that this constitutes an infringement of Community law. In so doing, the Court will not take into account any objective difficulty that may have prevented the institution from acting. As the Court has pointed out, 'under Article 175 the Court must find that there has been an infringement of the Treaty if the Council or the Commission fails to act when under an obligation to do so. Article 175 takes no account of how difficult it may be for the institution in question to comply with the obligation' (Case 13/83 *Parliament* v. *Council*, above, at p. 1596). The Court's judgment will be purely declaratory, but the institution whose failure to act has been declared contrary to the Treaty is required to take the necessary measures to comply with the judgment (Art. 176 EEC). Since this provision does not prescribe a time-limit for such compliance, the ECJ has held that the institution must take the necessary measures within a 'reasonable period' (ibid. at p. 1600). This obligation does not include an obligation to make good any damage caused by the institution's inaction, which may be recovered by means of separate proceedings under Arts. 178 and 215(2) EEC. Where the institution adopts the requested measure after the action has been brought but before judgment, the subject-matter of the action ceases to exist and there will no longer be any need for the Court to give a decision (Case 103/63 *Rhenania* v. *Commission*, above, at p. 429; Case 377/87 *Parliament* v. *Council* [1988] ECR paras. 10–11 and Case 383/87 *Commission* v. *Council* [1988] ECR paras. 10–11; see also the opinion of A.-G. Mischo in these two cases, paras. 114–35).

See also **Action against Member States, Action for annulment, Misuse of powers.**

Further reading 1. BOOKS: Bebr, *Development of Judicial Control of the European Communities* (1981), ch. 3; Hartley, *The Foundations of European Community Law*, 2nd edn. (1988), ch. 13; Schermers, *Judicial Protection in the European Communities*, 4th edn. (1987), ch. 2; Toth, *Legal Protection of Individuals in the European Communities* (1978), vol. ii, ch. 6.

2. ARTICLE: Toth, 'The Law as it Stands on the Appeal for Failure to Act' (1975/2) *LIEI* 65.

Adaptation decision

Admissibility of action

▶ **ADAPTATION DECISION** Council Decision of 1 January 1973 (*OJ* 1973 L2/1, *Bull. EC* 1–1973, p. 6), adopted under Art. 2 of the Accession Treaty 1972, adjusting the Act of Accession 1972, its Annexes, and Protocols as made necessary by the failure of Norway to ratify the Accession Treaty. The Adaptation Decision was accompanied by two further Council Decisions of the same date (*OJ* 1973 L2/28, L2/29), altering the number of members of the Commission (from fourteen to thirteen) and increasing the number of Advocates-General (from three to four), respectively.

See also **Accession Treaties**

▶ **ADMISSIBILITY OF ACTION** Concept implying that a set of requirements, mainly relating to jurisdiction, form, and procedure, must be satisfied before the ECJ may decide on the substantive issues of a case. Although these requirements are laid down in the Treaties in different terms for the different forms of action, generally speaking it may be stated that an action is admissible if the applicant possesses a right of action and the capacity to institute proceedings (or in reference proceedings the national court has the competence to refer), the application is made in the prescribed form and within the prescribed time-limits, and the ECJ has jurisdiction to grant what is requested (see e.g. Cases 9 and 11/71 *Compagnie d'Approvisionnement* v. *Commission* [1972] ECR 391 at p. 413 *per* A.-G. Dutheillet de Lamothe; Case 43/72 *Merkur* v. *Commission* [1973] ECR 1055 at pp. 1080–1 *per* A.-G. Mayras). The admissibility of an action must be assessed by reference to the situation prevailing when the application is lodged. If at that time the conditions of admissibility are not fulfilled, the action will be inadmissible, unless the defect is rectified within the period prescribed for the institution of proceedings (Case 50/84 *Bensider* v. *Commission* [1984] ECR 3991 at p. 3997).

As in principle every single action must be 'admissible' under one (or more) particular Treaty provision, the ECJ must always examine the question of admissibility, if raised, before it may deal with the merits of the case. Such question may be raised either by a party (the defendant in a direct action) or by the Court itself of its own motion (see e.g. Case 294/83 *Les Verts* v. *Parliament* [1986] ECR 1339 at p. 1364). It is normally examined as the first step in the proceedings, although it may be raised at any later stage (see e.g. Cases 67 to 85/75 *Lesieur* v. *Commission* [1976] ECR 391 at pp. 405–6 *per Curiam*, p. 419 *per* A.-G. Warner) or as a separate procedural issue (preliminary objection). It follows from this separation in principle of issues of admissibility and those of substance that an objection of inadmissibility will not be upheld where its consideration would involve an examination of the merits of the case (see e.g. Case 26/68 *Fux* v. *Commission* [1969] ECR 145 at p. 153; Cases 197 to 200/80 etc. *Ludwigshafener Walzmühle* v. *Council and Commission* [1981] ECR 3211 at p. 3244). Although the concept of admissibility mainly encompasses issues of jurisdiction, procedure, and form, in the system set up by the Community Treaties it acquires a much wider than merely procedural or formal significance. In their entirety, these issues essentially determine the scope of the judicial protection open to private individuals under Community law.

See also Absolute bar to proceedings, Absolute inadmissibility, Interest to sue, Jurisdiction, Preliminary objection, Right of action.

Further reading: Lasok, *The European Court of Justice: Practice and Procedure* (1984), ch. 7.

▶ **APPLICATION ORIGINATING PROCEEDINGS** Document whereby a direct action may be brought before the ECJ (Arts. 22 ECSC Statute, 19 EEC and Euratom Statutes, 37–8 RP; also referred to as 'originating application'). Although the Statutes expressly mention a 'written application addressed to the Registrar' the original of which has to be signed by the applicant's agent or lawyer, accompanied by a number of documents specified in Arts. 37–8 RP and lodged together with five copies for the Court and a copy for every other party to the proceedings, in Cases 281/85 etc. *Germany and Others* v. *Commission* [1987] ECR 3203 at p. 3249 the ECJ left open the question whether an application sent by telex satisfied these formal requirements and was compatible with the extension of time-limits on account of distance provided for in Art. 81(2) RP. A single application may challenge more than one measure of the institutions (Case 1/54 *France* v. *HA* [1954] ECR 1 at p. 6) and may contain various main heads of claim dealing with related matters, e.g. claims for annulment, for a declaration of failure to act, for an award of damages (Cases 7 and 9/54 *Industries Sidérurgiques Luxembourgeoises* v. *HA* [1956] ECR 175 at p. 189). Likewise, an application may include alternative conclusions for the event that the principal conclusions are dismissed (Cases 7/56 etc. *Algera* v. *Common Assembly* [1957] ECR 39 at p. 64; Case 42/71 *Nordgetreide* v. *Commission* [1972] ECR 105 at p. 110). A joint application by several applicants is also admissible, provided that the conclusions of all the applicants refer to the same measures or to measures which concern them all equally (Cases 18 and 19/64 *Alvino* v. *Commission* [1965] ECR 789 at p. 796) and that they all contest those measures on the same grounds and rely on the same submissions (Case 13/57 *Eisen- und Stahlindustrie* v. *HA* [1958] ECR 265 at p. 277).

An application must contain the name and permanent residence of the applicant; the name of the party against whom the application is made; the subject-matter of the dispute and the grounds on which the application is based (*causa petendi*); the 'form of order sought' by the applicant (*petitum*; referred to as 'submissions' in the English version of the Statutes and as 'conclusions' in the English-language *European Court Reports*); and the nature of any evidence founded upon by him (Art. 38(1) RP). In addition, the application must state an address for service in Luxembourg and the name of a person who is authorized and willing to accept service (Art. 38(2) RP). The lawyer acting for a party must lodge at the Registry a certificate that he is entitled to practise before a court of a Member State (Art. 38(3) RP). An application made by a legal person governed by private law must be accompanied by the instruments constituting and regulating that legal person and by proof that the authority granted to the applicant's lawyer has been properly conferred on him by someone authorized for the purpose (Art. 38(5) RP). Where appropriate, an application must also be accompanied by the measure the annulment of which is sought or, in the case of a failure to act, by documentary evidence of the date on which the institution was requested to act (Arts. 22(2) ECSC Statute, 19(2) EEC and Euratom Statutes, 38(4) RP). In appropriate cases, a copy of any arbitration clause contained in a contract or of any special agreement concluded between Member States, on which the application is based, must also be enclosed (Art. 38(6) RP).

If an application does not comply with the above formal requirements (i.e. those listed in Art. 38(2)–(6) RP), the Registrar must prescribe a reasonable period within which the applicant is to comply with them whether by putting the application itself in order or by producing any of the documents mentioned. If the applicant still fails to comply within the time prescribed, the Court may, after hearing the Advocate–General, dismiss the application as inadmissible on the ground of want of form (Art. 38(7) RP. For instances where the Court held applications to be inadmissible under this provision, see e.g. Case 289/83 *GAARM* v. *Commission* [1984] ECR 2789 at pp. 2790–1—failure to produce the instruments constituting the applicant companies and to supply proof of authority granted to their lawyers; Case 297/84 *Sahinler* v. *Commission* [1986] ECR 443 at pp. 444–5—failure to indicate an address for service in Luxembourg. The Court did not accept the financial reasons pleaded by the applicants as their application for legal aid had been refused. In both cases, the initial time-limits prescribed by the Registrar were considerably extended). The Registrar is required to publish details in the *Official Journal* of every new application (Arts. 16(6) RP; 25 IR).

Since the provisions governing the form of applications affect not only the interests of the parties but also the power of the ECJ to exercise judicial review, the Court will examine of its own motion whether those provisions have been complied with (Cases 19/60 etc. *Fives Lille Cail* v. *HA* [1961] ECR 281 at p. 294). It is particularly important that the subject-matter of the application, the grounds on which it is based, and the form of order sought (conclusions) should be stated adequately. These elements will be considered in turn below but, generally, the extent to which and the detail in which they must be specified depend on the nature of the application in question. On the whole, it may be said that the ECJ and its various Advocates-General do not insist on too rigid and formalistic requirements. They always attempt to give the terms in which an application is set out an interpretation which is reasonable, corresponds to the true intentions of the applicant, and satisfies the requirements of the law. In other words, they look for an interpretation that enables the Court to avoid, as far as possible, dismissing the application as inadmissible on the purely formal ground of defective drafting. The decisive consideration seems to be that an application should be held admissible on formal grounds as long as the alleged defects are not such as to prevent the defendant and any third parties concerned from effectively defending their interests, or to hinder the Court in the exercise of its judicial review (see Case 74/74 *CNTA* v. *Commission* [1975] ECR 533 at p. 544; see also the cases cited below).

As regards, more specifically, the subject-matter of the application, including the facts, this must be defined with sufficient precision to enable it to be examined properly. Any contested measures of the defendant institution, forming the subject-matter of the dispute, must be clearly indicated and enclosed. Non-compliance with these requirements will entail the inadmissibility of the application (Case 30/68 *Lacroix* v. *Commission* [1970] ECR 301 at pp. 310–11; by contrast, see Case 4/69 *Lütticke* v. *Commission* [1971] ECR 325 at pp. 335–6). The importance of these rules is that, since a party may not alter the actual subject-matter of the dispute during the course of the proceedings, the Court examines the substance of the application solely with reference to those matters contained in the originating application (Case 232/78 *Commission* v. *France* [1979] ECR 2729 at p. 2737).

As regards, secondly, the legal grounds on which the application is based (*causa petendi*), only a brief statement of these, and not an exhaustive treatment of all the issues, is required. Failure to designate the relevant Treaty provisions upon which the action is founded, or a mistake or inaccuracy made in that respect, will not entail the inadmissibility of the application (see e.g. Case 12/68 *X* v. *Audit Board* [1969] ECR 109 at p. 115). The ECJ will apply the correct provision, provided that it can ascertain that provision from the facts relied on and the arguments advanced (see e.g. Cases 7/56 etc. *Algera* v. *Common Assembly*, above, at p. 65; Cases 2 to 10/63 *San Michele* v. *HA* [1963] ECR 327 at p. 341). Nevertheless, in the case of an action for annulment the grounds must be set out with sufficient precision to enable the Court to establish whether they come within the four grounds of action listed in Arts. 33 ECSC, 173 EEC, 146 Euratom (Case 42/84 *Remia* v. *Commission* [1985] ECR 2545 at p. 2570). As the ECJ has stated, 'although it must be accepted that the statement of the grounds for instituting the proceedings need not conform with the phraseology or the list in [Art. 33 ECSC], it may be sufficient for the grounds for instituting the proceedings to be expressed in terms of their substance rather than of their legal classification provided, however, that it is sufficiently clear from the application which of the grounds referred to in the Treaty is being invoked. A mere abstract statement of the grounds in the application does not alone satisfy the requirements of the Protocol on the Statute of the Court of Justice or the Rules of Procedure. The words "brief statement of the grounds" used in those instruments mean that the application must specify the nature of the grounds on which the application is based. The ground of complaint relied upon must therefore be established in relation to the facts which have been set out' (Cases 19/60 etc. *Fives Lille Cail* v. *HA*, above, at p. 295, where the Court dismissed an application which merely accused the HA of acting *ultra vires* without specifying what constituted the *ultra vires* acts). A general reference to the grounds, submissions, and arguments put forward in another case is not admissible (Case 9/55 *Beeringen* v. *HA* [1956] ECR 311 at p. 325; Cases 19 and 65/63 *Prakash* v. *Commission* [1965] ECR 533 at p. 546). In the case of an action for damages, the grounds of the application must indicate the defendant institution's fault, i.e. the wrongful act or omission causing the injury, which is an element of non-contractual liability. Furthermore, the applicant must normally show, at least in broad outline, how the calculation of the amount of the damages is made up (Case 25/62 *Plaumann* v. *Commission* [1963] ECR 95 at pp. 119–20 *per* A.-G. Roemer; Case 40/75 *Produits Bertrand* v. *Commission* [1976] ECR 1 at p. 12 *per* A.-G. Reischl). Nevertheless, exact figures on which that calculation is based need not necessarily be produced; they may be presented at later stages in the proceedings (Cases 29/63 etc. *Usines de la Providence* v. *HA* [1965] ECR 911 at pp. 934–5).

As regards, finally, the conclusions or the form of order sought (*petitum*), they must be presented in an exact, unequivocal manner. They must specify the remedy sought, i.e. the precise result at which the applicant desires the Court to arrive on the basis of the grounds put forward. The ECJ is bound by the *ne ultra petita* rule, according to which it may not generally go beyond what is requested by the applicant. In the absence of an exact statement of the conclusions, the Court would risk either giving judgment *ultra petita* or failing to give judgment on all heads of claim. An imprecise statement of the conclusions would moreover prejudice the rights of the defence (Cases 46 and 47/59 *Meroni* v. *HA* [1962] ECR 411 at p. 419; see also Case 33/59 *Chasse* v. *HA* [1962] ECR 381 at pp. 387–8). Conclusions which have merely an abstract character will be dismissed as inadmissible (Case 15/67 *Bauer* v. *Commission* [1967] ECR 397 at p. 402). In certain circumstances, the Court has allowed the applicants to clarify the exact scope of imprecisely formulated conclusions (see e.g. Case 42/84 *Remia* v. *Commission*, above, at pp. 2569–70).

See also **Damage, Grounds of action, Judgment, Representation before the ECJ, Written procedure.**

Further reading: See under **Written procedure.**

▶ **ARBITRATION CLAUSE** Clause contained in a contract concluded by or on behalf of the European Communities, whether that contract be governed by public or private law, conferring jurisdiction on the ECJ to give judgment in disputes arising from that contract (Arts. 42 ECSC, 181 EEC, 153 Euratom). The jurisdiction conferred on the ECJ by an arbitration clause is unlimited or plenary (Case 1/56 *Bourgaux* v. *Common Assembly* [1956] ECR 361 at p. 367 *per Curiam*, pp. 374–5 *per* A.-G. Roemer; see also Case 1/55 *Kergall* v. *Common Assembly* [1955] ECR 151 at p. 155 *per Curiam*, pp. 164–5 *per* A.-G. Roemer). In determining the scope of that jurisdiction, the Court has stated that 'the jurisdiction of the Court, which is based on an arbitration clause, derogates from the ordinary rules of law and must therefore be given a restrictive interpretation. The Court may hear and determine only claims arising from a contract which was concluded with the Community and which contains the arbitration clause or [counter] claims that are directly connected with the obligations arising from that contract' (Case 426/85 *Commission* v. *Zoubek* [1986] ECR 4057 at p. 4069. The Court supported this view by reference to Art. 6(3) of the Convention on Jurisdiction and the Enforcement of Judgments in Civil and Commercial

Matters of 1968). Although the term refers to 'arbitration', the ECJ will not act as an 'arbitrator' making an 'award', but as a court proper giving a 'judgment'. The clause is therefore in the nature of a choice of jurisdiction clause in the sense of private international law. In the absence of such a clause, the dispute falls within the jurisdiction of the competent national courts of the Member States (Arts. 40(3) ECSC, 183 EEC, 155 Euratom; Case 43/84 *Maag* v. *Commission* [1985] ECR 2581 at p. 2603) or possibly of third countries. Under an arbitration clause, the ECJ is called upon to resolve a dispute in accordance with the substantive rules of the national law which governs the contract, as determined by the rules of private international law (Case 426/85 *Commission* v. *Zoubek*, above, at pp. 4067, 4069; see also Case 318/81 *Commission* v. *CO.DE.MI.* [1985] ECR 3693 at p. 3712). An application submitted to the ECJ under an arbitration clause must be accompanied by a copy of the clause itself (Art. 38(6) RP), which implies that the clause must be in writing. Nevertheless, the Court will not insist on any rigid requirements as to the form which the clause should take (see Case 23/76 *Pellegrini* v. *Commission* [1976] ECR 1807 at p. 1818 *per Curiam*, pp. 1825–7 *per* A.-G. Mayras).

See also **Contractual liability, Jurisdiction, Unlimited jurisdiction.**

▶ *AUDI ALTERAM PARTEM* General principle of law, recognized by the ECJ as forming part of Community law, according to which 'a person whose interests are perceptibly affected by a decision taken by a public authority must be given the opportunity to make his point of view known' (the right to be heard) (Case 17/74 *Transocean Marine Paint Association* v. *Commission* [1974] ECR 1063 at p. 1080 *per Curiam*, pp. 1088–9 *per* A.-G. Warner). This principle has been incorporated into, and reaffirmed by the ECJ in relation to, a number of provisions of written Community law of which the following three areas may be mentioned:

1. The right of the Member States to submit observations before the Commission may make a finding of a failure on their part to fulfil a Community obligation (Arts. 88 ECSC, 93(2) and 169 EEC, 141 Euratom). The ECJ has held that this right 'constitutes an essential guarantee required by the Treaty and amounts to an essential procedural requirement' (Case 31/69 *Commission* v. *Italy* [1970] ECR 25 at p. 33; see also Case 20/59 *Italy* v. *HA* [1960] ECR 325 at p. 342).

2. The right of interested parties to be heard before the Commission may impose sanctions or take certain measures, in particular in transport and competition matters, including competition in transport (Arts. 36(1), 46(2), 54(4), 66(5)(2) ECSC; Art. 25 of Reg. 11 (transport); Art. 19 of Reg. 17 and Reg. 99/63 (competition); Art. 26 of Reg. 1017/68 and Reg. 1630/69 (competition in transport); Art. 16 of Reg. 3975/87 (competition in air transport). See also Arts. 5(2) and 46(1)(2) Euratom). The ECJ has stated that 'observance of the right to be heard is in all proceedings in which sanctions . . . may be imposed a fundamental principle of Community law which must be respected even if the proceedings in question are administrative proceedings'

(Case 85/76 *Hoffmann-La Roche* v. *Commission* [1979] ECR 461 at p. 511).

3. The right of Community officials to be heard before a disciplinary measure may be imposed upon them. As the ECJ has observed: 'According to a generally accepted principle of administrative law in force in the Member States of the European Economic Community, the administrations of these States must allow their servants the opportunity of replying to allegations before any disciplinary decision is taken concerning them. This rule, which meets the requirement of sound justice and good administration, must be followed by Community institutions' (Case 32/62 *Alvis* v. *Council* [1963] ECR 49 at p. 55. See also Case 35/67 *Van Eick* v. *Commission* [1968] ECR 329 at pp. 344–5). Even outside disciplinary proceedings, the ECJ has upheld 'the general principle that when any administrative body adopts a measure which is liable gravely to prejudice the interests of an individual it is bound to put him in a position to express his point of view' (Case 121/76 *Moli* v. *Commission* [1977] ECR 1971 at p. 1979; Case 75/77 *Mollet* v. *Commission* [1978] ECR 897 at p. 908). In disciplinary proceedings the rights of the defence include, in addition to the right to be heard, the right of the official concerned to be assisted by counsel of his own choice who must have access to the disciplinary file (Case 115/80 *Demont* v. *Commission* [1981] ECR 3147 at p. 3158). Moreover, the principle of *audi alteram partem* also requires that the official charged or his representative should be given an opportunity to be present when witnesses are heard and to put to them any questions which the official considers useful for his defence (Case 141/84 *De Compte* v. *Parliament* [1985] ECR 1951 at p. 1966).

Measures taken in violation of the right to be heard will be annulled by the ECJ on the ground of infringement of an essential procedural requirement (see e.g. ibid. at p. 1967).

See also **Action against Member States, Administrative procedure*, General principles of law, Infringement of an essential procedural requirement, Natural justice.**

Further reading: See under **General principles of law.**

► **BUDGETARY TREATIES (1970 AND 1975)** 1. Treaty signed in Luxembourg on 22 April 1970, amending certain budgetary provisions of the Treaties establishing the European Communities and of the Merger Treaty. It entered into force on 1 January 1971 (*JO* 1971 L2/1). The conclusion of the Treaty followed the adoption of Council Decision 70/243 of 21 April 1970 (*OJ Sp. Edn.* 1970(I), p. 224), which provided for the replacement of financial contributions from the Member States by the Communities' own resources. This required strengthening of the budgetary powers of the European Parliament, mainly to establish democratic control over the Community budget at the Community level since such control could no longer be exercised at the national level. The Treaty made significant changes in Arts. 78 ECSC, 203 and 206 EEC, 177 and 180 Euratom, 20 Merger Treaty, which may be summarized as follows: (*a*) It increased Parliament's budgetary powers in two stages: the first, transitional, stage covered the years 1971 to 1974; the second, definitive, stage began with the budget for the financial year 1975. This corresponded to the stages by which the Communities were to acquire their own resources under the Council Decision of 21 April 1970. One of the major innovations introduced by the Treaty in the budgetary procedure from 1975 onwards was the distinction made between 'compulsory expenditure' and 'non-compulsory expenditure' (*see further under* **Community budget**). (*b*) The President of Parliament acquired the power, previously exercised by the President of the Council, to declare that the budget had been finally adopted. (*c*) The power to give a discharge to the Commission in respect of the implementation of the budget, previously within the competence of the Council, was conferred upon the Parliament and the Council acting jointly. It may be noted that, at the time of the signing of the Treaty, the Council adopted three resolutions and four declarations interpreting various aspects of the new budgetary procedure introduced by the Treaty (printed in *Treaties Establishing the European Communities* (1987), p. 1091).

2. Treaty signed in Brussels on 22 July 1975, amending certain financial provisions of the Treaties establishing the European Communities and of the Merger Treaty. It entered into force on 1 June 1977 (*OJ* 1977 L359/1). The conclusion of the Second Treaty was the consequence of the European Parliament's dissatisfaction with the First Budgetary Treaty of 1970 and of an undertaking given by the Commission at the time of its signing to present new proposals for a further extension of Parliament's budgetary powers (6th *Gen. Rep. EC* (1972), p. 5; Declaration No. 4 of the Council of 22 Apr. 1970 annexed to the 1970 Treaty, referred to above. For the draft Treaty presented by the Commission on 8 June 1973, with explanatory notes, see Suppl. 9/73—*Bull. EC*; for background information, see *Bull. EC* 6–1973, p. 6; for the EP's opinion and the Commission's amended proposals, see *Bull. EC* 10–1973, pp. 18 and 21; 7th *Gen. Rep. EC* (1973), pp. 45 and 497). The Treaty further amended and supplemented Arts. 7 and 78 ECSC, 4, 203 to 206 and 209 EEC, 3, 177 to 180 and 183 Euratom, 22 Merger Treaty, introducing the following major changes in the budgetary procedure. (*a*) It carried into the definitive stage, starting with the financial year 1975, the 'inverted majority' rule which in the Treaty of 1970 was provided for only

61

during the transitional stage (1971–4). (*b*) The Treaty expressly confirmed the power of Parliament to reject the draft budget and to ask for a new draft to be submitted to it 'if there are important reasons' for this (Art. 203(8) EEC). (*c*) The authority to give a discharge to the Commission in respect of the implementation of the budget was conferred exclusively on Parliament, acting on a recommendation from the Council (Art. 206b EEC). (*d*) A Court of Auditors was established which replaced the Audit Board of the Communities and the Auditor of the ECSC (Arts. 206–206a EEC, 22 Merger Treaty).

See also **Community budget, Conciliation procedure, Court of Auditors, European Parliament, Own resources.**

Further reading: Wooldridge and Sassella, 'Some Recent Legal Provisions Increasing the Budgetary Powers of the European Parliament, and Establishing a European Court of Auditors' (1976/2) *LIEI* 13. *See also under* **Community budget, European Parliament.**

▶ **CAPACITY TO INSTITUTE PROCEEDINGS** Legal capacity to appear as a party to, or to intervene in, proceedings before the ECJ. Such capacity is a necessary prerequisite for the exercise of a right of action which, in turn, is a precondition for any access to the Court. At the same time it must be distinguished from the right of action which is always a matter of an express conferment by Community law, while the capacity to institute proceedings is, in the case of natural persons, an inherent faculty recognized by law, and in the case of legal persons, a faculty attributed by law. The law that recognizes or grants such capacity is always the domestic law of a particular country, and not Community law. In the case of a natural person, this is usually the law of the country of which the person is a national or where he has his domicile; and in the case of a legal person (corporation), this is usually the law of the country where it is incorporated and/or where it has its registered office, central administration, or principal place of business. It follows that where a natural person enjoys full legal capacity according to his own personal law, or where a corporation has been properly constituted according to the relevant national law and recognized by it as a 'legal person', he/it will be regarded as having the consequent capacity to institute proceedings before the ECJ also (Case 18/57 *Nold* v. *HA* [1959] ECR 41 at pp. 48–9; Cases 16 and 17/62 *Producteurs de Fruits* v. *Council* [1962] ECR 471 at p. 483 *per* A.-G. Lagrange. For the capacity of associations to continue proceedings after dissolution and merger, see Case 294/83 *Les Verts* v. *Parliament* [1986] ECR 1339 at pp. 1362–3. See also Art. 38(5)(a) RP). Conversely, where a company is in formation but has not yet acquired legal personality under its national law at the time of bringing the action before the ECJ, the action will be inadmissible (Case 50/84 *Bensider* v. *Commission* [1984] ECR 3991 at p. 3997).

Nevertheless, possession of legal personality under national law is not always a necessary prerequisite for a body corporate to appear as a party to proceedings before the ECJ. The Court has recognized the capacity of bodies not having legal personality both to institute proceedings before it in their own name and to intervene in proceedings instituted by others, provided that they display at least the characteristics which are at the foundation of such personality, in particular the ability to undertake autonomous action and to assume liability. Thus, the ECJ has recognized that trade unions and other staff associations of European officials, which are endowed by their rules with the necessary independence to act as responsible bodies in legal matters and are sufficiently representative, have the capacity (though not necessarily the right of action) to institute proceedings even in the absence of formal legal personality (Case 175/73 *Union Syndicale* v. *Council* [1974] ECR 917 at p. 925; Case 18/74 *Syndicat Général du Personnel* v. *Commission* [1974] ECR 933 at pp. 943–4. See also Case 135/81 *Groupement des Agences de Voyages* v. *Commission* [1982] ECR 3799 at p. 3808). The ECJ has also recognized that a national union of consumers, an association formed to represent and protect the collective interests of its members, amongst other things, in judicial proceedings, but not deemed to have legal personality under national law, has the capacity to intervene in proceedings pending before the Court (Cases 41/73 etc. *S.A. Générale Sucrière* v. *Commission*

[1973] ECR 1465 at pp. 1468–9). On the other hand, the Court has denied such capacity to bodies lacking even a minimum of independence and responsibility (Case 15/63 *Lassalle* v. *Parliament* [1964] ECR 31 at p. 51).

See also Intervention, Right of action.

▶ **CAUSAL CONNECTION** One of the conditions for the establishment of the non-contractual liability of the Communities is that there must exist a direct, immediate, and exclusive causal connection between the damage alleged and the illegal act or omission with which the Community institutions or servants are charged (see in general Case 4/69 *Lütticke* v. *Commission* [1971] ECR 325 at p. 337; Case 153/73 *Holtz & Willemsen* v. *Council and Commission* [1974] ECR 675 at p. 693, etc.). Damage 'caused' not by such illegal conduct but by Treaties concluded by the Member States, such as the Treaties and Acts of Accession, cannot give rise to non-contractual liability on the part of the Communities (Case 169/73 *Compagnie Continentale* v. *Council* [1975] ECR 117 at p. 134; Cases 31 and 35/86 *LAISA* v. *Council* [1988] ECR 2285 at p. 2320).

The establishment of the necessary causality may give rise to difficult problems in practice. Although in theory it is true that any circumstance, near or remote, without which an injury would not have been produced may be considered to be its cause, the fact that a Community act or omission is one only of several such circumstances may not in itself be sufficient to establish a causal connection entailing non-contractual liability. As the ECJ has stated: 'In the field of non-contractual liability of public authorities for legislative measures, the principles common to the laws of the Member States to which the second paragraph of Article 215 of the EEC Treaty refers cannot be relied on to deduce an obligation to make good every harmful consequence, even a remote one, of unlawful legislation' (Cases 64 and 113/76 etc. *Dumortier* v. *Council* [1979] ECR 3091 at p. 3117). What is needed is that the damage complained of should be 'a sufficiently direct consequence of the unlawful conduct of the Council' or the Commission (ibid.). This will not be the case where a contributory (intervening) cause can also be shown to exist which is of such a nature as to break the chain of causation between the Community conduct and the damage.

Such a contributory (intervening) cause may consist in an act or omission of a Member State or in the conduct of the person suffering the injury himself. As regards the former, the ECJ has held that where the damage arises from an independent decision of the national authorities or from the legislative position in a Member State, the necessary relationship of cause and effect between the Community measure and the injury will be missing (Case 132/77 *Exportation des Sucres* v. *Commission* [1978] ECR 1061 at p. 1073; Cases 197 to 200/80 etc. *Ludwigshafener Walzmühle* v. *Council and Commission* [1981] ECR 3211 at p. 3255). Where, however, the conduct of the Member State has been made possible by an illegal failure of the Commission to exercise the supervisory powers conferred upon it by the Treaties, it is this failure that will be regarded as the direct cause of the damage. Thus, A.-G.

Roemer has stated that: 'The fact that conduct contrary to the Treaty on the part of a Member State is at the commencement of a chain of cause and effect does not prevent the subsequent omission of the High Authority [i.e. the Commission] from being regarded as the direct cause of the damage. If the High Authority has failed to exercise its functions of supervision with regard to a Member State it is liable for the damage which follows from the original behaviour of a Member State contrary to the Treaty' (Cases 9 and 12/60 *Vloeberghs* v. *HA* [1961] ECR 197 at p. 240; the Court adopted the same view at p. 216. See also Case 4/69 *Lütticke* v. *Commission*, above, at pp. 336 *et seq.*; Case 40/75 *Produits Bertrand* v. *Commission* [1976] ECR 1 at pp. 7–9). Where the cause of the damage can be traced back equally to an illegal action on the part of the Member State and to one on the part of the Communities (e.g. to a Community act illegally authorizing such a national action), the liability will be borne by the Member State and the Community jointly (Cases 5, 7, and 13 to 24/66 *Kampffmeyer* v. *Commission* [1967] ECR 245 at pp. 263 *et seq. per Curiam*, p. 279 *per* A.-G. Gand).

As regards the conduct of the person suffering the injury, negligence on his part involving a failure to recognize the possibility of the occurrence of the damage and an omission to take action to avoid or to limit it may operate as a contributory cause thereto and as such may break the chain of causation between the institutions' conduct and its harmful effects. Thus, where it can be shown that the applicant's own lack of foresight and circumspection has contributed to the damage, or, in other words, where he has not acted as a 'prudent and experienced person' (*bonus paterfamilias*), the causal connection will not be direct and exclusive or will be missing altogether. As a result, the Communities' liability will be diminished (and responsibility for the damage apportioned between the parties as in Case 145/83 *Adams* v. *Commission* [1985] ECR 3539 at p. 3592; see also Case 229/84 *Sommerlatte* v. *Commission* [1986] ECR 1805 at p. 1818), or will not be established at all (see e.g. Case 36/62 *Aciéries du Temple* v. *HA* [1963] ECR 289 at pp. 296–8; Case 169/73 *Compagnie Continentale* v. *Council*, above, at pp. 135–6 *per Curiam*, pp. 148 *et seq. per* A.-G. Trabucchi; Case 26/81 *Oleifici Mediterranei* v. *EEC* [1982] ECR 3057 at pp. 3079–80).

See also **Action for damages, Damage, Non-contractual liability.**

Further reading: See under **Action for damages, Non-contractual liability.**

▶ *CAUSA PETENDI* Cause of action; the grounds on which an application originating proceedings before the ECJ is based (see Case 238/78 *Ireks-Arkady* v. *Council and Commission* [1979] ECR 2955 at p. 2979 *per* A.-G. Capotorti). These must be clearly stated in the application (Art. 38(1) RP). The arguments put forward by the applicant in support of the grounds of action are dealt with in the grounds of the judgment (see Case 111/63 *Lemmerz-Werke* v. *HA* [1965] ECR 677 at p. 722 *per* A.-G. Roemer).

See also **Application originating proceedings, Judgment,** *Ne ultra petita,* **Petitum.**

▶ *CESSANTE RATIONE LEGIS, CESSAT ET IPSA LEX* General principle of law according to which 'when a rule loses its *raison d'être*, it must cease to be applied' (Case 34/74 *Roquette* [1974] ECR 1217 at p. 1238 *per* A.-G. Trabucchi). It seems that this principle, which achieves its full significance in the regulation of economic relationships which are subject to rapid changes, has never been expressly invoked by the ECJ.

▶ **COMMISSION** One of the four institutions of the European Communities, the others being the European Parliament, the Council, and the Court of Justice (Arts. 7 ECSC, 4 EEC, 3 Euratom). The present Commission was established by Art. 9 of the Merger Treaty of 1965 (MT), which provided for the merger of the former High Authority of the ECSC with the Commissions of the EEC and Euratom to form one single body serving all three Communities.

I. Organization and procedure

The Commission consists of seventeen members, who are chosen on the grounds of their general competence and whose independence is beyond doubt. Only nationals of Member States may be members of the Commission, and the Commission must include at least one but not more than two nationals of each Member State (Art. 10(1) MT as last amended by Art. 15 of the Act of Accession 1985). The members of the Commission are appointed by common accord of the Governments of the Member States for a renewable term of four years (Art. 11 MT). In practice, two Commissioners are appointed from each of the five larger Member States, i.e. France, Germany, Italy, Spain, and the United Kingdom, and one from each of the remaining seven Member States. The President and the six Vice-Presidents of the Commission are appointed from among its members, in consultation with the whole Commission, for a renewable term of two years in accordance with the same procedure (Art. 14 MT as last amended by Art. 16 of the Act of Accession 1985. For the appointment of the members, President, and Vice-Presidents of the Commission from 6 Jan. 1989, see *OJ* 1988 L351/38, L351/39, and *OJ* 1989 L31/28).

Since the Commission looks after the general interests of the Communities, it is of paramount importance that its members should be completely independent in the performance of their duties. They must therefore neither seek nor take instructions from any Government or from any other body. They are to refrain from any action incompatible with their duties. Each Member State has undertaken to respect this principle and not to seek to influence the members of the Commission in the performance of their tasks (Art. 10(2) MT). Nor may the Commissioners engage, during their term of office, in any other occupation, whether gainful or not. They are required to behave with integrity and discretion as regards the acceptance of certain appointments or benefits even after they have ceased to hold office. In the event of any breach of these obligations the Court of Justice may, on application by the Council or the Commission, compulsorily retire the member concerned or deprive him of his right to a pension or other benefits (ibid.). A Commissioner's term of office may be terminated by normal replacement, death, voluntary resignation, or compulsory retirement (Arts. 12–13 MT). The members of the Commission are required to resign as a body if the European Parliament passes a motion of censure on the activities of the Commission by the prescribed majority (Arts. 24 ECSC, 144 EEC, 114 Euratom). The Commissioners enjoy the same privileges and immunities as the officials and other servants of the Communities, in accordance with Arts. 12–15, 18, and 20 of the Protocol on Privileges and Immunities annexed to the Merger Treaty (*see further under* **Privileges and immunities**).

According to its Provisional Rules of Procedure (PRP) adopted on 6 July 1967 under Art. 16 of the Merger Treaty (*OJ Sp. Edn.* 2nd Ser. (VII), p. 14 incorporating parts of the Rules of Procedure of 1963, ibid. p. 9, as amended subsequently, see ibid. p. 22; *OJ* 1973 L7/1; *OJ* 1974 L34/28; *OJ* 1975 L199/43; *OJ* 1981 L8/16; *OJ* 1986 L72/34. See also the Decision of 6 Jan. 1973 on delegation of signature, Dec. 73/2, *OJ* 1973 L7/2), the Commission is required to act collectively and is in general governed by the principle of collegiate responsibility (Arts. 1 and 27 PRP). As the ECJ has pointed out, that principle is to be traced back to Art. 17 of the Merger Treaty, which provides that the Commission shall act by a simple majority of its members (which is nine, see Art. 2 PRP), and that its meetings are valid only if a prescribed number of members is present (which is also nine, ibid.). The principle of collegiate responsibility thus laid down 'is founded on the equal participation of the members of the Commission in the adoption of decisions and it follows from that principle, in particular, that decisions should be the subject of a collective deliberation and that all the members of the college of Commissioners bear collective responsibility on the political level for all decisions adopted' (Case 5/85 *AKZO Chemie* v. *Commission* [1986] ECR 2585 at p. 2614).

This does not mean, however, that the Commission is entirely prevented from delegating decision-making authority in certain cases. Thus, Art. 27 PRP provides that subject to the principle of collegiate responsibility being respected in full the Commission may empower its members to take, in its name and subject to its control, clearly defined measures of management or administration. Officials may also be authorized to take such measures if this is indispensable for the Commission properly to be able to fulfil its tasks. According to an internal decision adopted by the Commission, delegation of authority is subject to a number of procedural guarantees designed to ensure compliance with the principle of collegiate responsibility (these guarantees are discussed by the Court in the above-cited judgment at p. 2614). Moreover, in the particular field of competition law, the member of the Commission responsible for competition matters was granted the power to adopt in the name of the Commission certain procedural measures provided for in Reg. 17. He may decide, on his own, to initiate procedure, to seek information from undertakings, and to order an undertaking to submit to an investigation (ibid. at p. 2615).

This whole system of delegation of authority has been approved by the ECJ. Thus, the Court has held that the member of the Commission responsible for competition matters may authorize an official—the Director-General for Competition—to sign *per procurationem* statements of objections which he himself had previously approved in the exercise of the powers delegated to him by the Commission (see e.g. Case 48/69 *ICI* v. *Commission* [1972] ECR 619 at pp. 649–50; Case 8/72 *Cementhandelaren* v. *Commission* [1972] ECR 977 at pp. 988–9; Cases 43 and 63/82 *VBVB and VBBB* v. *Commission* [1984] ECR 19 at pp. 56–7). Also, the same Commissioner may adopt in the name of the Commission and subject to its control decisions ordering undertakings to submit to investigations, even although the decision of the Commission delegating such authority to him had not been published as, in principle, it should have been (Case 5/85 *AKZO Chemie* v. *Commission*, above, at pp. 2615–16). This settled case-law of the Court is based on two main considerations. First, such a system of delegation of authority does not have the effect of divesting the Commission of its powers. The Commission remains fully responsible for decisions adopted under delegated powers, which decisions may be challenged before the Court under the same conditions as if they had been considered by the full Commission. Moreover, certain measures may be reserved for the full Commission, which also has the right to reconsider any decision granting delegated powers. Secondly, such a system, which is restricted to measures of management or administration and which thus excludes policy decisions, is necessary to enable the Commission to perform its duties, having regard to the large number of decisions which it has to adopt. In its absence, the requirement of collective deliberation would have a paralysing effect on the decision-making process (ibid. at p. 2615. See also 1st *Gen. Rep. EC* (1967), p. 468). Another means serving the same purpose is the written procedure whereby proposals are circulated in writing to all members of the Commission and if no amendments or reservations are made within a fixed period, they are deemed to have been adopted by the Commission as a whole (Art. 11 PRP).

The measures adopted by the Commission must conform to certain formal and procedural requirements. These are set out in Arts. 15 ECSC, 190 EEC, 162 Euratom, 12 PRP, and Dec. 22/60 of 7 September 1960 (*OJ Sp. Edn.* 2nd Ser. (VIII), p. 13). All measures (i.e. decisions, recommendations, and opinions under the ECSC Treaty, regulations, directives, decisions, recommendations, and opinions under the EEC/Euratom Treaties) must be expressly named in their titles, must show the date of their adoption, and must be signed by the President, a Vice-President, or a member of the Commission (or, as seen above, by an official under delegated authority). All binding measures (i.e. ECSC decisions and recommendations, EEC/Euratom regulations, directives, and decisions) must contain (1) a reference to the provisions under which the measure has been adopted; (2) a reference to any proposals and opinions obtained in connection with it; and (3) a statement of the reasons on which the measure is based. ECSC general decisions and recommendations as well as EEC/Euratom regulations are to be published in the *Official Journal*. ECSC individual decisions and recommendations as well as EEC/Euratom directives and decisions are to be notified by the President of the Commission to those to whom they are addressed (see also Cases 275/80 and 24/81 *Krupp* v. *Commission* [1981] ECR 2489 at pp. 2511–12). Although Dec. 22/60 was adopted under the ECSC Treaty only, A.-G. Reischl described as 'patently untenable' the view that since the merger of the High Authority with the EEC and Euratom Commissions that decision has no longer been applicable, even though it has never been expressly repealed (ibid. at p. 2524). However, he did not state whether Dec. 22/60 also applies to measures which the Commission adopts under the EEC/Euratom Treaties.

In 1988, the Commission held 44 meetings. It adopted 6,799 instruments and sent the Council 696 proposals and 238 communications (see 22nd *Gen. Rep. EC* (1988), p. 40).

The administrative services of the Commission consist of Directorates-General (D.-G.) which are divided into Directorates which in turn are subdivided into Divisions (Art. 18 PRP). In addition, there are certain general and auxiliary services, such as the Secretariat-General, Legal Service, Spokesman's Service, Security, Statistical, and Publications Offices. There are 22 D.-G.s, each being responsible for a defined area of the Communities' activities. Each D.-G. is headed by a Director-General who is responsible to the particular Commissioner to whom the same field of responsibility ('portfolio') has been assigned by the full Commission (Art. 13 PRP. For the portfolios of individual Commissioners from 6 Jan. 1989, see 22nd *Gen. Rep. EC* (1988), p. 39). The departments of the Commission have no separate legal capacity or identity of their own and may act only under the responsibility of the Commission (Case 66/63 *Netherlands* v. *HA* [1964] ECR 533 at p. 546). In 1988, the Commission's establishment plan comprised 11,823 permanent and 505 temporary administrative posts as well as 404 permanent and 489 temporary research posts (see 22nd *Gen. Rep. EC* (1988), p. 40).

The composition, structure, and working methods of the Commission have been the subject of criticisms by the various bodies which have been set up to put forward proposals for reforming the Community institutions (see in particular the Vedel, Tindemans, Spierenburg, and Three Wise Men's Reports and the Report of the Committee on Institutional Affairs—the Dooge Committee). In 1985, the Commission endorsed a policy for the modernization of its civil service, which continued to be implemented during the course of 1986, 1987, and 1988 (see 20th, 21st, 22nd *Gen. Rep. EC* (1986, 1987, 1988), pp. 44, 38, 45, respectively).

II. Functions and powers

Art. 9 of the Merger Treaty provides that the Commission shall exercise the powers and jurisdiction conferred by the Community Treaties on the High Authority of the ECSC and on the Commissions of the EEC and Euratom. This means that the Commission is subject to three sets of jurisdictional rules and that its functions and powers vary according to the particular Treaty under which it acts in a given case. In this respect, there are considerable differences between the ECSC Treaty on the one hand, and the EEC and Euratom Treaties, on the other. These are considered separately below.

1. **Under the ECSC Treaty,** the Commission is both the chief decision-

making and the chief executive body. Its general duty is 'to ensure that the objectives set out in this Treaty are attained in accordance with the provisions thereof' (Art. 8). For this purpose, the Commission has been endowed with genuine law-making powers as it may adopt measures which are directly binding not only upon the Member States but also upon undertakings and private individuals (i.e. decisions and recommendations, see Art. 14). Before taking decisions, the Commission is normally required to consult the Council and/or the Consultative Committee, and in certain cases to receive the assent of the Council. The Commission also has a number of diverse executive tasks and powers conferred upon it: it may obtain information and carry out inspections (Arts. 46, 47); it may procure the funds which it requires to perform its tasks by imposing levies on the production of coal and steel and by contracting loans (Art. 49); it may itself grant or guarantee loans (Art. 54); it has considerable powers as regards investment (Art. 54), research (Art. 55), production (Arts. 57–9), prices (Arts. 60–4), competition (Arts. 65–7), wages (Art. 68), transport (Art. 70), commercial policy (Arts. 71–5), external relations (Arts. 93–4), and the enforcement of Treaty obligations against the Member States (Art. 88). In the words of A.-G. Roemer, under the ECSC Treaty the Commission 'groups together powers which on a national level are divided between various authorities and are subject to special rules and distinct powers' (Case 31/59 *Acciaieria di Brescia* v. *HA* [1960] ECR 71 at p. 88).

2. **Under the EEC and Euratom Treaties,** the Commission is chiefly an executive body whose main powers lie in the fields of initiating, implementing, and enforcing legislation, while the actual decision-making is primarily carried out by the Council, in many instances acting in co-operation with the European Parliament or after consulting that body and/or the Economic and Social Committee. The main task of the Commission is, under the EEC Treaty, 'to ensure the proper functioning and development of the Common Market' (Art. 155 EEC), and, under the Euratom Treaty, 'to ensure the development of nuclear energy within the Community' (Art. 124 Euratom). To enable it to perform these general tasks, both of these provisions confer on the Commission, in essentially similar terms, certain powers and entrust to it certain specific functions. These are as follows:

(*a*) To '*ensure that the provisions of this Treaty and the measures taken by the institutions pursuant thereto are applied*'. This function has two distinct aspects. First, the Commission is required to ensure that Community law is properly applied by all those subject to it, i.e. the Member States, the other Community institutions, as well as private individuals and undertakings. Secondly, the Commission is itself required to apply Community law.

Under the first aspect, the Commission acts as the 'guardian' of the Treaties, as a 'watchdog' of the Communities. It has important powers to investigate alleged violations of Community law (acting either on its own initiative or as a result of a complaint from a Member State or from a private individual), to take enforcement actions against the violator, and to impose sanctions where necessary. However, the scope of these powers varies according to the person of the violator. Thus, while the Commission may investigate non-compliance with Community law by the Member States, generally it has no power to take binding measures of enforcement against them or to impose sanctions on them. Its power lies in bringing the matter before the ECJ, and it is the judgment of the Court that will achieve the desired result since the Member States are required to comply with it, should the Court decide against them (Arts. 169, 171 EEC; 141, 143 Euratom; see also Arts. 93(2), 100A(4), 225 EEC; 38(3), 82(4) Euratom). Likewise, the Commission may institute legal proceedings before the Court against the Council (and perhaps also against the European Parliament), should these institutions act, or fail to act, contrary to the Treaties (Arts. 173, 175 EEC; 146, 148 Euratom). With regard to private individuals and undertakings, the powers of the Commission are of a quite different nature. Not only can it investigate alleged infringements of Community provisions, but it may also prescribe binding measures requiring the termination of the infringement and impose fines and other forms of sanction in certain areas such as competition, transport, competition in transport including air transport, and under the Euratom Treaty (Arts. 79(3) and (4), 87(2) EEC and measures adopted under them; Arts. 83, 145 Euratom).

Under the second aspect, the Commission acts as the executive arm of the Communities. It plays a vital role in the day-to-day implementation of Community law in a number of different areas, such as the administration of the Customs Union, the Common Agricultural Policy, the competition rules including State aids, the Common Commercial Policy. It has important powers with regard to transport, taxation, application of the various safe-guard clauses. It is required to draft and implement the Community budget and to administer four special Funds which form part of it, i.e. the European Social Fund, the European Development Fund (not yet fully integrated in the budget), the European Agricultural Guidance and Guarantee Fund, and the European Regional Development Fund. Under the Euratom Treaty, the Commission has supervisory responsibilities concerning such matters as the supply and use of fissile materials, protection of health and safety, inspection of nuclear plants, dissemination of technical information. It is in charge of a Community research and training programme including a Joint Nuclear Research Centre. It is also as the chief executive body that the Commission is required to publish annually a General Report on the Activities of the Communities (Art. 18 MT).

(b) To 'formulate recommendations or deliver opinions on matters dealt with in this Treaty, if it expressly so provides or if the Commission considers it necessary'. Since recommendations and opinions have no binding force (Arts. 189 EEC, 161 Euratom), this provision entrusts a mainly advisory or consultative function to the Commission (see e.g. Arts. 109(3), 153, 188, 237 EEC). In some cases recommendations or equivalent measures may be used in the performance of supervisory tasks (see e.g. Art. 93(1) EEC concerning State aids) or to initiate a Community procedure (see e.g. Art. 105(1) EEC concerning co-ordination of economic policies; Art. 113(3) EEC concerning the opening of treaty negotiations with third States).

71

(c) To '*have its own power of decision and [to] participate in the shaping of measures taken by the Council and by the Assembly [i.e. the European Parliament] in the manner provided for in this Treaty*'. This provision again has two distinct aspects. Firstly, it confers on the Commission a decision-making power of its own. Although, as seen above, it is true to say that under the EEC (and Euratom) Treaty the Council is the chief decision-making body, this does not mean that all original law-making power is vested in that institution while the Commission has only powers of supervision and implementation. Such a view, based on an alleged clear-cut division of powers and responsibilities between the two institutions, has been definitely rejected by the ECJ (see Cases 188 to 190/80 *France, Italy and United Kingdom* v. *Commission* [1982] ECR 2545 at pp. 2572–6). Thus, the Court has not accepted the argument that the Commission can legislate only within the limits of a specific and express power delegated to it by the Council and that its law-making measures are not of the same nature as those of the Council. The Court has pointed out, in particular, that under Art. 4 EEC the Commission is to participate in carrying out the tasks entrusted to the Community on the same basis as the other institutions; that Art. 155 confers on it the power of decision in terms almost identical to those used in Art. 145 to describe the same function of the Council; and that in defining the effects and contents of measures of the institutions Art. 189 makes no distinction between those adopted by the Council and those adopted by the Commission. The fact that most Treaty provisions confer the power to adopt general (i.e. law-making) measures on the Council is in itself not decisive and in any case such a general power cannot prevent the Commission from having concurrent powers in the same field under other provisions of the Treaty. Thus, the general power of the Council to legislate under Art. 94 EEC in relation to State aids does not preclude the Commission from adopting directives in the same field under powers granted it by Art. 90(3) EEC (ibid. at p. 2575). Moreover, the Court has recognized that where in a case falling within its competence the Council fails to legislate, contrary to the Treaty, the Commission may take emergency measures in co-operation with the Member States to meet urgent Community needs (Case 804/79 *Commission* v. *United Kingdom* [1981] ECR 1045 at pp. 1075–6 concerning the adoption of conservation measures necessary to protect fish stocks). However, in the absence of co-operation on the part of the Member States, the Commission still has no power unilaterally to lay down binding Community rules on behalf of the Council (Case 325/85 *Ireland* v. *Commission* [1987] ECR 5041 at pp. 5087–8 concerning the same matter). In practice, the original decision-making powers of the Commission, derived directly from the Treaty, are fairly restricted as compared with those delegated to it by the Council (see below under (d)).

Secondly, the Commission plays a vital part in the Community law-making process by virtue of its power to initiate legislation. Apart from a few exceptional situations where the Council may act upon its own initiative (see e.g. Arts. 73(1), 109(3), 114 EEC), in most cases the EEC Treaty provides that it shall act 'on a proposal from the Commission' (see e.g. Arts. 20, 28, 38(3),

49, 54(2), 56(2), 57). In these cases the Commission has an exclusive right of initiative, which it may have to exercise within a specified time-limit (see e.g. Arts. 21(2), 43(2)) or which it may exercise according to its own discretion (see e.g. Art. 94). However, the Council may request the Commission to submit to it any appropriate proposals (Arts. 152 EEC, 122 Euratom). In preparing its proposals, the Commission usually consults with representatives of the Member States; it may, and where required by the Treaties it must, also consult the Economic and Social Committee and/or the Euratom Scientific and Technical Committee (Arts. 198 EEC, 134, 170 Euratom; see e.g. Art. 43(2) EEC). Where the Council acts on a proposal from the Commission, it may adopt an act constituting an amendment to that proposal only by unanimity (Arts. 149(1) EEC, 119(1) Euratom). As long as the Council has not acted, the Commission may itself alter or withdraw its proposal (Arts. 149(3) EEC, 119(2) Euratom).

(d) To *'exercise the powers conferred on it by the Council for the implementation of the rules laid down by the latter'*. This provision gives effect to the distinction made between basic measures directly based on the Treaty itself and usually adopted by the Council, and derived law normally enacted by the Commission to ensure their implementation. The ECJ has in principle upheld the validity of delegation of powers to the Commission, subject to certain conditions. Thus, the Council, acting under a Treaty provision, must itself lay down the main rules and general principles (something which it may not delegate to the Commission), while leaving to the Commission the task of drawing up the necessary details. The delegation of powers must be sufficiently precise in the sense that the Council must clearly indicate the limits of the competence conferred on the Commission. On its part, the Commission may not go beyond those limits in the implementation of the basic rules and principles (Case 25/70 *Köster* [1970] ECR 1161 at pp. 1170–1; Case 291/86 *Central-Import Münster* [1988] ECR para. 13). Within the legislative framework defined by the Council, the Commission need not be restricted to the adoption of purely individual measures; it may equally be authorized to enact implementing regulations (Case 41/69 *Chemiefarma* v. *Commission* [1970] ECR 661 at p. 688 *per Curiam*, p. 708 *per* A.-G. Gand, approving delegation of powers in competition law under Reg. 17). As the ECJ has put it, 'in the exercise of its [delegated] powers, the Commission is authorised to adopt all the measures which are necessary or appropriate for the implementation of the basic legislation, provided that they are not contrary to such legislation or to the implementing legislation adopted by the Council' (Case 121/83 *Zuckerfabrik Franken* [1984] ECR 2039 at p. 2058).

In assessing the extent of the Commission's implementing powers in regard to the Common Agricultural Policy, the ECJ has held that 'the concept of implementation must be given a wide interpretation. Since only the Commission is in a position to keep track of agricultural market trends and to act quickly when necessary, the Council may confer on it wide powers of discretion and action in that sphere, and when it does so the limits of those powers must be determined in the light of the essential general aims of the market organisation' (Cases 279/84 etc. *Rau* v. *Commission* [1987] ECR

73

1069 at pp. 1120–1, confirming the Commission's power to lay down detailed rules for the implementation of the 'Christmas butter' scheme. See also Case 23/75 *Rey Soda* [1975] ECR 1279 at pp. 1300–1). Where, however, the wording of the provision conferring implementing powers does not clearly disclose an intention to grant a wide discretion, the Commission's power must be interpreted narrowly. Any measure going beyond that power thus interpreted will be annulled on the ground of lack of competence (Case 61/86 *United Kingdom* v. *Commission* [1988] ECR 431 at pp. 463–4; Case 264/86 *France* v. *Commission* [1988] ECR 973 at p. 998).

The Council is free to determine any detailed rules and procedures to which the Commission is subject in exercising the powers conferred on it. In practice, the rules which the Council has laid down in this respect provide for the consultation by the Commission of committees consisting of national experts. These committees fall into three main groups. First, Advisory Committees whose opinion is not legally binding. Secondly, Management Committees, set up for each organization of the agricultural market, whose favourable opinion reached by a qualified majority, or failure to deliver an opinion within a given time-limit (see Case 35/78 *Schouten* [1978] ECR 2543 at p. 2558; Case 128/86 *Spain* v. *Commission* [1987] ECR 4171 at p. 4196), enables the Commission to adopt measures which are immediately applicable. In the case of an adverse opinion, the Commission may also adopt measures but must communicate them to the Council. The Council, acting by a qualified majority, may take a different decision within a certain period which is usually one month. The ECJ has upheld the legality of the Management Committee procedure as established in the various agricultural regulations. In the opinion of the Court, since the Committees' sole function is to ensure permanent consultation and they themselves do not have the power to take decisions in place of the Commission or the Council, they cannot distort the institutional balance. In fact, the Court has held, this procedure enables the Council to delegate to the Commission wide implementing powers subject to its own power to take the decision if necessary (Case 25/70 *Köster*, above, at p. 1171; see also Case 16/88 *Commission* v. *Council* [1989] ECR). Thirdly, Regulatory Committees, used mainly in the field of approximation and harmonization of laws, which operate in the same way as the Management Committees except that in the case of an adverse opinion, or failure to deliver an opinion, the Commission must submit a proposal for a measure to the Council. If the Council fails to reach a decision within a certain time-limit (usually three months), the Commission may adopt the proposed measure. (For a complete list of the various Committees set up by the Council and the Commission, see Suppl. 2/80—*Bull. EC.*)

In practice, over the years the Council has not made sufficient use of the possibility of delegating powers to the Commission. Where it has, it has subjected the exercise of delegated powers to more and more complex and stultifying procedures involving a growing number of different committees (some 300 at present). To accelerate the decision-making process with a view to completing the internal market by 1992, Art. 10 of the Single European Act of 1986 (SEA) has added a new provision to Art. 145 EEC. This requires the

Council, as a matter of principle, to confer on the Commission powers for the implementation of the rules which the Council lays down. Delegation of powers has thus become a legal obligation for the Council, which may reserve to itself the right to exercise directly implementing powers only in 'specific cases', i.e. exceptionally. While the Council may impose certain requirements in respect of the use of delegated powers, it was itself required to lay down in advance the principles, rules, and procedures for the exercise of implementing powers conferred on the Commission (see Declaration No. 1 of the Inter-governmental Conference annexed to the SEA). The decision adopted by the Council for this purpose on 13 July 1987 (Dec. 87/373, *OJ* 1987 L197/33) provides that the Commission is to exercise its implementing and management powers in one of three ways: (i) independently; (ii) by one of three procedures which largely correspond to the Advisory, Management, and Regulatory Committee procedures although they contain certain new rules; or (iii) by a special emergency procedure to be used in the case of safeguard measures (e.g. under the Common Commercial Policy). The decision of the Council, which significantly departed from the Commission's original proposal (*OJ* 1986 C70/6) and from Parliament's opinion (*OJ* 1986 C297/94, see also *OJ* 1987 C190/75), was criticized by the Commission (see *Bull. EC* 6–1987, pp. 103–4) and challenged for annulment by the European Parliament before the Court of Justice, but the action was held inadmissable on account of Parliament's lack of *locus standi* (Case 302/87 *Parliament* v. *Council* (1988) ECR. See also 22nd *Gen. Rep. EC* (1988), p. 33).

(*e*) In addition to the four functions listed in Arts. 155 EEC, 124 Euratom, the Commission has important tasks assigned to it in the field of the Communities' *external relations*. It is responsible for the maintenance of all appropriate relations with other international organizations (Arts. 229 EEC, 199 Euratom). It negotiates, and under the Euratom Treaty also concludes, treaties and agreements with third States (Arts. 113, 228 EEC, 101 Euratom). The President of the Commission, acting jointly with the President of the Council, receives the credentials of Heads of Mission of non-Member States accredited to the Community (Luxembourg Compromise of 1966, point (a)(3)). The Commission represents the Communities as legal persons in the Member States (Arts. 211 EEC, 185 Euratom). (*See further under* **External relations, Treaty-making procedure.**)

See also **Committee on Institutional Affairs, Consultative Committee, Council, Economic and Social Committee, European Parliament, European Union, External relations, Institutional balance, Institutions, Luxembourg Compromise, Privileges and immunities, Scientific and Technical Committee, Secondary legislation, Single European Act, Spierenburg Report, Three Wise Men's Report, Tindemans Report, Treaty-making procedure, Vedel Report.**

Further reading 1. ʙᴏᴏᴋ: Lasok and Bridge, *Law and Institutions of the European Communities*, 4th edn. (1987), ch. 5.

2. ᴀʀᴛɪᴄʟᴇs: Noël, 'The Commission's Power of Initiative' (1973) 10 *CML Rev.* 123; id., 'The Functioning of the Commission of the European Communities', in Bates *et al.* (eds.), *In Memoriam J. D. B. Mitchell* (1983), p. 107; van Miert, 'The

Appointment of the President and the Members of the European Commission' (1973) 10 *CML Rev.* 257.

3. OFFICIAL PUBLICATIONS: House of Lords, Select Committee on the European Communities, Session 1985–6, 19th Report, 'Delegation of Powers to the Commission' (1986); id., Session 1986–7, 3rd Report, 'Delegation of Powers to the Commission (Final Report)' (1986).

See also under Community law; Institutions, Single European Act.

▶ **COMMITTEE OF PERMANENT REPRESENTATIVES (COREPER)** Committee formally set up by Art. 4 of the Merger Treaty of 1965 with responsibility for preparing the work of the Council and for carrying out the tasks assigned to it by the Council (see also Art. 16 of the Council's Rules of Procedure of 24 July 1979 (CRP), *OJ* 1979 L268/1). In reality, such a Committee had already existed since January 1958. Since the original EEC and Euratom Treaties made no provision for it (they only authorized the Council to set up such a Committee by its Rules of Procedure, see Arts. 151(2) EEC, 121(2) Euratom), its legal existence was based on Art. 16 of the Provisional Rules of Procedure adopted by the Council on 18 March 1958 (see *Bull. EC* 10–1980, p. 24). A similar Committee, called Co-ordinating Committee (COCOR), had assisted the ECSC Council since 1953. Since the coming into force of the Merger Treaty in 1967, a single Committee of Permanent Representatives has been serving all three Communities, incorporating its two predecessors.

The Committee consists of the Permanent Representatives of the Member States accredited to the Communities, who are civil servants with the rank of Ambassador. It itself is assisted by a network of working parties and committees—currently more than fifty—composed of senior national officials and experts, which carry out such preparatory work and studies as the Committee may assign to them. As at Council meetings, the Commission is generally represented at all meetings of the Committee and of the working parties. The General Secretariat of the Council assists the Committee and its subsidiary bodies in carrying out their tasks. The Committee and the working parties are presided over by the delegate of that Member State whose representative is President of the Council (Art. 16 CRP). To meet its increasing workload, the Committee has divided itself into two parts: COREPER I, composed of Deputy Permanent Representatives who generally discuss matters of a more technical nature, and COREPER II, composed of the Ambassadors (Permanent Representatives), who deal with politically important matters (see *Bull. EC* 10–1980, p. 24).

The Committee fulfils three important tasks. First, it prepares all the meetings of the Council which, consisting of members who are full-time active Ministers in their own countries, meets relatively infrequently and would otherwise not be able to cope with the volume of legislation needed by the Communities. Secondly, it acts as liaison between the national Governments and the Community institutions, informing both sides of each other's viewpoints. Thirdly, it acts as mediator or interface between the Council and the Commission, thus making the smooth passage of legislation possible.

The Committee has no decision-making powers of its own. It is not a Committee of Ministers' Deputies and the Council cannot delegate to it the powers conferred upon it by the Treaties. Nevertheless, it does exert considerable influence on the legislative process in two different ways. First, once the Permanent Representatives have reached agreement on a proposal from the Commission, the matter is put on the Council's agenda as a 'Part A' item and as such may be approved by the Council without further discussion (although this does not exclude the possibility of any member of the Council or of the Commission initiating discussion on the subject, see Art. 2(6) and (7) CRP). Most legislation of a technical nature is adopted in this way. Secondly, where the conflict of national interests is such that reaching agreement in the Council seems unlikely, COREPER may 'freeze' Commission proposals by not putting them on the agenda or by constantly referring them to the various committees. Many proposals have ended up in this way.

See also **Council, Privileges and immunities.**

Further reading: Noël, 'The Committee of Permanent Representatives' (1967) 5 JCMS 219. *See also under* **Council.**

▶ **COMMITTEE OF PRESIDENTS** Committee set up by the original Art. 78 ECSC, consisting of the Presidents of the four institutions—the Court of Justice, the High Authority, the Assembly, and the Council—and presided over by the President of the Court. The Committee acted as a kind of budgetary authority in respect of the administrative expenditure of the ECSC. It had the power to adopt the general estimate incorporating the estimate of the administrative expenditure of each institution, which had the effect of authorizing and requiring the High Authority to collect the corresponding revenue as provided in Art. 49 ECSC. The Committee could also determine the number of the Community's servants and the scale of their salaries, allowances, and pensions, where not already fixed by or under the Treaty; it could adopt the Staff Regulations (see the original Art. 7(3) of the Convention on the Transitional Provisions annexed to the ECSC Treaty, subsequently repealed and replaced by Art. 24 of the Merger Treaty); it could determine any extraordinary expenditure; authorize the transfer of appropriations within or between chapters; and deal with any supplementary estimates. The annual report drawn up by the auditor was also to be submitted to the Committee. Art. 78 ECSC was substantially amended by the Budgetary Treaties of 1970 and 1975, which introduced a uniform budgetary procedure for the three Communities, and the Committee of Presidents ceased to exist upon the former Treaty's coming into force on 1 January 1971.

See also **Community budget.**

▶ **COMMITTEE ON A PEOPLE'S EUROPE (ADONNINO COMMITTEE)** One of two *ad hoc* Committees set up by the European Council at Fontainebleau on 25 and 26 June 1984 to establish practical means of moving towards closer European Union (the other *ad hoc* Committee set up was that on

Institutional Affairs, also known as the Dooge Committee). The Committee consisted of the representatives of the Heads of State or Government of the Member States and of the President of the Commission and was chaired by Mr Pietro Adonnino, representative of Mr Bettino Craxi, Prime Minister of Italy. Its terms of reference were to prepare and co-ordinate action 'to strengthen and promote the identity and image [of the Community] both for its citizens and for the rest of the world' (*Bull. EC* 6–1984, p. 11; 18th *Gen. Rep. EC* (1984), p. 26). The Committee submitted an interim Report to the European Council in Brussels on 29 and 30 March 1985 (*Bull. EC* 3–1985, pp. 13, 21, text at p. 111), and a final Report to the European Council in Milan on 28 and 29 June 1985 (*Bull. EC* 6–1985, pp. 14, 21. Full text of both Reports with covering letters in Suppl. 7/85—*Bull. EC*. See also 19th *Gen. Rep. EC* (1985), p. 122).

The interim Report focuses on measures which are of direct relevance to Community citizens and which offer them tangible benefits in their everyday lives. Emphasis is laid on arrangements which may be implemented in the short term. Proposals are made for easing the rules and practices which cause irritation to the citizen and undermine the credibility of the Community. These proposals include simplified frontier formalities; a uniform European passport (the introduction of which had long been accepted by the European Council); periodical increases in tax-free allowances; new exemptions for books and periodicals; avoidance of double taxation on personal goods; easing of the formalities of currency controls; special treatment of frontier workers; improved services for tourists; etc. The Report also deals with Community citizens' rights, in particular with the still remaining difficulties in respect of employment, establishment, and residence. Amongst other things, it recommends the mutual recognition of diplomas and other qualifications without prior harmonization and the recognition of a general right of residence in any Member State for all citizens of the Community, subject to certain conditions.

The final Report contains both specific proposals to be implemented without delay and longer-term objectives to make the Community more of a reality for its citizens. These proposals relate to such matters as the special rights of citizens; culture and communication; information; youth, education, exchanges, and sport; volunteer work in Third World development; health, social security, and drugs; twinning; and strengthening of the Community's image and identity.

The European Council approved the proposals contained in the Reports of the Committee and instructed the Council, the Commission, and the Member States to take the necessary implementing measures. It also decided that the Intergovernmental Conference convened to draw up amendments to the EEC Treaty should follow the recommendations of the Adonnino and the Dooge Committees (*Bull. EC* 3–1985, p. 13; *Bull. EC* 6–1985, pp. 13–14). These Committees were thus instrumental in the coming into existence of the Single European Act of 1986, which was the outcome of that Conference.

See also **Committee on Institutional Affairs, European Union, Single European Act.**

► **COMMITTEE ON INSTITUTIONAL AFFAIRS (DOOGE COMMITTEE)**
One of two *ad hoc* Committees set up by the European Council at Fontaine-bleau on 25 and 26 June 1984 to establish practical means of moving towards closer European Union (the other *ad hoc* Committee set up was that on a People's Europe, also known as the Adonnino Committee). The Committee consisted of the personal representatives of the Heads of State or Government of the Member States and of the President of the Commission and was chaired by Mr James Dooge, President of the Irish Senate and former Minister of Foreign Affairs. Its terms of reference were 'to make suggestions for the improvement of the operation of European cooperation in both the Community field and that of political, or any other, cooperation' (*Bull. EC 6–1984*, p. 11; 18th *Gen. Rep. EC* (1984), p. 25). By resolution, the European Parliament asked to be involved in the Committee's discussions and urged the Committee to base its work on the Draft Treaty establishing the European Union, which Parliament adopted in February 1984 (*Bull. EC 7/8–1984*, p. 83). The Committee submitted an interim Report to the European Council in Dublin on 3 and 4 December 1984 (*Bull. EC 11–1984*, p. 70, text at p. 101), and a final Report to the European Council in Brussels on 29 and 30 March 1985 (*Bull. EC 3–1985*, p. 14, text at p. 102. See also 19th *Gen. Rep. EC* (1985), p. 29).

The final Report begins by stressing the need to make a qualitative leap ahead by the creation of a genuine political entity in the form of a European Union. For this purpose, the Report suggests the following priority objectives:

- the creation of a fully integrated internal market by the end of the decade on the basis of a precise timetable, including the creation of a technological Community and the strengthening of the European Monetary System (EMS);
- the promotion of the common values of civilization, including measures to protect the environment, the establishment of a European social area and of a homogeneous judicial area, and the promotion of common cultural values;
- the development of an external identity by the strengthening of European Political Co-operation (EPC), including questions of security and defence.

To achieve these objectives, the Report proposes a number of institutional changes and adjustments, such as:

- the European Council should play a purely strategic role by giving direction and political impetus to the Community rather than being involved in its day-to-day business. It should hold only two meetings a year;
- the decision-making in the Council should be improved. The 'General Affairs' Council should play a pre-eminent role of co-ordination and guidance. A new general principle on voting should be adopted according to which decisions should be taken by a qualified or simple majority while unanimity should be restricted to certain exceptional cases, distinctly fewer in number than those specified in the EEC Treaty. The

79

Presidency should, in the spirit of the Treaties, call a vote if the Commission or three Member States so request;

- the powers of the Commission should be increased, in particular through greater delegation of executive responsibility by the Council. Its President should be designated by the European Council and its members appointed on a proposal from the President-designate. It should not include more than one national from any Member State. Being the linchpin of the Communities, the Commission should have full powers of initiative, implementation, and administration;
- the role of the European Parliament should be enhanced, in particular (1) by effective participation in the legislative process in the form of joint decision-making with the Council; (2) by increasing its supervision of the various policies of the Union and its political control over the Commission and over co-operation in the external policy field: the association and accession agreements negotiated by the Union should be submitted to Parliament for approval; (3) by giving it responsibility in decisions on revenue: decisions on own resources should be taken jointly by the Council and Parliament;
- the Court of Justice should be relieved of staff cases and should be given jurisdiction for the interpretation of Community agreements by means of a standard clause.

As regards the methods of implementing the above proposals, the Report recommends that an Intergovernmental Conference should be convened to negotiate a draft European Union Treaty based on the *acquis communautaire*, the present Report, the Stuttgart Solemn Declaration on European Union of 1983, and guided by the spirit and method of the Draft Treaty on European Union adopted by the European Parliament. In addition to the Member States, including Spain and Portugal, the Commission should also participate in the negotiations and the outcome of the Conference should be submitted to the European Parliament. The very decision of convening such a Conference would represent the initial act of European Union.

While the Report contained a series of reservations mainly by the British, Danish, and Greek members of the Committee, it was favourably received by the European Council (*Bull. EC* 3–1985, p. 14), which at its meeting in Milan on 28 and 29 June 1985 decided to convene an Intergovernmental Conference to implement its proposals (*Bull. EC* 6–1985, p. 13; 19th *Gen. Rep. EC* (1985), p. 29). The outcome of that Conference was the Single European Act which was formally adopted in February 1986 and came into force on 1 July 1987. Thus, the proposals of the Dooge Committee, although less ambitious than the Parliament's Draft Treaty on European Union, played, together with those of the Adonnino Committee, an important part in the reform of the Community institutions.

See also Acquis communautaire, Commission, Committee on a People's Europe, Council, European Council, European Parliament, European Union, Institutional balance, Institutions, Single European Act, Solemn

Declaration on European Union, Spierenburg Report, Three Wise Men's Report, Tindemans Report.

Further reading: Editorial, 'The Dooge Committee and Majority Voting on the Council' (1985) 10 *EL Rev.* 85.

▶ *COMMON MARKET LAW REPORTS (CMLR)* Unofficial publication in existence since 1962 which reports a selection of:

- cases before the ECJ;
- cases before the Commission and the Council;
- cases before national courts (whether of Member States or of non-Member States);
- European Community legislation and draft legislation.

Since 1985, the editorial policy has been:

1. to report all of the following: Commission decisions on competition; UK decisions of courts, tribunals, ombudsman, etc. on Community law; ECJ decisions on competition, State aids, anti-dumping, Art. 30 EEC, sex discrimination, VAT, treaties and international law, banking and insurance, establishment and services, aliens, human rights, copyright and communications, patents and trade marks, company law, transport, Convention on Jurisdiction and Enforcement of Judgments;

2. not to report: staff cases, customs classification, monetary compensatory amounts (except in special cases);

3. to report an *ad hoc* selection of the remaining categories of cases before the ECJ and before national courts other than UK courts.

ECJ cases are reported in the official English translation where this is available; where not, they are reported in own translation and, occasionally, also in the original foreign language version. The operative part is always reported in official translation (see Editor's Note in [1985] 1 CMLR 1). The *CMLR* has no official standing before the ECJ.

See also European Court Reports.

▶ COMMUNITY BUDGET Instrument which 'sets out forecasts of, and authorises in advance, the expected revenue and expenditure of the Communities for each year' (Art. 1(1) of the Financial Regulation of 21 Dec. 1977 (FR), *OJ* 1977 L356/1). It is 'an accounting document which contains two statements relating to the revenue to be realised and to the expenditure to be provided for within a given period of time' and which is endowed with binding force *vis-à-vis* the Community institutions and the Member States by the act which promulgates it, i.e. a declaration by the President of the European Parliament that the budget has been finally adopted (Case 34/86 *Council* v. *Parliament* [1986] ECR 2155 at p. 2175 *per* A.-G. Mancini, p. 2202 *per Curiam.* See further below).

The single Community budget, known as the 'general budget of the European Communities', was created by Art. 20 of the Merger Treaty of 1965 (MT), as amended by Art. 10 of the Budgetary Treaty of 1970, and took

81

the place of (1) the administrative budget of the ECSC, (2) the budget of the EEC, (3) the operating budget, and (4) the research and investment budget of the Euratom, which had existed as four separate budgets between 1958 and the end of 1968. The general budget thus incorporates the administrative expenditure of the ECSC and the revenue relating thereto, the revenue and expenditure of the EEC, and the revenue and expenditure of the Euratom, with the exception of that of the Supply Agency and the Joint Undertakings (Art. 20(1) MT; Art. 1(1) FR). It does not include the following:

1. The operating budget of the ECSC which is, strictly speaking, not a real budget but an economic plan without binding effect. It consists of two columns headed 'requirements' and 'resources', respectively. The resources are, for the most part, made up of levies which the Commission is empowered to impose on the production of coal and steel under Art. 49 ECSC. These levies are assessed annually on the various products according to their average value but their rate may not exceed 1 per cent unless previously authorized by the Council (Art. 50(2) ECSC). The mode of assessment and collection of the levies was laid down in Dec. 2–52, which is still in force in an amended form (*OJ Sp. Edn.* 1952–8, p. 3, last amended by Dec. 3565/83, *OJ* 1983 L355/19). The amount of and methods for applying the levies was first determined by Dec. 3–52 (*OJ Sp. Edn.* 1952–8, p. 4). This decision is annually amended by a decision which fixes the rate of the levies for the following financial year and which contains, in the Annex, the operating budget for that year, extending over less than a page (for 1989, see Dec. 4031/88, *OJ* 1988 L355/33, fixing the rate of the levies at 0.31 per cent. See also 22nd *Gen. Rep. EC* (1988), p. 71. The operating budget for 1989 was 329 million ECU). In addition to levies and other ordinary resources (such as net balance from previous year, fines and surcharges for late payment, cancellation of commitments), the ECSC resources also include extraordinary revenue in the form of a sum transferred from the general budget subject to the agreement of the Council. The requirements include the following items (see Art. 50(1) ECSC): administrative expenditure (which is incorporated in the general budget), aid for redeployment (Art. 56 ECSC), aid for research (Art. 55 ECSC), interest subsidies on ECSC loans (Arts. 54 and 56 ECSC), and social measures connected with the restructuring of the steel industry (to be financed from the extraordinary revenue referred to above). In spite of continuing pressure from the European Parliament, not all the financial activities of the ECSC are included in the budget. Thus, borrowing and lending operations are still not entered into the budget; nor was, prior to the 1988 budgetary reform, the revenue raised by customs duties on imports of ECSC products channelled directly and exclusively to the ECSC but it accrued to the Member States (see Res. of 20 Nov. 1987 on the 1988 operating budget, *OJ* 1987 C345/214). As regards procedure, the sole budgetary authority is the Commission, which alone adopts the budget, although it does seek Parliament's opinion on a voluntary basis (see the above Res.). Parliament has repeatedly called for the drawing up of a Financial Regulation in respect of the ECSC operating budget and for the integration of this budget with the general budget of the Communities (ibid.).

2. The activities of the European Investment Bank, which enjoys independent status and financial autonomy (although EIB loans to Mediterranean countries guaranteed by the general budget are shown for information purposes in Annex II to Part B of Section III of the budget; for the 1988 budget, see *OJ* 1988 L226/1264).

3. EEC and Euratom borrowing and lending operations. Commission guarantees are given token entries in the budget while the operations are shown, by way of indication, in Annex II to Part B of Section III (ibid. p. 1071; see Art. 16(3) FR).

4. The operational activities of the European Development Fund which grants aid to associated African, Caribbean, and Pacific (ACP) countries and is financed from contributions paid by the Member States (see the conclusions of the Brussels European Council of 11–13 Feb. 1988, *Bull. EC* 2–1988, p. 12).

5. The European Schools and the University Institute in Florence.

6. The activities of certain entities set up under and governed by Community law, which enjoy legal personality and financial autonomy, such as the European Centre for the Development of Vocational Training—Cedefop (Reg. 337/75, *OJ* 1975 L39/1); the European Foundation for the Improvement of Living and Working Conditions (Reg. 1365/75, *OJ* 1975 L139/1); and the European Agency for Co-operation (Reg. 3245/81, *OJ* 1981 L328/1). The statements of revenue and expenditure of the first two of these bodies are published for information purposes in the *Official Journal* (for 1988, see *OJ* 1988 L227/1 and L227/25, respectively) and a subsidy allocated to them is entered in the general budget (for the 1988 budget, see *OJ* 1988 L226/630 and L226/640, respectively).

7. The revenue and expenditure of the Euratom Supply Agency, which has legal personality and financial autonomy and operates in accordance with commercial principles. This revenue and expenditure is to be budgeted for in a special account (Arts. 171(1) and (2) Euratom, 20(1) MT). Any participation in the capital of the Agency and in its investment expenditure must be included in the expenditure shown in the budget (Art. 174(2) Euratom). Euratom subsidy for operation of the Supply Agency is included in the budget (for the 1988 budget, see *OJ* 1988 L226/370).

8. The revenue and expenditure of Euratom Joint Undertakings (such as the Joint European Torus—JET), which have legal personality (Arts. 171(1) and (3) Euratom, 20(1) MT). Any participation in Joint Undertakings must be included in the expenditure shown in the budget (Art. 174(2) Euratom).

I. Contents and structure of the budget

The most important rules and principles relating to the contents and structure of the general budget may be summarized as follows (see Arts. 78–78h ECSC, 199–209 EEC, 171–83 Euratom as amended by the Budgetary Treaties of 1970 and 1975. Only the EEC provisions will be cited):

1. All items of revenue and expenditure of the Communities are to be included in estimates to be drawn up for each financial year, and are to be

83

shown in the budget (Arts. 199 EEC, 3(1) FR)—*the principle of unity or comprehensiveness*, also known as *the principle of 'complete and authentic budgetization'* (see Case 34/86 *Council* v. *Parliament*, above, at p. 2209 *per Curiam*, pp. 2180–1 *per* A.-G. Mancini. In that case Parliament charged the Council with having infringed this principle by not entering all expenditure in the budget; see also Res. of 14 Nov. 1985, *OJ* 1985 C345/74, point 11, also cited in the judgment). The principle of comprehensiveness is, however, not fully observed as there are certain special sources of finance and corresponding expenditure which are not included in the general budget (these are listed above). The European Parliament and the Commission have repeatedly urged the complete incorporation in the budget, in particular, of all borrowing and lending operations and of the European Development Fund, but the Council has so far been unwilling to agree to this (see e.g. the Commission's proposal of 15 June 1978 for amending the Financial Regulation of 1977, *OJ* 1978 C160/11 and EP Res. of 10 Apr. 1981, *OJ* 1981 C101/107. The failure of the Council to meet this demand was one of the reasons for rejecting the draft budget for 1980, see *Bull. EC* 12–1979, p. 120).

2. All revenue must be used without distinction to finance all expenditure entered in the budget, in other words, revenue may not be allocated to particular items of expenditure in advance; nor may any adjustment be made between revenue and expenditure—*the principle of universality or non-assignment* and *the gross budget principle* (see Arts. 3(1) FR and 6(1) of Dec. 88/376 of 24 June 1988 on the system of the Communities' own resources, *OJ* 1988 L185/24). This principle, too, is subject to certain exceptions. Thus, Art. 6(2) of Dec. 88/376 allows the financing of expenditure relating to supplementary research programmes, entered in the budget, by means of financial contributions from the Member States. Art. 3(2) FR provides that revenue earmarked for a specific purpose, such as income from foundations, subsidies, gifts, and bequests (which the Commission may accept on behalf of the Communities), shall not be used for any other purpose. Art. 22 FR allows netting-off and adjustment between particular items of revenue and expenditure in certain specific cases.

3. The expenditure shown in the budget is to be authorized for one financial year, which runs from 1 January to 31 December. The revenue of a financial year is to be entered in the accounts for that financial year on the basis of the amounts collected during that year, and the allotted appropriations are to be used solely to cover expenditure properly entered into and paid in the financial year for which they were granted—*the principle of annuality* (see Arts. 202(1) and 203(1) EEC, 1(2) and 5 FR). Nevertheless, there are some important exceptions to this principle also. Thus, under Art. 202(2) EEC, any appropriations, other than those relating to staff expenditure, that are unexpended at the end of the financial year may be carried forward to the next financial year only. Detailed provisions for the application of this rule have been laid down in Art. 6 FR as amended by Reg. 1252/79, *OJ* 1979 L160/1.

Another exception to the principle of annuality was created by the Financial Regulation of 21 Dec. 1977, which introduced a distinction between *commit-*

ment appropriations and *payment appropriations* in respect of multi-annual activities and projects (so-called '*differentiated*' *appropriations*). Commitment appropriations cover, for the current financial year, the total cost of the legal obligations entered into for activities whose implementation extends over more than one financial year. Payment appropriations cover, up to the limit of the amount entered in the budget, expenditure arising from commitments entered into in the current and/or preceding financial years (Art. 1(3) FR). Only the payment appropriations must be covered by revenue and their total amount is equal to the total amount of revenue, with which they must be balanced (see under (5) below). Under Art. 6(2) of the 1977 FR, commitment appropriations not committed at the end of the financial year remained available for the following financial year. Payment appropriations not used at the end of the financial year were carried over automatically to the next financial year only. These provisions were, however, amended by Reg. 2049/88 of 24 June 1988, *OJ* 1988 L185/3, which was adopted by the Council as part of the budgetary reforms introduced in 1988 (see section IV below). In order to strengthen the principle of annuality, Reg. 2049/88 discontinues automatic carryovers by providing that commitment and payment appropriations which have not been used at the end of the financial year for which they were entered shall, as a rule, lapse. Nevertheless, the Commission may decide by 15 February of the following year to carry over certain commitment and payment appropriations subject to strictly defined criteria provided that it informs the budgetary authority by 15 March. Reg. 2049/88 also provides that commitment appropriations shall, as a rule, lapse as a result of total or partial cancellation of the corresponding projects. However, the Commission may decide by 15 February to make these appropriations available again when it is essential to carry out the programme originally planned and the budget does not contain sufficient funds for this purpose. The Commission must inform the budgetary authority by 15 March.

4. Appropriations must be classified under different chapters grouping items of expenditure according to their nature or purpose and subdivided as necessary (Arts. 202(3) EEC, 21(1) FR)—*the principle of specification* intended to ensure that the appropriations available are not aggregated but allocated to specific destinations. Nevertheless, the Commission may transfer appropriations from one chapter to another or from one article to another within a chapter, subject to the detailed rules laid down in Art. 21 FR (Art. 205(3) EEC). In the event of unavoidable, exceptional, or unforeseen circumstances, amending and/or supplementary budgets may be adopted according to the ordinary procedure (Art. 1(5) FR, see e.g. amending and supplementary budget No. 1 for 1988, *OJ* 1988 L265/1, amending the 1988 budget to bring it into line with Council Dec. 88/376 on the new own resources system, adopted on the same day, see further section IV below). Amending budgets do not alter the total amount of the annual budget but merely the distribution of expenditure and/or revenue; supplementary budgets alter the overall amount of expenditure and revenue.

5. The revenue and expenditure shown in the budget must be in balance (Arts. 199(2) and 203(10) EEC, 20(1) MT)—*the principle of equilibrium*

between revenue and expenditure. Originally, the revenue was provided by the Member States by way of financial contributions on a scale laid down in the Treaty (see Art. 200 EEC). These financial contributions were replaced by the Communities' own resources by virtue of Council Dec. 70/243 of 21 Apr. 1970, *OJ Sp. Edn.* 1970(I), p. 224, according to which the budget was to be financed entirely from the Communities' own resources as from 1 January 1975 (in practice, this happened for the first time only in the 1980 financial year, see 14th *Gen. Rep. EC* (1980), pp. 42, 56–7. On financing the budget in general, see Suppl. 8/78—*Bull. EC*). The Decision of 21 Apr. 1970 was replaced by Dec. 85/257 of 7 May 1985, *OJ* 1985 L128/15, which in turn was replaced by Dec. 88/376 of 24 June 1988, *OJ* 1988 L185/24, which created a new system of the Communities' own resources as part of the budgetary reforms introduced in 1988 (see further section IV below *and under* **Own resources**). In addition to own resources, the revenue of the Communities includes any financial contributions based on GNP that may be payable instead of VAT (Art. 2(7) of the Dec. of 24 June 1988; in 1988 only Portugal paid such contributions); surpluses, such as balance from previous year; miscellaneous Community taxes, levies, and dues including taxes on the salaries, wages, and allowances of the members and officials of the Community institutions and of the European Investment Bank (EIB) (see Arts. 13 and 22 of the Protocol on Privileges and Immunities; Arts. 9 and 12 of Reg. 260/68, *OJ Sp. Edn.* 1968(I), p. 37, and Case 85/86 *Commission* v. *Board of Governors of the EIB* [1988] ECR 1281 at p. 1321); proceeds from the administrative operation of the institutions; contributions to Community programmes; interest on late payments; fines, periodic penalty payments, and other penalties; borrowing and lending operations; miscellaneous revenue. For the financial year 1988, the estimated total revenue was in excess of 43,820 million ECU, which was of course also the amount of total expenditure (see amending and supplementary budget No. 1 for 1988, *OJ* 1988 L265/5 and L265/16. The general budget for 1988 was published in *OJ* 1988 L226/1). For the same financial year, the main items of expenditure were (in million ECUs, rounded-up figures): agricultural market guarantees (28,500); agricultural structures (1,219); fisheries (282); regional policy and transport (3,211); social policy (2,841); research, energy, and industry (1,121); co-operation with developing and other third countries (893); repayments and reserves (3,779); staff and administrative expenditure of the Community institutions (1,974) (see *OJ* 1988 L265/16).

6. Art. 203 EEC and the corresponding provisions in the other Treaties, as amended by the Budgetary Treaties of 1970 and 1975, make a distinction between *compulsory expenditure (CE)* and *non-compulsory expenditure (NCE)*. CE is referred to in Art. 203 as 'expenditure necessarily resulting from this Treaty or from acts adopted in accordance therewith'. In a Joint Declaration adopted on 30 June 1982 (*OJ* 1982 C194/1), the European Parliament, the Council, and the Commission defined CE as expenditure which 'the budgetary authority is obliged to enter in the budget to enable the Community to meet its obligations, both internally and externally, under the Treaties and acts adopted in accordance therewith'. All other expenditure is

NCE. An Annex attached to the Joint Declaration contains classification of all headings in the 1982 budget into CE and NCE. It appears from this that all expenditure of the institutions other than the Commission, and most administrative expenditure of the Commission, is NCE. Of the operating appropriations, most expenditure relating to the Common Agricultural Policy is CE, while most other expenditure is NCE, with the exception of guarantees and aids which fall into both categories. However, this classification is neither precise nor rigid, and may be altered by agreement between the two institutions which make up the budgetary authority, i.e. the Council and the Parliament, on a proposal from the Commission. New items are classified in the same way. Declaration No. 1 of the Council of 22 Apr. 1970, annexed to the Budgetary Treaty of 1970, also recognizes that this classification may change 'in the light of the operational requirements of the Communities' (printed in *Treaties Establishing the European Communities* (1987), p. 1093). In fact, the Commission proposed new classification in the 1989 preliminary draft budget. The volume of NCE has increased over the years from an initial 3 per cent of the budget to 25.6 per cent in 1988 (*Bull. EC* 6–1988, p. 110; see further section IV below).

The distinction between CE and NCE is important in two main respects. First, the power to determine the budget is divided between the Council and the European Parliament (EP) in such a way that the Council has the right of decision in respect of CE, while the EP has the right of decision in respect of NCE (see further section II(6) below). Secondly, NCE is limited to a maximum rate of increase in relation to NCE in the previous financial year, which is to be fixed annually in the course of the budgetary procedure. This maximum rate is declared by the Commission on the basis of three objective factors, namely, the trend of the GNP within the Community, the average variation in the budgets of the Member States, and the trend of the cost of living during the preceding financial year. The maximum rate is communicated to all the institutions, which are required to conform to it during the budgetary procedure subject to two qualifications. First, the EP enjoys what is called the 'margin for manœuvre'. This means that if the increase in NCE appearing in the draft budget established by the Council is over half the maximum rate as indicated by the Commission, the EP may, exercising its right of amendment, further increase the total amount of that expenditure but only to a limit not exceeding half the maximum rate. Secondly, where the EP, the Council, or the Commission considers that the activities of the Communities require that the rate determined by the Commission should be exceeded, another rate may be fixed by agreement between the Council, acting by a qualified majority, and the EP, acting by a majority of its members and three-fifths of the votes cast (Art. 203(9) EEC).

In practice, these provisions have given rise to a continuous power conflict between the Council and the EP in the matter of determining and, in particular, increasing the NCE. This conflict culminated in Case 34/86 *Council* v. *Parliament*, above, which concerned the 1986 budget. The cause of the dispute was that the EP increased NCE in excess of the maximum rate as fixed by the Commission, without obtaining the consent of the Council. In

Parliament's opinion, this was necessary since the draft budget submitted by the Council had 'illegally' failed to provide sufficient appropriations for certain items of expenditure. The Council was willing to enter into a compromise solution, but only on its own terms. The Court held that all types of NCE fell within the scope of the rule relating to the maximum rate of increase and that in view of its importance, the agreement required by Art. 203(9) between the Council and Parliament could not be inferred on the basis of the presumed intention of one or the other of those institutions (ibid. at pp. 2208–9). Since the President of the EP had declared the budget for 1986 finally adopted in the absence of an agreement between the two institutions, this act was illegal and had to be annulled (ibid. at pp. 2210, 2211). However, such annulment did not have retroactive effect, and the Council and the EP were required to resume the budgetary procedure with a view to coming to an agreement on the new rate of increase (ibid. at pp. 2211–12). Such an agreement was in fact reached, and a new budget for 1986 adopted, within a week of the delivery of the judgment (see *Bull. EC* 7/8–1986, pp. 7, 9). In addition to the Council, five Member States also brought actions for the annulment of the 1986 budget. These were subsequently withdrawn, although the Court made an order in one of them (see Case 23/86R *United Kingdom* v. *Parliament* [1986] ECR 1085).

7. As regards the *structure of the budget*, it consists of a general statement of the revenue of the Communities, followed by separate sections, subdivided into statements of revenue and expenditure, dealing with the European Parliament, the Council, the Commission, the Court of Justice, and the Court of Auditors. The revenue and expenditure of the Economic and Social Committee is entered in the section dealing with the Council. The statement of expenditure in the section dealing with the Commission is subdivided into two parts entitled, respectively, administrative appropriations and operating appropriations. The latter includes all non-administrative expenditure of the EEC and Euratom which is entered in the budget. It has two annexes attached to it; one deals with research and investment activities, the other with borrowing and lending operations. Within each section, the items of revenue and expenditure are classified, according to their type or the use to which they are assigned, under titles, chapters, articles, and items, and are accompanied by appropriate remarks. In the 1988 budget, the part dealing with operating appropriations in the Commission's section was divided into 10 titles and 102 chapters, chapter 102 being a new chapter containing appropriations intended to cover any additional expenditure arising from significant fluctuations in the US dollar–ECU exchange rate. The budgetary nomenclature is decided during the budgetary procedure (Arts. 15–16 FR, 202(4) EEC).

8. Until 31 December 1977, the budget was drawn up in units of account based on gold parity (Art. 207(1) EEC). From 1 January 1978, the unit of account in the budget was replaced by the European unit of account (EUA) based on a basket of Community currencies as defined by Art. 10 FR. However, from 1 January 1981, the EUA was in turn replaced by the European currency unit (ECU) by virtue of the Financial Regulation of 16 December 1980 (*OJ* 1980 L345/23) which amended the Financial Regulation

of 21 December 1977 by providing that the budget shall be established in ECU. The ECU is composed of the sum of specified amounts of the currencies of the Member States as originally set out in Reg. 3180/78, *OJ* 1978 L379/1, changing the value of the unit of account used by the European Monetary Cooperation Fund. This regulation was subsequently amended by Reg. 2626/84, *OJ* 1984 L247/1, to include the Greek drachma in the ECU with effect from 17 September 1984, and by Reg. 1971/89, *OJ* 1989 L189/1, to include the Spanish peseta and the Portuguese escudo in the ECU with effect from 21 September 1989. Any change in the composition of the ECU applies automatically to the budget (*see further under* **European Currency Unit***).

II. The budgetary procedure

The power to determine the various elements of the budget and the general responsibility to ensure that Community public expenditure is executed correctly are assigned to the budgetary authority which comprises the Council and the European Parliament. However, all three political institutions, the Council, the EP, and the Commission, participate in the budgetary procedure, which consists of the following consecutive stages (see Arts. 203 EEC, 11–14 FR, Rule 66 and Annex IV of the EP's Rules of Procedure, consolidated version published by the EP in June 1987 (4th edn.). The procedure discussed below was introduced by the Budgetary Treaties of 1970 and 1975, which amended Art. 203 EEC and considerably increased the budgetary power of the EP. The procedure was first applied to the budget for 1975; for transitional provisions, see Art. 203a EEC):

1. After consulting the Economic Policy Committee, the Commission fixes the maximum rate of increase in relation to NCE and communicates it to all the institutions before 1 May each year (see section I(6) above).

2. Subject to that rate of increase, each institution, including for this purpose the Court of Auditors and the Economic and Social Committee, draws up before 1 July an estimate of its revenue and expenditure which the Commission consolidates in a preliminary draft budget to be submitted to the Council by 1 September.

3. Acting by a qualified majority, the Council establishes the draft budget which it is required to place before the EP not later than 5 October for its first reading. It seems that this time-limit is mandatory, and when in 1987 the Council was unable to reach agreement on the new own resources system proposed by the Commission for 1988 and, for the first time, failed to submit the draft budget by 5 October, both the EP and the Commission brought an action for failure to act against it under Art. 175 EEC (see Case 377/87 *Parliament* v. *Council* [1988] ECR and Case 383/87 *Commission* v. *Council* [1988] ECR. In both cases, the Court declared that there was no need for it to give a decision since the budget for 1988 had been adopted before the date of the judgment). Although the Council may depart from the preliminary draft budget prepared by the Commission, it has undertaken to make no amendments to the estimate of expenditure of the EP (see Res. No. 1 of 22 Apr.

89

1970, text in *Treaties Establishing the European Communities* (1987), p. 1091). In return, the EP has in practice refrained from amending the Council's expenditure estimates. Thus, each arm of the budgetary authority has complete independence regarding its own budget.

4. Within forty-five days of the draft budget being placed before it, the EP may: (*a*) give its approval, in which case the budget shall stand as finally adopted; (*b*) make no amendments or propose no modifications, in which case the budget shall be deemed to be finally adopted; (*c*) amend the draft budget in respect of NCE, acting by a majority of its members; or (*d*) propose to the Council modifications relating to CE, acting by an absolute majority of the votes cast. In cases (*c*) and (*d*), the draft budget is referred back to the Council for a second reading.

5. Within fifteen days of the draft budget being placed before it and acting on a qualified majority, the Council may: (*a*) modify any of the amendments adopted by the EP; (*b*) reject any proposed modification which does not have the effect of increasing the total amount of the expenditure of an institution. In the absence of a decision to reject it, the proposed modification shall stand as accepted (the so-called 'inverted majority rule'); (*c*) accept any proposed modification which has the effect of increasing the total amount of the expenditure of an institution. In the absence of a decision to accept it, the proposed modification shall stand as rejected. In both cases (*b*) and (*c*), where the Council has rejected a proposed modification, it may either retain the amount shown in the draft budget or fix another amount. The draft budget will be modified on the basis of the proposed modifications accepted by the Council; (*d*) make no modifications to any of the amendments adopted by the EP and accept all the modifications proposed by the EP. In case (*d*), the budget shall be deemed to be finally adopted, and the EP will be informed by the Council accordingly. In cases (*a*), (*b*), and (*c*), the modified draft budget is again forwarded to the EP for a second reading. The Council is required to inform the EP of the results of its deliberations.

6. Within fifteen days of the draft budget being placed before it, the EP may: (*a*) acting by a majority of its members and three-fifths of the votes cast, amend or reject the modifications to its amendments made by the Council and adopt the budget accordingly. Thus, as regards NCE, to which these amendments relate, the EP has the power of decision. However, this power is subject to two qualifications: the EP may not exceed its 'margin for manœuvre', corresponding to at least half the maximum rate of increase established by the Commission, and may not exceed that maximum rate except in agreement with the Council (see section I(6) above); (*b*) not modify the CE as fixed by the Council; in this respect, therefore, the Council has the last word; (*c*) take no action, in which case the budget shall be deemed to be finally adopted; (*d*) acting by a majority of its members and two-thirds of the votes cast, reject the draft budget and ask for a new draft to be submitted to it, 'if there are important reasons'. This is, clearly, an important power which enables Parliament to wield its political authority *vis-à-vis* the Council, and thus to influence the direction of Community policies. The EP for the first time made use of this power in 1979 when it rejected the 1980 budget (for background,

see *Bull. EC* 12–1979, pp. 93 and 120) and subsequently in 1984 when it rejected the 1985 budget (for reasons, see *Bull. EC* 12–1984, p. 28).

7. When the above procedure has been completed, it is for the President of the EP to declare that the budget has been finally adopted. Prior to 1975, this task was entrusted to the President of the Council (see Art. 203a(6) EEC), and its transfer to the President of the Parliament was intended to mark the increased powers of Parliament as a budgetary authority. It is this declaration which endows the budget with binding force *vis-à-vis* the institutions and the Member States. In exercising that function, the President acts, not as a distinct authority but in his capacity as an organ of the EP. Being a binding legal act, the declaration of the President, and, through it, the budget of the Communities itself, is subject to judicial review by the ECJ as there is no provision in the Treaties which would exempt the acts of the budgetary authority from such review. Thus, as seen above, in Case 34/86 *Council* v. *Parliament* the Court annulled the act of the President declaring the budget for 1986 finally adopted. The effect of that annulment was to deprive the 1986 budget of its validity and to require the two institutions to resume the budgetary procedure (see [1986] ECR at pp. 2201–3 and 2210–12 *per Curiam*, pp. 2175–6 *per* A.-G. Mancini). It may be noted that not only the budget as such may be the subject of annulment proceedings, but any binding act of the Parliament in the budgetary field which is designed to produce legal effects *vis-à-vis* third parties (Case 294/83 *Les Verts* v. *Parliament* [1986] ECR 1339 at pp. 1366–7, where the Court held that decisions of the Bureau and Enlarged Bureau of the EP concerning the allocation and use of certain appropriations entered in the budget to cover the cost of preparations for the 1984 European elections were subject to challenge). Nevertheless, the various steps in the budgetary procedure are not challengeable by natural or legal persons who can be directly concerned only by the measures taken to implement the budget (Case 216/83 *Les Verts* v. *Commission and Council* [1984] ECR 3325 at p. 3328).

8. If, at the beginning of a financial year, the budget has not yet been adopted, a sum equivalent to not more than one-twelfth of the budget appropriations for the preceding financial year may be spent each month in respect of any chapter of the budget, subject to the provisions of the Treaty (Arts. 204 EEC, 8 FR). These so-called 'provisional-twelfths' arrangements were applied in 1980 and 1985, due to the rejection of the draft budget by the EP (see 14th *Gen. Rep. EC* (1980), p. 42 and 19th *Gen. Rep. EC* (1985), p. 52), and again in 1988, due to the failure of the Council to present a draft budget by the end of 1987 (see 21st *Gen. Rep. EC* (1987), p. 60; *Bull. EC* 12–1987, p. 102).

9. The budgetary procedure as laid down in Art. 203 EEC, which divides the budgetary power between the Council and the EP on the basis of an ill-defined distinction between CE and NCE, inherently carries with it the seeds of tensions and conflicts between the two institutions (see the opinion of A.-G. Mancini in Case 34/86 *Council* v. *Parliament*, above, at pp. 2160–1 and 2186). In the words of the EP, these conflicts have, over the years, created a 'political and financial crisis . . . preventing the achievement of

91

Community objectives and policies, jeopardizing the normal operation of the Community and distorting the balance of interinstitutional power' (Res. of 15 Oct. 1987, *OJ* 1987 C305/126). On several occasions, the EP proposed a revision of Art. 203 EEC with a view to abolishing the 'artificial distinction' between CE and NCE (see Res. of 5 Oct. 1973, *OJ* 1973 C87/8; Res. of 23 May 1984, *OJ* 1984 C172/101; Res. of 15 Nov. 1984, *OJ* 1984 C337/404). To prevent such conflicts from arising, at the time of the signing of the Budgetary Treaty of 1970 the Council adopted a resolution providing that 'in matters of budgetary procedure everything possible should be done by common agreement between the Council and the EP to ensure close co-operation at all levels between the two institutions' (Res. No. 3 of 22 Apr. 1970, text in *Treaties Establishing the European Communities* (1987), p. 1091). However, the 'close co-operation' envisaged in the resolution had not materialized, and in 1981 the EP, supported by the Commission, called for improvements in the methods of collaboration between the two institutions (Res. of 10 Apr. 1981, *OJ* 1981 C101/107; Suppl. 3/82—*Bull. EC*, pp. 10–11).

The result was the adoption, on 30 June 1982, of a Joint Declaration by the EP, the Council, and the Commission on various measures to improve the budgetary procedure (*OJ* 1982 C194/1; for the background to this 'inter-institutional trialogue', see *Bull. EC* 6–1982, p. 7). The Declaration begins by laying down rules for the classification of expenditure under all existing and new budget items into CE and NCE (see further section I(6) above). It then establishes a procedure for interinstitutional budgetary collaboration, often referred to as '*budgetary conciliation*' to distinguish it from 'legislative conciliation', which is the subject of an earlier Joint Declaration (*see under* **Conciliation procedure**). The procedure consists of a meeting of the Presidents of Parliament, of the Council, and of the Commission, under the chairmanship of the President of the Commission. (In Case 34/86 *Council* v. *Parliament*, above, at pp. 2186–7 A.-G. Mancini suggested that the President of the Court of Justice might be better suited to preside over this body. Not being involved in the budgetary procedure, he possesses the necessary impartiality and authority to perform the tasks of mediation and conciliation. It may be noted that the original text of Art. 78(3) ECSC, no longer in force, did provide for a 'Committee of Presidents', presided over by the President of the Court, to be in charge of the administrative expenditure of the ECSC.) The 'Tripartite Dialogue' created by the Joint Declaration of 1982 may be used: (*a*) to resolve any disagreement between the Council and the EP regarding the classification of budget items into CE and NCE; (*b*) to bring about agreement between them on the fixing of a maximum rate of increase in the NCE; (*c*) to assess the results of the application of the Declaration; and (*d*) to consider unresolved problems in order to submit joint proposals for solutions to the institutions.

While the Declaration was ratified by the EP with approval (see Res. of 8 July 1982, *OJ* 1982 C238/64), it failed, contrary to expectations, to eliminate the conflicts and difficulties in the budgetary procedure (see e.g. Case 34/86 *Council* v. *Parliament*, above, at p. 2212, where the Court reminded the parties that they should resolve their disagreement regarding the delimitation of CE/NCE under the conciliation procedure set up by the Joint Declaration. See also Case 204/86 *Greece* v. *Council* [1988] ECR paras. 15–17). As part of the budgetary reforms introduced in 1988, a new Interinstitutional Agreement was reached between the EP, the Council, and the Commission concerning budgetary discipline and the improvement of the budgetary procedure (*OJ* 1988 L185/33), which the EP regards as a continuation of the Joint Declaration of 1982 (Res. of 15 June 1988, point D, *OJ* 1988 C187/94, see further section IV below).

III. Implementation of the budget

The implementation of the budget is the task of the Commission, which is required to act, in accordance with the Financial Regulation, on its own responsibility and within the limits of the appropriations (Art. 205 EEC, Title III FR. See also Reg. of 11 Dec. 1986 laying down detailed rules for the implementation of the FR, *OJ* 1986 L360/1 and Case 16/88 *Commission* v. *Council* [1989] ECR, holding that the Commission's implementing power, even where it has budgetary implications, may be subject to conditions imposed by the Council under Art. 145 (3) EEC, such as a Management Committee procedure). The main principle of implementation is that the authorizing officers and accounting officers must be different individuals. Their duties (and those of the financial controller) are mutually incompatible (Art. 17 FR). The requisite powers for the implementation of the sections of the budget relating to the EP, the Council, the ECJ, and the Court of Auditors are conferred upon those institutions by the Commission (Art. 18(2) FR). Each institution is to appoint a financial controller who is responsible for monitoring the commitment and authorization of all expenditure and also for monitoring all revenue (Art. 19 FR). In each institution, the collection of revenue and the payment of expenditure is carried out by an accounting officer who is appointed by the institutions (Art. 20 FR). The appropriations are administered by the authorizing officer, who alone is empowered to enter into commitments regarding expenditure and to establish entitlements to be collected (Art. 17 FR. See also Title V FR).

The Commission is required to submit annually to the Council and to the EP the accounts of the preceding financial year relating to the implementation of the budget, together with a financial statement of the assets and liabilities of the Communities (Art. 205a EEC). It is the task of the Court of Auditors to examine the accounts of all revenue and expenditure of the Communities and of the bodies set up by the Communities unless their constituent instruments provide otherwise (Art. 206a(1) EEC; *see further under* **Court of Auditors**). Acting on a recommendation from the Council adopted by a qualified majority, the EP alone has the power to give a discharge to the Commission in respect of the implementation of the budget (Art. 206b EEC. See also Title VI FR and Rule 68 and Annex V of the EP's Rules of Procedure, 4th edn. (1987)).

IV. The budgetary reforms of 1988

By the financial year 1987, the Communities had exhausted the resources made available to them by the 1985 own resources decision. At the same time, the Single European Act of 1986 (SEA), which was to come into force during the course of 1987, set the Communities a number of major new objectives with considerable financial implications. These included the completion of the frontier-free internal market by 1992; increased economic and social cohesion; a common scientific and technological development policy; further development of the European Monetary System; a new European social dimension; and co-ordinated action on the environment. To enable the Communities to have the resources needed for the achievement of these objectives, early in 1987 the Commission presented to the European Parliament and the Council a comprehensive package of proposals containing a number of closely related reforms (known as the 'Delors package', COM (87) 100 final, published in Suppl. 1/87—*Bull. EC*; see also *Bull. EC* 2–1987, p. 7 and Suppl. 1/88—*Bull. EC*, p. 19). These proposals were accepted in principle by the Brussels European Council of 11–13 February 1988 and the Council meeting of 22 February 1988 (see *Bull. EC* 2–1988, p. 8; for the opinions of the EP, see Res. of 18 Nov. 1987, *OJ* 1987 C345/43 and Res. of 21 Jan. 1988, *OJ* 1988 C49/116) and were subsequently incorporated into a number of legally binding measures, adopted by the Council on 24 June 1988 (comprising six regulations, two decisions, and an Interinstitutional Agreement, all published in *OJ* 1988 L185). The adoption of these important measures represents a major breakthrough in the field of Community finances. Together they create a financial framework which should be sufficient to cover Community expenditure for the next five years, and also lay down rules for controlling expenditure and introduce financial planning to avoid budgetary crises and institutional conflicts. The measures relate to the following five closely connected matters:

1. *Reform of the Common Agricultural Policy (CAP)* aimed at the adjustment of agricultural production to the needs of the market. In order to stabilize production as well as to ensure budgetary discipline, amongst other things the following measures have been adopted: production stabilizers, such as increased co-responsibility levies, restrictions on intervention, and automatic price reductions if production in a marketing year exceeds the maximum guaranteed quantity ('guarantee threshold') fixed in advance (these stabilizers have been incorporated in the basic regulations governing the individual market organizations with effect from the marketing year 1988/9, see *OJ* 1988 L110 and L132); limitation on supply by withdrawing agricultural land from production (set-aside, see Reg. 1094/88, *OJ* 1988 L106/28); promotion of early retirement of and income support for farmers (see Reg. 1096/88, *OJ* 1988 L110/1 and also Regs. 2048/88, 2050/88, and 2051/88 of 24 June 1988, *OJ* 1988 L185/1, 6, 8; see also the measures discussed under point (5) below and *see further under* **Common Agricultural Policy***).

2. *Reform of the structural Funds*, i.e. the European Agricultural Guidance and Guarantee Fund (EAGGF), Guidance Section, the European Social Fund (ESF), and the European Regional Development Fund (ERDF), with a view to clarifying and rationalizing their tasks, increasing their efficiency, and co-

ordinating their activities between themselves and with the operations of
other existing financial instruments and of the European Investment Bank
(EIB), as required by Art. 130D EEC, inserted by the SEA. The purpose is to
achieve some of the aims set by the SEA, i.e. strengthening the Communities'
economic and social cohesion and redressing the principal regional imbalances. Five priority objectives have been laid down: promoting the
development and structural adjustment of the regions whose development is
lagging behind (i.e. whose per caput GDP is less than 75 per cent of the
Community average); converting the regions seriously affected by industrial
decline; combating long-term unemployment; facilitating the occupational
integration of young people; and, with a view to reform of the CAP, speeding
up the adjustment of agricultural structures and promoting the development
of rural areas. Commitment appropriations for the three Funds will be
doubled in real terms by 1993 as compared with the 1987 level, thus bringing
their share of the budget from 16 per cent to about 25 per cent. This will also
restore the balance between compulsory and non-compulsory expenditure,
since the proportion of the latter is expected to rise from 25.6 per cent in 1988
to 30.7 per cent in 1989 (see *Bull. EC* 6–1988, p. 110. On the reform of the
structural Funds, see Framework Reg. 2052/88 of 24 June 1988, *OJ* 1988
L185/9. This Reg. was implemented by Regs. 4253/88, 4254/88, 4255/88,
and 4256/88 of 19 Dec. 1988, *OJ* 1988 L374, governing operations under
each Fund. They all entered into force on 1 Jan. 1989. See also Reg. 2053/88
of 24 June 1988, *OJ* 1988 L185/21 on financial assistance for Portugal.
See further under **European Agricultural Guidance and Guarantee Fund***,
European Regional Development Fund*, **European Social Fund***).

3. *New system of the Communities' own resources*, involving a substantial
increase in the volume, and a change in the structure, of own resources. In
addition to the three existing sources of finance, i.e. agricultural levies,
customs duties, and up to 1.4 per cent of national VAT, a new, open-ended
fourth resource has been introduced expressed as a percentage—to be
determined under the budgetary procedure in the light of the total of all other
revenue—of the Member States' Gross National Product (GNP). The overall
ceiling on the Communities' own resources has been defined as a percentage
of the Communities' total GNP—1.2 per cent for payment appropriations
and 1.3 per cent for commitment appropriations—irrespective of the limitations on the individual sources of finance. This is one of the major
advantages of the new system, calculated to ensure stability of finance
irrespective of developments concerning the individual components. It is
expected that the new system will provide adequate, stable, and guaranteed
resources at least until 1992, enabling the Communities to implement and
finance all their political, economic, and social measures in accordance with
the SEA. As a result, for the first time in several years, the 1989 budget is
based on sufficient resources (see *Bull. EC* 6–1988, p. 110). The conclusions
of the Fontainebleau European Council of 25–6 June 1984 on the grant of a
correction to the United Kingdom in respect of budgetary imbalances (see
Bull. EC 6–1984, p. 10) remain applicable, with certain modifications to
take account of the fourth resource, for as long as the new own resources

decision remains in force. Special provisions apply to Germany, Spain, and Portugal. The new own resources decision (Dec. 88/376 of 24 June 1988, *OJ* 1988 L185/24) was to be ratified by all the Member States by the end of 1988, after which it would take effect retroactively from 1 January 1988. During the interim period, Member States agreed to make available any funds required in excess of the existing ceiling on own resources to cover the 1988 budget expenditure, in the form of non-repayable advances on payments due after the entry into force of the decision (*Bull. EC* 2–1988, p. 13; see amending and supplementary budget No. 1 for 1988, *OJ* 1988 L265/10. *See further under* **Own resources**).

4. *Revision of the Financial Regulation of 1977* with a view to improving budgetary management, ensuring greater transparency of appropriations, and strengthening the principle of annuality by discontinuing automatic carryovers of commitment and payment appropriations (Reg. 2049/88 of 24 June 1988, *OJ* 1988 L185/3; see section I(3) above *and under* **Financial Regulation**).

5. *Budgetary discipline.* In order to contain the ever-increasing agricultural expenditure, on 4 December 1984 the Council adopted certain 'conclusions' on budgetary and financial discipline providing for a 'reference framework', i.e. the maximum level of expenditure to be fixed by the Council each year, and for 'financial guidelines' concerning the CAP (*Bull. EC* 12–1984, p. 24). However, the implementation of these conclusions has not been satisfactory (see Suppl. 1/87—*Bull. EC*, p. 20), and at its meetings in Brussels in 1987 and 1988, the European Council agreed to submit the use of the Communities' own resources to effective and legally binding discipline parallel to the efforts made by the Member States in connection with their own budgets. The conclusions of the European Council have been implemented by way of an Interinstitutional Agreement on budgetary discipline and improvement of the budgetary procedure, reached between the European Parliament, the Council, and the Commission on 29 June 1988 and entered into force on 1 July 1988 (*OJ* 1988 L185/33), and by a Council Decision of 24 June 1988 (Dec. 88/377, *OJ* 1988 L185/29).

The conclusion of the Interinstitutional Agreement shows that planning of expenditure and the fixing of priorities between the various categories of non-compulsory expenditure is only possible through co-operation between the Commission and the two arms of the budgetary authority. Budgetary discipline under the Agreement covers all expenditure and is binding on all the institutions involved, but without altering their respective budgetary powers as laid down in the Treaties. The Agreement is based on the 'financial perspective 1988–92', which is annexed to and forms an integral part of it. The financial perspective is basically a set of financial estimates indicating, in commitment appropriations, the volume and breakdown of foreseeable Community expenditure during that period, including expenditure for the development of new policies. The overall annual totals of compulsory and non-compulsory expenditure are also shown in both commitment and payment appropriations. The three institutions have recognized that each of the financial objectives laid down in the perspective represents an annual expenditure ceiling for the Community, and have undertaken to observe the different ceilings during the corresponding budgetary procedure. They have also agreed that any revision of the compulsory expenditure figure will not result in a reduction in the amount of non-compulsory expenditure shown.

Another important aspect of the Agreement is the mutual undertakings to accept, for the financial years 1988–92, the maximum rates of increase for NCE established within the ceilings set by the financial perspective and to comply, within those maximum rates, with the financing objectives set by the European Council for certain priority policy areas, such as the structural Funds, the Integrated Mediterranean Programmes (IMPs), the Specific Industrial Development Programme for Portugal (PEDIP), and the Research and Technology Development (RTD) framework programme. The institutions have also undertaken to comply with the European Council's conclusions concerning control of compulsory expenditure in the agricultural sector (the 'agricultural guideline').

The Council Decision on budgetary discipline stipulates that the rate of increase in agricultural guarantee expenditure between 1988 and a given year must not exceed 74 per cent of the rate of increase in Community GNP during the same period. This maximum progression for guarantee expenditure (the 'agricultural guideline'), which would correspond to 80 per cent if maximum EAGGF financing of set-aside were taken into consideration, must be respected each year. The Decision fixes the 1988 base of expenditure from which the agricultural guideline for each subsequent year is to be calculated at 27,500 million ECU. The agricultural guideline includes costs relating to depreciation of newly created (but not the existing) agricultural stocks. To cover significant and unforeseen fluctuations in the US dollar–ECU market rate as compared to the rate used in the budget, the Decision creates a monetary reserve of 1,000 million ECU, not included in the agricultural guideline. Compulsory expenditure other than EAGGF guarantee expenditure is subject to a reference framework to be adopted by the Council each year at the start of the budget procedure. It includes the maximum amounts for both commitment and payment appropriations which the Council considers to be necessary to cover the Community's legal obligations. Non-compulsory expenditure is subject to budgetary discipline on the basis of the Interinstitutional Agreement.

As a result of a new spirit of co-operation between the Parliament, Council, and Commission created by the Interinstitutional Agreement, it was possible, for the first time since 1983, to adopt the budget for 1989 before the end of the preceding financial year (on 15 Dec. 1988, published in OJ 1989 L26 and L27). The 1989 budget totalled 2,000 million ECU less than the ceiling set in the Agreement, the main reason being a substantial reduction in agricultural expenditure which, for the first time in the history of the Communities, constituted less than 60 per cent of the total budget.

See also Budgetary Treaties, Committee of Presidents, Common Agricultural Policy*, Conciliation procedure, Court of Auditors, European Agricultural Guidance and Guarantee Fund*, European Currency Unit*, European Parliament, European Regional Development Fund*, European Social Fund*, Financial Regulation, Own resources.

Further reading 1. B O O K S : Commission of the European Communities, *Thirty Years of Community Law* (1983), part I, ch. 8; Denton, *The Future of the EEC Budget* (1983); Druker, *Financing the European Communities* (1975); Strasser, *The Finances of Europe* (1981); Wallace, *Budgetary Politics: The Finances of the European Communities* (1980).

2. A R T I C L E S : Arnull, 'The Budget Case' (1986) 11 *EL Rev.* 431; Avery, 'Agricultural Policy: The Conclusions of the European Council' (1988) 25 *CML Rev.* 523; Dankert, 'The Joint Declaration by the Community Institutions of 30 June 1982 on the Community Budgetary Procedure' (1983) 20 *CML Rev.* 701; Editorial, 'The 1980/81 Budget Wrangle' (1981) 18 *CML Rev.* 5; id., 'Financing the Single Act' (1988) 13 *EL Rev.* 221; id., 'The Delors Package: The Result of a Successful Commission Strategy' (1988) 25 *CML Rev.* 479; Ehlermann, 'Applying the New Budgetary Procedure for the First Time' (1975) 12 *CML Rev.* 325; Kapteyn, 'The European Parliament, the Budget and Legislation in the Community' (1972) 9 *CML Rev.* 386; Kolte, 'The Community Budget: New Principles for Finance, Expenditure Planning and Budget Discipline' (1988) 25 *CML Rev.* 487; Lowe, 'The Reform of the Community's Structural Funds' (1988) 25 *CML Rev.* 503; Nichol, 'From Rejection to Repudiation: EC Budgetary Affairs' (1986) 25 *JCMS* 31; Pipkorn, 'Legal Implications of the Absence of the Community Budget at the Beginning of a Financial Year' (1981) 18 *CML Rev.* 141; Sopwith, 'Legal Aspects of the Community Budget' (1980) 17 *CML Rev.* 315; Wallace, 'A European Budget Made in Strasbourg and Unmade in Luxembourg' (1986) 6 *YEL* 263; Williamson, 'The Package, "Making a Success of the Single Act" ' (1988) 25 *CML Rev.* 483, Zangl, 'The Interinstitutional Agreement on Budgetary Discipline and Improvement of the Budgetary Procedure' (1989) 26 *CML Rev.* 675.

3. O F F I C I A L P U B L I C A T I O N S : Court of Auditors, 'Study of the Financial Systems of the European Communities (1981)', *OJ* 1981 C342/1; House of Lords, Select Committee on the European Communities, Session 1985–6, 21st Report, 'Community Budget 1986–87' (1986); id., Session 1987–8, 14th Report, 'Reform of the Structural Funds' (1988).

See also under **European Parliament, Own resources.**

▶ **COMMUNITY LAW** Body of legal rules and principles establishing, created by, and relating to the European Communities and governing their organization, powers, and activities.

Community law is, accordingly, an amalgamation of a number of rules and principles of different and distinct origin. First, the provisions establishing the Communities themselves being laid down in international Treaties, the basis of Community law is to be found in international law, with the founding Treaties as its primary source. Secondly, in contrast to ordinary international agreements, the Community Treaties have created more than mutual rights and obligations between the contracting States only. As the ECJ has stated in a series of leading cases, the Treaties have established their own legal system, Community law, which 'constitutes a new legal order of international law for the benefit of which the States have limited their sovereign rights, albeit within limited fields, and the subjects of which comprise not only Member States but also their nationals' (Case 26/62 *Van Gend en Loos* [1963] ECR 1 at p. 12; Case 6/64 *Costa* [1964] ECR 585 at p. 593; Case 28/67 *Molkerei-Zentrale Westfalen* [1968] ECR 143 at p. 152, etc.). This new system is characterized by the setting up of common institutions, to which the Member States have transferred sovereign powers, in particular legislative, executive, and judicial powers, enabling them to lay down legally binding provisions. Thus, in its second aspect, Community law is a self-generated (and self-generating) system of rules constantly in the process of being created by the institutions set up by the Treaties. The legal acts of these institutions ('secondary legislation'), as interpreted and applied in the case-law of the ECJ, form its secondary source. Thirdly, there are certain matters in respect of which the Treaties have not conferred decision-making powers upon the institutions, or which they have deliberately entrusted to the Member States. These matters are dealt with by the Representatives of the Governments of the Member States, and their decisions, agreements, and other acts form a third source of Community law. Fourthly, in addition to written rules, the Communities are also governed by a set of unwritten principles derived mainly (although not exclusively) from the national laws of the Member States. These principles have been incorporated in the body of Community law chiefly through the case-law of the ECJ and form its fourth source. Finally, as international organizations created by Treaties and entering into treaty (and other) relations themselves, the Communities are clearly bound by the rules of public international law. The relevant customary and conventional rules and principles of that law make up the fifth source of Community law.

Community law is an original and unique system of law which is peculiar to the European Communities. Issuing from an 'independent source of law' (Case 11/70 *Internationale Handelsgesellschaft* [1970] ECR 1125 at p. 1134; see also the cases cited above), it is distinct both from international law and from the national laws of the Member States. It is a supranational legal system whose subjects are not merely States (which is the position under international law), nor merely individuals (which is the case under national law), but both the Member States *and* their nationals. As the ECJ has stated, Community law 'not only imposes obligations on individuals but is also intended to confer upon them rights which become part of their legal heritage' (Case 26/62 *Van Gend en Loos*, above). These rights are enforceable before the national courts by virtue of the doctrine of direct effect, which forms one of the essential theoretical foundations of Community law as a supranational legal order (*see further under* **Direct effect**). Thus, Community law is closely integrated into the laws of the Member States (Case 6/64 *Costa*, above) and the national authorities, including the courts, must give priority to its provisions over conflicting provisions of national law. This follows from the principle of the supremacy or primacy of Community law, which forms another of its essential bases as a supranational legal system (*see further under* **Supremacy of Community law**).

Community law is, moreover, a self-contained system in that not only does it define the substantive powers, rights, and obligations of its subjects, but it has also created a 'complete system of legal remedies and procedures' as well as sanctions, enabling those subject to it to enforce their rights and to defend themselves against illegally imposed obligations. It also enables the ECJ to

99

review the legality of the conduct of the institutions and of the Member States (see Case 294/83 *Les Verts* v. *Parliament* [1986] ECR 1339 at p. 1365). This excludes any notion of self-help. As the ECJ has pointed out in a series of cases, the rule of customary international law which allows a party to an agreement, injured by the failure of another party to perform its obligations, to withhold performance of its own obligations is not applicable. Community law does not suffer from the traditional weakness of international law in respect of sanctions. Member States, therefore, may not take the law into their own hands, and even the fact that the Community institutions or other Member States fail to carry out their obligations cannot exempt them from performing theirs. They must resort, instead, to the appropriate remedy (Cases 90 and 91/63 *Commission* v. *Luxembourg and Belgium* [1964] ECR 625 at p. 631; Cases 52 and 55/65 *Germany* v. *Commission* [1966] ECR 159 at p. 172; Case 78/76 *Steinike und Weinlig* [1977] ECR 595 at p. 612; Cases 31 and 53/77R *Commission* v. *United Kingdom* [1977] ECR 921 at p. 924; etc.).

Since all the Member States adhered to the Treaties on the same conditions, definitely, and without reservations, Community law must apply in the whole territory of the Communities uniformly, i.e. unconditionally, at the same time, and with identical effects. Its executive force cannot vary from one State to another without jeopardizing the attainment of the common objectives and, ultimately, undermining the very foundations of the Communities. National law therefore cannot be invoked to determine the validity of Community law, to restrict the scope of its application, or in any way to override its provisions (Case 6/64 *Costa*, above, at pp. 593–4; Cases 9 and 58/65 *San Michele* v. *HA* [1967] ECR 1 at p. 30; Case 11/70 *Internationale Handelsgesellschaft*, above; Case 48/71 *Commission* v. *Italy* [1972] ECR 527 at p. 532; Case 106/77 *Simmenthal* [1978] ECR 629 at pp. 643–4; Case 149/79 *Commission* v. *Belgium* [1980] ECR 3881 at p. 3903; etc.).

Finally, as regards its subject-matter, Community law consists of two distinct categories of provisions. The first category lays down the institutional or constitutional law of the Communities and deals with such matters as the legal personality, legal capacity, status, administration, finances, privileges, immunities, and external relations of the Communities; the composition, organization, functions, and powers of their institutions; and legal remedies and procedures. These rules are either broadly similar or identical for all three Communities (ECSC, EEC, Euratom). The second category contains the substantive or economic law of the Communities and determines the scope of their activities, the subject-matters placed within their competence, and the powers transferred to them to deal with those subject-matters. These rules are basically different in respect of each of the three Communities which, moreover, have separate legal identity. Thus, strictly speaking, each Community is subject to a set of rules peculiar to itself. Nevertheless, these rules possess far too many common features and are based on far too many common principles and objectives to be regarded as three separate legal systems. They are, furthermore, adopted and administered by one set of common institutions. It is, therefore, more appropriate to treat Community law as a unitary system of rules with three distinct spheres of application.

Thus, in summary, it may be stated that Community law as a whole constitutes a new, independent (autonomous), supranational, self-contained, uniform, and unitary legal system of a *sui generis* nature, with a limited field of application.

See also **Community Treaties, Direct effect, European Communities, External relations, General principles of law, Institutional balance, Institutions, Representatives of the Governments of the Member States meeting in Council, Secondary legislation, Supremacy of Community law.**

Further reading 1. BOOKS: Collins, *European Community Law in the United Kingdom*, 4th edn. (1990); Commission of the European Communities, *Thirty Years of Community Law* (1983), part I, chs. 4–5; Donner, *The Role of the Lawyer in the European Communities*, (1968); Kapteyn and VerLoren van Themaat, *Introduction to the Law of the European Communities*, 2nd edn. by Gormley (1989); Lasok, *The Law of the Economy in the European Communities* (1980); Lasok and Bridge, *Law and Institutions of the European Communities*, 4th edn. (1987); Louis, *The Community Legal Order* (1980); Mathijsen, *A Guide to European Community Law*, 4th edn. (1985); Parry and Hardy, *EEC Law*, 2nd edn. (1981); Pescatore, *The Law of Integration* (1974); Plender, *A Practical Introduction to European Community Law* (1980); Smit and Herzog (eds.), *The Law of the European Economic Community: A Commentary on the EEC Treaty*, 6 vols. with regular supplements (1976); Steiner, *Textbook on EEC Law*, 2nd edn. (1990); Usher, *European Community Law and National Law: The Irreversible Transfer?* (1981); Vaughan (ed.), *Law of the European Communities*, 2 vols. (1986); White and Smythe (eds.), *Current Issues in European and International Law* (1990); Wyatt and Dashwood, *The Substantive Law of the EEC*, 2nd edn. (1987). *See also under* **European Court of Justice.**

2. ARTICLES: Aurrecoechea, 'The Role of the Autonomous Communities in the Implementation of European Community Law in Spain' (1989) 38 *ICLQ* 74; Bieber, 'On the Mutual Completion of Overlapping Legal Systems: The Case of the European Communities and the National Legal Orders' (1988) 13 *EL Rev.* 147; Bothe, 'Regional Autonomy and Independence: The Consequences for the Legal Order of the Communities' (1978) 15 *CML Rev.* 393; Dashwood and Arnull, 'English Courts and Article 177 of the EEC Treaty' (1984) 4 *YEL* 255; Dowrick, 'Overlapping International and European Laws' (1982) 31 *ICLQ* 59; id., 'A Model of the European Communities' Legal System' (1983) 3 *YEL* 169; Forman and Stevens, 'The Attitude of British Courts to Community Law: The First Three Years' (1976) 13 *CML Rev.* 388; Gormley, 'The Application of Community Law in the United Kingdom, 1976–1985' (1986) 23 *CML Rev.* 287; Hilf, 'The Application of Rules of National Administrative Law in the Implementation of Community Law' (1983) 3 *YEL* 79; Konstadinidis, 'Five Years of Application of Community Law in Greece' (1986/2) *LIEI* 101; Koopmans, 'The Role of Law in the Next Stage of European Integration' (1986) 35 *ICLQ* 925; Lord Mackenzie Stuart, 'Problems of the European Community: Transatlantic Parallels' (1987) 36 *ICLQ* 183; Meessen, 'The Application of Rules of Public International Law within Community Law' (1976) 13 *CML Rev.* 485; Monaco, 'The Limits of the European Community Order' (1975–6) 1 *EL Rev.* 269; Pescatore, 'International Law and Community Law: A Comparative Analysis' (1970) 7 *CML Rev.* 167; Schermers, 'Community Law and International Law' (1975) 12 *CML Rev.* 77; Sorensen, 'Autonomous Legal Orders: Some Considerations Relating to a Systems

Analysis of International Organisations in the World Legal Order' (1983) 32 *ICLQ*
559; Usher, 'The Influence of National Concepts on Decisions of the European Court'
(1975–6) 1 *EL Rev.* 359; Warner, 'The Relationship between European Community
Law and the National Laws of Member States' (1977) 93 *LQR* 349; Wyatt, 'New
Legal Order, or Old?' (1982) 7 *EL Rev.* 147.

▶ **COMMUNITY PREFERENCE** Principle of Community law derived from
the EEC Treaty, according to which in all essential respects 'intra-Community
trade must develop in more favourable conditions than trade with third
countries' (Case 6/78 *Union Française de Céréales* [1978] ECR 1675 at
p. 1691 *per* A.-G. Capotorti). The principle constitutes an important element
in the rules governing trade between Member States (ibid.) and is expressly
mentioned by Art. 44(2) EEC which, in the context of agriculture, refers to
the 'development of a natural preference between Member States'. The ECJ
and its various Advocates-General have considered and applied it in various
situations, holding that the principle of Community preference:

- must be taken into account by the Council in balancing the various
  interests of farmers and consumers (Case 5/67 *Beus* [1968] ECR 83 at
  p. 98);
- must be ensured in the system of advance fixing of levies and refunds
  (Case 73/69 *Oehlmann* [1970] ECR 467 at pp. 473–4 *per Curiam*,
  pp. 480–1 *per* A.-G. Roemer, p. 471 *per* plaintiff and Commission);
- justifies the granting of relief to products of a Member State in preference
  to products from third countries (Case 5/73 *Balkan-Import-Export*
  [1973] ECR 1091 at p. 1133 *per* A.-G. Roemer);
- justifies a different assessment of the question whether the importation
  of agricultural products may cause a 'disturbance' depending on whether
  the products involved come from another Member State or from a third
  country (Case 55/75 *Balkan-Import-Export* [1976] ECR 19 at p. 32);
- justifies the granting of 'accession' compensatory amounts where goods
  exported from an old Member State to a new Member State have
  perished in transit as a result of *force majeure*, because otherwise the
  exporter would be in an unfavourable competitive position in relation
  to a seller in a third country, and because the very purpose of the system
  of 'accession' compensatory amounts was to ensure the observance of
  the principle of Community preference in trade between the original
  Community and the new Member States before the full and complete
  integration of the latter into the common organization of agricultural
  markets (Case 6/78 *Union Française de Céréales*, above, at pp. 1683–4
  per Curiam, p. 1691 *per* A.-G. Capotorti; see also Case 38/79 *Butter-
  und Eier-Zentrale Nordmark* [1980] ECR 643 at pp. 653–5);
- protects the Community agriculture as a whole by preventing, through
  the system of levies and refunds, products from third countries from
  reaching the Community market at an abnormally low price (Case 4/79
  Providence Agricole de la Champagne [1980] ECR 2823 at p. 2845 *per
  Curiam*, p. 2859 *per* A.-G. Mayras).

See also Accession compensatory amount*, Common Agricultural Policy*, *Force majeure*, Freedom of movement for goods*, General principles of law.

▶ **COMMUNITY TREATIES** Treaties establishing, relating to, and concluded by the European Communities. Thus, in its broadest sense the term 'Community treaties' encompasses three categories of international agreements, each of which has a different place in the structure of Community law and a different importance as one of its sources. They are as follows:

- Treaties establishing the Communities as supplemented or amended by other treaties and acts ('basic' Treaties);
- other treaties concluded by the Member States between themselves or, exceptionally, with third States and relating to the functioning of the Communities or connected with their activities;
- treaties concluded by the Communities, with or without the participation of the Member States, with third States or international organizations.

Each of these three categories is further considered below.

I. Basic Treaties

These include the following three instruments:

- Treaty establishing the ECSC of 1951;
- Treaty establishing the EEC of 1957;
- Treaty establishing the Euratom of 1957;

as supplemented or amended by the following main instruments:

- Convention on Certain Institutions Common to the European Communities of 1957;
- Merger Treaty of 1965;
- Budgetary Treaties of 1970 and 1975;
- Treaties of Accession of 1972, 1979, and 1985;
- Treaty amending the Community Treaties with regard to Greenland of 1984;
- Single European Act of 1986.

Some of these Treaties are accompanied by various Annexes, Protocols, and Declarations. The Annexes and Protocols (but not the Declarations) form an integral part of the Treaty to which they are annexed (Arts. 84 ECSC, 239 EEC, 207 Euratom, 158, 150, and 400 of the Acts of Accession of 1972, 1979, and 1985, respectively. Arts. 239 EEC and 207 Euratom only mention the Protocols). For that reason, all those instruments are equally binding and must be applied in conjunction with the relevant Treaty (Cases 7 and 9/54 *Industries Sidérurgiques Luxembourgeoises* v. *HA* [1956] ECR 175 at p. 194).

The three basic Treaties are regarded as the 'basic constitutional charters' of the Communities (Case 8/55 *Fédération Charbonnière de Belgique* v. *HA* [1956] ECR 245 at p. 277 *per* A.-G. Lagrange; Case 6/64 *Costa* [1964] ECR 585 at p. 605 *per* A.-G. Lagrange; Case 294/83 *Les Verts* v. *Parliament* [1986] ECR 1339 at p. 1365) and therefore as the primary sources of Community law. Their mutual relationship is determined by the rule that the provisions of the EEC Treaty 'shall not affect' the provisions of the ECSC Treaty and 'shall not derogate' from those of the Euratom Treaty (Art. 232 EEC). It follows that the rules of the ECSC Treaty and all the provisions adopted to implement that Treaty remain in force as regards the functioning of the Common Market in coal and steel, despite the adoption of the EEC Treaty (Case 239/84 *Gerlach* [1985] ECR 3507 at p. 3517 holding that the EEC anti-dumping rules do not apply to products falling within the ambit of the ECSC Treaty). Thus, the relations between the EEC Treaty and each of the two other Treaties are rather like the relations between a *lex generalis* and a *lex specialis*. On account of its general scope, the EEC Treaty and the provisions adopted for its implementation may apply also to the coal and steel and the nuclear sectors where these are not governed by one or the other of the two corresponding Treaties or measures adopted under them. Otherwise, the relevant provisions of the ECSC and Euratom Treaties take precedence over those of the EEC Treaty. This principle has particular importance in the context of the basic rules relating to the free movement of goods, persons, services, and capital (Cases 188 to 190/80 *France, Italy and United Kingdom* v. *Commission* [1982] ECR 2545 at p. 2580; Case 328/85 *Deutsche Babcock Handel* [1987] ECR 5119 at p. 5139. See also 2nd *Gen. Rep. EC* (1968), pp. 467–8).

II. Other treaties between Member States or between Member States and third States

Treaties concluded between the Member States prior to the establishment of the Communities do not form part of Community law even if dealing with a subject-matter in itself within Community law (e.g. social security) and even if listed in a Community instrument (e.g. regulation) as forming an integral part thereof. They are outside the scope of the ECJ's jurisdiction. Thus, the Court has no power to interpret them by means of a preliminary ruling (Case 28/68 *Torrekens* [1969] ECR 125 at p. 134; Case 130/73 *Vandeweghe* [1973] ECR 1329 at p. 1333).

As the Member States have, following the establishment of the Communities, retained their treaty-making power in respect of matters not within the competence of the institutions, they may at any time enter into further agreements amongst themselves for a variety of purposes, such as:

- to supplement or amend the basic Treaties (the most important of these agreements are listed under (I) above);
- to regulate certain Community matters where the institutions lack the requisite powers (see e.g. the Convention for Mutual Assistance between the Customs Administrations of the Member States of 1967);
- to regulate matters which were expressly left within the Member States' competence (see e.g. the Agreement relating to the Determination of Part of the Common Customs Tariff in respect of the products in List G as provided for in Art. 20 EEC, dated 1960, and the Agreement relating to the Establishment of a Common Customs Tariff for certain products under Art. 94 Euratom, dated 1958);

- to bring new matters within the scope of Community law (see e.g. the Protocol of Agreement concerning Problems of Energy of 1964);
- to comply with Art. 220 EEC, which requires Member States to conclude agreements on specified subjects, such as the protection of persons, abolition of double taxation, mutual recognition of companies, and reciprocal enforcement of judgments. Only two of these subjects have so far been covered by conventions (see the Convention on the Mutual Recognition of Companies and Legal Persons of 1968, not yet in force, and the Convention on Jurisdiction and the Enforcement of Judgments in Civil and Commercial Matters of 1968, in force). Two more conventions have been signed which, although not strictly based on Art. 220, serve similar objectives (see the Convention for the European Patent for the Common Market of 1975, not yet in force, and the Convention on the Law Applicable to Contractual Obligations of 1980);
- in general, to co-ordinate the activities of the Member States so as to contribute to the proper functioning of the Communities (see e.g. the Statute of the European School of 1957 and the related Protocol of 1962).

The status of these agreements within the system of Community law is not quite clear. It seems that this depends in each case on the legal basis on which an agreement was concluded. Where an agreement is based on a provision in the basic Treaties, it must be regarded as part of Community law. Even so, it may be subject to the jurisdiction of the ECJ only by virtue of a specific provision or additional agreement, and not automatically (see e.g. Art. 30 of the Merger Treaty, Art. 31 of the Single European Act, the two Protocols of 3 June 1971 relating to the two Conventions concluded under Art. 220 EEC, Art. 73 of the Community Patent Convention of 1975), unless it merely supplements or amends the basic Treaties in which case no special provision is needed (see e.g. the Budgetary Treaties). Where, however, an agreement between the Member States does not have its legal basis in the Treaties, it cannot be regarded as part of Community law. As a result, the provisions of the Treaties do not apply to it. As the ECJ has stated, 'the mere fact that agreements [concluded between Member States] are linked to the Community and to the functioning of its institutions does not mean that they must be regarded as an integral part of Community law, the uniform interpretation of which throughout the Community falls within the jurisdiction of the Court. The Court therefore does not have jurisdiction to give a preliminary ruling . . . on the interpretation of such instruments' (Case 44/84 *Hurd* [1986] ECR 29 at p. 77; the instruments in question were the two agreements setting up the European School which the Court held were concluded between the Member States outside the scope of the Treaties. The Court also held that Art. 5 EEC did not apply to them, ibid. at p. 81).

The question of the relationship between the EEC Treaty and the pre-existing agreements of the Member States has two aspects. The first concerns agreements which the Member States had concluded between themselves.

The principle here is that in matters governed by the EEC Treaty, that Treaty takes precedence over such prior agreements, including agreements made within the framework of GATT (Case 10/61 *Commission* v. *Italy* [1962] ECR 1 at p. 10; Case 235/87 *Matteucci* [1988] ECR para. 22). This principle is of course subject to exceptions expressly authorized by the EEC Treaty. Thus, the EEC Treaty does not preclude the existence or completion of regional unions between Belgium and Luxembourg, or between Belgium, Luxembourg, and the Netherlands, to the extent that the objectives of these regional unions cannot be attained under the EEC Treaty (Art. 233 EEC, see also Art. 202 Euratom).

The second aspect concerns agreements concluded before the entry into force of the EEC Treaty between one or more Member States, on the one hand, and one or more third States, on the other. Art. 234 of the EEC Treaty provides that 'the rights and obligations arising from [such] agreements . . . shall not be affected by the provisions of this Treaty'. Nevertheless, the Member States are required to take all appropriate steps to eliminate any incompatibilities that may exist between such agreements and the Treaty. The ECJ has held that 'Article 234 is of general scope and it applies to any international agreement, irrespective of subject-matter, which is capable of affecting the application of the Treaty' (Case 812/79 *Burgoa* [1980] ECR 2787 at p. 2802). The terms 'rights and obligations' in Art. 234 refer, as regards the 'rights', to the rights of third countries and, as regards the 'obligations', to the obligations of Member States. Therefore, the real purpose of Art. 234 is to ensure, in accordance with the principles of international law, that the application of the EEC Treaty 'does not affect either the duty to observe the rights of non-member countries under an agreement concluded with a Member State prior to the entry into force of the Treaty . . . or the observance by that Member State of its obligations under the agreement and that, consequently, the institutions of the Community are bound not to impede the performance of those obligations by the Member State concerned' (ibid. at p. 2803, see also Case 10/61 *Commission* v. *Italy*, above, at p. 10).

It follows from the foregoing that Art. 234 concerns only the rights and obligations established between Member States and non-member countries and that it does not concern agreements made solely between the Member States (Case 235/87 *Matteucci*, above, para. 21). Prior agreements to which both Member States and third countries are parties cannot therefore be relied upon in the relations between the Member States themselves in order to justify, for example, restrictions on trade within the Community (Case 121/85 *Conegate* [1986] ECR 1007 at pp. 1024–5) or, more generally, as a ground for not applying the provisions of Community law in the sector to which they relate (Cases 110 and 111/78 *Van Wesemael* [1979] ECR 35 at pp. 53–4. Here the prior agreement invoked was ILO Convention No. 96 concerning Fee-charging Employment Agencies; in the *Conegate* case, above, the agreements in question were the Geneva Convention for the Suppression of Traffic in Obscene Publications of 1923 and the Universal Postal Convention). A pre-existing international agreement to which all the Member States are parties may, however, justify the adoption of implementing measures in the

Member States the purpose of which is to encourage, rather than hinder, trade and the free movement of goods within the Community (Case 89/76 *Commission* v. *Netherlands* [1977] ECR 1355 at pp. 1364–5 endorsing phytosanitary inspections carried out on the basis of the International Plant Protection Convention of 1951).

As seen, in Case 812/79 *Burgoa*, above, at p. 2803 the ECJ has held that Art. 234 imposes a duty on the Community institutions not to impede the performance of the obligations of Member States arising from a prior agreement with a third country. However, the Court has added that that duty 'does not bind the Community as regards the non-member country in question'. It would seem to follow from this that the Community itself is not bound by way of succession, at least under Art. 234, by agreements previously concluded by the Member States (*in casu*: the London Fisheries Convention of 1964 which was concluded by Ireland prior to her becoming a Member State). This is so even if an agreement deals with a subject-matter which falls within Community competence (*in casu*: sea fisheries).

There are, however, certain exceptions to this principle. Thus, in Cases 21 to 24/72 *International Fruit Company* [1972] ECR 1219 at p. 1227 the Court has said that 'in so far as under the EEC Treaty the Community has assumed the powers previously exercised by Member States in the area governed by the General Agreement [on Tariffs and Trade, GATT], the provisions of that agreement have the effect of binding the Community'. The Court has based this conclusion on at least four considerations. First, the fact that all the Member States were parties to GATT at the time when they concluded the EEC Treaty. Secondly, the intention of the Member States to bind the Community by the obligations arising from GATT since the Community pursues the same aims as GATT. This intention is shown by the fact that the Member States have conferred on the Community the powers and functions inherent in the tariff and trade policy. Thirdly, the fact that the Community, acting through its own institutions, has appeared as a partner in the tariff negotiations and as a party to the agreements of all types concluded within the framework of GATT. Fourthly, the fact that the transfer of powers from the Member States to the Community has been recognized by the other contracting parties (ibid. at pp. 1226–7). Subsequently, these considerations have been interpreted as representing the four requirements that must be satisfied before it may be assumed that the Community has succeeded to prior agreements concluded by the Member States with third countries (see the opinions of A.-G. Capotorti in Case 812/79 *Burgoa*, above, at pp. 2815–16 and in Case 181/80 *Arbelaiz-Emazabel* [1981] ECR 2961 at p. 2987). Later the Court has recognized that the Community has 'replaced' the Member States, so far as fulfilment of the commitments is concerned, not only in relation to GATT, but also in relation to the Convention on Nomenclature for the Classification of Goods in Customs Tariffs of 1950 and the Convention establishing a Customs Co-operation Council of the same date (Case 38/75 *Nederlandse Spoorwegen* [1975] ECR 1439 at p. 1450). The substitution of the Community for the Member States in relation to commitments under GATT took place on 1 July 1968, the date of the introduction of the Common

107

Customs Tariff. It was on that date that the Community assumed its full powers in relation to the sphere covered by GATT (Cases 21 to 24/72 *International Fruit Company*, above, at p. 1227; Cases 267 to 269/81 *SPI and SAMI* [1983] ECR 801 at p. 829). The legal effects of that 'substitution' or 'replacement' are:

- since that date the ECJ has jurisdiction to interpret the provisions of GATT by way of a preliminary ruling under Art. 177 EEC, while with regard to the period prior to that date, such interpretation is a matter exclusively for the courts of the Member States (ibid. at p. 829);
- the Community is obliged to ensure that the provisions of GATT are observed in its relations with non-Member States which are parties to GATT (Case 266/81 *SIOT* [1983] ECR 731 at p. 780);
- the mandatory effect, in law, of the commitments arising from GATT must be determined by reference to the Community legal system and not to the national legal systems (Case 38/75 *Nederlandse Spoorwegen*, above, at p. 1450);
- the provisions of GATT (Arts. II, III, V, VI, VIII, and XI) do not produce direct effects within the Member States (see the cases cited above and Case 9/73 *Schlüter* [1973] ECR 1135 at pp. 1157–8. *See further under* **Direct effect**, point 3).

As regards agreements concluded between some of the Member States after the coming into force of the EEC Treaty, it seems that these may not validly exclude or otherwise affect the application of the EEC Treaty (see Case 33/64 *Koster* [1965] ECR 97 at p. 104). Under Art. 5(2) EEC the Member States are required to abstain from 'any measure' (including international agreements) which could jeopardize the attainment of the objectives of the Treaty. Of course, by 'common accord' they are free to amend the Treaty in accordance with the procedure laid down in Art. 236. The relationship between the treaties of the Member States and the ECSC and Euratom Treaties is governed by Art. 75 ECSC and Arts. 103–6 Euratom, respectively.

III. Treaties between the Communities and third States or international organizations

By virtue of their treaty-making power, the Communities are able to enter into bilateral and multilateral treaties and agreements with third States and international organizations, acting either on their own as contracting parties (exclusive Community agreements) or jointly with the Member States as co-signatories (mixed agreements) (*see further under* **Mixed agreement, Treaty-making power, Treaty-making procedure**). These treaties possess a dual character. On the one hand, they are ordinary international agreements governed by the general rules of public international law. They are binding upon the Communities and the other contracting parties who are responsible for their bona fide performance (Case 104/81 *Kupferberg* [1982] ECR 3641 at p. 3663; see also Case 40/72 *Schroeder* [1973] ECR 125 at p. 146, dealing with the Association Agreement between the EEC and Greece; Case 87/75 *Bresciani* [1976] ECR 129 at p. 140, dealing with the Yaoundé Convention).

It follows that any secondary legislation adopted by the Community institutions must be compatible with international agreements binding upon the Communities and that the ECJ has jurisdiction to review that compatibility in actions properly brought before it. Any incompatibility may affect the validity of the acts of the institutions. Thus, just as Community law enjoys precedence or supremacy over the national laws of the Member States, so international agreements enjoy supremacy over (secondary) Community law (Cases 21 to 24/72 *International Fruit Company*, above, at pp. 1226, 1229 *per Curiam*, pp. 1233–4 *per* A.-G. Mayras).

On the other hand, the international agreements of the Communities, being concluded by means of an act of an institution (under the EEC Treaty: a regulation or a decision of the Council), form an integral part of Community law (Case 181/73 *Haegeman* [1974] ECR 449 at pp. 459–60, dealing with the EEC–Greece Association Agreement; see also Case 104/81 *Kupferberg*, above, at p. 3662, dealing with the EEC–Portugal Free Trade Agreement), even if they are concluded in the form of a 'mixed' agreement (Opinion 1/76 *Laying-up Fund* [1977] ECR 741 at p. 760 dealing with the Draft Agreement establishing a European Laying-up Fund for Inland Waterway Vessels; Ruling 1/78 *Protection of Nuclear Materials* [1978] ECR 2151 at p. 2180, dealing with the Draft Convention on the Physical Protection of Nuclear Materials, negotiated under the Euratom Treaty). They are therefore binding not only *upon* but also *within* the Communities. They produce important legal effects within Community law which may be summarized as follows:

1. According to Art. 228(2) EEC, the agreements concluded by the EEC are binding on the institutions of the Community and on the Member States. Consequently, it is incumbent upon the Community institutions, as well as upon the Member States, to ensure compliance with the obligations arising from such agreements. The measures needed to implement them must be adopted, according to the state of Community law for the time being in the areas affected by the agreements, either by the Community institutions or by the Member States. Nevertheless, their effects in the Community may not vary according to whether their application is in practice the responsibility of the institutions or of the Member States. In the latter case, their effect may not depend on the status and effects of international agreements within the internal legal order of each Member State. They must be applied uniformly throughout the Community, and it is for the ECJ to ensure this (see Case 104/81 *Kupferberg*, above, at pp. 3662–3). The application of mixed agreements entails particularly close co-operation between the institutions and the Member States, each side being responsible for the implementation of matters falling within its own competence (Ruling 1/78 *Protection of Nuclear Materials*, above, at p. 2180).

2. Since Community agreements are binding upon the Member States, they limit the freedom of action of the Member States in relation to matters covered by them (see e.g. Case 52/77 *Cayrol* [1977] ECR 2261 at p. 2278, dealing with the EEC–Spain Trade Agreement of 1970). Thus, the conclusion of an agreement by the Community precludes the adoption or application of

any conflicting national provisions by the Member States (Case 61/77 *Commission* v. *Ireland* [1978] ECR 417 at p. 448, dealing with sea fisheries; Case 17/81 *Pabst & Richarz* [1982] ECR 1331 at p. 1350, dealing with the EEC–Greece Association Agreement; see also Case 270/80 *Polydor* [1982] ECR 329 at p. 346, dealing with the EEC–Portugal Free Trade Agreement). It would thus seem that Community agreements, being an integral part of Community law, enjoy its supremacy over national law.

3. Where Community agreements fulfil the general conditions of direct effect, they may produce direct effects within the national legal systems of the Member States and thus create individual rights which the national courts must protect and enforce against the Member States (Case 87/75 *Bresciani*, above, at pp. 141–2; Case 17/81 *Pabst & Richarz*, above, at p. 1350; Case 104/81 *Kupferberg*, above, at p. 3665. *See further under* **Direct effect**, point 3).

4. Since, so far as the Community is concerned, Community agreements are 'acts of an institution' within the meaning of Art. 177(1)(b) EEC, the ECJ has jurisdiction, within the context of the Community legal order, to give preliminary rulings on the interpretation of such agreements (Case 181/73 *Haegeman*, above, at pp. 459–60; Opinion 1/76 *Laying-up Fund*, above, at p. 760; Cases 267 to 269/81 *SPI and SAMI*, above, at p. 829). Clearly, such interpretation is binding on the Community and the Member States only, but cannot have binding effect with regard to the other contracting party or parties. In fact, an international agreement is always a bilateral or multilateral instrument and therefore its identification with a unilateral act of a Community institution has been questioned (see the opinion of A.-G. Trabucchi in Case 87/75 *Bresciani*, above, at p. 147). It seems certainly doubtful whether the Court may also review the validity of Community agreements on the basis that they are 'acts of an institution' within the meaning of Art. 177(1)(b) (see further below).

The question of the relationship between treaties concluded by the (Economic) Community and the pre-existing treaty obligations of the Member States towards third countries raises intricate problems involving the interaction of public international law and Community law. In Case 812/79 *Burgoa*, above, at p. 2807 the ECJ held that the treaty relations which were then being established between the Community and Spain in the form of the EEC–Spain Fisheries Agreement were 'superimposed' on the regime which had previously applied under international fisheries agreements to which some of the Member States were parties. In Case 181/80 *Arbelaiz-Emazabel*, above, at p. 2982, in Cases 180 and 266/80 *Tome* [1981] ECR 2997 at pp. 3016–17, and in subsequent cases, the Court held that the relations which were developed with the concurrence of Spain and subsequently confirmed by the EEC–Spain Fisheries Agreement of 1980 'replaced' the prior international obligations existing between certain Member States, such as France, and Spain. Consequently, Spanish fishermen could not rely on previous international agreements between France and Spain in order to prevent the application of the Community regime in the event of any incompatibility between the two sets of provisions. It thus seems that the Court based the theory that Community agreements had replaced incompatible agreements of the Member States on the (implied) consent of the other contracting party, Spain. However, it should be noted that these decisions were given within the context of internal Community proceedings brought under Art. 177 EEC, without the participation of the other party, Spain, and therefore state the legal position under Community law only. They do not determine the issue under general international law, which could only be done by a court or tribunal adjudicating on the basis of public international law and in proceedings to which the other State involved is a party. Such a court acting in such proceedings might well arrive at the conclusion that a Community agreement cannot abrogate previous agreements concluded by the Member States (unless the other party consents, in which case there would be no cause for a dispute), even if the subject-matter of the agreement has, under internal Community law, passed from the treaty-making competence of the Member States into that of the Community, as in the above-mentioned fisheries cases.

Finally, the relationship between Community treaties and the EEC Treaty itself is governed (to some extent) by Art. 228(1) EEC. This enables the ECJ to give an opinion, at the request of the Council, the Commission, or a Member State, as to whether an agreement which the Community intends to conclude is compatible with the EEC Treaty. Where the opinion of the Court is adverse, the agreement may enter into force only after the EEC Treaty has been amended (*see further under* **Treaty-making procedure**, point 2(*d*). There are no corresponding provisions in the ECSC and Euratom Treaties).

While this provision clearly establishes the primacy of the EEC Treaty over intended future treaties of the Community, it is silent on the question whether the ECJ is competent to review the 'validity' (i.e. compatibility with the EEC Treaty) of treaties actually concluded by the Community. From the view that such treaties are acts of the institutions (see above) it would seem to follow that in theory their validity may be reviewed by the Court in accordance with the various provisions under which the Court has jurisdiction to review Community acts. These include Arts. 173 (action for annulment), 177 (preliminary ruling), 178 in conjunction with 215(2) (action for damages), and 184 (plea of illegality). The ECJ has itself stated that 'the question whether the conclusion of a given agreement is within the power of the Community and whether, in a given case, such power has been exercised in conformity with the provisions of the Treaty is, in principle, a question which may be submitted to the Court of Justice, either directly, under Article 169 or Article 173 of the Treaty, or in accordance with the preliminary procedure ... of Article 228' (Opinion 1/75 *Local Cost Standard* [1975] ECR 1355 at p. 1361).

Nevertheless, in the same opinion the Court has also stressed the complications and difficulties which would result from such a review. It has pointed out that a possible decision of the Court to the effect that an agreement which is binding upon the Community is incompatible with the Treaty 'could not fail to provoke, not only in a Community context but also in that of international relations, serious difficulties and might give rise to adverse consequences for all interested parties, including third countries' (ibid.). The purpose of Art. 228(1) is, the Court has said, precisely to forestall such complications. It may therefore be equally argued that the inclusion of Art. 228(1) in the Treaty indicates that the drafters did not envisage (or even intended to exclude) the possibility of judicial review once a treaty has been formally concluded. Moreover, such review cannot lead to the 'invalidity' or 'annulment' of the treaty itself but only to that of the act (decision or regulation) whereby it was concluded and incorporated into Community law. A treaty, being a bilateral or multilateral instrument governed by international law, cannot be terminated by an internal organ of one of the contracting parties as a result of an internal procedure in which the other contracting parties have no standing to participate and therefore no opportunity to defend their rights and interests. Nor may a party to a treaty invoke its internal law (including domestic judicial decisions) as justification for its failure to perform the treaty (see Art. 27 of the Vienna Convention on the Law of Treaties between States and International Organizations or between International Organizations of 1986). Therefore, a possible decision of the ECJ that a Community treaty is incompatible with the EEC Treaty could only mean that the treaty cannot be given effect within Community law, but the treaty itself would continue to bind the Community under international law and the Community would be internationally responsible towards the other parties for breach of its treaty obligations. A Community treaty could be validly terminated only in accordance with the procedures laid down by international law, and only on one of the grounds recognized by international law. One of these grounds is that consent to be bound by the treaty has been expressed by an international organization in 'manifest violation' of one of its rules of 'fundamental importance' regarding competence to conclude treaties, which ground the Community would be free to invoke (see Art. 46(2) of the Vienna Convention of 1986, cited above. For the various grounds of invalidity and termination of treaties, as well as the procedure to be followed, see Part V of the Convention). Nevertheless, given the fact that the Community's treaty-making competence is not always clearly defined and that the distribution of that competence between the Community and the Member States is not easily ascertainable by third States, the number of cases in which the Community could successfully invoke treaty-making incompetence (which has to be 'manifest') as a ground for terminating a treaty necessarily remains small.

In spite of these considerations, it seems that the ECJ does not hesitate to review an act of the Council concluding an international agreement and to declare it null and void in appropriate cases, even after the agreement has come into force. However, the Court has not so far had the opportunity to state the precise legal consequences, in Community law as well as in international law, of such annulment (see Case 165/87 *Commission* v. *Council* [1988] ECR paras. 18–19 *per Curiam*, paras. 35–6 *per* A.-G. Lenz, where the Court held that the decision of the Council concerning the conclusion of the International Convention on the Harmonised Commodity Description and Coding System of 1983, which came into force on 1 January 1988 and replaced the Convention on Nomenclature of 1950, was incorrectly based on Art. 235 EEC and was, to that extent, illegal. However, in the circumstances of the case, such illegality constituted a 'purely formal defect' which did not entail the annulment of the decision. Both the Commission and the Advocate-General submitted that in the case of the annulment of the decision the Court should apply Art. 174(2) EEC, thus ensuring that the Convention remained in force with regard to the Community).

See also **Community law, Direct effect, External relations, Legal personality, Mixed agreement, Treaty-making power, Treaty-making procedure.**

Further reading 1. BOOK: Groux and Manin, *The European Communities in the International Order* (1985).

2. ARTICLES AND PAPERS: Bebr, 'Agreements Concluded by the Community and their Possible Direct Effect: From International Fruit Company to Kupferberg' (1983) 20 *CML Rev.* 35; Churchill and Foster, 'European Community Law and Prior Treaty Obligations of Member States: The Spanish Fishermen's Cases' (1987) 36 *ICLQ* 504; Hartley, 'International Agreements and the Community Legal System: Some Recent Developments' (1983) 8 *EL Rev.* 383; Meessen, 'The Application of Rules of Public International Law Within Community Law' (1976) 13 *CML Rev.* 485; Pescatore, 'International Law and Community Law: A Comparative Analysis' (1970) 7 *CML Rev.* 167; id., 'External Relations in the Case-Law of the Court of Justice of the European Communities' (1979) 16 *CML Rev.* 615; Schermers, 'Community Law and International Law' (1975) 12 *CML Rev.* 77; id., 'The Internal Effect of Community Treaty-Making', in O'Keeffe and Schermers (eds.), *Essays in European Law and Integration* (1982), p. 167; van Panhuys, 'Conflicts between the Law of the European Communities and Other Rules of International Law' (1965–6) 3 *CML Rev.* 420; Völker, 'The Direct Effect of International Agreements in the Community's Legal Order' (1983/1) *LIEI* 131.

▶ **COMPULSORY JURISDICTION** Jurisdiction of a court or tribunal which is not subject to the special consent of the defendant to submit a dispute to it. While international courts and tribunals do not normally possess compulsory jurisdiction, the ECJ has been granted such jurisdiction in certain disputes between Member States. Under the ECSC Treaty, any dispute between Member States concerning the application of that Treaty which cannot be settled by another procedure provided for in the Treaty may be submitted to the Court on application by one of the States which are parties to the dispute (Art. 89(1) ECSC). Under the EEC and Euratom Treaties, a Member State which considers that another Member State has failed to fulfil an obligation under those Treaties may bring the matter before the Court, subject only to the completion of a compulsory preliminary procedure before the Commission (Arts. 170 EEC, 142 Euratom; see e.g. Case 141/78 *France* v. *United Kingdom* [1979] ECR 2923 at pp. 2938–9). Even this preliminary procedure may be dispensed with in certain specified cases (i.e. under Arts. 93(2), 100A(4), and 225(2) EEC; 38(3) and 82(4) Euratom).

See also **Action against Member States, Jurisdiction, Optional jurisdiction.**

113

Conciliation procedure

▶ **CONCILIATION PROCEDURE** Procedure established between the European Parliament and the Council, with the active participation of the Commission, aimed at involving Parliament more effectively in the adoption of certain important Community acts with major financial implications. The procedure was set up by a Joint Declaration of the European Parliament, the Council, and the Commission of 4 March 1975 (*OJ* 1975 C89/1; also known as 'legislative conciliation' to distinguish it from 'budgetary conciliation', which is the subject of another Joint Declaration, dated 30 June 1982, *OJ* 1982 C194/1, *see under* **Community budget**, section II(9)). The need for such a procedure arose from the recognition that the increased budgetary powers which were conferred upon Parliament by the Budgetary Treaties of 1970 and 1975 would remain largely illusory so long as Parliament was unable effectively to participate in the preparation and adoption of decisions which automatically determine important items of expenditure or revenue making up the budget of the Communities (for legislative history, see Suppl. 9/73— *Bull. EC*, p. 4; *Bull. EC* 6–1973, p. 6 and 10–1973, pp. 18, 21–2).

Under the Joint Declaration, the conciliation procedure may be set in motion only for 'Community acts of general application which have appreciable financial implications, and of which the adoption is not required by virtue of acts already in existence' (point 2). It must also be followed when adopting or amending the Financial Regulation itself (Preamble and Art. 107 of the Financial Regulation of 21 Dec. 1977, *OJ* 1977 L356/1). When submitting its legislative proposal, the Commission is required to indicate whether the act in question is, in its opinion, capable of being the subject of the conciliation procedure. The procedure may then be initiated at the request of the EP, made when giving its opinion, or at the request of the Council. It will be initiated if the criteria mentioned above are met and if the Council intends to depart from Parliament's opinion. The conciliation takes place in a 'Conciliation Committee' consisting of the Council and of a corresponding number of representatives of the EP led by the President or a Vice-President of the EP (Rule 43 of Parliament's Rules of Procedure (1987)). The Commission participates in the work of the Committee and is required to provide 'active assistance'. The aim of the procedure is to seek an agreement between the EP and the Council. The procedure normally takes place during a period not exceeding three months, although in urgent cases the Council may fix an appropriate time limit. When the positions of the two institutions are sufficiently close, the EP may give a new opinion, after which the Council is required to take definitive action. This procedure is to be followed also when the Council adopts measures to implement the Decision and Act of 20 September 1976 concerning the election of the representatives of the EP by direct universal suffrage (see Art. 13 and Annex III of the Act, *OJ* 1976 L278/1).

Although on a few occasions the conciliation procedure was used successfully to bring the Parliament's and the Council's positions closer together (see e.g. the adoption of the Financial Regulation of 1977 when the procedure was used for the first time and enabled the two institutions to find solutions to the majority of disputed points, *Bull. EC* 11–1977, p. 101, or see the adoption of the regulation reforming the European Regional Development Fund in June 1984, *Bull. EC* 6–1984, p. 18), it is generally recognized that in most cases it has not operated satisfactorily. In particular, it has not given Parliament the feeling of being part of a real dialogue with the Council. Therefore, in October 1981, the Commission put forward proposals for a second Joint Declaration of the three institutions concerning a new and improved conciliation procedure (Suppl. 3/82—*Bull. EC*, p. 15; see also *Bull. EC* 12–1981, p. 10). In accordance with the wishes expressed by the directly elected Parliament, the draft provides for an extension of the procedure to cover all important legislative acts of general application, with or without major financial implications, whose adoption is not required by acts already in existence. While the Commission's proposals were approved by Parliament (Res. of 14 Dec. 1983, *OJ* 1984 C10/34, see also Res. of 15 Nov. 1984, *OJ* 1984 C337/404), the Council was unable to adopt them because of the opposition of one Member State (18th *Gen. Rep. EC* (1984), p. 28; *Bull. EC* 6–1984, p. 90). The European Parliament has since called upon the Commission to submit new proposals for the revision of the 1975 Joint Declaration (Res. of 15 June 1988, point 4, *OJ* 1988 C187/94; Res. of 16 Feb. 1989, *OJ* 1989 C69/151).

See also **Budgetary Treaties, Community budget, European Parliament.**

Further reading: Forman, 'The Conciliation Procedure' (1979) 16 *CML Rev.* 77. *See also under* **Budgetary Treaties, European Parliament.**

▶ **CONFIDENTIALITY** General principle of law, also forming part of Community law, which requires that certain types of information concerning private individuals and undertakings should be protected from disclosure and from use in administrative or judicial proceedings. In Community law, the principle of confidentiality covers the following matters:

1. **Communications between lawyer and client (legal professional privilege).** In so far as written communications between a lawyer and a client undertaking have a bearing on the market activities of the latter, they form part of its 'business records' and thus fall within the category of documents of which the Commission is entitled to require production when requesting information or carrying out investigations in competition matters under Arts. 11 and 14 of Reg. 17 (*OJ Sp. Edn.* 1959–62, p. 87). Nevertheless, this rule does not exclude the possibility that, subject to certain conditions, some business records may be of a confidential nature and therefore protected from disclosure even although Reg. 17 is silent on this matter. Thus, relying on the principles and concepts common to the laws of the Member States concerning the observance of confidentiality, in Case 155/79 *AM & S.* v. *Commission* [1982] ECR 1575 at pp. 1610–13 the ECJ ruled that Reg. 17 must be interpreted as protecting the confidentiality of written communications between lawyer and client subject to two conditions. First, that such communications are made for the purposes and in the interests of the client's rights of defence. Secondly, that they emanate from independent laywers, i.e. lawyers who are not bound to the client by a relationship of employment. (As

115

regards the laws of the Member States, see the opinions of A.-G. Warner at pp. 1630–7 and of A.-G. Slynn at pp. 1648–58.)

Since the protection of confidentiality is an essential corollary to the rights of the defence, the ECJ has held that it must be extended to all written communications exchanged between lawyer and client after the initiation of the administrative procedure under Reg. 17, and also to earlier written communications which have a relationship to the subject-matter of that procedure. Moreover, the protection must apply without distinction to any lawyer entitled to practise his profession in one of the Member States, regardless of the Member State in which the client lives, but it may not be extended beyond those limits as determined by Dir. 77/249 (*OJ* 1977 L78/17), which lays down the common rules on the exercise of the legal profession. Nevertheless, the client remains free to disclose confidential communications if he considers that it is in his interests to do so (ibid.).

As regards the practical application of the principle, an undertaking claiming confidentiality must satisfy the Commission's agents that the communications in question fulfil the above conditions, although it is not bound to reveal their actual contents. If the Commission is not satisfied, it is entitled to order production of the documents. On its part, the undertaking has the right to challenge such a decision before the ECJ and in so doing it may obtain interim protection from the Court in the form of an order suspending the application of the Commission's decision pending final judgment. Thus, ultimately, the Court is the only body competent to decide any dispute concerning the application of the principle in a particular case (ibid. at pp. 1613–14).

The principle of confidentiality, as established by the Court in the *AM & S.* case, is restricted to independent lawyers who are entitled to practise their profession in one of the Member States. It has been claimed that the Commission should extend legal professional privilege to in-house lawyers, who are subject to the same professional rules as independent lawyers, and to independent lawyers from non-Community countries. However, since the judgment of the Court represents the authentic interpretation of Regulation 17, any such extension would require an amendment of that Regulation. After careful consideration, the Commission has decided not to propose any amendment to Regulation 17 in respect of in-house lawyers. As far as independent lawyers from non-Community countries are concerned, denial of the benefit of confidentiality to them can lead to an undesirable inequality of treatment, at least in the case of those countries whose legal systems afford corresponding privilege in a non-discriminatory manner to all lawyers, including Community lawyers. Therefore, the Commission has proposed to conclude bilateral agreements with interested third countries with the aim of extending, on the basis of reciprocity, the principle of confidentiality to their lawyers. The Commission has already sought the necessary authorization from the Council to open negotiations for this purpose (*Bull. EC* 6–1983, p. 43; 13th *Comp. Rep. EC* (1983), pp. 65–6; 14th *Comp. Rep. EC* (1984), p. 52).

Finally, it should be noted that in the *AM & S.* case the Court confirmed the principle of confidentiality 'in particular in the context of Regulation 17', i.e. in administrative proceedings in the field of competition law only. It therefore remains to be seen whether the same principle also applies to other areas of Community law in which the Commission has powers of investigation and of obtaining information, such as transport, competition in transport including air transport, dumping and subsidization, Art. 213 EEC, and in general to procedures under the ECSC and Euratom Treaties. It is also uncertain whether and, if so, to what extent the principle of confidentiality applies to judicial proceedings before the ECJ itself. The use of the words 'in particular' would seem to indicate that the Court has envisaged (or at least has not excluded) the possibility that the principle may also be applicable outside competition proceedings.

2. **Medical findings.** Because of the confidential nature of the relationship which exists between a patient and his doctor, the confidentiality of medical findings is protected, within certain limits, in all the Member States. Likewise, the ECJ has recognized that in staff recruitment cases the obligation to state the reasons for a refusal to appoint a candidate on grounds of physical unfitness must be mitigated by the confidentiality of medical secrets. The appointing authority is therefore neither obliged nor entitled to disclose medical findings; these must be communicated by the examining doctor either to the person concerned or to a doctor of his choice (Case 121/76 *Moli* v. *Commission* [1977] ECR 1971 at pp. 1978–9; Case 75/77 *Mollet* v. *Commission* [1978] ECR 897 at p. 907; Case 155/78 *M* v. *Commission* [1980] ECR 1797 at pp. 1810–11). However, in judicial proceedings before the ECJ, the doctor who carried out the medical examinations may not rely on the confidentiality of his findings in order to refuse to provide information to the Court where: (*a*) the person concerned has expressly given his consent; (*b*) the doctor's involvement takes place in the context of administrative checking procedures so that the spontaneous confidential relationship which is the basis of professional secrecy does not exist; (*c*) reliance on such confidentiality would have the result of obstructing the normal course of justice. In these circumstances, reliance on the principle of confidentiality as a ground for withholding indispensable information from the Court would make judicial review impossible (Case 155/78 *M* v. *Commission*, above, at p. 1811 *per Curiam*; pp. 1820–1 *per* A.-G. Capotorti).

3. **Professional secrecy and business secrets.** (*a*) *Under the ECSC Treaty*, the Commission is required not to disclose information 'of the kind covered by the obligation of professional secrecy, in particular information about undertakings, their business relations or their cost components' (Art. 47 ECSC). Subject to this reservation, the Commission is to publish such data as could be useful to Governments or to any other parties concerned (ibid.). Any breach of professional secrecy by the Commission which has caused damage to an undertaking may be the subject of an action for compensation before the ECJ (ibid.). The obligation contained in Art. 47 applies both to information lawfully obtained and, *a fortiori*, to information obtained unlawfully (Case 31/59 *Acciaieria di Brescia* v. *HA* [1960] ECR 71 at p. 100).

Although, in accordance with the principle of publicity—an important

117

feature of the ECSC Treaty—the Commission is under a duty to publish certain information (including information obtained from undertakings), Art. 47 is intended to guarantee that business secrecy is respected. It thereby ensures protection of the legitimate interests of undertakings and provides a quid pro quo for the obligation to supply information to the Commission. As a result, the Commission is required 'to balance the need for transparency of the Common Market in [coal and] steel products against the need to protect the business secrecy of individual undertakings' (Case 27/84 *Wirtschaftsvereinigung Eisen- und Stahlindustrie* v. *Commission* [1985] ECR 2385 at p. 2398). Where publication of information (e.g. production quota adjustments granted in cases of 'exceptional difficulties') might seriously affect the operation of an undertaking or even its continued existence, the Commission must not disclose the identity of the undertaking concerned. Where, however, this is not the case, protection of business secrets may not be relied on as a ground for refusing to disclose information the publication of which is obligatory under Art. 47 (ibid.).

(*b*) *Under the EEC Treaty*, the members of the institutions, the members of committees, the officials and other servants of the Community are required, even after their duties have ceased, not to disclose information 'of the kind covered by the obligation of professional secrecy, in particular information about undertakings, their business relations or their cost components' (Art. 214 EEC). It appears from the wording of this provision that it does not purport to lay down an exhaustive definition of the concept of 'professional secrecy'. Indeed, as A.-G. Lenz has pointed out in his opinion in Case 53/85 *AKZO Chemie* v. *Commission* [1986] ECR 1965 at p. 1977 the very term 'professional secrecy' is too narrow since, at least in some of the Member States, it covers only the obligation of secrecy imposed on the 'liberal' professions by their own professional rules. The more general expression 'official secrecy' might perhaps have been a more appropriate designation. In his view, the range of information covered by professional or official secrecy clearly goes beyond the industrial and business secrets of undertakings and includes all information acquired by the officials of the institutions in the exercise of their duties, whether in the course of formal investigations or informally, which is confidential and is inaccessible to the general public, whatever its nature. Nevertheless, the information must be of some importance to the undertaking and must concern matters which may be withheld without placing third parties at a disadvantage. In determining its significance, the opinion of the undertaking to which it relates is an important, although not of itself decisive, consideration (ibid.).

Moreover, the ECJ has held that while Art. 214 primarily refers to information gathered from undertakings, the expression 'in particular' shows that the principle in question is a general one which applies also to information supplied by natural persons, if the information is confidential. That is particularly so in the case of information provided on a purely voluntary basis and accompanied by a request for confidentiality in order to protect the informant's anonymity. An institution which accepts such information is bound to comply with such a request. Breach of the duty of confidentiality may establish the Community's non-contractual liability towards the supplier of information in respect of any damage caused him thereby (Case 145/83 *Adams* v. *Commission* [1985] ECR 3539 at p. 3587. For measures taken by the Commission in the light of this judgment, see 15th *Comp. Rep. EC* (1985), pp. 56–7).

The general rule or principle laid down in Art. 214 EEC has been implemented in various areas of Community law by means of specific provisions. Thus, for example, provisions protecting confidentiality exist in the fields of transport (Arts. 14(3) and 15 of Reg. 11, *OJ Sp. Edn.* 1959–62, p. 60), competition (Arts. 19(3), 20, and 21(2) of Reg. 17), competition in transport (Arts. 26(3), 27, and 28(2) of Reg. 1017/68, *OJ Sp. Edn.* 1968(I), p. 302), competition in air transport (Arts. 16(3), 17, and 18(2) of Reg. 3975/87, *OJ* 1987 L374/1), dumping and subsidization (Art. 8 of Reg. 2176/84, *OJ* 1984 L201/1 as corrected, *OJ* 1984 L227/35, and Art. 8 of Dec. 2177/84, *OJ* 1984 L201/17), etc. Generally, these provisions require both the Community institutions, their servants, and the competent authorities of the Member States not to disclose information acquired by them as a result of the application of the relevant regulation and of the kind covered by the obligation of professional secrecy. Information may only be used for the purpose for which it was obtained. Moreover, in publishing its decisions the Commission must have regard to the legitimate interests of undertakings in the protection of their business secrets. In addition, Community officials are under the general obligation not to disclose 'in any manner whatsoever' to any un-authorized person information acquired in connection with the performance of their duties, which has not already been made public. Nor may they publish without the permission of the appointing authority any matter dealing with the work of the Communities. The prohibition also applies to officials appearing in 'any legal proceedings' except when giving evidence before the ECJ (Arts. 17 and 19 of the Staff Regulations).

However, in a number of cases the ECJ has held that the obligation of professional secrecy must be reconciled with certain other rights and interests also protected by Community law. Thus, that obligation cannot be invoked to justify (i) deficiencies in the statement of reasons for Community acts (Cases 296 and 318/82 *Netherlands and Leeuwarder Papierwarenfabriek* v. *Commission* [1985] ECR 809 at pp. 825–6); (ii) a refusal to disclose information which must be made available to interested parties, such as information collected in anti-dumping proceedings (Case 264/82 *Timex* v. *Council and Commission* [1985] ECR 849 at pp. 868–9, 870); (iii) a claim that decisions imposing fines should not be published (Case 41/69 *Chemiefarma* v. *Commission* [1970] ECR 661 at p. 692; Case 54/69 *Francolor* v. *Commission* [1972] ECR 851 at pp. 872–3). But, perhaps most importantly, the duty of professional secrecy must be reconciled with the right to be heard (the rights of the defence). Thus, the ECJ has stated that the Commission may not use, to the detriment of undertakings involved in competition proceedings, 'facts, circumstances or documents which it cannot in its view disclose if such a refusal of disclosure adversely affects that undertaking's opportunity to make known effectively its views on the truth or implications of those

119

circumstances, on those documents or again on the conclusions drawn by the Commission from them' (Case 85/76 *Hoffmann-La Roche* v. *Commission* [1979] ECR 461 at pp. 512–13).

Likewise, the obligation of professional secrecy is relaxed in regard to third parties on whom Art. 19(2) of Reg. 17 confers the right to be heard in competition proceedings. These include, in particular, a third party who has made a complaint to the Commission under Art. 3 of Reg. 17. The Commission may communicate to such a party certain information covered by professional secrecy in so far as this is necessary for the proper conduct of the investigation. However, that power does not extend to business secrets, which enjoy very special protection. Thus, there is a mandatory requirement applicable during the whole course of the administrative procedure that a third party who has submitted a complaint may not in any circumstances be given access to documents containing business secrets. Art. 19(2) of Reg. 17 gives such a party a right to be heard and not a right to receive confidential information. Any other solution would lead to the unacceptable consequence that an undertaking might lodge a complaint with the Commission solely in order to gain access to its competitors' business secrets (Cases 209 to 215 and 218/78 *Van Landewyck* v. *Commission* [1980] ECR 3125 at pp. 3238–9— 'FEDETAB' cases; Case 53/85 *AKZO Chemie* v. *Commission*, above, at pp. 1991–2). In the case of a dispute, it is for the Commission to assess whether or not a particular document contains business secrets. After hearing the undertaking concerned, the Commission must adopt a reasoned decision on the matter. However, having regard to the extremely serious damage which could result from improper communication of business secrets to a competitor, the Commission must, before implementing its decision, give the undertaking an opportunity to bring an action before the ECJ to have the assessment reviewed and to prevent disclosure of the information in question (Case 53/85 *AKZO Chemie* v. *Commission*, above, at p. 1992). In the absence of such an opportunity, disclosure of the documents will be illegal, irrespective of whether or not they in fact contain business secrets (ibid. at pp. 1992–3).

(*c*) *Under the Euratom Treaty*, information the disclosure of which is liable to harm the defence interests of one or more Member States is subject to a security system (Art. 24 Euratom). Such information must be kept secret from any unauthorized person and from the general public (Art. 194(1) Euratom). Member States are required to prosecute anyone within their jurisdiction who infringes this obligation, in accordance with their laws relating to acts prejudicial to the security of the State or to disclosure of professional secrets (ibid.).

(*d*) *In proceedings before the ECJ*, the Court may require the parties to produce all documents and to supply all information which the Court considers desirable. It may also require the Member States and institutions not being parties to the case to supply all information which it considers necessary for the proceedings (Arts. 24 ECSC Statute, 21 EEC Statute, 22 Euratom Statute, 45(2)(b) RP). It seems that, in the absence of any qualifications or exceptions, these provisions enable the Court to order production of *any* document or information whether confidential or not. In practice, however, the Court has been willing to authorize a party to erase, omit, or withdraw information of a confidential nature. This may be necessary, for example, to preserve the secrecy of the deliberations of an institution (see e.g. Case 2/54 *Italy* v. *HA* [1954] ECR 37 at p. 42; Case 28/65 *Fonzi* v. *Commission* [1966] ECR 477 at pp. 492, 506–7); to protect third parties not involved in the proceedings (ibid. at p. 493); to enable an institution to observe professional secrecy (see e.g. Cases 36 to 38 and 40/59 *Geitling* v. *HA* [1960] ECR 423 at p. 437); or to protect the business secrets of an undertaking (see e.g. Case 30/78 *Distillers Company* v. *Commission* [1980] ECR 2229 at p. 2237). The Court also has power to withhold secret or confidential documents from an intervener (Art. 93(4) RP). Where an intervener (or a party) does not wish confidential information which is in its possession and on which it itself relies as evidence to be disclosed to the other parties and interveners (even if it is willing to make it available to the Court or to any person bound by professional secrecy), the Court will not order the production of that information but will simply ignore its existence as evidence. The reason is that 'it would infringe a basic principle of law to base a judicial decision on facts and documents of which the parties themselves, or one of them, have not been able to take cognisance and in relation to which they have not therefore been able to formulate an opinion' (Cases 42 and 49/59 *SNUPAT* v. *HA* [1961] ECR 53 at p. 84). Similarly, where the Court grants confidential treatment to certain documents containing business secrets, in the sense that they may only be disclosed to the principal parties and to the officers of the Court but not to third parties, the Court will exclude these documents from the file of the case if their confidentiality would conflict with the requirements that the Court should give a public statement of reasons for its judgments and that the Advocate-General should deliver his opinions in public. In other words, confidential information cannot be used as a basis for the Court's decisions (Case 236/81 *Celanese* v. *Council and Commission* [1982] ECR 1183 at pp. 1186–7, involving anti-dumping proceedings).

Where, on the other hand, the Court does order a party to produce confidential documents, the question arises whether such documents should be disclosed to the other party. In Case 110/75 *Mills* v. *Investment Bank* [1976] ECR 1613 at pp. 1634–5 A.-G. Warner suggested that in such a situation the Court itself should look at the documents in question and decide whether or not their evidentiary value outweighed the harm that their disclosure might do. If not, justice did not require their disclosure. The Court seems to have followed this opinion.

See also **Administrative procedure*, General principles of law, Investigation procedure*, Preparatory inquiries.**

Further reading: Boyd, 'A.M. & S. and the In-house Lawyer' (1982) 7 *EL Rev.* 493; Christoforou, 'Protection of Legal Privilege in EEC Competition Law: The Imperfections of a Case' (1985/2) *LIEI* 1; Editorial, 'The AKZO Case: A Boost to Due Process' (1986) 11 *EL Rev.* 245; Edward, 'The Professional Secret, Confidentiality and Legal Professional Privilege in the Nine Member States of the European Community', Report prepared for the Consultative Committee of the Bars and Law

121

Societies of the European Community (1976); Faull, 'A.M. & S.: The Commission's Practice Note' (1983) 8 *EL Rev.* 411; id., 'Legal Professional Privilege (A.M. & S.): The Commission Proposes International Negotiations' (1985) 10 *EL Rev.* 119; Forrester, 'Legal Professional Privilege: Limitations on the Commission's Powers of Inspection Following the A.M. & S. Judgment' (1983) 20 *CML Rev.* 75; Ghandhi, 'Legal Professional Privilege in European Community Law' (1982) 7 *EL Rev.* 308; Hunnings, 'The Stanley Adams Affair or the Biter Bit' (1987) 24 *CML Rev.* 65; Pagone, 'Legal Professional Privilege in the European Communities: The A.M. & S. Case and Australian Law' (1984) 33 *ICLQ* 663; Riesenfeld, 'The Treatment of Confidential Information in Anti-Dumping Cases: A Comment on the Celanese Case' (1984) 21 *CML Rev.* 553; Von Heydebrand und der Lasa, 'Confidential Information in Anti-Dumping Proceedings before United States Courts and the European Court' (1986) 11 *EL Rev.* 331. *See also under* **Administrative procedure***, **Investigation procedure***.

▶ **CONSULTATIVE COMMITTEE** Committee set up by Arts. 18–19 ECSC to advise and assist the Commission when acting under the ECSC Treaty (Art. 7 ECSC). Its functions are comparable to those of the Economic and Social Committee serving the EEC and Euratom. The Committee consists of not less than 72 and not more than 96 members comprising equal numbers of producers, of workers, and of consumers and dealers in the coal and steel industries (Art. 18 ECSC as last amended by Art. 22 of the Act of Accession 1985. The present membership is 96, see below). The members of the Committee are appointed by the Council, in the case of the producers and workers from lists drawn up by representative organizations designated by the Council. The 96 members are allocated on a national basis as follows: Belgium 8, Denmark 3, France 13, Germany 19, Greece 3, Ireland 3, Italy 9, Luxembourg 4, Netherlands 5, Portugal 3, Spain 8, United Kingdom 18. The members are appointed in their personal capacity for two years (for the appointments made on 18 Apr. 1988, see *OJ* 1988 C118/1). They are not bound by any mandate or instructions from the organizations which nominated them. They enjoy the privileges and immunities laid down in Art. 11 of the Protocol on Privileges and Immunities annexed to the Merger Treaty. The Committee elects its chairman and officers from among its members for a term of one year. It adopts its Rules of Procedure which determine its organization and functioning (called 'Internal Regulations'; for the latest version adopted on 6 Mar. 1981, see *OJ* 1981 C286/1).

The Commission must consult the Consultative Committee whenever such consultation is prescribed by the ECSC Treaty; it may consult the Committee in all cases in which it considers this appropriate. In certain cases (i.e. under Arts. 54, 65, and 66 ECSC), the Commission is required to keep the Committee informed of the broad lines of its action. The Commission may set the Committee a time-limit for the submission of its opinion, which may not be less than ten days. The Committee must forward the minutes of its proceedings to the Commission and to the Council together with its opinions (in practice, they are also sent to Parliament). As a rule, the opinions and resolutions of the Committee are published in the *Official Journal*. Although the Committee's opinions are not legally binding, they do have considerable impact on the decisions of the Commission and the Council owing to the expertise of its members. Moreover, failure to consult the Committee where consultation is mandatory constitutes infringement of an essential procedural requirement and may lead to the annulment of the measure concerned by the Court of Justice.

See also **Commission, Economic and Social Committee, Infringement of an essential procedural requirement, Privileges and immunities.**

Further reading: 'The Consultative Committee of the European Coal and Steel Community', *Bull. EC* 3–1986, p. 100.

▶ **CONTINUITY OF THE LEGAL SYSTEM** General principle of law, common to the legal systems of the Member States, according to which 'when legislation is amended, unless the legislature expresses a contrary intention, continuity of the legal system must be ensured' (Case 23/68 *Klomp* [1969] ECR 43 at p. 50). Accordingly, 'in the absence of any express provision, laws governing jurisdiction and procedure are immediately applicable; it follows that as soon as a law of this kind is repealed by another law it is no longer possible to apply the former law for the resolution of disputes, even if such disputes relate to facts or legal relationships which arose while the former law was still in force. This rule . . . is, however, qualified by . . . the doctrine of vested rights and . . . by a concern for legal certainty; hence proceedings begun under a given law may be continued even if such proceedings are no longer possible under a new law' (ibid. at p. 55 *per* A.-G. Gand).

See also **General principles of law, Retroactive effect.**

▶ **CONTRACTUAL LIABILITY** Liability of the European Communities for breach of a contract concluded by them or on their behalf. Such liability is governed by the law applicable to the contract in question (Arts. 215(1) EEC, 188(1) Euratom; there is no corresponding provision in the ECSC Treaty). This law can only be the national law of a particular country, which need not be a Member State of the Communities, but not Community law since Community law does not have its own law of contracts. This may be contrasted with the non-contractual liability of the Communities which is to be determined in accordance with Community law, it being the task of the ECJ to develop the relevant rules and principles from the 'general principles common to the laws of the Member States' (Arts. 215(2) EEC, 188(2) Euratom; the same applies also under Art. 40(1) ECSC).

The question which national law is applicable to the contract is to be decided in accordance with the rules of private international law. If the contract itself contains a provision specifying the national law governing it, as virtually all the contracts concluded by the Community institutions do, that provision must be given absolute priority. As the ECJ has stated in this respect, 'contractual provisions expressing the common intention of the parties must take precedence over any other criterion which might be used

123

only where the contract is silent on a particular point' (Case 318/81 *Commission* v. *CO.DE.MI.* [1985] ECR 3693 at p. 3712, where the Court accepted that, in accordance with their own terms and conditions, the contracts at issue were governed by Belgian law. See also Case 426/85 *Commission* v. *Zoubek* [1986] ECR 4057 at pp. 4067, 4069, where the law governing the contract was also Belgian law, and Case 23/76 *Pellegrini* v. *Commission* [1976] ECR 1807 at p. 1819, where it was Italian law). In the absence of a choice of law clause, other criteria that may be relevant in determining the applicable law include the place of conclusion or of performance of the contract, the implied intention of the parties, etc.

Not only is the contractual liability of the Communities governed by national law in a substantive sense, but any dispute concerning such liability falls in principle within the jurisdiction of the national courts (ibid. at p. 1825 *per* A.-G. Mayras). These may be the national courts of the Member States since disputes to which any of the Communities is a party are not on that ground alone excluded from their jurisdiction (Arts. 40(3) ECSC, 183 EEC, 155 Euratom). They may also be the national courts of third States since, in the absence of an international agreement between the Communities and a third State to the contrary, the Communities do not seem to enjoy *ipso jure* immunity from lawsuit in the domestic courts of such a State (*see further under* **Legal personality**, point 3). The ECJ itself has jurisdiction in contractual disputes only if jurisdiction has been expressly conferred upon it by an 'arbitration clause' contained in the contract in question (Arts. 42 ECSC, 181 EEC, 153 Euratom). In practice, most contracts concluded by the Community institutions (including the European Investment Bank, which has a quasi-institutional status) contain such a clause establishing the Court's jurisdiction, just as most contracts contain a choice of law clause (see above). However, the ECJ has held that since the jurisdiction based on an arbitration clause derogates from the ordinary jurisdictional rules, its scope must be interpreted restrictively (Case 426/85 *Commission* v. *Zoubek*, above, at p. 4069; *see further under* **Arbitration clause**). By contrast, disputes involving the non-contractual liability of the Communities fall in principle within the exclusive jurisdiction of the ECJ (Arts. 40 ECSC, 178 EEC, 151 Euratom). A dispute which originates in a contractual relationship does not fall within the scope of this exclusive jurisdiction (Case 232/84 *Tordeur* [1985] ECR 3223 at pp. 3233–4).

In practice, by virtue of the legal capacity which they enjoy in each Member State (Arts. 6 ECSC, 211 EEC, 185 Euratom; *see further under* **Legal personality**, point 2), the Communities are party to a wide range of contracts covering a variety of matters, such as renting and construction of buildings, administration of funds, supply of goods and services, banking, insurance, copyright, public utility services, transportation, research. Nevertheless, the ECJ has held, applying the principles which it has developed in respect of non-contractual liability, that where national intervention agencies conclude contracts for the purpose of giving effect to Community law (e.g. regarding food aid), only those agencies, and not the Communities, can incur contractual liability towards private traders with whom the contracts have been made, even though the contracts are ultimately financed by the Communities (Case 109/83 *Eurico* [1984] ECR 3581 at p. 3602).

As regards the employment relationships of Community officials, prior to the coming into force of the Staff Regulations of Officials and the Conditions of Employment of Other Servants, the staff of the institutions were engaged on a contractual basis (see the original Art. 7(3) of the Convention on the Transitional Provisions annexed to the ECSC Treaty and Arts. 246(3) EEC, 214(3) Euratom). The ECJ has held that a contract of employment entered into during this period between an institution of the ECSC and an official, even if concluded for a limited period, constituted a contract *sui generis*, being a precursor of the Staff Regulations. It created a legal relationship which was wider than that arising under a contract of employment governed by private law. In fact, such a contract was governed by public law since it concerned entry into the service of a public authority and involved the performance of duties appertaining to public law. Such an official thereby became a public official who was entitled to a right to permanent tenure (Case 1/55 *Kergall* v. *Common Assembly* [1955] ECR 151 at pp. 156–8).

The position was quite different under the EEC Treaty. Contracts of employment entered into during this interim period under the EEC Treaty were also governed by public law since one of the parties, the EEC, was endowed with legal personality under public law. These contracts were subject to the general rules and principles of administrative law (and not to those of any particular country). However, since Art. 246(3) EEC expressly provided for the conclusion of contracts of limited duration, these contracts did not give rise to a claim to security of tenure, even if they were concluded for an indefinite period (Cases 43, 45, and 48/59 *Lachmüller* v. *Commission* [1960] ECR 463 at pp. 472–4. The position was the same under the Euratom Treaty).

The first Staff Regulations of the ECSC came into force on 1 July 1956, while the Staff Regulations and the Conditions of Employment of the EEC and Euratom on 1 January 1962 (Council Reg. 31 (EEC), 11 (Euratom) of 18 Dec. 1961, *OJ Sp. Edn.* 1959–62, p. 135). Similar Staff Regulations and Conditions of Employment were adopted for the ECSC by the Committee of Presidents on 15 February 1962, which also came into force on 1 January 1962 (unpublished). With the merger of the Councils and the Commissions of the three Communities on 1 July 1967, the officials and other servants of the ECSC, EEC, and Euratom became officials and other servants of the European Communities and formed part of the single administration of those Communities (Art. 24 of the Merger Treaty). New Staff Regulations and Conditions of Employment were adopted on 29 February 1968, replacing the previous ones, applicable from 5 March 1968 to the officials and other servants of the European Communities (Council Reg. 259/68, *OJ Sp. Edn.* 1968(I), p. 30). With numerous amendments, these Regulations and Conditions are still in force (see the consolidated text published in Apr. 1986).

The Staff Regulations apply to the officials of the Communities. 'Official' means any person who has been appointed under the Staff Regulations to an established post on the staff of one of the institutions of the Communities by an instrument issued by the appointing authority of that institution. In addition to the four institutions (i.e. the European Parliament, the Council, the Commission, and the Court of Justice), the Economic and Social Committee and the Court of Auditors are also treated as institutions for the purposes of the Staff Regulations (Art. 1). The ECJ has ruled that the legal situation of an official who is subject to the provisions of the Staff Regulations 'is not derived from a contract concluded between two parties but [is] governed by statute and regulation and to his benefit and his detriment is governed by the general and impersonal provisions of the Staff Regulations' (Cases 27 and 39/59 *Campolongo* v. *HA* [1960] ECR 391 at p. 402). Any dispute between the Communities and their officials falls within the exclusive jurisdiction of the ECJ, subject to the limits and conditions laid down in the Staff Regulations (Arts. 179 EEC, 152 Euratom, 90–1 Staff Regs. The same applies to the ECSC by virtue of Art. 24 of the Merger Treaty. *See further under* **Staff cases**).

The Conditions of Employment apply to 'servants' who are engaged under contract by the Communities. Such servants fall into four categories: temporary staff, auxiliary staff, local staff, and special advisers (Art. 1). The rights and obligations of temporary and auxiliary staff are similar to those of officials appointed under the Staff Regulations. Disputes between the Communities and temporary and auxiliary staff and special advisers are governed by the same rules as disputes concerning officials and fall within the exclusive jurisdiction of the ECJ (Arts. 46, 73, and 83 of the Conditions of Employment which make Arts. 90–1 of the Staff Regs. applicable to these three categories of servants). However, the position of local staff is different. They are engaged 'according to local practice for manual or service duties', and their conditions of employment are determined by each institution 'in accordance with current rules and practice in the place where they are to perform their duties'. Any dispute between the institution and a member of the local staff is to be submitted to the competent national court 'in accordance with the laws in force in the place where the servant performs his duties', and not to the ECJ (Arts. 4, 79, 81 of the Conditions of Employment). Thus, the rules governing the employment relationships of members of the local staff are 'hybrid' in nature inasmuch as they are derived from both Community law and national private (contract) law (see Case 105/80 *Desmedt* [1981] ECR 1701 at pp. 1715–16 *per* A.-G. Capotorti).

The contract of employment, which is the basis of the service relationship between the Communities and their servants (into whichever of the four categories they fall), can only come into existence as a result of a decision of the designated competent authority of the institution concerned, but not by virtue of a national law or of a decision of a national court (Art. 6 of the Conditions of Employment; Case 65/74 *Porrini* [1975] ECR 319 at p. 329; Case 232/84 *Tordeur*, above, at p. 3235). Since the Staff Regulations and the Conditions of Employment constitute two complementary acts applicable to different categories of persons, it is in principle not possible for a person to come simultaneously within the scope of both of those acts. Therefore, the acquisition by a 'servant' of the status of 'official' automatically causes the contract of employment entered into on the basis of the Conditions of Employment to cease to have effect (Case 105/80 *Desmedt*, above, at p. 1712).

Finally, it may be noted that the Treaties only lay down rules in respect of the contractual and non-contractual liability of the Communities. They are entirely silent on the question, what substantive and jurisdictional rules govern certain other forms of liability which arise, strictly speaking, neither from contract nor from delict (or tort), but from quasi-contract or quasi-delict, such as unjust enrichment or management without mandate. It may be assumed that the Treaties intended to create a complete system of remedies in respect of the Communities' liability, just as they established 'a complete system of legal remedies and procedures' in respect of judicial review of the legality of their conduct (see Case 294/83 *Les Verts* v. *Parliament* [1986] ECR 1339 at p. 1365). Therefore, any such atypical or transitional form of liability must be classified, for the purposes of Community law, either as contractual or as non-contractual liability. Such classification is of decisive importance for those, admittedly few, cases in which the question of liability arises since it determines both the substantive law applicable and the courts having jurisdiction to deal with the question. If a quasi-contract or quasi-delict gives rise to contractual liability, the matter will be governed by national law and falls within the jurisdiction of national courts. If it engages the Communities' non-contractual liability, it will be governed by Community law and is subject to the exclusive jurisdiction of the ECJ. So far, these questions have not been directly raised before, and determined by, the ECJ. In those, relatively few, cases in which unjust enrichment was relied on as the basis of a claim, which cases came before the ECJ under various heads of its jurisdiction, the Court treated unjust enrichment as a 'general principle of law' forming part of Community law, without dealing with the questions whether it was to be regarded as a quasi-contract or quasi-delict and whether it gave rise to contractual or non-contractual liability.

See also Arbitration clause, Legal personality, Non-contractual liability, Staff cases, Unjust enrichment.

▶ CO-OPERATION PROCEDURE A new procedure introduced by Art. 6 of the Single European Act of 1986 (SEA), designed to increase the influence of the European Parliament in the Community legislative process but without going so far as to give it a real power of co-decision. The procedure applies only to those acts which are exhaustively listed in Art. 6 SEA and which may be adopted by the Council by a qualified majority (i.e. acts based on Arts. 7, 49, 54(2), 56(2), 57, 100A, 100B, 118A, 130E, and 130Q(2) EEC). However, it does not apply to all the cases in which qualified majority has been substituted for the previous unanimity requirement in order to enable the internal market to be established by 31 December 1992 (see Art. 16 SEA). The co-operation procedure is laid down in Art. 149(2) EEC, as amended by Art. 7 SEA, and applies only under the EEC Treaty. Basically, it involves a

127

second reading in both the Council and the Parliament and consists of the following successive steps.

The Council, acting by a qualified majority on a proposal from the Commission and after obtaining the opinion of the European Parliament, adopts a 'common position' (first reading). This common position, together with the reasons leading to its adoption and the Commission's opinion of it, is then communicated to the European Parliament for a second reading. Within a period of three months, Parliament may (1) approve the common position; (2) take no decision on it; (3) propose amendments to it by an absolute majority; or (4) reject it by the same majority. In cases (1) and (2), the Council will definitively adopt the act in question in accordance with the common position. In case (4), unanimity is required for the Council to act on a second reading against the rejection by Parliament (the Council must act within a period of three months). In case (3), the Commission is required, within a period of one month, to re-examine its original proposal by taking into account the amendments proposed by the European Parliament. It will then forward to the Council its revised proposal together with those amendments of Parliament which it has not accepted and its opinion on them. Thereafter the Council may (1) acting unanimously, adopt those amendments of Parliament which the Commission has not accepted; (2) acting by a qualified majority, adopt the revised proposal of the Commission; (3) acting unanimously, amend the revised proposal of the Commission; and (4) fail to act. In all these cases, the Council is required to act within a period of three months. This period, as well as the three-month period within which Parliament is required to act (see above), may be extended by a maximum of one month by common accord between the Council and the European Parliament. If the Council takes no decision within the three-month period, the Commission's proposal will be deemed not to have been adopted. This means that the Council will be unable to take a decision at a later stage. As long as the Council has not acted, the Commission may alter or withdraw its proposal at any time during the whole procedure.

It seems that in practice the co-operation procedure has, in general, worked satisfactorily so far and, although certain problems have arisen, the results have been encouraging (see 22nd *Gen. Rep. EC* (1988), p. 32).

See also **Commission, Council, European Parliament, Single European Act.**

Further reading: Bieber, 'Legislative Procedure for the Establishment of the Single Market' (1988) 25 *CML Rev.* 711. *See also under* **Single European Act.**

▶ COSTS (BEFORE THE ECJ) Sums and fees payable, and expenses incurred, in connection with litigation before the ECJ.

Since proceedings before the Court are, in principle, free of charge (Art. 72 RP), only the following items are regarded as constituting recoverable costs:

1. 'Avoidable costs' which a party has caused the Court to incur (Art. 72(a) RP). The party concerned may be ordered by the Court to refund these costs.

2. Registry charges in respect of copying or translation work (Arts. 16(5), 62(2), and 72(b) RP). These are payable according to a scale fixed by the Court (see Arts. 17–22 IR).

3. Sums payable to witnesses and experts (Art. 73(a) RP). These include travel and subsistence expenses as well as compensation for loss of earnings, in the case of witnesses, and fees for their services, in the case of experts (Art. 51 RP). Since these sums are usually paid out by the cashier of the Court either in advance or after the witnesses and experts have carried out their respective duties and tasks (ibid.; see also Art. 47(2) and (3) RP), they are in most cases recoverable by the Court itself rather than by one of the parties.

4. Expenses necessarily incurred by the parties for the purpose of the proceedings, in particular travel and subsistence expenses (Art. 73(b) RP). 'Proceedings' in this context means proceedings before the Court and does not include any prior stage, such as any compulsory preliminary procedures of an administrative nature (Case 75/69 *Hake* v. *Commission* [1970] ECR 901 at pp. 902–3). Costs relating to any such pre-litigation procedural steps are therefore not recoverable (ibid.). In general, the travel and subsistence expenses which are recoverable are those incurred by agents, advisers, or lawyers. However, the travel and subsistence expenses of the applicant himself are also recoverable if his presence at the hearing is necessary for the purpose of the proceedings, either because the Court has requested it, or because the hearing is concerned with the taking of evidence relating to events experienced by the applicant, or because the course of such events is extremely complicated and is the main point at issue before the Court (Case 24/79—Costs *Oberthür* v. *Commission* [1981] ECR 2229 at p. 2230). Where the agent, adviser, or lawyer is involved in several cases heard on the same day, travelling expenses are recoverable only once (Case 238/78 *Ireks-Arkady* v. *EEC* [1981] ECR 1723 at p. 1726), although in view of the importance of the cases and the large number of applicants, travelling expenses may be provided for more than one lawyer (Cases 241/78 etc. *DGV* v. *EEC* [1981] ECR 1731 at p. 1734, where there were six applicants and the Court awarded travelling expenses to two lawyers). In addition to travelling expenses, postal, telephone, telex, and photo-copying charges are also recoverable (see the two cases cited immediately above).

5. Remuneration of agents, advisers, or lawyers (Art. 73(b) RP). In dealing with this item, in a number of cases the Court has stated that: '. . . the Court is not called upon to tax the fees due by the parties to their own lawyers but to determine the extent to which such remuneration may be recovered from the party ordered to bear the costs. It follows that the Court is not required to have regard to a national scale fixing lawyers' fees [nor to any agreement reached between the parties and their lawyers]. As Community law has not laid down any provisions in the nature of a scale, the Court must undertake a free appreciation of the facts of the dispute having regard to its object and nature, its

129

importance from the point of view of Community law and the difficulties of the proceedings, the amount of work which the litigation may have caused the lawyer and what the dispute may have meant to the parties in financial terms' (Case 238/78 *Ireks-Arkady* v. *EEC*, above, at p. 1725; Cases 241/78 etc. *DGV* v. *EEC*, above, at p. 1734. See also Case 75/69 *Hake* v. *Commission*, above, at p. 903; Case 6/72 *Continental Can* v. *Commission* [1975] ECR 495 at p. 496; Case 4/73 *Nold* v. *Commission* [1975] ECR 985 at p. 987). In addition, the Court may take into account special circumstances, such as the fact that an intervener to a large extent relied on the arguments of the party which it supported (Case 4/73 *Nold* v. *Commission*, above, at p. 987); that all the applicants in several joined cases raising identical legal problems were represented by the same lawyers (Cases 241/78 etc. *DGV* v. *EEC*, above, at p. 1734; see also Case 238/78 *Ireks-Arkady* v. *EEC*, above, at pp. 1725–6); that a case raised new and important questions of Community law, that it had considerable financial importance, and that it involved a considerable extent of the lawyers' work (Cases 241/78 etc. *DGV* v. *EEC*, above, at p. 1734).

While the above considerations apply generally, in some respects private parties (i.e. natural or legal persons) on the one hand, and Community institutions and Member States, on the other, are subject to different rules on account of the different requirements relating to their representation before the Court. Thus, private parties are only required to be represented or assisted by 'a lawyer' (Arts. 20 ECSC Statute, 17 EEC and Euratom Statutes), and the ECJ has deduced from this that only the remuneration of the lawyer representing a private party in an action before the Court may be regarded as necessary expenses of legal assistance. Therefore, while a party is free to employ an adviser in addition to the lawyer representing him before the Court, the additional expenses incurred as a result of so doing are not recoverable (Cases 20 and 21/63 *Maudet* v. *Commission* [1964] ECR 621 at pp. 622–3). It follows that the fees of the lawyer compulsorily engaged in Luxembourg for the purpose of accepting service of documents (see Arts. 38(2) and 40(1) RP) are recoverable only in so far as they represent remuneration for that particular service (in principle, office and correspondence expenses), and not in so far as additional services (e.g. receiving the party, giving him legal advice and information) are also involved (ibid.).

By contrast, Community institutions and Member States are to be represented before the Court by an agent, who may be assisted by an adviser or by a lawyer (Arts. 20 ECSC Statute, 17 EEC and Euratom Statutes). The institutions are free to decide whether they will have recourse to the assistance of a lawyer or to appoint as an agent either one of their officials or a person who is not a member of their staff. When they are represented by a lawyer or appoint as agent a person who is not a member of their staff and who must be paid, such remuneration comes within the concept of expenses necessarily incurred for the purpose of the proceedings. When, on the other hand, they are represented by one of their officials, such representation is covered by the remuneration which is allotted to the official under the Staff Regulations, so that expenses in connection with his work are not recoverable (although his travelling expenses and a daily subsistence allowance are) (Case 126/76—Costs *Dietz* v. *Commission* [1979] ECR 2131 at pp. 2134–5).

6. Costs necessarily incurred by a party in enforcing a judgment or order of the Court (Art. 71 RP). These are to be refunded by the opposite party on the scale in force in the State where the enforcement takes place.

7. Expenses occasioned by letters rogatory (Arts. 26 EEC Statute, 27 Euratom Statute, 3 SR). Although the Court is required to defray these expenses, it has the right to charge them, where appropriate, to the parties.

8. The whole or any part of the amounts advanced as legal aid (Art. 76(5) RP). In its decision as to costs, the Court may order their payment to the cashier, and it is for the Registrar to take steps to obtain their recovery from the party ordered to pay them.

The Court is required to adjudicate upon costs in every case, even if the parties have not asked for them (Arts. 32 ECSC Statute, 35 EEC Statute, 36 Euratom Statute; Case 5/55 *ASSIDER* v. *HA* [1955] ECR 135 at p. 144). The Court gives its decision as to costs in its final judgment or in the order which closes the proceedings (Art. 69(1) RP). Such a decision is enforceable in the national courts in the usual way (see Case 4/73—Enforcement *Nold* v. *Ruhrkohle* [1977] ECR 1 at p. 3). As a matter of practice, the judgment or order of the Court merely states who is to bear the costs, without quantifying them. The taxation of the costs takes place either by agreement between the parties or, in the absence thereof, by a subsequent order of the Court (see below). Generally speaking, there are three main rules as to how costs are to be disposed of between the parties. These are as follows:

First, the normal rule is that the unsuccessful party must pay the costs, but only if they have been asked for in the successful party's pleading (Art. 69(2) RP). Where the successful party has not asked for costs, he must bear his own costs (see e.g. Cases 23, 24, and 52/63 *Usines Henricot* v. *HA* [1963] ECR 217 at p. 225; Case 23/76 *Pellegrini* v. *Commission* [1976] ECR 1807 at p. 1822; Case 138/79 *Roquette* v. *Council* [1980] ECR 3333 at p. 3361). Likewise, where neither party has asked for costs, each must pay his own costs (see e.g. Case 30/67 *Molitoria Imolese* v. *Council* [1968] ECR 115 at p. 121; Case 22/70 *Commission* v. *Council* [1971] ECR 263 at p. 283). Where there are several unsuccessful parties, it is for the Court to decide how the costs are to be shared (Art. 69(2) RP; see e.g. Cases 41, 43, and 44/73— Interpretation *S.A. Générale Sucrière* v. *Commission* [1977] ECR 445 at p. 464; Cases 32/78 etc. *BMW* v. *Commission* [1979] ECR 2435 at p. 2483).

The unsuccessful party is to pay also the costs of the intervener who has supported the successful party (see e.g. Case 14/61 *Hoogovens* v. *HA* [1962]

ECR 253 at p. 276; Case 19/61 *Mannesmann* v. *HA* [1962] ECR 357 at p. 378; Case 130/75 *Prais* v. *Council* [1976] ECR 1589 at p. 1600). A person whose application to intervene is dismissed (see e.g. Case 111/63 *Lemmerz-Werke* v. *HA* [1965] ECR 677 at p. 718) or who has intervened in support of the unsuccessful party (see e.g. Cases 3 to 18, 25, and 26/58 *Barbara Erzbergbau* v. *HA* [1960] ECR 173 at p. 198; Case 113/77 *Toyo Bearing* v. *Council* [1979] ECR 1185 at p. 1211) must bear his own costs as well as those incurred by the other party on account of his application or intervention, as the case may be. Nevertheless, in special circumstances, even an unsuccessful intervener may be ordered to bear his own costs only, if this appears 'fair and reasonable' (Cases 40 to 48/73 etc. *Suiker Unie* v. *Commission* [1975] ECR 1663 at pp. 2024–5—'Sugar' cases. See also Case 24/71 *Meinhardt* v. *Commission* [1972] ECR 269 at p. 279; Case 40/79 *Mrs P* v. *Commission* [1981] ECR 361 at p. 375). The costs of an application for the suspension of the operation or enforcement of an act or for the adoption of other interim measures are normally dealt with in the same way as the costs in the main action (see e.g. Cases 19 and 65/63 *Prakash* v. *Commission* [1965] ECR 533 at p. 561), i.e. the unsuccessful party must bear these costs as well, even though the successful party failed in respect of the interlocutory proceedings (see e.g. Case 68/63 *Luhleich* v. *Commission* [1965] ECR 581 at pp. 606–7; Cases 59 and 129/80 *Turner* v. *Commission* [1981] ECR 1883 at p. 1921). Nevertheless, there are cases where the successful party was ordered to pay the costs of his unsuccessful application for the adoption of interim measures (see e.g. Case 67/63 *SOREMA* v. *HA* [1964] ECR 151 at pp. 166–7). Special considerations may, of course, justify the application of either of the two rules to be discussed immediately below (see e.g. Cases 16 to 18/59 *Geitling* v. *HA* [1960] ECR 17 at p. 26).

Secondly, where each party succeeds on some and fails on other heads, or where the circumstances are exceptional, the Court may apportion the costs, i.e. order that the parties bear their own costs in whole or in part (Art. 69(3) RP; see e.g. Case 1/54 *France* v. *HA* [1954] ECR 1 at p. 16; Case 2/54 *Italy* v. *HA* [1954] ECR 37 at p. 55; Case 16/61 *Modena* v. *HA* [1962] ECR 289 at p. 307). Such will be the case, in particular, where the applicant is successful as to admissibility, while the defendant is successful as to substance (see e.g. Case 3/54 *ASSIDER* v. *HA* [1955] ECR 63 at p. 71; Case 8/57 *Aciéries Belges* v. *HA* [1958] ECR 245 at p. 263; Case 13/57 *Eisen-und Stahlindustrie* v. *HA* [1958] ECR 265 at p. 287), or where a party fails on the head on which witnesses were examined and is ordered to pay the costs of the examination (see e.g. Cases 40 to 48/73 etc. *Suiker Unie* v. *Commission*, above, at p. 2025). By way of example, the Court has regarded as an 'exceptional circumstance' justifying apportionment of the costs the following: the complexity of the questions raised concerning the admissibility of the application (Cases 2 and 3/60 *Niederrheinische Bergwerks* v. *HA* [1961] ECR 133 at p. 148; Cases 55 to 59/63 etc. *Modena* v. *HA* [1964] ECR 211 at p. 230); the fact that it was the defective drafting of the challenged measure that caused the (unsuccessful) applicant to bring the action (Case 14/63 *Clabecq* v. *HA* [1963] ECR 357 at p. 374; Case 26/66 *Hoogovens* v. *HA* [1967] ECR 115 at

p. 127); belated production by the defendant institution of a document which, if it had been lodged with the defence, might have led the applicant to discontinue the proceedings (Case 135/81 *Groupement des Agences de Voyages* v. *Commission* [1982] ECR 3799 at p. 3810); the existence of a wrongful act or omission on the part of the defendant institution giving rise to an action for damages, even if the action fails (Cases 5, 7, and 13 to 24/66 *Kampffmeyer* v. *Commission* [1967] ECR 245 at p. 267; Case 169/73 *Compagnie Continentale* v. *Council* [1975] ECR 117 at p. 136); or, quite simply, that the applicant had 'good reason' or 'sufficient reason' to bring the matter before the Court (Case 153/73 *Holtz & Willemsen* v. *Council and Commission* [1974] ECR 675 at p. 697; Case 23/76 *Pellegrini* v. *Commission*, above, at p. 1822; see also Cases 46 and 47/59 *Meroni* v. *HA* [1962] ECR 411 at p. 423; Cases 56 to 60/74 *Kampffmeyer* v. *Commission and Council* [1976] ECR 711 at p. 747).

Thirdly, the Court may order even a successful party to pay costs which the Court considers that party to have unreasonably or vexatiously caused the opposite party to incur (Art. 69(3) RP). Such is the case, for example, where it is some blameworthy conduct on the part of the defendant institution that has induced the applicant to institute, in safeguarding his rights, what in the end turns out to be an unnecessary and unsuccessful action. Such blameworthy conduct may consist for example in giving to a non-binding measure the appearance of a binding decision (Cases 16 to 18/59 *Geitling* v. *HA*, above, at p. 26; Cases 23, 24, and 52/63 *Usines Henricot* v. *HA*, above, at p. 225; etc. See also Case 88/76 *Exportation des Sucres* v. *Commission* [1977] ECR 709 at pp. 726–7); the adoption of two measures where one would have been sufficient and thereby causing the applicant to bring two actions instead of one (Cases 15 and 29/59 *Knutange* v. *HA* [1960] ECR 1 at p. 10; Cases 35/62 and 16/63 *Leroy* v. *HA* [1963] ECR 197 at p. 208; etc.); arbitrary conduct creating legal ambiguity (Case 148/79 *Korter* v. *Council* [1981] ECR 615 at p. 629); etc. Conversely, the applicant may cause unreasonable or vexatious costs by failing to discontinue an action after the defendant institution has revoked the contested measure (Cases 5, 7, and 8/60 *Meroni* v. *HA* [1961] ECR 107 at pp. 111–12) or after the Court has rendered a judgment clarifying an important disputed issue in a similar case (Cases 55 to 59/63 etc. *Modena* v. *HA*, above, at p. 238 *per* A.-G. Roemer); by bringing an action without establishing a real interest or in spite of its manifest inadmissibility (Cases 122 and 123/79 *Schiavo* v. *Council* [1981] ECR 473 at pp. 491–2; Case 204/85 *Stroghili* v. *Court of Auditors* [1987] ECR 389 at p. 403); or by negligently failing to produce certain documents prior to the adoption of the disputed measure, which could have convinced the institution not to take that measure (Case 18/62 *Barge* v. *HA* [1963] ECR 259 at p. 282); etc.

In addition to the foregoing general rules, the following provisions apply in special situations:

First, a party who discontinues or withdraws from proceedings is ordered to pay the costs, unless the discontinuance or withdrawal is justified by the conduct of the opposite party. If the opposite party has not asked for costs, the parties bear their own costs (Art. 69(4) RP, see e.g. Case 13/57 *Eisen-und Stahlindustrie* v. *HA*, above, at p. 287; Cases 29/63 etc. *Usines de la Providence* v. *HA* [1966] ECR 139 at pp. 142–3).

Secondly, where a case does not proceed to judgment, the costs are in the discretion of the Court (Art. 69(5) RP, see e.g. Cases 5, 7, and 8/60 *Meroni* v. *HA*, above, at p. 111). Although in such cases the Court does not have to consider to what extent the application was admissible and well founded (Case 103/63 *Rhenania* v. *Commission* [1964] ECR 425 at p. 429), it may, and usually does, take into account, in favour of the applicant, the fact that he was justified in believing that the bringing of the action was necessary (see e.g. Cases 7 and 9/54 *Industries Sidérurgiques Luxembourgeoises* v. *HA* [1956] ECR 175 at p. 203; Case 75/69 *Hake* v. *Commission* [1970] ECR 535 at p. 543).

Thirdly, in proceedings commenced by Community officials and servants against the institutions (staff cases), the institutions must always bear their own costs, including the expenses of witnesses heard in their capacity as Community officials, except where the costs have been caused unreasonably or vexatiously by the opposite party (Art. 70 RP; Cases 19 and 65/63 *Prakash* v. *Commission*, above, at p. 561; Case 34/65 *Mosthaf* v. *Commission* [1966] ECR 521 at p. 532, but see also Case 43/74 *Guillot* v. *Commission* [1977] ECR 1309 at p. 1338 where the applicant—an official—was ordered to pay the costs of hearing the witnesses).

Fourthly, in references for preliminary rulings, it is for the national court or tribunal to decide as to the costs of the reference as between the parties to the main action (Art. 104(3) RP), while the costs incurred by the institutions and the Member States which have participated in the proceedings before the ECJ (but without being parties) are not recoverable (see Case 13/61 *Bosch* [1962] ECR 45 at p. 54, where the Court for the first time laid down this rule, which it has applied ever since. For alternative solutions, see the opinion of A.-G. Lagrange, ibid. at p. 71. The present text of Art. 104(3) RP referred to above was introduced in 1979). The ECJ has held that the recovery of costs and the recoverability of expenses necessarily incurred by the parties to the main action are governed by the provisions of national law and that it is for the competent national courts to consider the extent to which matters incidental to an application for a preliminary ruling should be taken into account (Case 62/72 *Bollmann* [1973] ECR 269 at pp. 275–6).

As regards the taxation of costs, this usually takes place by agreement between the parties. If, however, there is a dispute between them concerning the costs to be recovered, the Chamber to which the case has been assigned will, on application by the party concerned and after hearing the opposite party and the Advocate-General, make an order, from which no appeal lies (Art. 74(1) RP). An application for the taxation of costs is admissible whenever one of the parties to the main action disputes the costs (Cases 9 and 58/65 *San Michele* v. *HA* [1968] ECR 259 at p. 260) but, conversely, is inadmissible where there is no dispute between the parties regarding either the amount of the costs to be recovered or their payment (ibid. at p. 259; Case

25/65 *Simet* v. *HA* [1967] ECR 113 at p. 114). The making of the application is not subject to any time-limit (Cases 9 and 58/65 *San Michele* v. *HA*, above, at p. 260) but the party awarded costs should send a detailed account of the costs claimed to the opposite party within a 'reasonable period' to avoid any possible allegation of an implied waiver of his rights that might arise from a long delay (see Case 126/76—Costs *Dietz* v. *Commission*, above, at p. 2133, where three months was held to be such a 'reasonable period'). The order on costs is enforceable (Art. 74(2) RP).

See also **Enforcement procedure, Legal aid, Letters rogatory, Representation before the ECJ.**

Further reading 1. BOOKS: Lasok, *The European Court of Justice: Practice and Procedure* (1984), ch. 11; Usher, *European Court Practice* (1983), chs. 15 and 17.
2. ARTICLE: Bierry and Dal Ferro, 'The Practice Followed by the Court of Justice with Regard to Costs' (1987) 24 *CML Rev.* 509.

▶ **COUNCIL** One of the four institutions of the European Communities, the others being the European Parliament, the Commission, and the Court of Justice (Arts. 7 ECSC, 4 EEC, 3 Euratom). The present Council was established by Art. 1 of the Merger Treaty of 1965 (MT), which provided for the merger of the former Special Council of Ministers of the ECSC with the Councils of the EEC and Euratom to form one single body serving all three Communities.

I. Organization and procedure

The Council consists of representatives of the Member States, each Government delegating to it one of its members (Art. 2(1) MT). While this provision implies that the members of the Council must be members of the national Governments, it is quite possible for a Council member who is prevented from attending a meeting to be represented by someone other than a Minister, for example by a Permanent Representative who is a civil servant with the rank of Ambassador. However, such a person does not have the right to vote since that right may only be delegated to another member of the Council (Arts. 4 and 5(3) of the Council's Rules of Procedure of 24 July 1979 (CRP) adopted under Art. 5 MT, *OJ* 1979 L268/1 as amended on 20 July 1987, *OJ* 1987 L291/27). No member of the Council may act on behalf of more than one other member (Arts. 28 ECSC, 150 EEC, 120 Euratom).

The Treaties do not specify which member of a Government should be delegated to the Council. This depends on the particular subject-matter to be discussed at any given meeting. A distinction is made between the so-called 'General Affairs' Council, consisting of Foreign Ministers and dealing with matters of general importance including external relations, and 'Specialized' Councils composed of Ministers responsible for particular subject-areas such as agriculture, transport, industry, finance. It is thus quite possible to hold two or more Council meetings at the same time. While this type of internal organization is perhaps inevitable, it carries with it the danger of the disintegration of the decision-making process. Each Council being free to adopt its own positions and measures, in the absence of an arbitration body

135

within the Council the various Councils dealing with different aspects of the same matter (e.g. the financing of the Common Agricultural Policy) may arrive at conflicting or incompatible decisions (see Suppl. 1/87—*Bull. EC*, p. 9). Perhaps in recognition of such a danger since 1976 joint Council meetings have occasionally been organized, attended by Ministers having different portfolios, so as to deal with complex problems extending over various sectors (see 10th *Gen. Rep. EC* (1976), p. 33). Since, however, the Treaty refers to the delegation by each Government of 'one' of its members, each Member State may have only one vote on the Council.

Although the Council consists of 'representatives' of the Member States who inevitably represent national interests, it is a Community institution, not an intergovernmental conference. It takes decisions in the name and on behalf of the Communities which decisions, once formally adopted, are fully valid and binding in law even if they are contrary to the mandates of individual Council members, to reservations and objections expressed by them, and to the national interests of their States (Case 38/69 *Commission* v. *Italy* [1970] ECR 47 at pp. 56–7; Case 39/72 *Commission* v. *Italy* [1973] ECR 101 at pp. 114–15; Case 128/78 *Commission* v. *United Kingdom* [1979] ECR 419 at pp. 428–9—'Tachographs' case). The Council, as a Community institution, must therefore be strictly distinguished both from occasional meetings and conferences of the Representatives of the Governments of the Member States which are held to take decisions by 'common accord' on certain matters which the Treaties deliberately left within the competence of the Member States (see e.g. Arts. 167, 216, and 236 EEC, 11, 14, and 37 MT), and from meetings of the 'Representatives of the Governments of the Member States meeting in Council', which are not provided for in the Treaties but have developed in practice. The Council of the European Communities must also be distinguished from the European Council and the meetings of the Foreign Ministers within the framework of European Political Co-operation, which again are distinct bodies.

The office of President of the Council is held in turn by each Member State for a term of six months in strict alphabetical order as laid down in Art. 2(2) MT (as last amended by Art. 11 of the Act of Accession 1985). The meetings of the Council are convened by the President acting either on his own initiative or at the request of one of its members or of the Commission (Art. 3 MT; Art. 1 CRP). There are some 75–80 meetings a year (80 in 1986, 78 in 1987, 77 in 1988, see 20th, 21st, 22nd *Gen. Rep. EC* (1986, 1987, 1988) pp. 39, 34, 38, respectively). The meetings are not normally public but the Commission is as a rule invited to attend (Art. 3 CRP). The deliberations of the Council are covered by the obligation of professional secrecy (Art. 18 CRP). It is the task of the President to draw up the provisional agenda for each meeting at least fourteen days in advance, indicating the items to be voted on. The agenda is adopted by the Council at the beginning of each meeting. The provisional agenda is divided into Part A and Part B. Part A contains items for which the approval of the Council is possible without discussion, although an 'A' item may be withdrawn from the agenda (and placed as a 'B' item on the agenda of the next meeting) if a member of the Council or the Commission so requests (Art. 2 CRP). The purpose of the Part A procedure is to speed up the decision-making process where an agreement has already been reached on the matter by the Committee of Permanent Representatives, a body set up to prepare the work of the Council (Art. 4 MT; Art. 16 CRP. *See further under* **Committee of Permanent Representatives**). In urgent cases, acts of the Council may be adopted by a written vote provided that all the members of the Council agree to that procedure (Art. 6 CRP). As the ECJ has pointed out, this procedural requirement of unanimity is independent of the question whether the act itself has to be adopted by unanimity or a majority vote. Recourse to the written procedure where one or more Member States have expressly opposed it constitutes an infringement of an essential procedural requirement which may entail the annulment of the act in question by the ECJ (Case 68/86 *United Kingdom* v. *Council* [1988] ECR 855 at pp. 901–2).

The texts of the acts adopted by the Council must be signed by the President-in-office at the time of their adoption and by the Secretary-General who is in charge of the General Secretariat set up to assist the Council (Arts. 9 and 17 CRP). Regulations must be published in the *Official Journal* (Art. 13 CRP). Directives, decisions, and recommendations may also be so published for information purposes, but generally they must be notified to the addressees by the President, who may entrust this task to the Secretary-General (Art. 15 CRP). However, neither the Secretary-General nor his staff may make any alterations or corrections to texts adopted by the Council, other than simple corrections of spelling and grammar. Alterations made to the notified and published version of an act which affect its content, including its preamble containing the statement of reasons, may lead to the annulment of the act by the ECJ (see Case 131/86 *United Kingdom* v. *Council* [1988] ECR 905 at pp. 934–5 *per Curiam*; pp. 921–4 *per* A.-G. Mischo).

In 1988, there were 1,986 permanent and 4 temporary posts on the Council's establishment plan (22nd *Gen. Rep. EC* (1988), p. 38).

II. Functions and powers

Art. 1 of the Merger Treaty provides that the Council shall exercise the powers and jurisdiction conferred by the Community Treaties on the Special Council of Ministers of the ECSC and on the Councils of the EEC and Euratom. This means that the Council is subject to three sets of jurisdictional rules and that its functions and powers vary according to the particular Treaty under which it acts in a given case. In this respect, there are considerable differences between the three Treaties, particularly between the ECSC Treaty and the EEC/Euratom Treaties. These are considered separately below.

1. **Under the ECSC Treaty**, the Commission is both the chief decision-making and the chief executive body, while the main task of the Council is 'to harmonise the action of the Commission and that of the Governments, which are responsible for the general economic policies of their countries' (Art. 26). To this end, the Council and the Commission are required to exchange information and to consult each other. The Council may also request the Commission to examine any proposals or measures which the Council

may consider appropriate or necessary for the attainment of the common objectives (ibid.). The Council deals with the Member States through its President (Art. 28).

The Council participates in the decision-making process in three different ways. First, in a number of cases the Treaty requires the Commission to consult the Council before taking a decision. In such cases, the Council may consider the matter without necessarily taking a vote but must forward the minutes of its proceedings to the Commission. Secondly, in a number of cases, the Commission must obtain the assent of the Council to a proposed measure. In some of these cases, the Treaty requires unanimous assent, in others assent by an absolute majority, counted in a special way (see Art. 28 as last amended by Art. 12 of the Act of Accession 1985). Thirdly, the Council may itself adopt decisions, in certain cases acting on a proposal from the Commission and after consulting the European Parliament, for example to alter the number of Commissioners, to increase the number of Judges and Advocates-General, to appoint the members of the Court of Auditors and of the Consultative Committee, to make financial regulations, in connection with the budget. Decisions are taken by majority, qualified majority, or unanimity. Majority vote is determined in a special way while qualified majority is subject to the same rules as under the EEC/Euratom Treaties (Art. 28 as amended). In specified cases, abstention does not prevent the adoption of acts which require unanimity (ibid.).

2. **Under the Euratom Treaty**, the main task of the Council is 'to co-ordinate the actions of the Member States and of the Community' (Art. 115). Nevertheless, it has also been given considerable powers of decision which it is required to exercise in accordance with the provisions of the Treaty (ibid.). These provisions (see in particular Arts. 116–23 Euratom as amended by the Merger Treaty) are in many respects similar to those of the EEC Treaty (see below).

3. **Under the EEC Treaty**, the Council is the main decision-making body, although it also has certain executive functions. Initially, Art. 145 EEC only specified two tasks for the Council, i.e. to ensure co-ordination of the general economic policies of the Member States and to take decisions. This provision has been supplemented by Art. 10 of the Single European Act of 1986 (SEA), which now requires the Council to confer implementing powers on the Commission. In addition, the Treaty entrusts a number of specific tasks to the Council, the most important of which will be discussed below.

(*a*) *Co-ordination of economic policies*. This is a function which is more of an executive (or political) than legislative nature. The economic policy, which in the EEC Treaty is dealt with under three headings (conjunctural policy, balance of payments, and commercial policy), in principle remains within the competence of the Member States except to the extent that the Treaty confers powers on the Community (as in the case of commercial policy). The Member States are only required to 'co-ordinate their economic policies' and for this purpose to ensure 'co-operation' between their appropriate administrative departments (Art. 105(1)). This co-ordination is to be achieved through consultations in the Council and through non-binding declarations, resolutions, recommendations, programmes, etc. rather than through legally enforceable measures. The Member States may, of course, enter into intergovernmental agreements through their representatives meeting in the Council but, as mentioned above, this does not involve the Council as a Community institution.

(*b*) *Power to take decisions.* This, of course, is the most important aspect of the Council's role under the EEC Treaty. In a wider sense, this power involves both policy-making and law-making since the Council may take both political and legal decisions. Quite apart from the co-ordination of economic policies, the Council is responsible for giving general political direction to the Community, although this role has increasingly been taken over by the European Council. As regards law-making, the Council is the chief legislator but its power is not unlimited. It may act only (i) 'in accordance with the provisions of this Treaty'; (ii) 'to ensure that the objectives set out in this Treaty are attained'; and (iii) 'within the limits of the powers conferred upon it by this Treaty' (Arts. 4, 145, 189). The combined effect of these provisions is to restrict the decision-making powers of the Council in three main respects.

First, apart from a few exceptional situations where the Council may act upon its own initiative (see e.g. Arts. 73(1), 109(3), 114 EEC), in most cases the EEC Treaty provides that it shall act 'on a proposal from the Commission' (see e.g. Arts. 20, 28, 38(3), 49, 54(2), 56(2), 57). In these cases the Commission has an exclusive right of initiative, although the Council may request the Commission to submit to it any appropriate proposals (Art. 152, see under (*d*) below). To enhance the importance of the Commission's power of initiative, Art. 149(1) provides that the Council may amend a Commission proposal only by acting unanimously. According to the prevailing opinion, the amendment may not be such as to distort the original proposal (see the opinions of A.-G. Mancini in Case 20/85 *Roviello* [1988] ECR 2805 at pp. 2826, 2838). As long as the Council has not acted, the Commission may itself alter its proposal (Art. 149(3)). In practice, since virtually all Commission proposals are amended by the Council, a vote by a qualified majority is possible only if the Commission first alters its proposal so that it becomes identical to the text which the Council intends to adopt. This is usually effected by an oral statement by the member of the Commission taking part in the discussion, who must of course have been empowered by the Commission to take such action (see the opinion of A.-G. Mischo in Case 131/86 *United Kingdom* v. *Council*, above, at p. 923).

Secondly, in a number of instances, the EEC Treaty requires the Council to consult the European Parliament and/or the Economic and Social Committee before adopting a measure. These instances include most important matters such as agriculture, free movement of persons and services, right of establishment, transport, competition (see e.g. Arts. 43(2), 49, 54(1) and (2), 56(2), 63(1) and (2), 75(1), 87(1)). Although the opinions of these bodies are not legally binding, failure to obtain them may lead to the annulment of the measure by the Court of Justice on the ground of infringement of an essential procedural requirement (see e.g. Case 138/79 *Roquette* v. *Council* [1980] ECR 3333 at pp. 3360–1. *See further under* **European Parliament, Infringement of an essential procedural requirement**). It seems that if the Commission's proposal is substantially amended after Parliament has been consulted, the Council is required to reconsult Parliament (Case 41/69 *Chemiefarma* v. *Commission* [1970] ECR 661 at pp. 688–9 and 701–2; Case 828/79 *Adam* v. *Commission* [1982] ECR 269 at p. 290 *per Curiam*, [1981] ECR 1512 at p. 1545 *per* A.-G. Capotorti; Case 20/85 *Roviello*, above, at pp. 2827–9, 2838–42 *per* A.-G. Mancini). In addition to consultation, in a number of specified cases the Council is now required to follow a new co-operation procedure, introduced by Art. 6 SEA. This involves a second reading designed to increase the influence of the European Parliament in the legislative process but without giving it a real power of co-decision (see Art. 149(2) EEC as amended by Art. 7 SEA. *See further under* **Co-operation procedure**).

Thirdly, the Council may normally exercise only such decision-making powers as have been expressly conferred upon it by the Treaty (the principle of 'conferred powers' or *compétences d'attribution, Enumerationsprinzip*, see e.g. Case 22/70 *Commission* v. *Council* [1971] ECR 263 at p. 273 *per Curiam*, p. 293 *per* A.-G. Dutheillet de Lamothe; Case 18/74 *Syndicat Général du Personnel* v. *Commission* [1974] ECR 933 at p. 949 *per* A.-G. Trabucchi). Thus, the Council has not been endowed with a general authorization to legislate as it wishes, but must base its acts on specific authority granted by a particular provision (or provisions) of the Treaty (*see further under* **Institutional balance**). It is true that, in addition to or in the absence of expressly conferred powers, the Council may exercise limited implied powers as well as supplementary (or gap-filling) powers (i.e. under Art. 235). Nevertheless, the Council is still subject to the restriction that in so doing it may not go beyond the objectives of the Community as laid down in the Treaty (*see further under* **Implied powers, Supplementary powers**).

To ensure that the Council complies with the above requirements, its Rules of Procedure provide, in accordance with Art. 190 EEC, that all binding measures, i.e. regulations, directives, and decisions, must contain (i) a reference to the provisions under which the measure has been adopted; (ii) a reference to any proposals and opinions obtained and consultations held in connection with it; and (iii) a statement of the reasons on which the measure is based (Arts. 11 and 14 CRP).

In 1988, the Council adopted 434 regulations, 63 directives, and 131 decisions (22nd *Gen. Rep. EC* (1988), p. 38).

(*c*) *Delegation of powers to the Commission.* In accordance with Art. 10 SEA, which has amended Art. 145 EEC, the Council is now expressly required to confer on the Commission powers for the implementation of the rules which the Council lays down. Nevertheless, the Council may impose certain conditions in respect of the exercise of these powers, and may also reserve the right, in specific cases, to exercise directly implementing powers itself. In the latter case, the Council is bound to observe its own basic legislation. Any implementing measure which the Council adopts cannot derogate from the basic regulation to which it is subordinate (Case 38/70 *Tradax* [1971] ECR 145 at pp. 154–5; Case 81/72 *Commission* v. *Council*

[1973] ECR 575 at pp. 582–5; Case 113/77 *Toyo Bearing* v. *Council* [1979] ECR 1185 at p. 1209. *See further under* **Commission**, section II(2*d*)).

(*d*) *Initiation of Commission action.* Although the Commission has an almost exclusive right to initiate legislation, Art. 152 enables the Council to request the Commission to undertake any studies which the Council considers desirable for the attainment of the common objectives, and to submit to it any appropriate proposals. The purpose of this provision is to prevent inaction by the Commission from blocking the decision-making process. Although the Commission as an independent institution is not subordinated to the Council, it cannot refuse to comply with such a request. Failure to carry out the studies requested and to submit proposals may give rise to an action by the Council before the Court of Justice under Art. 175. On the other hand, the Council does not seem to have the power to specify the contents of the proposals concerned since this would be contrary to the Commission's right of initiative.

(*e*) *External relations.* The Council also plays an important part in the Community's external relations. Although international agreements are negotiated by the Commission, they are concluded by the Council (Arts. 114, 228, 238). In the case of tariff and trade agreements, the opening and conduct of negotiations are subject to a mandate from the Council (Art. 113(3)). The President of the Council, acting jointly with the President of the Commission, receives the credentials of Heads of Mission of non-Member States accredited to the Community (Luxembourg Compromise of 1966, point (a)(3). *See further under* **External relations**, section III; **Treaty-making procedure**).

(*f*) *Other tasks.* A further task entrusted to the Council is to determine the rules ('statutes') governing the various committees provided for in the Treaty (Art. 153). It is also for the Council to fix the salaries, allowances, and pensions of the members of the Commission and of the Judges, Advocates-General, and Registrar of the Court of Justice (Art. 6 MT). The Council has power to alter the number of Commissioners (Art. 10 MT), to increase the number of Judges and Advocates-General (Arts. 165, 166), to set up a new Court of First Instance to be attached to the Court of Justice (Art. 168A inserted by Art. 11 SEA), to amend the Court's Statute and to approve its Rules of Procedure (Art. 188 as amended by Art. 12 SEA), and to appoint the members of the Court of Auditors (Art. 206) and of the Economic and Social Committee (Art. 194). Finally, the Council plays an important role in the procedures for the amendment of the Treaty (Art. 236) and for the admission of new Member States to the Community (Art. 237).

III. Rules of voting

Under the EEC and Euratom Treaties, the Council may take decisions in one of three ways: by a simple majority, by a qualified majority, and unanimously. Although voting by simple majority is stated to be the general rule which applies unless the Treaty otherwise provides, most of the provisions do provide otherwise. Thus, simple majority is really an exception which is used mainly, although not exclusively, in procedural matters. Where the Council is required to act by a qualified majority, the votes of its members are weighted as follows: Belgium 5, Denmark 3, Germany 10, Greece 5, Spain 8, France 10, Ireland 3, Italy 10, Luxembourg 2, Netherlands 5, Portugal 5, United Kingdom 10. Where the Council acts on a proposal from the Commission (which is the normal case), 54 votes in favour are required (out of a total of 76), which cannot be produced by less than seven States. Where the Council acts on its own initiative, still 54 votes are required but they must be cast by at least eight States, representing a two-thirds majority. When the Treaty requires unanimity, the rule is that abstentions by members present in person or represented cannot prevent the adoption of measures (Arts. 148 EEC, 118 Euratom as last amended by Art. 14 of the Act of Accession 1985).

The above rules have been designed so as to ensure smooth and efficient decision-making while at the same time protecting the interests of the Member States, particularly of the smaller ones, by preventing them from being outvoted by the larger States. Moreover, while during the first two stages of the transitional period (from 1958 to the end of 1965) most decisions had to be taken unanimously, from the third stage onwards (in some cases already from the second stage onwards) the EEC Treaty provided for a change from unanimity to qualified majority in a number of fields. From the end of the transitional period (1 Jan. 1970), most decisions ought to have been taken by a qualified majority, unanimity being retained for a relatively small number of cases only (see e.g. Arts. 51, 99, 100, 138, 149, 157, 165, 166, 235, 238. For a complete list of Treaty Articles requiring qualified or simple majority voting, see 20th *Gen. Rep. EC* (1986), p. 29).

These arrangements have been considerably upset by the Luxembourg Compromise of 1966 which introduced the principle that where very important national interests are at stake, decisions should be taken by unanimous agreement even if the Treaty requires a (qualified) majority vote only (*see further under* **Luxembourg Compromise**). The Compromise, which in practice amounts to the recognition of a right of veto for any Member State, has had a most serious disruptive effect on the development of the Communities and the process of integration. It has slowed down, in some cases has almost completely paralysed, the whole decision-making process since in practice unanimity has become the general rule. For years, votes have hardly ever been taken in the Council (except on procedural issues and budgetary matters) because at all levels—Ministers, Permanent Representatives, national experts, etc.—all procedures except that of unanimous agreement have been rejected in advance, without any reference to important national interests. The decision-making process has thus been turned into diplomatic-style nego-tiations, leaving a number of important matters unsettled for months and even years. Moreover, the institutional balance as envisaged by the Treaty has been greatly distorted. The Commission's power of initiative has been weakened as a result of constant search for compromise solutions acceptable to all the Member States. Its legislative proposals have lost the privileged position which they were intended to enjoy under Art. 149 since the difference between the votes needed for their adoption (qualified majority) and their amendment (unanimity) has disappeared in most cases.

The above developments have been criticized by the various bodies which have been set up to put forward proposals for reforming the Community institutions (see, in particular, the Vedel, Tindemans, and Three Wise Men's Reports and the Report of the Committee on Institutional Affairs—the Dooge Committee). The Commission itself has consistently expressed concern about the Council's practice and has urged it to return to the use of majority voting (see e.g. 2nd *Gen. Rep. EC* (1968), pp. 15, 18; 3rd *Gen. Rep. EC* (1969), pp. 335, 485; Suppl. to *Bull. EC* 9/10–1969, pp. 33–4; 8th *Gen. Rep. EC* (1974), p. 9; *Bull. EC* 4–1978, p. 10; Suppl. 2/78—*Bull. EC*, p. 12; *Bull. EC* 10–1981, p. 56; Suppl. 3/82—*Bull. EC*, p. 7). At the Paris Summit Conference of 19 to 21 October 1972, the Heads of State or Government recognized that the decision-making procedures and the functioning of the institutions should be improved and instructed the Council to take practical steps to this end (6th *Gen. Rep. EC* (1972), pp. 15–16). During 1973 and 1974, the Council in fact adopted various measures to improve its working methods (*Bull. EC* 7/8–1973, p. 76; *Bull. EC* 2–1974, p. 103; *Bull. EC* 6–1974, p. 122). Nevertheless, at the Paris Summit meeting of 9–10 December 1974, the Heads of State or Government still felt it important to emphasize that 'in order to improve the functioning of the Council . . . it is necessary to renounce the practice which consists of making agreement on all questions conditional on the unanimous consent of the Member States, whatever their respective positions may be regarding the conclusions reached in Luxembourg on 28 January 1966' (8th *Gen. Rep. EC* (1974), p. 298. See also the Solemn Declaration on European Union of Stuttgart of 19 June 1983, point 2.2, *Bull. EC* 6–1983, p. 24). In spite of all these statements, the Luxembourg Compromise has never been officially renounced or declared invalid by a legally binding instrument.

The Single European Act, which came into force on 1 July 1987, has however introduced certain changes in the voting rules of the Treaty. To enable measures necessary for the completion of the internal market by 31 December 1992 to be adopted without long delays, the Act has amended certain Articles of the EEC Treaty by substituting qualified majority for the previous unanimity requirement (see Art. 16 SEA amending Arts. 28, 59, 70(1), and 84(2) EEC). The Act has also inserted a number of new provisions into the EEC Treaty, most of which require the Council to act by a qualified majority (Arts. 13 to 25 SEA). Moreover, in a Declaration annexed to the Final Act, the Presidency declared its intention to improve the decision-making procedures. As a result, the Rules of Procedure of the Council were amended on 20 July 1987. The new Art. 5(1) provides that the Council shall vote on the initiative of the President but that the President is required to call for a vote at the request of a member of the Council or of the Commission, provided that a simple majority of Council members supports the request (*OJ* 1987 L291/27; see also 21st *Gen. Rep. EC* (1987), p. 31). While the SEA has not formally abolished the Luxembourg Compromise, this new rule makes it virtually impossible for a single Member State (or a group of States not being able to form a blocking minority) to stop the legislative process, provided that a majority of Council members is willing to put to the vote a proposed measure which may be adopted by a qualified majority. It seems that this

143

new arrangement has already produced a considerable improvement in the Council's decision-making procedure (see 22nd *Gen. Rep. EC* (1988), p. 32).

See also **Commission, Committee of Permanent Representatives, Committee on Institutional Affairs, Co-operation procedure, Economic and Social Committee, European Council, European Parliament, European Political Co-operation, European Union, External relations, Implied powers, Infringement of an essential procedural requirement, Institutional balance, Institutions, Luxembourg Compromise, Privileges and immunities, Representatives of the Governments of the Member States meeting in Council, Secondary legislation, Single European Act, Solemn Declaration on European Union, Supplementary powers, Three Wise Men's Report, Tindemans Report, Treaty-making procedure, Vedel Report.**

Further reading 1. BOOK: Lasok and Bridge, *Law and Institutions of the European Communities*, 4th edn. (1987), ch. 6.

2. ARTICLES: Editorial, 'Voting in the Council of Ministers' (1987) 12 *EL Rev.* 2; id., 'Majority Voting' (1987) 12 *EL Rev.* 405; Mortelmans, 'The Extramural Meetings of the Ministers of the Member States of the Community' (1974) 11 *CML Rev.* 62.

See also under **Community law, Institutions, Single European Act.**

▶ **COURT OF AUDITORS (CA)** Body established by the Second Budgetary Treaty of 22 July 1975 with responsibility for the external audit of the general budget of the European Communities and of the operating budget of the ECSC, the internal audit being the task of the Financial Controller of each institution. The Court exercises the powers and jurisdiction conferred upon it by the ECSC, EEC, and Euratom Treaties, as amended, and those previously vested in the Audit Board of the Communities (which had been responsible for the general budget) and in the Auditor of the ECSC (who had been responsible for the ECSC operating budget), which bodies it replaced upon coming into existence on 25 October 1977 (Arts. 7, 78e, 78f ECSC; 4, 206, 206a EEC; 3, 180, 180a Euratom; 22 Merger Treaty, as amended by the Budgetary Treaty of 1975, *OJ* 1977 L359/1. See also *Bull. EC* 10–1977, p. 22. Only the EEC provisions will be cited below). The creation of the Court was due partly to the desire of some (particularly the new) Member States to strengthen the then existing audit arrangements, and partly to the growing pressure of the European Parliament for greater power in the financial affairs of the Communities, for which purpose it needed the assistance of an independent audit body.

The CA is organized and acts as a corporate body and enjoys a quasi-institutional status (see Art. 1 of the CA's Rules of Procedure of 21 May 1981 (CARP), consolidated version of 24 July 1986). It enjoys a measure of financial and administrative independence, having its own administrative budget and staff establishment plan. Nevertheless, it is neither a 'court' nor an 'institution' in the strict sense. Although it is treated, together with the Economic and Social Committee, as an 'institution' for the specific purposes of the Staff Regulations and of the Financial Regulation (see Art. 1(2) of the

Staff Regulations and the Preamble and Art. 18(4) of the Financial Regulation of 21 Dec. 1977, *OJ* 1977 L356/1), it is in fact not given the full status of a Community institution. As the ECJ has pointed out, the Court is not listed in Arts. 7 ECSC, 4 EEC, and 3 Euratom as an institution (although it is mentioned in the amended versions of those Articles). Its treatment as an institution for the purposes of the Staff Regulations only has the object of ensuring that those Regulations are applied to its officials and of identifying the appointing authority for them, but does not imply similar treatment for the general purposes of the Treaties. Thus, the requirement laid down in Art. 24 of the Merger Treaty, that the Council shall consult the 'other institutions' when adopting or amending the Staff Regulations, does not apply to the Court of Auditors and the Economic and Social Committee (Case 828/79 *Adam* v. *Commission* [1982] ECR 269 at pp. 290–1). Nevertheless, it follows from Art. 1(2) of the Staff Regulations that the CA has the capacity to appear before the ECJ in proceedings between it and one of its officials (see e.g. Case 184/80 *Van Zaanen* v. *Court of Auditors* [1981] ECR 1951).

The CA consists of twelve full-time members (Art. 206(2) EEC as last amended by Art. 20 of the Act of Accession 1985) who are chosen from among persons who have had relevant auditing experience and qualifications and whose independence is beyond doubt. They are appointed for a renewable term of six years by the Council, acting unanimously after consulting the European Parliament (Art. 206(4) EEC, see also Rule 67 of the EP's Rules of Procedure, 4th edn. (1987)). The members elect the President of the Court for a term of three years; he may be re-elected (for the election, replacement, and functions of the President, see Arts. 5–7 CARP). The members of the Court must be completely independent in the performance of their duties; they must neither seek nor take instructions from any Government or from any other body. During their term of office they may not engage in any other occupation, whether gainful or not. Even after they have ceased to hold office, they must behave with integrity and discretion as regards the acceptance of certain appointments or benefits (Art. 206(5) and (6) EEC; Arts. 2–4 CARP). Their term of office may come to an end by reason of normal replacement, death, resignation, or compulsory retirement ordered by the Court of Justice if they no longer fulfil the conditions of their office. They enjoy the same privileges and immunities as the Judges of the Court of Justice enjoy under the Protocol on Privileges and Immunities annexed to the Merger Treaty (Art. 206(7)–(10) EEC). Decisions are taken by a majority of the members (Art. 20 CARP). Although the Court acts as a collective body, each member is assigned responsibility for an agreed sector of the Court's work (Art. 8 CARP. For the internal administration and organization of the Court, see further Arts. 8–24 CARP). At the end of 1988, there were 319 permanent posts and 56 temporary posts on the Court's establishment plan (22nd *Gen. Rep. EC* (1988), p. 43).

The main responsibility of the CA is to examine the accounts of all revenue and expenditure of the Communities and of any body set up by the Communities whose constituent instrument does not preclude such examination. These bodies include such entities as the European Centre for the Development of Vocational Training, the European Foundation for the Improvement of Living and Working Conditions, the European Agency for Co-operation, the Euratom Supply Agency, the Joint European Torus, and the European Schools, but do not include the European Investment Bank. An annex to the Budgetary Treaty of 1975 states that the Court is also to have jurisdiction to audit the operations of the European Development Fund (see *Treaties Establishing the European Communities* (1987), p. 958). In particular, the Court is required to examine not only whether all revenue has been received and all expenditure incurred in a lawful and regular manner, but also whether the financial management has been sound (Art. 206a(1) and (2) EEC. See also Art. 78f ECSC). Nevertheless, the CA's power of review does not preclude judicial review by the Court of Justice. As the ECJ has pointed out, the CA only has power to examine the legality of expenditure with reference to the budget and the secondary provision on which the expenditure is based (known as the 'basic measure'). Its review is thus distinct from that exercised by the ECJ, which concerns the legality of the basic measure (Case 294/83 *Les Verts* v. *Parliament* [1986] ECR 1339 at p. 1367).

The audit is based on records and, if necessary, performed on the spot in the Community institutions and in the Member States. In the Member States, the audit is carried out in close co-operation with the national audit bodies or, if these do not have the necessary powers, with the competent departments. Both the institutions and the national bodies are required to forward to the Court, at its request, any document or information necessary to carry out its task (Art. 206a(3) EEC; see also Arts. 78–82 FR). After the close of each financial year, the Court is required to draw up an Annual Report which is forwarded to the institutions and published, together with their comments, in the *Official Journal* (for the financial year 1988, see *OJ* 1989 C312/1). It includes an assessment of the soundness of the financial management. The Court may also, at any time, submit observations on specific matters on its own initiative, which are referred to as Special Reports. It may deliver opinions at the request of any of the institutions. The Court is required to assist the European Parliament and the Council in exercising their powers of control over the implementation of the budget. On its part, the Council must obtain the (non-binding) opinion of the Court before enacting Financial Regulations and taking certain other measures (Arts. 206a(4) and 209 EEC; see also Arts. 83–5 FR and Arts. 25–37 CARP. For the subjects on which the Court delivered opinions and issued Special Reports in 1988, see 22nd *Gen. Rep. EC* (1988), pp. 42–3).

See also **Budgetary Treaties, Community budget, European Parliament, Financial Regulation, Institutions, Privileges and immunities.**

Further reading: Price, 'The Court of Auditors of the European Communities' (1982) 2 *YEL* 239. *See also under* **Budgetary Treaties, Community budget.**

▶ **COURT OF FIRST INSTANCE (CFI)** Court attached to the ECJ with jurisdiction to hear and determine at first instance certain classes of action brought by natural or legal persons and requiring close examination of complex facts, subject to a right of appeal to the ECJ on points of law only. The setting up of such a Court was prompted by the need to reduce the workload of the ECJ and to shorten the duration of proceedings before it; to improve the judicial protection of individual interests, particularly in cases involving complex issues of fact; and, generally, to maintain the quality and effectiveness of judicial review in the Community legal order by enabling the ECJ to concentrate its activities on its fundamental task of ensuring uniform interpretation of Community law (see Proposal for a Decision of the Council establishing a Court of First Instance, Doc. 11191/86, prepared by the ECJ in 1986, General explanatory note; a printed version appears at [1988] 1 CMLR 185 but without the General explanatory note. In 1987 the ECJ submitted to the Council a formal Proposal which amended the 1986 informal Proposal in certain respects, Doc. 8770/87, unpublished. See also Preamble to Council Dec. 88/591 of 24 Oct. 1988 establishing a Court of First Instance of the European Communities, *OJ* 1988 L319/1, as corrected, see *OJ* 1989 L241/4 and *OJ* 1989 C215/1).

The idea to create a first instance Court to relieve the ECJ of some of its workload was not new. Already at its meeting of 26 November 1974, the Council agreed in principle with a German suggestion that a CFI be set up to deal with actions between the Communities and their civil servants and instructed the Commission to submit specific proposals on the subject (*Bull. EC* 11–1974, pp. 8 and 100). In August 1978, the Commission formally proposed the establishment of an Administrative Tribunal of the European Communities (*OJ* 1978 C225/6). At its meeting of 9 October 1978, the Council took note of the Commission's proposal and of a letter sent by the ECJ in July 1974 also proposing the setting up of such a Tribunal by amending the Staff Regulations, and requested the Committee of Permanent Representatives to start discussions on these proposals (*Bull. EC* 10–1978, p. 14). In July 1978 and January 1979, the ECJ put forward proposals, amongst other things, for the transfer of staff cases to an Administrative Tribunal and for the creation of a new CFI. No action was taken, however, until November 1985, when the ECJ submitted a new proposal for a CFI to the Intergovernmental Conference which was convened to draw up what became the Single European Act of 1986 (SEA). As a result, Arts. 4–5, 11– 12, and 26–7 of the SEA inserted identical new Arts. 32D and 45(2), 168A and 188(2), 140A and 160(2) into the ECSC, EEC, and Euratom Treaties, respectively, empowering the Council, acting at the request of the ECJ, to establish a CFI to deal with certain classes of case, to determine its composition, and to lay down the necessary amendments to the Statutes of the ECJ. These provisions were adopted by the Council in its Decision of 24 October 1988 (see above), which established the CFI and inserted an identical new Title IV in each of the three Statutes of the ECJ, adding new Arts. 44–54 to the ECSC and EEC Statutes and new Arts. 45–55 to the Euratom Statute (only the EEC provisions will be cited below). The Decision entered into force on 26 November 1988, the day following its publication in the *Official Journal* (see Art. 13), and the new CFI commenced exercising its jurisdiction on 31 October 1989, the date of the publication in the *Official Journal* of the

147

decision of the President of the ECJ that the CFI was constituted in accordance with law (*OJ* 1989 L317/48).

I. Composition and organization

The CFI consists of twelve members to be chosen from persons whose independence is beyond doubt and who possess the ability required for appointment to judicial office; they are to be appointed by common accord of the Governments of the Member States for a term of six years. The membership is to be partially renewed every three years, but retiring members are eligible for reappointment (Art. 2(1) of the Dec. of 24 Oct. 1988; Art. 168A(3) EEC. For the appointment of the first members of the CFI as from 1 Sept. 1989, see *OJ* 1989 L220/76). It thus seems that the qualifications required of the members of the CFI are lower than those of the members of the ECJ, who must possess the qualifications necessary for appointment to the 'highest judicial offices' in their respective countries (see Art. 167(1) EEC). Nevertheless, this is not necessarily a disadvantage in a Court dealing with cases which require expertise in special fields. The President of the CFI is elected by its members from among their number for a term of three years; he may be re-elected (Art. 2(2) of the Dec. of 24 Oct. 1988; under Art. 11 the first President was appointed by the Member States, see *OJ* 1989 L220/77). No separate Advocates-General are to be appointed, but the members of the CFI (i.e. the Judges) may be called upon to perform the task of an Advocate-General in certain cases which are to be selected in accordance with the criteria laid down in the CFI's Rules of Procedure. A Judge so called upon may not take part in the judgment of the case. The tasks of an Advocate-General of the CFI are basically the same as those of an Advocate-General of the ECJ, although the former may deliver his reasoned opinion in writing (Art. 2(3) of the Dec. of 24 Oct. 1988; new Art. 46(3) EEC Statute). The CFI is required to sit in Chambers of three or five Judges but in certain cases to be determined by its Rules of Procedure it may sit in plenary session (Art. 2(4) of the Dec. of 24 Oct. 1988. On 4 Oct. 1989, the CFI set up five Chambers; for their composition, Presidents and the assignment of cases to them, see *OJ* 1989 C281/12). It may be noted that the Commission recommended that the CFI should have two autonomous sections, one for economic cases and the other for staff cases, composed of Judges having specific qualifications; that its members should be persons of senior rank; and that Advocates-General should also be appointed (*Bull. EC* 5–1988, pp. 92–3). The European Parliament, too, proposed that the CFI should be assisted by three Advocates-General (see Res. of 17 June 1988, *OJ* 1988 C187/223 and 227). It seems that none of these recommendations was adopted.

The CFI appoints its own Registrar (see *OJ* 1989 C281/12) and lays down the rules governing his service. Although so far as its judicial functions are concerned the CFI is entirely independent of the ECJ, which will exercise no supervisory authority over it, it has no administrative departments of its own. It is closely attached to the ECJ, its seat being at the ECJ in Luxembourg (Art. 1 of the Dec. of 24 Oct. 1988). It is envisaged that the CFI will make use of the administration, documentation, library, translation, and interpretation services of the ECJ. There will be no officials of the CFI as such, but the officials of the ECJ will render their services to the CFI under conditions to be determined by common accord by the Presidents of the two Courts. Certain officials will be responsible to the Registrar of the CFI under the authority of its President (Art. 45 EEC Statute). The members and the Registrar of the CFI enjoy the same privileges and immunities as the members and the Registrar of the ECJ (Art. 2(5) of the Dec. of 24 Oct. 1988; Art. 44 EEC Statute. *See further under* **Privileges and immunities**).

II. Jurisdiction

The jurisdiction of the CFI covers only such classes of action, listed exhaustively, as have been transferred to it from the ECJ; it does not cover new areas of jurisdiction. In actions so transferred, the jurisdiction of the CFI is exclusive. The actions falling within its jurisdiction are as follows (see Art. 3 of the Dec. of 24 Oct. 1988):

1. disputes between the Communities and their servants ('staff cases' brought under Arts. 179 EEC and 152 Euratom);
2. actions for annulment and for failure to act brought against the Commission by undertakings and their associations under Arts. 33 and 35 ECSC and which concern individual acts relating to levies, production, prices, restrictive agreements, decisions or practices, and concentrations (Arts. 50 and 57–66 ECSC);
3. actions for annulment and for failure to act brought against a Community institution by natural or legal persons under Arts. 173 and 175 EEC relating to the implementation of the competition rules applicable to undertakings.

Wherever the same natural or legal person brings an action which the CFI has jurisdiction to hear under the above rules and a related action for compensation for damage caused by the act or failure to act which is the subject of the first action, the CFI also has jurisdiction to hear and determine the action for compensation. The Council has moreover reserved the right to review the situation after two years of operation of the CFI and to confer jurisdiction on it also in respect of actions in the fields of dumping and subsidies (Arts. 74 ECSC and 113 EEC), as proposed by the ECJ. On the other hand, the CFI has no jurisdiction (1) in cases brought by natural or legal persons under the Euratom Treaty; (2) in cases brought by Member States or by Community institutions; and (3) in references for preliminary rulings, under any of the Treaties (Arts. 32D(1) ECSC, 168A(1) EEC, 140A(1) Euratom). The rules of the Treaties relating to actions for annulment and for failure to act apply to the CFI (i.e. Arts. 172, 174, 176, 184 to 187 and 192 EEC, see Art. 4 of the Dec. of 24 Oct. 1988).

The CFI and the ECJ have the power mutually to transmit to each other applications and other procedural documents mistakenly lodged with them. Likewise, either Court may refer to the other actions brought before it but falling within that other Court's jurisdiction. Where both Courts are seised of cases in which the same relief is sought, the same issue of interpretation is raised, or the validity of the same act is called in question, the CFI may stay proceedings until the ECJ has delivered judgment. Where actions are brought for the annulment of the same act, the CFI may decline jurisdiction in favour of the ECJ. In all of these cases, the ECJ, too, may decide to stay proceedings, allowing the CFI to continue the proceedings before it (Art. 47 EEC Statute). These provisions are obviously designed to avoid conflicting judgments being given in parallel proceedings involving different parties (e.g. Member States and individuals) but the same legal issues. However, they can only achieve their objective fully if it is assumed that each Court will follow the decision of the other. This leads to the strange result that the ECJ—a superior Court— will have to follow the ruling of the CFI—a lower Court—where that ruling is not appealed against. (Where an appeal is brought against the decision of the CFI, the ECJ will of course be able to quash that decision if it disagrees with it.) Moreover, in the absence of an express provision it is difficult to see on what legal basis either Court can be bound by the decision of the other rendered in a different case, given that the two Courts are judicially independent of one another and that no doctrine of precedent exists in Community law (see further below).

III. Appeals

An appeal may be brought before the ECJ against final decisions of the CFI and against decisions disposing of the substantive issues in part only or disposing of a procedural issue concerning a plea of lack of competence or inadmissibility. Such an appeal may be brought within two months of the notification of the decision by any party which has been unsuccessful, in whole or in part, in its submissions. Interveners other than the Member States and the Community institutions may bring an appeal only where the decision 'directly affects them'. With the exception of staff cases, an appeal may also be brought by Member States and institutions which did not intervene in the proceedings; these will be in the same position as Member States and institutions which intervened at first instance (Art. 49 EEC Statute). In special cases, the right of appeal is restricted. Thus, only the person whose application to intervene has been dismissed by the CFI may appeal against that decision; the time-limit is two weeks. Only the parties to the proceedings may appeal against decisions concerning suspension of operation of an act, interim measures, and suspension of enforcement of an act (Arts. 185, 186, and 192(4) EEC). In these cases the time-limit is two months. The ECJ is to hear and determine these special appeals by way of summary procedure under Art. 36 EEC Statute (Art. 50 EEC Statute). No appeal lies against acts of 'judicial administration' (e.g. extensions of time-limits, preparatory inquiries, decisions on legal aid) and regarding only the amount of the costs or the party ordered to pay them (Art. 51(2) EEC Statute; see also the Explanatory note to Art. 48 in the ECJ Proposals). It may be asked whether, to prevent the development in the CFI of a case-law inconsistent with itself or with that of the ECJ, it might not have been advisable to confer on the ECJ the right to review of its own motion any decision of the CFI not appealed against, with the power to give a ruling on issues of law only but without altering the decision of the CFI with regard to the parties (something which the ECJ may do where an appeal is brought by a Member State or institution not party to the case, see below).

An appeal to the ECJ must be limited to points of law. It lies only on three types of grounds: lack of competence of the CFI; a breach of procedure before it which adversely affects the interests of the appellant; and the infringement of Community law by the CFI (Art. 51 EEC Statute). The last ground corresponds to the third ground of action listed in Art. 173(1) EEC but is more broadly drafted. It presumably includes infringement not only of primary and secondary Community law but also of any general principle of law which the ECJ has recognized as part of Community law. The often delicate distinction between questions of law and of fact will be made by the ECJ in its decisions (see Explanatory note to Art. 48 EEC Statute in the 1986 ECJ Proposal). It is, however, not quite clear whether the failure of the CFI to follow a previous decision of the ECJ given in a different case in itself constitutes an infringement of Community law and thus a ground of appeal, given that the decisions of the ECJ do not constitute binding precedents under Community law.

On appeal, the procedure before the ECJ consists of a written and an oral part but, after hearing the Advocate-General and the parties, the Court may dispense with the oral procedure on certain conditions laid down in its Rules of Procedure (Arts. 52 EEC Statute, 120RP). An appeal has no suspensory effect. However, decisions of the CFI declaring a regulation to be void take effect only after the expiry of the two-month period within which ￢n appeal may be brought or, if an appeal has been brought, after its dismissal by the ECJ. Nevertheless, this does not affect the right of a party to apply to the ECJ for the suspension of the operation of the regulation or for any other interim measure under Arts. 185 and 186 EEC, which provisions remain fully available on appeal (Art. 53 EEC Statute). The purpose of the above rule is to avoid the clearly undesirable consequences which would otherwise arise from a judgment of the ECJ quashing a decision of the CFI which has annulled a regulation. Such a judgment would create legal uncertainty by restoring retroactively a legislative act annulled at first instance. A similar solution is not necessary where the CFI merely declares a regulation inapplicable under Art. 184 EEC, since such a finding does not have the same effects as an annulment (see Explanatory note to Art. 51 EEC Statute in the 1986 ECJ Proposal).

If the appeal is well founded, the ECJ will quash the decision of the CFI. The ECJ may then itself give final judgment in the matter, even on questions of fact, where the facts are simple and the state of the proceedings so permits, or refer the case back to the CFI for judgment, which is likely to happen particularly where complex facts need to be examined. In the latter case, the CFI is bound by the decision of the ECJ on points of law. When an appeal brought by a Member State or a Community institution, which has not intervened in the proceedings before the CFI, is well founded the ECJ may, if it considers this necessary, confirm some of the effects of the decision of the CFI which has been quashed as being definitive in respect of the parties to the case (Art. 54 EEC Statute). This rule is an application by analogy of the principle laid down in Art. 174 EEC in respect of regulations. Its purpose is to avoid prejudicing the position of the parties, who have both acquiesced in the decision of the CFI, as a result of an appeal brought by non-parties.

It may be noted that subject to the amendments introduced by the SEA and the Council Decision of 24 October 1988, summarized above, the provisions of the Treaties relating to the ECJ and those of the Court's Statutes apply to the CFI also (Art. 168A(2) EEC; see also Art. 4 of the Council Dec. of 24 Oct. 1988 and Art. 44 EEC Statute). The procedure before the CFI is governed by Title III of the ECJ's Statutes (with certain exceptions). Further and more detailed provisions are to be laid down in the Rules of Procedure which the CFI is required to adopt in agreement with the ECJ and subject to the unanimous approval of the Council. Until the entry into force of those Rules, the Rules of Procedure of the ECJ apply *mutatis mutandis* (Arts. 168A(4) EEC, 46 EEC Statute, 11 of the Dec. of 24 Oct. 1988. By mid-1990, only draft Rules of Procedure were published, see *OJ* 1990 C136/1). The procedure on appeal is governed by the ECJ's amended Rules of Procedure (see *OJ* 1989 L241/1). The parties must seek the same form of order as that sought at first instance and they may not change the subject-matter of the proceedings (Arts. 113 and 116 RP). Apart from the provisions on costs and a few other matters, most of the rules of the ordinary procedure apply also to the procedure on appeal (see Art. 118 RP).

IV. Comments

Clearly, at this stage it is impossible to comment in detail on the system created by the Council Decision of 24 October 1988. Any initial doubts that may exist, in particular as to the advisability of mixing the tasks of Judge and Advocate-General, or as to the possibility of conflicting decisions being given by the two Courts in unforeseen situations which have not been provided for, may easily be dispelled after both Courts have had the opportunity to interpret and apply the new rules in practice. One fundamental question still remains, however. Has the setting up of a new Court of First Instance been the best solution to achieve the main objectives set out at the beginning of this entry, in particular that of reducing the workload of the ECJ? Given the fact that twelve new Judges have been appointed, would it not have been a better proposition to increase the number of Judges of the ECJ by the same number and at the same time to authorize the Court freely to assign any type of case to Chambers? This would have resulted in a total of twenty-five Judges, which would have enabled the Court to dispose of a considerably larger number of cases than at present by forming Chambers in various combinations. Thus, five Chambers of five Judges, four Chambers of six Judges, eight Chambers of three Judges, etc. would have been possible. Some of these could have been designated as specialist Chambers dealing with staff or competition cases only. With a quorum of seven, three full Courts could have been constituted simultaneously. Even the most important cases, making the participation of Judges from all the twelve Member States desirable, could have been dealt with by two parallel benches. Most of the advantages of having a separate CFI could have been attained without the disadvantages of a two-tier system.

Thus, individual interests in complex cases could have been protected by assigning such cases to specialist Chambers consisting of Judges with the relevant qualification and expertise. As regards workload and the duration of proceedings, it seems reasonable to assume that a given number of Judges (say, twenty-five) can dispose of a larger number of cases during the same period if they have to hear each case normally only once rather than hear a probably very high proportion of them twice or even three times (i.e. those referred back for retrial). Although the possibility of a second appeal is not expressly mentioned in the Decision, it is not excluded either. For example, in cases where on first appeal the ECJ quashes a decision of the CFI on the sole ground that it has incorrectly declared the action inadmissible and returns the case to the Court below, a second appeal must surely be available against the second decision dealing with the substance of the case, which was not the subject of the first appeal (other situations requiring two appeals are conceivable). In such cases, a number of hearings will become necessary. The consistency of the case-law is undoubtedly better ensured in a single instance system than in a system involving two different Courts, particularly because it is not quite clear to what extent the CFI is bound by the case-law of the ECJ in general, given that it is a judicially independent body (see above). As regards the quality of judicial review, it is difficult to envisage that this would be enhanced by the addition of a new Court consisting of Judges with lower qualifications, particularly since the ultimate decision lies with the present court. Finally, a simple enlargement of the existing ECJ would have avoided all the costs and trouble involved in the setting up of a new organization, not to mention the inevitable multiplicity of complex legal texts and procedures which is a necessary consequence of the two-tier system.

See also **European Court of Justice, Single European Act.**

Further reading 1. BOOK: Millett, *The Court of First Instance of the European Communities* (1990).
  2. ARTICLES: Dué, 'The Court of First Instance' (1988) 8 *YEL* 1; Dué and da Cruz Vilaça, 'Formal Sitting of the European Court on Setember 25, 1989' (1990) 15 *EL Rev.* 3; Editorial, 'The British Suggestions Concerning the Court of Justice' (1979) 16 *CML Rev.* 3; id., 'The Re-organisation of the Court: A British View' (1980) 17 *CML Rev.* 154; id., 'Report on the Re-organisation of the European Court' (1980) 5 *EL Rev.* 1; id., 'What Kind of First Instance Court?' (1986) 11 *EL Rev.* 329; id., 'The Proposal for a European Court of First Instance' (1987) 12 *EL Rev.* 77; Kennedy, 'The Essential Minimum: The Establishment of the Court of First Instance' (1989) 14 *EL Rev.* 7; Millett, 'The New European Court of First Instance' (1989) 38 *ICLQ* 811; Schermers, 'The European Court of First Instance' (1988) 25 *CML Rev.* 541; Toth, 'The Court of First Instance of the European Communities', in White and Smythe (eds.), *Current Issues in European and International Law* (1990), p.19.
  3. OFFICIAL PUBLICATIONS: House of Lords, Select Committee on the European Communities, Session 1978–9, 17th Report, 'Staff Administrative Tribunal' (1979); id., Session 1979–80, 23rd Report, 'European Court of Justice' (1979); id., Session 1987–8, 5th Report, 'A European Court of First Instance' (1987).

D

▶ **DAMAGE** One of the conditions for the establishment of the non-contractual liability of the Communities is that there must exist an actual, certain, and specific damage which is, in principle, quantifiable and definitive (see in general Case 4/69 *Lütticke* v. *Commission* [1971] ECR 325 at p. 337; Case 153/73 *Holtz & Willemsen* v. *Council and Commission* [1974] ECR 675 at p. 693; etc. See also Cases 9 and 25/64 *FERAM* v. *HA* [1965] ECR 311 at p. 320 and the cases cited below). As A.-G. Capotorti has explained, 'the legal concept of "damage" covers both a material loss *stricto senso*, that is to say, a reduction in a person's assets, and also the loss of an increase in those assets which would have occurred if the harmful act had not taken place (these two alternatives are known respectively as *damnum emergens* and *lucrum cessans*). . . . The object of compensation is to restore the assets of the victim to the condition in which they would have been apart from the unlawful act, or at least to the condition closest to that which would have been produced if the unlawful act had not taken place: the hypothetical nature of that restoration often entails a certain degree of approximation . . . These general remarks are not limited to the field of private law, but apply also to the liability of public authorities, and more specifically to the non-contractual liability of the Community' (Case 238/78 *Ireks-Arkady* v. *Council and Commission* [1979] ECR 2955 at pp. 2998–9—'Quellmehl' case; see also Cases 29/63 etc. *Usines de la Providence* v. *HA* [1965] ECR 911 at pp. 938–9 *per Curiam*, pp. 943–4 *per* A.-G. Lagrange).

The requirement that the damage must be specific means that it must affect the applicant's interests and assets in a special and individual way. Thus, the normal disadvantages inherent in a legislative measure which affect every Community undertaking in a more or less similar manner cannot give rise to a claim for compensation (see e.g. Cases 14/60 etc. *Meroni* v. *HA* [1961] ECR 161 at pp. 166–7; Cases 9 and 58/65 *San Michele* v. *HA* [1967] ECR 1 at p. 12). Also, as the ECJ has held in a consistent line of cases, an action for damages brought for unlawful legislative action cannot succeed unless 'the damage alleged by the applicant exceeds the limits of the economic risks inherent in operating in the sector concerned' (Case 59/83 *Biovilac* v. *EEC* [1984] ECR 4057 at pp. 4080–1).

According to the above definition, the ECJ determines the quantum of damages so as to grant full compensation for the loss actually sustained (see in particular Cases 5, 7, and 13 to 24/66 *Kampffmeyer* v. *Commission* [1967] ECR 245 at pp. 263–5; Case 238/78 *Ireks-Arkady* v. *Council and Commission*, above, at p. 2974). The Court is also prepared in principle to award compensation for loss of profits, although it seems to be more conservative in quantifying this owing to the essentially speculative nature of commercial transactions (Cases 5, 7, and 13 to 24/66 *Kampffmeyer* v. *Commission*, above, at p. 266. See, however, Case 74/74 *CNTA* v. *Commission* [1975] ECR 533 at p. 550 where the Court restricted the amount of compensation to the loss actually suffered). Where it is possible for the applicant to pass on the loss to his customers (e.g. by increasing his selling prices), the amount of compensation must, in principle, be reduced correspondingly (Case 238/78 *Ireks-Arkady* v. *Council and Commission*, above, at p. 2974). Any advantages which the applicant may derive from the measure causing the damage must be taken into account in determining the quantum of damages (Case 229/84 *Sommerlatte* v. *Commission* [1986] ECR 1805 at p. 1818).

The Court assesses the damage as it stands at the date of the judgment, and it is the rate of exchange prevailing at that date which must be applied for the purpose of converting into national currency the amount of damages payable (Cases 64 and 113/76 etc. *Dumortier* v. *Council* [1982] ECR 1733 at p. 1746; Cases 256/80 etc. *Birra Wührer* v. *Council and Commission* [1984] ECR 3693 at p. 3731). Where the amount of the compensation cannot be determined at a given stage of the proceedings although the liability of the Community has already been established, the Court will lay down by interlocutory judgment the criteria for the assessment of damages, while leaving the amount of compensation to be fixed either by agreement between the parties or by the Court, at a later stage, in the absence of such agreement (see e.g. Case 74/74 *CNTA* v. *Commission*, above, at pp. 550–1; for the final judgment in that case, see [1976] ECR 797. See also Case 238/78 *Ireks-Arkady* v. *Council and Commission*, above, at pp. 2974–5; Cases 256/80 etc. *Birra Wührer* v. *Council and Commission*, above, at p. 3732).

The applicant is, in principle, required to state the nature and the extent of the alleged damage in the originating application (Art. 38(1) RP). However, in the interests of procedural economy, the ECJ is willing to accept an application which is incomplete in this respect where the question of the legal basis of the Community's liability is appropriate for separate treatment. Deciding on this question first, the Court will reserve consideration of the damage itself for a later stage (Case 74/74 *CNTA* v. *Commission*, above, at p. 544; Case 90/78 *Granaria* v. *Council and Commission* [1979] ECR 1081 at pp. 1090–1). Also, the ECJ is willing to give a declaratory judgment on the Community's liability for imminent damage foreseeable with sufficient certainty even if the damage cannot at that stage be precisely assessed (Cases 56 to 60/74 *Kampffmeyer* v. *Commission and Council* [1976] ECR 711 at p. 741).

The onus to provide conclusive evidence as to the existence and exact amount of the damage lies with the applicant. Overall statistical figures showing disadvantageous trends in trade, purely subjective economic considerations which cannot be verified, will not suffice (Case 26/74 *Roquette* v. *Commission* [1976] ECR 677 at pp. 687–8; Cases 197 to 200/80 etc. *Ludwigshafener Walzmühle* v. *Council and Commission* [1981] ECR 3211 at p. 3254). Nevertheless, the defendant institution is required to collaborate with the applicant by producing relevant documents and information which it alone possesses (Cases 29/63 etc. *Usines de la Providence* v. *HA*, above, at pp. 943–4 *per* A.-G. Lagrange). The ECJ itself has an unfettered discretion in assessing all the evidence submitted to it (Case 261/78 *Interquell Stärke-Chemie* v. *EEC* [1982] ECR 3271 at p. 3280).

See also **Action for damages, Causal connection, Interest, Interlocutory judgment, Non-contractual liability, Non-material damage.**

Further reading: See under **Action for damages, Non-contractual liability.**

155

▶ **DECISION** One of the binding acts which the Council and the Commission may adopt within the scope of secondary legislation.

1. **Under the ECSC Treaty,** decisions adopted by the Commission are 'binding in their entirety' (Art. 14 ECSC). They may be addressed to both Member States and undertakings. Those addressed to undertakings are normally directly applicable to the addressees, i.e. applicable without the need for national implementing measures. The Treaty makes a distinction between 'general' decisions and decisions which are 'individual in character'. The importance of such a distinction is that it is the general or individual nature of a decision which determines (*a*) whether it has to be published in the *Official Journal* or notified to the addressee (Art. 15 ECSC), and (*b*) whether it may be challenged by undertakings before the ECJ (Art. 33 ECSC) (*see further under* **General decision, Individual decision**).

The ECSC Treaty places two different courses of action at the Commission's disposal to enable it to carry out the tasks assigned to it. Whenever the Commission has been given law-making (regulatory) power by the Treaty, it exercises that power by means of a decision. This is usually the case in those sectors of the economy of the Member States which have been placed entirely within Community competence. By contrast, in cases where legislative power is withheld from the Commission and remains with the Member States, the Commission may act only by means of a recommendation. The ECJ has held that the Commission may adopt regulatory decisions only where the Treaty has expressly granted legislative powers to it (Case 20/59 *Italy* v. *HA* [1960] ECR 325 at pp. 336, 338; Case 9/61 *Netherlands* v. *HA* [1962] ECR 213 at p. 232).

In considering whether an act of the Commission is a binding decision within the meaning of Art. 14 ECSC or a measure that has no binding force, in a series of cases the ECJ has stated that 'a decision must appear as a measure taken by the High Authority [i.e. the Commission], acting as a body, intended to produce legal effects and constituting the culmination of procedure within the High Authority, whereby the High Authority gives its final ruling in a form from which its nature can be identified. Any measure, therefore, which, in particular, does not appear to have been debated and adopted by the High Authority and authenticated by the signature of one of its members, cannot be regarded as a decision' (Cases 23, 24, and 52/63 *Usines Henricot* v. *HA* [1963] ECR 217 at p. 224; Cases 53 and 54/63 *Lemmerz-Werke* v. *HA* [1963] ECR 239 at p. 248; Case 54/65 *Forges de Chatillon* v. *HA* [1966] ECR 185 at p. 195; etc.). In the light of this definition, the ECJ has held that informal acts of the Commission, such as letters, communications, notifications, statements, internal instructions, originating from an internal division (e.g. Directorate-General, Directorate) and signed by mere officials or Heads of Department acting in personal capacity and not in the name and on behalf of the Commission, cannot normally be regarded as binding decisions within the meaning of Art. 14 and are not, therefore, challengeable for annulment under Art. 33 ECSC (see the cases cited immediately above, and also Case 20/58 *Phoenix-Rheinrohr* v. *HA* [1959] ECR 75 at pp. 81–2; Cases 16 to 18/59 *Geitling* v. *HA* [1960] ECR 17 at pp. 24–6; Cases 42 and 49/59

SNUPAT v. *HA* [1961] ECR 53 at p. 72; Cases 35/62 and 16/63 *Leroy* v. *HA* [1963] ECR 197 at p. 204; etc.).

2. **Under the EEC and Euratom Treaties,** a decision taken by the Council or the Commission 'shall be binding in its entirety upon those to whom it is addressed' (Arts. 189 EEC, 161 Euratom). The addressees may be one, several, or all the Member States or one or more natural or legal persons. Moreover, the Council may adopt decisions for the purpose of laying down binding rules of conduct for itself (Case 81/72 *Commission* v. *Council* [1973] ECR 575 at pp. 582–4) or for the Commission, or of giving instructions to the latter. Decisions must be notified to those to whom they are addressed and take effect upon such notification (Arts. 191 EEC, 163 Euratom). Decisions addressed to private individuals create rights and obligations for the addressees; decisions imposing a pecuniary obligation on private persons are enforceable in the national courts (Arts. 192 EEC, 164 Euratom).

It follows from the above provisions that a decision is an act which is different from both a regulation and a directive. As the ECJ has stated, 'Article 189 makes a clear distinction between the concept of a "decision" and that of a "regulation" . . . The criterion for the distinction must be sought in the general "application" or otherwise of the measure in question. The essential characteristics of a decision arise from the limitation of the persons to whom it is addressed, whereas a regulation, being essentially of a legislative nature, is applicable not to a limited number of persons, defined or identifiable, but to categories of persons viewed abstractly and in their entirety' (Cases 16 and 17/62 *Producteurs de Fruits* v. *Council* [1962] ECR 471 at p. 478; see also Case 25/62 *Plaumann* v. *Commission* [1963] ECR 95 at p. 107). It is precisely this limited scope of a decision that makes it suitable for use as an implementing act whereby the Commission, in its executive role, can apply the general provisions of the Treaty or of a regulation to individual persons, cases, or situations (see e.g. Case 16/65 *Schwarze* [1965] ECR 877 at p. 887). Thus a 'decision' under the EEC/Euratom Treaties largely corresponds to an 'individual decision' under the ECSC Treaty.

Nevertheless, it is possible for a decision, too, to have a very wide field of application (Cases 16 and 17/62 *Producteurs de Fruits* v. *Council*, above, at p. 479), so wide, in fact, that it may assume the character and effects of a general law-making measure. In that case it will differ from a regulation by name only (see e.g. Case 15/71 *Mackprang* v. *Commission* [1971] ECR 797 at pp. 803–4). There are also certain decisions of a *sui generis* type which are subject to different rules regarding notification and coming into effect. These must normally be published in the *Official Journal* and enter into force in accordance with their own provisions rather than upon notification. Into this category fall, for example, Council Decisions 70/243, 85/257, and 88/376 on the Communities' own resources (*OJ Sp. Edn.* 1970(I), p. 224, *OJ* 1985 L128/15, and *OJ* 1988 L185/24); Council Decision 76/787 on direct elections to the European Parliament (*OJ* 1976 L278/1); and Council Decision 88/591 establishing a Court of First Instance of the European Communities (*OJ* 1988 L319/1). The Decisions on own resources and direct elections almost have the character of an international agreement between the Member States, being subject to ratification by them in accordance with their respective constitutional requirements. Also, where a decision is addressed to a Member State, it may have genuine normative effects by requiring for its implementation the taking of legislative measures at the national level. In practice, therefore, the distinction between decisions and regulations is not always easy to make. Such a distinction is of primary importance in the context of an action for annulment under Arts. 173 EEC, 146 Euratom. Private individuals may only challenge decisions of the Council and the Commission, while they have no *locus standi* to bring annulment proceedings against regulations (*see further under* **Action for annulment**).

A decision differs from a directive in that it is 'binding in its entirety', while a directive is binding only as to the result to be achieved. In principle, therefore, a decision leaves no margin of discretion to the Member State to which it is addressed as to the choice of form and method of its implementation. The position is different where a decision grants an authorization to a Member State (e.g. to take protective measures). Such a decision normally leaves to the State concerned complete freedom to decide whether or not to make use, wholly or partially, of the authorization and also a measure of discretion as to the way (i.e. form and method) in which to make such use. Such a decision is binding only in the sense that the Member State may not go beyond the limits of the authorization granted.

At the same time, there are certain similarities between directives and decisions addressed to Member States. In the first place, such decisions are often used as an alternative means to directives (see e.g. Arts. 90(3), 97(2), and 108(2) EEC), particularly for the purpose of giving instructions to the Member States to harmonize, co-ordinate, or approximate their laws (for detailed lists of harmonization decisions adopted under the EEC Treaty, see Suppls. 9/72 and 3/75—*Bull. EC*).

Secondly, like directives, decisions addressed to Member States are binding on all the authorities of the Member States, including the courts. It follows that by virtue of the principle of the supremacy of Community law, national courts must refrain from applying all national measures whose application could hinder the proper implementation of Community decisions (Case 249/85 *ALBAKO* [1987] ECR 2345 at p. 2360).

Finally, like directives, decisions addressed to Member States normally require implementing measures on the part of the national authorities to become applicable to individuals. For a long time it was not clear whether, in the absence of implementing measures, such decisions could produce direct effects in the sense of creating rights for individuals enforceable in the national courts. Already in Case 38/69 *Commission* v. *Italy* [1970] ECR 47 at p. 57 the ECJ held that the Acceleration Decision of 26 July 1966 (*JO* 1966, p. 2971), although addressed to the Member States alone, was capable of producing direct effects within those States in conjunction with Art. 9(1) EEC and any measures taken in their implementation (see also Case 33/70 *SACE* [1970] ECR 1213 at pp. 1221–3). In Case 9/70 *Grad* [1970] ECR 825 at p. 837 the Court recognized that 'it would be incompatible with the binding effect attributed to decisions by Article 189 to exclude in principle the possibility that persons affected may invoke the obligations imposed by a decision. Particularly in cases where, for example, the Community authorities by means of a decision have imposed an obligation on a Member State ... to act in a certain way, the effectiveness ("*l'effet utile*") of such a measure would be weakened if the nationals of that State could not invoke it in the courts and the national courts could not take it into consideration as part of Community law. ... Therefore, in each particular case, it must be ascertained whether the nature, background and wording of the provision in question are capable of producing direct effects in the legal relationships between the addressee of the act and third parties.' Thus, where a decision imposes a mandatory obligation upon the Member States which is 'unconditional and sufficiently clear and precise', it will be 'capable of producing direct effects in the legal relationships between the Member States and those subject to their jurisdiction and of creating the right for the latter to invoke these obligations before the courts' (ibid. at pp. 838–9). On the other hand, it would seem that a decision addressed to the Member States cannot produce direct effects in the legal relationships between individuals ('horizontal direct effect'), nor can it impose obligations on individuals in their relationships with the Member States in the absence of implementing measures (see Case 30/75 *Unil-It* [1975] ECR 1419 at pp. 1427–8). These conclusions would appear to follow from the Court's case-law on directives, the direct effect of which is based on the same considerations as that of decisions (see in particular Case 152/84 *Marshall* [1986] ECR 723 at p. 749. *See further under* Directive).

See also Acceleration decisions, Action for annulment, Direct effect, Directive, General decision, Individual decision, Notification, Publication, Reasoned decision, Regulation, Secondary legislation, Statement of reasons.

Further reading: See under Secondary legislation.

▶ **DENIAL OF JUSTICE** Refusal by a court to give judgment on the ground that the law is silent, obscure, or insufficient. Denial of justice is expressly prohibited in certain national legal systems (see e.g. Art. 4 of Code Napoléon). The ECJ and its Advocates-General consider it to be their duty to fill any lacunae that may occur in the body of Community law so as to avoid denial of justice. Thus, should a problem arise for the solution of which the Treaties contain no rules, 'unless the Court is to deny justice it is ... obliged to solve the problem by reference to the rules acknowledged by the legislation, the learned writing and the case-law of the member countries' (Cases 7/56 etc. *Algera* v. *Common Assembly* [1957] ECR 39 at p. 55) or by resorting to various methods of judicial interpretation (Case 8/55 *Fédération Charbonnière de Belgique* v. *HA* [1956] ECR 245 at pp. 277–8 *per* A.-G. Lagrange).

It may be noted that the term 'denial of justice' is also used in public international law where it means, generally, any failure by a State to do justice to an alien wronged within its territory. Such denial of justice may establish the international responsibility of that State.

See also Non liquet.

▶ **DIRECT ACTION** Action instituted before the ECJ by means of an 'originating application' for a final and binding determination of the disputed issues between the parties within the framework of contentious proceedings and for the grant of any appropriate relief. Owing to the very wide scope of the Court's jurisdiction, there are a number of different forms of direct action, the most important being: action for annulment; action for failure to act; action for damages; action against sanctions; action against Member States; and action brought by Community officials against the employing institution (staff cases).

Direct actions may be contrasted with references for preliminary rulings which come before the ECJ from the courts or tribunals of the Member States. In reference proceedings the ECJ does not decide the disputed issues between the parties but merely gives an abstract ruling upon a point of Community law that has been referred to it while the referring court or tribunal retains its jurisdiction to determine the dispute in the light of the Court's ruling.

See also **Jurisdiction, Preliminary ruling, Reference proceedings.**

▶ **DIRECT APPLICABILITY** 1. **Under the ECSC Treaty:** term used by the ECJ to describe the effect of that Treaty, or of certain provisions of it, both *upon* and *within* the Member States. Thus, the term has been used in two different senses, although neither has been clearly defined nor elaborated on in detail by the Court.

In the first of these senses, the concept of direct applicability is based on the premiss that Arts. 2 to 5 of the Treaty, which constitute fundamental provisions establishing the Common Market and laying down the common objectives of the Community, are legally self-sufficient and capable of standing by themselves. They are therefore 'directly' applicable to or by the Commission and the Member States, i.e. applicable independently of any particular provisions that may appear later on in the Treaty, unless they are further elaborated on in such particular provisions. Where they are referred to, restated, or elaborated on in other parts of the Treaty, the general and the specific provisions relating to one and the same subject-matter must be considered as a whole and applied simultaneously (Cases 7 and 9/54 *Industries Sidérurgiques Luxembourgeoises* v. *HA* [1956] ECR 175 at p. 195; Case 8/57 *Aciéries Belges* v. *HA* [1958] ECR 245 at p. 253). Directly applicable are, moreover, such provisions of the Treaty as impose, both on the Commission and on the Member States, a 'substantive and binding rule' as opposed to a mere programme for action (Cases 3 to 18, 25, and 26/58 *Barbara Erzbergbau* v. *HA* [1960] ECR 173 at p. 190, confirming the direct applicability—in this sense—of Art. 70(1) ECSC).

In a second sense, the term 'direct applicability' refers to those rules of the Treaty which, like provisions laid down by the national legislature, are capable of 'being directly implemented in the Member States, such implementation taking place *ipso iure* as a result of their acceptance into the law of the Member States by the ratification of the Treaty' (Case 20/59 *Italy* v. *HA* [1960] ECR 325 at p. 335). These rules may therefore be applied to undertakings and associations in the same way as national legislation. By contrast, rules which are not directly applicable require implementing measures before they may be so applied. This is the case, for example, with regard to Art. 70(3) ECSC which, 'although it establishes a concrete rule with regard to transport valid both for the Member States and for the High Authority, requires implementing measures for it to be applied to the subjects of the ECSC', i.e. to coal- and steel-producing undertakings and their associations (ibid.; see also Case *25/59 Netherlands* v. *HA* [1960] ECR 355 at p. 371).

2. **Under the EEC Treaty:** term used to describe the way in which regulations become operative within the Member States. Thus, Art. 189 EEC provides that regulations shall be 'directly applicable in all Member States', which implies that they are automatically, i.e. without national ratification or any other specific act of approval, confirmation, reception, transformation, etc., incorporated into the national legal systems and therefore binding on the authorities of the Member States, including the courts (*see further under* **Regulation**).

Since the Treaty uses the term in relation to regulations only, the question arises whether the provisions of the Treaty itself or of the other binding acts of the institutions, such as directives and decisions, are or may ever be directly applicable. To answer that question, it is first of all necessary to make a clear distinction between the concept of direct applicability, a creation of the Treaty, and the related concept of direct effect, which has been gradually developed by the ECJ in its case-law. Direct effect means that certain provisions of the Treaty and of the acts of the institutions are capable of producing legal effects in the Member States without the need for any implementing measures, in the sense of conferring rights and in some cases imposing obligations upon individuals which are enforceable in the national courts (*see further under* **Direct effect**). It is thus clear that while 'direct applicability' concerns the way in which a Community provision (a regulation) comes into operation within the Member States, 'direct effect' describes the effects of such a provision in the national legal systems *after* it has come into operation therein. Strictly speaking, therefore, they refer to two different aspects of the relationship between Community law and national law, although they are closely related in that they both deal with the same relationship.

While according to a now prevailing view the two concepts ought to be distinguished, some confusion still arises from the fact that the Court does not follow a consistent and uniform terminology in this respect, and has (perhaps deliberately?) never attempted to determine their respective scope and mutual relationship. Thus, for example, the Court often uses the term 'direct applicability', whereas what it means is, clearly, 'direct effect' (see e.g. Case 106/77 *Simmenthal* [1978] ECR 629 at pp. 643–4, dealing with the consequences of the 'direct applicability' of Community law in the case of a conflict with national law; see also the opinion of A.-G. Reischl, ibid. at pp. 651 *et seq.*, who uses the two terms interchangeably; Case 2/74 *Reyners* [1974] ECR 631 at p. 652, deciding that Art. 52 EEC is a 'directly applicable' provision and repeating this in the operative part at p. 656; Case 17/81 *Pabst*

161

& *Richarz* [1982] ECR 1331 at pp. 1349, 1350, holding that Art. 95(1) EEC and the similar Art. 53(1) of the Association Agreement with Greece are 'directly applicable', having previously established that Art. 95(1) EEC produced 'direct effects', see e.g. Case 57/65 *Lütticke* [1966] ECR 205 at p. 211). Occasionally, the Court uses the two terms synonymously within the same case (see e.g. Case 48/71 *Commission* v. *Italy* [1972] ECR 527 at p. 532, where the Court refers to Art. 16 EEC both as producing 'direct effects' and as being 'directly applicable', or Case 43/75 *Defrenne* [1976] ECR 455 where at p. 471 the Court sets out to examine the 'direct effect' of Art. 119 EEC and at p. 474 arrives at the conclusion that Art. 119 is 'directly applicable') or equates the direct applicability of a Treaty Article with that of a regulation (see e.g. Case 167/73 *Commission* v. *France* [1974] ECR 359 at pp. 371, 372, holding that both Art. 48 EEC and Reg. 1612/68 are 'directly applicable'). Sometimes the Court even uses other terms (see e.g. Case 34/73 *Variola* [1973] ECR 981 at p. 990 and Case 65/75 *Tasca* [1976] ECR 291 at p. 308, both stating that a regulation has 'immediate effect'). In some cases the inconsistency—at least in the English version—clearly results from divergent translations of the same text (see e.g. Case 34/73 *Variola*, above, at p. 990, where the Court refers to the 'direct applicability' inherent in regulations and other rules of Community law. When the Court cites this passage in Case 50/76 *Amsterdam Bulb* [1977] ECR 137 at p. 146, the term 'direct effect' appears instead of 'direct applicability').

It is submitted that in spite of this seeming terminological confusion the following distinction can properly be made between the concepts of direct applicability and direct effect. The term 'directly applicable' as defined above should be applied to regulations alone. As far as the Treaty is concerned, the use of the term is clearly inappropriate. As an instrument of international law, the Treaty was required to be ratified before it could enter into force (Art. 247). Prior to ratification, the Treaty was applicable neither directly nor indirectly. Following ratification and entry into force, it 'became an integral part of the legal systems of the Member States' (Case 6/64 *Costa* [1964] ECR 585 at p. 593; see also Cases 9 and 58/65 *San Michele* v. *HA* [1967] ECR 1 at pp. 29–30, Order in Case 9/65), and therefore binding on, or applicable to, the Member States under general international law *and* their respective internal organs under its own law, in particular under Art. 5 EEC. No further measures were required to make its provisions internally binding (the necessary measures having already been taken prior to or as part of the ratification process) although in some instances implementing acts (by the institutions and/or by the Member States) were clearly necessary to make them more specific. In addition to being binding on the Member States and their various organs, the ECJ also established by way of Treaty interpretation that some of its provisions were capable of creating enforceable rights in favour of individuals or, to use the terminology that appears in the majority of cases, 'capable of producing direct effects in the legal relationship between Member States and their subjects' (see e.g. Case 26/62 *Van Gend en Loos* [1963] ECR 1 at p. 13). To refer to this ability of the Treaty as 'direct applicability' would be to attribute to the latter term a meaning which is different from that which it was intended to have under Art. 189. It is to avoid the confusion that might arise from one term having two different meanings that the use of 'direct effect' alone is suggested in the context of the Treaty.

As regards directives (and the same considerations would seem to apply to decisions addressed to Member States), these can never be 'directly applicable' since by definition they always require further measures of implementation (or transformation) to become part of national law. If they are properly implemented, they reach individuals through the implementing measures only. If they are not correctly implemented, or not implemented by the prescribed time-limit, they may produce 'direct effects' for individuals in the form of enforceable rights (but not obligations), although the legal basis of the direct effect is not the direct applicability of the directive/decision but the default of the Member State in performing its obligation arising from the Treaty. By contrast, the legal basis of the direct effect of a regulation is always its direct applicability which in turn follows from Art. 189 (see, in particular, the opinion of A.-G. Reischl in Case 148/78 *Ratti* [1979] ECR 1629 at pp. 1650–3, and the opinions of A.-G. Warner in Case 38/77 *Enka* [1977] ECR 2203 at p. 2226 and in Case 131/79 *Santillo* [1980] ECR 1585 at pp. 1608–11. *See further under* **Directive**).

To sum up:

(*a*) certain provisions of the EEC Treaty may have direct effects, without the question arising whether or not they are directly applicable;

(*b*) regulations are by definition always directly applicable and may, in consequence, produce direct effects;

(*c*) directives and decisions addressed to Member States are by definition never directly applicable although they may have direct effects; the legal basis of their direct effect is different from that of regulations;

(*d*) the question whether a provision of the Treaty or of a regulation, directive, or decision is capable of producing direct effect is always a matter of judicial interpretation and depends, in each case, on the nature, general scheme, and wording of the provision concerned.

See also **Decision, Direct effect, Directive, Regulation.**

Further reading: Winter, 'Direct Applicability and Direct Effect: Two Distinct and Different Concepts in Community Law' (1972) 9 *CML Rev.* 425. *See also under* **Direct effect, Directive.**

▶ **DIRECT CONCERN** One of two prerequisites (the other being individual concern) for the institution of annulment proceedings before the ECJ by a private individual (a natural or legal person) under the EEC/Euratom Treaties against a decision or other binding measure which is addressed to another person or taken in the form of a regulation (Arts. 173(2) EEC, 146(2) Euratom). In challenging such a measure, a private individual has *locus standi* only if he can prove that the measure is of 'direct and individual concern' to him.

As interpreted by the ECJ, a measure not addressed to a person is of direct concern to him if it constitutes 'a complete set of rules which are sufficient in themselves and which require no implementing provisions, since [their implementation] is automatic and leaves no room for any discretion' (Case 294/83 *Les Verts* v. *Parliament* [1986] ECR 1339 at p. 1367). In other words, the measure must produce immediate, automatic, and inevitable (not merely possible) disadvantageous legal effects upon the person. Such will be the case only if neither the addressee nor any other person is in a position to interpose his own autonomous power of decision between the measure and the results that follow from it. Accordingly, where a decision is addressed to a Member State or taken in the form of a regulation, private individuals will not be directly concerned by it if the decision leaves any margin of discretion to the Member State in the matter of implementation. In such a case, it is only the implementing national measure, and not the Community act, that will produce direct legal effects for individuals (see e.g. Case 222/83 *Municipality of Differdange* v. *Commission* [1984] ECR 2889 at pp. 2896–7; Case 333/85 *Mannesmann-Röhrenwerke* v. *Council* [1987] ECR 1381 at p. 1410). This is the position, in particular, where the Community act is not mandatory but merely enabling, i.e. contains an authorization of which the Member State is entirely free to avail itself or not, or contains a refusal to grant an authorization. Thus, in Case 69/69 *Alcan* v. *Commission* [1970] ECR 385 at pp. 393–4 the Court held that the applicants, three Belgian firms which imported and refined aluminium, were not directly concerned by a Commission decision refusing to authorize Belgium to open a tariff quota for unwrought aluminium. The Court said that even if the authorization had been granted, it would not have conferred enforceable rights upon the applicants as Belgium was free to make use, or not to make use, of it. For similar reasons in Cases 103 to 109/78 *Société des Usines de Beauport* v. *Council* [1979] ECR 17 at p. 25 the applicants, sugar producers in Guadeloupe and Martinique, were found not to be directly concerned by a Council regulation enabling France to reduce the basic quotas for sugar.

By contrast, a Community decision addressed to a Member State or taken in the form of a regulation will directly concern individuals where it leaves no discretion to the Member State in the matter of implementation so that implementation by the national agencies is purely and entirely automatic. Thus, in Cases 41 to 44/70 *International Fruit Company* v. *Commission* [1971] ECR 411 at pp. 422–3 the Court held that a Commission decision taken in the form of a regulation, laying down the conditions for the grant of import licences for table apples, was of direct concern to the applicants since the national authorities were required to issue or to refuse to issue import licences by mechanically applying those conditions, without having any independent power of evaluation or decision. (See also Case 92/78 *Simmenthal* v. *Commission* [1979] ECR 777 at pp. 797–8; Case 113/77 *Toyo Bearing* v. *Council* [1979] ECR 1185 at p. 1205; Cases 239 and 275/82 *Allied Corporation* v. *Commission* [1984] ECR 1005 at p. 1030; etc.)

The position is the same where a Member State, although given a discretionary power, had already exercised that power, or had already committed itself to exercise that power in a certain way, before the Community decision was taken and the decision does no more than merely confirm or authorize the national measure. Thus, in Cases 106 and 107/63 *Toepfer* v. *Commission* [1965] ECR 405 at p. 411 the Court held that a Commission decision retroactively confirming protective measures taken by Germany regarding import of maize was of direct concern to certain importers, including the applicants, since it simply validated a measure already taken, i.e. a discretion already exercised. In Case 62/70 *Bock* v. *Commission* [1971] ECR 897 at p. 908 the Court held that the applicant, a German importer, was directly concerned by a Commission decision authorizing Germany to exclude from Community treatment mushrooms originating in China and already in free circulation in the Benelux countries. Although in theory Germany was free to make use or not to make use of the authorization, the German authorities had already informed the applicant that they would reject its application for an import licence as soon as the Commission had granted them the requisite authorization. They had requested that authorization precisely with reference to the applications already pending before them at that time. This established the applicant's direct concern in the matter. In Case 11/82 *Piraiki-Patraiki* v. *Commission* [1985] ECR 207 at pp. 241–2 the Court went considerably further by accepting that a Commission decision authorizing France to impose a quota system on imports of cotton yarn from Greece under Art. 130 of the Act of Accession 1979 was of direct concern to the applicants. The reason was simply that in the circumstances of the case the possibility that France might decide not to make use of the authorization granted to it (which, in the absence of any advance commitment, she was free to do) was 'entirely theoretical, since there could be no doubt as to the intention of the French authorities to apply the decision'. This ruling may indicate a change in the Court's case-law towards a more relaxed interpretation of the requirement of direct concern. (See also Case 730/79 *Philip Morris* v. *Commission* [1980] ECR 2671 at p. 2687, where a potential recipient of a proposed investment aid was able to challenge a Commission decision refusing to approve the aid, and Case 169/84 *COFAZ* v. *Commission* [1986] ECR 391 at p. 416, where a decision whereby the Commission terminated a State aid procedure initiated under Art. 93(2) EEC against the Netherlands was held to be of direct concern to certain French undertakings which were in competition with the recipients of the aid.)

The criteria for establishing direct concern are essentially the same also in cases where the decision is addressed not to a Member State, but to another natural or legal person. Thus, in Case 26/76 *Metro* v. *Commission* [1977] ECR 1875 at p. 1901 *per Curiam*, p. 1922 *per* A.-G. Reischl, the Court held that a Commission decision granting an undertaking exemption under Art. 85(3) EEC in respect of a selective distribution system was of direct concern to another undertaking against which the system was applied in practice and which had made a complaint to the Commission under Art. 3(2)(b) of Reg. 17. (See also Cases 228 and 229/82 *Ford* v. *Commission* [1984] ECR 1129 at p. 1159 and Case 75/84 *Metro* v. *Commission* [1986] ECR 3021 at pp. 3079–80.) However, the mere fact that by conferring certain advantages (e.g. aid) on certain undertakings only a decision is likely to influence existing conditions of competition in the relevant market is not sufficient for every

165

market participant having a competitive relationship with the addressee to be regarded as being directly and individually concerned (see e.g. Cases 10 and 18/68 *Eridania* v. *Commission* [1969] ECR 459 at pp. 480–2, where the Court dismissed as inadmissible applications by certain Italian sugar refineries for the annulment of three Commission decisions granting aid to other refineries from the European Agricultural Guidance and Guarantee Fund).

(For comprehensive lists of cases in which the ECJ has so far established the existence of direct concern, *see* **Action for annulment.**)

See also **Action for annulment, Individual concern.**

Further reading: Barav, 'Direct and Individual Concern: An Almost Insurmountable Barrier to the Admissibility of Individual Appeal to the EEC Court' (1974) 11 *CML Rev.* 191. *See also under* **Action for annulment.**

▶ **DIRECT EFFECT** Concept developed by the ECJ to determine the effects of Community law within the domestic legal systems of the Member States. It implies that certain provisions of the EEC Treaty, of the acts of the institutions, and of Treaties concluded by the EEC with third countries are capable of producing legal effects in the Member States without the need for any implementing measures, in the sense of conferring rights and in some cases imposing obligations upon individuals which are enforceable in the national courts. These rights and obligations may arise in legal relationships between individuals and Member States ('vertical direct effect'), or between individuals *inter se* ('horizontal direct effect'). Provisions which are not directly effective can give rise to enforceable individual rights and obligations only through further implementing measures taken by the Community institutions or the national authorities, or both.

To some extent the concept of direct effect raises different problems, and is subject to different considerations, in the context of the EEC Treaty, the acts of the institutions, and treaties concluded with third countries. These are discussed below in turn.

1. The question whether certain provisions of the **EEC Treaty,** an international agreement concluded between sovereign States, were capable of producing enforceable rights in favour of individuals was first raised in Case 26/62 *Van Gend en Loos* [1963] ECR 1. In that case the ECJ stated that the answer to that question depended on the 'spirit, the general scheme and the wording' of those provisions (ibid. at p. 12). The Court pointed out that since the objective of the EEC Treaty was to establish a Common Market of direct concern to the private citizen, it amounted to more than a set of mutual obligations between the contracting States only. In contrast to ordinary treaties, the EEC Treaty set up a Community which constituted 'a new legal order of international law for the benefit of which the States have limited their sovereign rights, albeit within limited fields, and the subjects of which comprise not only Member States but also their nationals. Independently of the legislation of Member States, Community law therefore not only imposes obligations on individuals but is also intended to confer upon them rights which become part of their legal heritage. These rights arise not only where

they are expressly granted by the Treaty, but also by reason of obligations which the Treaty imposes in a clearly defined way upon individuals as well as upon the Member States and upon the institutions of the Community' (ibid.).

Regarding the general scheme and the wording of the provision the direct effect of which was in question (Art. 12 EEC), the Court observed that it contained a 'clear and unconditional prohibition' which was 'not a positive but a negative obligation' in that it required Member States to refrain from introducing any new customs duties and from increasing existing ones. This obligation was not qualified by any reservation and its implementation was not conditional upon any legislative measure to be enacted under national law. Therefore, the Court concluded that 'the very nature of this prohibition makes it ideally adapted to produce direct effects in the legal relationship between Member States and their subjects' in the sense of 'creating individual rights which national courts must protect' (ibid. at p. 13). These rights were in fact a necessary counterpart or corollary of the obligation imposed by Art. 12 on the Member States. As a result, where Member States introduced or increased customs duties contrary to Art. 12, any interested individual might challenge such duties before the competent national courts which were required to give effect to the Treaty.

The full implications of the concept of direct effect were subsequently explained by the Court in Case 106/77 *Simmenthal* [1978] ECR 629 at p. 643. In that case the Court stated that direct effect means that 'rules of Community law must be fully and uniformly applied in all the Member States from the date of their entry into force and for so long as they continue in force. These provisions are therefore a direct source of rights and duties for all those affected thereby, whether Member States or individuals, who are parties to legal relationships under Community law. This consequence also concerns any national court whose task it is as an organ of a Member State to protect, in a case within its jurisdiction, the rights conferred upon individuals by Community law.' Then, referring to the principle of the precedence or supremacy of Community law, the Court pointed out that the relationship between directly effective provisions of Community law and the national law of the Member States is such that the former 'not only by their entry into force render automatically inapplicable any conflicting provision of current national law but—in so far as they are an integral part of, and take precedence in, the legal order applicable in the territory of each of the Member States—also preclude the valid adoption of new national legislative measures to the extent to which they would be incompatible with Community provisions.'

Nevertheless, the Court has also made it clear that although the directly effective provisions of the Treaty must be applied by all the authorities of the Member States without national implementing measures, the right of individuals to rely on these provisions before national courts is only a minimum guarantee. It is not sufficient in itself to ensure the full and complete implementation of the Treaty. Consequently, in order to avoid any ambiguity and uncertainty, Member States are obliged to amend provisions of national law which are incompatible with a provision of the Treaty even if the latter is

167

directly effective (see Case 168/85 *Commission* v. *Italy* [1986] ECR 2945 at pp. 2960–1 and the cases cited therein).

The doctrine of direct effect, as formulated in the above decisions and refined in a number of other cases (see below), forms one of the two essential foundations of Community law as a supranational legal system (the other being the closely related doctrine of the supremacy of Community law). Its importance lies in the fact that:

- it enables legal provisions of an extraneous, i.e. Community origin automatically to penetrate into and form an integral part of national law;
- it ensures the full and uniform application of Community law in all the Member States;
- it makes the individual a subject of Community law alongside the Member States by creating substantive rights and obligations for him;
- it increases the legal protection of individuals by ensuring them access to the national courts and remedies in matters governed by Community law;
- it prevents conflicting national measures being applied to them.

The EEC Treaty itself contains only a relatively few provisions which may be said, without any doubt, to have been intended to create a direct relationship between Community law and the individual (see Arts. 85, 86, 187, 189, 191, and 192 EEC) or which expressly call upon the national authorities, including the courts, to co-operate with the Community institutions in the application and enforcement of Community law (see Arts. 88, 177, 187, 192 EEC; Arts. 26 and 27 EEC Statute). For the most part, it is therefore a matter of Treaty interpretation to establish whether a particular provision is capable of producing direct effect. This task falls within the exclusive jurisdiction of the ECJ (see e.g. Case 2/74 *Reyners* [1974] ECR 631 at p. 659 *per* A.-G. Mayras), whose decision on the matter must be regarded as definitive (see e.g. Case 41/74 *Van Duyn* [1974] ECR 1337 at pp. 1354–5 *per* A.-G. Mayras). The legal nature of a directly effective provision, once established, cannot change and is therefore no longer subject to successful challenge even if its application may give rise to certain difficulties in the Member States (see e.g. Case 28/67 *Molkerei-Zentrale Westfalen* [1968] ECR 143 at p. 154; Case 13/68 *Salgoil* [1968] ECR 453 at p. 462). The judgment of the Court establishing direct effect has retroactive application in the sense that the provision to which it relates must be regarded as having produced direct effects from the time of its coming into force. The Court may restrict this retroactive effect only in exceptional circumstances (see Case 43/75 *Defrenne* [1976] ECR 455 at pp. 480–1 as interpreted and applied in Case 61/79 *Denkavit Italiana* [1980] ECR 1205 at pp. 1223–4 and in Cases 66, 127, and 128/79 *Salumi* [1980] ECR 1237 at pp. 1260–1).

The question whether a particular provision of the EEC Treaty can produce direct effect depends on the nature and wording of that provision and its place in the general scheme of the Treaty. According to the case-law of the ECJ, a provision must satisfy the following three requirements before it

may be regarded as being directly effective (see in general the opinions of
A.-G. Mayras in Case 2/74 *Reyners*, above, at pp. 659–63 and in Case 41/74
Van Duyn, above, at p. 1354).

First, it must be sufficiently clear and precise, imposing on the Member
States an obligation the scope of which is perfectly determined. This is usually
the case where the obligation is a 'negative' one, i.e. an obligation to refrain
from doing something, a prohibition. Such are the so-called 'stand-still
provisions' of the EEC Treaty. These prohibit the introduction of new
measures which are more restrictive or more discriminatory than those which
had already been in force in the Member States at the time of the coming into
force of the Treaty. Thus, the ECJ has confirmed the direct effect of all of the
following stand-still provisions as from 1 January 1958, the date on which
the EEC Treaty came into force:

- Art. 12: elimination of customs duties (see e.g. Case 26/62 *Van Gend en
  Loos*, above, at pp. 12–13);
- Arts. 31 and 32(1): elimination of quantitative restrictions (see e.g. Case
  13/68 *Salgoil*, above, at pp. 460–1);
- Art. 37(2): adjustment of State commercial monopolies (see e.g. Case
  6/64 *Costa* [1964] ECR 585 at pp. 597–8);
- Art. 53: freedom of establishment (see e.g. Case 6/64 *Costa*, above, at
  pp. 596–7);
- Art. 93(3) (last sentence): State aids (see e.g. Case 6/64 *Costa*, above, at
  p. 596);
- Art. 95(1): discriminatory taxation (see e.g. Case 57/65 *Lütticke* [1966]
  ECR 205 at p. 210);
- Art. 95(2): protective taxation (see e.g. Case 27/67 *Fink-Frucht* [1968]
  ECR 223 at pp. 231–2).

Provisions imposing a 'positive' obligation, i.e. a duty to abolish existing
restrictions and discriminations or to repeal or amend national provisions
which conflict with Community rules, may also produce direct effects if the
Member States have no discretion as to the date by which such obligation
must be performed. Upon the expiry of the date set, the 'positive' obligation
in fact transforms itself into a 'negative' obligation, i.e. a prohibition on the
imposition of the restrictions or discriminations which were to be abolished
(even if they were not). As from that date, individuals may directly enforce the
Treaty provisions themselves in the national courts. The ECJ has declared the
following provisions falling within this category to be directly effective as
from the dates indicated:

- Art. 13(2): abolition of charges having equivalent effect to customs
  duties on imports, as from 1 January 1970 (see e.g. Case 33/70 *SACE*
  [1970] ECR 1213 at p. 1222);
- Art. 16: abolition of customs duties on exports and charges having
  equivalent effect as from 1 January 1962 (see e.g. Case 18/71 *Eunomia*
  [1971] ECR 811 at p. 816);
- Art. 48: freedom of movement for workers, as from 1 January 1970 (see

169

e.g. Case 167/73 *Commission* v. *France* [1974] ECR 359 at p. 371; Case 41/74 *Van Duyn*, above, at p. 1347);

- Art. 95(3): elimination of discriminatory taxation, as from 1 January 1962 (see e.g. Case 57/65 *Lütticke*, above, at pp. 210–11);
- Art. 119: equal pay for equal work, as from 1 January 1962 (within certain areas only, see Case 43/75 *Defrenne*, above, at pp. 471–81).

The above considerations apply *a fortiori* to the expiry of the transitional period which, by virtue of a mandatory provision of the Treaty (Art. 8(7) EEC), constituted the latest date by which all the rules laid down in the Treaty had to enter into force and all the measures required for establishing the Common Market had to be implemented. Thus, the ECJ has confirmed that the following provisions became directly effective on 1 January 1970, as a result of the expiry of the transitional period on 31 December 1969:

- Art. 9: prohibition of customs duties and charges having equivalent effect, in general (see e.g. Case 251/78 *Denkavit* [1979] ECR 3369 at p. 3384);
- Art. 30: prohibition of quantitative restrictions on imports and measures having equivalent effect (see e.g. Case 74/76 *Iannelli* [1977] ECR 557 at p. 575);
- Art. 37(1): adjustment of State commercial monopolies (see e.g. Case 59/75 *Manghera* [1976] ECR 91 at p. 101);
- Art. 52: freedom of establishment (see e.g. Case 2/74 *Reyners*, above, at pp. 651–2);
- Arts. 59(1) and 60(3): freedom to provide services (see e.g. Case 33/74 *Van Binsbergen* [1974] ECR 1299 at pp. 1310–12).

In contrast with the above provisions, obligations which the Member States have undertaken unequivocally towards the Community only, e.g. the obligation to consult or to inform the Commission before taking certain measures, are binding upon them solely as States in their relationship with the Community and do not create individual rights which the national courts must protect (see Case 174/84 *Bulk Oil* [1986] ECR 559 at p. 594). For this reason, the ECJ has declared the following provisions not to be directly effective:

- Art. 92(1): State aids (unless implemented under Arts. 93(2) or 94, see e.g. Case 77/72 *Capolongo* [1973] ECR 611 at pp. 621–2; Case 74/76 *Iannelli*, above, at pp. 574–5);
- Art. 93: State aids (except the last sentence of Art. 93(3), see e.g. Case 6/64 *Costa*, above, at pp. 595–6);
- Art. 102: approximation of laws (see e.g. Case 6/64 *Costa*, above, at p. 595).

Also, obligations which, not being sufficiently precise in scope or as to the methods applicable or make several alternative solutions possible, usually enable Member States to exercise such a measure of discretion in performing them as to prevent direct effect wholly or in part. The ECJ has held the following provisions to fall within this category:

- Arts. 32(2) (last sentence) and 33: elimination of quantitative restrictions (see e.g. Case 13/68 *Salgoil*, above, at p. 461);
- Art. 97: discriminatory or protective taxation (see e.g. Case 57/65 *Lütticke*, above, at p. 211; Case 28/67 *Molkerei-Zentrale Westfalen*, above, at pp. 155–6).

The foregoing considerations apply also to the introductory provisions of the EEC Treaty which lay down the fundamental principles and objectives of the Community (Arts. 2, 3, 5, 6, and 7). On account of their general wording, they impose on the Member States general obligations only, the precise content and extent of which can only be ascertained from the subsequent, more detailed provisions of the Treaty which give effect to, and must be interpreted in the light of, these principles and objectives. While clearly amounting to more than a mere non-binding general programme (see e.g. Case 6/72 *Continental Can* v. *Commission* [1973] ECR 215 at p. 244), the introductory Articles do not contain in themselves sufficiently clear and specific legal rules and legal consequences to give rise to subjective rights in favour of individuals. For this reason, the following provisions have been held not to produce direct effects:

- Arts. 2, 3(f), and 5 (see Case 155/73 *Sacchi* [1974] ECR 409 at p. 435 *per* A.-G. Reischl; Case 31/74 *Galli* [1975] ECR 47 at pp. 60 *et seq. per Curiam*, pp. 71–2 *per* A.-G. Warner; Case 126/86 *Giménez Zaera* [1987] ECR 3697 at pp. 3715–16);
- Art. 5 (see Case 78/70 *Deutsche Grammophon* [1971] ECR 487 at p. 499; Case 44/84 *Hurd* [1986] ECR 29 at p. 83);
- Arts. 5, 40(3), and 98 (except in conjunction with implementing regulations, see Case 2/73 *Geddo* [1973] ECR 865 at pp. 878–9);
- Art. 7 (except in conjunction with particular provisions of the Treaty, such as e.g. Arts. 48, 52, 59(1), or 60(3), or of acts of institutions, which are clearly intended to implement the general rule of non-discrimination, see e.g. Case 2/74 *Reyners*, above, at pp. 650–2; Case 36/74 *Walrave* [1974] ECR 1405 at pp. 1420–1; Case 13/76 *Donà* [1976] ECR 1333 at p. 1341; Case 1/78 *Kenny* [1978] ECR 1489 at pp. 1496–7. However, in Case 29/84 *Commission* v. *Germany* [1985] ECR 1661 at p. 1675 the Court referred to the direct effect of the 'Community principle of non-discrimination on grounds of nationality', and in Case 24/86 *Blaizot* [1988] ECR 379 at p. 407 to the direct effect of Art. 7 EEC).

A second requirement for direct effect is that the provision concerned must impose an unconditional obligation, the implementation of which is not subject to any exception or reservation on the part of the Member States (see the cases cited above establishing the direct effect of various Treaty Articles). This requirement is not met where a provision merely authorizes, rather than obligates, Member States to do something, or lays down an objective as opposed to a legal rule, thus giving them a discretion or choice of which they may or may not avail themselves. Such a provision implies the interposition between the Community rule and its implementation of further discretionary measures, which excludes the direct effect of the provision. The proper use of

171

the power made available to the Member States is subject to the Commission's supervision at Community level which further precludes the possibility of its being challenged in the national courts. The same applies where the implementation of a provision depends on an assessment of the requirements and interests of the Community or of the economic and monetary policies of the Member States, which assessment, too, is a matter for the Community institutions rather than for the national courts. For these reasons, the ECJ has declared the following provisions not to be directly effective:

- Arts. 5 and 107: balance of payments (see Case 9/73 *Schlüter* [1973] ECR 1135 at pp. 1160–1);
- Arts. 67(1) and 71: freedom of movement for capital (see Case 203/80 *Casati* [1981] ECR 2595 at pp. 2613–16);
- Art. 90(2): public undertakings (see Case 10/71 *Muller* [1971] ECR 723 at p. 730);
- Art. 97: discriminatory or protective taxation (see e.g. Case 28/67 *Molkerei-Zentrale Westfalen*, above, at pp. 155–6; Case 25/67 *Milch-, Fett- und Eier-Kontor* [1968] ECR 207 at pp. 217–18);
- Art. 220: negotiation of certain conventions (see Case 137/84 *Mutsch* [1985] ECR 2681 at pp. 2694–5).

A third condition for direct effect is that the provision in question must be self-sufficient and legally complete so that no action is required on the part either of the Community institutions or of the Member States for its implementation or its entry into force (see the cases cited above establishing the direct effect of various Treaty Articles). Strictly speaking, it should follow from this requirement that a provision cannot be considered to be directly effective where its implementation is expressly made subject by the Treaty to measures to be taken by the Community institutions (see e.g. Art. 48 in conjunction with 49, Art. 52 in conjunction with 54 and 57, Arts. 59 and 60 in conjunction with 63 and 66) or by the Member States (see e.g. Art. 37(1)). If, however, the provision imposes an obligation to attain a precise result by a particular date, e.g. by the end of the transitional period, upon the expiry of that period the provision becomes legally complete and unconditional and thus directly effective, even in the absence of the implementing measures. These measures now become legally superfluous, although from a practical point of view they may still be useful (see in particular Case 2/74 *Reyners*, above, at pp. 648–52; Case 48/75 *Royer* [1976] ECR 497 at pp. 511–12; Case 11/77 *Patrick* [1977] ECR 1199 at pp. 1204–6, dealing with Arts. 48, 52, 59 EEC). Thus, in particular, all the provisions of the Treaty requiring the Member States to abolish all discrimination based on nationality within a specified period became directly effective upon the expiry of that period (see the cases cited above in connection with the expiry of the transitional period).

The concept of direct effect can operate not only in the relationship between the Member States and individuals, but also between individuals themselves (the so-called 'horizontal direct effect'). Thus, the ECJ has confirmed that the following provisions of the Treaty are capable of creating directly enforceable rights, obligations, and prohibitions in relations between individuals to which the national courts must give effect:

- Art. 7 in conjunction with Arts. 48–51 or Arts. 59–66: prohibition of discrimination on grounds of nationality in respect of employed persons and persons providing services (see Case 36/74 *Walrave*, above, at pp. 1418–19; Case 13/76 *Donà*, above, at p. 1341);
- Art. 30: prohibition of quantitative restrictions on imports and measures having equivalent effect (see Case 58/80 *Dansk Supermarked* [1981] ECR 181 at p. 195);
- Arts. 85(1), 85(2), and 86: competition rules (see Case 48/72 *Brasserie de Haecht* [1973] ECR 77 at p. 86; Case 127/73 *BRT* [1974] ECR 51 at p. 62; Case 155/73 *Sacchi*, above, at p. 430; Case 37/79 *Marty* [1980] ECR 2481 at p. 2500);
- Art. 119: prohibition of discrimination on grounds of sex: equal pay for equal work (see Case 43/75 *Defrenne*, above, at p. 476).

2. In addition to the EEC Treaty, the binding **acts of the institutions** or any particular provision of such acts can also produce direct effects if they satisfy the criteria which the Court established in respect of the Treaty. Thus, a provision is directly effective if it lays down a clear and precise obligation which is not subject to any reservation or condition and which does not require the intervention of any further act on the part of either the Community institutions or the Member States (*see further under* **Decision, Directive, Regulation**).

3. The question whether **treaties concluded by the EEC with third countries** are capable of having direct effect within the Member States raises complex issues of the relationship between public international law, European Community law, and national law. In his opinion in Cases 21 to 24/72 *International Fruit Company* [1972] ECR 1219 at p. 1235 A.-G. Mayras submitted that the concept of direct effect, which is applied in the relationship between Community law and national law, should in principle also be applied in the relationship between international law and Community law. It appears from the case-law of the ECJ itself that the answer to the question whether a Community treaty may produce direct effect depends on two factors. First, the nature, subject-matter, and wording of the treaty concerned as a whole, and secondly, the nature, structure, and wording of the particular provision the direct effect of which is in question. As regards the former, Community treaties in general have a 'dual nature'. Although governed by public international law, they also form an 'integral part' of the Community legal system (see Case 181/73 *Haegeman* [1974] ECR 449 at pp. 459–60). According to Art. 228(2) EEC, they are binding on both the Community institutions and the Member States, which are equally responsible for their proper performance. The Court deduced from this that 'it follows from the Community nature of such [treaties] that their effect in the Community may not be allowed to vary according to whether their application is in practice the responsibility of the Community institutions or of the Member States and, in the latter case, according to the effects in the internal legal order of each

173

Member State which the law of that State assigns to international agreements concluded by it. Therefore it is for the Court, within the framework of its jurisdiction in interpreting the provisions of agreements, to ensure their uniform application throughout the Community' (Case 104/81 *Kupferberg* [1982] ECR 3641 at pp. 3662–3, dealing with the Free Trade Agreement between the EEC and Portugal of 1972, see below). The Court concluded that treaties entered into by the Community may in principle have direct effect within a Member State even if treaties in general cannot, according to the law of that State, normally produce such effect. It is for the ECJ to decide this issue, but only if the treaty itself is silent on this point. The fact that a treaty set up a special institutional framework for consultations and negotiations in relation to its own performance, or that it did not create complete reciprocity between the obligations of all the parties, does not in itself prevent it from having direct effect. Nor does it make any difference whether the treaty is concluded and incorporated in Community law by means of a regulation or a decision of the Council (ibid. at pp. 3663–5; see also Case 87/75 *Bresciani* [1976] ECR 129 at pp. 139–42 dealing with the First Yaoundé Convention of 1963, see below), or whether it is concluded in the form of a 'mixed agreement' involving the participation of the Member States (ibid.; Case 12/86 *Demirel* [1987] ECR 3719 at pp. 3752–4, where the Court did not exclude the direct effect of the Association Agreement between the EEC and Turkey of 1963 on the ground that it was a mixed agreement, although certain provisions of the Agreement were found not to have direct effect on other grounds, see below).

As regards the nature, structure, and wording of the particular provision in question, it is capable of producing direct effects if it contains 'a clear and precise obligation' which is 'not subject, in its implementation or effects, to the adoption of any subsequent measure' or to any implied or express reservation (Case 17/81 *Pabst & Richarz* [1982] ECR 1331 at p. 1350 dealing with the Association Agreement between the EEC and Greece of 1961; Case 12/86 *Demirel*, above, at p. 3752. See also the two cases cited immediately above).

On the basis of these twofold considerations, the ECJ has so far confirmed the (vertical) direct effect of the following provisions:

- Art. 2(1) of the First Yaoundé Convention of 1963, providing for the abolition of customs duties and charges having equivalent effect in respect of goods imported from the Associated States into the Member States and expressly referring to Art. 13 EEC, as from 1 January 1970 (Case 87/75 *Bresciani*, above, at pp. 141–2);
- Art. 53(1) of the Association Agreement between the EEC and Greece of 1961, prohibiting discriminatory or protective taxation in terms similar to those of Art. 95 EEC, as from the beginning of the third year after the entry into force of the Agreement (Case 17/81 *Pabst & Richarz*, above, at p. 1350);
- Art. 21 of the Free Trade Agreement between the EEC and Portugal of 1972, prohibiting discriminatory taxation in terms somewhat different from those of Art. 95 EEC (Case 104/81 *Kupferberg*, above, at p. 3665).

On the other hand, the ECJ has held that the following provisions of the General Agreement on Tariffs and Trade (GATT) are not capable of producing direct effect, partly because GATT is based on the principle of negotiations undertaken on a reciprocal and mutually advantageous basis, and partly because of the great flexibility of its provisions, especially those concerning derogations, exceptional measures, and the settlement of disputes:

- Art. II (Case 9/73 *Schlüter*, above, at pp. 1157–8);
- Arts. II, III, VI, and VIII (Cases 267 to 269/81 *SPI and SAMI* [1983] ECR 801 at p. 830);
- Art. V (Case 266/81 *SIOT* [1983] ECR 731 at p. 780);
- Art. XI (Cases 21 to 24/72 *International Fruit Company*, above, at pp. 1227–8).

Likewise, the ECJ has ruled that Art. 12 of the Association Agreement between the EEC and Turkey of 1963 and Art. 36 of the Additional Protocol of 1970, in conjunction with Art. 7 of the Agreement, being essentially in the nature of a programme and not being sufficiently precise and unconditional to regulate the movement of workers directly, are not capable of producing direct effects (Case 12/86 *Demirel*, above, at pp. 3753–4).

In the United Kingdom, the direct effect of Community law is ensured by section 2(1) of the European Communities Act 1972, which gives the force of law in the United Kingdom to all present and future, primary and secondary, Community provisions which under Community law are directly effective. By contrast, section 2(2) provides for subordinate legislation for the purpose of implementing Community provisions which are not directly effective but which create rights and obligations for the United Kingdom as a Member State. Although the Act frequently uses the term 'directly applicable Community provisions' (see sections 5(1), 6(4), 7(1) and (2), 10(1) and (2); Schedule 1, Part II, Schedule 4 paras. 3(2)(a), 9(1), and 10 (Sections 7(1) and (2), 10(1) and (2) have since been repealed)), it gives no definition of it, owing probably to the recognition that since that expression relates to a concept of Community law (presumably meaning 'directly effective Community provisions'), only Community law can define its meaning.

See also **Community Treaties, Decision, Direct applicability, Directive, Regulation, Supremacy of Community law, Transitional period.**

Further reading 1. BOOKS: Bebr, *Development of Judicial Control of the European Communities* (1981), ch. 13; Commission of the European Communities, *Thirty Years of Community Law* (1983), part I, ch. 6; Hartley, *The Foundations of European Community Law*, 2nd edn. (1988), chs. 7–8; Schermers, *Judicial Protection in the European Communities*, 4th edn. (1987), ch. 1, part III/D; Toth, *Legal Protection of Individuals in the European Communities* (1978), vol. i, ss. 104–5.

2. ARTICLES AND PAPERS: Bebr, 'Directly Applicable Provisions of Community Law: The Development of a Community Concept' (1970) 19 *ICLQ* 257; id., 'Agreements Concluded by the Community and their Possible Direct Effect: From International Fruit Company to Kupferberg' (1983) 20 *CML Rev.* 35; Collins, 'Remedies in the United Kingdom: Some Practical Problems of Direct Applicability', in Jacobs (ed.), *European Law and the Individual* (1976), p. 161; Dashwood, 'The Principle of Direct Effect in European Community Law' (1978) 16 *JCMS* 229;

Hartley, 'International Agreements and the Community Legal System: Some Recent Developments' (1983) 8 *EL Rev.* 383; Llavero, 'The Possible Direct Effect of the Provisions on Competition in the EEC–EFTA Free Trade Agreements in the Light of the Kupferberg Decision' (1984/2) *LIEI* 83; Pescatore, 'The Doctrine of "Direct Effect": An Infant Disease of Community Law' (1983) 8 *EL Rev.* 155; Schermers, 'The Direct Application of Treaties with Third States: Note Concerning the Polydor and Pabst Cases' (1982) 19 *CML Rev.* 563; Steiner, 'Direct Applicability in EEC Law: A Chameleon Concept' (1982) 98 *LQR* 229; Völker, 'The Direct Effect of International Agreements in the Community's Legal Order' (1983/1) *LIEI* 131; Weiss, 'Self Executing Treaties and Directly Applicable E.E.C. Law in French Courts' (1979/1) *LIEI* 51; Winter, 'Direct Applicability and Direct Effect: Two Distinct and Different Concepts in Community Law' (1972) 9 *CML Rev.* 425; Wyatt, 'Directly Applicable Provisions of EEC Law' (1975) 125 *NLJ* 458, 575, 669, 793; id., 'The Direct Effect of Community Social Law: Not Forgetting Directives' (1983) 8 *EL Rev.* 241.

▶ **DIRECTIVE** One of the binding acts which the Council and the Commission may adopt under the EEC and Euratom Treaties within the scope of secondary legislation. According to those Treaties, 'a directive shall be binding, as to the result to be achieved, upon each Member State to which it is addressed, but shall leave to the national authorities the choice of form and methods' (Arts. 189 EEC, 161 Euratom).

It follows from this definition that the legal nature of a directive is different from that of a regulation. Thus, while a regulation creates rights and obligations for Member States and individuals alike, and is applicable in the same way in all the Member States of the Community, a directive can only be addressed to, and therefore binding upon, (one, some, or all) Member States (Cases 188 to 190/80 *France, Italy and United Kingdom* v. *Commission* [1982] ECR 2545 at pp. 2573–4) but may not of itself impose obligations on individuals (Case 148/78 *Ratti* [1979] ECR 1629 at p. 1645; Case 152/84 *Marshall* [1986] ECR 723 at p. 749. See further below).

Moreover, while a regulation is binding in its entirety, a directive is only binding as to the result to be achieved, leaving the choice of form and methods to the national authorities. The main purpose of directives is, therefore, not to lay down uniform common rules applicable throughout the whole Community, but to call upon the Member States to exercise their own legislative powers either for the purpose of adapting their laws to common standards and requirements set by the institutions, or for the purpose of carrying out the obligations arising from the Treaties. Thus, one of the primary uses of directives is to approximate, co-ordinate, or harmonize national laws in areas where the diversity of those laws could adversely affect the establishment or functioning of the Common Market. These include the following: agriculture, insurance, energy, external trade, taxation, public contracts, monetary and financial matters, company law, transport, free movement of employed and self-employed persons and of services, production methods and characteristics of marketed products, customs legislation, statistics, etc. (see Arts. 43, 49, 54, 56, 57, 63, 66, 75, 99, 100, 101, 103, 112, 113, 213, 235 EEC. For detailed lists of harmonization directives adopted under the EEC Treaty, see

Suppls. 9/72 and 3/75—*Bull. EC*). Also, directives are often used to lay down time-limits and other provisions for the abolition by the Member States of restrictions on the free movement of goods, persons, services, and capital (see Arts. 10, 13, 14, 21, 33, 49, 54, 57, 63, 69, 70 EEC) and may also be employed in the fields of transport, competition law, taxation, and balance of payments (see Arts. 75, 87, 90, 97, 108 EEC). The Council may issue 'directives' to the Commission, for example concerning the negotiation of tariff and trade agreements with third countries (see Arts. 111 and 113 EEC). In general, Commission directives are of the same legal nature as those adopted by the Council. The ECJ has expressly rejected the argument that only Council directives may contain general legislative provisions, including the imposition of new obligations on Member States, while the directives of the Commission may merely lay down specific measures for one or more Member States (Cases 188 to 190/80 *France, Italy and United Kingdom* v. *Commission*, above, at p. 2573. *See further under* **Commission**, section II(2c)).

It also follows from·the above definition that directives always require the adoption of implementing measures by the Member States to which they are addressed. At the same time, they leave to the national authorities a certain degree of freedom in the matter of selecting those measures. They therefore both impose an obligation (i.e. to achieve a specific result) and grant a discretion (i.e. to decide how to achieve it). One of the most difficult problems arising in connection with directives is to determine the precise relationship between these two aspects, i.e. between the obligation and the discretion, the result and the choice of forms and methods. In a consistent line of cases, the ECJ has held that 'the choice of form and methods can only operate in compliance with the stipulations and prohibitions in Community law ... The Member States are consequently obliged to choose, within the bounds of the freedom left to them by Article 189, the most appropriate forms and methods to ensure the effective functioning of the directives, account being taken of their aims' (Case 48/75 *Royer* [1976] ECR 497 at p. 518; Case 14/83 *Von Colson and Kamann* [1984] ECR 1891 at p. 1906). Although each Member State is free to delegate powers for the purpose of implementing directives to its various domestic authorities, whether legislative or executive and whether central, regional, or local, that does not release it from the obligation to give effect to a directive by means of a legally binding provision if it is apparent from the nature, aim, and wording of the directive that it was meant to be transformed into binding national rules. It is therefore essential that 'each Member State should implement ... directives ... in a way which fully meets the requirements of clarity and certainty in legal situations which directives seek for the benefit of [those individuals concerned]. Mere administrative practices, which by their nature can be changed as and when the authorities please and which are not publicised widely enough cannot in these circumstances be regarded as a proper fulfilment of the obligation imposed by Article 189 on Member States to which the directives are addressed' (Case 102/79 *Commission* v. *Belgium* [1980] ECR 1473 at p. 1486; Case 96/81 *Commission* v. *Netherlands* [1982] ECR 1791 at pp. 1804–5; Case 160/82

177

Commission v. *Netherlands* [1982] ECR 4637 at p. 4642; Case 300/81 *Commission* v. *Italy* [1983] ECR 449 at p. 456; etc.).

Nevertheless, the implementation of a directive does not necessarily require legislative action in each Member State. Thus, no new legislation is needed where the law in force at the time when the directive becomes binding on a State already complies with its provisions (Case 131/79 *Santillo* [1980] ECR 1585 at p. 1611 *per* A.-G. Warner, referring to Case 21/78 *Delkvist* [1978] ECR 2327 at p. 2339). Also, the ECJ has pointed out that the existence of general principles of constitutional or administrative law may render implementation of specific legislation superfluous. This is, however, subject to the proviso that (1) those principles guarantee that the national authorities will in fact apply the directive fully; (2) where the directive is intended to create rights for individuals, the legal position arising from those principles is sufficiently precise and clear; (3) the persons concerned are made fully aware of their rights and, where appropriate, afforded the possibility of relying on them before the national courts. The last condition is of particular importance where the directive in question is intended to accord rights to the nationals of other Member States because those nationals are not normally aware of such principles (Case 29/84 *Commission* v. *Germany* [1985] ECR 1661 at p. 1673). Nevertheless, reliance on too broad and general principles of law may not guarantee compliance with a directive the provisions of which are of a precise and detailed nature (ibid. at p. 1675).

The fact that in certain circumstances a directive may produce direct effect in favour of individuals (see further below) does not exempt the Member States from their obligation to implement the directive by adopting positive measures. As the ECJ has observed, the right of individuals to rely in law on a directive against a Member State constitutes a 'minimum guarantee' and 'cannot justify a Member State's absolving itself from taking in due time implementing measures sufficient to meet the purpose of each directive' (Case 102/79 *Commission* v. *Belgium*, above, at p. 1487; Case 301/81 *Commission* v. *Belgium* [1983] ECR 467 at p. 478). Nor can the direct effect of a Community rule or principle be used to evade the obligation of implementation (Case 29/84 *Commission* v. *Germany*, above, at p. 1675).

To be effective, the implementing measures must be taken within the time-limit laid down by the directive. Compliance with these time-limits is particularly important since the existence of differences in the laws of the Member States following their expiry might result in discrimination. If they prove to be too short, the correct course of action for a Member State is to apply for their extension rather than commit a breach of a Community obligation by failing to implement (see e.g. Case 79/72 *Commission* v. *Italy* [1973] ECR 667 at p. 672; Case 52/75 *Commission* v. *Italy* [1976] ECR 277 at p. 284; Case 301/81 *Commission* v. *Belgium*, above, at p. 478). Such a failure cannot be justified by invoking domestic difficulties, practices, legal— or even constitutional—provisions, similar failures of other Member States (ibid.; Case 100/77 *Commission* v. *Italy* [1978] ECR 879 at p. 887; Case 102/79 *Commission* v. *Belgium*, above, at p. 1487; Case 160/82 *Commission* v. *Netherlands*, above, at p. 4642; etc.), or the argument that the failure to implement has had no adverse effect on the functioning of the Common Market (Case 95/77 *Commission* v. *Netherlands* [1978] ECR 863 at p. 871).

The contents and form of implementing measures depend, in each case, on the result which the directive is intended to achieve. Subject to the general requirement that 'Member States are obliged to ensure the full and exact application of the provisions of any directive' (Case 91/79 *Commission* v. *Italy* [1980] ECR 1099 at p. 1105), in some cases the national authorities may enjoy a fairly wide discretion in selecting the appropriate means for implementation (see e.g. Case 51/76 *Nederlandse Ondernemingen* [1977] ECR 113 at p. 125, interpreting the Second VAT Directive; Case 152/79 *Lee* [1980] ECR 1495 at pp. 1507–8, interpreting the directive on the modernization of farms; Case 8/81 *Becker* [1982] ECR 53 at p. 72, interpreting the Sixth VAT Directive; Case 163/82 *Commission* v. *Italy* [1983] ECR 3273 at pp. 3286–7 and Case 14/83 *Von Colson and Kamann*, above, at pp. 1907–9, both dealing with the implementation of the equal treatment directive).

In other cases, however, the provisions of a directive may be so detailed, and the result which it is intended to achieve so precise, that it leaves virtually no area of discretion to the Member States in the matter of implementation. Where, for example, a directive itself implements a regulation, its provisions may have to be given identical application in the whole Community (just like the provisions of the regulation), which can only be achieved if all the Member States implement it in exactly the same way. In such circumstances a directive, having general and uniform application, comes very close to a regulation (see e.g. Case 38/77 *Enka* [1977] ECR 2203 at pp. 2212–13, dealing with the directive on customs warehousing procedure; see also Case 5/84 *Direct Cosmetics* [1985] ECR 617 at p. 643, interpreting Art. 27 of the Sixth VAT Directive).

A directive is different from a regulation not only as regards its *legal nature*, but also as to its *legal effect* within the national legal systems of the Member States. By virtue of Art. 189 EEC, a regulation is always directly applicable and may therefore produce direct effect in the legal relations between Member States and individuals, or between individuals. By contrast, Art. 189 does not provide that a directive, too, shall be directly applicable, nor is a directive suited to be such since, as seen above, it always requires implementing measures by the Member States. For this reason, it was for a long time not clear whether a directive could also have direct effect in the sense of conferring rights (and perhaps even imposing obligations) upon individuals, which the national courts must protect and enforce. In a series of cases, however, the ECJ has clarified the position by stating that:

It would be incompatible with the binding effect attributed to a directive by Article 189 to exclude, in principle, the possibility that the obligation which it imposes may be invoked by those concerned. In particular, where the Community authorities have, by directive, imposed on Member States the obligation to pursue a particular course of conduct, the useful effect of such an act would be weakened if individuals were prevented from relying on it before their national courts and if the latter were prevented from taking it into consideration as an element of Community law ... It is necessary to examine, in every case, whether the nature, general scheme and wording of the provision in question are capable of having direct effects on the relations between Member States and individuals . . . [That is the case where] the provision lays down an obligation which is not subject to any exception or condition and which, by its very nature, does not require the intervention of any act on the part either of the institutions of the Community or of Member States. (Case 41/74 *Van Duyn* [1974] ECR 1337 at p. 1348. The Court has repeated this statement in most of the cases cited below.)

Subsequently, the Court recognized that individuals might invoke the provisions of a directive before a national court not only to enforce rights directly arising from the directive, but also 'in order that the [national court] shall rule whether the competent national authorities, in exercising the choice which is left to them as to the form and the methods for implementing the directive, have kept within the limits as to their discretion set out in the directive' (Case 51/76 *Nederlandse Ondernemingen*, above, at p. 127) or, to put it in another way, 'for the purpose of verifying whether the national measures adopted for its implementation are in accordance with it' (Case 38/77 *Enka*, above, at p. 2213). While the actual area of discretion itself (e.g. whether or not the legislative or administrative authorities have exercised the power to make derogations or exceptions authorized by the directive and the material contents of such derogations or exceptions) is not subject to judicial review, it is the duty of the national courts to determine whether the disputed implementing measure falls outside the margin of discretion (and cannot therefore be considered as a legitimate derogation or exception) (Case 51/76 *Nederlandse Ondernemingen*, above, at p. 127; see also Case 126/82 *Smit* [1983] ECR 73 at pp. 88–9).

While the above cases established that directives were in principle capable of having direct effect, two closely related questions still remained to be clarified. First, what was the basis of this direct effect? Secondly, did the direct effect of directives operate also as between individuals ('horizontal direct effect') and, in particular, could directives impose obligations upon individuals? The subsequent case-law of the Court has provided the answer to these questions.

Following the advice of various Advocates-General (see, in particular, the opinion of A.-G. Reischl in Case 148/78 *Ratti*, above, at pp. 1650–3, and the opinions of A.-G. Warner in Case 38/77 *Enka*, above, at p. 2226 and in Case 131/79 *Santillo*, above, at pp. 1608–11), the Court has gradually recognized that in the case of a directive the basis of direct effect is not direct applicability (thereby making an implicit distinction between the two concepts), but the failure of the Member State concerned to comply with the obligation to implement the directive correctly within the prescribed time-limit. Thus, in Case 148/78 *Ratti*, above, at p. 1642, the Court stated:

. . . a Member State which has not adopted the implementing measures required by the directive in the prescribed periods may not rely, as against individuals, on its own failure to perform the obligations which the directive entails. . . . Therefore . . . *after the expiration of the period fixed for the implementation of a directive* a Member State may not apply its internal law—even if it is provided with penal sanctions—which has not yet been adapted in compliance with the directive, to a person who has complied with the requirements of the directive. (emphasis added)

On the other hand, where that period has not yet expired and the Member State may still comply with its obligations in time, the directive cannot produce direct effect (ibid. at p. 1645).

The fact that the direct effect of a directive arises from the binding nature of the obligation which it imposes on the Member States under Art. 189, in conjunction with the principle that a State may not plead its own failure to comply with that obligation, has subsequently been confirmed by the ECJ in a number of cases (see e.g. Case 102/79 *Commission* v. *Belgium*, above, at p. 1487; Case 8/81 *Becker*, above, at p. 72; Case 152/84 *Marshall*, above, at p. 749; Case 286/85 *McDermott and Cotter* [1987] ECR 1453 at pp. 1466–7). From this explanation of the concept of direct effect, a number of important consequences follow which may be summarized as follows:

First, while in the case of a regulation direct effect is a 'natural' consequence which flows from the essence of a regulation as a directly applicable legislative measure, in the case of a directive it signifies an 'unnatural' state of affairs, an exceptional situation which can only arise in special circumstances as a 'minimum guarantee' in favour of individuals (Case 102/79 *Commission* v. *Belgium*, above, at p. 1487; see also Case 148/78 *Ratti*, above, at p. 1650 *per* A.-G. Reischl). Thus, a directive is capable of having direct effect only where (1) it has not been correctly implemented or (2) it has not been implemented at all by the end of the prescribed period. On the other hand, wherever a directive is correctly implemented (i.e., ideally, in the majority of cases), it constitutes a rule of national law and 'its effects extend to individuals through the medium of the implementing measures adopted by the Member State concerned' (Case 8/81 *Becker*, above, at p. 70; Case 270/81 *Felicitas* [1982] ECR 2771 at pp. 2786–7; Case 5/84 *Direct Cosmetics*, above, at p. 643; Case 222/84 *Johnston* [1986] ECR 1651 at p. 1690). In other words, it will not then produce direct effects.

Of course, a Member State's failure to implement a provision of a directive does not of itself mean that that provision may be directly invoked by private persons. As the ECJ has stated in Case 41/74 *Van Duyn*, cited above, 'it is necessary to examine, in every case, whether the nature, general scheme and wording of the provision in question are capable of having direct effects'. That is the case only where the provision is, as far as its subject-matter is concerned, 'unconditional and sufficiently precise' (see e.g. Case 8/81 *Becker*, above, at p. 71; Case 14/83 *Von Colson and Kamann*, above, at p. 1909; Case 222/84 *Johnston*, above, at pp. 1691–2; and the other cases cited in connection with direct effect).

Secondly, the Member States' obligation to achieve the result envisaged by a directive is binding on all the national authorities including the courts. It follows that national courts are required to interpret national law, and in particular the law introduced to implement a directive, in the light of the wording and the purpose of that directive so as to help achieve its purpose. This requirement exists even where the directive leaves a certain margin of

181

discretion to the Member States to choose between different solutions (Case 14/83 *Von Colson and Kamann*, above, at p. 1909; see also Case 222/84 *Johnston*, above, at p. 1690; Case 80/86 *Kolpinghuis Nijmegen* [1987] ECR 3969 at p. 3986).

Thirdly, since under Art. 189 a directive is only binding on the Member States, the ECJ has confirmed that it 'may not of itself impose obligations on an individual and that a provision of a directive may not be relied upon as such against such a person' (Case 152/84 *Marshall*, above, at p. 749; see also Case 148/78 *Ratti*, above, at p. 1645). It is therefore clear that a directive, unlike a regulation, is not capable of having direct effect in the relationships between individuals ('horizontal direct effect'). Nor can it impose obligations on an individual in his relationship with a Member State. In particular, a directive cannot, of itself and independently of a national law adopted for its implementation, have the effect of determining or aggravating the criminal liability of persons who act in breach of its provisions (Case 14/86 *Pretore di Salò* [1987] ECR 2545 at p. 2570; Case 80/86 *Kolpinghuis Nijmegen*, above, at p. 3986). Thus, a directive can only operate *in favour of individuals* and against Member States. Moreover, a person may rely on a directly effective provision of a directive against the State 'regardless of the capacity in which the latter is acting, whether employer or public authority. In either case it is necessary to prevent the State from taking advantage of its own failure to comply with Community law' (Case 152/84 *Marshall*, above, at p. 749). Although in the case of directives which create rights for employed persons this may put State employees in a more advantageous position than private employees (or, conversely, may put the State as an employer in a more vulnerable position than a private employer), such a distinction may easily be avoided if the State concerned correctly implements the directive in national law (ibid.; see also Case 222/84 *Johnston*, above, at p. 1691).

Fourthly, the directly effective provisions of a directive enjoy the same supremacy over national law, including both legislative acts and individual administrative decisions, as is attributed to all directly effective provisions of Community law. Thus, in a number of cases the ECJ has stated that 'the national courts must give [such a directive] precedence over any national measures which may prove incompatible with its terms' (Case 38/77 *Enka*, above, at p. 2213; see also Case 36/75 *Rutili* [1975] ECR 1219 at pp. 1229–30) or that 'a national authority may not apply to a person legislative or administrative measures which are not in accordance with an unconditional and sufficiently clear obligation imposed by the directive' (Case 158/80 *Rewe* [1981] ECR 1805 at p. 1838; see also e.g. Case 148/78 *Ratti*, above, at pp. 1641–4; Case 8/81 *Becker*, above, at p. 71; Case 271/82 *Auer* [1983] ECR 2727 at pp. 2744–5; Case 5/83 *Rienks* [1983] ECR 4233 at pp. 4245–6; Case 5/84 *Direct Cosmetics*, above, at p. 643).

To sum up, the direct effect of directives enables individuals:

- to derive enforceable rights from directives, which they may assert against the Member States;

- to oppose incompatible national legislative and administrative measures, including the institution of criminal proceedings;
- to verify the conformity with the directive of national implementing measures;
- to have national law interpreted in accordance with the directive.

See also **Commission, Decision, Direct applicability, Direct effect, Harmonization of laws*, Notification, Regulation, Secondary legislation, Supremacy of Community law.**

Further reading: Arnull, 'The Direct Effect of Directives: Grasping the Nettle' (1986) 35 *ICLQ* 939; Barents, 'Some Remarks on the "Horizontal" Effect of Directives', in O'Keeffe and Schermers (eds.), *Essays in European Law and Integration* (1982), p. 97; Curtin, 'Effective Sanctions and the Equal Treatment Directive: The Von Colson and Harz Cases' (1985) 22 *CML Rev.* 505; Easson, 'Can Directives Impose Obligations on Individuals?' (1979) 4 *EL Rev.* 67; id., 'The "Direct Effect" of EEC Directives' (1979) 28 *ICLQ* 319; id., 'EEC Directives for the Harmonisation of Laws: Some Problems of Validity, Implementation and Legal Effects' (1981) 1 *YEL* 1; Editorial, 'The Cohn Bendit Decision of the Conseil d'État' (1979) 4 *EL Rev.* 65; id., 'Another Court Baulks at the Direct Effect of Directives' (1981) 6 *EL Rev.* 426; id., 'The Direct Effect of Directives—Vertical and Horizontal' (1982) 7 *EL Rev.* 81; Green, 'Directives, Equity and the Protection of Individual Rights' (1984) 9 *EL Rev.* 295; Simmonds, '*Van Duyn* v. *The Home Office*: The Direct Effectiveness of Directives' (1975) 24 *ICLQ* 419; Timmermans, 'Directives: Their Effect within the National Legal Systems' (1979) 16 *CML Rev.* 533; Wyatt, 'The Direct Effect of Community Social Law—Not Forgetting Directives' (1983) 8 *EL Rev.* 241. *See also under* **Secondary legislation.**

▶ **DISCONTINUANCE OF PROCEEDINGS** Termination of proceedings pending before the ECJ by a voluntary, unilateral, and written act of the applicant, resulting in the removal of the case from the register (Art. 78 RP; see however Cases 109 and 114/75 *National Carbonising Company* v. *Commission* [1977] ECR 381, where the other parties were first allowed to express their views). Discontinuance (or withdrawal) of one only of several claims is also possible (Cases 16 to 18/59 *Geitling* v. *HA* [1960] ECR 17 at p. 26). A party who discontinues or withdraws from proceedings will normally be ordered to pay the costs, unless the discontinuance or withdrawal is justified by the conduct of the opposite party (Art. 69(4) RP; Cases 5, 7, and 8/60 *Meroni* v. *HA*, below; Cases 123/81 and 123/81R *Krupp* v. *Commission* [1981] ECR 2391 at p. 2392). Discontinuance must be distinguished both from the abandonment of claims, which implies a common agreement between the parties (settlement), and from a decision by the ECJ that the application has lost its purpose and that therefore there is no ground for proceeding to judgment, which is a decision on the substance of the case (Cases 16 to 18/59 *Geitling* v. *HA*, above; Cases 5, 7, and 8/60 *Meroni* v. *HA* [1961] ECR 107 at pp. 111–12 *per Curiam*, p. 113 *per* A.-G. Lagrange; Case 74/81 *Flender* v. *Commission* [1982] ECR 395 at p. 404).

See also **Abandonment of claims, Settlement.**

Further reading: Usher, *European Court Practice* (1983), ch. 9.

E

▶ **ECONOMIC AND SOCIAL COMMITTEE (ESC)** Committee set up by Arts. 193 EEC and 165 Euratom to assist the Council and the Commission, acting in an advisory capacity. The functions which the two Treaties confer upon the ESC are to be exercised by a single body (Art. 5 of the Convention on Certain Institutions Common to the European Communities of 1957). These functions are comparable to those of the Consultative Committee of the ECSC.

The Committee has a quasi-institutional status in that it enjoys a measure of financial and administrative independence, having its own administrative budget and staff establishment plan (at the end of 1988, there were 485 permanent posts on its establishment plan, see 22nd *Gen. Rep. EC* (1988), p. 44). Nevertheless, it is not a Community 'institution' in the strict sense. Although it is treated, together with the Court of Auditors, as an 'institution' for the specific purposes of the Staff Regulations and of the Financial Regulation (see Art. 1(2) of the Staff Regulations and Art. 18(4) of the Financial Regulation of 21 Dec. 1977, *OJ* 1977 L356/1), it is in fact not given the full status of a Community institution. As the ECJ has pointed out, the ESC is not listed in Arts. 4 EEC and 3 Euratom as an institution (although it is mentioned in those Articles). Its treatment as an institution for the purposes of the Staff Regulations only has the object of ensuring that those Regulations are applied to its officials and of identifying the appointing authority for them, but does not imply similar treatment for the general purposes of the Treaties. Thus, the requirement laid down in Art. 24 of the Merger Treaty that the Council shall consult the 'other institutions' when adopting or amending the Staff Regulations, does not apply to the ESC and the Court of Auditors (Case 828/79 *Adam* v. *Commission* [1982] ECR 269 at pp. 290–1). Nevertheless, it follows from Art. 1(2) of the Staff Regulations that the ESC has the capacity to appear before the ECJ in proceedings between it and one of its officials (Case 79/70 *Müller* v. *Economic and Social Committee* [1971] ECR 689 at p. 696; Case 307/85 *Gavanas* v. *Economic and Social Committee and Council* [1987] ECR 2435 at p. 2459).

The ESC consists of representatives of the various categories of economic and social activity, in particular, representatives of producers, farmers, carriers, workers, dealers, craftsmen, professional occupations, and of the general public. The members of the Committee are appointed by the Council, acting unanimously, for renewable terms of four years. The 189 members are allocated on a national basis as follows: Belgium 12, Denmark 9, Germany 24, Greece 12, Spain 21, France 24, Ireland 9, Italy 24, Luxembourg 6, Netherlands 12, Portugal 12, United Kingdom 24 (Arts. 194 EEC and 166 Euratom as last amended by Art. 21 of the Act of Accession 1985. For the composition of the ESC during the period 21 Sept. 1986 to 20 Sept. 1990, see *OJ* 1986 C244/2). The appointment of members is from a list of candidates provided by each Member State and is to take account of the need to ensure adequate representation of the various categories of economic and social activity. The ECJ has held that adequate representation must be ensured at Community level but that, because of the limited number of seats available, it is not possible to guarantee that all the elements from every category of economic and social activity are represented by nationals from each Member State (Case 297/86 *CIDA* v. *Council* [1988] ECR 3531 at p. 3554). Before making the appointments, the Council is required to consult the Commission and may also obtain the opinion of European organizations representative of the various sections. While the former is an obligation, the latter is only an option (ibid. at pp. 3556–7). The members of the Committee are appointed in their personal capacity and may not be bound by any mandatory instructions (Arts. 194–5 EEC, 166–7 Euratom). They enjoy the privileges and immunities laid down in Art. 11 of the Protocol on Privileges and Immunities annexed to the Merger Treaty (Art. 54 of the ESC's Rules of Procedure, see below).

The organs and officers of the Committee are as follows: Bureau, Chairman (normally elected, for a term of two years, in turn from among the members representing employers, workers, and other categories of activity), specialized Sections, Sub-Committees, Rapporteur-General, three roughly equal Groups formed on a voluntary basis (i.e. Employers', Workers', and General Interests Groups), and a General Secretariat headed by a Secretary-General (see Arts. 196–7 EEC, 168–9 Euratom, Art. 5 of the Convention on Common Institutions, and Title I of the ESC's Rules of Procedure (Revised), which entered into force in Sept. 1986, *OJ* 1986 L354/1).

In the words of the ECJ, the function of the ESC is 'to advise the Council and Commission on the solutions to be adopted with regard to practical problems of an economic and social nature and to deliver opinions based on its specific competence and knowledge' (Cases 281/85 etc. *Germany and Others* v. *Commission* [1987] ECR 3203 at p. 3256). The Council and the Commission must consult the Committee where the Treaties so provide; they may consult it in all cases in which they consider it appropriate (Arts. 198 EEC, 170 Euratom). However, it follows from the above definition of the Committee's function that consultation is mandatory only where its purpose is the implementation of practical measures. By contrast, consultation is not mandatory in connection with making studies, compiling information, or organizing meetings, for the decisions involved then are purely preparatory and procedural and, by definition, do not touch on substantive questions which are liable to involve the ESC in making assessments of a socio-economic nature (ibid., dealing with the consultation requirement laid down in Art. 118 EEC).

Initially, the ESC could only produce opinions at the request of the Council or the Commission. However, at the Paris Summit Conference of October 1972, the Heads of State or Government invited the Community institutions to recognize the right of the Committee to deliver opinions on its own initiative on any question pertaining to the tasks assigned to the EEC or the Euratom (6th *Gen. Rep. EC* (1972), p. 16). At its session of 11–12 February 1974, the Council formally recognized this right (see *Bull. EC* 2–1974, pp. 97 and 104), which was subsequently incorporated in the Committee's Revised Rules of Procedure of 13 June 1974 (Art. 20(4), *OJ* 1974 L228/1) and has been retained unchanged in the current Rules of Procedure of September 1986 (Art. 20(4)). At the same session, the Council also adopted a

185

set of measures to improve its relations with the ESC, including an undertaking that the President-in-office of the Council would make an annual statement to the Committee on the Council's work (*Bull. EC* 2–1974, p. 104). However, it was only in May 1987 that the President of the Council addressed a plenary session of the Committee for the first time (*Bull. EC* 5–1987, p. 101).

The opinions of the Committee are prepared by a Section designated by the Chairman and then discussed and adopted at plenary sessions of the full Committee which are as a rule held during the last seven days of the month (see Title II of the ESC's Rules of Procedure. In 1988, the Committee held ten sessions. For the subjects on which the Committee delivered opinions and own-initiative opinions and adopted resolutions in 1988, see 22nd *Gen. Rep. EC* (1988), p. 43). The Council and the Commission may set the Committee a time-limit for the submission of its opinion, which may not be less than ten days. Failure to deliver an opinion within the time-limit cannot prevent further action by the institutions. Opinions adopted by the Committee, Section opinions, Section reports, and minutes of Committee sessions are sent to the Council and the Commission. Opinions are published in the *Official Journal*. Although the Committee's opinions are not legally binding, they do have considerable impact on the decisions of the two institutions owing to the expertise of its members. Moreover, failure to consult the Committee where consultation is mandatory in the above-discussed sense constitutes infringement of an essential procedural requirement and may lead to the annulment of the measure concerned by the Court of Justice.

See also **Commission, Consultative Committee, Council, Infringement of an essential procedural requirement, Institutions, Privileges and immunities.**

Further reading 1. ARTICLE: Zellentin, 'The Economic and Social Committee' (1962) 1 *JCMS* 22.

2. OFFICIAL PUBLICATIONS: Economic and Social Committee, 'The Right of Initiative of the Economic and Social Committee of the European Communities', 2nd edn. (1982); id., 'Basic Documents' (1986).

▶ **EFFECTIVE JUDICIAL CONTROL** General principle of law, recognized by the ECJ as forming part of Community law, according to which 'all persons have the right to obtain an effective remedy in a competent court against [national] measures which they consider to be contrary to [Community law]. It is for the Member States to ensure effective judicial control as regards compliance with the applicable provisions of Community law and of national legislation intended to give effect to the rights for which [it] provides' (Case 222/84 *Johnston* [1986] ECR 1651 at p. 1682).

The Court has derived this principle from the constitutional traditions common to the Member States and from various provisions of the European Convention on Human Rights of 1950. It has stated that in Community law this principle is reflected in Art. 6 of Dir. 76/207 on equal treatment for men and women (*OJ* 1976 L39/40), which requires Member States to introduce into their national legal systems such measures as are necessary to enable all persons who consider themselves wronged by discrimination 'to pursue their claims by judicial process'. The Court has held that a national provision which has the effect of depriving an individual of the possibility of asserting by judicial process the rights conferred by the directive is contrary to the principle of effective judicial control (ibid. at pp. 1682–3, 1692. See also Case 222/86 *UNECTEF* [1987] ECR 4097 at p. 4117).

See also **Equal treatment***, **General principles of law, Human rights, Procedural safeguards***.

▶ **ENFORCEMENT PROCEDURE** Procedure for the enforcement of the following Community measures:

- judgments and orders of the ECJ, including penalties imposed and other measures ordered in respect of witnesses and the recovery of sums owed to the Court on various grounds (Arts. 44 and 92 ECSC; 187 and 192 EEC; 159 and 164 Euratom; 48(4), 71, 74(2), 86(2), 90(2) RP; 22(2) IR);
- final decisions of the Euratom Arbitration Committee (Arts. 18(3) and 164 Euratom);
- decisions of the Commission imposing certain sanctions under the Euratom Treaty (Arts. 83(2) and 164 Euratom);
- decisions of the Commission imposing pecuniary obligations under the ECSC Treaty (Art. 92 ECSC);
- decisions of the Council and of the Commission imposing pecuniary obligations on persons other than States under the EEC Treaty (Art. 192 EEC).

Enforcement falls within the jurisdiction of the national courts and is governed by the rules of civil procedure in force in the State in the territory of which it is carried out.

Before enforcement may be commenced, the authenticity of the judgment or decision in question must be verified by the national authority which the Government of each Member State has designated for this purpose and has made known to the ECJ and to the Commission. This is the only formality required for the issue of an order for enforcement (writ of execution) which the designated national authority must append to the judgment or decision. When this has been done, the party concerned may proceed to enforcement in accordance with national law, by bringing the matter directly before the competent court. From this moment on the national rules of civil procedure apply and the national courts have jurisdiction over any question which the enforcement may raise (see e.g. Case 108/63 *Merlini* v. *HA* [1965] ECR 1 at p. 10; Case 4/73—Enforcement *Nold* v. *Ruhrkohle* [1977] ECR 1 at pp. 3–4). Nevertheless, enforcement may be suspended only by a decision of the ECJ made in accordance with the general rules on suspension of operation of Community measures (Art. 89 RP).

See also **Limitation periods, Suspension of operation.**

187

▶ EQUALITY General principle of law recognized by the ECJ as forming part of Community law (also known as the principle of non-discrimination). Thus, in a number of cases the Court has stated that 'the general principle of equality, of which the prohibition of discrimination on grounds of nationality is merely a specific expression, is one of the fundamental principles of Community law. That principle requires that comparable situations should not be treated differently [and different situations should not be treated in the same way] unless such differentiation is objectively justified. Clearly it requires that [persons] who are in identical situations should be governed by the same rules, but it does not prevent the Community legislature from taking into account objective differences in the conditions or situations in which those concerned are placed' (Case 147/79 *Hochstrass* v. *Court of Justice* [1980] ECR 3005 at p. 3019; see also Case 810/79 *Überschär* [1980] ECR 2747 at pp. 2764–5; the bracketed phrase appears in Case 106/83 *Sermide* [1984] ECR 4209 at p. 4231. Substantially similar definitions are given in most of the cases referred to below). It follows from this definition that the different treatment of non-comparable situations does not automatically involve prohibited discrimination. As the Court has pointed out, 'an appearance of discrimination in form may . . . correspond in fact to an absence of discrimination in substance. Discrimination in substance would consist in treating either similar situations differently or different situations identically' (Case 13/63 *Italy* v. *Commission* [1963] ECR 165 at pp. 177–8; see also the opinion of A.-G. Lagrange, ibid. at pp. 182–3, 190). The distinction made by the Court between discrimination in form and discrimination in substance corresponds to the distinction between the concepts of equality in law and equality in fact. As the Permanent Court of International Justice stated in the *Minority Schools in Albania* case, 'equality in law precludes discrimination of any kind; whereas equality in fact may involve the necessity of different treatment in order to attain a result which establishes an equilibrium between different situations' (Advisory Opinion of 6 Apr. 1935, Series A/B, No. 64, p. 19, cited by A.-G. Lagrange in the case mentioned immediately above, at p. 190). It is equality in fact, which prohibits discrimination in substance, no less than equality in law, that Community law strives to achieve. Moreover, discrimination in a legal sense implies a difference in treatment arising from human activity, and especially from measures taken by public authorities (Community institutions or national authorities) or, less frequently, by private individuals and organizations. Differences which are due to purely natural phenomena cannot be described as 'discrimination' within the meaning of Community law (Case 52/79 *Debauve* [1980] ECR 833 at p. 858).

In national law, the principle of equality is guaranteed by constitutional provisions, usually in the framework of the protection of fundamental human rights. Nevertheless, with the development of State intervention in the economy, the principle has increasingly been applied also in economic law in order to restrict the freedom of public authorities to intervene and to protect undertakings from unwarranted differences in treatment (see the opinion of A.-G. Capotorti in Cases 117/76 and 16/77 *Ruckdeschel* [1977] ECR 1753 at pp. 1777–80—'Quellmehl' cases).

In international law, equality or non-discrimination is regarded as a fundamental human right (possibly the most important one), and is accordingly given a prominent place in most treaties and conventions on the subject. Thus, for example, Art. 26 of the International Covenant on Civil and Political Rights of 1966 provides that 'all persons are equal before the law' and that 'the law shall prohibit any discrimination'. Art. 14 of the European Convention on Human Rights requires that the enjoyment of the rights and freedoms set forth in the Convention should be secured 'without discrimination on any ground' whatsoever. (On the concept of equality in international law, see in particular the Dissenting Opinion of Judge Tanaka in the *South West Africa Cases* (Second Phase), ICJ Reports 1966, p. 6, 250 at pp. 284 *et seq.*)

In Community law, the basic Treaties do not contain a single general rule, similar to those quoted above, guaranteeing equality of treatment in a comprehensive manner. Instead, there are a number of unconnected individual provisions, scattered over the ECSC and EEC Treaties, ensuring equal treatment in relation to specific matters (see below). It has been through the interpretation and application of these provisions, in cases dealing with the most diverse issues, that the ECJ has developed a uniform and coherent principle of equality. At the same time, the Court has also recognized the existence of a 'general principle of equality' of which the individual Treaty provisions are only 'specific expressions' or 'specific enunciations' (see most of the cases cited above and below). This has been significant in two main respects. First, as part of unwritten Community law, such a general principle of equality applies to all situations comprehensively, even in the absence of any particular Treaty provision requiring equal treatment (see e.g. Cases 66, 127, and 128/79 *Salumi* [1980] ECR 1237 at pp. 1262–3, holding that the fixing and collection of the financial charges making up the Community's own resources are governed by the general principle of equality; Case 131/73 *Grosoli* [1973] ECR 1555 at p. 1566 and Case 199/84 *Migliorini* [1985] ECR 3317 at p. 3331, confirming that the allocation of Community tariff quotas by the Member States is subject to the principle of equal treatment; Case 165/84 *Krohn* [1985] ECR 3997 at pp. 4022, 4023, referring to the general principle of equal treatment of traders). Secondly, the concept of a general principle of equality has in turn served as an instrument in defining the precise meaning and scope of the many disparate provisions of primary and secondary Community law which prohibit discrimination, thereby ensuring their uniform and coherent operation. It has thus been as a result of a two-way process, both inductive and deductive, that the Court has established the criteria for the application of the principle of equality in Community law.

It follows from the criteria laid down by the Court that, in establishing whether there exists a prohibited discrimination, the following three circumstances must be considered: (1) whether the measure or conduct in question is by itself of a discriminatory nature; (2) whether the situations which are subject to different treatment are comparable; and (3) whether the differentiation is objectively justified (see in general the opinion of A.-G. Capotorti in Cases 117/76 and 16/77 *Ruckdeschel*, above, at pp. 1777–80). These questions are considered below in turn.

1. Dealing with the *concept of discrimination* in the context of Arts. 2(2), 3(b), 60, and 67 of the ECSC Treaty (for which see further below), the ECJ has held that there may be considered as discriminatory in principle and, accordingly, prohibited by the Treaty 'measures or interventions . . . which are calculated, by substantially increasing differences in production costs otherwise than through changes in productivity, to give rise to an appreciable disequilibrium in the competitive position of the undertakings concerned. In other words, any intervention attempting to distort or actually distorting competition artificially and significantly must be regarded as discriminatory and incompatible with the Treaty . . .' (Cases 32 and 33/58 *SNUPAT* v. *HA* [1959] ECR 127 at p. 143). Nevertheless, the ECJ has recognized that the prohibition of discriminatory measures and practices laid down in Art. 4(b) of the ECSC Treaty (for which see below) could not have the effect of creating absolute equality in the conditions of competition of the coal and steel industries, nor of eliminating all interference with the conditions of competition by the Member States. The persistence of differences in conditions of competition is in fact a necessary and inevitable consequence of the partial nature of the integration brought about by the Treaty and does not necessarily involve prohibited discrimination (Cases 7 and 9/54 *Industries Sidérurgiques Luxembourgeoises* v. *HA* [1956] ECR 175 at p. 198).

Also, the general prohibition of discrimination on grounds of nationality under Art. 7 of the EEC Treaty (for which see below) does not aim at the complete elimination of disparities in treatment which may result from divergences existing between the laws of the various Member States. Non-discrimination cannot be equated with prior and complete harmonization of the national laws. Therefore, the fact that one Member State applies stricter legislation in a certain area than other Member States cannot be regarded as prohibited discrimination, even if this detrimentally affects the competitiveness of undertakings established in that State, so long as the law affects all persons subject to it in accordance with objective criteria and without regard to their nationality (Case 14/68 *Wilhelm* [1969] ECR 1 at p. 16 *per Curiam*, p. 29 *per* A.-G. Roemer; Case 1/78 *Kenny* [1978] ECR 1489 at p. 1498; Cases 185 to 204/78 *Van Dam* [1979] ECR 2345 at p. 2361; Case 155/80 *Oebel* [1981] ECR 1993 at p. 2007; Case 126/82 *Smit* [1983] ECR 73 at pp. 92–3; etc.). Even the fact that certain laws apply to foreign nationals only (e.g. rules concerning the entry, residence, control, and expulsion of aliens) does not necessarily constitute prohibited discrimination, provided that the essential freedoms of the individual protected by Community law (freedom of movement, employment, establishment, etc.) are not infringed and that the application of such laws is based on objective factors and is not arbitrary. In fact, so long as there is no Community nationality, nationals of other Member States will always have a different status from that of the nationals of the State concerned even where all of them enjoy the same basic rights on equal conditions (Case 118/75 *Watson and Belmann* [1976] ECR 1185 at p. 1199 *per Curiam*, p. 1210 *per* A.-G. Trabucchi; Case 8/77 *Sagulo, Brenca and Bakhouche* [1977] ECR 1495 at pp. 1505–6; Cases 115 and 116/81 *Adoui and Cornuaille* [1982] ECR 1665 at p. 1707).

The concept of discrimination implies that a person, undertaking, or group suffers some form of disadvantage as opposed to others. As the ECJ has said, for an authority to be accused of discrimination 'it must be shown to have treated like cases differently, thereby subjecting some to disadvantage as opposed to others, without such differentiation being justified by the existence of substantial objective differences' (Cases 17 and 20/61 *Klöckner* v. *HA* [1962] ECR 325 at p. 345). It follows that there is no prohibited discrimination where it is apparent from a comparison of the different treatments, assessed in the light of the objective differences in the situations to which they are applied, that those subject to one treatment are not placed at a disadvantage as compared with those subject to the other treatment (Case 152/73 *Sotgiu* [1974] ECR 153 at p. 165; Case 810/79 *Überschär*, above, at p. 2765). On the other hand, the concept of discrimination does not imply, by definition, the fact that direct damage is caused. The meaning of that concept is, primarily, that 'unequal conditions are laid down for comparable cases'. Although the application of such unequal conditions may bring about damage (which may then be used as evidence of discrimination), this does not mean that the concept of discrimination may be reduced solely to those cases of unequal treatment in which the interested parties in fact suffer damage (Cases 3 to 18, 25, and 26/58 *Barbara Erzbergbau* v. *HA* [1960] ECR 173 at p. 192). Moreover, discrimination may result not only from a positive act, but also from a silence of a text or from a failure to act, for example, where the Community institutions fail to adopt measures necessary to bring to an end a situation which produces discriminatory effects (Cases 56 to 60/74 *Kampff-meyer* v. *Commission and Council* [1976] ECR 711 at pp. 743–5; see also Case 300/86 *Van Landschoot* [1988] ECR 3443 at pp. 3461, 3464).

2. As regards the *comparability of the situations* which are subject to different treatment, the ECJ has rejected the view that any comparison between several undertakings must take into account all the circumstances in which they are placed. The Court has pointed out that this would lead to the result that an undertaking is only comparable with itself, and thus the concept 'comparably placed' and, therefore, that of 'discrimination' would become devoid of all meaning (Cases 3 to 18, 25, and 26/58 *Barbara Erzbergbau* v. *HA*, above, at p. 191).

It is clear, therefore, that the requirement that the situations should be comparable does not mean that they shoud be exactly identical. In principle, comparability must be determined by two main factors. The first is the objectives of the measure at issue. It is mainly in the light of those objectives that it is possible to evaluate whether certain differences existing between undertakings are sufficient to regard them as non-comparable and therefore to subject them to different treatment (see Cases 117/76 and 16/77 *Ruck-deschel*, above, at p. 1779 *per* A.-G. Capotorti). Secondly, comparability must be determined against the background of competition. Thus, for example, in Case 14/59 *Fonderies de Pont-à-Mousson* v. *HA* [1959] ECR 215 at pp. 231–2 the Court established that there was no discrimination on the part of the High Authority in exempting certain foundries from the payment of compulsory contributions while at the same time refusing to grant a similar exemption to other foundries of a different type since the categories of undertakings involved did not operate with the same production plant or use the same raw materials and therefore their competitive positions were not comparable. In Cases 17 and 20/61 *Klöckner* v. *HA*, above, at p. 345, again dismissing a complaint of discrimination made in the context of the scrap equalization scheme, the Court said that 'in this case, in spite of identical circumstances as regards production, the applicants by reason of their legal structure incorporating several undertakings were not in a similar position to that of their competitors who formed a single legal entity. This difference is of importance in law and is therefore capable of justifying different treatment.'

The Court used the criterion of competition also in the 'Quellmehl', 'Gritz', and 'Isoglucose' cases. In examining whether various agricultural products (quellmehl and starch in the 'Quellmehl' cases; maize groats and meal—called gritz—and maize starch in the 'Gritz' cases; isoglucose and starch as well as isoglucose and sugar in the 'Isoglucose' cases) were in a comparable situation the Court considered whether the one could be substituted for the other in the specific use to which the latter product was traditionally put and whether there was therefore competition between them. Where this was the case, the different products had to be treated in the same manner unless differentiation was objectively justified (Cases 117/76 and 16/77 *Ruckdeschel*, above, at p. 1770—'Quellmehl' cases; Cases 124/76 and 20/77 *Moulins de Pont-à-Mousson* [1977] ECR 1795 at p. 1812—'Gritz' cases; Cases 103 and 145/77 *Royal Scholten-Honig* [1978] ECR 2037 at p. 2078—'Isoglucose' cases). On the other hand, where the products had different applications so that there was no possibility of interchangeability between them and therefore they could not be in comparable competitive positions with regard to one another, their different treatment did not amount to unlawful discrimination (Case 125/77 *Koninklijke Scholten-Honig* [1978] ECR 1991 at pp. 2003–4; Cases 103 and 145/77 *Royal Scholten-Honig*, above, at p. 2073—'Isoglucose' cases. For other cases in which the Court found—for various reasons—that a difference in treatment was justified by a difference between the underlying situations, see e.g. Case 8/57 *Aciéries Belges* v. *HA* [1958] ECR 245 at pp. 256–7: dissimilar operating conditions; Case 230/78 *Eridania* [1979] ECR 2749 at pp. 2767–8: differences in the economic situations of Member States; Case 8/82 *Wagner* [1983] ECR 371 at pp. 387–8: different location of warehouses; Case 283/83 *Racke* [1984] ECR 3791 at pp. 3800–2: different application of countervailing charges on wines; Cases 279/84 etc. *Rau* v. *Commission* [1987] ECR 1069 at p. 1125: essential differences between the butter and margarine markets).

3. Even where the two situations are comparable, there is no illegal discrimination if the difference in treatment is *objectively justified*. Thus, in a number of cases the Court has held that different treatment could be regarded as constituting prohibited discrimination only if 'it appears to be arbitrary, or in other words . . . devoid of adequate justification and not based on objective criteria' (Case 106/81 *Kind* v. *EEC* [1982] ECR 2885 at p. 2921; see also e.g. Case 8/57 *Aciéries Belges* v. *HA*, above, at p. 256; Case 11/74 *Union des*

Minotiers de la Champagne [1974] ECR 877 at pp. 886–7; Cases 117/76 and 16/77 *Ruckdeschel*, above, at p. 1770; Cases 103 and 145/77 *Royal Scholten-Honig*, above, at p. 2079; Case 139/77 *Denkavit* [1978] ECR 1317 at p. 1333). Clearly, what is or is not 'arbitrary' and 'objectively justified' depends on the circumstances of each individual case. Generally speaking, the Court has tended to interpret the latter concept fairly broadly, almost using it as an exception or derogation clause to the principle of equality. Thus, the Court has accepted that the different treatment of comparable situations is not discriminatory where:

- it is justified by the aims which the institutions may lawfully pursue as part of a Community policy (Case 250/83 *Finsider* v. *Commission* [1985] ECR 131 at pp. 152–3, dealing with steel quotas and aids);
- its purpose is to obviate special difficulties in one sector of industry (Case 166/78 *Italy* v. *Council* [1979] ECR 2575 at p. 2600, dealing with bonuses granted to potato starch to the exclusion of maize starch);
- it is not arbitrary in the sense that the measure adopted does not exceed the scope of the broad discretion enjoyed by the Community institutions in implementing common policies and is not based on manifestly erroneous considerations (Case 43/72 *Merkur* v. *Commission* [1973] ECR 1055 at pp. 1073–4, dealing with compensatory amounts; Case 106/81 *Kind* v. *EEC*, above, at p. 2921, dealing with intervention methods in the market in mutton and lamb; Case 106/83 *Sermide*, above, at p. 4233, dealing with production levy in the sugar sector);
- it is based on 'objective differences arising from the economic circumstances underlying the common organisation of the market in [the relevant] products' (Case 59/83 *Biovilac* v. *EEC* [1984] ECR 4057 at p. 4079, holding that the granting of greater subsidies to skimmed-milk powder than to whey was 'objectively justified' owing to the market-supporting role of the former; see also Case 15/83 *Denkavit Nederland* [1984] ECR 2171 at p. 2185) or it is based on 'objective criteria which ensure a proportionate division of the advantages and disadvantages for those concerned without distinction between the territories of the Member States' (Case 106/83 *Sermide*, above, at p. 4231, holding that the calculation of the production levy for sugar was 'objectively justified' notwithstanding the use of different reference periods in the different Member States; see also Case 153/73 *Holtz & Willemsen* v. *Council and Commission* [1974] ECR 675 at p. 695).

As a general principle of law, the principle of equality is binding upon the Community institutions, the authorities of the Member States, and private individuals, organizations, and undertakings alike. As regards the institutions, failure to observe the principle may constitute a misuse of powers (Case 8/57 *Aciéries Belges* v. *HA*, above, at p. 256) and may entail the invalidity or the annulment of the measure in question (see e.g. Case 114/76 *Bela-Mühle* [1977] ECR 1211 at p. 1221—'Skimmed-milk powder' case; Cases 117/76 and 16/77 *Ruckdeschel*, above, at pp. 1771–2—'Quellmehl' cases; Cases 103 and 145/77 *Royal Scholten-Honig*, above, at p. 2081—'Isoglucose' cases; Case 224/82 *Meiko-Konservenfabrik* [1983] ECR 2539 at p. 2550—in all these cases the Court declared invalid various agricultural regulations; Case 41/84 *Pinna* [1986] ECR 1 at pp. 25–6, declaring invalid Art. 73(2) of Reg. 1408/71 on social security). Moreover, the ECJ has recognized that the principle of equality 'occupies a particularly important place among the rules of Community law intended to protect the interests of the individual' (Case 238/78 *Ireks-Arkady* v. *Council and Commission* [1979] ECR 2955 at p. 2973—'Quellmehl' case). In fact, it constitutes a 'superior rule of law' for the protection of the individual, the infringement of which may establish the non-contractual liability of the Communities in respect of a legislative measure involving choices of economic policy (ibid.; Cases 83 and 94/76 etc. *HNL* v. *Council and Commission* [1978] ECR 1209 at p. 1224). As regards the Member States, the Court has stated that 'in applying Community rules the Member States cannot unilaterally adopt additional measures which are such as to compromise the equality of treatment of traders throughout the Community and thus to distort competitive conditions between the Member States' (Cases 15 and 16/76 *France* v. *Commission* [1979] ECR 321 at p. 340). As regards, finally, private persons and organizations, the Court has pointed out that 'prohibition of . . . discrimination does not only apply to the action of public authorities but extends likewise to rules of any other nature aimed at regulating in a collective manner gainful employment and the provision of services. The . . . fundamental objectives of the Community . . . would be compromised if the abolition of barriers of national origin could be neutralised by obstacles resulting from the exercise of their legal autonomy by associations or organisations which do not come under public law' (Case 36/74 *Walrave* [1974] ECR 1405 at pp. 1418–19; Case 13/76 *Donà* [1976] ECR 1333 at p. 1341, applying the principle of non-discrimination to rules of sporting organizations; Case 90/76 *Van Ameyde* [1977] ECR 1091 at p. 1127, applying the same principle to measures of the Italian national insurers' bureau, a company formed under private law; Case 43/75 *Defrenne* [1976] ECR 455 at p. 476, extending the application of the prohibition on discrimination between men and women even to contracts between individuals, see below).

Nevertheless, the principle of equality is binding on the Community in its internal affairs only. In its external relations, there exists no general principle obliging the Community to accord equal treatment to third countries. Nor is there a right on the part of traders to rely on the prohibition of discrimination where the difference of treatment between traders is an automatic consequence of the different treatment of non-member countries. In this respect the Community institutions enjoy broad discretion within the framework of the Common Commercial Policy (Case 55/75 *Balkan-Import-Export* [1976] ECR 19 at p. 32; Case 245/81 *Edeka* [1982] ECR 2745 at p. 2756; Case 236/84 *Malt* [1986] ECR 1923 at pp. 1946–7).

As mentioned above, a number of provisions of the basic Community Treaties and of secondary legislation contain prohibitions on discrimination in respect of specific matters. The most important of these provisions and the case-law of the ECJ relating thereto may be summarized as follows:

1. Under the ECSC Treaty

(*a*) *Art. 3(b)* requires the institutions of the Community to ensure that 'all comparably placed consumers in the Common Market have equal access to the sources of production'.

(*b*) *Art. 4(b)* abolishes and prohibits within the Community 'measures or practices which discriminate between producers, between purchasers or between consumers'. (Arts. 3(b) and 4(b) have been interpreted and applied in Case 8/57 *Aciéries Belges* v. *HA*, above, at pp. 256–7; Case 14/59 *Fonderies de Pont-à-Mousson* v. *HA*, above, at pp. 231–2; Cases 17 and 20/61 *Klöckner* v. *HA*, above, at pp. 344–6; see also Case 250/83 *Finsider* v. *Commission*, above, at pp. 152–3 and the cases under (*d*) below.)

(*c*) *Art. 60(1)* prohibits pricing practices contrary to Arts. 2, 3, and 4, in particular 'discriminatory practices involving, within the Common Market, the application by a seller of dissimilar conditions to comparable transactions, especially on grounds of the nationality of the buyer'.

(*d*) *Art. 67* enables the High Authority (i.e. Commission) to take various steps in respect of 'any action by a Member State which is liable to have appreciable repercussions on conditions of competition in the coal or the steel industry'. (Arts. 3(b), 4(b), 60, and 67 have been interpreted and applied in Cases 7 and 9/54 *Industries Sidérurgiques Luxembourgeoises* v. *HA*, above, at pp. 197–9; Cases 32 and 33/58 *SNUPAT* v. *HA*, above, at pp. 143–5.)

(*e*) *Art. 70* prohibits in traffic between Member States 'any discrimination in rates and conditions of carriage of every kind which is based on the country of origin or destination of products'. (Art. 70 has been interpreted and applied in Cases 3 to 18, 25, and 26/58 *Barbara Erzbergbau* v. *HA*, above, at pp. 190–3.)

2. Under the EEC Treaty

(*a*) *Art. 7* provides that 'within the scope of application of this Treaty, and without prejudice to any special provisions contained therein, any discrimination on grounds of nationality shall be prohibited'. In a number of cases, the ECJ has stated that Art. 7 is merely a 'specific expression' or a 'specific enunciation' of the general principle of equality (see the cases cited at the beginning of this entry). As such, it contains a 'general prohibition' and it 'must be applied in every respect and in all circumstances governed by Community law to any person established in a Member State' (Case 36/75 *Rutili* [1975] ECR 1219 at p. 1229 and Case 137/84 *Mutsch* [1985] ECR 2681 at p. 2695). The Court has also pointed out that the rule on equal treatment with nationals is 'one of the fundamental legal provisions of the Community', and in particular 'the fundamental principle in the context of the rules on freedom of movement' (Case 2/74 *Reyners* [1974] ECR 631 at p. 651 and Case 249/83 *Hoeckx* [1985] ECR 973 at p. 989). However, the general principle of Art. 7 must be applied in conjunction with and subject to the special provisions of the Treaty which implement it in the various areas of the Treaty's operation, such as, in particular, the freedom of movement for workers (Arts. 48 to 51), freedom of establishment (Arts. 52 to 58), and freedom to provide services (Arts. 59 to 66), and subject to the measures of the Community institutions adopted on the basis of those provisions (such as Reg. 1612/68, Reg. 1251/70, Reg. 1408/71, Dir. 64/221, Dir. 68/360). All these provisions, read in conjunction with Art. 7, 'are intended to eliminate all measures which, in the fields [mentioned], treat a national of another Member State more severely or place him in a situation less advantageous, from a legal or factual point of view, than that of one of the Member State's own nationals in the same circumstances' (Case 251/83 *Haug-Adrion* [1984] ECR 4277 at p. 4288. See also, in particular, Case 2/74 *Reyners*, above, at pp. 650–2; Case 36/74 *Walrave*, above, at pp. 1417–19; Case 13/76 *Donà*, above, at pp. 1339–40; Case 90/76 *Van Ameyde*, above, at pp. 1126–7; Case 8/77 *Sagulo, Brenca and Bakhouche*, above, at pp. 1505–6; Case 1/78 *Kenny*, above, at pp. 1496–7; etc.).

The principle of non-discrimination on grounds of nationality may only be invoked in situations which come within one of the areas (basic freedoms) covered by Community law. As the ECJ has put it, 'unequal treatment based on nationality must be regarded as discrimination prohibited by Article 7 of the Treaty *if it falls within the scope of the Treaty*' (Case 293/83 *Gravier* [1985] ECR 593 at p. 611, emphasis added). It follows that where unequal treatment is applied in relation to a matter which falls outside the scope of the EEC Treaty, it does not constitute prohibited discrimination under Art. 7 (see in particular Case 39/86 *Lair* [1988] ECR 3161 at pp. 3194–5 and Case 197/86 *Brown* [1988] ECR 3205 at pp. 3242–3. In these cases the Court held that the payment by a Member State to or on behalf of students of tuition fees charged by a university falls within the scope of the EEC Treaty and is, consequently, subject to the rule of non-discrimination, whereas the payment of grants for students' maintenance does not fall within the scope of the Treaty and is, therefore, not subject to Art. 7). Nor can Art. 7 be applied to 'situations which are wholly internal to a Member State and which are in no way connected to any situations envisaged by Community law'. The mere fact that nationals of a Member State are employed by an employer situated in the territory of that State is not sufficient to confer on those persons the benefit of the Community rules on the free movement of workers. It follows that in these circumstances the principle of non-discrimination cannot prevent a Member State from adopting measures which are more restrictive or less favourable to its own nationals than to the nationals of other Member States (Case 44/84 *Hurd* [1986] ECR 29 at p. 85; see also Case 175/78 *Saunders* [1979] ECR 1129 at pp. 1134–5; Cases 35 and 36/82 *Morson and Jhanjan* [1982] ECR 3723 at p. 3736). Nor does the same principle prohibit un-favourable treatment of domestic products as compared with imported products or of traders selling domestic products as compared with those selling imported products, when the treatment is applied by a Member State in a sector not subject to Community rules or to the harmonization of national legislation (Case 355/85 *Cognet* [1986] ECR 3231 at p. 3242; Cases 80 and 159/85 *Edah* [1986] ECR 3359 at p. 3384). On the other hand, within the sphere of application of Art. 7 discrimination is prohibited even if it constitutes only an obstacle of secondary importance as regards the equality of access to, and other conditions of, work, employment, establishment, provision of services, etc. (Case 167/73 *Commission* v. *France* [1974] ECR 359 at p. 373).

Art. 7 only prohibits discrimination on grounds of nationality. It follows that rules of Member States which differentiate between traders not on the basis of their nationality but on the basis of their location or on the basis of the goods which they sell do not infringe Art. 7, even if they affect the competitiveness of the traders covered by them (Case 155/80 *Oebel*, above, at p. 2007; Case 355/85 *Cognet*, above, at p. 3241; Cases 80 and 159/85 *Edah*, above, at p. 3383; see also Case 90/76 *Van Ameyde*, above, at p. 1127; Case 31/78 *Bussone* [1978] ECR 2429 at p. 2446). Nor does Art. 7 prohibit discrimination between the nationals of the same State (Case 223/86 *Pesca Valentia* [1988] ECR 83 at p. 109). Nevertheless, in a consistent line of decisions the Court has also held that the rules regarding equality of treatment, both in the Treaty and in the related secondary legislation, forbid not only overt discrimination by reason of nationality but also 'all covert forms of discrimination which, by the application of other criteria of differentiation lead in fact to the same result'. The reason is that Community law strives to ensure equality of treatment both 'in fact and in law'. Therefore, criteria of differentiation such as the place of origin or residence of a person may, according to the circumstances, be tantamount, as regards their practical effect, to discrimination on the grounds of nationality and thus prohibited by Community law (Case 152/73 *Sotgiu*, above, at p. 164; Case 71/76 *Thieffry* [1977] ECR 765 at p. 777. For instances of covert or disguised or indirect discrimination, see e.g. Case 61/77 *Commission* v. *Ireland* [1978] ECR 417 at pp. 450–1—sea fisheries; Case 237/78 *Toia* [1979] ECR 2645 at pp. 2653–4—social security; Case 68/79 *Just* [1980] ECR 501 at p. 519—taxation of spirits; Case 96/80 *Jenkins* [1981] ECR 911 at pp. 925–6—pay for part-time work; Case 249/83 *Hoeckx*, above, at p. 989—social advantage; Case 41/84 *Pinna*, above, at pp. 25–6—family allowances; Case 20/85 *Roviello* [1988] ECR 2805 at pp. 2852–3—social security. See however Case 22/80 *Boussac* [1980] ECR 3427 at pp. 3436–7, where a covert form of discrimination was found not to be real discrimination prohibited by Art. 7).

The prohibition of discrimination on the basis of nationality contained in Arts. 48 *et seq.* EEC is subject to certain reservations and limitations justified on grounds of public policy, public security, or public health (Arts. 48(3), 56(1), 66 EEC). These reservations permit Member States to adopt, with respect to the nationals of other Member States, measures which they cannot apply to their own nationals (e.g. measures concerning the entry, residence, control, and expulsion of aliens). Although such a difference of treatment is allowed, the Member States are required, when exercising their powers, not to make arbitrary distinctions to the detriment of foreign nationals (Cases 115 and 116/81 *Adoui and Cornuaille*, above, at p. 1707).

The rules relating to the abolition of discrimination based on nationality with regard to employment (Art. 48(2) EEC), establishment (Art. 52 EEC), and provision of services (Arts. 59, 60, and 65 EEC) have been implemented, in turn, by secondary legislation in a number of different areas. Thus, discrimination is prohibited, in particular, in the field of social security (Art.

3(1) of Reg. 1408/71, see e.g. Case 63/76 *Inzirillo* [1976] ECR 2057 at p. 2067; Case 1/78 *Kenny*, above, at p. 1496); in relation to any 'social advantage' (Preamble and Art. 7(1) and (2) of Reg. 1612/68; Art. 7 of Reg. 1251/70, see e.g. Case 32/75 *Cristini* [1975] ECR 1085 at pp. 1094–5; Case 249/83 *Hoeckx*, above, at p. 989; Case 94/84 *Deak* [1985] ECR 1873 at pp. 1886–7; Case 137/84 *Mutsch*, above, at pp. 2695–6; Case 235/87 *Matteucci* [1988] ECR para. 16); in the field of education and vocational training including, in general, university studies (Arts. 7(3) and 12 of Reg. 1612/68, see e.g. Case 9/74 *Casagrande* [1974] ECR 773 at pp. 778–9; Case 152/82 *Forcheri* [1983] ECR 2323 at p. 2336; Case 293/83 *Gravier*, above, at pp. 611–14; Case 24/86 *Blaizot* [1988] ECR 379 at pp. 404–5; Case 39/86 *Lair*, above; Case 197/86 *Brown*, above), etc.

(*b*) *Art. 36* provides that prohibitions and restrictions on imports and exports which may be permissible on various grounds 'shall not . . . constitute a means of arbitrary discrimination' (see e.g. Case 4/75 *Rewe-Zentralfinanz* [1975] ECR 843 at p. 860).

(*c*) *Art. 37(1)* requires the Member States to adjust State monopolies of a commercial character so as to ensure that 'no discrimination regarding the conditions under which goods are procured and marketed exists between nationals of Member States' (see e.g. Case 13/70 *Cinzano* [1970] ECR 1089 at p. 1096; Case 59/75 *Manghera* [1976] ECR 91 at pp. 100–1; Case 45/75 *Rewe-Zentrale* [1976] ECR 181 at pp. 197–8, where the Court said that the rule in Art. 37(1) constituted a 'basic principle'; Case 91/75 *Miritz* [1976] ECR 217 at pp. 229–30).

(*d*) *Art. 40(3)* lays down the rule that the common organization of agricultural markets 'shall exclude any discrimination between producers or consumers within the Community'. In a number of cases, the ECJ has held that this provision is 'merely a specific enunciation of the general principle of equality which is one of the fundamental principles of Community law' and that therefore Art. 40(3) prohibits discrimination not only between producers of the same product but also between different industrial or trade sectors in the sphere of processed agricultural products, provided that the products are in a comparable situation (see e.g. Cases 117/76 and 16/77 *Ruckdeschel*, above, at p. 1769; Cases 124/76 and 20/77 *Moulins de Pont-à-Mousson*, above, at p. 1811; Case 125/77 *Koninklijke Scholten-Honig*, above, at p. 2003; Cases 103 and 145/77 *Royal Scholten-Honig*, above, at p. 2072; see also Case 245/81 *Edeka*, above, at p. 2754; Case 281/82 *Unifrex* v. *Commission and Council* [1984] ECR 1969 at p. 1986). In three sets of cases, the Court has established discrimination contrary to Art. 40(3), and has declared the relevant Council regulations null and void or invalid, on the following grounds: (i) compulsory purchase of certain animal feed products at such a disproportionate price that it amounted to a 'discriminatory distribution of the burden of costs between the various agricultural sectors' without being justified by the object in view, namely, the disposal of stocks of skimmed-milk powder ('Skimmed-milk powder' cases: Case 114/76 *Bela-Mühle*, above, at p. 1221; Case 116/76 *Granaria* [1977] ECR 1247 at pp. 1265–6; Cases 119 and 120/76 *Ölmühle and Becher* [1977] ECR 1269 at pp. 1286–7); (ii) abolition of the production refund for quellmehl and gritz while maintaining it for starch ('Quellmehl' cases: Cases 117/76 and 16/77 *Ruckdeschel*, above, at p. 1771; 'Gritz' cases: Cases 124/76 and 20/77 *Moulins de Pont-à-Mousson*, above, at p. 1812); (iii) the introduction of a system of production levies for isoglucose for the purpose of making up the marketing losses incurred by the sugar sector ('Isoglucose' cases: Cases 103 and 145/77 *Royal Scholten-Honig*, above, at pp. 2078–81).

The rule of non-discrimination applies also to the fisheries sector which is treated as part of agriculture under Art. 38 EEC (see Case 61/77 *Commission* v. *Ireland*, above, at p. 451, and Case 88/77 *Schonenberg* [1978] ECR 473 at pp. 490–1, applying Art. 7 EEC in conjunction with Art. 2(1) of Reg. 101/76; see also Cases 185 to 204/78 *Van Dam*, above, at pp. 2360–1, where the Court held that certain national protective measures were not discriminatory). Moreover, the ECJ has held that Art. 40(3) is also binding on the Member States when they are implementing the agricultural provisions. Consequently, where Community rules leave Member States a certain discretion to choose between various methods of implementation, they may not opt for measures which are liable to create discrimination within the meaning of Art. 40(3) (Cases 201 and 202/85 *Klensch* [1986] ECR 3477 at pp. 3507–8).

(*e*) *Arts. 48(2), 52, 59, 60, and 65* abolish any discrimination based on nationality as regards employment, establishment, and the provision of services—see above under (*a*).

(*f*) *Art. 67(1)* requires the Member States to abolish all restrictions on the movement of capital belonging to persons resident in Member States and 'any discrimination based on the nationality or on the place of residence of the parties or on the place where such capital is invested'. Under *Art. 68(2)*, where a Member State applies to the movements of capital the domestic rules governing the capital market and the credit system, 'it shall do so in a non-discriminatory manner'.

(*g*) *Art. 79(1)* provides for the abolition, in the case of transport within the Community, of 'discrimination which takes the form of carriers charging different rates and imposing different conditions for the carriage of the same goods over the same transport links on grounds of the country of origin or of destination of the goods in question'. However, as regards Government measures, in the absence of a Common Transport Policy disparities may still exist in the way in which undertakings of different Member States are treated as a result of differences between national legislation. The fact that one Member State applies more severe restrictions to transport undertakings established in its territory than other Member States cannot be regarded as prohibited discrimination (Case 126/82 *Smit*, above, at pp. 92–3).

(*h*) *Arts. 85 and 86* prohibit undertakings from applying 'dissimilar conditions to equivalent transactions with other trading parties, thereby placing them at a competitive disadvantage'.

(*i*) *Art. 95* prohibits any Member State from imposing on the products of other Member States discriminatory taxation. This provision is intended to ensure equality of treatment in internal taxation and the prohibition therefore concerns not only the rate but also the basis of taxation (Case 54/72 *FOR* [1973] ECR 193 at p. 204; Case 74/76 *Iannelli* [1977] ECR 557 at p. 578; see also e.g. Case 45/75 *Rewe-Zentrale*, above, at pp. 193–6; Case 78/76 *Steinike und Weinlig* [1977] ECR 595 at p. 613).

(*j*) *Art. 119* lays down the principle of non-discrimination based on sex by providing that 'men and women should receive equal pay for equal work'. The ECJ has stated that 'the principle of equal pay forms part of the foundations of the Community' (Case 43/75 *Defrenne*, above, at p. 472). However, the Court has made a distinction between, 'first, direct and overt discrimination which may be identified solely with the aid of the criteria based on equal work and equal pay referred to by [Art. 119] and, secondly . . . indirect and disguised discrimination which can only be identified by reference to more explicit implementing provisions . . .' (ibid. at p. 473). Direct discrimination includes discrimination which has its origin in legislative provisions or in collective labour agreements and in particular situations where men and women receive unequal pay for equal work carried out in the same establishment or service, whether public or private. In such situations, Art. 119 may give rise to enforceable individual rights which the national courts must protect (ibid. at pp. 473–4). In this context, the Court has pointed out that since Art. 119 is mandatory in nature, 'the prohibition on discrimination between men and women applies not only to the action of public authorities, but also extends to all agreements which are intended to regulate paid labour collectively, as well as to contracts between individuals' (ibid. at p. 476). The principle of equal pay for men and women has been implemented by Dir. 75/117.

Art. 119 only concerns equal pay and does not prescribe equality of treatment in respect of working conditions in general. However, this does not mean that Community law does not contain any general principle prohibiting discrimination based on sex as regards the conditions of employment and working conditions of men and women. Thus, the ECJ has repeatedly stated that 'respect for fundamental personal human rights is one of the general principles of Community law, the observance of which [the Court] has a duty to ensure', and that 'there can be no doubt that the elimination of discrimination based on sex forms part of those fundamental rights' (Case 149/77 *Defrenne* [1978] ECR 1365 at p. 1378, referring to the European Social Charter and ILO Convention No. 111). In several cases, the Court has recognized the need to ensure equality in the matter of working conditions for men and women employed by the Community itself, within the context of the Staff Regulations of Officials (see e.g. Case 20/71 *Sabbatini* v. *Parliament* [1972] ECR 345 at p. 351; Case 32/71 *Bauduin* v. *Commission* [1972] ECR 363 at p. 370; Case 21/74 *Airola* v. *Commission* [1975] ECR 221 at p. 228). However, as regards the relationships of employer and employee governed by national law, enforceable rules prohibiting discrimination between men and women in the matter of working conditions can only be found in the relevant implementing legislation (i.e. Dir. 76/207 and Dir. 79/7) and not in the Treaty itself or in the general principles of Community law (Case 149/77 *Defrenne*, above, at pp. 1378–9 *per Curiam*, pp. 1382–8 *per* A.-G. Capotorti).

3. In staff cases

Art. 5(3) of the Staff Regulations of Officials provides that 'identical conditions of recruitment and service career shall apply to all officials belonging to the same category or the same service'. In several cases, the Court has stated in relation to this provision that 'although the principle of equality of treatment is a general rule forming part of the law applicable to the employees of the Communities, discrimination occurs only where identical or comparable situations are treated in an unequal way' and that 'a breach of the prohibition of discrimination occurs only in cases of unequal treatment where the discrimination is not objectively justified' (Cases 198 to 202/81 *Micheli* v. *Commission* [1982] ECR 4145 at p. 4157; Case 147/79 *Hochstrass* v. *Court of Justice*, above, at p. 3019). Moreover, the Court has interpreted Art. 5(3) as a rule of 'fundamental importance' or a 'superior rule of law' which applies not only to appointment procedures (see e.g. Cases 129 and 274/82 *Lux* v. *Court of Auditors* [1984] ECR 4127 at p. 4142; Case 119/83 *Appelbaum* v. *Commission* [1985] ECR 2423 at pp. 2454, 2456; Case 143/84 *Vlachou* v. *Court of Auditors* [1986] ECR 459 at p. 478; in all these cases the Court annulled decisions appointing officials in infringement of the principle of equality), but to the whole body of law relating to the employment of Community officials, and includes the principle of equal pay for officials in comparable positions and performing duties of the same nature (Case 156/78 *Newth* v. *Commission* [1979] ECR 1941 at pp. 1952–3; Case 91/85 *Christ* v. *Commission* [1986] ECR 2853 at pp. 2869, 2871; see also Case 7/87 *Commission* v. *Council* [1988] ECR 3401 at p. 3440; in all three cases the Court established a breach of this principle).

See also **Common Agricultural Policy*, Common Fisheries Policy*, Common Transport Policy*, Common Vocational Training Policy*, Discriminatory price*, Discriminatory selling conditions*, Equal pay*, Equal treatment*, Freedom of establishment*, Freedom of movement for capital*, Freedom of movement for goods*, Freedom of movement for persons*, Freedom to provide services*, General principles of law, Human rights, Social advantage*, Social security*, Staff cases, State commercial monopolies*, Taxation*.**

Further reading 1. BOOKS: Sundberg-Weitman, *Discrimination on Grounds of Nationality: Free Movement of Workers and Freedom of Establishment under the EEC Treaty* (1977). *See also under* **General principles of law.**

2. ARTICLES AND REPORTS: FIDE, 'The Principle of Equality in Economic Law', *Reports of the Eleventh FIDE Congress* (1984) vol. ii, ch. 3, also in (1985) 22 *CML Rev.* 135; Herdegen, 'The Relation between the Principles of Equality and Proportionality' (1985) 22 *CML Rev.* 683; Kon, 'Aspects of Reverse Discrimination in Community Law' (1981) 6 *EL Rev.* 75; Pickup, 'Reverse Discrimination and Freedom of Movement for Workers' (1986) 23 *CML Rev.* 135; Schmitthoff, 'The Doctrines of Proportionality and Non-Discrimination' (1977) 2 *EL Rev.* 329; Steiner, 'The Right to Welfare: Equality and Equity under Community Law' (1985) 10 *EL Rev.* 21; Sundberg-Weitman, 'Addressees of the Ban on Discrimination Enshrined in Article 7 of the EEC Treaty' (1973) 10 *CML Rev.* 71.

▶ **EQUITY** Concept derived from English law where it implies justice and fairness. It is based on the principle that 'people should not make unconscionable use of their legal rights' (Case 102/75 *Petersen* v. *Commission* [1976] ECR 1777 at p. 1799 *per* A.-G. Warner). In several cases, the ECJ has resorted to equity to temper what would have been the rigours of a rigid and literal interpretation or application of Community law (see e.g. Case 94/75 *Süddeutsche Zucker* [1976] ECR 153 at p. 159; Case 34/80 *Authié* v. *Commission* [1981] ECR 665 at p. 676), sometimes going so far as to fill gaps by reference to equity (see e.g. Case 64/74 *Reich* [1975] ECR 261 at pp. 268–9, dealing with a plea of *force majeure*). Often the Court refers to the rules of 'fairness' to achieve similar results (see e.g. Case 31/75 *Costacurta* v. *Commission* [1975] ECR 1563 at p. 1570; Case 102/75 *Petersen* v. *Commission*, above, at p. 1793; Case 94/77 *Zerbone* [1978] ECR 99 at p. 114; Case 87/78 *Welding* [1978] ECR 2457 at p. 2466; see also Case 37/72 *Marcato* v. *Commission* [1973] ECR 361 at p. 368).

See also Force majeure, **General principles of law, Interpretation of Community law, Natural justice.**

▶ *ERGA OMNES* EFFECT General effect, usually meaning the binding effect of a legal provision or judicial decision on everyone, i.e., in the Community context, on the institutions, on the various authorities of the Member States including the courts, and on private individuals. As regards the acts of the institutions, ECSC general decisions and EEC/Euratom regulations, being legislative measures, by definition produce *erga omnes* effects. As to the judgments of the ECJ, owing to the *res judicata* rule, only those declaring an act of an institution void in a direct action for annulment under Arts. 33, 34 and 37, 38 ECSC, 173, 174 EEC, and 146, 147 Euratom have, strictly speaking, *erga omnes* effects.

See also **Action for annulment, General decision,** *Inter partes* **effect, Plea of illegality, Preliminary ruling, Regulation,** *Res judicata.*

▶ **EUROPEAN ACT (DRAFT)** Document presented by the German and Italian Governments to the European Council, the European Parliament, and the Commission in November 1981 containing proposals to revitalize the Communities by strengthening political and security co-operation as a way of progressing towards European Union (also known variously as the 'Bonn–Rome', 'German–Italian' or 'Genscher–Colombo' initiative on European Union). Although solemn in form, the Draft European Act was neither a new treaty nor a legally binding instrument; its objective was to formulate principles and outline adjustments to existing structures as a further contribution to the establishment of European Union. It was accompanied by a draft declaration on economic integration (*Bull. EC* 11–1981, p. 10, texts at pp. 87 and 91).

The document presented by the two Governments has three main aims. First, to spotlight the prime political objective of European unification. Secondly, to establish an overall framework for co-operation among the Community institutions; in that context it calls for greater convergence in the decision-making structures of the Community and of political co-operation under the responsibility of the European Council; it stresses the need for strengthening Parliament's decision-making and review powers; it urges the Council to revert to the rule of majority decision as provided for by the Treaties and to plead 'vital interests' in exceptional cases only; and underlines the particular importance of the Commission as guardian of the Treaties and as a driving force in the process of European integration. The third aim is to include the political and economic aspects of European security within the common foreign policy of the Communities. Provision is made for a general review of the Act five years after its signing with a view to incorporating the progress achieved in a Treaty on European Union.

The Draft European Act received cautious approval from the Commission and mixed reaction from the European Parliament (*Bull. EC* 11–1981, pp. 11–12), while the European Council invited the Foreign Ministers in co-operation with the Commission to examine and clarify its proposals and to report back to a future meeting (ibid. p. 8). The report of the Foreign Ministers was presented to the Stuttgart European Council on 17–19 June 1983 and resulted in the signing by the ten Heads of State or Government of the 'Solemn Declaration on European Union' (*Bull. EC* 6–1983, p. 23, text at p. 24).

See also **European Union, Institutions, Solemn Declaration on European Union.**

Further reading: Neville-Jones, 'The Genscher–Colombo Proposals on European Union' (1983) 20 *CML Rev.* 657; Weiler, 'The Genscher–Colombo Draft European Act: The Politics of Indecision' (1983) 6 *Journal of European Integration* 129.

▶ **EUROPEAN COMMUNITIES** (EC) Organizations established by six European States (Belgium, France, Germany, Italy, Luxembourg, and the Netherlands) by Treaties under public international law, as follows:

- *European Coal and Steel Community (ECSC)* established by the Treaty of Paris of 18 April 1951; the Treaty was concluded for a period of fifty years (Art. 97) and entered into force on 25 July 1952;
- *European Economic Community (EEC)* established by the Treaty of Rome of 25 March 1957; the Treaty was concluded for an unlimited period (Art. 240) and entered into force on 1 January 1958;
- *European Atomic Energy Community (EAEC or Euratom)* established by the Treaty of Rome of 25 March 1957; the Treaty was concluded for an unlimited period (Art. 208) and entered into force on 1 January 1958.

The creation of the first Community, the ECSC, was prompted by the determination of the Member States 'to substitute for age-old rivalries the merging of their essential interests' and 'to create, by establishing an economic community, the basis for a broader and deeper community among peoples long divided by bloody conflicts' (Preamble to the ECSC Treaty). The setting up of the EEC was motivated by even more ambitious and far-reaching ideals, namely, 'to lay the foundations of an ever closer union among the peoples of

Europe' and to ensure 'the economic and social progress of their countries by common action to eliminate the barriers which divided Europe' (Preamble to the EEC Treaty). The purpose of the Euratom was to create the conditions 'necessary for the development of a powerful nuclear industry which will provide extensive energy resources' (Preamble to the Euratom Treaty).

Under the *ECSC Treaty*, integration is partial and limited to the coal and steel sectors only, as defined in Annexes I, II, and III to the Treaty (see Art. 81 ECSC). The rules of the Treaty apply primarily to coal- and steel-producing undertakings and their associations as referred to in Arts. 48(1) and 80 ECSC, but do not cover those sectors of the economy of the Member States and those economic activities of undertakings which have not been included within the scope of Community competence. Such are, for example, the general economic, social, transport, fiscal, and commercial policies of the Member States and any action by them affecting conditions of competition, and the activities of distributing undertakings in the coal and steel industry (see Arts. 26(1), 67, 68(1), 70(5), 71(1), and 80 ECSC, the latter subject to Arts. 65 and 66 ECSC). The Member States remain fully responsible for all such economic sectors and activities (see Case 20/59 *Italy* v. *HA* [1960] ECR 325 at pp. 335 *et seq.*; Case 30/59 *Steenkolenmijnen* v. *HA* [1961] ECR 1 at p. 23; Case 9/61 *Netherlands* v. *HA* [1962] ECR 213 at p. 232), subject to the Community's considerable co-ordinating and supervisory powers (see Arts. 26, 57, 67, 68, 69, 70, 71–5 ECSC). On the other hand, the ECSC is founded on a Common Market for coal and steel, which includes the free movement of goods, as well as on common objectives and common institutions (Art. 1 ECSC). Although there is no Common Customs Tariff, the ECJ has held that the ECSC does not constitute a free-trade area in which the origin of a product is a determining factor, but is more akin in its structure to the principle of a Customs Union (Case 36/83 *Mabanaft* [1984] ECR 2497 at p. 2523; for an analysis of the various tasks and objectives laid down in Arts. 2–5 ECSC, see Cases 154/78 etc. *Valsabbia* v. *Commission* [1980] ECR 907 at pp. 1002–4, 1008–10).

Integration is likewise limited under the *Euratom Treaty*, the scope of which is restricted to the nuclear energy sector (see Art. 197 Euratom), and which in the main applies to a limited category of 'persons' and 'undertakings' as defined in Art. 196. The Treaty has set up a nuclear Common Market involving the free movement of specialized materials and equipment, the establishment of a Common Customs Tariff, the free movement of capital for investment in the field of nuclear energy, and freedom of employment for specialists (Arts. 2(g) and 92–100 Euratom; Annex IV to the Treaty. For an analysis of the scope of the Euratom Treaty and of the powers of its institutions, see Ruling 1/78 *Protection of Nuclear Materials* [1978] ECR 2151 at pp. 2170 *et seq.*).

In contrast with the two previous Communities, integration under the *EEC Treaty* is in principle of a comprehensive nature and is not to take place separately according to the economic sectors. The Treaty applies generally to all 'natural and legal persons' carrying on activities falling within its scope, although for certain purposes such persons must be nationals of or established in a Member State, or satisfy some other criterion. The establishment of the

Common Market under the EEC Treaty, unlike those under the ECSC and Euratom Treaties, thus refers to the whole of the economic activities in the Community and involves the creation of a Customs Union with a Common Customs Tariff and a Common Commercial Policy towards third countries (Arts. 3(a) and (b), 9–37, 110–16 EEC; see also Case 167/73 *Commission* v. *France* [1974] ECR 359 at p. 369 *per Curiam*, p. 378 *per* A.-G. Reischl). The Treaty aims at full economic and social integration (see Case 152/73 *Sotgiu* [1974] ECR 153 at pp. 169–70 *per* A.-G. Mayras; Case 43/75 *Defrenne* [1976] ECR 455 at p. 472), but political integration has not, so far, developed beyond mere co-operation (*see further under* **European Political Co-operation**). The aims of the Treaty are to be achieved through the creation of a single economic region, a unification of the national markets into a large single market without internal frontiers in which the free movement of goods, persons, services, and capital is fully ensured (see Case 9/73 *Schlüter* [1973] ECR 1135 at p. 1161; Case 192/73 *Van Zuylen* [1974] ECR 731 at p. 744). Such an internal market, which should have been established already by 31 December 1969 (Art. 8(7) EEC), is now to be completed by 31 December 1992 under the Single European Act of 1986 (SEA) (Art. 13, inserting a new Art. 8A into the EEC Treaty). But until these objectives have been fully achieved, there remain certain areas of the economic life (e.g. conjunctural policy, balance of payments, rates of exchange) that are not subject to common rules. Here the Member States retain their freedom of decision to a considerable extent although they are required to regard their various policies as a matter of common concern (Arts. 103–9 EEC; see Case 9/73 *Schlüter*, above, at pp. 1152–3, 1161). They are also under an obligation to co-ordinate, in close co-operation with the institutions of the Communities, their respective economic and monetary policies (Arts. 3(g), 6, and 102A EEC, the latter being added by Art. 20 of the SEA).

The three Communities were established as distinct legal entities, each having its own separate legal personality both in international law and in the national laws of the Member States (Arts. 6 ECSC, 210 EEC, 184 Euratom; *see further under* **Legal personality**). Although their unification had long been envisaged (see the Preamble and Art. 32 of the Merger Treaty of 1965; the latter actually refers to a 'Treaty establishing a Single European Community'), so far only the merger of the four institutions has been achieved (*see further under* **Institutions**). It seems that the idea of merging the Communities themselves has now given way to an effort to transform the relations between the Member States into a European Union, which must however take place 'with the fullest respect for the Treaties already signed' (Declaration of the Paris Summit Conference of 19–21 Oct. 1972, point 16, 6th *Gen. Rep. EC* (1972), p. 7. See also Preamble to the SEA, and *see further under* **European Union**). The relations between the three Communities are determined by the principle that the provisions of the EEC Treaty shall not affect those of the ECSC Treaty and shall not derogate from those of the Euratom Treaty (Art. 232 EEC; *see further under* **Community Treaties**).

The legal nature of the European Communities has been described by the ECJ in the following terms: 'By creating a Community of unlimited duration, having its own institutions, its own personality, its own legal capacity and capacity of representation on the international plane and, more particularly, real powers stemming from a limitation of sovereignty or a transfer of powers from the States to the Community, the Member States have limited their sovereign rights, albeit within limited fields, and have thus created a body of law which binds both their nationals and themselves' (Case 6/64 *Costa* [1964] ECR 585 at p. 593). It thus seems that the legal existence of the Communities is based on a definitive and irreversible transfer to them of sovereign powers from the Member States. This transfer is definitive in that it is for an unlimited period and no longer subject to reservations by the Member States or to challenge by their nationals in legal proceedings (see Cases 9 and 58/65 *San Michele* v. *HA* [1967] ECR 1 at pp. 29–30). It is also irreversible because 'powers thus conferred could not . . . be withdrawn from the Community, nor could the objectives with which such powers are concerned be restored to the field of authority of the Member States alone, except by virtue of an express provision of the Treaty' (Case 7/71 *Commission* v. *France* [1971] ECR 1003 at p. 1018. See also Case 804/79 *Commission* v. *United Kingdom* [1981] ECR 1045 at p. 1073, where the same principle is stated in regard to the Common Fisheries Policy).

The foregoing explanation has important consequences both for the Communities and for the Member States. For the Communities, it means that they can exercise only such powers as have been expressly or by implication conferred on them by the founding Treaties; they possess only derived or 'attributed' competences (*compétences d'attribution*; *Enumerationsprinzip*; see Case 22/70 *Commission* v. *Council* [1971] ECR 263 at pp. 273, 275–6, 278 *per Curiam*, p. 293 *per* A.-G. Dutheillet de Lamothe—'ERTA' case). They cannot, on their own authority, assume additional powers, nor can they bring entirely new matters (i.e. matters not covered by the objectives of the Communities as laid down in the Treaties) within the scope of their competence. This can be done only by the Member States acting through their Representatives meeting in Council, or by Treaty amendment (under Arts. 95, 96 ECSC, 236 EEC, 204 Euratom), or by the conclusion of new Treaties. Accordingly, any action taken by the Community institutions in a field which falls within the exclusive competence of the Member States will 'lack all legal basis in the Community legal system' (Cases 6 and 11/69 *Commission* v. *France* [1969] ECR 523 at p. 539; see also Case 30/59 *Steenkolenmijnen* v. *HA*, above, at p. 23).

For the Member States, the transfer of powers to the Communities has as a consequence 'a permanent limitation of their sovereign rights, against which a subsequent unilateral act incompatible with the concept of the Community cannot prevail' (Case 6/64 *Costa*, above, at p. 594). In general, Member States must by all means at their disposal facilitate the performance of the Communities' tasks. They must take all appropriate measures to ensure fulfilment of the obligations arising from the Treaties or from action taken by the institutions. Conversely, they must abstain from any measure which would jeopardize the attainment of Community objectives (Arts. 86 ECSC, 5 EEC, 192 Euratom). As the ECJ has stressed in a series of cases, these obligations are, indeed, only a natural corollary to the benefits which the Member States derive from the existence of the Communities. The balance of mutual advantages and obligations flowing from the establishment of the Communities has created a 'duty of solidarity' for the Member States, any unilateral breach of which in the national interests brings into question their equality before Community law, creates discriminations at the expense of their nationals, and ultimately strikes at the fundamental basis of the Community legal order (see Case 39/72 *Commission* v. *Italy* [1973] ECR 101 at p. 116; Case 128/78 *Commission* v. *United Kingdom* [1979] ECR 419 at p. 429—'Tachographs' case; etc.). As A.-G. Darmon has put it succinctly, 'formed of States based on the rule of law, the European Community is necessarily a Community of law. It was created and works on the understanding that all Member States will show equal respect for the Community legal order' (Case 222/84 *Johnston* [1986] ECR 1651 at p. 1656). The fact that the Community is a 'Community based on the rule of law' also means that both the Member States and the institutions are subject to judicial review by the ECJ regarding the question whether the measures adopted by them are in conformity with the 'basic constitutional charter', the founding Treaties (Case 294/83 *Les Verts* v. *Parliament* [1986] ECR 1339 at p. 1365).

Finally, it follows from the transfer of powers that the authority of the Communities over matters falling within their competence is exclusive, and leaves no room for any concurrent authority on the part of the Member States. Any initiative taken outside the Community framework in these matters is incompatible with the unity of the Common Market and the uniform application of Community law (see e.g. Case 30/59 *Steenkolenmijnen* v. *HA*, above, at p. 22, dealing with the powers of the ECSC; Case 22/70 *Commission* v. *Council*, above, at pp. 274, 276, dealing with the treaty-making powers of the EEC. The ECJ has confirmed and applied this principle in a long line of cases concerning a variety of matters transferred to Community competence, e.g. tariff matters, the Common Agricultural Policy, treaty-making power, see e.g. Case 40/69 *Bollmann* [1970] ECR 69 at p. 79; Case 18/72 *Granaria* [1972] ECR 1163 at p. 1171; Case 131/73 *Grosoli* [1973] ECR 1555 at pp. 1565–6).

In view of the foregoing characteristic features, it may be stated that the European Communities represent a novel, *sui generis* type of international organization. They are distinguished from all other existing forms of international organization not only by the unique division of competences between the Communities and their Member States but also, and even more importantly, by the setting up of common institutions endowed with sovereign legislative, executive, and judicial powers the exercise of which affects not only the Member States (as may be the case in a 'traditional' type of international organization), but also their nationals. These features show a certain degree of resemblance to the internal structure of federal States. At the same time, the external appearance of the Communities, their legal personality, status, and treaty-making powers under international law approximate them more closely to international organizations. It is, therefore, perhaps more appropriate to regard them, at the present stage of their

207

development, not as a State-like entity or as a federal State, but as a new public authority of a special and original nature, a supranational organization in the process of progressive integration with an autonomous source of sovereign power within a limited sphere of action.

See also **Accession Treaties, Action against Member States, Community law, Community Treaties, European Political Co-operation, European Union, External relations, Implied powers, Institutions, Judicial review, Legal personality, Representatives of the Governments of the Member States meeting in Council, Single European Act, Supplementary powers, Treaty-making power.**

Further reading 1. BOOKS: Commission of the European Communities, *Twenty-five Years of the Common Market in Coal, 1953–1978* (1978); id., *The Community Today* (1980); id., *Thirty Years of Community Law* (1983), part I, chs. 2–3; Lasok and Soldatos (eds.), *The European Communities in Action* (1981); Noël, *The European Community: How It Works* (1979). *See also under* **Community law, European Court of Justice.**

2. ARTICLES: Bleckmann, 'The Personal Jurisdiction of the European Community' (1980) 17 *CML Rev.* 467; Collins, 'Personal Jurisdiction of the European Community: Some Comments on the Application of Civil and Penal Jurisdiction' (1980) 17 *CML Rev.* 487; Gillies, 'West Berlin and the European Communities' (1987/2) *LIEI* 33; Heusdens and de Horn, 'Crisis Policy in the European Steel Industry in the Light of the ECSC Treaty' (1980) 17 *CML Rev.* 31; Hütte, 'Berlin and the European Communities' (1983) 3 *YEL* 1; Rees and Thomas, 'Harmonisation in the Western European Context: A Case Study of European Coal and Steel Community (ECSC) Readaptation Aid' (1986/2) *LIEI* 45; Schepers, 'The Legal Force of the Preamble to the EEC Treaty' (1981) 6 *EL Rev.* 356; Weiler, 'The Community System: The Dual Character of Supranationalism' (1981) 1 *YEL* 267.

3. OFFICIAL PUBLICATIONS: (*a*) On the *ECSC*: *Bull. EC* 2–1978, p. 22; 2–1981, p. 13; 3–1981, p. 87; 5–1981, p. 7. (*b*) On the *Euratom*: *Bull. EC* 7/8–1977, p. 10; 3–1978, p. 14; 12–1982, p. 17; 11–1984, p. 11.

▶ **EUROPEAN COUNCIL** Name under which the Heads of State or Government of the Member States of the European Communities have been holding regular meetings since 1975 which replaced earlier occasional Summit Conferences. Initially, the European Council was not provided for in any of the Community Treaties but was *de facto* established at the Paris Summit Conference of 9 and 10 December 1974 when the Heads of State or Government decided 'to meet, accompanied by the Ministers of Foreign Affairs, three times a year and, whenever necessary, in the Council of the Communities and in the context of political co-operation'. To ensure consistency in Community activities, the Ministers of Foreign Affairs, meeting in the Council of the Communities, would act as initiators and co-ordinators. They might hold political co-operation meetings at the same time. These arrangements were not to affect the rules and procedures laid down in the Treaties or the provisions on European Political Co-operation (EPC), nor the powers vested in the Commission by those texts (Communiqué of 10 Dec. 1974, 8th *Gen. Rep. EC* (1974), p. 297).

The setting up of the European Council was intended to achieve several objectives, such as the strengthening of the decision-making process; to ensure at the highest level an overall and coherent approach to the problems facing the Communities; to provide political impetus to the construction of the European Union; and to ensure consistency between the activities of the Communities and EPC by bringing them both under the authority of one supreme political body.

The organization, procedure, functions, and powers of the European Council are not set out in any legally binding instrument. However, two declarations made by the European Council itself deal with some of these matters. First, the Declaration of London of 30 June 1977 lays down the framework for the organization of European Council meetings (*Bull. EC 6–1977*, p. 83). Generally, the European Council can hold three types of discussion:

1. Informal and unminuted exchanges of view of a wide-ranging nature held in the greatest privacy and not designed to lead to formal decisions or public statements.
2. Discussions which are designed to produce decisions, set guidelines for future action, or lead to the issue of public statements expressing the agreed view of the European Council ('Conclusions of the Presidency').
3. Exceptionally, the European Council can also settle issues outstanding from discussions at a lower level. However, in dealing with matters within Community competence the European Council must conform to the appropriate procedures laid down in the Treaties and other agreements and must, in particular, observe the powers vested in the Commission.

While informal exchanges of view need little advance preparation, discussions aimed at reaching decisions or issuing statements must be adequately prepared. This is the responsibility of the Foreign Ministers acting either in the Council or within the EPC machinery or holding a special meeting for this purpose if necessary. The European Council is presided over by the Head of State or Government of the Member State whose representative holds the office of President of the Council. Its meetings are also attended by the President and a member (a Vice-President) of the Commission. The Secretariat is provided by the General Secretariat of the Council.

Secondly, the Solemn Declaration on European Union signed in Stuttgart on 19 June 1983 by the ten Heads of State or Government sets out the most important functions and tasks of the European Council, particularly in the context of European Union (*Bull. EC 6–1983*, p. 24). These include the provision of a general political impetus to the construction of Europe; issuing general political guidelines for both the European Communities and EPC; deliberating upon matters concerning European Union; initiation of co-operation in new areas of activity and expressing the common position on external relations. The Declaration also states that when the European Council acts in matters within the scope of the Communities, it does so in its capacity as the Council within the meaning of the Treaties. The President of

209

the European Council is required to report to the European Parliament on the outcome of each meeting (this had already been the practice since Dec. 1981 following the precedent set by Mrs Thatcher, see *Bull. EC* 12–1981, p. 73). The Presidency addresses the Parliament at the beginning of its term of office and presents its programme. At the end of its term, it reports on the progress achieved. The European Council is also to address a written annual report to the European Parliament on progress towards European Union.

The particular importance and leading role of the European Council in Community affairs have been recognized in all the other Reports and documents that have been produced on institutional reform and European Union (see in particular the Tindemans and Three Wise Men's Reports, the Draft European Act, the European Parliament's Draft Treaty on European Union, and the Report of the Committee on Institutional Affairs—the Dooge Committee). Nevertheless, the precise position of the European Council within the institutional structure of the Communities is still not clear. While Art. 2 of the Single European Act of 1986 (SEA) has given it formal Treaty status—something which it was lacking before—it only deals with its composition. It simply provides that the European Council shall bring together the Heads of State or Government of the Member States and the President of the Commission, who are to be assisted by the Ministers for Foreign Affairs and by a member of the Commission, and that it shall meet at least twice a year. Art. 2 is thus entirely silent as to the functions and powers of the European Council and its relationship to the other institutions. It does not confer upon it the status of a Community institution within the meaning of Arts. 7 ECSC, 4 EEC, 3 Euratom. Nor does Art. 2, or any of the other provisions of the SEA, create a legal link between the European Council and the Council of the Communities or between the European Council and EPC. It would seem to follow from this that the Community institutions proper— the Council, Commission, and European Parliament—are not legally bound by the political acts of the European Council although in practice they do take the necessary measures, where so requested, to implement the decisions of the European Council, thereby giving them binding legal effect. There is, of course, nothing to prevent the latter from acting as the Council of the Communities since its composition largely corresponds to that of the Council as laid down in the Treaties (see Art. 2 of the Merger Treaty. Strictly speaking, however, the French President is a Head of State and not a Member of Government as required by Art. 2 MT). In such a case, the European Council may adopt legally binding measures on the basis of the Treaties but subject to their rules as to competence, form, and procedure. Although the European Council as such is not subject to the jurisdiction of the European Court of Justice (see Art. 31 SEA), when acting as the Council it would presumably be subject to it in the same way as the Council is.

So far, the European Council has refrained from embarking upon legislative activities, confining itself to its initial task of providing general political impetus and guidance to the Communities. While not always successful in resolving major issues, it has nevertheless produced some quite important results, such as the establishment of the European Monetary System (EMS),

Resolution of the Brussels European Council of 4 and 5 December 1978 (*Bull. EC* 12–1978, p. 10; *Bull. EC* 2–1979, p. 7); the adoption of the Solemn Declaration on European Union, cited above; the settlement of budgetary issues by the Fontainebleau European Council of 25 and 26 June 1984 (*Bull. EC* 6–1984, p. 7); the convening of the Intergovernmental Conference to amend the Treaties by the Milan European Council of 28 and 29 June 1985 (*Bull. EC* 6–1985, p. 13); the agreement on the reform of the institutions and the completion of the internal market by the Luxembourg European Council of 2 and 3 December 1985 (*Bull. EC* 11–1985, p. 7) subsequently incorporated in the Single European Act of 1986; the reform of the Community budget by the Brussels European Council of 11–13 February 1988 (*Bull. EC* 2–1988, p. 8).

See also **Commission, Committee on Institutional Affairs, Council, European Act, European Parliament, European Political Co-operation, European Union, Institutions, Secondary legislation, Single European Act, Solemn Declaration on European Union, Three Wise Men's Report, Tindemans Report.**

Further reading 1. BOOK: Bulmer and Wessels, *The European Council: Decision-making in European Politics* (1987).
   2. ARTICLES: Editorial, 'The Solemn Declaration on European Union' (1983) 8 *EL Rev.* 295; Lauwaars, 'The European Council' (1977) 14 *CML Rev.* 25. *See also under* **Single European Act.**

▶ **EUROPEAN COURT OF JUSTICE (ECJ)** One of the four institutions of the European Communities, the others being the European Parliament, the Council, and the Commission (Arts. 7 ECSC, 4 EEC, 3 Euratom). The present Court was established by Arts. 3 and 4 of the Convention on Certain Institutions Common to the European Communities of 1957, which set up a single Court of Justice to serve all three Communities, taking the place of the former Court of Justice of the ECSC and of the Courts of Justice created by the EEC and Euratom Treaties. This single Court exercises the jurisdiction conferred by each of the three founding Treaties upon each of the Courts which they set up, in accordance with the provisions of those Treaties (the main provisions governing the ECJ are as follows: Arts. 31–45 ECSC, 164–88 EEC, 136–60 Euratom, as amended; ECSC, EEC, and Euratom Statutes as amended; Rules of Procedure (RP), Supplementary Rules (SR), and the Instructions to the Registrar (IR), all dated 4 Dec. 1974, as amended, codified versions in *OJ* 1982 C39/1, as further amended on 8 May 1987, *OJ* 1987 L165/1, and on 7 June 1989, *OJ* 1989 L241/1. Since the provisions of the ECSC, EEC, and Euratom Treaties and Statutes relating to the composition and organization of the Court are very similar, for ease of reference only the EEC provisions will be cited below).

I. Composition

The ECJ consists of thirteen *Judges* and is assisted by six *Advocates-General*. Both the Judges and the Advocates-General are chosen from persons whose independence is beyond doubt and who possess the qualifications required for appointment to the highest judicial offices in their respective countries or

who are jurisconsults of recognized competence. They are appointed by
common accord of the Governments of the Member States for a term of six
years. Every three years there is a partial replacement of the Judges and of the
Advocates-General. Seven and six Judges are replaced alternately, while
three Advocates-General are replaced on each occasion. Retiring Judges and
Advocates-General are eligible for reappointment. Immediately after the
partial replacement, the Judges elect, by secret ballot, the President of the
Court from among their number for a term of three years; he may be re-
elected (Arts. 165–7 EEC as last amended by Arts. 17–19 of the Act of
Accession 1985; Art. 7 RP). Although the Treaties lay down no provisions
regarding the nomination and nationality of Judges and Advocates-General,
in practice each Member State nominates one Judge who is its national and
each of the four larger Member States (Germany, France, Italy, and the
United Kingdom) nominates one Advocate-General, who is also its national.
The thirteenth Judge is nominated by the larger Member States (including
Spain) in rotation and the fifth and sixth Advocates-General by the smaller
Member States in rotation (see *Bull. EC* 3–1981, p. 63; for the partial
replacement of Judges and Advocates-General for the period from 7 Oct.
1988 to 6 Oct. 1994, see *OJ* 1988 L273/11; for the appointment of the
thirteenth Judge for the same period, see *OJ* 1988 L279/19. For the election
of the President for the period from 7 Oct. 1988 to 6 Oct. 1991, see *OJ* 1988
C285/11).

Before taking up his duties, each Judge is required to take an oath to
perform his duties impartially and conscientiously and to preserve the secrecy
of the deliberations of the Court. At the same time, he is to sign a solemn
declaration by which he undertakes that he will respect the obligations arising
from his office, and in particular the duty to behave with integrity and
discretion as regards the acceptance, after he has ceased to hold office, of
certain appointments and benefits (Arts. 2 and 4 EEC Statute, 3 RP). The
Judges may not hold any political or administrative office and may not engage
in any occupation, whether gainful or not, unless exemption is exceptionally
granted by the Council (Art. 4 EEC Statute). No Judge may take part in the
disposal of any case in which he has previously taken part as agent or adviser
or has acted for one of the parties, or on which he has been called upon to
pronounce as a member of a court or tribunal, of a commission of inquiry, or
in any other capacity (Art. 16 EEC Statute). The Judges are immune from
legal proceedings. They continue to enjoy such immunity even after they have
ceased to hold office, but only in respect of acts performed by them in their
official capacity, including words spoken or written. The Court may waive
the immunity (Art. 3 EEC Statute). In addition, Judges enjoy the same
privileges and immunities as the officials and other servants of the Communities, in accordance with Arts. 12–15, 18, and 21 of the Protocol on
Privileges and Immunities annexed to the Merger Treaty (*see further under*
Privileges and immunities). A Judge's term of office may be terminated
by normal replacement, death, voluntary resignation, or by a unanimous
decision of the other Judges and the Advocates-General that he no longer
fulfils the requisite conditions or meets the obligations arising from his office

(Arts. 5–6 EEC Statute; 4 RP). All the above rules apply in a corresponding manner to Advocates-General (Arts. 8 EEC Statute, 5 RP. Arts. 7 and 13 of the ECSC Statute, laying down the rules whereby Judges and Advocates-General may be deprived of their office, are slightly different).

The main task of the *Advocates-General* is to deliver an oral and reasoned opinion in each case brought before the Court. In so doing, they do not represent the parties to the case, nor do they defend the Communities' interests. Rather, they are required to act 'with complete impartiality and independence', the purpose of their opinion being to assist the Court in the performance of the task assigned to it (Arts. 166 EEC, 59 RP). In addition to the opinion on the substance of the case, the Advocates-General are also required to deliver opinions on a large number of procedural issues (*see further under* **Opinion**, point 6). Judges and Advocates-General rank equally in precedence according to their seniority in office. Where there is equal seniority in office, precedence is determined by age (Art. 6 RP). Nevertheless, only Judges may take part in the deliberations of the Court, with the exception of deliberations concerning questions of the Court's own administration in which the Advocates-General also participate and have a vote (Art. 27 RP). Each year, the Court appoints the *First Advocate-General* whose main task is to assign each case to an Advocate-General. He is also required to take the necessary steps if an Advocate-General is absent or prevented from attending (Art. 10 RP. For the appointment of the First Advocate-General from 7 Oct. 1989, see *OJ* 1989 C274/3).

The principal duties of the *President of the Court* are to direct the judicial business and the administration of the Court and to preside at hearings and at deliberations in the Deliberation Room (Art. 8 RP). In addition, a number of specific functions have been entrusted to him, such as e.g. to assign new cases to one of the Chambers and to designate the Judge-Rapporteur from that Chamber (Art. 9(2) RP, see further below). He also has power to order the suspension of operation or enforcement of Community acts and to prescribe any necessary interim measures (Arts. 36 EEC Statute, 83–90 RP; see also Art. 81(3) and (4) Euratom), etc. When the President of the Court is absent or prevented from attending or when the office of President is vacant, the functions of President are exercised by a President of a Chamber according to the order of precedence laid down in Art. 6 RP (see above).

The Treaties enable the Court to form *Chambers* either to undertake certain preparatory inquiries or to adjudicate on particular categories of cases in accordance with rules laid down for these purposes (Art. 165 EEC). Art. 9 RP in fact provides for the setting up of Chambers, the number and composition of which have altered several times over the years. The third enlargement of the Communities in 1986 made it possible to increase the number of Chambers to six: since 3 October 1986 there have been four Chambers of three Judges each and two Chambers of six Judges each (see *OJ* 1986 C286/4; for the composition of the Chambers during the period from 7 Oct. 1989 to 6 Oct. 1990, see *OJ* 1989 C274/3). The Court appoints for a period of one year the Presidents of the Chambers (see ibid.), who exercise the powers of the President of the Court in cases assigned to or devolving upon the Chambers (Art. 9(4) and 10 RP).

Initially, the main function envisaged for the Chambers was to conduct any necessary preparatory inquiries, and this is still one of their tasks (see Arts. 9(2), 44(2), and 46(1) RP). However, over the years they have been used to an increasing extent to relieve the full Court of its growing workload by adjudicating over certain categories of cases. For this purpose, Art. 165(3) EEC was amended in 1974 (by Council Dec. 74/584, OJ 1974 L318/22, see also *Bull. EC* 11–1974, p. 8), and the Court's Rules of Procedure were amended twice (in 1974 and 1979). Under the 1979 amendments, currently in force, the following types of case may be assigned to Chambers for hearing and determination, as distinct from the initial assignment by the President under Art. 9(2) RP (see Art. 95 RP):

1. references for a preliminary ruling;
2. direct actions instituted by natural or legal persons for annulment, for failure to act, for damages, against sanctions, or under an arbitration clause;
3. proceedings commenced by officials or other servants of the Communities (staff cases);

provided that, under (1) and (2), the difficulty or the importance of the case or particular circumstances are not such as to require that the Court decide it in plenary session. The decision to assign a case to a Chamber for hearing is taken by the full Court at the end of the written procedure. However, a case may not be so assigned if a Member State or a Community institution which is a party to or an intervener in the proceedings, or which has submitted written observations in reference proceedings, has requested that the case be decided in plenary session. Nor may cases brought by a Member State or a Community institution be assigned to a Chamber (Art. 165 EEC). Staff cases are always heard by a Chamber; they are allocated in rotation amongst the first four Chambers, i.e. those composed of three Judges (this system has been used since 1981, see OJ 1981 C265/3; for 1988–9, see OJ 1988 C285/12). However, a Chamber may at any stage refer to the full Court any case assigned to it, including staff cases (Art. 95(4) RP).

When the President of the Court initially allocates a new case to a Chamber, he is also required to designate a *Judge-Rapporteur* from that Chamber (Art. 9(2) RP; see also Arts. 76(3), 105(3), and 108(1) RP dealing with special proceedings). The principal function of the Judge-Rapporteur is to prepare the Report for the Hearing (see Art. 18 EEC Statute). This sets out the facts of the case as well as the procedure followed and summarizes the conclusions, submissions, and arguments of the parties. Prior to January 1985, the Report for the Hearing was incorporated in the Court's judgment as its 'Facts and Issues' part; since September 1986 it is published separately, together with the judgment, in the *European Court Reports*. In addition, the Judge-Rapporteur has certain other tasks. At the end of the written procedure, he is to present a preliminary report to the Court containing recommendations as to whether a preparatory inquiry is necessary and whether the case should be referred to the Chamber for determination (Art.

44(1) RP). He may be entrusted with measures of inquiry (Art. 45(3) RP) or with the supervision of experts (Art. 49(2) RP). Most importantly, however, it is the Judge-Rapporteur who drafts the judgment of the Court in the case assigned to him, although this task is not specifically mentioned in the Court's Statutes or Rules of Procedure.

The Statutes and the Rules of Procedure also provide that on a proposal from the Court the Council may appoint *Assistant Rapporteurs* 'in particular' to assist the President in connection with applications for interim measures and to assist the Judge-Rapporteurs in their work (Arts. 12 EEC Statute; 24 RP). No such appointment has been made so far.

II. Organization and procedure

The Court of Justice is assisted by the *Registrar*, who is appointed for a term of six years in accordance with the same procedure as the President of the Court (Arts. 168 EEC, 9 EEC Statute, 12 RP). He is assisted by an *Assistant Registrar* (Art. 13 RP) and by two *administrators* (Art. 23 RP). The Registrar is responsible, under the authority of the President, for the administration of the Court, its financial management, and its accounts (Art. 23 RP); for the work of the Registry (Art. 16 RP); for the acceptance, transmission, and custody of documents (Art. 17(1) RP); for the records and the publications of the Court (of which the most important is the *Reports of Cases before the Court* or *European Court Reports*); and for the custody of the seals (Art. 18 RP). He is also required to assist the Court, the Chambers, the President, and the Judges in all their official functions (Art. 17(2) RP) and hence to attend the sittings of the Court and of the Chambers, except the deliberations (Art. 19 RP). The Register is kept in the *Registry* and initialled by the President; in it are entered all pleadings and supporting documents (Art. 16(1) RP). Detailed rules for keeping the Register are laid down in the Instructions to the Registrar.

In addition to the Registry, the Court has the following departments: *Library, Research and Documentation Directorate*, which includes the Library Division and the Research and Documentation Division; *Legal Data-processing Department*; *Translation Directorate*; *Interpretation Division*; and *Information Service* (see *Synopsis of the Work of the Court of Justice*, listed below under Official Publications, p. 137). The officials and other servants of the Court are appointed in accordance with the Staff Regulations; they are responsible to the Registrar under the authority of the President (Arts. 11 EEC Statute; 20 RP). At the end of 1988, there were 626 permanent and 46 temporary posts on the Court's establishment plan (see 22nd *Gen. Rep. EC* (1988), p. 42).

The Court remains permanently in session and determines the duration of its vacations having regard to its workload (Art. 14 EEC Statute). At present the vacations run from 18 December to 10 January, from the Sunday before Easter to the second Sunday after Easter, and from 15 July to 15 September. During the vacations, the functions of the President are exercised in Luxembourg by the President himself, or by a President of a Chamber or by a Judge selected by the President. In case of urgency, the President may convene the

Judges and the Advocates-General during the vacations (Art. 28 RP). The official holidays of the Court are laid down in Annex I to the Rules of Procedure; the Court also observes the official holidays in Luxembourg (Art. 28(3) RP).

When the Court sits in plenary session (full Court), the quorum is seven; when it sits in Chambers, the quorum is three (Art. 15 EEC Statute). Since decisions of the Court are valid only when an uneven number of Judges is sitting in the deliberations (ibid.), the full Court may be validly constituted with seven, nine, eleven, or thirteen Judges. In practice, only the most important cases are dealt with by the full Court composed of all thirteen Judges. If an even number of Judges is present, the most junior Judge in office must abstain from taking part in the deliberations (Art. 26(1) RP). Only those Judges who were present at the oral proceedings may take part in the deliberations (with the exception of deliberations concerning questions of the Court's own administration, in which the Advocates-General also take part and have a vote and at which the Registrar is also present unless the Court decides otherwise). Every Judge participating in the deliberations must give his view and the reasons for it. The decision of the Court is determined by a majority vote; votes are cast in reverse order of seniority in office (Art. 27 RP). A single judgment is always given and no separate or dissenting opinions are made public since the deliberations of the Court are and must remain secret (Art. 32 EEC Statute). The composition of the full Court or of the Chambers may not be challenged by a party on the grounds of the nationality of a Judge or the absence of a Judge of the party's nationality (Art. 16(4) EEC Statute).

The procedure before the Court generally consists of two main parts: written and oral; where preparatory inquiries are ordered by the Court they are undertaken after the end of the written and before the beginning of the oral procedure. The written procedure consists of the communication by the Registrar to the parties and to the relevant Community institutions of applications, defences, replies, rejoinders, statements of case, written observations, and any supporting papers and documents. The oral procedure consists of the hearing by the Court of the parties (through their agents, advisers, or lawyers) and of the opinion of the Advocate-General. The Court also has the power to hear witnesses and experts at this stage, although these are usually examined during the course of the preparatory inquiries (Art. 18 EEC Statute). Depending on the nature and the subject-matter of the proceedings, the procedure is concluded by a judgment, order, opinion, ruling, or, exceptionally, by some other form of decision by the Court. In specific cases, the Court is to follow one or the other of the special forms of procedure laid down in the Rules of Procedure. In 1988, 372 cases were brought before the Court, of which 173 were references for preliminary rulings, 59 staff cases, and 140 others. The Court delivered 311 judgments, of which 133 were preliminary rulings, 45 were in staff cases, and 133 in other cases (see 22nd *Gen. Rep. EC* (1988), p. 42).

(For specific issues of jurisdiction and procedure, see the relevant entries listed below.)

See also Action against Member States, Action against sanctions, Action for annulment, Action for damages, Action for failure to act, Admissibility of action, Application originating proceedings, Arbitration clause, Capacity to institute proceedings, Compulsory jurisdiction, Costs, Court of First Instance, Denial of justice, Direct action, *European Court Reports,* Judgment, Judicial review, Jurisdiction, Language of the case, Legal aid, Limited jurisdiction, *Lis pendens,* Opinion, Optional jurisdiction, Oral procedure, Order, Preliminary ruling, Preparatory inquiries, Privileges and immunities, Reference proceedings, Representation before the ECJ, Special forms of procedure, Staff cases, Unlimited jurisdiction, Written procedure.

Further reading 1. BOOKS: Bebr, *Development of Judicial Control of the European Communities* (1981); Brown and Jacobs, *The Court of Justice of the European Communities*, 3rd edn. (1989); Commission of the European Communities, *Thirty Years of Community Law* (1983), part I, ch. 7; Feld, *The Court of the European Communities: New Dimension in International Adjudication* (1964); Green, *Political Integration by Jurisprudence: The Work of the Court of Justice of the European Communities in European Political Integration* (1969); Hartley, *The Foundations of European Community Law*, 2nd edn. (1988); Lasok, *The European Court of Justice: Practice and Procedure* (1984); Lasok and Bridge, *Law and Institutions of the European Communities*, 4th edn. (1987), ch. 9; Mann, *The Function of Judicial Decision in European Economic Integration* (1972); Lord Mackenzie Stuart, *The European Communities and the Rule of Law* (1977); Rasmussen, *On Law and Policy in the European Court of Justice* (1986); Schermers, *Judicial Protection in the European Communities*, 4th edn. (1987); Toth, *Legal Protection of Individuals in the European Communities*, 2 vols. (1978); Usher, *European Court Practice* (1983); Valentine, *The Court of Justice of the European Communities*, 2 vols. (1965); Wall, *The Court of Justice of the European Communities: Jurisdiction and Procedure* (1966).

2. ARTICLES AND PAPERS: Arnull, 'Reflections on Judicial Attitudes at the European Court' (1985) 34 *ICLQ* 168; Borgsmidt, 'The Advocate General at the European Court of Justice: A Comparative Study' (1988) 13 *EL Rev.* 106; Cappelletti, 'The "Mighty Problem" of Judicial Review and the Contribution of Comparative Analysis' (1979/2) *LIEI* 1; id., 'Is the European Court of Justice "Running Wild"?' (1987) 12 *EL Rev.* 3; Dashwood, 'The Advocate General in the Court of Justice of the European Communities' (1982) 2 *Legal Studies* 202; Donner, 'The Constitutional Powers of the Court of Justice of the European Communities' (1974) 11 *CML Rev.* 127; Editorial, 'The British Suggestions Concerning the Court of Justice' (1979) 16 *CML Rev.* 3; id., 'The Re-organisation of the Court: A British View' (1980) 17 *CML Rev.* 154; id., 'Report on the Re-organisation of the European Court' (1980) 5 *EL Rev.* 1; id., 'Changes at the European Court' (1981) 6 *EL Rev.* 137; id., 'Trends in the European Court' (1988) 13 *EL Rev.* 85; Jacobs, 'The Working of the European Court in the Enlarged Communities' (1975–6) 1 *EL Rev.* 43; id., 'Amendments to the Rules of Procedure' (1980) 5 *EL Rev.* 52; Lenz, 'The Court of Justice of the European Communities' (1988/2) *LIEI* 1, also in (1989) 14 *EL Rev.* 127; Lord Mackenzie Stuart, 'The European Court: A Personal View', in Bates *et al.* (eds.), *In Memoriam J. D. B. Mitchell* (1983), p. 118; Plender, 'The European Court as an International Tribunal' (1983) 42 *Cambridge Law J.* 279; id., 'In Praise of Ambiguity' (1983) 8 *EL Rev.* 313; Rasmussen, 'Between Self-Restraint and Activism: A Judicial Policy for the European Court' (1988) 13 *EL Rev.* 28; Slynn, 'The Court of Justice of

217

the European Communities' (1984) 33 *ICLQ* 409; Usher, 'Presenting a Case before the European Court' (1975–6) 1 *EL Rev.* 109; Warner, 'The Role of the Advocate-General' (1975) 20 *J. of the Law Soc. of Scotland* 47; id., 'Some Aspects of the European Court of Justice' (1976) 14 *J. of the Soc. of Public Teachers of Law* 15.

3. OFFICIAL PUBLICATIONS: Court of Justice, 'Selected Instruments relating to the Organization, Jurisdiction and Procedure of the Court' (1990); id., 'Synopsis of the Work of the Court of Justice of the European Communities in 1986 and 1987 and Record of Formal Sittings in 1986 and 1987' (1988); House of Lords, Select Committee on the European Communities, Session 1979–80, 23rd Report, 'European Court of Justice' (1979).

▶ **EUROPEAN COURT REPORTS (ECR)** Official publication of the ECJ having the full title *Reports of Cases before the Court*. It is the duty of the Registrar to arrange for the publication of these *Reports* (Arts. 68 RP; 23 IR). Subject to a decision to the contrary, they must contain 'the judgments of the Court together with the submissions [i.e. opinions] of the Advocates-General and the opinions given and the interim orders made in the course of the calendar year' (Art. 24 IR). In addition, the *Reports* usually contain other orders dealing with matters such as: costs (see e.g. Case 126/76—Costs *Dietz* v. *Commission* [1979] ECR 2131); intervention (see e.g. Cases 56 and 58/64 *Consten and Grundig* v. *Commission* [1966] ECR 299 at pp. 382, 385); interpretation (see e.g. Case 9/81—Interpretation *Court of Auditors* v. *Williams* [1983] ECR 2859), rectification (see e.g. Case 27/76 *United Brands* v. *Commission* [1978] ECR 207 at pp. 345, 349), supplementation (see e.g. Case 13/67 *Becher* [1968] ECR 187 at p. 196), or enforcement of judgments and orders (see e.g. Case 4/73—Enforcement *Nold* v. *Ruhrkohle* [1977] ECR 1); objection of inadmissibility (see e.g. Cases 106 and 107/63 *Toepfer* v. *Commission* [1965] ECR 405 at p. 429); lack of jurisdiction (see e.g. Case 138/80 *Borker* [1980] ECR 1975); reopening of the oral procedure (see e.g. Case 155/79 *AM & S.* v. *Commission* [1982] ECR 1575 at p. 1616); confidential treatment of documents (see e.g. Case 236/81 *Celanese* v. *Council and Commission* [1982] ECR 1183); rescission of a joinder and removal of a case from the Register (see e.g. Cases 19 and 65/63 *Prakash* v. *Commission* [1965] ECR 533 at p. 574); legal aid (see e.g. Case 233/82 *K* v. *Germany and Parliament* [1982] ECR 3637); letters rogatory (see e.g. Case 160/84 *Oryzomyli Kavallas* v. *Commission* [1985] ECR 675); etc. While the *Reports* are to be published in all the nine official languages (Arts. 30(2) RP, 24 IR), only the version drawn up in the language of the case is authentic (Art. 31 RP). This language is always indicated in a footnote in the *Reports*. In order to facilitate use of the *Reports*, pagination is the same in every language edition. The decisions are published in chronological order. Except for the first five years (1954 to 1958), each volume in the English edition covers a full calendar year, although a volume consists of several parts. Since the *ECR* are the only official reports of cases, they alone should be cited in proceedings before the Court.

Until the end of January 1985, the practice was to publish the complete text of judgments, i.e. the 'Facts and Issues', the 'Decision', and the operative part (in heavy type) including the order on costs. This was followed by the opinion of the Advocate-General. Since the end of January 1985, the 'Facts and Issues' part of the judgment is no longer published (except in special cases), its essential contents being incorporated in the 'Decision' part. Since the beginning of 1985, the opinion of the Advocate-General is printed before the judgment and since September 1986 the Report for the Hearing is also published, to which usually reference is made in the text of the judgment. From January 1989, certain cases are published only in summary form.

The report of a case begins with a summary of the main points and provisions dealt with in the judgment or order, normally followed by a more detailed summary of the principal issues decided by the Court. However, these summaries have no binding force and are in no way to be regarded as an authentic interpretation of the decision. Unlike judgments, orders are not reported according to a uniform scheme; some are structured like judgments (see e.g. Case 292/84R *Scharf* v. *Commission* [1984] ECR 4349), others contain no 'Facts and Issues' part (see e.g. Case 258/84R *Nippon Seiko* v. *Council* [1984] ECR 4357), while yet others are based on a very brief summary of the facts and relevant provisions (see e.g. Cases 259/84 and 259/84R *Strack* v. *Parliament* [1985] ECR 453). Opinions and rulings are drafted differently from both judgments and orders, but generally they are preceded by a summary of the facts and arguments and the reasoning of the Court on which they are based. Opinions of the Advocates-General relating to orders are only very rarely, while those relating to opinions and rulings are never, reported.

See also Common Market Law Reports, **Judgment, Language of the case,** *Official Journal*, **Official languages, Opinion, Order.**

▶ **EUROPEAN INVESTMENT BANK (EIB)** Body established by Art. 129 EEC 'to facilitate the economic expansion of the Community by opening up fresh resources' (Art. 3(j) EEC). It has its own legal personality, which is distinct from that of the EEC (see Arts. 129 and 210 EEC); its members are the Member States and its functions and activities are governed by its own Statute which is laid down in a Protocol annexed to the EEC Treaty (subsequently amended by Art. 28 of the Merger Treaty of 1965; by the Treaty of 10 July 1975, *OJ* 1978 L91/1; by decisions of the Board of Governors of the EIB of 30 Dec. 1977, *OJ* 1978 L199/1, 19 June 1978, *OJ* 1978 L199/3, 13 May 1981, *OJ* 1981 L311/1, and 15 June 1981, *OJ* 1981 L311/2; by Protocols No. 1 annexed to each of the Acts of Accession of 1972, 1979, and 1985).

It follows from the foregoing that the Bank is not a Community 'institution' in the strict sense; it is certainly not listed as one in Art. 4 EEC. It is an autonomous legal entity having its own resources independently of the Community budget and its own decision-making, managing, and supervisory bodies, which are distinct from, and in no way under the control of, those of the Community. Nevertheless, this does not mean that the Bank is totally detached from the Community structure. It was set up by and is subject to the EEC Treaty of which its Statute forms an integral part (Art. 239 EEC). It pursues a Community objective and is required to act in the interest of the

Community (Arts. 3(j) and 130 EEC). Disputes concerning the fulfilment by the Member States of their obligations under the Bank's Statute as well as those concerning measures adopted by the Bank's organs (the Board of Governors and the Board of Directors) are subject to the jurisdiction of the Court of Justice (Art. 180 EEC). The Bank, the members of its organs, and its staff enjoy the same privileges and immunities as the Community institutions and their officials, including exemption from national taxes on salaries (Arts. 28 of the Merger Treaty and 13, 22 of the Protocol on Privileges and Immunities annexed to it; *see further under* **Privileges and immunities**). The staff of the Bank are thereby placed in a special legal situation identical to that of the staff of the institutions and any dispute between them and the Bank falls within the jurisdiction of the ECJ under Art. 179 EEC (Case 110/75 *Mills* v. *Investment Bank* [1976] ECR 955 at pp. 968–9; see also the opinion of A.-G. Warner at pp. 973–5).

Considering all these factors in Case 85/86 *Commission* v. *Board of Governors of the EIB* [1988] ECR 1281 at p. 1320, which concerned the question whether the proceeds of the income tax levied by the Bank on the salaries of its staff in lieu of national taxes should be entered as revenue in the general budget of the Communities as required by Arts. 9 and 12 of Reg. 260/68, *OJ Sp. Edn.* 1968(I), p. 37, the Court has come to the conclusion that the position of the Bank is 'ambivalent'. On the one hand, it is characterized by a measure of operational and institutional autonomy in the management of its own affairs, acting with complete independence in financial matters like any other bank. On the other hand, as regards its objectives, it is closely connected with the Community and forms part of the Community structure. Referring to its earlier judgment in the *Mills* case (above), the Court has stated that the Bank is a 'Community body [*organisme communautaire*] established and endowed with legal personality by the Treaty' (ibid. at p. 1319) and that it cannot be completely separated from the Communities and exempted from the rules of Community law (ibid. at p. 1320). Since the privileges and immunities under the Protocol have been conferred on the Bank only in its capacity as a body acting in the interest of the Communities, the tax on salaries which replaces national taxes is also levied for the benefit of the Communities and not for the Bank's own benefit. It must therefore be transferred to the Community budget. Since such transfer does not affect the Bank's own resources or the amounts of capital payable to the Member States in the event of suspension of the activity or liquidation of the Bank, it cannot prejudice the Bank's financial position (ibid. at pp. 1319, 1321).

I. Organization

The Bank is directed and managed by the following organs (see Arts. 8–14 EIB Statute, as amended; for the composition of the organs and the organizational structure of the Bank as at 1 June 1989, see EIB Annual Report for 1988):

Board of Governors, consisting of the Ministers designated by the Member States, generally the Finance Ministers. It lays down general directives for the credit policy of the Bank and ensures their implementation; decides whether to increase the Bank's subscribed capital; appoints the members of the Board of Directors, Management Committee, and Audit Committee; authorizes loans for projects to be carried out outside the Community territory; approves the annual report of the Board of Directors, the annual balance sheet, and profit and loss account; has power to take decisions concerning the suspension of the operations of the Bank and its liquidation. Where the Board decides by a majority of its members, this majority must represent at least 45 per cent of the subscribed capital. Voting is in accordance with Art. 148 EEC. The Presidency of the Board rotates among its members on an annual basis.

Board of Directors, consisting of 22 directors and 12 alternates appointed by the Board of Governors for renewable terms of five years, 21 and 11, respectively, being nominated by the Member States, 1 and 1 by the Commission. Members are chosen from persons whose independence and competence are beyond doubt; they are responsible only to the Bank. Alternates may take part in the Board's meetings but have no right of vote except when they replace a director. Each director has one vote and decisions are normally taken by a simple majority; a qualified majority requires 15 votes in favour. Meetings of the Board are presided over by the President of the Management Committee or, in his absence, by one of the Vice-Presidents, who has no right of vote. The Board of Directors has sole power to take decisions in respect of granting loans and guarantees and raising loans; it fixes the interest rates on loans granted and the commission on guarantees; it ensures that the Bank is properly run and managed in accordance with the Treaty, its Statute, and the general directives laid down by the Board of Governors. It submits an annual report to the latter.

Management Committee, consisting of a President and six Vice-Presidents appointed for a renewable period of six years by the Board of Governors on a proposal from the Board of Directors. The Board of Governors may vary this number. The Committee and the staff of the Bank are responsible only to the Bank and are completely independent in the performance of their duties. The Management Committee is responsible for the current business of the Bank, under the authority of the President and the supervision of the Board of Directors. It prepares the decisions of the Board of Directors, in particular decisions on the raising of loans and the granting of loans and guarantees, and ensures that these decisions are implemented.

Audit Committee, consisting of three members appointed on the grounds of their competence by the Board of Governors. Its task is annually to verify that the operations of the Bank have been conducted and its books kept in a proper manner.

At the end of 1988, the total number of staff at the Bank was 710, of whom 357 were in executive positions and 353 were secretarial, clerical, and support staff (EIB Annual Report for 1988, p. 82).

Originally, the Bank was set up with a capital of 1,000 million units of account subscribed by the six Member States. This amount has been increased several times, and at the accession of Spain and Portugal the Bank's capital was set at 28,800 million ECU, subscribed by the twelve Member States in agreed proportions (see Art. 4(1) EIB Statute, as amended). As mentioned above, the Board of Governors has the power to increase the subscribed capital (Art. 4(3) EIB Statute). The Bank is required to build up a reserve fund of up to 10 per cent of the subscribed capital, and it may set aside additional reserves (Art. 24 EIB Statute). Nevertheless, the Bank raises most of the funds necessary for the performance of its tasks by borrowing on the international capital markets. It may also borrow on the capital market of a Member State (Art. 22 EIB Statute).

II. Functions

The functions of the Bank may broadly be divided into two parts: (1) those arising directly from the provisions of the EEC Treaty and its Statute; and (2) those entrusted to it in practice outside those provisions. These will be discussed in turn below.

1. Under the EEC Treaty, the task of the Bank is to contribute, by having recourse to the capital markets and utilizing its own resources, to the balanced and steady development of the Common Market in the interest of the Community. Operating on a non-profit-making basis, the Bank furthers this objective by granting loans and giving guarantees which facilitate the financing of the following projects in all sectors of the economy (in practice, energy, the manufacturing industry, services, agriculture, telecommunications, and transport are the main beneficiaries): (*a*) projects for developing less-developed regions; (*b*) projects for modernizing or converting undertakings or for developing fresh activities called for by the progressive establishment of the Common Market; (*c*) projects of common interest to several Member States or benefiting the Community as a whole (projects of common European interest). In cases (*b*) and (*c*), the projects must be of such a size or nature that they cannot be entirely financed by the various means available in the individual Member States (Art. 130 EEC). While the Bank was established primarily to finance public or private investment projects within the European territories of the Member States, the Board of Governors may authorize, by way of derogation, the grant of loans for projects to be carried out outside the Community. Thus, loans from EIB own resources with interest rate subsidy from the European Development Fund are granted to ACP, OCT, and Mediterranean countries, often in conjunction with financing from Community or Member States' budgetary resources (see further points 2(*a*), (*b*), (*c*) below). As far as possible, however, loans within the Community are granted only on the condition that other sources of finance are also used, and the aggregate amount outstanding at any time of loans and guarantees granted by the Bank may not exceed 250 per cent of its subscribed capital (Art. 18 EIB Statute). In its loan and guarantee operations, the Bank is required to observe a number of rules and principles including the requirement that its funds must be employed as rationally as possible in the interests of the Community (Art. 20 EIB Statute). Interest rates on loans and commission on guarantees are adjusted to conditions prevailing on the capital market and are calculated in such a way that the income therefrom should enable the Bank to meet its obligations, to cover its expenses, and to build up a reserve fund (but without making any profits). The Bank may not grant any reduction in

interest rates (Art. 19 EIB Statute). All loans provided from the Bank's own resources, whether within or outside the Community, are included in the Bank's balance sheet.

Applications for loans or guarantees may be made to the Bank either directly, or through the Commission or the Member State in whose territory the project will be carried out. The Member State concerned and the Commission are required to give an opinion on the application within two months. It is the task of the Board of Directors to rule on the applications, after the Management Committee has examined whether they comply with the Statute (Art. 21 EIB Statute).

Loans granted may be divided into three categories: direct individual loans, indirect individual loans, and global loans. Direct individual loans are granted directly to the firm or public authority which has submitted the project to be financed. Indirect individual loans are granted to a specialized financial institution which is responsible for forwarding the funds in order to finance a specific project submitted by a firm or public authority. Global loans are granted to financial intermediaries (banks, other financial institutions, or Government agencies) which allocate (on-lend) the funds, after approval of the Bank, to a number of small and medium-sized investment projects. The Bank normally finances no more than half the cost of a project. In general, it prefers not to lend less than 1 million ECU per project but it may grant individual loans under the global loan system ranging between 50,000 (in some cases 25,000) and 4 million ECU, although the total cost may not exceed 12 million ECU. The term of loans varies between 7 and 12 years for industrial projects and up to 20 years for infrastructure projects, including those in the energy sector.

2. In addition to granting loans from its own resources (principally from the proceeds of its borrowings on capital markets) and furnishing guarantees, the EIB also acts as agent for the Community in providing financing from Community funds in non-member countries in furtherance of the Community's policy of economic and financial co-operation and development aid, and also in Member States by making Euratom loans and loans from the resources of the New Community Instrument for borrowing and lending (NCI). These operations, the decision to mount which is the responsibility of the Board of Directors, are accounted for off balance sheet in the Special Section which was set up in 1963. This contains a record of the operations carried out by the EIB for the account of and under mandate from third parties (e.g. the Communities). The following operations fall into this category:

(*a*) Loans in the African, Caribbean, and Pacific (ACP) States under the Lomé Conventions, made from Community or Member States' budgetary resources in the form of risk capital assistance. This type of financing is provided by the Bank under mandate from, on behalf, for the account, and at the risk of the EEC with the Bank's responsibility being limited to proper performance of the mandate entrusted to it.

(*b*) Loans in the Overseas Countries and Territories (OCT) under the

223

relevant decision of the Council (Dec. 86/283 of 30 June 1986, *OJ* 1986 L175/1), subject to the same conditions as (*a*) above.

(*c*) Loans in the Mediterranean countries (Maghreb and Mashreq countries, Israel, Turkey, Cyprus, Malta) under financial protocols, from Community budgetary resources, subject to the same conditions as (*a*) above.

(*d*) Euratom loans for the purpose of contributing to the financing of nuclear power stations, issued by the Commission on behalf of the Euratom under various Council decisions (see Dec. 77/270, *OJ* 1977 L88/9; Dec. 77/271, *OJ* 1977 L88/11; Dec. 82/170, *OJ* 1982 L78/21; Dec. 85/537, *OJ* 1985 L334/23).

(*e*) Loans under the New Community Instruments (NCI) for the purpose of financing investment projects of small and medium-sized enterprises (SMEs) within the Community, which contribute to the industrial adjustment and competitiveness of the Community in particular by means of the application of new technologies and innovation. The funds are borrowed by the Commission and then entrusted to the Bank, which is to manage them in accordance with the terms of a co-operation agreement drawn up between the Bank and the Commission. The Bank is to carry out transactions under the mandate contained in the agreement, on behalf of, for, and at the risk of the Community (four such Instruments have been made so far: NCI I: Dec. 78/870, *OJ* 1978 L298/9; NCI II: Dec. 82/169, *OJ* 1982 L78/19; NCI III: Dec. 83/200, *OJ* 1983 L112/26; NCI IV: Dec. 87/182, *OJ* 1987 L71/34). Similarly, the Bank has been entrusted to grant loans from Community resources for the reconstruction of the regions affected by earthquake in Italy and Greece, under mandate, for the account and at the risk of the Community (see Dec. 81/19, *OJ* 1981 L37/21; Dec. 81/1013, *OJ* 1981 L367/27).

(*f*) In co-operation with Community grants of up to 4,100 million ECU, the EIB participates, with loans from its own resources and from NCI resources, in the Integrated Mediterranean Programmes (IMPs), which are applicable in Greece, Italy, and France for a seven-year period beginning on 1 August 1985 (Art. 12(3) of Reg. 2088/85, *OJ* 1985 L197/1).

(*g*) EIB financing combined with EEC grant aid: a project benefiting from Community grant aid may also be eligible for EIB loan finance. Particularly in the case of the European Regional Development Fund (ERDF), there are many instances of projects being implemented through the use of both EIB loans from own resources and grants from Community budgetary funds. EIB loans combined with Community grant aid may cover up to 70 per cent or, exceptionally, even more of the investment cost of a project. Effective co-ordination between the different structural Funds (ERDF, European Agricultural Guidance and Guarantee Fund (EAGGF), Guidance Section, and the European Social Fund (ESF)) and the EIB is now expressly required by Reg. 2052/88 of 24 June 1988, *OJ* 1988 L185/9, providing for reform of the structural Funds, which was adopted by the Council under Art. 130D EEC, inserted by the Single European Act of 1986 (SEA). In order to achieve the general objectives of the SEA, i.e. strengthening the economic and social cohesion of and redressing the principal regional imbalances in the Community, as well as the particular objectives laid down in the regulation, the

EIB is required to co-operate with the three Funds in accordance with Arts. 129–30 EEC, with its Statute and with the practical arrangements to be established with the Commission by mutual agreement (see in particular Arts. 2(2) and 3(5) of Reg. 2052/88. See also Reg. 4253/88 of 19 Dec. 1988, *OJ* 1988 L374/1, laying down provisions for implementing Reg. 2052/88 as regards co-ordination between the Funds and the EIB).

In 1988, financing provided by the Bank amounted to 10,175 million ECU, of which 9,638.4 million came from own resources and 536.6 million from Special Section operations. Lending in the Community in 1988 totalled 9,474.8 million, comprising 9,118.3 million from the Bank's own resources and 356.5 million from NCI resources. Financing outside the Community amounted to 700.2 million, comprising 520.1 million from own resources and 180.1 million from budgetary resources. The Bank raised a total of 7,666.1 million ECU (see 22nd *Gen. Rep. EC* (1988), pp. 83–5 and EIB Annual Report for 1988, pp. 19–20).

See also **European Agricultural Guidance and Guarantee Fund*, European Regional Development Fund*, European Social Fund*, New Community Instrument*, Privileges and immunities.**

Further reading 1. BOOK: Strasser, *The Finances of Europe* (1981), ch. 10.

2. ARTICLES: Käser, 'The European Investment Bank: Its Role and Place within the European Community System' (1984) 4 *YEL* 303; Schermers, Case-note on Case 85/86 *Commission* v. *Board of Governors of the EIB* (1988) 25 *CML Rev.* 617.

▶ **EUROPEAN PARLIAMENT (EP)** One of the four institutions of the European Communities, the others being the Council, the Commission, and the Court of Justice (Arts. 7 ECSC, 4 EEC, 3 Euratom). The present Parliament was established by Arts. 1 and 2 of the Convention on Certain Institutions Common to the European Communities of 1957, which set up a single Assembly to serve all three Communities, taking the place of the former Common Assembly of the ECSC and of the Assemblies created by the EEC and Euratom Treaties. In 1958, this single Assembly decided to call itself 'European Parliamentary Assembly' (*JO* 1958, p. 6), and in 1962 it changed its title to 'European Parliament' (Res. of 30 Mar. 1962, *JO* 1962, p. 1045). This designation has been officially confirmed by Art. 3(1) of the Single European Act of 1986 (SEA).

I. Organization and procedure

The EP consists of 'representatives of the peoples of the States brought together in the Communities', who are referred to as 'Members of the European Parliament' (MEPs) (Arts. 20 ECSC, 137 EEC, 107 Euratom; Rule 1(2) of the EP's Rules of Procedure (EPRP), consolidated version published by the EP in June 1987 (4th edn.); the amendments adopted since June 1987 were published in Jan. 1989). Originally, the MEPs were not directly elected but delegated by the respective national Parliaments from among their Members. However, the Treaties required the EP to draw up proposals for elections by direct universal suffrage in accordance with a uniform procedure in all Member States. On this basis the Council was to lay down the appropriate provisions for direct elections to be adopted by the Member States in accordance with their respective constitutional requirements (Arts. 21 ECSC, 138 EEC, 108 Euratom). The first Draft Convention on Direct Elections produced by the EP in 1960 (*JO* 1960, p. 834, based on the 'Dehousse Report') was not acted upon by the Council. Following the decision of the Paris Summit Conference of 9–10 December 1974 to hold direct elections as soon as possible and preferably in or after 1978 (point 12 of the Communiqué of 10 Dec. 1974, 8th *Gen. Rep. EC* (1974), p. 297), the EP prepared a second Draft Convention (Res. of 14 Jan. 1975, *OJ* 1975 C32/15, based on the 'Patijn Report'), on the basis of which the Council adopted a Decision and Act laying down provisions for the election of MEPs by direct universal suffrage (Dec. 76/787 of 20 Sept. 1976, *OJ* 1976 L278/1. For the legislative history of the Decision and Act, see *Bull. EC* 6–1976, p. 5; 7/8– 1976, p. 6; and 9–1976, p. 79). Upon the completion of the national ratification procedures and the passing of the necessary implementing legislation as required by the Council Decision of 1976 (see 12th *Gen. Rep. EC* (1978), pp. 31 and 360), the first direct elections took place on 7 and 10 June 1979, followed by the second direct elections on 14 and 17 June 1984 (for the results of the elections and the distribution of seats in and the officers and committees of the 1979 and 1984 Parliaments, see 13th *Gen. Rep. EC* (1979), p. 27; *Bull. EC* 6–1979, p. 19 and 18th *Gen. Rep. EC* (1984), p. 29; *Bull. EC* 6–1984, p. 13, respectively). The third direct elections were held from 15 to 18 June 1989 (for the results and the distribution of seats, see 23rd *Gen. Rep. EC* (1989), p. 33; *Bull. EC* 6–1989, p. 18). In the United Kingdom, the Council Decision of 1976 was implemented by the European Assembly Elections Act 1978, subsequently renamed by the European Communities (Amendment) Act 1986, section 3(2), as the European Parliamentary Elections Act 1978.

According to the Act annexed to the Decision of 1976, MEPs are to be elected by direct universal suffrage for a term of five years (Arts. 1 and 3). The number of MEPs elected in each Member State is as follows: Belgium 24, Denmark 16, Germany 81, Greece 24, Spain 60, France 81, Ireland 15, Italy 81, Luxembourg 6, Netherlands 25, Portugal 24, United Kingdom 81; a total of 518 MEPs (Art. 2 as last amended by Art. 10 of the Act of Accession 1985). Within the United Kingdom, the 81 seats are distributed as follows: England 66, Scotland 8, Wales 4, Northern Ireland 3 (European Parliamentary Elections Act 1978, section 2). MEPs are required to vote on an individual and personal basis; they are not bound by any instructions and are not to receive a binding mandate. They enjoy the privileges and immunities provided for in Arts. 8–10 of the Protocol on Privileges and Immunities annexed to the Merger Treaty (Art. 4; Rule 2 EPRP. *See further under* **Privileges and immunities**). While MEPs may be Members of their own national Parliaments (Art. 5), their office is incompatible with membership of a national Government, of the Commission, of the Court of Justice (whether as Judge, Advocate-General, or Registrar), of the Court of Auditors, of the Consultative Committee of the ECSC or the Economic and Social Committee of the EEC and Euratom, and with a number of other posts. In addition, the Member States may lay down rules at national level relating to incompatibility (Art. 6; see also Rule 7 EPRP).

Both the Treaties and the Act of 1976 (Art. 7(1)) envisaged that direct elections would take place in accordance with a uniform electoral procedure in all the Member States and required the EP to draw up proposals for that purpose. The 1976 Act also provided that pending the entry into force of such a procedure, the electoral procedure should be governed in each Member State by its own national provisions (Art. 7(2)). National provisions would apply also to the filling of vacant seats during the five-year term of office (Art. 12(1)). Since the Member States were unable to agree on a uniform procedure, all three direct elections were held in accordance with the various voting systems in force in the Member States, the most common being some form of proportional representation (see *Bull. EC* 6–1979, p. 19; 6–1984, p. 13; 6–1989, p. 18). In the United Kingdom, the simple majority ('first-past-the-post') system was used in England, Scotland, and Wales, and the single transferable vote system in Northern Ireland (European Parliamentary Elections Act 1978, section 3). On the other hand, the elections took place in all Member States during the same period starting on a Thursday morning and ending on the following Sunday (Art. 9(1) of the 1976 Act).

The ECJ has interpreted the concept of 'electoral procedure' within the meaning of Art. 7(2) of the 1976 Act as including *inter alia* the rules designed to ensure that the electoral procedure is properly conducted and that the various candidates are afforded equal opportunities during the election campaign. Rules providing for the reimbursement of election campaign expenses belong to that category and are therefore not covered by the Act of 1976. As Community law stands at present, these rules remain, by virtue of Art. 7(2), within the competence of the Member States and are beyond the powers of the EP (Case 294/83 *Les Verts* v. *Parliament* [1986] ECR 1339 at p. 1372; see also Case 221/86R *Group of the European Right* v. *Parliament* [1986] ECR 2969 at pp. 2977–8).

The Treaties provide that the EP shall hold an annual session and that it shall meet, without requiring to be convened, on the second Tuesday in March. The EP may also meet in extraordinary session at the request of a majority of its members or at the request of the Council or of the Commission (Arts. 22 ECSC, 139 EEC, 109 Euratom; see also Rule 9 EPRP). The annual session is divided into part-sessions which are convened as a rule each month and are subdivided into daily sittings (Rule 9(1) EPRP). Thus, the EP normally holds 12 part-sessions each year (see 20th, 21st, 22nd *Gen. Rep. EC* (1986, 1987, 1988) pp. 38, 33, 36, respectively). Plenary sittings are held for one week of each month (with the exception of August), while one week a month is set aside for committee meetings and one week for meetings of political groups. In the absence of any provision in the Treaties determining the precise duration of the annual session, the ECJ has held that this is a matter which falls within the EP's power to adopt rules for its own internal organization (see below) and that the decision on the date of closure of each annual session is therefore within the EP's discretion. According to consistent practice, a session lasts for the whole year and is closed only on the eve of the opening of a new session. An extraordinary session may be convened where the EP decides to close its annual session early. It follows that the EP must be considered to be in session, even if it is not actually sitting, until the decision is taken closing its annual or extraordinary sessions (Case 149/85 *Wybot* [1986] ECR 2391 at pp. 2408–10, interpreting Art. 10 of the Protocol on Privileges and Immunities which grants MEPs immunity 'during the sessions of the EP'. See also Case 101/63 *Wagner* [1964] ECR 195 at p. 201).

The Treaties authorize the EP to adopt its Rules of Procedure, acting by a majority of its Members (Arts. 25 ECSC, 142 EEC, 112 Euratom). The ECJ has interpreted these provisions in the broadest possible sense, holding that they confer on Parliament the power 'to determine its own internal organisation . . . [and] to adopt appropriate measures to ensure the due functioning and conduct of its proceedings'. They form the basis of 'the right inherent in the Parliament to discuss any question concerning the Communities, to adopt resolutions on such questions and to invite the Governments to act' (Case 230/81 *Luxembourg* v. *Parliament* [1983] ECR 255 at p. 287). In the exercise of its 'independent powers', the EP thus could lawfully decide to hold plenary sessions in Strasbourg, to organize the meetings of its committees and political groups as a general rule in Brussels, and, in the absence of a seat or even a single place of work, to maintain in the various places of work (i.e. Luxembourg, Brussels, and Strasbourg) the infrastructure necessary for fulfilling in all those places the tasks entrusted to it by the Treaties (ibid. at pp. 289–90; see also Rule 10 EPRP). Similarly, the ECJ has confirmed that Parliament's power to determine its own internal organization comprises the power to hold, exceptionally, special or additional plenary sessions outside Strasbourg, i.e. in Brussels, and to order, for that purpose, the construction of a suitable building there (Cases 358/85 and 51/86 *France* v. *Parliament* [1988] ECR paras. 36–41). On the other hand, the EP is obliged to respect the power of the Member States to determine the seat of the institutions, and in particular their Decision of 8 April 1965 on the provisional location of certain institutions and departments of the Communities (*JO* 1967 152/18), Art. 4 of which provides that the General Secretariat of the EP and its departments shall remain in Luxembourg. The decision to transfer the General Secretariat from Luxembourg to Strasbourg and Brussels was therefore beyond the powers of Parliament (Case 108/83 *Luxembourg* v. *Parliament* [1984] ECR 1945 at pp. 1960–1).

The ECJ has further held that the rules adopted by the EP governing the reimbursement of travel and subsistence expenses incurred by MEPs in the exercise of their mandates also fall within the scope of measures of internal organization intended to ensure Parliament's proper functioning, with which the Member States must not interfere (Case 208/80 *Lord Bruce of Donington* [1981] ECR 2205 at pp. 2219–20). So does the determination of the duration of its sessions (Case 149/85 *Wybot*, above, at p. 2408). By contrast, as seen above, the reimbursement of election campaign expenses does not come within Parliament's power of internal organization but remains within the competence of the Member States (Case 294/83 *Les Verts* v. *Parliament*, above, at pp. 1370, 1372).

The officers of the EP are the President, fourteen Vice-Presidents, and five Quaestors who are elected by Parliament, in that order, by secret ballot for a term of two and a half years (Arts. 23(1) ECSC, 140(1) EEC, 110(1) Euratom; Rules 11–20 EPRP. For the names of officers elected in July 1989, see 23rd *Gen. Rep. EC* (1989), p. 34). The duties of the President are to direct all the activities of Parliament and of its bodies, to preside over the proceedings and to ensure that they are properly conducted, to open, suspend, and close sittings, to maintain order, etc. He also represents Parliament in international relations, on ceremonial occasions, and in administrative, legal, or financial (e.g. budgetary) matters (Rule 18). If the President is absent or unable to discharge his duties or if he wishes to take part in a debate, he is replaced by one of the Vice-Presidents (Rule 19). The Quaestors are responsible for administrative and financial matters directly concerning MEPs (Rule 20). The President and the fourteen Vice-Presidents make up the Bureau of Parliament of which the Quaestors are also members in an advisory capacity. The function of the Bureau is to take financial and organizational decisions on matters concerning MEPs, the EP, and its bodies (Rules 21–2). The Enlarged Bureau consists of the Bureau and the chairmen of the political groups (see below), while non-attached MEPs may delegate two of their number to attend meetings without the right to vote. The Enlarged Bureau takes decisions on questions relating to the internal organization of the EP, and on matters affecting relations with non-Community institutions and organizations. It may also deliberate on relations with the other institutions and bodies of the Communities (Rules 23–5).

The EP is assisted by a Secretary-General who is appointed by the Bureau. He is the Head of a Secretariat the composition and organization of which is determined by the Bureau, which 'has the power to organise its Secretariat as it wishes and in the interests of the service' (Case 1/55 *Kergall* v. *Common Assembly* [1955] ECR 151 at p. 158; Cases 7/56 etc. *Algera* v. *Common Assembly* [1957] ECR 39 at p. 57. See also Rule 133). At the end of 1988, the Secretariat comprised 2,975 permanent and 392 temporary posts (22nd *Gen. Rep. EC* (1988), p. 36).

The ECJ has held that the decisions adopted by these various organs of the EP must be regarded as measures adopted by the EP itself (Case 294/83 *Les Verts* v. *Parliament*, above, at p. 1364; see also Case 149/85 *Wybot*, above, at p. 2409). Thus, when the President, in accordance with the Treaties, formally declares that the Community budget has been finally adopted (see Art. 203(7) EEC), he acts not as a distinct authority but in his capacity as an organ of the EP (Case 34/86 *Council* v. *Parliament* [1986] ECR 2155 at p. 2202; *see further under* **Community budget**).

In addition to the officers and organs discussed above, the internal organization of the EP comprises *political groups and committees*. Political groups are formed by MEPs according to their political affinities. A minimum of 23 MEPs may form a group if all of them come from a single Member State, 18 if they come from two Member States, and 12 if they come from three or more

229

States (Rule 26). Non-attached MEPs are those who do not belong to a group (Rule 27). Seats in the Chamber are allocated among political groups, non-attached Members, and Community institutions by the enlarged Bureau (Rule 28). After the third direct elections in June 1989, the 518 seats were distributed among ten groups and 10 non-affiliated Members (see 23rd *Gen. Rep. EC* (1989), pp. 33–4).

The EP may set up standing committees, temporary committees, and committees of inquiry (Rule 109); standing and temporary committees may appoint subcommittees (Rule 114). The composition of committees and subcommittees must be such as to ensure fair representation of both Member States and political views (Rule 110). Standing committees play an extremely important part in every aspect of Parliament's work (see further below). Their task is to examine questions referred to them by the EP (Rule 112) and, in particular, to prepare reports containing draft legislative resolutions on Commission proposals (Rule 117), non-legislative reports (Rule 118), opinions (Rule 120), or own-initiative reports (Rule 121). A committee may approve proposals without report or in accordance with a simplified procedure (Rule 116). The committees may decide to hold Question Time (Rule 122). A committee may be convened at any time by its chairman or at the request of the President. The Commission and Council may take part in committee meetings if invited to do so; by special invitation any other person may attend and speak at a meeting (Rule 124). The duties of temporary committees and committees of inquiry are defined when they are set up (Rule 112). The task of the latter is to investigate alleged contraventions of Community law or incidents of maladministration (Rule 109). In 1989, there were 18 standing committees, each covering one or more aspects of the Communities' activities, e.g. Political Affairs, Agriculture, Budgets, Legal Affairs, Institutional Affairs (for the powers and responsibilities of standing committees, see Annex VI to EPRP; for their composition after the third direct elections, see 23rd *Gen. Rep. EC* (1989), p. 34).

The plenary sittings of the EP itself may be attended by members of the Commission and the Council who must, at their request, be heard on behalf of their institutions (Arts. 23 ECSC, 140 EEC, 110 Euratom; see also Rules 56 and 78 and Art. 19 of the Council's Rules of Procedure of 24 July 1979). Debates are public unless the EP decides otherwise (Rule 81). All documents are drawn up in, and speeches simultaneously interpreted into, all the official languages (Rule 79). Save as otherwise provided in the Treaties, the EP acts by an absolute majority of the votes cast (Arts. 141 EEC, 111 Euratom). A quorum exists when one-third of the current MEPs are present in the Chamber. However, all votes are valid whatever the number of voters unless the President, acting on a request made by at least 13 MEPs, ascertains that the quorum is not present. In that case, the vote is placed on the agenda of the next sitting. If fewer than 13 MEPs are present, the President may rule that there is no quorum (Rule 89). The right to vote is a personal right. Voting by proxy is prohibited (Rule 93). The minutes of proceedings are published within one month in the *Official Journal*, while verbatim reports of proceedings are published as annexes to the *Official Journal* (Rules 107–8).

II. Functions and powers

Arts. 1 and 2 of the Convention on Certain Institutions Common to the European Communities of 1957 provide that the single Assembly (i.e. the Parliament) shall exercise the powers and jurisdiction conferred by the Community Treaties on the Common Assembly of the ECSC and on the Assemblies of the EEC and Euratom. The ECSC Treaty confers upon Parliament 'supervisory powers' (Art. 20), while the EEC and Euratom Treaties confer upon it 'advisory and supervisory powers' (Arts. 137 EEC, 107 Euratom). Thus, with one exception (the so-called 'minor revision' of the ECSC Treaty under Art. 95(3) and (4), see below), the original Treaties gave the EP no power to adopt legally binding measures, whether in the legislative or in the budgetary field, limiting its functions to those of consultation and political control only (see also Case 294/83 *Les Verts* v. *Parliament*, above, at pp. 1365–6). Community legislation was entrusted to non-elected and non-representative bodies such as the Council and the Commission.

This state of affairs, aggravated by the absence of direct elections to Parliament prior to 1979, cast grave doubt upon the democratic legitimacy of the whole constitutional structure of the Communities and has been criticized by the various reports and proposals which have been put forward for reforming the institutions (see, in particular, the Vedel, Tindemans, and Three Wise Men's Reports, the various Reports and proposals on European Union, and the Report of the Committee on Institutional Affairs—the Dooge Committee). All of these documents came down in favour of increasing the supervisory, legislative, and budgetary powers of the EP. These views were shared by the European Council (see e.g. 6th, 7th, and 8th *Gen. Rep. EC* (1972, 1973, and 1974), pp. 16, 489, and 299, respectively, and in particular the Solemn Declaration on European Union of 19 June 1983, point 2.3, *Bull. EC* 6–1983, p. 24); the Council (see the practical measures adopted by the Council to improve its relations with the EP, *Bull. EC* 10–1973, p. 89; see also 7th *Gen. Rep. EC* (1973), pp. 41, 55–6); the Commission (see its communication to the EP of 8 June 1973, *Bull. EC* 6–1973, p. 8; see also 6th *Gen. Rep. EC* (1972), pp. 4–5; 9th *Gen. Rep. EC* (1975), p. xx; Suppl. 5/75—*Bull. EC*, p. 39; Suppl. 3/82—*Bull. EC*, esp. at pp. 8 *et seq*; etc.); and, of course, by the EP itself (see e.g. Suppl. 9/75—*Bull. EC*, p. 11; the Draft Treaty on European Union of 14 Feb. 1984, *OJ* 1984 C77/33, *Bull. EC* 2–1984, p. 8; more recently Res. of 8 Oct. 1986 on relations between the EP and the Council, *OJ* 1986 C283/36; Res. of 8 Oct. 1986 on relations between the EP and the Commission, *OJ* 1986 C283/39 and the numerous previous Resolutions cited therein; Res. of 9 Oct. 1986 on the position of the EP in actions for annulment brought under Art. 173 EEC, *OJ* 1986 C283/85). As a result of these various pressures and other developments, the powers of the EP have been gradually enlarged in four main directions: with regard to the budget (through the Budgetary Treaties of 1970 and 1975), in the fields of legislation and treaty-making (through the Single European Act of 1986), and as to its standing before the ECJ (through the Court's case-law).

As Community law stands at present, the functions and powers of the EP

231

extend over four main areas: Community legislation, external relations, control over the other institutions, and the Community budget. These will be considered in turn below.

1. **Participation in Community legislation.** Although the EP still has no legislative powers of its own, it participates in the Community legislative process in three different ways: through the consultation and the co-operation procedures and through its own initiatives.

(a) In a number of cases, the EEC and Euratom Treaties require the Council to consult the EP before adopting a binding measure. These cases include most important matters such as e.g. agriculture, free movement of persons and services, right of establishment, transport, competition, etc. under the EEC Treaty (see e.g. Arts. 43(2), 49, 54(1) and (2), 56(2), 63(1) and (2), 75(1), 87(1)); the protection of health and safety, the amendment of certain Treaty provisions, etc. under the Euratom Treaty (see e.g. Arts. 31, 76, 85, 90). Although the opinion of the EP is not legally binding, consultation is still an essential aspect of the law-making process. As the ECJ has pointed out, consultation 'is the means which allows the Parliament to play an actual part in the legislative process of the Community. Such power represents an essential factor in the institutional balance intended by the Treaty. Although limited, it reflects at Community level the fundamental democratic principle that the peoples should take part in the exercise of power through the intermediary of a representative assembly. Due consultation of the Parliament in the cases provided for by the Treaty therefore constitutes an essential formality disregard of which means that the measure concerned is void.' This requirement is therefore not satisfied by the Council's simply asking for an opinion; Parliament must actually express its opinion on the matter (Case 138/79 *Roquette* v. *Council* [1980] ECR 3333 at p. 3360; see also Case 828/79 *Adam* v. *Commission* [1982] ECR 269 at pp. 287–8).

It is the Council which is required to consult the EP once it has received a legislative proposal from the Commission. However, to involve Parliament in the decision-making process at a much earlier stage, the Commission has expressed its intention to consult the House in advance on important issues, such as decisions affecting the future of the Communities, before it makes formal proposals. In the case of major initiatives with political implications, the Commission normally sends Parliament and the Council advance communications and takes into account the views of the former in shaping its proposals (see Suppl. 3/82—*Bull. EC*, p. 9). Also, in addition to the mandatory consultations prescribed by the Treaties, both the Commission and the Council normally seek the EP's opinion on an optional basis on a wide range of measures having determining effect on policy, even including matters falling within the scope of the ECSC Treaty (see *Bull. EC* 6–1973, pp. 9–10; *Bull. EC* 10–1973, p. 90). The ECJ has expressly confirmed the validity of such optional consultations (Case 165/87 *Commission* v. *Council* [1988] ECR para. 20). However, a constant complaint of the EP is that it is not consulted on implementing measures even where the Treaty requires consultation on the basic legislation (see Res. of 8 Oct. 1986, *OJ* 1986 C283/36, Preamble and point 11(d), and the opinion of the Legal Affairs

Committee, EP Working Doc. A 2–103/86, Annex IV, 29 Sept. 1986). It would seem, however, that Community law does not impose the requirement of consultation in respect of implementing measures where the basic act (regulation) itself lays down no such requirement, provided that the implementing measure adopted without consultation respects the 'basic elements' laid down in the basic regulation adopted after consultation of the EP (Case 46/86 *Romkes* [1987] ECR 2671 at pp. 2685–6; Case 203/86 *Spain* v. *Council* [1988] ECR para. 34; Case 230/78 *Eridania* [1979] ECR 2749 at pp. 2764–5; see also Case 828/79 *Adam* v. *Commission*, above, and the opinion of A.-G. Capotorti in [1981] ECR 1512 at p. 1544).

Requests received from the Council or the Commission for an opinion or for advice are referred by the President to the appropriate committee for consideration. Parliament then discusses the Commission's proposal in plenary sitting on the basis of the report drawn up by the committee and adopts a legislative resolution which may approve, reject, or propose amendments to the proposal. This concludes the consultation procedure (Rule 36). Alternatively, Parliament may delegate to the appropriate committee the power to take a decision (Rule 37 as amended). At any time during the procedure, the Commission may withdraw or amend its proposal, particularly to give effect to Parliament's opinion (Arts. 149(3) EEC, 119(2) Euratom. As to the procedure to be followed by the EP if the Commission does not withdraw a rejected proposal or does not intend to adopt the EP's amendments, see Rules 39 and 40). Although the EP's opinions are not legally binding, both the Commission and the Council have expressed their intention to take them duly into account in their deliberations and to inform Parliament on the action taken on them (*Bull. EC* 6–1973, p. 10; *Bull. EC* 10–1973, p. 90). The EP itself has laid down provisions for monitoring the progress of proposals following the adoption of its opinion (Rule 41). In the case of certain important Community measures having appreciable financial implications, the Council has undertaken to maintain the closest co-operation with the EP and to explain to it the reasons if it intends to depart from the EP's opinion (Council Res. No. 2 of 22 Apr. 1970, text in *Treaties Establishing the European Communities* (1987), p. 1091). In such a case, a conciliation procedure may also be initiated by the EP or by the Council to bring about agreement between the two institutions (Rules 41(4) and 43; *OJ* 1975 C89/1; *see further under* **Conciliation procedure**).

Where the proposal on which Parliament expressed an opinion is subsequently amended by the Commission or the Council, it is not necessary to reconsult Parliament if 'considered as a whole the substance of the draft... on which the Parliament was consulted has not been altered' (Case 41/69 *Chemiefarma* v. *Commission* [1970] ECR 661 at p. 702; see also pp. 688–9) or, in other words, if the 'amendment to the initial proposal constitutes in reality a change of method rather than of substance' and the amended text 'corresponds broadly to the wish expressed by the Parliament' (Case 828/79 *Adam* v. *Commission*, above, at p. 290; Case 68/86 *United Kingdom* v. *Council* [1988] ECR 855 at pp. 887–8 *per* A.-G. Lenz; the Court did not consider this question, see p. 902). It seems to follow from this (although the

ECJ has never ruled to this effect so far) that renewed consultation is required where the amendments to the Commission's initial draft are 'so radical as to render the first consultation outdated and irrelevant' (Case 828/79 *Adam* v. *Commission, per* A.-G. Capotorti in [1981] ECR 1512 at p. 1545; see also Rule 42 EPRP and EP Res. of 21 Jan. 1988, *OJ* 1988 C49/117, point 4). It seems that failure to reconsult Parliament in such a situation constitutes an infringement of an essential procedural requirement and may entail the nullity of the measure (Case 20/85 *Roviello* [1988] ECR 2805 at pp. 2827–9, 2838–42 *per* A.-G. Mancini. The Court did not consider this question, see p. 2853).

(*b*) The co-operation procedure was introduced by Art. 6 SEA with a view to increasing the influence of the EP in the legislative process but without giving it a real power of co-decision. The procedure applies only to those acts which are exhaustively listed in Art. 6 SEA and which may be adopted by the Council by a qualified majority (i.e. acts based on Arts. 7, 49, 54(2), 56(2), 57, 100A, 100B, 118A, 130E, and 130Q(2) EEC). The co-operation procedure itself is laid down in Art. 149(2) EEC, as amended by Art. 7 SEA, and applies only under the EEC Treaty (*see further under* **Co-operation procedure**). Basically, it involves two readings both in the Council and in the EP. In the EP, the procedure for the first reading is identical with the consultation procedure (Rule 44 EPRP). The second reading begins with the communication of the 'common position' of the Council to Parliament, which is then referred automatically to the committee responsible. This committee submits a recommendation on the second reading as to the decision which Parliament should take (Rules 45, 47). The co-operation procedure is concluded by Parliament approving, rejecting, or amending the common position (Rule 48). If the common position is rejected, or if the Commission fails to accept Parliament's amendments in its re-examined proposal, Parliament may request the Commission to withdraw its proposal (Rules 50, 52). As long as the Council has not acted, the Commission may alter or withdraw its proposal at any time during the procedure (Art. 149(3) EEC), but neither it nor the Council is legally bound by Parliament's decision on the second reading. It may be noted that the EP has called upon the Council to extend the co-operation procedure to spheres of major importance to the Community and the Member States, such as the Common Agricultural Policy and the fixing of farm prices (see Res. of 8 Oct. 1986, *OJ* 1986 C283/36, point 11(e). On the application of the co-operation procedure to proposals which were already pending before the Council when the SEA came into effect, see Res. of 9 Apr. 1987, *OJ* 1987 C125/137 and Res. of 21 Jan. 1988, *OJ* 1988 C49/117).

(*c*) In addition to opinions given in the context of the formal consultation and co-operation procedures, the EP may adopt resolutions on its own initiative on any matter 'falling within the sphere of activities of the Communities' (Rule 63 as amended). It may also debate any 'topical and urgent subject of major importance' (Rule 64 as amended). As seen above, the ECJ has expressly confirmed Parliament's inherent right 'to discuss any question concerning the Communities, to adopt resolutions on such questions and to invite the Governments to act' (Case 230/81 *Luxembourg* v. *Parliament*, above, at p. 287). On its part, the Commission considers it quite legitimate for a directly elected Parliament to put forward initiatives to develop the Communities and to expect the implementation of its findings. The Commission attaches great importance to legislative proposals submitted by the EP and is willing to act on them provided that there are no objections of substance (see Suppl. 3/82—*Bull. EC*, p. 10. See also Res. of 8 Oct. 1986, *OJ* 1986 C283/39, point 3). The European Council has also confirmed that the Council and the Commission will respond to Parliament's resolutions concerning matters of major importance and general concern (see the Solemn Declaration on European Union, point 2.3.3).

In 1988, the EP adopted 605 resolutions and decisions, including 210 resolutions embodying its opinions (45 on first reading and 42 on second reading under the co-operation procedure) and 32 own-initiative resolutions (22nd *Gen. Rep. EC* (1988), p. 36).

2. **External relations.** Apart from the sphere of the Community budget, the most important increase in the powers of the EP has occurred in the field of the negotiation and conclusion of international agreements. Developments in this area, which had taken place over a long period of time, culminated in Arts. 8 and 9 SEA amending Arts. 237 and 238 EEC, respectively. Under these provisions, the EP has been granted a real power of co-decision with regard to the conclusion of accession treaties and association agreements— the only field where, outside the budgetary procedure, the EP enjoys such power. These treaties and agreements may only be concluded with the assent of the EP, acting by an absolute majority of its component Members. In addition, Parliament is consulted by the Council on the negotiation and conclusion of trade, co-operation, and other 'significant' international agreements and is kept informed by the Commission and the Council, through the appropriate committees, of progress in such negotiations (Rules 32 to 35 EPRP. *See further under* **Treaty-making procedure**, point 2(*c*)). The EP has called upon the Council to extend co-decision to all international agreements concluded by the Community in respect of which national Parliaments have lost their powers (see Res. of 8 Oct. 1986, *OJ* 1986 C283/36, point 11(b) and (c), and also Res. of 17 June 1988 on the role of the EP in external policy within the framework of the SEA, *OJ* 1988 C187/233). Indeed, Rule 34(2) EPRP has already extended the assent procedure, laid down for association agreements, to other 'significant' agreements, thus going beyond the terms of Art. 9 SEA.

It may be noted that, under Art. 95(3) and (4) ECSC, Parliament enjoys a real power of decision of its own in so far as amendments jointly proposed by the Commission and the Council to the ECSC Treaty and approved by the Court of Justice may enter into force only if adopted by Parliament acting by a three-quarters majority of the votes cast, representing a two-thirds majority of its current Members (the so-called 'minor revision' of the Treaty). The EP may itself pass a resolution proposing to the Commission and Council amendments under Art. 95 (Rule 31 EPRP. Art. 95(4) ECSC has last been amended by Art. 13 of the Act of Accession 1985).

In addition to its role in the treaty-making process, the EP participates in the external relations of the Communities in several other ways. Thus, for example, Art. 27 of the EEC–Turkey Association Agreement of 1963 provides for co-operation and contact between the EP and the Turkish Parliament (*JO* 1964, p. 3687, English text in *OJ* 1973 C113/1), while Art. 25 of the Third ACP–EEC Convention of 1984 (Lomé III) set up a Joint Assembly composed of equal numbers of MEPs on the Community side and of MPs or representatives designated by the ACP States (*OJ* 1986 L86/3; in 1988 the Joint Assembly held two sessions, see 22nd *Gen. Rep. EC* (1988), p. 400). The EP has set up a number of interparliamentary delegations (see Rule 126 EPRP) and maintains close relations with the Parliamentary Assembly of the Council of Europe, to which it sends an annual report (Rule 127 EPRP; see also the Protocol on Relations with the Council of Europe annexed to the ECSC Treaty, esp. Art. 2).

3. **Control over the other institutions.** While the EP's role in the Community legislative process is still limited, its real powers lie, apart from the budgetary sphere, in the field of parliamentary control over the other institutions, in the first place over the Commission. There are a number of ways in which Parliament may exercise its supervisory powers; these may be summarized as follows.

(*a*) A political group or one-tenth of the current MEPs may table a motion of censure on the activities of the Commission which, if carried by a two-thirds majority of the votes cast, representing a majority of MEPs, means that the Commission must resign as a body (Arts. 24 ECSC, 144 EEC, 114 Euratom, Rule 30 EPRP). This power, which is unique in the field of international organizations, clearly has great symbolic value even although it has never been exercised so far. (Several motions have been tabled over the years but none carried, see e.g. the motion tabled in Nov. 1972 on account of the Commission's failure to submit proposals for the enlargement of Parliament's budgetary powers. After a satisfactory explanation from the Commission, the motion was withdrawn, see 6th *Gen. Rep. EC* (1972), pp. 342–3.) However, the scope of the power is somewhat limited in that it may only be used against the Commission while the Council, which is the chief decision-making body, is not subject to Parliament's control. Moreover, even if a motion of censure is carried, the members of the Commission continue to deal with current business until they are replaced in accordance with the normal procedure, i.e. a new Commission is appointed by the Member States, over which the EP has only a limited influence (see point (*e*) below). Also, the dismissal of the Commission would lead to a major political crisis within the Communities which might cause more problems than it could possibly solve. In practice, therefore, it is the mere existence, rather than the exercise, of this power that is important.

(*b*) The Commission is required to publish annually, not later than one month before the opening of the session of the EP, a General Report on the Activities of the Communities (Art. 18 of the Merger Treaty). After the various parts of the Report have been considered by the appropriate committees, the Report as a whole is discussed by Parliament in open plenary sitting (Arts. 24 ECSC, 143 EEC, 113 Euratom, Rule 29B). In addition to the General Report, the Commission also prepares a number of Reports dealing with special matters such as the Agricultural Situation, Social Developments, Competition Policy (see 22nd *Gen. Rep. EC* (1988), p. 3. See also the Fifth Annual Report to the EP on Commission monitoring of the application of Community Law, *OJ* 1988 C310/1). Moreover, the Commission presents an annual programme (for 1990, see Suppl. 1/90—*Bull. EC*) which is debated in Parliament, after which the Enlarged Bureau and the Commission agree on an annual legislative programme (Rule 29(4); see also the Draft Joint Declaration annexed to Res. of 8 Oct. 1986, *OJ* 1986 C283/39). The President of the Commission reports regularly to the chairmen of the committees on the execution of the annual programme so that Parliament is in a position to exert, through its committees, considerable influence on legislative matters (*Bull. EC* 6–1973, p. 9).

(*c*) The EP maintains close contacts with European Political Co-operation (EPC), with the European Council, and with the Council. Thus, the Presidency of EPC reports regularly to Parliament on the foreign policy matters examined in EPC and also on the extent to which the views of Parliament on these matters have been taken into account. The EP may hold a debate during which the Commission will also be heard. The Presidency also presents an annual report on progress in EPC and four colloquies are held each year between the Foreign Ministers and the Political Affairs Committee (Rule 57). The Presidency of the European Council is likewise required to report to the EP after each meeting, at the beginning and end of its term of office and once a year (see the Solemn Declaration on European Union, points 2.1.4 and 2.3.4. *See further under* **European Council, European Political Co-operation**). The President of the Council customarily presents to Parliament a programme and a report at the beginning and at the end, respectively, of his six-month term of office (see e.g. *Bull. EC* 1–1988, p. 87; 6–1988, p. 175; 7/8–1988, p. 167; 1–1989, p. 84; 23rd *Gen. Rep. EC* (1989), p. 35). The Council is usually represented at, and participates in, important parliamentary debates (see *Bull. EC* 10–1973, p. 91). Parliament has requested the Council to present, as the Commission does, a half-yearly report on action taken on Parliament's own-initiative resolutions (Res. of 8 Oct. 1986, *OJ* 1986 C283/36, point 7).

(*d*) One of the most important ways in which the EP exercises its supervisory powers is through its right to put questions to the Commission, to the Council, and to the Foreign Ministers meeting in EPC. Questions may be put by a committee, a political group, a group of MEPs, or an individual Member, and may call for an oral answer with or without debate, a written answer, or an oral answer at Question Time. Question Time is held at each part-session, during which any Member may put oral question to the above institutions. This may be followed by debate. Written questions and answers are published in the *Official Journal* (Rules 58 to 62 and Annex II). Question Time may also be held in committee (Rule 122). Under the Treaties, only the Commission is required to reply to questions (see Arts. 23 ECSC, 140 EEC, 110 Euratom) since the EP has no political control over the Council. However, early in 1973 the Council agreed to take part in Question Time which had just been introduced by Parliament, and later in that year it confirmed its decision to reply (on a voluntary basis) to all written and oral questions put to it (7th *Gen. Rep. EC* (1973), p. 64; *Bull. EC* 10–1973, p. 89. See also the Solemn Declaration on European Union, point 2.3.3). In 1988, a total of 2,842 written questions (2,512 to the Commission, 159 to the Council, and 171 to EPC) and 1,091 oral questions (723 to the Commission, 213 to the Council, and 155 to EPC) were put (22nd *Gen. Rep. EC* (1988), p. 36).

(*e*) Although the appointment of the members of the Commission is within the powers of the Member States (Arts. 11 and 14 of the Merger Treaty), the European Council has decided that before the appointment of the President of the Commission, the President of the Representatives of the Governments of the Member States should seek the opinion of the Enlarged Bureau of the EP (Solemn Declaration on European Union, point 2.3.5. See the new Rule 29A inserted in EPRP on 15 June 1988. This also requires the EP to pass a vote of confidence in the new Commission upon its appointment and renewal, *OJ* 1988 C187/81. See also *Bull. EC* 1–1989, p. 10). Parliament would like to be consulted on the appointment of the whole Commission (Res. of 8 Oct. 1986, *OJ* 1986 C283/36, point 9).

(*f*) An important supervisory power of the EP is its competence to receive petitions. Under Rule 128 EPRP every citizen of the European Community has the right, individually or jointly with others, to address written requests or complaints (petitions) to the EP. Petitions must fall within the sphere of activities of the Communities. They are examined by the Committee on Petitions, which may organize hearings, dispatch fact-finding missions, and collect any necessary information. It may submit motions for resolutions to Parliament and monitors action taken by the Council and the Commission on petitions referred to them by the EP (Rules 129, 130). In practice, the EP receives a growing number of petitions each year, mostly relating to injustices suffered as a result of infringement of Community law or of Community interest. Parliament would like to strengthen the right of citizens by enabling them to submit petitions also to the other Community institutions through the EP (see Res. of 9 Oct. 1986, *OJ* 1986 C283/86, point 1).

(*g*) In addition to political control, the EP may exercise legal control over the institutions by initiating or participating in proceedings against them before the ECJ. In this respect, by broad interpretation of the relevant Treaty provisions, the Court has considerably improved the standing of Parliament. Thus, the Court has confirmed that Parliament has the right to intervene in cases on the same basis as the other institutions (i.e. without establishing a specific legal interest in the case) as 'it is not possible to restrict the exercise of that right by one of [the institutions] without adversely affecting its institutional position as intended by the Treaty' (Case 138/79 *Roquette* v. *Council*, above, at pp. 3357–8). Relying on exactly the same argument, the Court has also accepted that Parliament has the right to challenge any unlawful inaction of the Council (and, by implication, also of the Commission) by bringing an action for failure to act against it under Art. 175 EEC (or Art. 148 Euratom). In particular, the Court has pointed out that the fact that the EP's primary task to exercise a political review of the activities of the institutions cannot lead to a restrictive interpretation of its right of action (Case 13/83 *Parliament* v. *Council* [1985] ECR 1513 at p. 1588).

This recognition of the power of Parliament to exercise legal control over the Council is potentially of great importance precisely because of the restricted nature of its political control over that institution. Use has been made of this power in Rule 54 EPRP, which provides that where, in the context of the co-operation procedure, the Council fails to adopt the proposed legislation in accordance with the common position which the EP has neither rejected nor amended, the President may, on behalf of Parliament, bring an action for failure to act against the Council under Art. 175 EEC. Provision has also been made for a systematic examination in committee of all Community legislation to ensure that Parliament's rights have been fully respected (Rule 55). It seems, however, that in the case of a breach of its rights Parliament only envisages the possibility of intervention rather than that of instituting proceedings itself (ibid.), although the latter would provide a more effective remedy. The EP may also be invited by the Court to state its opinion on any matter which concerns it in preliminary ruling proceedings under Arts. 177 EEC, 150 Euratom, although it is not automatically entitled to submit observations in those proceedings (see e.g. Case 149/85 *Wybot*, above, at p. 2407).

In several cases, the ECJ has ruled that the EP is capable of adopting measures intended to have legal effects *vis-à-vis* third parties, for example, in the budgetary field or with regard to its internal organization or direct elections. While Art. 38 ECSC allows these measures to be challenged for annulment, Arts. 173 EEC and 146 Euratom contain no express provision for active or passive participation of the EP in annulment proceedings (i.e. either as an applicant or as a defendant). Nevertheless, the ECJ has held that an action for annulment may be brought against the EP not only under Art. 38 ECSC (see Case 230/81 *Luxembourg* v. *Parliament*, above, at pp. 282–3; Case 108/83 *Luxembourg* v. *Parliament*, above, at p. 1958), but also under Art. 173 EEC or Art. 146 Euratom (Case 294/83 *Les Verts* v. *Parliament*, above, at p. 1366; Case 34/86 *Council* v. *Parliament*, above, at pp. 2201–3). The justification put forward by the Court for such a broad interpretation of those Articles has been that the Treaties intended to establish a complete system of legal remedies designed to permit the Court to review the legality of all binding measures of the institutions. In the absence of such judicial review, measures adopted by the EP could encroach on the powers of the Member States or of the other institutions, or exceed the limits of Parliament's powers (Case 294/83 *Les Verts* v. *Parliament*, above, at pp. 1365–6).

While Parliament has accepted and welcomed the Court's ruling, it has claimed that it should in turn itself have the right to bring actions for the annulment of acts of the Council and the Commission under Art. 173 EEC (ibid. at pp. 1364–5; see also Res. of 9 Oct. 1986, *OJ* 1986 C283/85, point 3). In Parliament's opinion, such a right of action is necessary (i) in order to maintain the institutional balance; (ii) to enable it effectively to control the other institutions; (iii) to defend its prerogatives against them; and (iv) to complement its right to challenge their inaction (Case 302/87 *Parliament* v. *Council* [1988] ECR paras. 12 *et seq.*; see also the Report for the Hearing—the first case to be brought by Parliament against the Council under Art. 173 EEC). However, the ECJ has not accepted Parliament's arguments and has held that the actual text of Art. 173 does not enable the Court to recognize the *locus standi* of Parliament to bring an action for annulment under that provision (ibid. para. 28). To preserve the autonomy of Parliament, the ECJ has decided that where a measure concerns only the internal organization of Parliament's work and does not produce any legal effects with regard to third parties, it is not subject to an action for annulment (Case 78/85 *Group of the European Right* v. *Parliament* [1986] ECR 1753 at p. 1757; Case 190/84 *Les Verts* v. *Parliament* [1988] ECR 1017 at p. 1035. See also Res. of 9 Oct. 1986, *OJ* 1986 C283/85, point 4. *See further under* **Action for annulment, Action for failure to act**).

4. **Budgetary powers.** Undoubtedly, the most significant increase in the powers of the EP has taken place in the budgetary sphere. Orginally, under the EEC and Euratom Treaties, the Council was the sole budgetary authority having the power to determine and to adopt the budget, and to give a discharge to the Commission in respect of its implementation. Parliament only had the right to propose non-binding modifications to the draft budget submitted to it by the Council, which the Council hardly ever took into account (see the original Arts. 203, 206 EEC, 177, 180 Euratom). By contrast, under the ECSC Treaty, the budgetary power was essentially entrusted to the Commission, which only consulted Parliament on a voluntary basis. These arrangements were due to the fact that under the EEC and Euratom Treaties the budget revenue was originally made up of financial contributions from the Member States, while the ECSC procured its own funds by imposing levies on the production of coal and steel (see Arts. 200 EEC, 172 Euratom, 49–50 ECSC).

When at the Hague Summit Conference of 1 and 2 December 1969 the Heads of State or Government agreed progressively to replace, in accordance with Art. 201 EEC, the financial contributions of Member States by the Communities' own resources, they also recognized that this would require the strengthening of the budgetary powers of the EP (see Final Communiqué of 2 Dec. 1969, point 5, 3rd *Gen. Rep. EC* (1969), p. 486). This was in fact necessary in order to establish democratic control over the Community budget at the Community level, since such control could no longer be exercised at the national level. Thus, following the adoption by the Council of Dec. 70/243 on 21 April 1970 creating the Communities' own resources, which were gradually to replace the financial contributions of Member States (*OJ Sp. Edn.* 1970(I), p. 224), the First Budgetary Treaty was signed on 22 April 1970 (*JO* 1971 L2/1). This increased Parliament's budgetary powers in two stages, the first, transitional, stage covering the years 1971 to 1974, the second, definitive, stage beginning with the budget for the financial year 1975. This corresponded to the stages by which the Communities were to acquire their own resources under the Council Decision of 21 April 1970.

However, the Treaty of 1970 failed to satisfy the European Parliament, and on the occasion of its signing the Commission undertook to present new proposals for a further extension of Parliament's budgetary powers (6th *Gen. Rep. EC* (1972), p. 5; 7th *Gen. Rep. EC* (1973), p. 45). These proposals resulted in the signing on 22 July 1975 of the Second Budgetary Treaty, which entered into force on 1 June 1977 (*OJ* 1977 L359/1). The Treaty further amended and supplemented the financial provisions of the original Treaties and established a Court of Auditors which replaced the previous Audit Board of the Communities and the Auditor of the ECSC.

The various amendments introduced by the two Budgetary Treaties had the effect of conferring upon the EP a real power of co-decision in the budget procedure, establishing it as one arm of the budgetary authority on a footing of equality with the Council (this has also been confirmed by the ECJ in Case 34/86 *Council* v. *Parliament*, above; *see further under* **Community budget**). Accordingly, the EP now exercises the following powers in respect of the draft budget drawn up and submitted to it by the Council on the basis of a preliminary draft prepared by the Commission. Parliament may: (*a*) approve the draft budget without amendments; (*b*) reject the draft budget and ask for a new draft to be submitted to it 'if there are important reasons' for this; (*c*) propose to the Council modifications to the draft budget relating to 'expenditure necessarily resulting from this Treaty or from acts adopted in accordance therewith' (the so-called 'compulsory expenditure'); however, these modifications are not binding upon the Council, which may accept, reject, or modify them, having the last word in respect of this part of the budget; (*d*) amend the draft budget in relation to 'non-compulsory expenditure'; in this respect the EP has a genuine power of decision in that, subject to certain limits, it may determine this part of the budget by overriding any contrary decision of the Council; (*e*) through its President, declare that the budget has been finally adopted; (*f*) give a discharge to the Commission in respect of the implementation of the budget (Arts. 78, 78g ECSC; 203, 206b EEC; 177, 180b Euratom. The ECSC provisions apply only to the administrative budget of that Community. *See further under* **Budgetary Treaties, Community budget**).

It is clear, however, that the increased budgetary powers of the EP cannot be viewed in isolation. Since the major part of budgetary expenditure is incurred automatically pursuant to decisions of principle and other multi-annual commitments adopted by the Council, Parliament's increased powers remain largely illusory so long as Parliament is unable to influence the making of those decisions. It is therefore essential that Parliament should be associated with the preparation of decisions determining the major annual budget items and those reflecting Community policies. In other words, its increased powers in the budgetary field should be accompanied by more effective participation in the legislative process (see EP Res. of 5 Oct. 1973, point 2, *OJ* 1973 C87/8). In the absence of a right of legislative co-decision corresponding to budgetary co-decision, the above objective has to a limited extent been achieved through a conciliation procedure which was established between the Parliament and the Council in 1975 during the course of the negotiation of the

Second Budgetary Treaty (*OJ* 1975 C89/1; *see further under* **Conciliation procedure**).

See also **Action for annulment, Action for failure to act, Budgetary Treaties, Commission, Committee on Institutional Affairs, Community budget, Conciliation procedure, Co-operation procedure, Council, Court of Auditors, European Council, European Political Co-operation, European Union, Institutional balance, Institutions, Own resources, Privileges and immunities, Secondary legislation, Single European Act, Solemn Declaration on European Union, Three Wise Men's Report, Tindemans Report, Treaty-making procedure, Vedel Report.**

Further reading 1. BOOKS: Cocks, *The European Parliament: Structure, Procedure and Practice* (1973); Fitzmaurice, *The European Parliament* (1978); Herman and Hagger, *The Legislation of Direct Elections to the European Parliament* (1980); Herman and Lodge, *The European Parliament and the European Community* (1978); Kirchner, *The European Parliament: Performance and Prospects* (1984); Lasok and Bridge, *Law and Institutions of the European Communities*, 4th edn. (1987), ch. 7; Lodge (ed.), *Direct Elections to the European Parliament 1984* (1986); Palmer, *The European Parliament* (1981); Sasse *et al.*, *The European Parliament: Towards a Uniform Procedure for Direct Elections* (1981).

2. ARTICLES AND PAPERS: Allott, 'The Democratic Basis of the European Communities' (1974) 11 *CML Rev.* 298; Bangemann, 'Preparations for Direct Elections in the Federal Republic of Germany' (1978) 15 *CML Rev.* 321 and (1979) 16 *CML Rev.* 241; Baviera, 'Preparations for Direct Elections in Italy' (1978) 15 *CML Rev.* 199; Bieber, 'Legal Developments in the European Parliament', Annual Surveys in (1982) 2 *YEL* 259, (1983) 3 *YEL* 371, (1984) 4 *YEL* 341, (1985) 5 *YEL* 341, (1986) 6 *YEL* 357, (1987) 7 *YEL* 285, (1988) 8 *YEL* 189 (by Bradley); id., 'Achievements of the European Parliament, 1979–1984' (1984) 21 *CML Rev.* 283; Bieber, Pantalis, and Schoo, 'Implications of the Single European Act for the European Parliament' (1986) 23 *CML Rev.* 767; Bosscher, 'Preparations for Direct Elections in the Netherlands' (1978) 15 *CML Rev.* 465; Bradley, 'Maintaining the Balance: The Role of the Court of Justice in Defining the Institutional Position of the European Parliament' (1987) 24 *CML Rev.* 41; id., 'The Variable Evolution of the Standing of the European Parliament in Proceedings Before the Court of Justice' (1988) 8 *YEL* 27; Brown, 'Judicial Control of Acts of the European Parliament' (1983/1) *LIEI* 75; Cohen, 'The Development of Question Time in the European Parliament' (1979) 16 *CML Rev.* 41; Conference Report, 'Direct Elections and the Future of the European Parliament' (1978) 15 *CML Rev.* 69; Editorial, 'Tindemans, Vedel and the European Parliament' (1975–6) 1 *EL Rev.* 183; id., 'Direct Elections: Agreement at Last' (1975–6) 1 *EL Rev.* 429; id., 'The European Parliament before the Court of Justice?' (1979) 16 *CML Rev.* 175; id., 'Isoglucose Gives More Power to the Parliament's Elbow' (1980) 5 *EL Rev.* 431; id., 'Mixed Legal Fortunes for the European Parliament' (1988) 13 *EL Rev.* 293; Forman, 'Direct Elections to the European Parliament' (1977) 2 *EL Rev.* 35; id., 'Preparations for Direct Elections in the United Kingdom' (1978) 15 *CML Rev.* 347 and (1979) 16 *CML Rev.* 235; Gulmann and Vesterdorf, 'Preparations for Direct Elections in Denmark' (1979) 16 *CML Rev.* 119; Hartley, 'Where Should the European Parliament Meet?' (1984) 9 *EL Rev.* 44; Herman, 'Direct Elections to the European Parliament: Comparative Perspectives' (1979) 16 *CML Rev.* 209; Jacobs, 'Isoglucose Resurgent: Two Powers of the European Parliament upheld by the Court' (1981) 18 *CML Rev.* 219; Kovar and Simon, 'Some Reflections on the Decision of the French Constitutional Council of December 30,

1976' (1977) 14 *CML Rev.* 525; Lodge, 'The Significance of Direct Elections for the European Parliament's Role in the European Community and the Drafting of a Common Electoral Law' (1979) 16 *CML Rev.* 195; Neels, 'Preparations for Direct Elections in Belgium' (1978) 15 *CML Rev.* 337 and (1979) 16 *CML Rev.* 243; Robinson, 'Preparations for Direct Elections in Ireland' (1978) 15 *CML Rev.* 187; Schermers, 'The Powers of the European Parliament', in Bates *et al.* (eds.), *In Memoriam J. D. B. Mitchell* (1983), p. 128; Simon, 'Preparations for Direct Elections in France' (1979) 16 *CML Rev.* 127; Stewart, 'Direct Elections to the European Parliament' (1976) 13 *CML Rev.* 283; Thill, 'Preparations for Direct Elections in the Grand Duchy of Luxembourg' (1978) 15 *CML Rev.* 473; van den Berghe, 'Direct Elections in Accordance with a Uniform Procedure' (1979) 4 *EL Rev.* 331.

3. OFFICIAL PUBLICATIONS: European Parliament, 'Elections to the European Parliament by Direct Universal Suffrage', Report, Resolutions, and Debates of the European Parliament (1977); House of Lords, Select Committee on the European Communities, Session 1982–3, 5th Report, 'Uniform Electoral Procedure for the Election of Members of the European Parliament' (1983).

See also under **Community law, Institutions, Single European Act.**

▶ **EUROPEAN POLITICAL CO-OPERATION** (EPC) Framework within which the Member States of the European Communities co-ordinate their activities in the spheres of foreign policy and international diplomacy by the adoption of common positions and the implementation of joint action.

The need for EPC arises from the fact that foreign policy matters remain, for the most part, outside the scope of the Community Treaties which pursue, primarily, economic and social objectives. Prior to the coming into force of the Single European Act of 1986 (SEA), EPC had no legal foundation in primary or secondary Community law, but developed gradually on an entirely voluntary basis through a series of reports, declarations, undertakings, and practices. A distinction was therefore made between the political co-operation machinery, which dealt on the intergovernmental level with problems of international politics, and the activities of the institutions of the Communities, which were based on the legal commitments undertaken by the Member States in the Treaties. Nevertheless, both sets of machinery had the common aim of contributing to the process of European unification. The setting up of EPC was prompted by the realization that the implementation of the common policies of the Communities, particularly those affecting their external relations (e.g. the Common Commercial Policy), required corresponding developments in the political sphere. There was a need for a coherent and united approach to international affairs by the Member States since it was imperative that while the Community was acting as one trading bloc they should be able to speak with one voice towards the outside world. It was also realized that the Member States were far from playing a role in the world appropriate to their combined influence; instead of shaping events they could merely react to them.

Apart from declarations made at various Summit Conferences, the objectives, methods, and procedures of EPC are laid down in the following six documents:

- the Luxembourg Report of 27 October 1970 (First Report on EPC, also known as the Davignon Report, *Bull. EC* 11–1970, p. 9);

243

- the Copenhagen Report of 23 July 1973 (Second Report on EPC, 7th *Gen. Rep. EC* (1973), p. 502);
- the London Report of 13 October 1981 (Third Report on EPC, Suppl. 3/81—*Bull. EC*, p. 14);
- the Solemn Declaration on European Union of 19 June 1983 (adopted by the European Council in Stuttgart, *Bull. EC* 6–1983, p. 24);
- Title III of the Single European Act of 1986 (Suppl. 2/86—*Bull. EC*; *OJ* 1987 L169);
- Decision adopted by the Foreign Ministers on 28 February 1986 on the occasion of the signing of the SEA (*Bull. EC* 2–1986, p. 115).

The Luxembourg Report, which was prepared at the request of the Hague Summit Conference of 1–2 December 1969 (see point 15 of the Final Communiqué of 2 Dec. 1969, 3rd *Gen. Rep. EC* (1969), p. 486), laid the foundations of EPC. It set out the main objectives of EPC and provided for twice-yearly meetings of the Foreign Ministers, assisted by a Political Committee comprising the Political Directors of the Member States. The Copenhagen Report implemented the decision of the Paris Summit Conference of 19–21 October 1972 that EPC should be intensified at all levels (see point 14 of the Declaration of 21 Oct. 1972, 6th *Gen. Rep. EC* (1972), p. 7). It increased the number of ministerial meetings to four a year and set up the Group of Correspondents. It also provided for the participation in the implementation of EPC by the diplomatic missions of the Member States. Finally, the Report defined in more detail the methods of co-operation and the relationship between EPC and the activities of the Community institutions. The London Report made further improvements in the co-operation machinery and procedures. The Solemn Declaration of Stuttgart emphasized the need for the reinforcement of EPC and the importance of greater coherence and closer co-ordination between EPC and the existing structures of the Communities (in this respect see also the Tindemans Report, the (Draft) European Act, and the Report of the Committee on Institutional Affairs—the Dooge Committee).

The above developments have been codified and, for the first time, given a Treaty basis in Title III of the SEA. Nevertheless, Art. 1(3) SEA makes it clear that Title III is not intended to replace but rather to 'confirm and supplement' the procedures agreed in the various Reports and Declarations and the practices gradually established among the Member States. The decision of the Foreign Ministers of 28 February 1986, which concerns the practical application of certain aspect of Title III, also affirms that those procedures remain in force and that the provisions of the decision are supplementary to them.

This raises the questions whether the various texts mentioned have thereby acquired binding force and whether EPC itself has thus become an integral part of Community law. To deal with the second question first, in its opinion delivered on the convening of the Intergovernmental Conference to draft what became the SEA, the Commission emphasized the need for a unified institutional framework for Community and EPC activities (*Bull. EC* 7/8–

1985, p. 9). While such a framework has, strictly speaking, not been created, the Intergovernmental Conference at least decided to incorporate both the provisions amending the existing Community Treaties and those relating to EPC in a 'Single' Act (see 19th *Gen. Rep. EC* (1985), p. 34; *Bull. EC* 12–1985, p. 11). However, it does not follow from this that both sets of provisions have thereby acquired equal status and binding force as part of the Community legal order. While Art. 1(1) SEA states that the European Communities and EPC share the common objective of contributing to European unity, Art. 3 makes a clear distinction between the institutions of the Communities, whose powers and jurisdiction are governed by the Treaties as amended by Title II of SEA, and the 'institutions and bodies responsible for EPC', whose powers and jurisdiction are subject to Title III of SEA and to the documents referred to above (see also the Preamble, second indent). Moreover, the jurisdiction of the ECJ is not extended to EPC (Art. 31 SEA), nor do the provisions relating to EPC affect the Treaties establishing the Communities (Art. 32 SEA). It therefore seems that EPC has not been made an integral part of Community law in a strict sense but is now based on a Treaty which is binding upon the Member States under general international law only. While the provisions of Title III are undoubtedly binding in this sense, they are not enforceable before the ECJ; nor are they drafted in a sufficiently precise manner to enable a breach of those provisions to be judicially established except perhaps in the most exceptional situations. Political co-operation thus continues to be based, ultimately, more on mutual consent than on enforceable legal obligation. Nevertheless, EPC still forms part of the *acquis communautaire* in a wider sense so that new Member States cannot refuse to participate in it upon acceding to the Communities.

In defining the substantive and procedural aspects of EPC, Art. 30 SEA, which makes up Title III, for the most part restates the established practices arising from the three Reports previously mentioned. The main undertaking of the Member States is to 'endeavour' jointly to formulate and implement a European foreign policy (Art. 30(1)). The objective of co-operation is to ensure the effective exercise of the combined influence of the Member States. Co-operation takes place through regular exchanges of information and consultations on any foreign policy matters of general interest; through co-ordination, the adoption of common positions, and the implementation of joint action (Art. 30(2)(a)). Consultations are to take place before the States decide on their final positions in the adoption of which the positions of the other States and the common European position must be fully taken into account (Art. 30(2)(b) and (c)). The Member States are required not to impede the formation of consensus and the implementation of joint action (Art. 30(3)(c)). For the first time, questions of European security are brought within the scope of EPC in so far as the States have expressed their readiness to co-ordinate their positions more closely on the political and economic aspects of security (Art. 30(6)(a), see also EP Res. of 16 Nov. 1988, *OJ* 1988 C326/65). The co-operation between the Member States is to extend also to their activities within international institutions and at international conferences (Art. 30(7)).

As regards its organs and procedures, EPC takes place within the framework of a complex structure involving the following main organs:

- the European Council;
- the meetings of the Foreign Ministers;
- the Presidency;
- the Political Committee;
- the European Correspondents' Group;
- working groups;
- a Secretariat;
- the Heads of diplomatic missions.

The apex of the whole system is the *European Council*, which may deal with both Community issues and matters falling within EPC (*see further under* **European Council**).

The *Ministers for Foreign Affairs* and a member of the Commission meet at least four times a year within the framework of EPC to deal with items of major importance. They may also discuss foreign policy matters falling within EPC on the occasion of meetings of the Council of the European Communities. In addition, the Foreign Ministers gather once every six months for informal so-called 'Gymnich-type' meetings, called after the castle near Bonn where the first meeting of this type took place in 1974 (Art. 30(3)(a) SEA; see also point 1 of the London Report).

The *Presidency* of EPC is held by the Member State which holds the Presidency of the Council of the European Communities. The duties of the Presidency are quite considerable. It is responsible in general for the management of political co-operation and in particular for drawing up the timetable of meetings and for convening and organizing meetings. It is also responsible for initiating action and co-ordinating and representing the positions of the Member States. It acts as spokesman for all the Member States in the European Parliament, in international organizations such as the United Nations, and in contacts with third countries (Art. 30(10)(a) and (b) SEA). To lighten its workload, the London Report decided to provide operational support for the Presidency in the form of a small team of officials seconded from the current, preceding, and succeeding Presidencies, but without setting up a permanent Secretariat (see point 10 of the Report). Such a Secretariat is provided for in the SEA (see below).

The *Political Committee*, comprising the Political Directors of the Foreign Ministries of the Member States, is one of the central organs of EPC. It meets regularly, normally at least once a month, in order to give the necessary impetus, maintain the continuity of EPC, and prepare Ministers' discussions. It is also responsible for supervising and directing the work of the working groups. The Political Committee or, if necessary, a ministerial meeting is to convene within 48 hours at the request of at least three Member States to deal with crisis situations (Art. 30(10)(c) and (d) SEA; see also points 2 and 13 of the London Report).

The *European Correspondents' Group*, consisting of European 'Correspondents' (senior officials) in the Foreign Ministries, is responsible, under the direction of the Political Committee, for monitoring the implementation of EPC and for studying general organizational problems (Art. 30(10)(e) SEA; see also point 3 of the London Report).

Working groups bring together, under the direction of the Political Committee, senior officials (experts) of the Foreign Ministries to deal with particular problems and to undertake medium- and long-term studies (Art. 30(10)(f) SEA, see also Part II of the Copenhagen Report and points 4 and 5 of the London Report).

A *Secretariat* based in Brussels and acting under the authority of the Presidency was set up by the SEA. It is responsible for assisting the Presidency in preparing and implementing EPC activities and in administrative matters, and for a number of other tasks assigned to it. Following on from the support team arrangement introduced by the London Report, the Secretariat consists of five officials seconded from the current, two preceding, and two succeeding Presidencies for a term of two and a half years. They enjoy the same privileges and immunities as members of the diplomatic missions of the Member States based in Brussels, to which they are administratively attached (Art. 30(10)(g) and (11) SEA; Part III of the Ministerial Decision of 28 Feb. 1986).

The *Heads of diplomatic missions* of the Member States participate closely in the political co-operation process. Those accredited to third countries meet regularly to exchange information and co-ordinate views. Those accredited to other Member States likewise hold regular meetings with the Political Director of the host Government. There are other forms of co-operation as well (see Part II of the Copenhagen Report and points 7–9 of the London Report). The SEA has called for increased co-operation between the Member States' missions and Commission delegations accredited to third countries and to international organizations. Such co-operation extends over a whole range of subjects and takes the form of regular meetings between the Member States' Heads of Mission and the Commission's representative to co-ordinate their views and to prepare joint reports, and any other suitable form (Art. 30(9) SEA; Part II of the Ministerial Decision of 28 Feb. 1986).

As regards, finally, the relations between EPC and the activities and institutions of the European Communities, the fundamental principle is that the external policies of the Communities and the policies agreed in EPC must be consistent. It is the special responsibility of the Presidency and of the Commission, each acting within its own sphere of competence, to ensure that such consistency is sought and maintained (Art. 30(5) SEA). As for the Community institutions, the Commission is now fully associated with the proceedings of EPC at all levels (Art. 30(3)(b) SEA; see also Part II of the Copenhagen Report and point 12 of the London Report). The Presidency maintains the necessary link and co-ordination between the work of EPC and the Council (ibid.). The European Parliament is likewise closely associated with EPC, mainly through frequent contacts with the Presidency. These take the form of regular Presidency addresses to Parliament on foreign policy issues being discussed within EPC, answers to parliamentary questions on EPC, the annual report on EPC, the Presidency speeches at the beginning and end of its term of office, and four annual colloquies with the Political Affairs

Committee. The views of the European Parliament, as expressed in its resolutions, are also required to be duly taken into account in EPC work (Art. 30(4) SEA; Part I of the Ministerial Decision of 28 Feb. 1986. See also point 11 of the London Report and points 15–17 of EP Res. of 8 Oct. 1986, *OJ* 1986 C283/36).

See also Acquis communautaire, **Commission, Committee on Institutional Affairs, Council, European Act, European Council, European Parliament, Single European Act, Solemn Declaration on European Union, Tindemans Report.**

Further reading 1. BOOKS: Allen, Rummel, and Wessels, *European Political Co-operation* (1982); De Vree, Coffey, and Lauwaars (eds.), *Towards a European Foreign Policy: Legal, Economic and Political Dimensions* (1987); Hill (ed.), *National Foreign Policies and European Political Co-operation* (1983); Ifestos, *European Political Cooperation: Towards a Framework of Supranational Diplomacy* (1987); Pijpers, Regelsberger, and Wessels (eds.), *European Political Co-operation in the 1980s* (1988).

2. ARTICLES: Brückner, 'European Political Co-operation: A Danish Perspective' (1985) 5 *YEL* 191; Freestone and Davidson, 'Community Competence and Part III of the Single European Act' (1986) 23 *CML Rev.* 793; Meynell, 'External Relations of the European Community' (1981) 1 *YEL* 347 at p. 368; Nuttall, 'European Political Co-operation', Annual Surveys in (1982) 2 *YEL* 249, (1983) 3 *YEL* 267, (1984) 4 *YEL* 327, (1985) 5 *YEL* 325, (1986) 6 *YEL* 313, (1987) 7 *YEL* 269; id., 'European Political Co-operation and the Single European Act' (1985) 5 *YEL* 203; id., 'Interaction between European Political Co-operation and the European Community' (1987) 7 *YEL* 211; Pijpers, 'European Political Co-operation and the CSCE Process' (1984/1) *LIEI* 135; von der Gablentz, 'Luxembourg Revisited or The Importance of European Political Co-operation' (1979) 16 *CML Rev.* 685. *See also under* **Single European Act.**

3. OFFICIAL PUBLICATIONS: 18th *Gen. Rep. EC* (1984), p. 304; 19th *Gen. Rep. EC* (1985), p. 349; 20th *Gen. Rep. EC* (1986), p. 365; 21st *Gen. Rep. EC* (1987), p. 347; 22nd *Gen. Rep. EC* (1988), p. 411; 23rd *Gen. Rep. EC* (1989), p. 387.

▶ **EUROPEAN UNION** Concept used to describe the ultimate goal towards which the European Communities are progressing, implying a new phase, a qualitatively higher stage, in the history of European integration. In the sense in which it is generally used today, the term 'European Union' is not susceptible of precise definition since it refers to a continuous process, to an evolving body of ideals, proposals, and measures, rather than to an entity having a definite legal, political, or institutional structure. For this reason, its meaning has been subject to a number of different interpretations over the years.

The origins of the concept may be traced back to the opening words of the Preamble to the EEC Treaty which express the determination of the signatory States 'to lay the foundations of an ever closer union among the peoples of Europe'. While the phrase 'ever closer union' clearly implies a dynamic, unceasing forward movement of integration, it does not cast light on the nature of the union to which it refers. The notion of an 'ever closer union' may be seen as both the ideological basis, the *raison d'être*, and the ultimate objective of the European Communities.

The idea of a European Union was formally launched at the Paris Summit Conference of 19 to 21 October 1972 where the Heads of State or Government of the enlarged Community set themselves the 'major objective of transforming, before the end of the present decade and with the fullest respect for the Treaties already signed, the whole complex of the relations of Member States into a European Union', and requested the institutions to draw up a report on this subject before the end of 1975 for submission to a later Summit Conference (point 16 of the Declaration made at the end of the Conference, 6th *Gen. Rep. EC* (1972), p. 7). What particular legal and political form the intended Union would take was not made clear but was left to the institutions to define. At the Copenhagen Summit of 14 and 15 December 1973, the Heads of State or Government decided to speed up the work required to define the European Union (point 2 of the Declaration issued at the end of the Conference, 7th *Gen. Rep. EC* (1973), p. 487). At the same time, they adopted a Declaration on European Identity, which contained frequent references to 'United Europe', 'European unification', and 'European Union' but without spelling it out whether these terms referred to one and the same or different concepts (ibid. p. 492). At the next Summit in Paris on 9 and 10 December 1974, the Heads of State or Government considered that the time had come for the nine 'to agree as soon as possible on an overall concept of European Union' and invited the institutions as well as Mr Tindemans, Prime Minister of Belgium, to submit comprehensive reports on the subject during the course of 1975 (8th *Gen. Rep. EC* (1974), pp. 299–300).

The Commission's 'Report on European Union' of 26 June 1975 (Suppl. *5/75—Bull. EC*) states that the achievement of European Union requires 'the definition of new objectives, the transformation of the institutional system and the explicit granting to the institutions of new competences and new powers' (p. 41). All these changes and commitments will be enshrined in an Act of Constitution, to be drawn up in the form of a new Treaty and to be ratified by all the Member States (ibid.). The Report thus envisages European Union as a new entity, having its own legal personality in international relations (p. 10), a set of defined competences (pp. 10–11), and direct decision-making, supervisory, and judicial powers (pp. 12–13). However, the Union is not to become a centralizing super-State: it will be given responsibility only for those tasks which the Member States cannot effectively accomplish (the principle of 'subsidiarity'). Formally, the Union will have competences of three types: exclusive, concurrent, and potential. Substantively, the fields of competence of the Union encompass economic, monetary, and budgetary matters (with the creation of an Economic and Monetary Union being the main objective), social affairs, common foreign policy including defence, and the protection of human rights (pp. 14–26). In this last respect, the Report recommends the incorporation of a list of specified basic rights in the Union's Act of Constitution (p. 26). With regard to the institutional structure of the Union, the Report outlines three possible models of which it gives preference to the second. According to this, executive power and the power to initiate legislation would be exercised by a European Government, a collegiate body whose members would be independent of the national Governments. This

249

would replace the present Commission. Legislative power would be allocated to a bicameral system consisting of a Chamber of Peoples and a Chamber of States, the latter to be designated by the national Governments (p. 31). The European Council would be dealing with the most difficult political problems only (p. 35). The judicial system should be subject to a single Supreme Court with power to review the legality and constitutionality of legislation and to declare invalid acts of the Member States which are contrary to Union law (pp. 36–7). Pending the setting-up of the new institutions, the European Council should act as a driving and guiding force and as a decision-making body on matters of major importance (p. 39. For a summary of the Commission's Report, see *Bull. EC* 6–1975, p. 6).

According to the Report of the European Parliament, presented in the form of a Resolution adopted on 10 July 1975 (Suppl. 9/75—*Bull. EC*, p. 10), European Union must be conceived as a pluralist and democratic Community whose priority aims are: to ensure strict respect for liberty and human dignity; to promote social justice and solidarity between the Member States and the citizens of the Community, through the establishment of an economic order ensuring full employment and equitable distribution of incomes and wealth; to oppose any cause of conflict or tension; and to settle disputes by peaceful means. The Union must be based on an institutional structure which will ensure its coherence. The powers and responsibilities of the Union must be progressively widened.

According to the Court of Justice, the European Union must be governed by the rule of law, it must have an effective decision-making body, a single Supreme Court with jurisdiction to cover any new powers to be exercised by the institutions, and a unified system of law characterized by homogeneity, coherence, and effectiveness (Suggestions on European Union, 15 July 1974, ibid. p. 17. For the Opinion of the Economic and Social Committee on European Union, see ibid. p. 25. For a summary of the positions taken by the three institutions, see *Bull. EC* 7/8–1975, p. 6).

The Tindemans Report, submitted on 29 December 1975 (Suppl. 1/76—*Bull. EC*), emphasizes the need to build European Union by strengthening the practical solidarity of the Member States and their peoples, both internally and in their relations with the outside world, and gradually to provide the Union with the instruments and institutions necessary for its operation (*see further under* **Tindemans Report**).

Having examined the above Reports, the European Council at its meeting in The Hague on 29 and 30 November 1976 announced its intention of establishing a comprehensive and coherent common political approach and reaffirmed its desire to increase the authority and efficiency of the Community institutions with the European Council as a driving force. At the same time, it invited the Foreign Ministers and the Commission to report to it once a year on the results obtained and the progress which could be achieved in the short term in the various sectors of the Union, 'thus translating into reality the common conception of European Union' (10th *Gen. Rep. EC* (1976), pp. 25–6; *Bull. EC* 11–1976, pp. 93–4).

In spite of this determination, it appears that, apart from the presentation of the Annual Reports on European Union from 1977 on (published as Suppls. 8/77, 1/79, 9/79, 4/80, 3/81, 7/82—*Bull. EC*) and the holding of direct elections to the European Parliament in 1979, no further action was taken during the next five years. Then, in an attempt to revitalize the Community and European Union, in October 1981 a memorandum was produced by the French Government (*Bull. EC* 11–1981, pp. 13, 92) and, more importantly, in November 1981 the Genscher–Colombo initiative was launched by the German and Italian Governments (*Bull. EC* 11–1981, pp. 10, 87. *See further under* **European Act**). The latter resulted in the signing by the ten Heads of State or Government of the 'Solemn Declaration on European Union' in Stuttgart on 19 June 1983 (*Bull. EC* 6–1983, p. 24. *See further under* **Solemn Declaration on European Union**). Not only does the Declaration reaffirm the determination of the signatories to transform the whole complex of relations between their States into a European Union, but it also mentions, for the first time in a document adopted at that level, the possibility of incorporating the progress achieved in a Treaty on European Union.

In the meantime, however, these developments were to some extent overtaken by events which took place in the first directly elected European Parliament. On the initiative of a group of MEPs known as the 'Crocodile Club' (after the name of the restaurant where they first met), founded by Mr Altiero Spinelli, on 9 July 1981 Parliament adopted a Resolution whereby it decided to take full initiative in giving fresh impetus to the establishment of European Union and to create a Committee on Institutional Affairs with the task of drawing up a modification to the existing Treaties (*OJ* 1981 C234/48; *Bull. EC* 7/8–1981, p. 66). As the Committee subsequently explained, the purpose of the new Treaty would be to take a qualitative step in the process of European integration going beyond the important but limited achievements of the existing Communities. This was necessary, in particular, to update the existing Treaties in order to include new areas of competence; to bring into a single clear institutional framework the various forms of co-operation that had grown up over the years (European Communities, European Political Co-operation, European Monetary System, etc.); and to render the Community institutions more democratic, more effective, and more accountable than before (Report of July 1983, EP Doc. 1–575/83/B, 4). After adopting the Committee's initial guidelines for the reform of the Treaties (Res. of 6 July 1982, *OJ* 1982 C238/25; *Bull. EC* 7/8–1982, p. 78) and the substance of the preliminary Draft Treaty (Res. of 14 Sept. 1983, *OJ* 1983 C277/95; *Bull. EC* 9–1983, pp. 7, 8), Parliament approved the final Draft Treaty establishing the European Union on 14 February 1984 by 237 votes to 31 with 43 abstentions (*OJ* 1984 C77/53, text at C77/33; *Bull. EC* 2–1984, p. 7, text at p. 8).

The Draft Treaty is cast in the form of an entirely new treaty rather than of one amending the existing Community Treaties. It incorporates many of the ideas and proposals that were put forward by the various Reports and other documents which preceded it. Nevertheless, it is characterized by a combination of continuity and change. This is clearly indicated in the opening words of the

251

Preamble which state that the Treaty was drafted 'with a view to continuing and reviving the democratic unification of Europe'. Moreover, while the Treaty establishes a new entity, the European Union (Art. 1), which has its own citizenship, territory, and legal personality (Arts. 3, 5, and 6), it also provides that the Union shall take over the 'Community patrimony', the *acquis communautaire* (Art. 7). Thus, the provisions of the Treaties establishing the European Communities and of the related instruments which are not explicitly or implicitly amended by the Draft Treaty shall constitute part of the law of the Union. The acts of the Communities and the measures adopted within the context of the European Monetary System and European Political Co-operation shall also continue to be effective until replaced by acts of the Union. The Union shall respect all the international commitments of the Communities. It shall protect the fundamental rights and freedoms of the individual (Art. 4).

The relationship between the Union and its Member States is determined by the principle of 'subsidiarity', according to which the Union is entrusted only with those tasks which it can carry out more satisfactorily than the States acting independently (Preamble, last indent). In every field of action entrusted to it, the Union is to act by one of two methods: either by common action, in the form of measures adopted by the Union institutions, or by co-operation, in the form of commitments undertaken by the Member States within the European Council. The fields within which each method applies are determined by the Treaty (Art. 10). The competences of the Union are either exclusive, in which case the Union institutions have sole power to act, or concurrent, in which case the Member States may continue to act so long as the Union has not legislated (Art. 12). The Member States are required to implement the law of the Union in good faith (Art. 13).

The institutional structure of the Union also shows a great degree of continuity as compared with that of the existing Communities. Nevertheless, the powers of the institutions, and in some cases their composition and method of appointment, have been altered so as to make them more efficient and more democratic, as indicated in the Preamble (second indent). The institutions include the European Parliament, the Council of the Union, the Commission, the Court of Justice, and the European Council (Art. 8). The legislative and budgetary powers and the power to conclude international agreements are shared between the Parliament and the Council (Arts. 16, 21, 36, 65, 70). In the Council, majority voting becomes the general rule although national veto is recognized in a restricted form for a period of ten years (Art. 23). The Commission becomes the sole executive body; it retains the power of initiative and plays an important role throughout the legislative procedure. It represents the Union externally (Art. 28). In addition to the five institutions and other bodies mentioned elsewhere in the Treaty (see e.g. Arts. 51, 54, 61), the Union has four organs: the Court of Auditors, the Economic and Social Committee, the European Investment Bank, and the European Monetary Fund (Art. 33).

The acts of the Union include laws, regulations, and decisions but, unlike the present system, do not include directives. Laws are the principal instruments of common action (Art. 34), while regulations and decisions are used for their implementation (Art. 40). The law of the Union is directly applicable in the Member States and takes precedence over national law (Art. 42). Judicial review of Union acts is carried out by the Court of Justice in accordance with the existing Community rules as supplemented by an organic law to be adopted on the basis of a number of principles laid down in the Treaty (Art. 43). The effect of these principles is, generally, to extend the right of action of individuals and to enlarge the jurisdiction of the Court of Justice which will include the power to impose sanctions on Member States. Specified sanctions may also be imposed by the European Council in cases of 'serious and persistent violations' by Member States of the Treaty or of fundamental rights (Arts. 4(4) and 44).

With regard to the policies of the Union, the Treaty makes it clear that, starting from the Community patrimony, the Union shall continue the actions already undertaken as well as undertake new actions (Art. 45). In addition to the rules relating to the creation of a homogeneous judicial area (Art. 46), the Treaty lays down a number of policies—both old and new— under three main headings: economic policy (Arts. 47–54), policy for society (Arts. 55–62), and international relations (Arts. 63–9). Economic policy incorporates the European Monetary System and a number of new sectoral policies, such as telecommunication and energy. Policy for society includes social and health policy, consumer protection, regional, environmental, education, and cultural policies. International relations cover commercial policy, development aid policy, and political co-operation. In most policy areas, the Union is to exercise concurrent rather than exclusive competence. The finances of the Union are governed by complex rules relating to revenue, expenditure, and the budget (Arts. 70–81).

One of the most difficult problems associated with the Draft Treaty concerns the way in which it is to enter into force. According to Arts. 96 ECSC, 236 EEC, and 204 Euratom, the original Treaties may be amended only through an Intergovernmental Conference and by the 'common accord' of all the Member States. The European Parliament decided to adhere to neither of these two requirements. Seeing the inability of intergovernmental negotiations in the framework of the European Council to make any real progress towards European Union, Parliament instructed its President to submit the Draft Treaty for ratification directly to the Parliaments (and Governments) of the Member States, calling upon its successor, the second directly elected Parliament, to arrange all appropriate contacts with, and to take into account the opinions and comments of, the national Parliaments (Res. of 14 Feb. 1984 approving the Draft Treaty, see above). Moreover, to prevent a minority of the Member States from blocking the coming into force of the Treaty, Art. 82 of the Draft makes it possible for the Treaty to enter into force once it has been ratified by a majority of the Member States whose population represents two-thirds of the total population of the Communities. While both measures may be politically justified, they raise a number of complex legal issues concerning, in particular, the power of the Parliament to draft treaties on its own initiative; the legal consequences of avoiding the amendment procedures laid down in the original Treaties; the relationship between the Union and the Communities should the former be established without the dissolution of the latter; and, in the absence of a unanimous agreement, the legal relationship between the majority States wishing to move forward towards the Union and those in the minority which refuse to consent to the dissolution of the Communities.

However, at the present time these problems seem to be more theoretical than real since the chances of the Draft Treaty being adopted by a majority of States are very small. This is not due to any inherent defects in the Draft, which is generally recognized as being a progressive and well-prepared instrument striking just about the right balance between continuity and gradual change. The reason is, rather, that the Draft Treaty itself has since been overtaken by events. Perhaps as a counter-measure, at its Fontainebleau meeting on 25 and 26 June 1984 the European Council decided to set up two *ad hoc* Committees to establish practical means of moving towards European Union (*see further under* **Committee on a People's Europe, Committee on Institutional Affairs**). In its Report to the Brussels European Council of 29 and 30 March 1985, the latter (Dooge) Committee envisaged European Union as a 'genuine political entity . . . with the power to take decisions in the name of all citizens, by a democratic process according to their common interest in political and social development, economic progress and security, and according to procedures which could vary depending on whether the framework is that of intergovernmental cooperation, the Community Treaties or new instruments yet to be agreed' (*Bull. EC* 3–1985, p. 102 at p. 103). The Committee also proposed that an Intergovernmental Conference be convened to negotiate a draft European Union Treaty based on the *acquis communautaire*, the Committee's Report, and the Stuttgart Solemn Declaration on European Union and 'guided by the spirit and method of the Draft Treaty voted by the European Parliament' (ibid. p. 110). Such a Conference was in fact convened in accordance with Art. 236 EEC in September 1985, and produced the Single European Act (SEA), which was formally adopted in February 1986 and came into force on 1 July 1987.

Although the Preamble to the SEA again reaffirms the determination of the Member States to transform their relations as a whole into a European Union, it also makes it clear that they intend to implement this Union on the basis of 'the Communities operating in accordance with their own rules' and of European Political Co-operation (see also Art. 1(1)). Thus, unlike the Parliament's Draft Treaty, the SEA is not a genuine European Union Treaty as suggested by the Dooge Committee. It contains certain amendments and additions to the existing Treaties which, although important in certain respects, do not go nearly so far as the Parliament's Draft. The fact that in the end the Member States gave preference to Treaty amendment over making a new Treaty does not in any way detract from the value of Parliament's efforts. Quite apart from crystallizing ideas on the nature, scope, and structure of a European Union, the main significance of the Draft Treaty is perhaps that it has acted as a catalyst in breaking the deadlock caused by the inertia of the Member States. (It may be noted that in its Res. of 17 June 1987, *OJ* 1987

C190/71, reaffirmed by Res. of 16 Feb. 1989, *OJ* 1989 C69/145, the European Parliament still considered it to be its duty to continue its campaign for European Union on the basis of the Draft Treaty, regardless of the success or failure of the Single European Act.)

In the light of all these developments, the question may be asked whether the term 'European Union' has any real meaning and significance at all. Nearly all the reports and proposals produced on this subject stress at least four features which distinguish a future 'Union' from the present 'Community'. These are as follows: (1) more efficient and more democratic institutions; (2) a more united front towards the outside world not only in economic but also in political matters, i.e. a common foreign policy, including questions of security and defence; (3) a fully integrated internal market, including Economic and Monetary Union, together with a homogeneous judicial area; (4) a people's Europe, i.e. a Europe which is of direct relevance to its citizens in all aspects of their everyday lives. Clearly, if these objectives are to be achieved by piecemeal Treaty amendments representing *ad hoc* improvements on the system, the replacement of the term 'European Community' by the term 'European Union' will have no more than symbolic or emotional value. A meaningful 'European Union' requires more than this: it implies a qualitative leap forward, a transformation of the nature and intensity of the relations between the Member States, which can hardly be accomplished within the existing legal, political, and institutional framework of the present Communities.

See also Acquis communautaire, **Committee on a People's Europe, Committee on Institutional Affairs, European Act, European Political Co-operation, Institutional balance, Institutions, Single European Act, Solemn Declaration on European Union, Spierenburg Report, Three Wise Men's Report, Tindemans Report, Vedel Report.**

Further reading 1. BOOKS: Bieber, Jacqué, and Weiler (eds.), *An Ever Closer Union: A Critical Analysis of the Draft Treaty Establishing the European Union* (1985); Capotorti, Hilf, Jacobs, and Jacqué, *The European Union Treaty: Commentary on the Draft Adopted by the European Parliament on 14 February 1984* (1986); Lodge (ed.), *European Union: The European Community in Search of a Future* (1986); Pryce (ed.), *The Dynamics of European Union* (1987).

2. ARTICLES: Edward and Lane, 'European Union and the Canadian Experience' (1985) 5 YEL 1; Hendry, '. . . of Cabbages and Kings' (1983) 8 EL Rev. 394; Jacqué, 'The Draft Treaty Establishing the European Union' (1985) 22 CML Rev. 19; Lodge, Freestone, and Davidson, 'Some Problems of the Draft Treaty on European Union' (1984) 9 EL Rev. 387; Nickel and Corbett, 'The Draft Treaty Establishing the European Union' (1984) 4 YEL 79; Weiler and Modrall, 'Institutional Reform: Consensus or Majority?' (1985) 10 EL Rev. 316.

3. OFFICIAL PUBLICATION: House of Lords, Select Committee on the European Communities, Session 1984–5, 14th Report, 'European Union' (1985).

▶ *EX NUNC* **EFFECT** Future effect, i.e. the effect of a legal provision or judicial decision upon acts, events, situations, or legal relationships which occur or arise after the entry into force of that provision or decision.

See also Ex tunc **effect, Retroactive effect.**

▶ *EXPRESSIO UNIUS EST EXCLUSIO ALTERIUS* Rule of interpretation
according to which the express application by a text of a provision to a certain
situation excludes the application of the same provision to any other situation
not expressly mentioned (*a contrario* argument). While the ECJ has never
explicitly rejected this rule, it and its various Advocates-General have been
reluctant to apply it in practice. Thus, the Court has stated that an *a contrario*
argument is 'acceptable only in the last resort when no other interpretation
appears to be adequate or compatible with the text, the context and their
objectives' (Case 8/55 *Fédération Charbonnière de Belgique* v. *HA* [1956]
ECR 292 at p. 300; Case 9/56 *Meroni* v. *HA* [1958] ECR 133 at p. 140).
A.-G. Lagrange has pointed out the weakness of the rule (Case 15/63 *Lassalle*
v. *Parliament* [1964] ECR 31 at p. 54), while A.-G. Warner has referred to it
as an 'unreliable maxim' (Case 155/79 *AM & S.* v. *Commission* [1982] ECR
1575 at p. 1620).

See also Interpretation of Community law.

▶ **EXTERNAL RELATIONS** Relations of the European Communities with
non-Member States and international organizations. By virtue of their international legal personality, the Communities maintain a variety of relations,
including legal, political, diplomatic, economic, commercial, cultural, etc.
relations, with a large number of countries and organizations, covering most
matters and activities falling within their competence. From a legal point of
view, the Communities' external relations may be divided into the following
categories:

- treaty relations;
- relations with international organizations;
- diplomatic relations;
- international responsibility;
- settlement of international disputes.

These will be considered in turn below.

I. Treaty relations

By virtue of their treaty-making power, the Communities have entered into a
large number of bilateral and multilateral treaties and agreements acting
either on their own as contracting parties (Community agreements) or jointly
with the Member States as co-signatories (mixed agreements). The internal
aspects of treaty-making competence and procedure are governed by Community law (*see further under* **Mixed agreement, Treaty-making power,
Treaty-making procedure**), and the external aspects by general international
law and practice (*see further under* **Legal personality**). Since the Communities
are not States, they are not normally entitled to participate in treaties on
exactly the same basis as the other (State) parties, unless this has been so
agreed from the start of the negotiations. So far, the Communities have been
allowed to participate on the same terms and conditions as States in all
bilateral agreements, but only in a relatively small number of multilateral
agreements. Apart from these exceptional cases, the general practice is to

insert a special participation or accession clause in the (multilateral) agreement enabling the Communities (i.e. the EEC, ECSC, Euratom, as the case may be) to become contracting parties. This clause may take a number of different forms. It may be general, allowing participation by 'customs or economic unions', 'regional economic integration organisations set up by sovereign States', or 'intergovernmental organisations set up by States', provided they have power to negotiate, conclude, and implement international agreements on the particular subject-matter concerned (see e.g. the Law of the Sea Convention of 1982). The purpose behind such general formulas, which are often used at the insistence of States like the Soviet Union and the other East European countries which until June 1988 did not recognize the Communities, is to avoid referring to the latter by name. Since it may not always be clear whether the relevant Community is in fact included in the category of organizations mentioned, it is not unusual for the Community concerned to make a unilateral statement to the effect that it considers itself so included. Alternatively, the clause may be specific, either expressly allowing the EEC (or ECSC or Euratom, as the case may be) to participate, or assimilating it to participating Governments. Sometimes the clause may extend not only to the EEC but also to 'similar' or 'comparable' organizations (even if there may not exist any organization which is 'similar' to the EEC). The clause, whether general or specific, may be an integral part of the agreement or may be incorporated in an additional protocol. Generally, the Communities may become party to international agreements by any of the methods used by States, i.e. by signature, exchange of instruments constituting the treaty, act of formal confirmation, acceptance, approval (which replaces the concept of ratification), or accession (see Art. 11(2) of the Vienna Convention on the Law of Treaties between States and International Organizations or between International Organizations of 1986), unless a particular agreement restricts them to the use of one or the other of these methods, such as e.g. accession.

The treaty relations of the three Communities cover a wide variety of subjects which, together with the relevant legal bases in the Treaties, may be summarized as follows:

1. *EEC bilateral agreements*:
   - commercial agreements (Art. 113), including the following categories:
     - framework agreements for commercial and economic co-operation (Arts. 113 and 235);
     - preferential and Free Trade Agreements for industrial and other products;
     - trade agreements in a variety of industrial and agricultural products;
     - textile agreements concluded under the Multifibre Arrangement;
     - simplification of trade formalities;
   - association agreements (Art. 238):
     - with individual Mediterranean countries;
     - with African, Caribbean, and Pacific States (Lomé III Convention);

257

- fisheries agreements providing for reciprocal rights and obligations (implied powers under Art. 43);
- transport agreements (implied powers under Arts. 74 and 75);
- environmental and consumer protection agreements (implied powers under Art. 235);
- miscellaneous agreements (implied powers under the Treaty generally and under Art. 235), concerning such matters as:
  - health and hygiene at work;
  - aid to refugees;
  - research and development;
  - exchange of information;
- privileges and immunities (Art. 7(1) of the Protocol on the Privileges and Immunities of the European Communities) concerning
  - recognition of *laissez-passer*.

2. *EEC multilateral agreements*:

- international commodity agreements (Art. 113);
- other commercial agreements including GATT and related agreements and the Multifibre Arrangement (Art. 113);
- fisheries conventions (implied powers under Art. 43);
- transport conventions (implied powers under Arts. 74 and 75);
- customs conventions (implied powers under Art. 9), including the Convention on the Harmonised Commodity Description and Coding System of 1983 (Arts. 28, 113, and 235, although reference to Art. 235 was found by the ECJ to be illegal, see Case 165/87 *Commission* v. *Council* [1988] ECR para. 18);
- conventions for the protection of animals (implied powers under Arts. 43 and 100);
- conventions for the protection of the environment (implied powers under Art. 235);
- miscellaneous agreements including the UN Convention on the Law of the Sea (implied powers under Art. 235).

3. *ECSC bilateral agreements*:

- voluntary limitation agreements in respect of iron and steel products;
- framework agreement for commercial and economic co-operation (with Canada);
- transport agreements;
- agreements supplementing, in respect of ECSC products, commercial co-operation agreements concluded by the EEC or the commercial sections of association or co-operation agreements concluded by the EEC.

4. *ECSC multilateral agreements*:

- the ECSC as such is not party to any multilateral agreement; the 1979 Geneva Protocols on tariffs resulting from the multilateral trade negotiations of 1973–9 (Tokyo Round) were concluded, in respect of ECSC products, by the Member States.

5. *Euratom bilateral agreements*:
- co-operation agreements (including the framework agreement with Canada);
- agreement on transfer of nuclear materials;
- agreements in the fields of thermonuclear fusion and plasma physics;
- verification agreement concerning Euratom safeguards.

6. *Euratom multilateral agreement*:
- physical protection of nuclear materials.

7. *Accession treaties (Arts. 237 EEC and 205 Euratom)*:
- strictly speaking, these are not 'Community' treaties but treaties between the applicant States and the existing Member States. However, their negotiation and conclusion does involve the Community institutions. Accession to the ECSC is by means of a Council decision (Art. 98 ECSC).

(For complete and up-to-date lists of Community treaties, showing the contracting parties, dates of signature and/or entry into force, references to the *Official Journal*, and any participation or accession clauses, see the publications listed below under Official Publications. See also Groux and Manin's work listed below under Books, part II, esp. at pp. 61–7. Sections I and II of this entry are based on information contained in these publications.)

II. Relations with international organizations

All three Treaties contain provisions for the establishment of relations with other international organizations. Thus, the Commission is entrusted with the task of maintaining 'all appropriate relations' with the organs of the United Nations, of its specialized agencies, of the General Agreement on Tariffs and Trade (GATT), and, in general, with all international organizations. The Communities are moreover required to establish 'all appropriate forms of co-operation' with the Council of Europe and 'close co-operation' with the Organization for European Economic Co-operation, which has since been replaced by the Organization for Economic Co-operation and Development (OECD) (Arts. 229–31 EEC, 199–201 Euratom, and the somewhat different Arts. 93–4 ECSC. See also the Protocol on Relations with the Council of Europe annexed to the ECSC Treaty). In accordance with these provisions, the Commission has concluded 'liaison agreements' or entered into other working arrangements with most of the existing universal or regional organizations. These agreements or arrangements generally take the form of exchange of letters providing for consultations, the exchange of documents and information, participation in meetings, in some cases even for joint working parties. In the case of the International Labour Organization (ILO), the arrangements are based on formal co-operation agreements. In the case of the Council for Mutual Economic Assistance (CMEA or COMECON), a Joint Declaration provides for the development of co-operation in areas of common interest, the forms and methods of which are to be determined by means of contacts and discussions between the parties (Joint Declaration on

259

the establishment of official relations between the EEC and the CMEA of 25 June 1988, approved by Council Dec. 88/345 of 22 June 1988, *OJ* 1988 L157/34. On EC–CMEA relations, see *Bull. EC* 6–1988, p. 13 and also the Res. of the European Parliament of 22 Jan. 1987, *OJ* 1987 C46/71. For a complete list of organizations with which arrangements have been made and the texts of the arrangements, see *The European Community, International Organisations and Multilateral Agreements*, listed below under Official Publications. See also Groux and Manin, op. cit.). In addition, the Commission has set up permanent delegations at a number of organizations, such as the United Nations (in New York and Geneva), UNESCO, OECD (in Paris), GATT, WHO, ILO, UNCTAD, etc. (in Geneva), OPEC, UNIDO, IAEA, etc. (in Vienna).

On the other hand, problems have arisen with regard to the right of access to, and participation in the work of the deliberative organs of, international organizations and conferences. In this respect, a distinction must be made between organizations which already existed when the Communities were established, and bodies which were set up by agreements to which the Communities are party, mainly for the purpose of supervising and implementing those agreements.

As regards the first group, the Communities have encountered difficulties similar to those which have arisen in the field of (multilateral) treaty-making. The constitutions of these organizations admit only sovereign States to full membership. Since the Communities are not States, and since it would have been extremely difficult or even impossible to amend those constitutions, in none of the pre-existing organizations nor in any conferences convened under their auspices have the Communities so far been able to participate as full members on equal footing with States. Owing mainly to resistance coming from the Soviet Union and its East European allies, in many organizations and conferences the Communities enjoy only observer status (or consultative status which is essentially the same). This implies a right to participate in the meetings and the work of the deliberative organs but without the right to vote and, in most cases, without the right to table proposals and amendments. The observer status may be permanent or based on *ad hoc* invitations. The EEC at present has observer status in virtually all the institutions related to the United Nations, such as the principal organs (General Assembly, Economic and Social Council), subsidiary organs (regional commissions, such as e.g. the Economic Commission for Europe, and technical organs, such as e.g. UNCTAD), specialized agencies (ILO, FAO, UNESCO, WHO, IMO, WIPO, IMF, etc.), autonomous agencies (IAEA), as well as in many other universal or regional organizations (OECD, Council of Europe, Customs Co-operation Council, Organization of American States, etc.). Since most of these organizations deal with matters which fall partly within Community competence and partly within the competence of the Member States, Community representation often takes place in the form of 'dual representation', whereby the Community is represented by both the Commission and the Member State holding the Presidency of the Council at the time. The Commission representative normally acts as the Community spokesman on matters falling within Community competence. This form of representation has been adopted, for example, for the United Nations General Assembly, the Economic and Social Council, and UNCTAD. In addition, there are many different formulas which are used for the purpose of establishing the representation of the Communities in international organizations and conferences, in multilateral treaty negotiations, and in organs set up by treaties to which the Communities are party (*see further under* **Mixed agreement**, point 3(*g*)).

While, by virtue of their observer status, in most international organizations the Communities are placed on the same footing as other intergovernmental organizations of the traditional type (even when the organization is discussing matters falling within exclusive Community competence), there are certain exceptions. Thus, although the Communities are not members of the OECD, their status there is higher than that of an observer. Supplementary Protocol No. 1 to the Convention establishing the OECD provides that the Commission shall participate as of right in the work of the Organization and that representation of the Communities to the OECD shall be determined in accordance with the institutional provisions of the Community Treaties. The Communities also enjoy a favourable position within GATT. Although the EEC has not formally replaced its Member States as 'contracting parties' to GATT (the Member States still sit in the deliberative organs), the EEC delegation's right to speak and to table proposals and amendments in its own name has now been fully recognized. The contracting parties to GATT have also recognized that the Member States have transferred exclusive competence to the EEC in the field of the Common Commercial Policy and in particular with regard to the conclusion of tariff and trade agreements (Art. 113 EEC). Accordingly, the EEC, acting through its own institutions, has been allowed to appear as a partner in the tariff negotiations and as a party to agreements of all types concluded within the framework of GATT (see Cases 21 to 24/72 *International Fruit Company* [1972] ECR 1219 at p. 1227; Case 38/75 *Nederlandse Spoorwegen* [1975] ECR 1439 at pp. 1449–50). Following the multilateral trade negotiations of 1973–9 (Tokyo Round), the EEC became a party, in its own name and without the Member States, to a number of trade agreements and a *de jure* member of the management committees set up to supervise the implementation of those agreements.

As regards, secondly, international organs and institutions established by agreements to which the Communities are party, the position of the Communities is more favourable than in pre-existing organizations. Thus, the Communities are full members, with or without the Member States, of the various bodies (joint committees, councils of association, co-operation councils, etc.) set up to supervise the implementation of most bilateral trade, association, and co-operation agreements to which the Communities are party, with or without the Member States. In the case of bodies set up by multilateral agreements, however, the Communities' position is not always wholly satisfactory. In some instances, it is not even clear whether the Communities are entitled to participate at all. Thus, for example, the participation clause included in the UN Law of the Sea Convention of 1982 does not specify whether, by becoming party to the Convention, the EEC would become a member of the International Seabed Authority and of the various other institutions created by the Convention, such as the Assembly and the Council. While in most cases the EEC has the status of full member of the deliberative assemblies of bodies set up by multilateral agreements to which it is party, it is not always entitled to be elected to membership of the more restricted executive committees. In bodies set up by 'Community agreements', i.e. agreements concluded without the participation of the Member States, where the EEC has a right to vote it exercises that right on the same terms and conditions as the States which are parties and has the same number of votes as a single State. In bodies set up by 'mixed agreements', the usual practice is that either the Community or the Member States, but not both, is/are entitled to vote, as determined in each case in accordance with the internal law of the Community. Where it is the Community which exercises the right to vote, it is usually allocated a number of votes equal to the total number of votes available to the participating Member States.

The number of international organizations in which the Communities enjoy the right to vote, and are thus able to participate in the actual decision-making, is relatively small. They include mainly the management bodies of international commodity agreements and the Commissions of regional fisheries organizations. In most other (pre-existing) organizations, the Communities are unable to take part in the actual adoption of binding decisions and in the conclusion of international agreements. While this state of affairs is perhaps inevitable in view of the reluctance (at least prior to June 1988) of the Eastern Bloc countries to grant the Communities higher than observer status, it does create difficulties from the point of view of internal Community law. The difficulty arises from the fact that the EEC has exclusive treaty-making competence in the field of the Common Commercial Policy under Arts. 113–14 EEC, in theory even if the treaty is made within the framework, or in the form of a decision, of an international organization in which the Community is unable fully to participate. Under Art. 116 EEC, the Member States are required, in respect of all matters of particular interest to the Common Market, to proceed within the framework of international organizations of an economic character only by common action. To this end, the Commission is to submit to the Council proposals concerning the scope and implementation of such common action. The ECJ has said that this provision 'was conceived with a view to evolving common action by the Member States in international organisations of which the Community is not part; in such a situation the only appropriate means is concerted, joint action by the Member States as members of the said organisations' (Opinion 1/78 *Natural Rubber Agreement* [1979] ECR 2871 at p. 2915). However, in the same opinion the Court has also stated that where 'negotiations undertaken within the framework of an international organisation are intended to lead to an "undertaking ... which has binding force", [then] it is the provisions of the Treaty relating to the negotiation and conclusion of agreements, in other words Articles 113, 114 and 228, which apply and not Article 116' (ibid. at pp. 2915–16). This means that, strictly speaking, only the EEC, and not the Member States, has competence to conclude agreements and to undertake other binding commitments even within the framework of an international organization of which it is not a member. It seems that until such time as the EEC is enabled to exercise that competence by being admitted to full membership of the relevant organization, the Member States are entitled, and even obliged, to proceed by common action under Art. 116. Nevertheless, they are under a duty, together with the Community institutions, 'to use all the political and legal means at their disposal in order to ensure the participation of the Community' in the organization at an early date and in any agreement concluded during its absence (Cases 3, 4, and 6/76 *Kramer* [1976] ECR 1279 at p. 1311).

Finally, it should be mentioned that the Communities are under an obligation to implement in internal Community law any binding measures of international organizations of which they are members and which measures fall within Community competence.

III. Diplomatic relations

By virtue of their international legal personality, the Communities enjoy the right of representation or the 'right of legation', which is the right to send and to receive diplomatic missions (termed 'active' and 'passive' right of legation, respectively). While this right has traditionally belonged to States as subjects of international law, in recent times it has been recognized that international organizations, too, may send and receive representatives to and from both their Member States and non-Member States. Nevertheless, in the case of international organizations, the 'active' and 'passive' right of legation do not exactly correspond to one another (as they do in the case of States). While it is fairly common today for States to establish so-called 'permanent missions' at organizations of which they are members, and 'permanent observer missions' at organizations of which they are not members (see the Vienna Convention on the Representation of States in their Relations with International Organizations of a Universal Character of 1975), it is only exceptionally that international organizations may exercise reciprocal rights by setting up representations to States enjoying the same kind of diplomatic status and measure of protection.

Since the European Communities represent a *sui generis* type of organization, their diplomatic relations resemble partly the diplomatic practices of States and partly those of traditional intergovernmental organizations. Nevertheless, strictly speaking they are subject neither to the above-mentioned Vienna Convention of 1975, which applies only to world-wide organizations, nor to the Vienna Convention on Diplomatic Relations of 1961, which governs relations between States only. Their diplomatic relations with States, which have developed mainly in response to practical necessities, may be summarized as follows.

1. *The right to receive missions.* Each Member State is represented at the Communities by a 'Permanent Representative' who is a high-ranking diplomat having the status of an Ambassador. His appointment is not subject to any accreditation or approval procedure on the part of the Communities. In addition to maintaining the necessary relations between the Communities and their own countries, the Permanent Representatives play an important

263

part in the internal institutional structure of the Communities. Their organ, the Committee of Permanent Representatives (COREPER), formally established by Art. 4 of the Merger Treaty, is responsible for preparing the work of the Council and for carrying out any other task assigned to it by the Council.

Non-Member States are represented by 'permanent missions' or, in the case of ACP States, by 'delegations'. States, other than ACP countries (i.e. African, Caribbean, and Pacific countries associated with the EEC under the Lomé Conventions), must obtain the agreement of the Communities both to the establishment of a mission and to the appointment of the person who is to be its Head. The credentials of Heads of Mission accredited to the EEC and Euratom are submitted jointly to the President of the Council and to the President of the Commission (this practice was introduced by the Luxembourg Compromise of 1966), while the credentials of those accredited to the ECSC are submitted to the President of the Commission only. 140 States have established diplomatic missions to the Communities so far (see *Bull. EC* 6–1989, p. 86), although most of the Heads of Mission are persons who are also accredited to the Kingdom of Belgium. Belgium is required to accord the customary diplomatic privileges and immunities to missions of third countries accredited to the Communities (Art. 17 of the Protocol on Privileges and Immunities). On the occasion of the establishment of 'official relations' between the EEC and the Council for Mutual Economic Assistance (CMEA or COMECON) in June 1988, the Soviet Union and a number of East European countries announced their intention to accredit diplomatic missions to the Community for the first time (*Bull. EC* 6–1988, p. 14. For the Joint Declaration of 25 June 1988 between the EEC and the CMEA and Council Dec. 88/345 of 22 June 1988 approving it, see *OJ* 1988 L157/34). In August and September 1988, diplomatic relations were in fact established between those countries and the EEC (see 22nd *Gen. Rep. EC* (1988), p. 356).

2. *The right to send missions.* The Communities are not represented in their Member States by separate missions, the necessary relations being maintained chiefly through the Member States' Permanent Representatives appointed to the Communities (see above). The Press and Information Offices which the Commission may establish in the Member States with the permission of the latter have no official diplomatic status or function.

In non-Member States, the Communities are represented by 'delegations' established by the Commission with the consent of the host State. Currently, there are some thirteen delegations (*inter alia* in Australia, Canada, Japan, USA) and three regional delegations (in Caracas for Latin America, in Bangkok for South-East Asia, and in New Delhi for South Asia). In addition, Commission delegations have been set up in the ACP countries under the Lomé Convention. The delegations may normally deal only with matters falling within Community competence, while matters falling within 'political co-operation' are entrusted to the diplomatic mission of the Member State which holds the Presidency of the Council at a given time. Community delegations enjoy such diplomatic privileges and immunities as are granted to them by the host State either by means of a bilateral agreement with the Communities or by a unilateral act (see e.g. United States, Executive Order of

5 Dec. 1972). Although there may thus be variations between receiving States, on the whole the Communities enjoy similar diplomatic privileges and immunities to those accorded to States under customary international law, covering the Head and staff of the mission, its premises, archives, communications, etc.

IV. International responsibility

International law has as yet developed few rules on the responsibility of international organizations. Nevertheless, it is clear that the European Communities, as subjects of international law, are bound by the rules and principles of that law (see e.g. Case 48/69 *ICI* v. *Commission* [1972] ECR 619 at p. 693 *per* A.-G. Mayras; Cases 21 to 24/72 *International Fruit Company*, above, at p. 1226 *per Curiam*, p. 1233 *per* A.-G. Mayras). One such principle is that 'any breach of an engagement involves an obligation to make reparation' (*Chorzow Factory (Indemnity) Case*, PCIJ (1928) Series A, No. 17, p. 29). Thus, the Communities are internationally responsible for any breach of an obligation binding upon them under international law. However, in dealing with questions of international responsibility, a distinction must be made between obligations arising from treaties to which the Communities are parties, and those arising from general (customary) international law.

As regards treaties, the PCIJ has said in the above-cited case that 'reparation is the indispensable complement of a failure to apply a convention, and there is no necessity for this to be stated in the convention itself' (ibid.). In the case of exclusive Community treaties, i.e. those concluded without the participation of the Member States, non-compliance will primarily entail the responsibility of the Communities. However, under Art. 228(2) EEC, Community treaties are binding 'on the institutions of the Community and on Member States', and it is therefore 'incumbent upon the Community institutions, as well as upon the Member States, to ensure compliance with the obligations arising from such agreements' (Case 104/81 *Kupferberg* [1982] ECR 3641 at p. 3662). In the same case, the ECJ has also stated that 'in ensuring respect for commitments arising from an agreement concluded by the Community institutions the Member States fulfil an obligation . . . in relation to the non-member country concerned' (ibid. at p. 3662). Unless the Court gives a different interpretation to this statement in a future case, it would seem to follow from it that the Member States may be held internationally responsible towards the other (non-member) party for the Communities' as well as their own non-compliance with a Community treaty to which they are not formally parties. This view appears to be confirmed by the comments and observations of the EEC on the draft articles of the Vienna Convention on the Law of Treaties between States and International Organizations or between International Organizations of 1986. These observations do not accept the view that Member States as such have absolutely nothing to do with treaties validly concluded by the organization to which they belong, since an international organization does not constitute an independent sovereign entity possessing original powers like a State. Accordingly, Art. 228(2) should be

265

interpreted as a provision 'which intends to give guarantees to non-Member States which those States assent to and accept' by entering into a treaty with the EEC (*YILC* 1981, Vol. II, Part Two, p. 201 at pp. 202–3). It would seem to follow from this interpretation that the responsibility of the Member States would be secondary to, rather than joint and several with, that of the Community and that it could be relied on only if a claim against the Community should fail. In the case of mixed agreements, both the Community and the Member States are in principle responsible for non-compliance since they are all contracting parties (*see further under* **Mixed agreement**, point 3(*f*)).

Where the responsibility of the Communities is based on a breach of an obligation arising under general (customary) international law, a further distinction is necessary between two situations. The first is where the Communities have caused a direct injury to a foreign State as State (e.g. transboundary pollution caused by a Community installation). The second is where the injury is caused to a private individual (or corporation) who is a national of the foreign State (e.g. imposition of a fine, damage to property or denial of a right, contrary to international law). The common feature of the two situations is that they are both covered by the rules of international law. Referring to the second situation, the PCIJ has stated in the *Chorzow Factory (Indemnity) Case* (above) that 'the rules of law governing the reparation are the rules of international law in force between the two States concerned, and not the law governing the relations between the State which has committed a wrongful act and the individual who has suffered damage'. The difference between the two situations is that the injured State can bring an international claim against the Communities, while the injured individual cannot. His case has to be presented by the State of which he is a national, according to the rules of diplomatic protection, although in taking up his case 'a State is in reality asserting its own rights—its right to ensure, in the person of its subjects, respect for the rules of international law' (*Mavrommatis Palestine Concessions (Jurisdiction) Case*, PCIJ (1924) Series A, No. 2, p. 12). However, it is a well-established rule of customary international law that before the State may institute international proceedings, local remedies must be exhausted. The reason is that 'the State where the violation occurred should have an opportunity to redress it by its own means, within the framework of its own domestic system' (*Interhandel Case*, ICJ Reports 1959, p. 6 at p. 27). In the context of the Communities, this means of course the Community legal system, and the exhaustion of local remedies means the institution of an action for damages before the ECJ. Where such an action does not redress the violation, the foreign State may proceed with its claim at the level of international law. Where the foreign State has suffered a direct injury to itself, international law does not require it to exhaust the local remedies, i.e. to bring an action before the ECJ, which in any case is not the proper forum to deal with disputes of this kind (see under section V below).

Where the damage is caused (either to a State or to an individual) by an act or omission of a Community institution, the responsibility is clearly the Communities'. Where, however, it is caused by an act of an authority or official of a Member State adopted in implementation of a Community provision, the question of responsibility is not so clear-cut. Applying the rules and principles of international law on State responsibility, it seems that where the national authority acts strictly in accordance with and for the purpose of implementing a Community provision which leaves no margin of discretion to the Member State, its action is imputable to the Communities and is capable of establishing their responsibility. Where, however, it acts *ultra vires* (i.e. in a way not required by Community law) or exercises a discretion left to the Member State, it will incur liability for its own State rather than for the Communities, although joint and several liability of the Member State and of the Community is also conceivable, for example where the Community provision itself is illegal (or is declared as such subsequently). Where the Member State's responsibility is involved, all the available national remedies must be exhausted before an international claim may be brought.

V. Settlement of international disputes

In its Advisory Opinion concerning *Reparation for Injuries Suffered in the Service of the United Nations* (ICJ Reports 1949, p. 174), the International Court of Justice has established the principle that international organizations as subjects of international law are capable of possessing international rights and duties and the necessary capacity to maintain their rights by bringing international claims. This means, in particular, the capacity to negotiate, to conclude a special agreement, and to prosecute a claim before an international tribunal (ibid. at pp. 179, 181). Relying on the concepts of functional protection (as opposed to diplomatic protection by the national State) and of objective international personality, the ICJ has held that the United Nations has the capacity to bring an international claim not only in respect of damage caused to itself but also in respect of damage caused to one of its agents when the ground of the claim is a breach of an international obligation which exists towards itself, and that the Organization can bring such a claim against both a Member State and a non-Member State (ibid. at pp. 180–7).

Applying these principles to the European Communities, it may be stated that as international organizations they have the capacity to bring an international claim and that they may, for this purpose, avail themselves of the various procedures established for the settlement of international disputes. They may bring a claim not only on their own behalf but also on behalf of their officials. Moreover, using the concept of functional protection, it may be argued that where a claim is based on a breach of an obligation owed to the Communities rather than to the Member States (e.g. breach of an exclusive Community treaty to which the Member States are not party), the Communities should be entitled to bring a claim on behalf of the nationals of the Member States who suffer damage as a result of the breach. Otherwise such nationals would be deprived of any possibility of redress since in these circumstances their own State cannot take up their case. This is because according to the principles of diplomatic protection only the party to whom an international obligation is due can bring a claim in respect of its breach (see ibid. at pp. 181–2). Since, however, the European Communities cannot be said to possess 'objective international personality', i.e. one that may be asserted *erga omnes*, they may bring an international claim only against States and international organizations which have recognized them as subjects of international law (*see further under* **Legal personality**).

Regarding the question what forums are available to or against the Communities for the settlement of international disputes, it is clear that the International Court of Justice is not open for this purpose. Under Art. 34(1) of its Statute, 'only States may be parties in cases before the Court', while a limited category of international organizations, such as the General Assembly, the Security Council, and in certain circumstances the other organs and specialized agencies of the United Nations, may request advisory opinions (Art. 96 of the UN Charter. Art. 66 of the Vienna Convention on the Law of Treaties between States and International Organizations or between International Organizations of 1986 provides for recourse to advisory opinions by international organizations in situations in which States may submit their disputes to the Court for a decision).

In considering whether the ECJ itself has jurisdiction to deal with the international disputes of the Communities, a distinction must again be made, as in the previous section, between disputes arising from treaties to which the Communities are party and other disputes. As regards the former, it seems that unless a treaty expressly provides that disputes may be referred to the ECJ (as in the case of the former Association Agreement with Greece and the still existing Association Agreement with Turkey), the Court has no jurisdiction to settle such disputes (see Cases 21 to 24/72 *International Fruit Company*, above, at p. 1234 *per* A.-G. Mayras). Even if a dispute should raise the question of the international responsibility of the Communities for breach of a treaty obligation, this is clearly an issue which concerns neither the contractual liability nor the non-contractual liability of the Communities within the meaning of Arts. 215 EEC or 188 Euratom and is therefore outside the Court's jurisdiction (a treaty is not a contract). Moreover, the ECJ being the domestic Court of one of the parties, its involvement in dispute settlement would offend against the principle *nemo judex in causa sua*. It is an entirely different matter that the Court may still be seized of internal disputes concerning the interpretation, application, or even enforcement of a Community treaty, through the ordinary remedies of Community law, such as references for a preliminary ruling or direct actions. Thus, an individual may be able to enforce a right arising from a directly effective provision of a Community treaty (*see further under* **Direct effect**, point 3), or an act of an institution may be challenged on the ground that it is incompatible with such a treaty (i.e. that the Community has committed a breach of the treaty). But these disputes are settled according to Community law, not international law, and do not directly involve the other contracting party.

Disputes concerning matters other than treaties are likewise beyond the limits of the ECJ's jurisdiction. Thus, for example, when the international responsibility of the Communities is raised in respect of damage caused to a foreign State, it would be impossible to equate this with the concept of 'non-contractual liability' and to bring the dispute before the Court under the provisions relating to non-contractual liability (Arts. 215(2) EEC, 188(2) Euratom). These provisions have been designed to deal with the internal liability of the Communities and instruct the Court to decide the matter 'in accordance with the general principles common to the *laws of the Member States*'. On the other hand, as seen in the previous section, the question of international responsibility is always governed by the substantive rules of *international law*, and any dispute relating to it must be submitted to a tribunal which adjudicates on the basis of international law. Where, however, the damage is caused to foreign nationals or corporations, they may (or even must) use the above provisions and, as a first step, bring an action for damages before the ECJ as required by the exhaustion of local remedies rule. Since ultimately even this situation raises the question of the Communities' international responsibility, the foreign State of which the individual is a national may bring the matter before an international tribunal if the action for damages is unsuccessful (see under section IV above).

Because of the non-availability (normally) of the ICJ and the ECJ, the international disputes of the Communities must be settled by one of the methods laid down in Art. 33 of the UN Charter, i.e. by negotiation, inquiry, mediation, conciliation, arbitration, judicial settlement. In a number of agreements to which they are parties or to which they are likely to accede, the Communities have accepted several of these methods. Thus, arbitration clauses have been included, for example, in the Lomé Convention, the Association Agreements with Greece and Turkey, some of the fisheries agreements, and other conventions. The UN Convention on the Law of the Sea of 1982 provides for dispute settlement by an International Tribunal for the Law of the Sea and by arbitral tribunals (Art. 287; Annex IX, Art. 7; see also Part XV). The Vienna Convention on the Law of Treaties of 1986 establishes procedures for judicial settlement, arbitration, and conciliation (Art. 66). Some agreements have set up their own institutions to which disputes may be referred. Thus, under all the commodity agreements and GATT, disputes may be submitted to the relevant Council, and under the Association Agreements with Greece and Turkey to the Association Council (which may decide to settle the dispute or refer it to the ECJ). However, in Opinion 1/76 *Laying-up Fund* [1977] ECR 741 at pp. 760–1 the ECJ has warned against the dangers that might arise from the setting up of an external tribunal with parallel jurisdiction to that of the Court itself. This might give rise to conflicts of jurisdiction and the possibility cannot be ruled out that such a tribunal and the ECJ might arrive at divergent interpretations of the same treaty, with consequential effect on legal certainty. Owing to the fact that, as seen above, the ECJ has jurisdiction to interpret Community treaties, such a possibility already exists with regard to most of the dispute settlement procedures discussed.

See also **Common Commercial Policy*, Community Treaties, Direct effect, Legal personality, Mixed agreement, Non-contractual liability, Privileges and immunities, Treaty-making power, Treaty-making procedure.**

Further reading 1. BOOKS: Bathurst *et al.* (eds.), *Legal Problems of an Enlarged European Community* (1972), part IV; Coffey and Wionczek (eds.), *The European Economic Community and Mexico* (1987); Commission of the European Communities, *Thirty Years of Community Law* (1983), part I, ch. 9; Groux and Manin, *The European Communities in the International Order* (1985); Henig, *The External Relations of the European Community: Associations and Trade Agreements* (1971); Parry and Hardy, *EEC Law*, 2nd edn. (1981), part 6; Steenbergen, de Clercq, and Foqueé, *Change and Adjustment: External Relations and Industrial Policy of the European Communities* (1983); Twitchett (ed.), *Europe and the World: The External Relations of the Common Market* (1976); Völker and Steenbergen (eds.), *Leading Cases and Materials on the External Relations Law of the EC* (1985); von Gesau (ed.), *The External Relations of the European Community: Perspectives, Policies and Responses* (1974).

2. ARTICLES AND PAPERS: Barents, 'The European Communities and the Commodity Organisations' (1984/1) *LIEI* 77; Bot, 'EEC–CMEA: Is a Meaningful Relationship Possible?' (1976) 13 *CML Rev.* 335; id., 'Co-operation between the Diplomatic Missions of the Ten in Third Countries and International Organisations' (1984/1) *LIEI* 149; Brinkhorst, 'Permanent Missions of the EC in Third Countries: European Diplomacy in the Making' (1984/1) *LIEI* 23; Cusack, 'External Relations of the European Atomic Energy Community in the Fields of Supply and Safeguards: Background and Developments in 1982 and 1983' (1983) 3 *YEL* 347; Czaplinski, 'International Legal Aspects of Relations between the GDR and the EEC: A Polish View' (1985) 22 *CML Rev.* 69; Editorial, 'The Community and the Council for Mutual Economic Assistance' (1988) 25 *CML Rev.* 663; Goldstajn, 'The Relationship of Yugoslavia and the EEC' (1981) 18 *CML Rev.* 569; Jackson, 'United States–EEC Trade Relations: Constitutional Problems of Economic Interdependence' (1979) 16 *CML Rev.* 453; Koers, 'The External Authority of the EEC in Regard to Marine Fisheries' (1977) 14 *CML Rev.* 269; id., 'The European Economic Community and International Fisheries Organisations' (1984/1) *LIEI* 113; Lay, 'Euro-American Relations' (1987) 7 *YEL* 171; Leenen, 'Participation of the EEC in International Environmental Agreements' (1984/1) *LIEI* 93; Le Lièvre and Houben, 'EC versus Japan: The Community's Legal Weapons' (1987) 24 *CML Rev.* 427; Lysén, 'EEC–CMEA/Eastern Europe: Legal Aspects on Trade and Co-operation' (1987/1) *LIEI* 83; Maslen, 'The European Community's Relations with the State-Trading Countries 1981–1983' (1983) 3 *YEL* 323; id., 'The European Community's Relations with the State-Trading Countries of Europe 1984–1986' (1986) 6 *YEL* 335; Meynell, 'External Relations of the European Community' (1981) 1 *YEL* 347; Nollkaemper, 'The European Community and International Environmental Co-operation: Legal Aspects of External Community Powers' (1987/2) *LIEI* 55; Ouchterlony, 'The European Communities and the Council of Europe' (1984/1) *LIEI* 59; Pescatore, 'External Relations in the Case-Law of the Court of Justice of the European Communities' (1979) 16 *CML Rev.* 615; Schermers, 'International Organisations as Members of Other International Organisations', in *Festschrift für Hermann Mosler* (1982); Schweisfurth, 'The Treaty-Making Capacity of the CMEA in Light of a Framework Agreement between the EEC and the CMEA' (1985) 22 *CML Rev.* 615; Sutton, 'Relations between the European Community and Japan in 1982 and 1983' (1983) 3 *YEL* 285; Tarullo, 'The US–EC Trade Relationship and the Uruguay Round' (1987) 24 *CML Rev.* 411; Wellenstein, 'Twenty-Five Years of European Community External Relations' (1979) 16 *CML Rev.* 407; id., 'The Relations of the European Communities with Eastern Europe', in O'Keeffe and Schermers (eds.), *Essays in European Law and Integration* (1982), p. 197; id., 'The Relations between the

European Communities and Finland' (1983) 20 *CML Rev.* 713; id., 'Participation of the Community in International Commodity Agreements', in Bates *et al.* (*eds.*), *In Memoriam J. D. B. Mitchell* (1983), p. 65.

3. OFFICIAL PUBLICATIONS: Commission of the European Communities, 'Agreements and Other Bilateral Commitments Linking the Communities with Non-Member Countries (as at 30 June 1986)'; id., 'The European Community, International Organizations and Multilateral Agreements', 3rd edn. (1983); id., 'Multilateral Conventions and Agreements: Signatures and/or Conclusions by the European Communities' (1987); House of Lords Select Committee on the European Communities, Session 1984–5, 16th Report, 'External Competence of the European Communities' (1985); 16th *Gen. Rep. EC* (1982), p. 227; 17th *Gen. Rep. EC* (1983), p. 247; 18th *Gen. Rep. EC* (1984), p. 235; 19th *Gen. Rep. EC* (1985), p. 263; 20th *Gen. Rep. EC* (1986), p. 291; 21st *Gen. Rep. EC* (1987), p. 279; 22nd *Gen. Rep. EC* (1988), p. 331; 23rd *Gen. Rep. EC* (1989), p. 307.

See also under **Treaty-making power.**

▶ *EX TUNC* EFFECT Retroactive effect, i.e. the effect of a legal provision or judicial decision upon acts, events, situations, or legal relationships which occurred or arose before the entry into force of that provision or decision.

See also **Ex *nunc*** **effect, Retroactive effect.**

F

▶ **FINANCIAL REGULATION (FR)** Council Regulation of 21 December 1977 applicable to the general budget of the European Communities (*OJ* 1977 L356/1). The FR entered into force on 1 January 1978, and repealed the previous FR of 25 April 1973 (*OJ* 1973 L116/1) and the FR of 18 March 1975 amending the latter (*OJ* 1975 L73/45). The FR of 1977 has been amended several times (see Reg. 1252/79, *OJ* 1979 L160/1; the FR of 16 Dec. 1980 concerning the use of the ECU in the general budget, *OJ* 1980 L345/23; Reg. 1600/88, *OJ* 1988 L143/1; Reg. 2049/88, *OJ* 1988 L185/3). The FR was further implemented by Comm. Reg. of 11 December 1986 (*OJ* 1986 L360/1), which took effect on 1 January 1987 and repealed the previous Comm. Reg. of 30 June 1975 implementing the 1973 FR (*OJ* 1975 L170/1).

The FR of 1977 was introduced mainly to lay down new provisions regarding the adoption of the budget as required by the entry into force on 1 June 1977 of the Second Budgetary Treaty of 1975. It was also necessary to adapt the provisions relating to the presenting and auditing of accounts to the new situation created by the establishment of a Court of Auditors by the Treaty of 1975. One of the innovations of the FR was that, in the case of projects lasting several years, it enabled a distinction to be made between commitment appropriations and payment appropriations ('differentiated' appropriations) in the course of the budgetary procedure itself. It also replaced the parity unit of account used in the FR of 1973 by a unit of account based on a basket of currencies (the European Unit of Account), although this was in turn replaced subsequently by the European Currency Unit (ECU). After laying down some general principles regarding the budget (Title I), the FR deals with the presentation, structure, and implementation of the budget (Titles II and III; see also Comm. Reg. of 11 Dec. 1986, above, laying down detailed rules for the implementation of certain provisions of the FR). Title IV relates to the conclusion of contracts, inventories, and accounts (see also Case 56/77 *Agence Européenne d'Intérims* v. *Commission* [1978] ECR 2215 at pp. 2233 *et seq.*, interpreting the corresponding provisions of the 1973 FR). The responsibilities of authorizing officers, financial controllers, accounting officers, and administrators of advance funds are set out in Title V, while Title VI deals with the presenting and auditing of accounts. Special provisions apply to research and investment appropriations (Title VII), to the Guarantee Section of the European Agricultural Guidance and Guarantee Fund (Title VIII), to Food Aid (Title IX), and to the Office for Official Publications (Title X). Title XI contains transitional and final provisions providing, amongst other things, for the periodic review of the FR (Art. 107). The Annex, which set out budgetary nomenclature, was deleted by Art. 1(6) of Reg. 1252/79.

The latest amendment to the FR of 1977, adopted by the Council on 24 June 1988 (Reg. 2049/88, above) gives effect to the conclusions of the Brussels European Council of 11–13 February 1988 (see *Bull. EC* 2–1988, p. 8) and forms an essential element of the budgetary reform which, together with a new system of the Communities' own resources, was introduced during the course of 1988. It aims to achieve improved budgetary management and greater transparency of appropriations. In particular, the changes relate to the following matters:

1. the introduction of a time-limit for the implementation of legal commitments entered into by the Commission for measures extending over more than one financial year;
2. strengthening of the principle of annuality by discontinuing automatic carryovers of commitment and payment appropriations;
3. official recognition of a 'negative reserve', limited to a maximum amount of 200 million ECU;
4. alteration of the special provisions applicable to the EAGGF Guarantee Section to take account of the amendments to the regulation on the financing of the Common Agricultural Policy.

(For background to the amendments introduced in 1988, see 20th *Gen. Rep. EC* (1986), p. 70; 21st *Gen. Rep. EC* (1987), p. 66; Suppl. 1/87—*Bull. EC*, p. 22; *Bull. EC* 7/8—1987, p. 12; *Bull. EC* 6–1988, p. 114. On 16 Dec. 1988, the Commission sent the Council a proposal for a general revision of the Financial Regulation, see *Bull. EC* 12–1988, p. 136.)

See also **Budgetary Treaties, Community budget, Court of Auditors, Own resources.**

▶ *FORCE MAJEURE* 1. *In the legal systems of the Member States*: external cause of such a nature as to 'exonerate an individual from the effects of non-observance of a positive obligation or of a prohibition by which he is bound' (Case 68/77 *IFG* v. *Commission* [1978] ECR 353 at p. 381 *per* A.-G. Capotorti). While the concept of *force majeure* is generally recognized in national law, it has different effects in the different branches of the law, such as criminal law, public law, and private law. Thus, in the relationship between an individual and the public administration, *force majeure* can only be relied on in order to avoid the consequences of the non-fulfilment of an obligation and not in order to remedy a situation which is detrimental to the interests of the individual (ibid. at p. 370 *per Curiam*, pp. 380–1 *per* A.-G. Capotorti).

2. *In Community law*: the existence of the concept of *force majeure* as a general principle of law has not so far been explicitly recognized by the ECJ. Various Advocates-General have expressed divergent views on the matter. Thus, in a series of cases A.-G. Capotorti pointed out that in Community law the concept of *force majeure* had been developed by reference to specific provisions of agricultural regulations, and that 'the existence of a general principle, begetting a uniform concept of *force majeure* applicable to all sectors of Community law' had not been, and could not be, established because of the 'diversity of the functions which the relieving effect of *force majeure* may perform' (Case 38/79 *Butter- und Eier-Zentrale Nordmark* [1980] ECR 643 at pp. 658–9; Cases 154/78 etc. *Valsabbia* v. *Commission* [1980] ECR 907 at p. 1067; see also Case 68/77 *IFG* v. *Commission*, above, at p. 380; Case 149/78 *Rumi* v. *Commission* [1979] ECR 2523 at p. 2547; Case 42/79 *Milch-, Fett- und Eier-Kontor* [1979] ECR 3703 at p. 3723). He in fact went so far as to suggest the adoption of a 'radical view to the effect that in the absence of an express provision, *force majeure* cannot be relied

273

upon in Community law' (Cases 154/78 etc. *Valsabbia* v. *Commission*, above, at p. 1068). By contrast, A.-G. Mayras thought that the concept of *force majeure* should be regarded as part of the general principles of law and, as such, could be invoked even in the absence of an express provision, for example to justify a failure to observe a time-limit (Case 32/72 *Wasaknäcke* [1972] ECR 1181 at p. 1197). A.-G. Warner was willing to recognize the concept of *force majeure* but only as a particular application of the general principle of proportionality (Case 64/74 *Reich* [1975] ECR 261 at p. 274).

The ECJ itself has not unequivocally followed any of these opinions. On the one hand, the Court has been willing to consider and even to accept pleas of *force majeure* in the absence of express provisions applicable to the situation in question, but has either failed to indicate the legal basis for this (Case 149/78 *Rumi* v. *Commission*, above, at p. 2537; Cases 154/78 etc. *Valsabbia* v. *Commission*, above, at p. 1022), or has justified it by reference to other concepts and principles, such as equity (Case 64/74 *Reich*, above, at pp. 268–9, where the Court held that the defence of *force majeure*, allowed for by the relevant agricultural regulations in the field of trade with third countries only, could equally apply to trade between Member States) or the principle of Community preference (Case 6/78 *Union Française de Céréales* [1978] ECR 1675 at pp. 1683–4, where the Court applied by analogy the *force majeure* provisions of the export refunds regulation to 'accession' compensatory amounts. See however Case 38/79 *Butter- und Eier-Zentrale Nordmark*, above, at p. 655, where the Court refused to apply the same *force majeure* provisions to monetary compensatory amounts). On the other hand, the Court has repeatedly stated that 'as the concept of *force majeure* is not identical in the different branches of law and the various fields of application, the significance of this concept must be determined on the basis of the legal framework within which it is intended to take effect' (Case 4/68 *Schwarzwaldmilch* [1968] ECR 377 at p. 385; Case 158/73 *Kampffmeyer* [1974] ECR 101 at p. 110). So far, the Court has given the following interpretations of the concept of *force majeure* in the different areas of Community law:

(*a*) In the context of agricultural regulations dealing with import and export licences and advance-fixing certificates, the Court has held that 'the concept of *force majeure* is not limited to absolute impossibility but must be understood in the sense of unusual circumstances, outside the control of the importer or exporter, the consequences of which, in spite of the exercise of all due care, could not have been avoided except at the cost of excessive sacrifice. This concept implies a sufficient flexibility regarding not only the nature of the occurrence relied upon but also the care which the exporter should have exercised in order to meet it and the extent of the sacrifices which he should have accepted to that end' (Case 11/70 *Internationale Handelsgesellschaft* [1970] ECR 1125 at pp. 1137–8; Case 4/68 *Schwarzwaldmilch*, above, at pp. 385–6; Case 158/73 *Kampffmeyer*, above, at pp. 110–11 holding that in certain circumstances the loss of an import licence may constitute a case of *force majeure*; Case 186/73 *Fleischkontor* [1974] ECR 533 at p. 544; Case 3/74 *Pfützenreuter* [1974] ECR 589 at p. 599; Case 64/74 *Reich*, above, at pp. 268–9; Case 71/82 *Brüggen* [1982] ECR 4647 at p. 4657; etc.). In all these cases, where the import or export transaction could not be carried out during the period of validity of the licence owing to *force majeure*, the consequence was either to release the trader from the obligation to import or to export and to release the security, or to extend the period of validity of the licence, even retroactively, to enable the trader to benefit from the rate of refund or levy fixed in advance.

(*b*) In the context of agricultural regulations dealing with the sale of butter from public storage, the Court has interpreted the concept of *force majeure* as referring to 'absolute impossibility caused by abnormal circumstances unrelated to the purchaser of the butter from storage, the consequences of which could not have been avoided except at the cost of excessive sacrifices, despite the exercise of all due care' (Case 42/79 *Milch-, Fett- und Eier-Kontor*, above, at p. 3716; Case 20/84 *De Jong* [1985] ECR 2061 at p. 2111. The Court refused to accept as *force majeure* the fraudulent misappropriation of the butter by a duly authorized agent or the failure by a subsequent buyer to comply with the processing obligation).

(*c*) In the context of agricultural regulations dealing with monetary compensatory amounts, the Court has defined *force majeure* as 'unusual and unforeseeable circumstances, beyond the trader's control, the consequences of which could not have been avoided even if all due care had been exercised', adding that that concept must be considered in relation to the provisions of each regulation in which the term *force majeure* appears (Case 266/84 *Denkavit France* [1986] ECR 149 at p. 170).

(*d*) In the context of a failure to comply with a decision fixing minimum prices under Art. 61 ECSC, the Court has held that 'recognition of circumstances of *force majeure* presupposes that the external cause relied on by individuals has consequences which are inexorable and inevitable to the point of making it objectively impossible for the persons concerned to comply with their obligations and . . . leaving them no alternative but to infringe [the] decision' in question (Cases 154/78 etc. *Valsabbia* v. *Commission*, above, at p. 1022. See also Case 149/78 *Rumi* v. *Commission*, above, at p. 2537, dealing with a failure to publish price lists under Art. 60 ECSC). The Court has given a similar definition of *force majeure* in the context of claims for the repayment or remission of import or export duties, emphasizing that the 'external cause' must amount to an 'unforeseeable and inevitable circumstance' having 'irresistible consequences' resulting in objective impossibility (Cases 98 and 230/83 *Van Gend & Loos* v. *Commission* [1984] ECR 3763 at p. 3779).

(*e*) Interpreting Art. 39(3) ECSC Statute, which provides that 'No right shall be prejudiced in consequence of the expiry of a time limit if the party concerned proves the existence of . . . *force majeure*' (Arts. 42(2) EEC Statute and 43(2) Euratom Statute are in identical terms), the Court has stated that 'apart from special cases in specific areas in which it is used, the concept of *force majeure* essentially covers unusual circumstances which make it impossible for the relevant action to be carried out. Even though it does not presuppose absolute impossibility it nevertheless requires abnormal difficulties, independent of the will of the person concerned and apparently inevitable even if all due care is taken' (Case 284/82 *Busseni* v. *Commission* [1984] ECR 557 at p. 566; Case 224/83 *Ferriera Vittoria* v. *Commission* [1984] ECR 2349 at p. 2356; Case 209/83 *Valsabbia* v. *Commission* [1984] ECR 3089 at pp. 3097–8. In all three cases the Court dismissed pleas based on *force majeure*). It would seem to follow from the introductory clause to the first sentence that the Court has intended this to be a general definition of *force majeure*, applicable in all cases which do not fall within one of the special situations discussed earlier. Nevertheless, it still remains to be seen whether the Court is willing to recognize the concept of *force majeure* as a general principle of law operating across the whole range of Community law, even in the absence of any express provision (see e.g. Case 71/87 *Inter-Kom* [1988] ECR 1979 at p. 1998, para. 15, where the Court deliberately left open this question).

See also **Accession compensatory amount*, Advance-fixing procedure*, Community preference, Equity, Export refund*, General principles of law, Minimum price*, Monetary compensatory amount*, Price list*, Proportionality, Recovery of import and export duties*.**

Further reading: Flynn, 'Force Majeure Pleas in Proceedings before the European Court' (1981) 6 *EL Rev.* 102; Thompson, 'Force Majeure: The Contextual Approach of the Court of Justice' (1987) 24 *CML Rev.* 259. *See also under* **General principles of law.**

▶ *FUMUS BONI JURIS* Strong presumption that an application instituting proceedings before the ECJ is well founded; the existence of factual and legal grounds establishing a prima-facie case. This is one of several conditions that must be fulfilled before suspension of operation of a Community act or other interim measures may be ordered by the Court (Art. 83(2) RP; see e.g. Cases 43, 45, and 48/59 *Lachmüller* v. *Commission* [1960] ECR 463 at p. 492; Case 292/84R *Scharf* v. *Commission* [1984] ECR 4349 at p. 4353).

See also **Interim measures, Suspension of operation.**

▶ *FUNCTUS OFFICIO* Court or tribunal which has exhausted its jurisdiction. Thus, the ECJ is said to become *functus officio* once it has given a final (as opposed to interlocutory) judgment in a case. This rule is however subject to certain exceptions, such as the power of the Court to interpret and revise its judgments (see Case 5/55 *ASSIDER* v. *HA* [1955] ECR 135 at p. 147 *per* A.-G. Lagrange; Case 110/63A *Willame* v. *Commission* [1966] ECR 287 at p. 295 *per* A.-G. Gand).

See also **Interlocutory judgment, Interpretation of judgments, Judgment, *Res judicata*, Revision of judgments, Third party proceedings.**

► **GENERAL DECISION** One of two types of decision (the other being individual decision) that the Commission may adopt under the ECSC Treaty. The Treaty makes a distinction between these two types of decision, without further defining them, in the context of the rules relating to their publication/ notification (Art. 15 ECSC) and in defining the right of undertakings and associations to bring an action for their annulment before the ECJ (Art. 33 ECSC). In the latter context the ECJ has held that the general or individual character of a decision results directly from the contents and not from the form of the decision, and that it must be determined by objective criteria. Thus, the Court has defined a general decision as a 'quasi-legislative measure adopted by a public authority with legislative effect *erga omnes*' (Case 8/55 *Fédération Charbonnière de Belgique* v. *HA* [1956] ECR 245 at p. 258; Case 18/57 *Nold* v. *HA* [1959] ECR 41 at p. 50). Such a general decision 'establishes a legislative principle, imposes abstract conditions for its implementation and sets out the legal consequences entailed thereby' (Case 13/57 *Eisen- und Stahlindustrie* v. *HA* [1958] ECR 265 at p. 276; Case 10/57 *Aubert et Duval* v. *HA* [1958] ECR 339 at p. 345). It 'contains general rules which . . . may be of importance in the same way for an indeterminate number of cases. Those rules are to be applicable to all persons finding themselves in the circumstances specified for the application of such rules' (Cases 36 to 38, 40, and 41/58 *Simet* v. *HA* [1959] ECR 157 at p. 166). It will not, therefore, individually and directly affect the legal position of the persons to whom it applies (Cases 55 to 59/63 etc. *Modena* v. *HA* [1964] ECR 211 at p. 228 *per Curiam*, pp. 234–5 *per* A.-G. Roemer). A general decision under the ECSC Treaty is, accordingly, comparable to a regulation under the EEC/Euratom Treaties.

The significance of the distinction between general and individual decisions is twofold. First, where a decision is general in character, undertakings and associations may challenge it before the ECJ only on the sole ground of misuse of powers affecting them (ibid.; Case 8/55 *Fédération Charbonnière de Belgique* v. *HA*, above; Art. 33 ECSC). Secondly, a general decision must be published in the *Official Journal* and it takes effect by the mere fact of publication (Art. 15 ECSC).

See also **Action for annulment, Decision, Individual decision, Publication, Regulation.**

► **GENERAL PRINCIPLES OF LAW** Legal concepts and principles of fundamental importance 'forming that philosophical, political and legal substratum common to the Member States from which through the case-law [of the ECJ] an unwritten Community law emerges' (Case 11/70 *Internationale Handelsgesellschaft* [1970] ECR 1125 at p. 1146 *per* A.-G. Dutheillet de Lamothe).

The Community Treaties and the Statutes of the ECJ contain no provisions similar to Art. 38(1)(c) of the Statute of the International Court of Justice, which directs the Court to apply, in deciding disputes submitted to it, the 'general principles of law recognised by civilized nations'. Nevertheless, it is universally accepted that the general principles of law form part of 'the law' the observance of which the ECJ is required to ensure (Arts. 31 ECSC, 164 EEC, and 136 Euratom). They may therefore be regarded as genuine sources of Community law. As the ECJ has stated: 'Community law, which derives from not only the economic but also the legal interpenetration of the Member States, must take into account the principles and concepts common to the laws of those States . . .' (Case 155/79 *AM & S. v. Commission* [1982] ECR 1575 at p. 1610, referring to the principle of confidentiality; see also the opinion of A.-G. Slynn, ibid. at pp. 1648–50, and the cases cited below).

As sources of Community law, the general principles of law may be resorted to by the ECJ for the following main purposes:

- to review the legality or the validity of the acts of the institutions: an act infringing a general principle recognized by the Court as part of Community law will be annulled or declared invalid (see e.g. Case 4/73 *Nold* v. *Commission* [1974] ECR 491 at p. 507; Case 114/76 *Bela-Mühle* [1977] ECR 1211 at p. 1221; Case 122/78 *Buitoni* [1979] ECR 677 at pp. 684–5; Case 224/82 *Meiko-Konservenfabrik* [1983] ECR 2539 at pp. 2548–50);
- to review the compatibility with Community law of the legislation or administrative practice of the Member States: a national law or practice infringing a general principle will be held incompatible with Community law (see e.g. Case 203/80 *Casati* [1981] ECR 2595 at p. 2618; Case 222/84 *Johnston* [1986] ECR 1651 at pp. 1682–3);
- to establish the non-contractual liability of the Economic and Euratom Communities (Arts. 215(2) EEC and 188(2) Euratom);
- to interpret provisions of written Community law (see e.g. Case 13/61 *Bosch* [1962] ECR 45 at p. 59 *per* A.-G. Lagrange; Case 15/63 *Lassalle* v. *Parliament* [1964] ECR 31 at p. 54 *per* A.-G. Lagrange; Case 53/81 *Levin* [1982] ECR 1035 at p. 1049);
- to supplement the provisions of written Community law (see e.g. Case 11/70 *Internationale Handelsgesellschaft*, above, at p. 1134 *per Curiam*, pp. 1146–7 *per* A.-G. Dutheillet de Lamothe; Case 7/72 *Boehringer* v. *Commission* [1972] ECR 1281 at pp. 1293 *et seq. per* A.-G. Mayras; Case 64/74 *Reich* [1975] ECR 261 at pp. 274–5 *per* A.-G. Warner; Case 155/79 *AM & S. v. Commission*, above).

The general principles of law are themselves derived from a number of different sources. Most frequently—and most importantly—they are derived from principles and concepts which are common to the legal systems of the Member States and the origins of which may very often be traced back to Roman law (see e.g. Case 23/68 *Klomp* [1969] ECR 43 at p. 50, dealing with the principle of the continuity of the legal system when legislation is amended; see also the principles of *res judicata, non bis in idem, audi alteram partem*, unjust enrichment, *cessante ratione legis cessat et ipsa lex, nullum crimen nulla poena sine legem*, etc.). In the context of the non-contractual liability of the Economic and Euratom Communities, the ECJ is expressly required to apply the 'general principles common to the laws of the Member States' (Arts. 215(2) EEC, 188(2) Euratom). To the extent to which general principles had been incorporated into Community law prior to the accession of the new Member States in 1973, they represent principles of the civil law system. With the enlargement of the Communities, however, the concept of general principles of law has become broader so as to take account of the laws of the new Member States and thus to accommodate principles of the common law system. While these laws cannot be relevant to the solution of disputes that had arisen before accession (see e.g. Case 81/72 *Commission* v. *Council* [1973] ECR 575 at p. 593 *per* A.-G. Warner; Cases 63 to 69/72 *Werhahn* v. *Council* [1973] ECR 1229 at p. 1259 *per* A.-G. Roemer), the principles of common law have, since the enlargement of the Communities, made considerable impact upon Community law, thus contributing to its development through the concept of general principles (see the cases cited immediately above, and—in particular—Case 17/74 *Transocean Marine Paint Association* v. *Commission* [1974] ECR 1063 at pp. 1079–80 *per Curiam*, pp. 1088–9 *per* A.-G. Warner, dealing with the principle of *audi alteram partem*—the right to be heard—and Case 155/79 *AM & S.* v. *Commission*, above, at pp. 1610–13 *per Curiam*, pp. 1620–4 and 1630–7 *per* A.-G. Warner, pp. 1648 *et seq. per* A.-G. Slynn, dealing with the principle of confidentiality or legal professional privilege).

For a legal concept or principle to be recognized as part of Community law it is not necessary for it to be unanimously accepted in the legal systems of all the Member States, nor to represent at least the 'lowest common denominator' or the 'lowest limit' of the national solutions. What is required is that a principle should be widely accepted and should provide a solution which is the best, the most appropriate, and the most progressive of all comparable solutions, if assessed by the methods of evaluative comparative law in the light of the particular objectives, nature, and structure of Community law. A general principle cannot therefore be obtained by 'adding up' all the special features of the twelve (or thirteen) different national legal systems, nor by taking into account their detailed rules and solutions. Rather, it is a matter of finding common underlying principles, even if broadly expressed, by eliminating the differences that separate the domestic laws of the Member States. It is thus through a comparative and creative process, carried out by the ECJ and its Advocates-General, that concepts and principles of national law re-emerge as general principles of unwritten Community law (see in particular Case 14/61 *Hoogovens* v. *HA* [1962] ECR 253 at pp. 283–4 *per* A.-G. Lagrange; Case 25/62 *Plaumann* v. *Commission* [1963] ECR 95 at pp. 116–17 *per* A.-G. Roemer; Cases 5, 7, and 13 to 24/66 *Kampffmeyer* v. *Commission* [1967] ECR 245 at p. 273 *per* A.-G. Gand; Case 5/71 *Zucker-fabrik Schöppenstedt* v. *Council* [1971] ECR 975 at pp. 989–90 *per* A.-G. Roemer; Case 155/79 *AM & S.* v. *Commission*, above, at pp. 1648–50 *per* A.-G. Slynn; etc.).

Therefore, while the domestic legal systems, taken individually, cannot be regarded as proper sources of Community law since—apart from certain special situations—they cannot normally be resorted to by the Court and the other institutions (see e.g. Case 1/58 *Stork* v. *HA* [1959] ECR 17 at p. 26; Cases 36 to 38 and 40/59 *Geitling* v. *HA* [1960] ECR 423 at p. 438), national rules and concepts—including constitutional traditions—which represent values common to the legal orders of all the Member States may be elevated to the rank of 'general principles of law' and thus incorporated into Community law (ibid. at p. 450 *per* A.-G. Lagrange, and see in particular Case 11/70 *Internationale Handelsgesellschaft*, above, at p. 1134 and Case 4/73 *Nold* v. *Commission*, above, at p. 507, both dealing with human rights). It has been in this way that the Court has developed a number of general principles of fundamental importance to the whole legal order of the Communities and in particular to the protection of the rights of the individual, such as the principles of confidentiality, effective judicial control, legal certainty, legitimate expectation, non-retroactivity, proportionality, and those relating to the non-contractual liability of the Communities and to the protection of fundamental human rights.

There are nevertheless certain limits to the extent to which principles of national law may be incorporated into Community law. In the first place, there is no common general principle to incorporate where the national laws vary to such a degree that it is impossible to extract from them a truly common meaning of a legal concept. Nor where a principle existing in one Member State is not at least generally known in the others (see e.g. Case 41/69 *Chemiefarma* v. *Commission* [1970] ECR 661 at p. 713 *per* A.-G. Gand; Case 5/73 *Balkan-Import-Export* [1973] ECR 1091 at p. 1130 *per* A.-G. Roemer; Cases 63 to 69/72 *Werhahn* v. *Council*, above, at p. 1274 *per* A.-G. Roemer; Case 72/74 *Union Syndicale* v. *Council* [1975] ECR 401 at p. 416 *per* A.-G. Reischl). In such cases, a principle of national law can only be adopted in Community law as a new and independent concept of the latter, having its own new and independent meaning, rather than as a general principle of law (see e.g. Case 4/68 *Schwarzwaldmilch* [1968] ECR 377 at p. 385 *per Curiam*, pp. 392–3 *per* A.-G. Gand; Case 158/73 *Kampffmeyer* [1974] ECR 101 at p. 110; both cases dealing with the concept of *force majeure*). In the second place, the ECJ is reluctant to incorporate general principles where this would amount to genuine legislative activity on its part, as opposed to the proper judicial function of interpreting and applying the law (see e.g. Case 41/69 *Chemiefarma* v. *Commission*, above, at p. 683; Case 48/69 *ICI* v. *Commission* [1972] ECR 619 at pp. 652–3; in both cases the Court refused to fix limitation periods in competition law by applying the relevant principles of national law). In the third place, a general principle of national law will not be adopted into Community law if the subject-matter to which it relates is already governed by an independent rule or principle of that law (Case 9/69 *Sayag* [1969] ECR 329 at pp. 339–40 *per* A.-G. Gand).

While the legal systems of the Member States are the main sources of the general principles of law, they are not the only ones. Thus, general principles may also be derived, although less frequently, from public international law (see Cases 21 to 24/72 *International Fruit Company* [1972] ECR 1219 at p. 1233 *per* A.-G. Mayras), including international treaties to which the Member States are signatories, such as the European Convention on Human Rights of 1950 (see in particular Case 4/73 *Nold* v. *Commission*, above, at p. 507; Case 44/79 *Hauer* [1979] ECR 3727 at pp. 3744–5; Case 222/84

Johnston, above, at p. 1682; etc.), and from Community law itself. As a new and independent legal order of a *sui generis* type, Community law has given rise to certain principles which are peculiar to itself and which have no exact parallel in either national or international law. These include the principles of Community preference, equality of treatment or non-discrimination, free movement and free competition, freedom of trade, etc. The main difference between these principles and those derived from national or international law is that the former normally have their basis in the provisions of written Community law (mainly in the Treaties), from which the Court has developed them by way of generalization and other methods of judicial interpretation, while the latter represent unwritten Community law.

*See also **Audi alteram partem**, **Cessante ratione legis cessat et ipsa lex**, Community law, Community preference, Confidentiality, Continuity of the legal system, Effective judicial control, Equality, Equity, **Force majeure**, Good faith, Human rights, Interpretation of Community law, Legal certainty, Legitimate expectation, Natural justice, **Non bis in idem**, Non-contractual liability, Proportionality, **Res judicata**, Retroactive effect, **Stare decisis**, Unjust enrichment, **Venire contra factum proprium**, Vested rights.*

Further reading 1. BOOKS: Bebr, Arnull, *The General Principles of EEC Law and the Individual* (1990); Hartley, *The Foundations of European Community Law*, 2nd edn. (1988), ch. 5; Schermers, *Judicial Protection in the European Communities*, 4th edn. (1987), ch. 1, part II/B; Toth, *Legal Protection of Individuals in the European Communities* (1978) vol. i, ss. 221, 303, 304.

2. ARTICLES: Akehurst, 'The Application of General Principles of Law by the Court of Justice of the European Communities' (1981) 52 *BYIL* 29; Lorenz, 'General Principles of Law: Their Elaboration in the Court of Justice of the European Communities' (1964) 13 *AJCL* 1.

▶ **GOOD FAITH** It is a fundamental principle of the Community legal system that the rights and obligations arising under it must at all times be exercised and performed in good faith. Thus, the ECJ has stated categorically that 'the conduct of an authority, in administrative as in contractual matters, is at all times subject to observance of the principle of good faith': the Community institutions cannot act arbitrarily, but their actions must always be justified on adequate legal grounds (Cases 43, 45, and 48/59 *Lachmüller* v. *Commission* [1960] ECR 463 at pp. 474–5; Case 44/59 *Fiddelaar* v. *Commission* [1960] ECR 535 at p. 547). Community law does not safeguard the interests of a person who acts in such a way that he cannot reasonably rely upon good faith worthy of protection (Case 14/61 *Hoogovens* v. *HA* [1962] ECR 253 at p. 273; Case 250/78 *DEKA* v. *EEC* [1983] ECR 421 at p. 431).

The principle of good faith is closely related to, and provides the ultimate basis for, certain other general principles of Community law, such as, in particular, the principles of the protection of legitimate expectations, of legal certainty, and of *venire contra factum proprium*. The first of these requires that 'assurances relied upon in good faith should be honoured' (Case 169/73 *Compagnie Continentale* v. *Council* [1975] ECR 117 at p. 140 *per* A.-G.

Trabucchi). The second requires that legal relationships established in good faith should, as far as possible, not be called in question (Case 61/79 *Denkavit Italiana* [1980] ECR 1205 at p. 1223, referring to Case 43/75 *Defrenne* [1976] ECR 455 at pp. 480–1). According to the third principle, no one may rely upon his own irregular conduct in order to gain an advantage or to escape an obligation, since this would be contrary to good faith, which governs the relations between the various subjects of Community law (see Case 36/72 *Meganck* v. *Commission* [1973] ECR 527 at p. 534; Case 156/80 *Morbelli* v. *Commission* [1981] ECR 1357 at p. 1372; Cases 59 and 129/80 *Turner* v. *Commission* [1981] ECR 1883 at p. 1912). Often these related principles are invoked together (see e.g. Case 127/78 *Spitta* [1979] ECR 171 at p. 180).

See also **General principles of law, Legal certainty, Legitimate expectation, Venire contra factum proprium.**

▶ **GROUNDS OF ACTION** Grounds on which binding acts of the Council, the Commission, and the European Parliament may be challenged before, and declared void by, the ECJ in the framework of annulment proceedings (Arts. 33 and 38 ECSC, 173 EEC, 146 Euratom).

Following the traditional classification used in French administrative law (see e.g. Case 3/54 *ASSIDER* v. *HA* [1955] ECR 63 at p. 75 *per* A.-G. Lagrange), the Treaties specify the following four grounds of action:

1. lack of competence;
2. infringement of an essential procedural requirement;
3. infringement of the Treaty or of any rule of law relating to its application; and
4. misuse of powers.

The main purpose of this classification is to help identify possible defects in an act that the Treaties recognize as being of such gravity as to entail the act's annulment. The distinction between the various grounds plays an important part under the ECSC Treaty, where in certain circumstances only the sole ground of misuse of powers may be relied on. No such restriction, however, exists under the EEC/Euratom Treaties which, generally, do not attach so much importance to the distinction between the four grounds (see Case 34/62 *Germany* v. *Commission* [1963] ECR 131 at p. 151 *per* A.-G. Roemer). The practice of the ECJ shows that under the EEC Treaty almost any well-substantiated infringement of Community law, other than a really minor one, may be invoked to establish the illegality of a measure and may in principle lead to its annulment. This is a consequence of the fact that the various grounds are drawn up in such wide terms that they encompass amongst themselves almost all conceivable cases of illegality. Moreover, they overlap considerably so that in certain situations the classification of an infringement according to the clear-cut terms used by the Treaties becomes not only unnecessary but virtually impossible (see e.g. Case 66/63 *Netherlands* v. *HA* [1964] ECR 533 at p. 553 *per* A.-G. Lagrange).

It follows from the foregoing that although an application originating

annulment proceedings must contain 'a brief statement of the grounds on
which the application is based' (Arts. 22(1) ECSC Statute, 19(1) EEC and
Euratom Statutes, 38(1) RP), such a statement need not conform to the
phraseology or the list used by the Treaties. As the ECJ has stated, '. . . it may
be sufficient for the grounds for instituting the proceedings to be expressed in
terms of their substance rather than of their legal classification provided,
however, that it is sufficiently clear from the application which of the grounds
referred to in the Treaty is being invoked. A mere abstract statement of the
grounds in the application does not alone satisfy the requirements of the
Protocol on the Statute of the Court of Justice or the Rules of Procedure . . .
The application must specify the nature of the grounds on which the
application is based. The ground of complaint relied upon must therefore be
established in relation to the facts which have been set out' (Cases 19/60 etc.
Fives Lille Cail v. *HA* [1961] ECR 281 at p. 295). Grounds which are not
mentioned in the application are inadmissible (Case 18/57 *Nold* v. *HA* [1959]
ECR 41 at p. 51).

In considering the substance of a case, the ECJ generally limits itself to
examining the particular grounds put forward by the applicant unless public
interest, public policy, or the need properly to fulfil its task of exercising
judicial review requires it to do otherwise. Thus, the Court will consider of its
own motion whether or not an act has been vitiated by a lack of competence
(see e.g. Case 14/59 *Fonderies de Pont-à-Mousson* v. *HA* [1959] ECR 215 at
p. 229) or by an infringement of an essential procedural requirement such as
lack of consultation of the (ECSC) Council (see e.g. Case 1/54 *France* v. *HA*
[1954] ECR 1 at p. 15) and/or the Consultative Committee (see e.g. Case 6/54
Netherlands v. *HA* [1955] ECR 103 at p. 112) or lack of reasoning (see e.g.
Case 18/57 *Nold* v. *HA*, above, at p. 52). By contrast, the Court will not of its
own motion examine a misuse of powers (see Cases 7 and 9/54 *Industries
Sidérurgiques Luxembourgeoises* v. *HA* [1956] ECR 175 at p. 199) although
it may consider an infringement of the Treaties or of any rule of law relating
to their application, depending on the circumstances of an individual case (see
Case 14/59 *Fonderies de Pont-à-Mousson* v. *HA*, above, at pp. 229–30; see
also Case 5/67 *Beus* [1968] ECR 83 at p. 109 *per* A.-G. Gand). Nevertheless,
the Court will not on its own initiative review the legality of a measure which
the applicant has evidently not intended to challenge in order not to interfere
with the scope which the applicant wished to give its action (Case 14/59
Fonderies de Pont-à-Mousson v. *HA*, above, at p. 231).

See also Action for annulment, Application originating proceedings, Infringement of an essential procedural requirement, Infringement of the Treaties,
Lack of competence, Misuse of powers, Statement of reasons.

Further reading: See under Action for annulment.

H

HUMAN RIGHTS Rights and freedoms recognized by national constitutions and international conventions as being 'fundamental' both in the sense that they protect and promote the most essential human values, such as the dignity, the personality, the intellectual and physical integrity, or the economic and social well-being of the individual, and in the sense that they are inseparably and permanently attached to man as a person. While an exhaustive cataloguing of these rights and freedoms is not possible (since their concept and range change with the progress of society), it may be stated that they fall within the following three broad categories. First, civil and political rights, such as the right to life, liberty, and security of person; prohibition of slavery, servitude, torture, and cruel, inhuman, or degrading treatment or punishment; equality before the law; prohibition of arbitrary arrest, detention, or exile; right to a fair trial; presumption of innocence; right to privacy, family life, home, and correspondence; freedom of thought, conscience, religion, opinion, and expression; freedom of assembly and association; right to free elections; right to property. Secondly, economic, social, and cultural rights, such as the right to work including the right to just, safe, and healthy working conditions and the right to fair and equal remuneration (equal pay for equal work to men and women); the right to form and join trade unions; right to collective bargaining; right to strike; right to social security and to an adequate standard of living; protection of the family, women, mother, and children; right to education and vocational training; right to take part in cultural life. Thirdly, collective or group rights, such as the right of self-determination, prohibition of all forms of racial discrimination, prohibition of apartheid.

In national law, human rights are protected by constitutional provisions and principles, whether written or unwritten. In international law, they are protected by a wide network of conventions which may be universal, such as the International Covenants on Civil and Political Rights and on Economic, Social and Cultural Rights of 1966, or regional, such as the European Convention for the Protection of Human Rights and Fundamental Freedoms of 1950 and the European Social Charter of 1961. In Community law, the basic Treaties themselves contain no specific provisions for the protection of human rights as such. This may perhaps be explained by the essentially economic character of the Communities which makes the possibility of their encroaching upon fundamental human values, such as life, personal liberty, freedom of opinion, speech, conscience, very unlikely. Only in so far as it was thought that in their normal course of business the Communities might interfere with certain basic economic and social interests of the individual, or in order to achieve a Community objective, were safeguards built into the Treaties. Thus, the EEC Treaty provides for a general prohibition of discrimination on grounds of nationality (Art. 7); for the protection of industrial and commercial property (Art. 36); for the protection of existing systems of property ownership (Art. 222); for the protection of business secrets (Art. 214); for the freedom of movement of persons (Arts. 48, 52); for the promotion of improved working conditions, improved standard of living, vocational training, social security, right of association, and collective bargaining (Arts. 117, 118); for the principle of the equality of sexes (equal pay for equal work, Art. 119).

The gap created by the absence of specific human rights provisions in the Treaties became apparent when certain German undertakings challenged Community measures on the ground that they infringed some of the fundamental rights protected by the German Constitution. In dismissing these complaints the ECJ pointed out that it was not the task of the Community institutions, including the Court itself, to ensure respect for rules of national law, including the constitutional provisions on human rights (Case 1/58 *Stork* v. *HA* [1959] ECR 17 at p. 26; Cases 36 to 38 and 40/59 *Geitling* v. *HA* [1960] ECR 423 at p. 438). Subsequently, the Court explained that 'recourse to the legal rules or concepts of national law in order to judge the validity of measures adopted by the institutions of the Community would have an adverse effect on the uniformity and efficacy of Community law. The validity of such measures can only be judged in the light of Community law. In fact, the law stemming from the Treaty, an independent source of law, cannot because of its very nature be overridden by rules of national law, however framed, without being deprived of its character as Community law and without the legal basis of the Community itself being called in question. Therefore the validity of a Community measure or its effect within a Member State cannot be affected by allegations that it runs counter to either fundamental rights as formulated by the constitution of that State or the principles of a national constitutional structure' (Case 11/70 *Internationale Handelsgesellschaft* [1970] ECR 1125 at p. 1134. The Court repeated these principles in subsequent cases, see e.g. Case 44/79 *Hauer* [1979] ECR 3727 at p. 3744; Case 234/85 *Keller* [1986] ECR 2897 at p. 2912).

While this decision was necessary to preserve the unity and supremacy of Community law, it also made it clear that in matters falling within Community competence, individuals were no longer under the protection of the guarantees enshrined in their national Constitutions. In order to fill the gap thus created, the ECJ felt itself obliged to look for 'analogous guarantee[s] inherent in Community law' (Case 11/70 *Internationale Handelsgesellschaft*, above, at p. 1134). In the absence of written provisions, the Court found that 'respect for fundamental rights forms an integral part of the general principles of law protected by the Court of Justice. The protection of such rights, whilst inspired by the constitutional traditions common to the Member States, must be ensured within the framework of the structure and objectives of the Community' (ibid. See also the opinion of A.-G. Dutheillet de Lamothe, ibid. at pp. 1146–7 and Case 29/69 *Stauder* [1969] ECR 419 at p. 425, where the Court first stated that 'fundamental human rights [were] enshrined in the general principles of Community law and protected by the Court'). Subsequently, the Court stated categorically that it 'cannot therefore uphold measures which are incompatible with fundamental rights recognised and protected by the Constitutions of [the Member] States', and added that 'similarly, international treaties for the protection of human rights on which the Member States have collaborated or of which they are signatories, can supply guidelines which should be followed within the framework of

Community law' Case 4/73 *Nold* v. *Commission* [1974] ECR 491 at p. 507; see also Case 44/79 *Hauer*, above, at pp. 3744–5; Cases 41, 121, and 796/79 *Testa* [1980] ECR 1979 at pp. 1996–7; Case 136/79 *National Panasonic* v. *Commission* [1980] ECR 2033 at p. 2057).

Relying on the general principles of law as derived from the Constitutions of the Member States and on relevant international treaties, in particular on the European Convention on Human Rights, the European Social Charter, and certain Conventions of the International Labour Organization, the ECJ has so far recognized that the following specific human rights are protected under Community law:

- the right to property and the freedom to choose and practise a trade or a profession, although subject to such limitations as are justified, in the light of the social function of these rights, by the public interest and by Community objectives provided that the substance of the rights is not affected (Case 4/73 *Nold* v. *Commission*, above, at p. 508; Case 44/79 *Hauer*, above, at pp. 3745–50, relying on and interpreting Art. 1 of the First Protocol to the European Convention on Human Rights and the constitutional rules and practices of the nine Member States, see also the opinion of A.-G. Capotorti, ibid. at pp. 3759–61; Cases 154/78 etc. *Valsabbia* v. *Commission* [1980] ECR 907 at pp. 1010–11; Cases 41, 121, and 796/79 *Testa*, above, at pp. 1997–8; Case 116/82 *Commission* v. *Germany* [1986] ECR 2519 at pp. 2545–6; Case 234/85 *Keller*, above, at p. 2912);
- the right to carry on an economic activity (Case 230/78 *Eridania* [1979] ECR 2749 at p. 2768);
- freedom of trade, although subject to restrictions justified by the general interest and Community objectives, provided that the substance of the right is not impaired (Case 240/83 *ADBHU* [1985] ECR 531 at pp. 548–9);
- the right to an effective judicial remedy before the national courts (Case 222/84 *Johnston* [1986] ECR 1651 at pp. 1681–3; Case 222/86 *UNECTEF* [1987] ECR 4097 at p. 4117; the Court derived this right from the constitutional traditions common to the Member States and from Arts. 6 and 13 of the European Convention on Human Rights and interpreted Art. 6 of Dir. 76/207, on equal treatment for men and women, in its light). In Case 98/79 *Pecastaing* [1980] ECR 691 at p. 718 A.-G. Capotorti expressed the opinion that, in interpreting Arts. 8 and 9 of Dir. 64/221 on movement and residence of foreign nationals, regard must be had to the right to a fair hearing as laid down in Art. 6 of the European Convention. However, the Court held that it was not necessary to refer to Art. 6 (ibid. at p. 716). In Cases 209 to 215 and 218/78 *Van Landewyck* v. *Commission* [1980] ECR 3125 at p. 3248— 'FEDETAB' cases—the Court stated that the requirements of Art. 6 of the European Convention concerning fair hearing did not apply to the Commission since it was not a 'tribunal');
- non-retroactivity of penal provisions (Case 63/83 *Kirk* [1984] ECR

2689 at p. 2718 relying on Art. 7 of the European Convention on Human Rights and on legal principles common to the Member States);

- the right to respect for private and family life, home, and correspondence as referred to in Art. 8(1) of the European Convention on Human Rights but subject to the restrictions laid down in Art. 8(2) (Case 136/79 *National Panasonic* v. *Commission*, above, at pp. 2056–8);

- the principle that Member States may impose on aliens, in the interests of national security or public safety, only such restrictions as are necessary for the protection of those interests 'in a democratic society' (Case 36/75 *Rutili* [1975] ECR 1219 at p. 1232, referring to Arts. 8, 9, 10, and 11 of the European Convention on Human Rights and to Art. 2 of the Fourth Protocol);

- the prohibition of discrimination based on sex as regards working conditions and conditions of employment—the principle of equal treatment (Case 149/77 *Defrenne* [1978] ECR 1365 at p. 1378 relying on the European Social Charter and ILO Convention No. 111. See also Case 20/71 *Sabbatini* v. *Parliament* [1972] ECR 345 at p. 351; Case 32/71 *Bauduin* v. *Commission* [1972] ECR 363 at p. 370; Case 21/74 *Airola* v. *Commission* [1975] ECR 221 at p. 228; Case 222/84 *Johnston*, above, at p. 1660 *per* A.-G. Darmon) and the prohibition of discrimination as regards pay—the principle of equal pay for equal work (Case 43/75 *Defrenne* [1976] ECR 455 at pp. 483 and 490 *per* A.-G. *Trabucchi*. The Court stated that 'the principle of equal pay forms part of the foundations of the Community' but did not refer to it as a fundamental human right, ibid. at p. 472);

- freedom of religion (Case 130/75 *Prais* v. *Council* [1976] ECR 1589 at pp. 1598–9);

- freedom of trade union activity including the right to form and join staff associations (Case 175/73 *Union Syndicale* v. *Council* [1974] ECR 917 at p. 925; Case 18/74 *Syndicat Général du Personnel* v. *Commission* [1974] ECR 933 at p. 944);

- the right to free elections to staff representative bodies (Case 54/75 *De Dapper* v. *Parliament* [1976] ECR 1381 at p. 1389).

The case-law of the ECJ has also been endorsed by the three political institutions. In a Joint Declaration of 5 April 1977, the European Parliament, the Council, and the Commission stressed the 'prime importance' which they attached to the protection of fundamental rights, 'as derived in particular from the constitutions of the Member States and the European Convention for the Protection of Human Rights and Fundamental Freedoms', and declared that in the exercise of their powers they would respect these rights (*OJ* 1977 C103/1). The importance of this statement is, first, that it specifically singled out the European Convention as one of the 'international treaties' on which the Court might rely (pointing out that all the Member States were contracting parties to the Convention) and, secondly, that it gave explicit support to the Court in the matter of protecting human rights, on which the Court has from time to time relied (see e.g. Case 44/79 *Hauer*, above, at p. 3745; Case 222/84 *Johnston*, above, at p. 1682).

Nevertheless, the fact that in the absence of written rules the protection of fundamental rights is based on extraneous, i.e. non-Community, sources has created certain problems which have not yet been fully resolved. In the first place, the question has arisen whether, in order that the Court may protect a particular right, it is necessary for that right to be enshrined in the Constitutions of *all* the Member States, or whether it is sufficient if it is guaranteed by *any one* of them. In Case 7/76 *IRCA* [1976] ECR 1213 at p. 1237 A.-G. Warner expressed the opinion that 'a fundamental right recognised and protected by the Constitution of any Member State must be recognised and protected also in Community law'. The reason was that no Member State could be presumed to have transferred to the Community the power to legislate in infringement of the basic rights protected by its own Constitution. While this view, which is often referred to as the 'maximum' theory (as it affords the maximum protection to fundamental rights), is strongly supported in academic writing, it has not been expressly accepted by the ECJ so far. On the contrary, in all the relevant cases the Court has consistently referred to the constitutional traditions, concepts, ideas, or precepts '*common* to the Member States' and to fundamental rights recognized and protected 'by the Constitutions of *those* States' (see in particular the *Internationale Handelsgesellschaft*, *Nold*, *Hauer*, *Testa*, and *National Panasonic* cases discussed above). In dealing with the right to property, in particular, the Court expressly mentioned 'the constitutional rules and practices of the nine Member States' (Case 44/79 *Hauer*, above, at p. 3746). This is in contrast with the approach which the Court adopts when recognizing other 'general principles of law' as part of Community law even if they have not been generally accepted in *all* the Member States.

A second question concerns the precise status of the European Convention on Human Rights in Community law. In several cases, the Commission put forward the argument that following its ratification by all the Member States, the Convention became an 'integral part' of Community law and was legally binding upon the Community. It applied both to measures adopted by the Community institutions and to actions of the Member States and their authorities in the field of Community law (see Case 48/75 *Royer* [1976] ECR 497 at pp. 506–7; Case 118/75 *Watson and Belmann* [1976] ECR 1185 at p. 1194). By contrast, A.-G. Mayras considered that the Convention could not be regarded as a Community instrument producing direct effect which had to be ensured by the national courts, athough it could be relied on to confirm a conclusion arrived at on the basis of Community law (Case 48/75 *Royer*, above, at p. 525). A.-G. Trabucchi was of the opinion that while the Convention was not incorporated as such in the Community legal order, it could be used to establish principles which were common to the Member States themselves. The protection of fundamental rights formed part of Community law and their infringement by the Member States (and not only by the institutions) could be raised before the ECJ at least to the extent to which it involved a right or freedom accorded to individuals by Community law (Case 118/75 *Watson and Belmann*, above, at pp. 1207–8. In neither case did the Court itself refer to the Convention).

While the view that the European Convention is binding on the Community has received strong support in academic writing (mainly on the ground that the Community, having acquired legislative and executive powers, has been substituted for the Member States), it has never been expressly endorsed by the ECJ. In the earlier cases, the Court only stated that international treaties on human rights could supply 'guidelines which should be followed within the framework of Community law' (see in particular the *Nold* and *Hauer* cases discussed above). Although in subsequent cases the Court has not used the word 'guidelines' (see the *Testa* and *National Panasonic* cases above), it has so far been unwilling to go any further than the statement that 'the principles on which [the European] Convention is based must be taken into consideration in Community law' (Case 222/84 *Johnston*, above, at p. 1682). On the other hand, the Court has clearly recognized that those principles may be resorted to not only in reviewing the legality of the acts of the Community institutions but also in assessing the compatibility with Community law of the conduct of the Member States in matters falling within Community competence (ibid.; see also Case 36/75 *Rutili*, above, at p. 1232). Neverthe-less, the Court has stated that it has no power to examine the compatibility with the European Convention of national legislation which concerns an area which is within the jurisdiction of the national legislator and falls outside the scope of Community law (Cases 60 and 61/84 *Cinéthèque* [1985] ECR 2605 at p. 2627; Case 12/86 *Demirel* [1987] ECR 3719 at p. 3754).

Since the principles underlying the European Convention have been recog-nized by all the Member States collectively (as they have all adhered to the Convention), it would seem that any particular right or freedom covered by those principles must be protected in Community law irrespective of the question whether it is, in addition, also protected by the Constitution of each Member State individually. Moreover, since the Convention represents a 'common denominator', a common standard of protection acceptable to all the Member States, this standard should be applied also to the Community irrespective of whether or not the Convention is formally binding on it. On the other hand, it is still not clear whether in applying the 'principles' and 'standards' of the Convention the ECJ is bound by the interpretations given to those principles and standards by the Convention organs, and in particular by the European Court of Human Rights. Quite apart from the difficult question of the relationship between the two Courts, each being the highest judicial body within its own field, problems are likely to arise whatever solution is finally adopted. Situations are conceivable in which the ECJ may have to 'reinterpret' human rights standards so as to suit the particular needs and requirements of the Community, but this may lead to discrepancies in the application of—ultimately—one and the same instrument (see e.g. Case 44/79 *Hauer*, above, at p. 3746 where the ECJ found that the text of Art. 1 of the First Protocol dealing with the right to property did not enable 'a sufficiently precise answer' to be given to the question raised in the particular case—i.e. whether a temporary prohibition on the new planting of vines was contrary to the right to property—and went on to interpret that Article in the light of the 'indications' provided by the constitutional rules and practices of the nine

Member States, rather than in the light of the case-law of the Convention organs. A.-G. Capotorti did refer briefly to the case-law of the Human Rights Commission but pointed out that it was at the time undergoing a significant change, ibid. at p. 3761).

As regards the future of the protection of human rights in Community law, it seems that the following three options are open:

- first, the formal accession of the Communities to the European Convention on Human Rights;
- secondly, the drawing up of a special Community catalogue of human rights adapted to the needs and requirements of the Communities;
- thirdly, leaving it to the ECJ to continue to guarantee the maximum level of protection within the existing institutional and legal frameworks.

Initially, the Commission was of the opinion that the existing standard of protection was satisfactory. Since in its view the Communities were—on the basis of the principle of substitution—already obliged to observe the rights and freedoms embodied in the European Convention, there was no need for them formally to become parties to the Convention (Report of 4 Feb. 1976, Suppl. 5/76—*Bull. EC*, pp. 14, 16–17; 10th *Gen. Rep. EC* (1976), pp. 288–9; 11th *Gen. Rep. EC* (1977), p. 280). Only in the context of the planned European Union did the Commission consider the incorporation of a codified catalogue of specific human rights in a future European Constitution to be a desirable, if not essential, objective (ibid.; see also the Report on European Union, Suppl. 5/75—*Bull. EC*, p. 26).

Later, however, the Commission examined more closely the disadvantages which arose from the lack of a written catalogue of human rights both for the image of the Communities in general and for the protection of the rights of the citizen in particular. It pointed out that by their very nature the Court's decisions could only operate *ex post facto* and could not therefore fully satisfy the requirement of legal certainty and the citizen's 'undeniable and legitimate demand: to see his rights established in advance' (*Bull. EC* 4–1979, p. 16; Memorandum of 4 Apr. 1979, Suppl. 2/79—*Bull. EC*, esp. at pp. 6–8). While recognizing that the ideal solution would be to supplement the Treaties with a catalogue of fundamental rights specially tailored to the needs of the Communities, the Commission realized that because of the conflicting opinions of the Member States, in particular on the precise definition of economic and social rights, this goal could not be attained in the short or medium term. For these reasons, the Commission recommended the formal accession of the Communities to the European Convention. The decisive factor was that the Convention and the case-law of the ECJ essentially had the same aim, namely, 'the protection of a heritage of fundamental and human rights considered inalienable by those European States organised on a democratic basis. The protection of this Western European heritage should ultimately be uniform and accordingly assigned, as regards the Community also, to those bodies set up specifically for this purpose' (Memorandum of 4 Apr. 1979, ibid. at p. 8). Nevertheless, the eventual accession to the Convention would not form an obstacle to the preparation of a special

290

Community catalogue in due course, nor would it prevent the ECJ from further developing its case-law on the subject (ibid. For detailed arguments both in favour of and against accession as well as for the institutional and technical aspects of accession, see ibid. at pp. 11 *et seq.* See also 13th *Gen. Rep. EC* (1979), p. 276).

For its part, the European Parliament first suggested an agreement between the Member States declaring the European Convention on Human Rights, the International Covenant on Civil and Political Rights, and the civil and political rights provided for in the Constitutions and laws of the Member States to be 'integral parts' of the Treaties establishing the Communities (Res. of 16 Nov. 1977, *OJ* 1977 C299/26). Subsequently, it declared itself entirely in favour of the accession of the Communities to the European Convention and called on the Council and Commission to make immediate preparations therefor (Res. of 27 Apr. 1979, *OJ* 1979 C127/69; Res. of 29 Oct. 1982, *OJ* 1982 C304/253).

In spite of an auspicious start, it seems that—owing to the reluctance or even outright opposition of some Member States—no final decision has ever been taken, one way or another, in the matter of accession (for initial difficulties following the Commission's Memorandum of 4 Apr. 1979, see 14th *Gen. Rep. EC* (1980), p. 304). Nor has a special Community catalogue of human rights ever been adopted. Instead, the various institutions have made a number of statements and declarations affirming their intention to protect and promote fundamental human rights within the Community. Of these, the following may be mentioned:

- Copenhagen Declaration on Democracy of 8 April 1978 adopted by the European Council, *inter alia* approving the Joint Declaration of 5 April 1977 (*Bull. EC* 3–1978, p. 5);
- Declaration against Racism and Xenophobia of 11 June 1986 adopted by the European Parliament, the Council, the Representatives of the Member States meeting within the Council, and the Commission (*OJ* 1986 C158/1) and approved by the European Parliament (Res. of 11 June 1986, *OJ* 1986 C176/63);
- Statement on Human Rights of 21 July 1986 adopted by the Foreign Ministers meeting in Political Co-operation (*Bull. EC* 7/8–1986, p. 100);
- Declaration of Fundamental Rights and Freedoms adopted by the European Parliament (Res. of 12 Apr. 1989, *OJ* 1989 C120/51).

However, the only legally binding instrument so far which mentions human rights is the Single European Act of 1986, the Preamble of which refers to the Member States' determination to promote democracy on the basis of the fundamental rights 'recognised in the Constitutions and laws of the Member States, in the Convention for the Protection of Human Rights and Fundamental Freedoms and the European Social Charter' (Suppl. 2/86—*Bull. EC*, p. 5; *OJ* 1987 L169/2).

Finally, the institutions have on several occasions made it clear that they are concerned with the promotion and protection of human rights not only within the Communities but also in non-member countries, particularly those with which the Communities have established relations. Thus, the Statement on Human Rights of 21 July 1986 (above) expressly declares that 'The Twelve seek universal observance of human rights' and that 'Respect for human rights is an important element in relations between third countries and the Europe of the Twelve'. Accordingly, the Foreign Ministers affirmed that 'in the development of their relations with non-Member States as well as in the administration of aid the European Community and its Member States will continue to promote fundamental rights' (*Bull. EC* 7/8–1986, pp. 100, 101. See also the fifth paragraph of the Preamble to the Single European Act and 20th *Gen. Rep. EC* (1986), pp. 369–72; 21st *Gen. Rep. EC* (1987), pp. 352–5; Res. of 12 Mar. 1987 of the European Parliament on human rights in the world and Community policy on human rights, *OJ* 1987 C99/157 and the documents referred to therein; 22nd *Gen. Rep. EC* (1988), p. 419; 23rd *Gen. Rep. EC* (1989), p. 398). Perhaps the most important example of this determination is the Third Lomé Convention of 1984 which, for the first time, established a link between development work and the promotion of human dignity by incorporating specific references to, and provisions for, the protection of human rights in the context of the ACP–EEC relations (see in particular the Preamble to and Art. 4 of the Convention, and Annex I to the Final Act containing a Joint Declaration on Art. 4). The new (Fourth) Lomé Convention, signed on 15 December 1989, also contains provisions dealing specifically with human rights and the rights of peoples, whereby the contracting states reaffirm their deep attachment to human dignity and human rights, as being a legitimate aspiration for individuals and peoples. The provisions cover non-discriminatory treatment, fundamental personal rights, civil and political rights, and also economic, social, and cultural rights (see 23rd *Gen. Rep. EC* (1989), pp. 400–1). Similarly, the Commission is intent on promoting the cause of human rights in developing countries which are not parties to the Lomé Convention (see 20th *Gen. Rep. EC* (1986), pp. 371–2).

See also **Effective judicial control, Equality, Equal pay*, Equal treatment*, European Union, General principles of law, Retroactive effect, Single European Act.**

Further reading 1. BOOKS: Betten, *The Right to Strike in Community Law: The Incorporation of Fundamental Rights in the Legal Order of the European Communities* (1985). *See also under* **General principles of law.**

2. ARTICLES, PAPERS, AND REPORTS: Addo, 'Some Issues in European Community Aid Policy and Human Rights' (1988/1) *LIEI* 55; Alkema, 'The EC and the European Convention of Human Rights: Immunity and Impunity for the Community?' (1979) 16 *CML Rev.* 501; Bridge, 'Fundamental Rights in the European Economic Community', in Bridge *et al.* (eds.), *Fundamental Rights* (1973), p. 291; Churchill and Foster, 'Double Standards in Human Rights? The Treatment of Spanish Fishermen by the European Community' (1987) 12 *EL Rev.* 430; Dauses, 'The Protection of Fundamental Rights in the Community Legal Order' (1985) 10 *EL Rev.* 398; Drzemczewski, 'Fundamental Rights and the European Communities: Recent Developments' (1977) 2 *Human R. Rev.* 69; id., 'The Domestic Application of the European Human Rights Convention as European Community Law' (1981) 30 *ICLQ*

118; Economides and Weiler, 'Accession of the Communities to the European Convention on Human Rights: Commission Memorandum' (1979) 42 *MLR* 683; Edeson and Wooldridge, 'European Community Law and Fundamental Human Rights: Some Recent Decisions of the European Court and of National Courts' (1976/1) *LIEI* 1; Editorial (concerning EP Declaration of 12 Apr. 1989), (1989) 26 *CML Rev.* 589; FIDE, 'The Individual and European Law', *Reports of the Seventh FIDE Congress* (1975); Finnie, 'The Location of Fundamental Rights in the Community Treaty Structure' (1982/1) *LIEI* 89; Forman, 'The Joint Declaration on Fundamental Rights' (1977) 2 *EL Rev.* 210; Foster, 'The European Court of Justice and the European Convention for the Protection of Human Rights' (1987) 8 *HRLJ* 245; Ghandi, 'Interaction between the Protection of Fundamental Rights in the European Economic Community and under the European Convention on Human Rights' (1981/2) *LIEI* 1; Hilf, 'The Protection of Fundamental Rights in the Community', in Jacobs (ed.), *European Law and the Individual* (1976), p. 145; McBride and Brown, 'The United Kingdom, the European Community and the European Convention on Human Rights' (1981) 1 *YEL* 167; Mendelson, 'The European Court of Justice and Human Rights' (1981) 1 *YEL* 125; id., 'The Impact of European Community Law on the Implementation of the European Convention on Human Rights' (1983) 3 *YEL* 99; Pescatore, 'Fundamental Rights and Freedoms in the System of the European Communities' (1970) 18 *AJCL* 343; id., 'The Protection of Human Rights in the European Communities' (1972) 9 *CML Rev.* 73; id., 'The Context and Significance of Fundamental Rights in the Law of the European Communities' (1981) 2 *HRLJ* 295; Rinck, 'Civil Liberties and the Common Market: A Study in Comparative Economic Law' (1976) *Juridical Rev.* 249; Schermers, 'The Communities under the European Convention on Human Rights' (1978/1) *LIEI* 1; Scheuner, 'Fundamental Rights in European Community Law and in National Constitutional Law' (1975) 12 *CML Rev.* 171; Schwarze, 'The Administrative Law of the Community and the Protection of Human Rights' (1986) 23 *CML Rev.* 401; Toth, 'The Individual and European Law' (1975) 24 *ICLQ* 659; id., 'Human Rights in a Changing World' (1986) 31 *J. of the Law Soc. of Scotland* 385 and 444; Weiler, 'Eurocracy and Distrust: Some Questions Concerning the Role of the European Court of Justice in the Protection of Fundamental Human Rights within the Legal Order of the European Communities' (1986) 61 *Washington Law Rev.* 1103; Zuleeg, 'Fundamental Rights and the Law of the European Communities' (1971) 8 *CML Rev.* 446.

3. OFFICIAL PUBLICATIONS: House of Lords, Select Committee on the European Communities, Session 1979–80, 71st Report, 'Human Rights' (1980); 'Report on European Union' submitted by the Commission on 26 June 1975, Suppl. *5/75—Bull. EC*; 'The Protection of Fundamental Rights in the European Community', Report of the Commission of 4 Feb. 1976, Suppl. *5/76—Bull. EC*; 'Accession of the Communities to the European Convention on Human Rights', Memorandum adopted by the Commission on 4 Apr. 1979, Suppl. *2/79—Bull. EC*.

▶ **IMPLIED POWERS (DOCTRINE OF)** Doctrine according to which every treaty or piece of legislation must be interpreted as providing, if not expressly then by implication, all the powers which are necessary for its effective application and for the attainment of its objectives.

In the context of Community law, the doctrine of implied powers has only a limited application owing to the fact that most of the powers necessary for the attainment of the Communities' objectives are either expressly provided for in the Treaties or may be derived from the general authorization to legislate contained in Arts. 95(1) ECSC, 235 EEC, 203 Euratom (*see further under* **Supplementary powers**). Nevertheless, in a few cases the ECJ has specifically endorsed the use of, or has itself relied on, implied powers. Thus, in interpreting the power of the High Authority (Commission) to fix the prices of Belgian coal under Art. 26 of the Convention on the Transitional Provisions annexed to the ECSC Treaty, the Court considered that it was possible to apply 'a rule of interpretation generally accepted in both international and national law, according to which the rules laid down by an international treaty or a law presuppose the rules without which that treaty or law would have no meaning or could not be reasonably and usefully applied'. Furthermore, the Court pointed out, under Art. 8 ECSC it was the duty of the High Authority to ensure that the objectives set out in the Treaty were attained in accordance with the provisions thereof. The Court concluded from this that it had to be assumed that the High Authority enjoyed the powers which were necessary for the attainment of the objectives of the provision in question, including the power to fix prices, even if such power was not expressly provided for (Case 8/55 *Fédération Charbonnière de Belgique* v. *HA* [1956] ECR 245 at pp. 299–300. See also Case 20/59 *Italy* v. *HA* [1960] ECR 325 at p. 336). Nevertheless, in the latter case, the Court also pointed out that powers could not be implied where it could not be shown that the Member States had, expressly or by implication, renounced competence in favour of the Communities (ibid. at p. 338).

In the context of the EEC Treaty, following the opinion of A.-G. Trabucchi, the Court accepted that the power of administering the Customs Union conferred by the Treaty on the institutions had to be widely interpreted and that it included by necessary implication the power to enact the rules which were necessary for the proper functioning of the Customs Union. Nevertheless, the Court saw no reason why the Council could not legitimately adopt Reg. 803/68 on the valuation of goods for customs purposes, an essential instrument of the Customs Union, on the basis of the general authorization contained in Art. 235, having regard to the interest of legal certainty (Case 8/73 *Massey-Ferguson* [1973] ECR 897 at p. 908 *per Curiam*, p. 913 *per* A.-G. Trabucchi). Subsequently, the Court confirmed that although neither Art. 28 nor Art. 113 EEC explicitly conferred on the Council the competence to establish a tariff nomenclature, an instrument which was indispensable for the functioning of the Customs Union, those two provisions taken together did provide, by necessary implication, the requisite legal basis for the Council to adopt such a nomenclature and to conclude an international convention for that purpose (i.e. the International Convention on the Harmonised Commodity Description and Coding System of 1983, replacing the Convention on Nomenclature of 1950). However, the Court added that the Council was not justified in relying, in addition to those two Articles, also on Art. 235 (Case 165/87 *Commission* v. *Council* [1988] ECR paras. 7–13, 18).

In the field of conjunctural policy, the Court held that the power conferred by Art. 103(2) EEC on the Council to decide upon 'the measures appropriate to the situation' included the power necessary to adopt, in principle, 'any conjunctural measures which may appear to be needed in order to safeguard the objectives of the Treaty. Without some such faculty, the natural concomitant of any kind of economic administration, the institutions of the Community would find it impossible to accomplish the tasks entrusted to them in this field' (Case 5/73 *Balkan-Import-Export* [1973] ECR 1091 at p. 1109). More recently, in dealing with the question whether Art. 118(2) EEC gave the Commission the power to adopt a binding decision with a view to 'arranging consultations' in the social field, the Court emphasized that 'where an article of the EEC Treaty—in this case Article 118—confers a specific task on the Commission it must be accepted, if that provision is not to be rendered wholly ineffective, that it confers on the Commission necessarily and *per se* the powers which are indispensable in order to carry out that task. Accordingly, the second paragraph of Article 118 must be interpreted as conferring on the Commission all the powers which are necessary in order to arrange the consultations' (Cases 281/85 etc. *Germany and Others* v. *Commission* [1987] ECR 3203 at p. 3253). Finally, in the field of external relations, in a series of cases the Court has stated that the Community's authority to enter into international agreements arises 'not only from an express conferment by the Treaty, but may equally flow implicitly from other provisions of the Treaty, from the Act of Accession and from measures adopted, within the framework of those provisions, by the Community institutions' (Cases 3, 4, and 6/76 *Kramer* [1976] ECR 1279 at p. 1308; see also Case 22/70 *Commission* v. *Council* [1971] ECR 263 at p. 274—'ERTA' case; Opinion 1/76 *Laying-up Fund* [1977] ECR 741 at p. 755. *See further under* **Treaty-making power**).

See also **Council, Supplementary powers, Treaty-making power.**

▶ **INDIVIDUAL CONCERN** One of two prerequisites (the other being direct concern) for the institution of annulment proceedings before the ECJ by a private individual (a natural or legal person) under the EEC/Euratom Treaties against a decision or other binding measure which is addressed to another person or taken in the form of a regulation (Arts. 173(2) EEC, 146(2) Euratom). In challenging such a measure, a private individual has *locus standi* only if he can prove that the measure is of 'direct and individual concern' to him.

According to the ECJ, 'persons other than those to whom a decision is addressed may only claim to be individually concerned if that decision affects them by reason of certain attributes which are peculiar to them or by reason of circumstances in which they are differentiated from all other persons and by virtue of these factors distinguishes them individually just as in the case of the person addressed' (Case 25/62 *Plaumann* v. *Commission* [1963] ECR 95 at p. 107. This definition has been repeated by the Court in a number of subsequent cases, some of which are cited below). In the *Plaumann* case the Court held that the applicant, a German importer of southern fruits, was not individually concerned by a Commission decision addressed to the German Government refusing to authorize it to lower the customs duty on imported clementines. The Court stated the reasons thus: 'In the present case the applicant is affected by the disputed Decision as an importer of clementines, that is to say, by reason of a commercial activity which may at any time be practised by any person and is not therefore such as to distinguish the applicant in relation to the contested Decision as in the case of the addressee' (ibid.).

It follows from the above definition that where a measure is intended to apply to a commercial activity or to affect a whole category of commercial operators defined in general and abstract terms, the fact that a person carries out that activity or belongs to that category is not sufficient to make him individually concerned. Even the fact that a single person alone happens to be in that position in a Member State at any given time subsequent to the adoption of the measure is not such as to distinguish him individually as long as it remains at least theoretically possible for others to join the class of persons affected. Thus, for example, in Case 1/64 *Glucoseries Réunies* v. *Commission* [1964] ECR 413 at p. 417 the Court held that the applicant, a Belgian firm producing glucose, was not individually concerned by a Commission decision authorizing France to levy countervailing charges on the importation of glucose because the decision affected imports from the whole Community in general, except Italy. This was so in spite of the fact that the applicant was the only Belgian undertaking willing and able to export glucose from Belgium to France during the period of validity of the decision. In Case 38/64 *Getreide-Import* v. *Commission* [1965] ECR 203 at p. 208 the Court held that the purely fortuitous fact that the applicant, a German importer of cereals, was the only firm to apply for an import licence *subsequent to* the adoption of the contested Commission decision fixing the c.i.f. prices for certain cereals was not sufficient to differentiate it from the other importers and to distinguish it individually as required by Art. 173(2) EEC. In Case 40/64 *Sgarlata* v. *Commission* [1965] ECR 215 at p. 227 the Court held that Commission regulations fixing reference prices for certain fruits affected the import trade in general and did not therefore individually concern the applicants, Italian producers of citrus fruit. As the ECJ has stated in Case 123/77 *UNICME* v. *Council* [1978] ECR 845 at p. 852, 'the possibility of determining more or less precisely the number or even the identity of the persons to whom a measure applies by no means implies that it must be regarded as being of individual concern to them'. Moreover, a professional association or organization (including trade unions), formed for the protection of the collective interests of a category of persons and acting in its capacity as the representative of its members, cannot be considered as being individually concerned by a measure affecting the general interests of that category (Cases

16 and 17/62 *Producteurs de Fruits* v. *Council* [1962] ECR 471 at pp. 479–80; Case 72/74 *Union Syndicale* v. *Council* [1975] ECR 401 at pp. 409–10; Case 117/86 *UFADE* v. *Council and Commission* [1986] ECR 3255 at p. 3260).

It follows from the ECJ's restrictive interpretation that a measure is of individual concern to an applicant only if the class of persons whom it may affect is closed on the date of its adoption and if the applicant belongs to that class. The class is closed if the number and identity of its members is in one way or another unalterably fixed and therefore ascertainable at the time when the measure is taken. The author of the measure is then in a position to know whose interests and position the measure will exclusively affect. Only in such circumstances are these persons differentiated from all other persons and singled out just as if they were the addressees. If this condition is satisfied, the small or large number of those affected or the territorial scope of application of the measure (i.e. whether it applies in one, some, or all the Member States) is of no relevance. Nor is it important whether or not the author of the measure actually knows the identity of those concerned.

The circumstance that is capable of so individualizing a person is usually a past act on his part, that is to say, an act preceding in time the adoption of the measure. Such an act may be, for example, the submission of an application for an import or export licence in situations where the measure applies exclusively to those who had submitted such applications during a certain period of time prior to its adoption. Thus, for example, in Cases 106 and 107/63 *Toepfer* v. *Commission* [1965] ECR 405 at pp. 411–12 a Commission decision retroactively authorizing Germany to retain certain protective measures concerning the importation of maize could only affect those importers who had applied for an import licence during the course of a particular day *prior to* the adoption of the decision. The number and identity of those importers had therefore become fixed and ascertainable before the decision was made. The Court held that the fact that the applicants in the case were amongst those importers who had applied for a licence differentiated them from all other persons and distinguished them individually as required by Art. 173(2) EEC. (Compare this case with Case 38/64 *Getreide-Import* v. *Commission*, above, where the applicants applied for an import licence *subsequent to* the adoption of the contested decision.) In Cases 41 to 44/70 *International Fruit Company* v. *Commission* [1971] ECR 411 at pp. 421–2 the contested regulation whereby the Commission refused to grant the applicants licences to import dessert apples from third countries applied only to the quantities of apples for which applications for import licences had been made during the course of a particular week prior to the adoption of the regulation. Thus, when the regulation was made the number of applications which could be affected by it was fixed. No new applications could be added. The Court held that the regulation was of individual concern to the applicants and that it was, in fact, a 'conglomeration of individual decisions' taken in the form of a regulation. In Case 100/74 *CAM* v. *Commission* [1975] ECR 1393 at pp. 1402–3 the circumstance that distinguished the applicants individually was the fact that they had applied for advance fixing of the export refund

297

during a particular period prior to the adoption of the contested regulation. They were therefore individually concerned by it. In Case 62/70 *Bock* v. *Commission* [1971] ECR 897 at p. 908 the applicant, a German importer, challenged a Commission decision authorizing Germany to exclude from Community treatment mushrooms originating in China and already in free circulation in the Benelux countries. However, he challenged the decision only 'to the extent to which it also covers imports for which applications for import licences were already pending at the date of its entry into force'. Since he had an application pending at that date, he was individually concerned by the decision. In Case 11/82 *Piraiki-Patraiki* v. *Commission* [1985] ECR 207 at pp. 242–6 the Court held that a Commission decision authorizing France to impose a quota system on imports of cotton yarn from Greece was of individual concern to those Greek undertakings which could show that before the date of the decision they had entered into contracts with French customers for the delivery of cotton yarn from Greece during the period of application of that decision. These undertakings were thus members of a limited class of traders identified or identifiable by the Commission and were, by reason of those contracts, particularly affected by the decision at issue which prevented the execution of their contracts.

The strict interpretation of the concept of individual concern, which implies a retrospective aspect, has to some extent been relaxed in the more recent case-law of the ECJ in respect of certain situations and certain categories of cases. Thus, in Case 294/83 *Les Verts* v. *Parliament* [1986] ECR 1339 at pp. 1368–9 the Court expressly refused to apply, at least in the unusual circumstances of that case, the traditional test according to which only persons who were 'identifiable at the date of the adoption of the contested measure are individually concerned by it'. The case concerned certain decisions of organs of the European Parliament granting aid to rival political groupings in connection with the 1984 European elections. Some of these groupings were, while others were not, represented in the organs which adopted the decisions. In these circumstances, the Court held, the traditional interpretation of the concept of individual concern, which would restrict the right of action to groupings which were represented and therefore identifiable, would give rise to inequality in the protection afforded by the Court. The fact that the applicant association was *in existence* at the time when the contested decisions were adopted, and was able to present candidates at the 1984 elections, was sufficient to establish its individual concern. Moreover, in a series of cases the Court has held that a measure is of individual concern to persons who are identified by name in the measure itself, even if the measure is a regulation (see Case 113/77 *Toyo Bearing* v. *Council* [1979] ECR 1185 at p. 1205; Case 138/79 *Roquette* v. *Council* [1980] ECR 3333 at p. 3356; Cases 239 and 275/82 *Allied Corporation* v. *Commission* [1984] ECR 1005 at p. 1030; Cases 87/77 etc. *Salerno* v. *Commission and Council* [1985] ECR 2523 at p. 2535; etc.).

The most important relaxation of the requirement of individual concern has, however, occurred in certain specific types of cases, such as competition, State aid, anti-subsidy, and anti-dumping proceedings. In these proceedings, the Court's overriding consideration seems to be to afford effective procedural guarantees and legal protection to all applicants who can establish a sufficiently important legitimate interest deserving such protection. Thus, in a series of cases the Court has recognized that a decision or a regulation may be of individual concern to an undertaking simply because that undertaking has played a certain part in the administrative proceedings leading to its adoption. In particular, the Court has accepted as evidence of individual concern the fact that the undertaking was at the origin of the complaint which led to the opening of the investigation procedure, the fact that its views were heard during that procedure, and the fact that the conduct of the procedure was largely determined by its observations. These circumstances were sufficient to differentiate that undertaking from all other persons in the sense of the *Plaumann* decision (see above). Thus, undertakings have been allowed to challenge measures not addressed to them but adversely affecting their legitimate interests by granting advantages to their competitors and thereby seriously jeopardizing their position on the market in question (see in particular Case 169/84 *COFAZ* v. *Commission* [1986] ECR 391 at pp. 414–16, which concerned State aid proceedings initiated under Art. 93(2), and the cases cited therein. See also Cases 228 and 229/82 *Ford* v. *Commission* [1984] ECR 1129 at p. 1159).

(For comprehensive lists of cases in which the ECJ has so far established the existence of individual concern, *see* **Action for annulment**.)

See also **Action for annulment, Direct concern.**

Further reading: Barav, 'Direct and Individual Concern: An Almost Insurmountable Barrier to the Admissibility of Individual Appeal to the EEC Court' (1974) 11 *CML Rev.* 191. *See also under* **Action for annulment.**

▶ **INDIVIDUAL DECISION** One of two types of decision (the other being general decision) that the Commission may adopt under the ECSC Treaty. The Treaty makes a distinction between these two types of decision, without further defining them, in the context of the rules relating to their notification/publication (Art. 15 ECSC) and in defining the right of undertakings and associations to bring an action for their annulment before the ECJ (Art. 33 ECSC). In the latter context the ECJ has held that the individual or general character of a decision results directly from the contents and not from the form of the decision, and that it must be determined by objective criteria. Thus, an individual decision may be defined as 'a decision which may be directly applied to individual undertakings described by name or ascertainable from the decision, the basis of which is a specific concrete situation existing in the case of these undertakings . . . The undertakings concerned have a direct and specific interest in the legality of such a decision even if the decision is formally directed to another addressee' (Cases 7 and 9/54 *Industries Sidérurgiques Luxembourgeoises* v. *HA* [1956] ECR 175 at p. 214 *per* A.-G. Roemer). A decision is individual if 'its provisions are likely to affect directly and individually the situation of the persons to whom they apply' (Cases 55 to 59/63 etc. *Modena* v. *HA* [1964] ECR 211 at p. 228). For the purposes of Art.

299

Infringement of an essential procedural requirement

33 ECSC, it is not necessary that a decision should be an individual one in relation to the applicant. Once a decision is individual in character in relation to any person (who may be the applicant, or another undertaking, or even a Member State), it is necessarily individual as regards all. It cannot, therefore, at the same time be considered to be a general decision with regard to third parties (Cases 7 and 9/54 *Industries Sidérurgiques Luxembourgeoises* v. *HA*, above, at p. 192 *per Curiam*; Case 18/57 *Nold* v. *HA* [1959] ECR 41 at p. 50). Thus, even a camouflaged individual decision, i.e. one taken under the external appearance of a general decision, remains an individual one, since its nature depends on its scope rather than on its form (Case 8/55 *Fédération Charbonnière de Belgique* v. *HA* [1956] ECR 245 at p. 257). An individual decision under the ECSC Treaty is, accordingly, comparable to a decision under the EEC/Euratom Treaties.

The significance of the distinction between individual and general decisions is twofold. First, where a decision is individual in character, undertakings and associations may challenge it before the ECJ on any or all of the four grounds of action, provided also that it 'concerns' the applicant, i.e. directly affects its position and interests (ibid. at pp. 258–9; Case 18/57 *Nold* v. *HA*, above, at p. 51; Case 30/59 *Steenkolenmijnen* v. *HA* [1961] ECR 1 at pp. 16–17; Art. 33 ECSC). Secondly, an individual decision becomes binding upon being notified to the party concerned (Art. 15 ECSC).

See also **Action for annulment, Decision, General decision, Notification.**

▶ **INFRINGEMENT OF AN ESSENTIAL PROCEDURAL REQUIREMENT**
One of four grounds of action on which binding acts of the Council, the Commission, and the European Parliament may be challenged before, and declared void by, the ECJ in the framework of annulment proceedings (Arts. 33 and 38 ECSC, 173 EEC, 146 Euratom).

This ground of action gives effect to the general requirement that, in the preparation, adoption, presentation, and communication of their acts, the Community institutions must observe certain basic rules relating to form and procedure laid down by Community law. The main purpose of these rules is to ensure that the measures of the institutions are taken 'with all due care and prudence' (Case 6/54 *Netherlands* v. *HA* [1955] ECR 103 at p. 112) and to enable all those concerned, whether Member States, other institutions, or private individuals, to identify these measures from their very form and by objective criteria (see e.g. Cases 23, 24, and 52/63 *Usines Henricot* v. *HA* [1963] ECR 217 at pp. 223–4). Infringement of these requirements may lead to the annulment of the measure by the ECJ. As this ground of action involves public interest, the Court may examine it of its own motion (see e.g. Case 6/54 *Netherlands* v. *HA*, above; Case 18/57 *Nold* v. *HA* [1959] ECR 41 at p. 52).

In order to have an effect on the validity of a measure, the infringement must be of an 'essential' procedural requirement (Cases 23, 24, and 52/63 *Usines Henricot* v. *HA*, above, at p. 223; Cases 275/80 and 24/81 *Krupp* v. *Commission* [1981] ECR 2489 at pp. 2511–12). To determine what constitutes such an infringement, A.-G. Warner put forward the following test in

Case 30/78 *Distillers Company* v. *Commission* [1980] ECR 2229 at p. 2290:
'In Community law a person challenging the validity of an administrative
decision cannot rely on an irregularity in the procedure leading to that
decision unless he can show at least a possibility that, but for the irregularity,
the decision would have been different'. The Court adopted and applied
this test in the case (at pp. 2264–5), and subsequently in Cases 209 to
215 and 218/78 *Van Landewyck* v. *Commission* [1980] ECR 3125 at
p. 3239—'FEDETAB' cases (see below).

Generally speaking, procedural requirements whose infringement usually
constitutes a ground of action may be divided into three categories, i.e. those
relating to the (1) preparation, (2) form, and (3) communication of a
measure. These are considered below in turn.

1. As regards the preparation and adoption of a measure, the ECJ has so far
recognized the following five main types of infringement as grounds of
invalidity. First, failure of the Commission to obtain the assent of the Council
where required to do so under the ECSC Treaty (e.g. under Art. 58(1) ECSC,
see Case 119/81 *Klöckner-Werke* v. *Commission* [1982] ECR 2627 at
p. 2648). Secondly, failure of the Council to comply with its own Rules of
Procedure requiring unanimity for the use of the written procedure (Art. 6(1),
see Case 68/86 *United Kingdom* v. *Council* [1988] ECR 855 at pp. 901–2).
Thirdly, failure to consult the various consultative bodies where consultation
is required by a provision of primary or secondary Community law. These
bodies include, as the case may be, the ECSC Council and Consultative
Committee (e.g. under Art. 60(1) ECSC, see Case 1/54 *France* v. *HA* [1954]
ECR 1 at p. 15; Case 6/54 *Netherlands* v. *HA*, above, at p. 112; or under Art.
61 ECSC, see Cases 154/78 etc. *Valsabbia* v. *Commission* [1980] ECR 907 at
pp. 997–1000); the European Parliament (e.g. under Art. 43(2) EEC, see the
cases cited below); the EEC/Euratom Economic and Social Committee (e.g.
under Art. 43(2) EEC); 'the other institutions concerned' (Art. 24 Merger
Treaty, which institutions however do not include, for the purposes of
consultation, the Economic and Social Committee and the Court of Auditors,
see e.g. Case 828/79 *Adam* v. *Commission* [1982] ECR 269 at pp. 290–1);
and, in EEC competition matters, the Advisory Committee on Restrictive
Practices and Monopolies (Art. 10 of Reg. 17, *OJ Sp. Edn.* 1959–62, p. 87;
see Case 41/6 *Chemiefarma* v. *Commission* [1970] ECR 661 at p. 710 *per*
A.-G. Gand). Undoubtedly, it is consultation with the European Parliament
to which the ECJ attaches the greatest importance. As the Court has stated:
'The consultation provided for in . . . the Treaty is the means which allows the
Parliament to play an actual part in the legislative process of the Community.
Such power represents an essential factor in the institutional balance intended
by the Treaty. Although limited, it reflects at Community level the fundamental democratic principle that the peoples should take part in the exercise
of power through the intermediary of a representative assembly. Due consultation of the Parliament in the cases provided for by the Treaty therefore
constitutes an essential formality disregard of which means that the measure
concerned is void' (Case 138/79 *Roquette* v. *Council* [1980] ECR 3333.at
p. 3360. In that case the Court declared a Council regulation void for the

301

Council's failure to obtain the opinion of the Parliament as required by Art. 43(2) EEC. See also Case 828/79 *Adam* v. *Commission*, above, at p. 287). To satisfy the requirement of consultation, the body consulted must actually express its opinion; a simple request for the opinion is not sufficient (Case 138/79 *Roquette* v. *Council*, above, at pp. 3360–1; see also Case 1/54 *France* v. *HA*, above). However, failure to obtain the opinion of a Management Committee does not amount to an infringement of an 'essential' procedural requirement where the Commission is authorized to adopt the measure in question even in the absence of a positive opinion (Case 128/86 *Spain* v. *Commission* [1987] ECR 4171 at p. 4196).

A fourth type of procedural defect that may occur during the course of the preparation of a measure consists of a failure to grant interested parties a hearing before the measure is finally adopted. A hearing may be prescribed by a provision of Community law (see e.g. Arts. 88 ECSC, 169 EEC, 141 Euratom; Case 20/59 *Italy* v. *HA* [1960] ECR 325 at p. 342; Case 31/69 *Commission* v. *Italy* [1970] ECR 25 at p. 33), or it may be required by the general principle of *audi alteram partem*, or both. Thus, in Case 17/74 *Transocean Marine Paint Association* v. *Commission* [1974] ECR 1063 at p. 1080 the ECJ held that the procedure for hearing in competition cases laid down in Art. 19 of Reg. 17 and in Reg. 99/63 was an application of 'the general rule that a person whose interests are perceptibly affected by a decision taken by a public authority must be given the opportunity to make this point of view known'. Since this requirement was not fulfilled in the case before it, the Court annulled in part the challenged decision of the Commission (see also Case 141/84 *De Compte* v. *Parliament* [1985] ECR 1951 at pp. 1966–7 and *see further under* **Audi alteram partem**).

Finally, an illegal disclosure by the Commission of confidential information (e.g. business secrets) during the course of a preparatory procedure might amount to a procedural irregularity, although this 'would involve the annulment in whole or in part of the decision only if it were shown that in the absence of such irregularity the contested decision might have been different' (Cases 209 to 215 and 218/78 *Van Landewyck* v. *Commission*, above, at p. 3239). A failure to disclose non-confidential information, where disclosure is explicitly required by Community law (e.g. in anti-dumping proceedings), is also regarded as an infringement of an essential procedural requirement which will lead to the annulment of the measure in question (Case 264/82 *Timex* v. *Council and Commission* [1985] ECR 849 at p. 870).

2. As regards the form of a measure, while insignificant formal irregularities remain irrelevant (see e.g. Cases 56 and 58/64 *Consten and Grundig* v. *Commission* [1966] ECR 299 at pp. 338–9; Cases 275/80 and 24/81 *Krupp* v. *Commission*, above, at pp. 2511–12 *per Curiam*, pp. 2524–5 *per* A.-G. Reischl), the giving of no or insufficient reasons will always constitute an infringement of an essential procedural requirement. In fact, on account of the strict requirements set by the ECJ in respect of the obligation to state the reasons for every binding measure, inadequate reasoning has so far been the most successful single ground of action under both the ECSC and EEC Treaties (*see further under* **Statement of reasons**).

302

3. As regards the communication of a measure, while publication of general law-making measures is an essential condition of their formal validity, irregularities in the procedure for notification of individual decisions are regarded as being extraneous to the acts themselves. Such irregularities cannot invalidate the act, but in certain circumstances they may prevent the time for bringing an action for annulment from starting to run (Case 48/69 *ICI* v. *Commission* [1972] ECR 619 at p. 652). By contrast, failure to communicate a measure in the proper language as required by Community law constitutes a legal defect which is, under given circumstances, capable of affecting the validity of the measure (Case 41/69 *Chemiefarma* v. *Commission*, above, at p. 686). Similarly, substantial alterations made by the Council's General Secretariat to the text of an act after its adoption by the Council, leading to discrepancies between the adopted version and the notified or published versions, will result in the annulment of the act (Case 131/86 *United Kingdom* v. *Council* [1988] ECR 905 at pp. 934–5).

See also **Administrative procedure***, *Audi alteram partem*, **Grounds of action, Notification, Official languages, Publication, Statement of reasons.**

▶ **INFRINGEMENT OF THE TREATIES** One of four grounds of action on which binding acts of the Council, the Commission, and the European Parliament may be challenged before, and declared void by, the ECJ in the framework of annulment proceedings (Arts. 33 ECSC, 173 EEC, 146 Euratom).

The purpose of this ground of action is to enable the ECJ to review the substantive legality of the acts of the institutions, i.e. their conformity with the material (as opposed to the formal and procedural) rules and principles of Community law. 'Community law' encompasses, for this purpose, not only the basic Treaties but also 'any rule of law relating to their application'. This term includes: (1) the whole body of secondary legislation; (2) such general principles of law as have been recognized by the ECJ as forming part of Community law (see e.g. Case 4/73 *Nold* v. *Commission* [1974] ECR 491 at p. 507; Case 112/77 *Töpfer* v. *Commission* [1978] ECR 1019 at p. 1033); and (3) such rules of general (customary) international law and such treaty obligations as are binding upon the Communities. Infringement of any of these rules and principles may lead to the annulment of the act by the ECJ (see e.g. Case 92/78 *Simmenthal* v. *Commission* [1979] ECR 777 at p. 811, where the Court annulled a Commission decision partly for infringement of a Council regulation; Case 45/86 *Commission* v. *Council* [1987] ECR 1493 at p. 1522 *per Curiam*, p. 1515 *per* A.-G. Lenz, where the adoption of certain regulations on the incorrect legal basis constituted an infringement of the Treaties and led to the annulment of the regulations).

See also **Community law, Community Treaties, General principles of law, Grounds of action, Judicial review, Secondary legislation.**

▶ **INSTITUTIONAL BALANCE** Principle of fundamental importance for the institutional (or constitutional) law of the European Communities, according to which, in carrying out the tasks entrusted to it, each of the four institutions (i.e. the European Parliament, the Council, the Commission, and the Court of Justice) is required to act within the limits of the powers conferred upon it by the Treaties and is required to observe the powers and prerogatives of the other institutions (also known as the principle of division or balance of powers). Although in the system of the Treaties the powers of the institutions differ, they must be kept 'in balance' in the sense that in principle no institution is allowed to arrogate to itself more powers at the expense of the others than allocated to it by the Treaties. As the ECJ has stated, 'in accordance with the balance of powers between the institutions provided for by the Treaties, the practice of [one institution] cannot deprive the other institutions of a prerogative granted to them by the Treaties themselves' (Case 149/85 *Wybot* [1986] ECR 2391 at p. 2409). The balance of powers, which is therefore characteristic of the institutional structure of the Communities, is important not only for the relations between the institutions. As the ECJ has stressed, it also constitutes a 'fundamental guarantee' granted by the Treaties to undertakings and private individuals intended to ensure that the sometimes wide discretionary powers conferred on the institutions are at all times exercised by them within the proper limits of their authority (Case 9/56 *Meroni* v. *HA* [1958] ECR 133 at p. 152).

The principle of institutional balance, which is expressly laid down in the Treaties (see Arts. 3 ECSC, 4 EEC, 3 Euratom), has been confirmed and applied by the ECJ in a number of situations covering the whole spectrum of the various interinstitutional relationships. The most important of these may be summarized as follows.

1. *As regards the relationship between the European Parliament (EP) and the other political institutions (Council and Commission)*, the Court has pointed out that the consultation of the EP required by the Treaty 'is the means which allows the Parliament to play an actual part in the legislative process of the Community. Such power represents an essential factor in the institutional balance intended by the Treaty' (Case 138/79 *Roquette* v. *Council* [1980] ECR 3333 at p. 3360; Case 828/79 *Adam* v. *Commission* [1982] ECR 269 at p. 287). With regard to the budgetary procedure, and in particular the classification of expenditure, the Court has remarked that the power of assessment of the institutions is 'limited by the division of powers between the institutions as provided for by the Treaty' (Case 204/86 *Greece* v. *Council* [1988] ECR para. 17). In confirming the right of the EP to intervene in proceedings before the Court and its right to bring an action for failure to act under Art. 175 EEC, the Court has stressed that 'all the institutions of the Community have [such right]. It is not possible to restrict the exercise of that right by one of them without adversely affecting its institutional position as intended by the Treaty and in particular Article 4(1)' (Case 138/79 *Roquette* v. *Council*, above, at p. 3357, confirming the right to intervene; Case 13/83 *Parliament* v. *Council* [1985] ECR 1513 at p. 1588, confirming the right to bring an action for failure to act). In ruling that binding acts of the EP were subject to judicial review, i.e. that the EP could appear as a defendant in an action for annulment under Art. 173 EEC even

although that Article does not expressly so provide, the Court relied on the reasoning that in the absence of such review 'measures adopted by the European Parliament . . . could encroach on the powers of the Member States or of the other institutions, or exceed the limits which have been set to the Parliament's powers' (Case 294/83 *Les Verts* v. *Parliament* [1986] ECR 1339 at p. 1366; Case 34/86 *Council* v. *Parliament* [1986] ECR 2155 at p. 2203— 'Budget' case). However, when in turn Parliament argued that the institutional balance also required that Parliament itself should be given the same status as the other institutions, not only as a defendant but also as an applicant, i.e. that it should be able to challenge acts of the Council and the Commission under Art. 173, the Court did not accept the argument. The Court held that in the scheme of the Treaties there was no necessary parallelism between the capacity to be a defendant and the right to appear as an applicant. Parliament was given the power to exercise political control over the Commission through its right to table a motion of censure, and the power to exert influence upon the legislative measures of the Council through the consultation and co-operation procedures, but was not given the right to exercise legal control by means of an action for annulment. Its prerogatives could be defended *vis-à-vis* the other institutions by various other means, including actions brought by the Commission in its capacity as the guardian of the Treaties (Case 302/87 *Parliament* v. *Council* [1988] ECR paras. 12–13, 19–21, 25–58). Thus, the Parliament was unable to challenge Council Dec. 87/373 laying down the procedures for the exercise of implementing powers conferred on the Commission, even although in Parliament's opinion by adopting this decision the Council encroached on Parliament's own supervisory powers over the Commission (ibid., Report for the Hearing).

2. *As to the relationship between the Council and the Commission*, the Court rejected the argument put forward by the United Kingdom that in accordance with the division of powers between the institutions created by the Treaties, all original law-making power was vested in the Council, while the Commission had only powers of supervision and implementation. The Court pointed out that the Commission was to participate in carrying out the Community's tasks on the same basis as the other institutions, having its own power of decision as laid down in the Treaty (Cases 188 to 190/80 *France, Italy and United Kingdom* v. *Commission* [1982] ECR 2545 at pp. 2572–3). On the other hand, when the Council delegates implementing power to the Commission under Art. 155 EEC, it is entitled to lay down certain conditions for the exercise of that power (e.g. the Management Committee procedure) without thereby jeopardizing the independence of the Commission or distorting the institutional balance (Case 25/70 *Köster* [1970] ECR 1161 at pp. 1170–1; Case 23/75 *Rey Soda* [1975] ECR 1279 at pp. 1300–1). Delegation of a law-making power to bodies set up not by the Treaties but by secondary legislation is not permissible (Case 98/80 *Romano* [1981] ECR 1241 at p. 1256, where the body in question was the Administrative Commission set up under Reg. 1408/71 on social security). Delegation of a discretionary power, i.e. other than a clearly defined executive power, to bodies established entirely outside the framework of Community law is contrary to the principle

305

of institutional balance and hence illegal (Case 9/56 *Meroni* v. *HA*, above, at pp. 152, 154; the bodies in question were the so-called 'Brussels agencies' set up to administer the scrap equalization system).

3. *As to the relationship between the Court of Justice itself and the other institutions*, the Court has consistently followed the principle that there is a clear division between the judicial and the legislative/executive functions and that the Court, having been assigned a purely judicial task by the Treaties, is not allowed to interfere with the legislative/executive process. The Court has applied this important principle in the following main situations:

- when, in exercising judicial review over the acts of the institutions, the Court annuls a measure, it may not enter the sphere of legislation by prescribing what measure the institution in question should take in replacement of the one annulled (see e.g., under the ECSC Treaty, Cases 42 and 49/59 *SNUPAT* v. *HA* [1961] ECR 53 at p. 88; under the EEC Treaty, Cases 142 and 156/84 *BAT and Reynolds* v. *Commission* [1987] ECR 4487 at p. 4571);
- likewise, in the context of procedures for interim measures, 'it is outside the jurisdiction of the Court . . . to substitute its own appraisal for that of the Commission' (Case 71/74R and RR *Fruit- en Groentenimport-handel* v. *Commission* [1974] ECR 1031 at p. 1034, under the EEC Treaty; see also Case 19/59R *Geitling* v. *HA* [1960] ECR 17, 34 at p. 37, under the ECSC Treaty);
- in reviewing the exercise of discretionary powers conferred on the Council and the Commission, the Court restricts itself to examining the strict legality of the measures adopted but refrains from entering the actual area of the discretion itself, i.e. the sphere of suitability or expediency. Otherwise the Court would replace the legislative discretion of the institutions by its own views of the economic policies to be pursued by the Communities (*see the cases cited under* **Judicial review**);
- in actions brought by the Commission against Member States under Arts. 169 EEC/141 Euratom, 'in the context of the balance of powers between the institutions laid down in the Treaty, it is not for the Court to consider what objectives are pursued' by the Commission, since the bringing of such actions 'is a matter for the Commission in its entire discretion' (Case 416/85 *Commission* v. *United Kingdom* [1988] ECR 3127 at p. 3151; see also Case 7/68 *Commission* v. *Italy* [1968] ECR 423 at p. 428);
- in a number of diverse situations, the Court has explicitly declined to fill obvious gaps in the body of Community law by laying down detailed rules, saying that this is the task of the Community legislature and beyond the proper judicial function (see e.g. Case 41/69 *Chemiefarma* v. *Commission* [1970] ECR 661 at p. 683; Case 92/71 *Interfood* [1972] ECR 231 at p. 242; Case 130/79 *Express Dairy Foods* [1980] ECR 1887 at p. 1900; Case 168/82 *Ferriere Sant'Anna* [1983] ECR 1681 at p. 1696).

The Community Treaties lay down very few provisions as to how the institutional balance, which they intended to create, should be maintained. Mention may be made of Art. 95(3) ECSC, which provides that amendments made to the ECSC Treaty under that Article (the so-called 'minor revisions') must not interfere, amongst other things, 'with the relationship between the powers of the High Authority [i.e. the Commission] and those of the other institutions of the Community'. In its *Opinion of 17 December 1959*, the ECJ held that a proposed amendment to Art. 56 ECSC was not compatible with Art. 95 in that, *inter alia*, it jeopardized the 'balance between the institutions of the Community, provided for by the Treaty' by impairing the High Authority's freedom of action and assessment ([1959] ECR 260 at p. 273). Art. 15 of the Merger Treaty, which replaced Art. 162 EEC, provides that the Council and the Commission 'shall consult each other and shall settle by common accord their methods of co-operation' (see also Art. 26(2) ECSC). On the basis of this provision, the Luxembourg Compromise of 1966 established certain 'practical methods of co-operation' without affecting the 'respective competences and powers of the two institutions' (*see further under* **Luxembourg Compromise**).

There are, however, no provisions in the Treaties creating a special procedure for settling jurisdictional conflicts between the institutions. In the absence of such a procedure, interinstitutional disputes have to be decided in the framework of the available actions, i.e. actions for annulment and actions for failure to act (see the opinion of A.-G. Lenz in Case 45/86 *Commission* v. *Council* [1987] ECR 1493 at p. 1506). In the context of these actions, the main means whereby the Court is able to assess whether the institutions have acted within the limits of their respective powers is the requirement that their measures must state the reasons on which they are based, including the Treaty provision(s) which served as their legal basis (Arts. 15 ECSC, 190 EEC, 162 Euratom; Arts. 11 and 14 of the Council's Rules of Procedure of 24 July 1979, *OJ* 1979 L268/1; see Case 131/86 *United Kingdom* v. *Council* [1988] ECR 905 at pp. 934–5—'Protection of battery hens' case). In a series of recent cases, the Court has pointed out that the choice of legal basis is an 'essential institutional problem' (ibid. at p. 935; Case 68/86 *United Kingdom* v. *Council* [1988] ECR 855 at p. 902—'Hormones' case), and that 'in the context of the organization of the powers of the Community the choice of the legal basis for a measure may not depend simply on an institution's conviction as to the objective pursued but must be based on objective factors which are amenable to judicial review' (Case 45/86 *Commission* v. *Council*, above, at p. 1520; see also the opinion of A.-G. Lenz at pp. 1505–6). Therefore, any dispute concerning the correct legal basis is not purely a formal or political one since the choice of the legal basis may affect (1) the procedure to be followed in the adoption of the measure; (2) the respective influence of the various institutions which participate in that procedure; and (3) the determination of the content of the measure (ibid. at p. 1520 *per Curiam*, pp. 1505–6, 1515 *per* A.-G. Lenz).

These effects become particularly apparent in the following two situations. First, where the choice as a possible legal basis is between two Articles of the

307

(EEC) Treaty, one of which requires the Council to act unanimously (e.g. Art. 100 or 235), the other by qualified majority (e.g. Art. 43 or 113), in the adoption of the measure. It is quite clear that the choice of the former Article will weaken the position of the Commission in the legislative process by ·compelling it to find a compromise solution for its proposal which is acceptable to all the Member States and not only to a majority of them. Precisely for this reason, the selection of the legal basis may also have a decisive influence on the content of the measure. The second situation is where the choice is between one Article which provides for a simple consultation of the European Parliament and another Article which requires recourse to the new co-operation procedure introduced by the Single European Act of 1986. It is again obvious that the choice of the former will give Parliament a less important role in the decision-making process than the latter. It is probably for these reasons that Parliament always examines the 'validity and appropriateness' of the chosen legal base for any draft measure on which it is consulted (see Rule 36(3) of its Rules of Procedure, 4th edn. (1987)).

For the above reasons, the ECJ has laid down some quite stringent requirements concerning the selection of the correct legal basis. These may be summarized as follows (all references are to the EEC Treaty):

1. Failure to refer to a precise provision of the Treaty in the preamble to the measure need not necessarily constitute an infringement of essential procedural requirements when the legal basis may be determined from other parts of the measure. However, such explicit reference is indispensable where, in its absence, the parties concerned and the Court are left uncertain as to the exact legal basis. Thus, the use of the phrase 'having regard to the Treaty' is as a rule insufficient, particularly where it is deliberately adopted with the aim of leaving the legal basis vague (Case 45/86 *Commission* v. *Council*, above, at pp. 1519–20 *per Curiam*, pp. 1513–14 *per* A.-G. Lenz).

2. Insufficiently precise statement of the legal basis constitutes an infringement of the requirement relating to the statement of reasons and hence an infringement of an essential procedural requirement, while the adoption of a measure on the incorrect legal basis (e.g. Art. 235 instead of Art. 113) constitutes a substantive infringement of the Treaty, both leading to the annulment of the measure (ibid. at p. 1522 *per Curiam*, pp. 1514–15 *per* A.-G. Lenz. The measures in question in this case were two Council regulations applying generalized tariff preferences to certain industrial products, which fell within the sphere of the Common Commercial Policy and therefore should have been adopted under Art. 113—requiring qualified majority—rather than under Art. 235—requiring unanimity).

3. Where a measure can be validly based on one legal basis (i.e. on one Treaty Article) alone, there is no need (and it is generally illegal) to have recourse to another legal basis (i.e. to another Treaty Article) as well. In the case, in particular, of harmonization measures (i.e. directives), the

general provision in Art. 100 should be resorted to only in the absence of any specific provision in the Treaty permitting the harmonization of national laws (Case 68/86 *United Kingdom* v. *Council*, above, at pp. 896–8; Case 131//86 *United Kingdom* v. *Council*, above, at pp. 930–3 *per Curiam*, pp. 917–18 *per* A.-G. Mischo, both holding that since certain directives falling within the Common Agricultural Policy could be properly adopted under Art. 43, which requires qualified majority, there was no need to rely, in addition, on Art. 100, which requires unanimity).

4. By contrast, where the powers of an institution are derived from two Articles of the Treaty, that institution is obliged to adopt the relevant measure on the basis of both of those Articles (Case 165/87 *Commission* v. *Council* [1988] ECR para. 11, holding that the Council was entitled to conclude the International Convention on the Harmonised Commodity Description and Coding System on the basis of both Arts. 28 and 113).

5. Where a measure can be validly based on one (or more) particular provision(s) of the Treaty, it may not be based on the general authorization contained in Art. 235 (ibid. para. 18. *See also under* **Supplementary powers**).

It must be stated, however, that owing to certain developments which occurred in the life of the Communities, the institutional balance has not been maintained in practice in the way in which it was originally envisaged by the Treaties. Thus, for example, there has been a pronounced shift in the balance of powers from the Commission to the Council. This has been due to at least three main reasons. First, the introduction of the practice of unanimous voting in the Council by the Luxembourg Compromise of 1966 has weakened the position of the Commission in the legislative process by depriving its proposals of the special importance granted them by Art. 149 EEC. Secondly, the reluctance of the Council to delegate implementing powers to the Commission under Art. 155 EEC, and its practice of subjecting those powers to various restrictions, has diminished the role of the Commission even as an executive body. Thirdly, by taking decisions as 'Representatives of the Governments of the Member States meeting in Council', the Council has blurred the dividing line between the Community and intergovernmental decision-making processes. As a result, as the Vedel Report pointed out as early as 1972, the shift in the balance of powers led to the predominance of the Council growing 'to such a point that the Council, acting in some instances as a Community body and in others as the States in concert, has become the sole effective centre of power in the system' (Suppl. 4/72—*Bull. EC*, p. 25). This in turn has weakened the position of the European Parliament both as a supervisory body (since it has no power of control over the Council) and as a consultative organ (since its opinions have lost their impact on the final decisions taken by the Council). Finally, the creation of the European Council has introduced an element of intergovernmental policy-making which was not envisaged by the Treaties and which is not subject to Community procedures.

309

These developments have been criticized by the various reports and proposals put forward over the years for reforming the Community institutions (see, in particular, the Vedel, Tindemans, and Three Wise Men's Reports and the Report of the Committee on Institutional Affairs—the Dooge Committee). These criticisms, combined with efforts made towards establishing a European Union, have ultimately led to the adoption of the Single European Act of 1986. Those provisions of the Act which deal with institutional reform mark a new starting-point in the process aimed at restoring the balance as envisaged by the Treaties.

See also **Commission, Committee on Institutional Affairs, Council, European Act, European Council, European Court of Justice, European Parliament, European Union, Institutions, Judicial review, Luxembourg Compromise, Representative of the Governments of the Member States meeting in Council, Single European Act, Solemn Declaration on European Union, Statement of reasons, Supplementary powers, Three Wise Men's Report, Tindemans Report, Vedel Report.**

Further reading 1. ARTICLES AND PAPERS: Bieber, 'The Settlement of Institutional Conflicts on the Basis of Article 4 of the EEC Treaty' (1984) 21 *CML Rev.* 505; Bradley, 'Maintaining the Balance: The Role of the Court of Justice in Defining the Institutional Position of the European Parliament' (1987) 24 *CML Rev.* 41; id., 'The European Court and the Legal Basis of Community Legislation' (1988) 13 *EL Rev.* 379; FIDE, 'Possible Areas of Conflict between Community Institutions in the Implementation of Community Law', *Reports of the Ninth FIDE Congress* (1980), vol. iii.

2. OFFICIAL PUBLICATION: Commission of the European Communities, 'The Institutional System of the Community: Restoring the Balance', Suppl. 3/82—*Bull. EC.*

▶ **INSTITUTIONS** Bodies set up by the ECSC, EEC, and Euratom Treaties to carry out the tasks entrusted to the Communities which they have established. Originally, each Treaty provided for its own four institutions, as follows:

- *ECSC Treaty*: High Authority, Common Assembly, Special Council of Ministers, Court of Justice (Art. 7);
- *EEC and Euratom Treaties*: Assembly, Council, Commission, Court of Justice (Arts. 4 EEC, 3 Euratom).

However, 'to limit the number of institutions responsible for carrying out similar tasks', a Convention on Certain Institutions Common to the European Communities was signed at the same time as the EEC and Euratom Treaties (25 Mar. 1957), which created a single Assembly and a single Court of Justice to exercise the powers and jurisdiction conferred on those institutions by the three Treaties. Subsequently, as a first step towards the intended unification of the three Communities themselves, a Treaty establishing a Single Council and a Single Commission of the European Communities (known as the Merger Treaty) was signed on 8 April 1965, which came into force on 1 July 1967. This merged the Special Council of Ministers of the ECSC and the Councils of the EEC and Euratom into a single Council, as well as the High

Authority of the ECSC and the Commissions of the EEC and Euratom into a single Commission, each to exercise the powers and jurisdiction conferred on those institutions by the three original Treaties. The Merger Treaty also provided for a general budget of the European Communities to replace the separate budgets of each Community, and created a single administration of the European Communities to be made up of the officials and other servants of the three Communities.

As a result of the above changes, since 1 July 1967 there have been four (and only four) institutions serving all three Communities: the Assembly (calling itself European Parliament since 1962, a title which has been officially recognized by Art. 3(1) of the Single European Act of 1986), the Council, the Commission, and the Court of Justice. They are all characterized by the fact that (1) their (non-elected) members are appointed directly by the Member States and not by other institutions; (2) they possess a set of (more or less clearly) defined powers; and (3) as regards their internal organization, they enjoy a certain degree of legal, financial, and administrative autonomy within the limits of their powers (see Cases 7/56 etc. *Algera* v. *Common Assembly* [1957] ECR 39 at p. 57).

In addition to the four institutions, the Treaties and subsequent amendments have also created certain other bodies, such as the ECSC Consultative Committee, the EEC/Euratom Economic and Social Committee, the Court of Auditors, the European Investment Bank, and the Court of First Instance. However, with the exception of the Court of First Instance, which is attached to the Court of Justice, these bodies are not 'institutions' *stricto sensu*. Thus, as the ECJ has ruled, although the Economic and Social Committee and the Court of Auditors are treated as 'institutions' for the specific purposes of the Staff Regulations and of the Financial Regulation, they are not listed as 'institutions' in Arts. 7 ECSC, 4 EEC, and 3 Euratom (although they are mentioned in those Articles), and do not possess the full status of a Community institution for the general purposes of the Treaties (Case 828/79 *Adam* v. *Commission* [1982] ECR 269 at pp. 290–1). The European Investment Bank has its own legal personality (which the institutions do not have), and is in an 'ambivalent' position in relation to the EEC (Case 85/86 *Commission* v. *Board of Governors of the EIB* [1988] ECR 1281 at p. 1320). As a result, these bodies may at best be described as 'quasi-institutional' bodies with the consequence that they do not enjoy the full powers and prerogatives which the four institutions enjoy under the Treaties and which are ensured through the fundamental principle of institutional balance (*see further under* **Institutional balance**). Finally, the European Council, not created by Treaty, is an intergovernmental body not a Community institution. Although its legal existence has been recognized in Art. 2 of the Single European Act, the European Council has not been integrated into the institutional structure of the Communities.

The Treaties provide that the seat of the institutions is to be determined by common accord of the Governments of the Member States (Arts. 77 ECSC, 216 EEC, 189 Euratom). However, the Member States have taken no decision so far determining the seat of the institutions; they have confined themselves to determining provisional places of work only (see the Decisions of the Foreign Ministers of 25 July 1952 and 7 Jan. 1958, referred to in Case 230/81 *Luxembourg* v. *Parliament* [1983] ECR 255 at p. 227; the Decisions of the Representatives of the Governments of the Member States of 8 Apr. 1965, signed at the same time as the Merger Treaty, *JO* 1967 152/18, and of 5 Apr. 1977 relating to the Court of Auditors, *OJ* 1977 L104/40. The status quo created by these decisions was confirmed unanimously by the Maastricht European Council of 23–4 Mar. 1981, *Bull. EC* 3–1981, p. 9 and subsequently by a Conference of the Representatives of the Member States, see Case 230/81 *Luxembourg* v. *Parliament*, above, at p. 280).

As a result of the above Decisions, the present position is as follows. Luxembourg, Brussels, and Strasbourg remain the provisional places of work of the institutions (Art. 1 of the Dec. of 8 Apr. 1965). The Council and the Commission are established in Brussels, but the Council is to hold certain meetings in Luxembourg and the Commission also has some of its departments in Luxembourg. The Court of Justice, the Court of First Instance, the Court of Auditors, the European Investment Bank, some financial departments, and the Office for Official Publications are all located in Luxembourg. The European Parliament has three different places of work: it holds its plenary sessions in Strasbourg, has its General Secretariat and its departments in Luxembourg, while the meetings of the committees and political groups are normally held in Brussels (for various attempts by Parliament to improve its working conditions, see Case 230/81 *Luxembourg* v. *Parliament*, above; Case 108/83 *Luxembourg* v. *Parliament* [1984] ECR 1945; Cases 358/85 and 51/86 *France* v. *Parliament* [1988] ECR. *See further under* **European Parliament**).

See also **Commission, Consultative Committee, Council, Court of Auditors, Court of First Instance, Economic and Social Committee, European Communities, European Council, European Court of Justice, European Investment Bank, European Parliament, Institutional balance, Single European Act.**

Further reading 1. B O O K S : Freestone and Davidson, *The Institutional Framework of the European Communities* (1988); Henig, *Power and Decision in Europe: The Political Institutions of the European Community* (1980); Lodge (ed.), *Institutions and Policies of the European Community* (1983); Noël, *Working Together: The Institutions of the European Community* (1985). *See also under* **Community law.**

2. ARTICLES: Ehlermann, 'Legal Status, Functioning and Probable Evolution of the Institutions of the European Communities' (1973) 10 *CML Rev.* 195; Stein, 'The European Community in 1983: A Less Perfect Union?' (1983) 20 *CML Rev.* 641; Weiler and Modrall, 'Institutional Reform: Consensus or Majority?' (1985) 10 *EL Rev.* 316.

▶ **INTEREST** 1. *Default interest*: (*a*) Interest payable on arrears of payments due to a person but unlawfully withheld by a Community institution. Thus, in a series of staff cases where the Commission has wrongly refused to pay sums owed to officials by virtue of the Staff Regulations, the ECJ has held that 'it is fair to place the applicant in the position in which he would have been if the [amount] which must now be paid to him had been paid in accordance with the relevant provisions, or in other words, in due time. Default interest must therefore be awarded to the applicant at 6% *per annum*, as claimed as from the various dates on which payment fell due, on the amounts to which he is entitled' (Case 185/80 *Garganese* v. *Commission* [1981] ECR 1785 at p. 1796. See also e.g. Case 158/79 *Roumengous* v. *Commission* [1985] ECR 39 at pp. 51–2. In Case 110/63 *Willame* v. *Commission* [1965] ECR 649 at p. 668 the Court awarded default interest at the rate of 4.5 per cent *per annum*. In Case 58/75 *Sergy* v. *Commission* [1976] ECR 1139 at p. 1155 the Court awarded interest at 8 per cent from the date of the complaint lodged by the applicant pursuant to Art. 90(2) of the Staff Regulations). However, in a series of subsequent cases the Court has stated that an obligation to pay default interest can arise only where the amount of the principal sum owed is certain or can at least be ascertained on the basis of established objective factors, and has refused to award interest with retroactive effect (see e.g. Case 174/83 *Amman* v. *Council* [1986] ECR 2647 at pp. 2665–6). In several non-staff cases, the Court has refused to award default interest on costs recoverable from the institutions (see e.g. Case 6/72 *Continental Can* v. *Commission* [1975] ECR 495 at p. 497; Case 238/78 *Ireks-Arkady* v. *EEC* [1981] ECR 1723 at p. 1726).

(*b*) Interest payable by the Member States in respect of 'any delay' in crediting the amount of own resources to the Commission's account (Art. 11 of Reg. 2891/77, OJ 1977 L336/1 as amended by Reg. 3760/86, OJ 1986 L349/1). The ECJ has held that this interest is payable regardless of the reason for the delay and at a flat rate which cannot be varied according to the particular circumstances of each individual case (Case 303/84 *Commission* v. *Germany* [1986] ECR 1171 at p. 1183; Case 93/85 *Commission* v. *United Kingdom* [1986] ECR 4011 at pp. 4035–6).

2. *Interest on damages*: Interest payable by the Communities on amounts which they are required to pay by way of compensation. As a claim for interest of this type arises from the non-contractual liability of the Community under Art. 215(2) EEC, the ECJ has held that 'it must be considered in the light of the principles common to the legal systems of the Member States, to which that provision refers. It follows that a claim for interest is in general admissible. Taking into account the criteria for the assessment of damages laid down by the Court, the obligation to pay interest arises on the date of this judgment, in that it establishes the obligation to make good the damage. The rate of interest which it is proper to apply is 6%' (Case 238/78 *Ireks-Arkady* v. *Council and Commission* [1979] ECR 2955 at p. 2975—'Quellmehl' case. See however Case 131/81 *Berti* v. *Commission* [1985] ECR 645 at p. 652, a staff case, where the Court ordered the Commission to pay interest at the rate of 12 per cent). As regards compensation for non-material damage, in one case the Court held that interest was not payable (Case 110/63 *Willame* v. *Commission*, above, at p. 668), while in another case it awarded interest at the rate of 8 per cent (Cases 169/83 and 136/84 *Leussink* v. *Commission* [1986] ECR 2801 at p. 2828).

3. *Interest on fines*: Interest payable, since December 1981, by an undertaking on the amount of a fine imposed by the Commission where, on appeal

313

to the ECJ, the Commission agrees to suspend collection of the fine pending judgment and the Court upholds the fine. The Court has confirmed the legality of such an interest as a means of discouraging manifestly unfounded actions brought with the sole object of delaying payment of the fine (Case 107/82 *AEG* v. *Commission* [1983] ECR 3151 at p. 3221). The interest is payable from the date on which the fine itself becomes payable and up to the date of the actual payment; the rate of interest is calculated at 1 per cent above the discount rate fixed by the Central Bank of the Member State where the undertaking is incorporated or has its registered office (Case 107/82R *AEG* v. *Commission* [1982] ECR 1549 at pp. 1552–3; Case 78/83R *Usinor* v. *Commission* [1983] ECR 2183 at p. 2190).

4. *Interest on undue payments*: Interest payable on sums which have been wrongly paid to or by the national authorities under Community law. In a series of cases the ECJ has held that in the absence of provisions of Community law on this point, it is at present for the national courts dealing with the recovery of such sums to decide, by applying their own domestic rules, whether such interest is payable and, if so, what the rate of interest is and from what date the interest must be calculated. However, the application of national legislation must be effected in a non-discriminatory manner (see e.g. Case 130/79 *Express Dairy Foods* [1980] ECR 1887 at pp. 1900–1; Case 54/81 *Fromme* [1982] ECR 1449 at pp. 1463–4).

See also **Damage, Fine*, Non-contractual liability, Non-material damage, Own resources, Recovery of undue payments*.**

▶ **INTEREST TO SUE** 1. A legally relevant interest, recognized by the law as worthy of protection, an infringement of which may give rise to a right of action. Although the requirement that an applicant must have an interest to protect in bringing legal proceedings forms the basis of the system of judicial protection in the European Communities, the founding Treaties have not explicitly made the proof of such a legal interest a general condition of admissibility of action before the ECJ. Instead, they regulate the question of admissibility in two different ways. Firstly, they grant certain privileged applicants (i.e. the Community institutions and the Member States) an almost unqualified right to institute proceedings for the judicial review of the institutions' conduct. These applicants, as representatives of the public interests, are presumed to have a general interest in the judicial control of the legality of any Community action. They are consequently not required to prove any particular legal interest in instituting any particular proceedings (Cases 2 and 3/60 *Niederrheinische Bergwerks* v. *HA* [1961] ECR 133 at p. 147 *per Curiam*; p. 154 *per* A.-G. Lagrange; Case 166/78 *Italy* v. *Council* [1979] ECR 2575 at p. 2596 *per Curiam*, pp. 2606 *et seq. per* A.-G. Reischl; Case 45/86 *Commission* v. *Council* [1987] ECR 1493 at p. 1518). Secondly, as regards other, non-privileged applicants (private individuals and corporations), the Treaties define the conditions of admissibility in strict and precise terms in respect of each category of challengeable Community acts or omissions. Here admissibility is made dependent not upon the infringement of a legitimate interest, but upon the nature of the act or omission challenged and upon the applicant's 'concern' (under the ECSC Treaty) or 'direct and individual concern' (under the EEC/Euratom Treaties) in it, i.e. upon the existence of a sufficiently close and specific relationship between the applicant and the act (Case 3/54 *ASSIDER* v. *HA* [1955] ECR 63 at p. 88 *per* A.-G. Lagrange; Cases 7 and 9/54 *Industries Sidérurgiques Luxembourgeoises* v. *HA* [1956] ECR 175 at pp. 212–13 *per* A.-G. Roemer; Cases 16 and 17/62 *Producteurs de Fruits* v. *Council* [1962] ECR 471 at pp. 485–6 *per* A.-G. Lagrange).

2. General requirement according to which a party may seize the ECJ of an action or of a particular submission only if and when he is genuinely and objectively in need of the Court's protection and if the Court is in the position to afford the kind of protection sought (see e.g. Case 53/85 *AKZO Chemie* v. *Commission* [1986] ECR 1965 at p. 1990). Accordingly, an interest to sue will not exist (and the action or submission will be dismissed as inadmissible) where, for example, the act or omission complained of is not capable of adversely affecting the legal position of the applicant (Cases 16 to 18/59 *Geitling* v. *HA* [1960] ECR 17 at p. 26; Case 88/76 *Exportation des Sucres* v. *Commission* [1977] ECR 709 at p. 726; Case 229/86 *Brother Industries* v. *Commission* [1987] ECR 3757 at pp. 3762–3; see also Cases 154/78 etc. *Valsabbia* v. *Commission* [1980] ECR 907 at pp. 991–2, and Art. 91 of the Staff Regulations) or where the applicant pursues an aim which is legally impossible to attain, or which is unreasonable, does not 'make sense', is purely academic, or amounts to an abuse of process (see e.g. Cases 42 and 49/59 *SNUPAT* v. *HA* [1961] ECR 53 at p. 73; Case 243/78 *Simmenthal* v. *Commission* [1980] ECR 593 at pp. 606–7; Case 179/80 *Roquette* v. *Council* [1982] ECR 3623 at pp. 3634–5).

See also Admissibility of action, Direct concern, Individual concern, Right of action.

Further reading: van Dijk, *Judicial Review of Governmental Action and the Requirement of an Interest to Sue* (1980), ch. 7.

▶ **INTERIM MEASURES** 1. Provisional protective measures ordered by the President of the ECJ or—exceptionally—by the full Court by way of summary procedure at the request of a party to a case pending before the Court and relating to that case. These measures are of a conservatory nature, their purpose being to preserve the status quo pending final judgment by the Court in the main action but without prejudice to it (Arts. 39 ECSC, 186 EEC, 158 Euratom, 33 ECSC Statute, 36 EEC Statute, 37 Euratom Statute, 83–90 RP. See, in general, the opinion of A.-G. Capotorti in Cases 24 and 97/80R *Commission* v. *France* [1980] ECR 1319 at p. 1337).

'Interim measures' must be distinguished from the 'suspension of operation' of a Community act, although the two are often applied for simultaneously and their grant is subject to basically similar conditions. The main differences are, first, that 'suspension of operation' by definition always implies a negative act and, secondly, that it may only be ordered against a Community

315

institution which is usually a party (the defendant) to the proceedings. By contrast, an interim measure may require positive action as well as an abstention and may be granted against an institution, a Member State, or even a private party (a natural or legal person), which/who need not be a party to the main action. (The distinct nature of the two measures may be illustrated, for example, by reference to Case 120/83R *Raznoimport* v. *Commission* [1983] ECR 2573 at pp. 2579–80, where the President, while finding that there were no grounds for suspending the operation of the contested measure, ordered the Commission to follow a certain course of action.)

The conditions for the grant of interim measures have been defined by the ECJ in the following terms: 'By virtue [of the Treaties] and Article 83 of the Rules of Procedure, as well as of a consistent line of decisions of the Court, measures of this kind may be adopted by the judge hearing the application for such measures if it is established that their adoption is *prima facie* justified in fact and in law, if they are urgent in the sense that it is necessary, in order to avoid serious and irreparable damage, that they should be laid down, and should take effect, before the decision of the Court on the substance of the action and if they are provisional in the sense that they do not prejudge the decision on the substance of the case, that is to say that they do not at this stage decide disputed points of law or of fact or neutralise in advance the consequences of the decision to be given subsequently on the substance of the action' (Case 20/81R *Arbed* v. *Commission* [1981] ECR 721 at pp. 730–1. For similar definitions, see e.g. Case 220/82R *Moselstahlwerk* v. *Commission* [1982] ECR 2971 at p. 2978; Cases 228 and 229/82R *Ford* v. *Commission* [1982] ECR 3091 at p. 3098; Case 120/83R *Raznoimport* v. *Commission*, above, at p. 2577; and the cases cited below).

It appears from the above definition that normally the following three conditions must be satisfied before interim measures may be granted: first, there must exist a prima-facie case; secondly, the measures must be urgent; and thirdly, they must be provisional. Since suspension of operation is subject in essence to the same three conditions, the discussion under that entry applies, *mutatis mutandis*, to interim measures also. The following text is therefore restricted to issues which require additional or special considerations.

As regards the first condition, in proceedings against a Community institution, it may be necessary for the applicant to establish prima facie that the defendant institution has competence under Community law to take the measures sought (see e.g. Case 809/79R *Pardini* v. *Commission* [1980] ECR 139 at p. 148, where the President of the Court held that the measure requested—the issue of a new export licence—fell, prima facie, within the discretionary powers of the Member States, not of the Commission). Moreover, although the applicant is normally required to show prima facie that the main action stands a reasonable chance of succeeding, he is also required to make out a prima-facie case for the adoption of the particular interim measure requested. Thus, the existence of 'serious and genuine doubts' concerning the proper application of Community law by the defendant institution may not, in itself, constitute sufficient justification for an interim measure which would entail 'grave consequences' for all those concerned. There is no prima-facie case for an interim measure which would be a 'disproportionate response' to the doubts raised by the applicant (see e.g. Case 118/83R *CMC* v. *Commission* [1983] ECR 2583 at pp. 2599–601). Where the Commission applies for interim measures against a Member State in the context of enforcement proceedings under Art. 169 of the EEC Treaty, a prima-facie case is established if the Commission produces evidence showing the existence of 'serious doubts' as to the compatibility with Community law of the national measures or practices which form the subject-matter of the principal proceedings (see e.g. Case 61/77R *Commission* v. *Ireland* [1977] ECR 937 at p. 941; Case 42/82R *Commission* v. *France* [1982] ECR 841 at p. 856). The Court will not, however, order interim measures the purpose of which is to compel the Member State to bring about a legal situation (e.g. by amending its legislation or practice) which it is already under an obligation to achieve by virtue of a previous judgment rendered under Art. 169. In such circumstances, the interim measure would serve no useful purpose (Cases 24 and 97/80R *Commission* v. *France*, above, at pp. 1331–3).

One particular problem that may arise in the context of establishing a prima-facie case concerns the extent to which the President (or the full Court) is required to deal with preliminary objections raised by the defendant regarding the jurisdiction of the Court and the admissibility of the main application. In Case 118/83R *CMC* v. *Commission*, above, at p. 2595 this question was dealt with in the following terms: '. . . since [these] preliminary objections . . . constitute a prerequisite for the decision on the admissibility of the application for the adoption of interim measures, the judge hearing that application cannot escape the necessity of resolving provisionally the various problems raised. From his point of view, it is sufficient if he can establish, with a sufficient degree of probability, that there is a basis, albeit partial, on which the Court may found its jurisdiction in order to enable him to acknowledge the existence of a legitimate interest in the adoption of interim measures designed to preserve the existing position pending a decision on the substance of the case.'

The second condition to which the grant of interim measures is subject is that there must exist an urgency 'which must be shown more particularly by the imminence of serious and irreparable damage' (Case 809/79R *Pardini* v. *Commission*, above, at p. 149). The interim measures must be necessary in order to prevent 'an irreversible *de facto* situation', a 'serious and irreparable harm' from arising while the main proceedings are pending (Case 118/83R *CMC* v. *Commission*, above, at p. 2599; Case 171/83R *Commission* v. *France* [1983] ECR 2621 at p. 2629). Accordingly, there is no urgency where there is no threat to the maintenance of the status quo (Cases 160 and 161/73R *Miles Druce* v. *Commission* [1973] ECR 1049 at pp. 1053–4; see also Cases 160, 161, and 170/73R II *Miles Druce* v. *Commission* [1974] ECR 281 at pp. 283–4). The expected damage may threaten the applicant himself (see e.g. the cases cited immediately above) or, where it arises from an act of a Member State, it may threaten the nationals of the other Member States, the other Member States as such, or the interests of the Community in general

317

(see e.g. Case 61/77R *Commission* v. *Ireland* [1977] ECR 937 and 1411 at pp. 942 and 1414). The cause of the damage is usually an act or omission of the defendant (which is the subject of the main action), but it may equally be an act or omission of a third person, not party to the proceedings. Consequently, interim measures may be ordered not only against the defendant but also against persons not party to the case (see e.g. Cases 160, 161, and 170/73R II *Miles Druce* v. *Commission*, above, at pp. 283–4, where no action threatening the applicant's interests was to be taken during a certain period by 'anyone whomsoever'. See also Case 109/75R *National Carbonising Company* v. *Commission* [1975] ECR 1193 at pp. 1201–2, where the interim measure requested by the applicant was an order to be addressed to the National Coal Board requiring it to refrain from implementing a certain policy on prices). In the latter situation, the interests of the third persons involved are protected by their being allowed to intervene in the proceedings for the adoption of interim measures (see the two cases cited immediately above). It follows from the foregoing that, in the absence of exceptional circumstances, an application for interim measures is not an appropriate procedure for obtaining measures which are akin to measures of inquiry (e.g. production of documents), which the Court may order under Art. 45 or 91 RP (see Cases 121/86R and 121 and 122/86R *Epichirisseon* v. *Council and Commission* [1986] ECR 2063 at p. 2068 and [1987] ECR 833 at p. 838).

Finally, the third condition, i.e. that the interim measures must be provisional, means that they must 'remain within the context of the main action: when the latter is concluded the measure has spent its force and it is the judgment which definitively determines the rights and obligations of the parties with an authority and effectiveness which are logically greater than that of the interim measure. Of course, the temporary character of this kind of measure implies that by its nature it may be varied or cancelled, as Article 87 of the Rules of Procedure provides, and does not give rise to an irreversible situation' (Cases 24 and 97/80R *Commission* v. *France*, above, at p. 1337 *per* A.-G. Capotorti). Unless the order provides otherwise, the interim measure lapses upon the delivery of the final judgment, and it must be without prejudice to the decision of the Court on the substance of the case (Art. 86(3) and (4) RP). In other words, 'the urgent interim measure cannot affect the judgment in the main action and cannot therefore be allowed to attain the results sought by the main action; otherwise the latter would be without purpose' (Cases 24 and 97/80R *Commission* v. *France*, above, at p. 1338 *per* A.-G. Capotorti; Case 231/86R *Breda-Geomineraria* v. *Commission* [1986] ECR 2639 at p. 2645).

One final point concerns the extent to which the Court (or its President) may order particular measures the adoption of which falls within the competence of the Community executive (usually the Commission). Basing themselves on the principle of institutional balance or division of powers, in a consistent line of cases various Presidents have stated that the interim measures provided for by the Treaties 'can only be of a conservatory nature and do not give the Court the power to substitute itself for the administration or take, even provisionally, administrative decisions in place of the executive'

(Case 19/59R *Geitling* v. *HA* [1960] ECR 17, 34 at p. 37; see also Case 25/62R 1 *Plaumann* v. *Commission* [1963] ECR 95, 123 at p. 124 and in particular Case 109/75R *National Carbonising Company* v. *Commission*, above, at pp. 1201–2).

As regards procedure, applications for interim measures are governed by the same general rules as applications for suspension of operation, the only difference being that in the former case the applicant need not be 'challenging' a measure before the Court; it is sufficient if the applicant is a party to a case before the Court and the application relates to that case (Art. 83(1) RP). It may be noted that, in practice, in proceedings involving applications for interim measures more use is made of the possibility of the President's referring the application to the full Court under Art. 85 RP. This is what normally happens where the application is brought against a Member State under Art. 169 EEC (see the cases cited above), or where it raises a novel point of law of general importance (see e.g. Case 792/79R *Camera Care* v. *Commission* [1980] ECR 119 at p. 128).

2. Provisional protective measures may be adopted not only by the ECJ but also by the Commission in competition matters, after receiving complaints under Art. 3 of Reg. 17 (First Regulation implementing Arts. 85 and 86 EEC, *OJ Sp. Edn.* 1959–62, p. 87) or when acting on its own initiative under the same provision, pending the final decision on the substance of the case. Although Reg. 17 does not expressly confer upon the Commission the power to adopt interim measures, the ECJ has confirmed that the powers which the Commission holds under Art. 3(1) of Reg. 17 include the power to take such interim measures as are 'indispensable for the effective exercise of its functions and, in particular, for ensuring the effectiveness of any decisions requiring undertakings to bring to an end infringements which it has found to exist'. The Court has also pointed out that in taking such measures the Commission must have regard to the legitimate interests of the undertakings concerned by them. Therefore, interim measures may be taken only 'in cases proved to be urgent in order to avoid a situation likely to cause serious and irreparable damage to the party seeking their adoption, or which is intolerable for the public interest. A further requirement is that these measures be of a temporary and conservatory nature and restricted to what is required in the given situation. When adopting them the Commission is bound to maintain the essential safeguards guaranteed to the parties concerned by Regulation No. 17, in particular by Article 19. Finally, the decisions must be made in such a form that an action may be brought upon them before the Court of Justice by any party who considers he has been injured' (Case 792/79R *Camera Care* v. *Commission*, above, at p. 131). The Court has added that it is in fact 'in accordance with the key principles of the Community that any interim measures which prove to be necessary should be taken by the Community institution which is given the task of receiving complaints by governments or individuals, of making inquiries and of taking decisions in regard to infringements which are found to exist, whilst the role of the Court of Justice consists in undertaking the legal review of the action taken by the Commission in these matters' (ibid. at p. 132).

319

Subsequently, the Court stated that since the legal basis of the Commission's interim measures is Art. 3(1) of Reg. 17, 'the interim measures must come within the framework of the final decision which may be adopted by virtue of Article 3', and annulled an interim decision on the ground that the measure ordered by it did not come within the framework of a final decision which the Commission was able to adopt in the particular case (Cases 228 and 229/82 *Ford* v. *Commission* [1984] ECR 1129 at pp. 1161–2. The Court held that the Commission had exceeded the limits of its powers. See also Cases 228 and 229/82R *Ford* v. *Commission*, above, at pp. 3101–3, where the President of the Court suspended the operation of the Commission's interim decision in part).

For its part, the Commission has summarized the conditions to be met for the granting of interim measures as follows:

- the establishment by sufficiently clear evidence of a likelihood of infringement,
- the likelihood of serious and irreparable harm to the applicant unless measures are ordered,
- proven urgency.

The interim measure must further be restricted to the measures necessary for ensuring the effectiveness of any final decision. They may comprise an order to perform some act or to desist from some act provided each measure is indispensable and restricted to what is necessary in the particular situation.

In considering the terms of any order which it may make the Commission will also have regard to the balance between the likely harm to the applicant if it does not act and the effect upon the alleged infringer of any order as well as the interests of third parties which may be affected . . .

The measures to be adopted must be of a temporary nature, designed to restore the status quo and restricted to what is required in the situation in question. In making any order the Commission must have regard to the effect of the order on the parties involved. (*ECS/AKZO*, Commission Dec. 83/462, *OJ* 1983 L252/13 at pp. 17, 19).

In certain cases the Commission is willing to accept an undertaking from the company against which the complaint is directed, in lieu of taking an interim measure decision. This enables the Commission to respond to the complaint in the shortest possible time without prejudging the outcome of the main proceedings (see 15th *Comp. Rep. EC* (1985), pp. 55–6).

See also **Administrative procedure***, **Costs, Special forms of procedure, Suspension of operation.**

Further reading 1. BOOKS: *See under* **Suspension of operation.**
2. ARTICLES AND COMMENTS: Temple Lang, 'The Powers of the Commission to Order Interim Measures in Competition Cases' (1981) 18 *CML Rev*. 49; Wainwright, 'Article 186 EEC: Interim Measures and Member States' (1977) 2 *EL Rev*. 349. *See also under* **Suspension of operation.**

▶ **INTERLOCUTORY JUDGMENT** Judgment given by the ECJ at a particular stage in the proceedings where the Court is as yet unable to give a final decision on the disputed issues between the parties. Such a judgment may be used for a number of different purposes, e.g. to settle a preliminary question relating to jurisdiction and/or admissibility (see e.g. Case 110/75 *Mills* v.

Investment Bank [1976] ECR 955 at p. 971), often in response to a formal objection of inadmissibility (see e.g. Case 51/81 *De Franceschi* v. *Council and Commission* [1982] ECR 117 at p. 135); or to obtain further evidence (see e.g. Cases 5, 7, and 13 to 24/66 *Kampffmeyer* v. *Commission* [1967] ECR 245 at p. 268); or to enable the parties to reach extra-judicial settlement or to clarify certain aspects of the case by mutual agreement (see e.g. Cases 156/79 and 51/80 *Gratreau* v. *Commission* [1980] ECR 3943 at p. 3956). Thus, in actions for damages the Court may, by interlocutory judgment, establish the liability of the Communities in principle while ordering the parties to produce to the Court within a certain period of time figures of the amount of the compensation arrived at by agreement between them or, in the absence of such agreement, a statement of their views with supporting figures (see e.g. Cases 29/63 etc. *Usines de la Providence* v. *HA* [1965] ECR 911 at pp. 940–1; Case 74/74 *CNTA* v. *Commission* [1975] ECR 533 at pp. 550–1; Case 238/78 *Ireks-Arkady* v. *Council and Commission* [1979] ECR 2955 at pp. 2974–6). In actions brought by the Commission against a Member State under Art. 169 EEC, the Court may, by interlocutory judgment, order the parties to re-examine the issues between them in the light of the legal considerations contained in the judgment and to report to the Court within a specified period, either on any solution to the dispute which they have reached or on their respective viewpoints, to enable the Court to give final judgment in the case (see e.g. Case 170/78 *Commission* v. *United Kingdom* [1980] ECR 417 at p. 438; Case 149/79 *Commission* v. *Belgium* [1980] ECR 3881 at pp. 3904–5).

See also **Damage, Judgment, Preliminary objection.**

▶ *INTER PARTES* **EFFECT** Relative effect, usually meaning the binding effect of a judicial decision as between the parties and in the particular case only. Owing to the *res judicata* rule, the judgments of the ECJ normally produce *inter partes* effects. Strictly speaking, the only exceptions are judgments declaring an act of an institution void in a direct action for annulment under Arts. 33, 34 and 37, 38 ECSC, 173, 174 EEC, and 146, 147 Euratom, which are said to have *erga omnes* effects.

See also **Action for annulment,** *Erga omnes* **effect, Plea of illegality, Preliminary ruling,** *Res judicata.*

▶ **INTERPRETATION OF COMMUNITY LAW** Process of determining the meaning, scope, and effects of provisions of Community law. Since interpretation and application of the law are inseparably connected, both the courts of the Member States and the ECJ are called upon to interpret Community law as part of their normal judicial functions. Nevertheless, to ensure the uniform application of Community law in all the Member States, only the ECJ has jurisdiction to interpret that law with final binding effect. This is ensured in practice by the system of obligatory references to the ECJ

321

for interpretative preliminary rulings under Art. 177(3) EEC and Art. 150(3) Euratom.

Interpretation of Community law gives rise to particular difficulties on account of its peculiar characteristic features. These difficulties, and how national courts should deal with them, have been summarized by the ECJ as follows:

> To begin with, it must be borne in mind that Community legislation is drafted in several languages and that the different language versions are all equally authentic. An interpretation of a provision of Community law thus involves a comparison of the different language versions. It must also be borne in mind, even where the different language versions are entirely in accord with one another, that Community law uses terminology which is peculiar to it. Furthermore, it must be emphasized that legal concepts do not necessarily have the same meaning in Community law and in the law of the various Member States. Finally, every provision of Community law must be placed in its context and interpreted in the light of the provisions of Community law as a whole, regard being had to the objectives thereof and to its state of evolution at the date on which the provision in question is to be applied. (Case 283/81 *CILFIT* [1982] ECR 3415 at p. 3430.)

In its practice, the ECJ has had occasion to have recourse to all principal methods of interpretation which have been developed by national and international jurisprudence. The aim of these methods is to discover, respectively, the objective meaning of the words actually used, in the context of the instrument as a whole (grammatico-logical and systematic interpretation); the subjective intention of the legislator or, in the case of a contract/treaty, the common intention of the contracting parties (historical interpretation); the object and purpose of the particular provision as well as of the instrument as a whole (teleological interpretation). While the ECJ has used all these traditional methods, either separately or in combination with one another (placing the main emphasis on the teleological and systematic methods), it has at the same time developed its own special brand of interpretation as necessitated by the special nature of Community law. In so doing, it has laid down a number of rules and principles, the most important of which may be summarized as follows:

1. Where terms are not expressly defined, it is necessary, in order to determine their meaning, 'to have recourse to the generally recognized principles of interpretation, beginning with the ordinary meaning to be attributed to those terms in their context and in the light of the objectives of the Treaty' (Case 53/81 *Levin* [1982] ECR 1035 at p. 1048). 'In the absence of working documents clearly expressing the intention of the draftsmen of a provision, the Court can base itself only on the scope of the wording as it is and give it a meaning based on a literal and logical interpretation' (Case 15/60 *Simon* v. *Court of Justice* [1961] ECR 115 at p. 125). Where, however, literal interpretation fails to give a definite answer or leads to a conclusion which runs counter to common sense, to the basic principles of Community law or its rational (logical) application, or which is otherwise unacceptable, it is necessary to go beyond the text and have recourse to equity (see e.g. Case

94/75 *Süddeutsche Zucker* [1976] ECR 153 at p. 159 *per Curiam*, pp. 164–5 *per* A.-G. Warner), to the 'spirit' of the law (*ratio legis*), to the intention of the Community legislature or of the High Contracting Parties, to the scheme, object, and purpose of the provision in question (see e.g. Case 803/79 *Roudolff* [1980] ECR 2015 at p. 2024; Case 67/79 *Fellinger* [1980] ECR 535 at p. 550 *per* A.-G. Mayras), or to the foundations and the system of the Communities, as established by the Treaties (see e.g. Case 231/78 *Commission* v. *United Kingdom* [1979] ECR 1447 at pp. 1459–60). Very often a literal interpretation is, in itself, not sufficient (even if leading to an otherwise acceptable result) but must be confirmed by one or more of these various criteria (see e.g. Case 6/60 *Humblet* v. *Belgium* [1960] ECR 559 at p. 575; Case 30/59 *Steenkolenmijnen* v. *HA* [1961] ECR 1 at p. 19; Case 118/79 *Knauf* [1980] ECR 1183 at pp. 1190–1). While the intention of the High Contracting Parties is difficult to ascertain as no preparatory work (*travaux préparatoires*) has been made public in respect of the basic Community Treaties, the intention of the Community institutions may be determined in the light of the legislative history of the act in question and in the light of its preamble stating the main reasons for its adoption (see e.g. Case 29/69 *Stauder* [1969] ECR 419 at p. 425; Case 72/69 *Bremer Handelsgesellschaft* [1970] ECR 427 at p. 435; Case 36/77 *Greco* [1977] ECR 2059 at p. 2071).

2. The relevant provisions of the Treaty being interpreted must be read together and, in so far as possible, reconciled with one another as they mutually complement and supplement each other (see e.g. Case 9/61 *Netherlands* v. *HA* [1962] ECR 213 at pp. 235–6; Case 6/72 *Continental Can* v. *Commission* [1973] ECR 215 at p. 245).

3. A provision must be interpreted in the light of its own object and purpose and in the light of the object and purpose of the Article, Chapter, Title, Part, and Treaty in which it appears. In particular, the introductory Articles to each Treaty (i.e. Arts. 1 to 5 ECSC, 1 to 8 EEC, and 1 to 3 Euratom) lay down obligatory general principles and objectives whose scope of application extends over the whole spectrum of that Treaty and which are decisive for the interpretation of those more detailed provisions which give effect to them (see e.g. Case 22/70 *Commission* v. *Council* [1971] ECR 263 at pp. 274–5, interpreting the EEC's treaty-making power in the field of transport; Case 6/72 *Continental Can* v. *Commission*, above, at pp. 243–5, interpreting Art. 86 EEC; Case 167/73 *Commission* v. *France* [1974] ECR 359 at pp. 369–71, interpreting Art. 84(2) EEC; Case 43/75 *Defrenne* [1976] ECR 455 at pp. 471 *et seq.*, interpreting the direct effect of Art. 119 EEC). Where the provision is one of an act of secondary legislation, it must be interpreted in the light of the object and purpose of both the act itself and the relevant Treaty provisions under which the act was adopted (see e.g. Case 22/67 *Goffart* [1967] ECR 321 at pp. 326–7; Case 17/76 *Brack* [1976] ECR 1429 at p. 1451). When the wording of secondary Community law is open to more than one interpretation, preference should be given to the interpretation which renders the provision consistent with the Treaty rather than the interpretation which leads to its being incompatible with the Treaty (Case 218/82 *Commission* v. *Council* [1983] ECR 4063 at p. 4075).

4. 'Terms used in Community law must be uniformly interpreted and implemented throughout the Community, except when an express or implied reference is made to national law' (Case 49/71 *Hagen* [1972] ECR 23 at p. 34; see also Case 327/82 *Ekro* [1984] ECR 107 at p. 119). Owing to its autonomous and supranational character, 'the Community legal order does not . . . aim in principle to define its concepts on the basis of one or more national legal systems without express provision to that effect' (Case 64/81 *Corman* [1982] ECR 13 at p. 24. See also Case 270/81 *Felicitas* [1982] ECR 2771 at p. 2784, etc.). It follows that, unless proved otherwise, undefined terms appearing in Community texts must be presumed to have an independent Community meaning which must be ascertained in the light of the principles and objectives of the Community legal order and which must prevail over any different or conflicting meaning attributed to them in the laws of the Member States. Otherwise the meaning, scope, and effect of a Community concept could be determined and modified unilaterally by the national authorities, without any control by the Community institutions, and could vary from Member State to Member State. This would endanger the unity and efficacy of Community law (see e.g. Case 75/63 *Hoekstra* [1964] ECR 177 at pp. 184–5 and Case 53/81 *Levin*, above, at p. 1049, both interpreting the terms 'worker' and 'wage-earner' as they appear in Arts. 48 to 51 EEC; Case 2/74 *Reyners* [1974] ECR 631 at pp. 654–5, interpreting the concept of 'official authority' appearing in Art. 55(1) EEC; Case 41/74 *Van Duyn* [1974] ECR 1337 at p. 1350 and Case 36/75 *Rutili* [1975] ECR 1219 at p. 1231, both interpreting the concept of 'public policy' as it appears in Arts. 48(3), 56(1), and 66 EEC; Case 149/79 *Commission* v. *Belgium* [1980] ECR 3881 at p. 3903, interpreting the concept of 'public service' within the meaning of Art. 48(4) EEC; Case 149/85 *Wybot* [1986] ECR 2391 at pp. 2407–8; interpreting the concept of a 'session' of the European Parliament).

5. 'The different language versions of a Community text must be given a uniform interpretation and hence in the case of divergence between the versions the provision in question must be interpreted by reference to the purpose and general scheme of the rules of which it forms part' (Case 30/77 *Bouchereau* [1977] ECR 1999 at p. 2010. See also Case 6/74 *Moulijn* v. *Commission* [1974] ECR 1287 at p. 1293). Where a measure is addressed to all the Member States, 'the necessity for uniform application and accordingly for uniform interpretation makes it impossible to consider one version of the text in isolation but requires that it be interpreted on the basis of both the real intention of its author and the aim he seeks to achieve, in the light in particular of the versions in all four languages. [In such a case] the most liberal interpretation must prevail, provided that it is sufficient to achieve the objectives pursued by the [measure] in question. It cannot, moreover, be accepted that the authors of the [measure] intended to impose stricter obligations in some Member States than in others' (Case 29/69 *Stauder*, above, at pp. 424–5. See also Case 19/67 *Van der Vecht* [1967] ECR 345 at p. 354; Case 80/76 *Kerry Milk* [1977] ECR 425 at pp. 434–5; etc.).

6. Provisions laying down the fundamental freedoms guaranteed by the EEC Treaty (i.e. the free movement of goods, persons, services, and capital) may not be interpreted restrictively (Case 53/81 *Levin*, above, at p. 1049). Conversely, the various exceptions to and derogations from these provisions permitted by the Treaty must be interpreted strictly in order to avoid the effectiveness of Community law being defeated by unilateral measures of Member States (see e.g. Case 29/72 *Marimex* [1972] ECR 1309 at p. 1318; Case 2/74 *Reyners*, above, at pp. 654–5; Case 41/74 *Van Duyn*, above, at p. 1350; Case 29/75 *Kaufhof* v. *Commission* [1976] ECR 431 at p. 443).

7. Provisions conferring substantive or procedural rights upon individuals must not be interpreted restrictively. Consequently, the silence or obscurity of a text in a matter which affects the rights of individuals may not be construed in a manner unfavourable to them (see e.g. Case 25/62 *Plaumann* v. *Commission* [1963] ECR 95 at p. 107; Cases 8 to 11/66 *Cimenteries* v. *Commission* [1967] ECR 75 at p. 92; Case 140/73 *Mancuso* [1973] ECR 1449 at p. 1456; Case 66/74 *Farrauto* [1975] ECR 157 at pp. 161–2; Case 32/75 *Cristini* [1975] ECR 1085 at pp. 1094–5; Case 104/76 *Jansen* [1977] ECR 829 at p. 842).

The combined application of the above rules and principles has enabled the ECJ to use interpretation as a powerful instrument in maintaining the unity and effectiveness of Community law. The Court has thus been able not only to fill lacunae in the body of the law but also to contribute to its progressive development (in this respect, see in particular Case 22/70 *Commission* v. *Council*, above, at pp. 274–5; Case 6/72 *Continental Can* v. *Commission*, above, at pp. 243–5; Case 167/73 *Commission* v. *France*, above, at pp. 369–71). A dynamic interpretation makes it possible for the Court, without exceeding the limits of its judicial function, to ensure the necessary evolution of the law that life demands.

See also Acte clair, Expressio unius est exclusio alterius, **Preliminary ruling, Reference proceedings,** *Travaux préparatoires, Ut res magis valeat quam pereat.*

Further reading 1. BOOKS: Bredimas, *Methods of Interpretation and Community Law* (1978); Marsh, *Interpretation in a National and International Context* (1974).
2. ARTICLES, PAPERS, AND REPORTS: Bridge, 'National Legal Tradition and Community Law: Legislative Drafting and Judicial Interpretation in England and the European Community' (1981) 19 *JCMS* 351; Chevallier, 'Methods and Reasoning of the European Court in its Interpretation of Community Law' (1964–5) 2 *CML Rev.* 21; McMahon, 'The Court of the European Communities: Judicial Interpretation and International Organisation' (1961) 37 *BYIL* 320; Plender, 'The Interpretation of Community Acts by Reference to the Intentions of the Authors' (1982) 2 *YEL* 57; Court of Justice of the European Communities, 'Methods of Interpretation of Community Law by the Court of Justice and National Courts', Reports presented to a Judicial and Academic Conference (1976); 'The Interpretation of Community Law and the Role of the European Court', Papers given at a Conference organized by the UK Association for European Law and the Centre of European Law at King's College, London (1976).

325

Interpretation of judgments	▶ **INTERPRETATION OF JUDGMENTS** A 'special form of procedure' before the ECJ, the purpose of which is to have the Court construe the 'meaning or scope' of one of its judgments (Arts. 37 ECSC Statute, 40 EEC Statute, 41 Euratom Statute, 102 RP). In the words of A.-G. Lagrange, 'the application for interpretation is a special legal remedy making it possible to obtain an interpretation of an obscure or ambiguous provision contained in a judgment from the very court which gave that judgment: it is one of the rare applications in modern law of the maxim *"ejus est interpretari cujus est condere"* and is an exception to the principle according to which the Court is *functus officio*—that it has exhausted its jurisdiction—once it has given judgment' (Case *5/55 ASSIDER* v. *HA* [1955] ECR 135 at p. 147).

Interpretation by the Court of its own judgments is subject to three sets of conditions relating, respectively, to the application for, the interest in, and the subject-matter of, the interpretation. These are discussed below in turn.

First, an application for interpretation may only be made by a person who was a party to the case in which the judgment was given, or by a Community institution. An application by third parties is inadmissible (Case 24/66 *bis Getreidehandel* v. *Commission* [1973] ECR 1599 at p. 1603), although a third party who establishes an interest in the result of the interpretation may be allowed to intervene (Case 9/81—Interpretation *Court of Auditors* v. *Williams* [1983] ECR 2859 at p. 2861). The Court has interpreted the term 'party' broadly, holding that 'where several actions are brought against the same decision of [an institution] and where, as the result of one of those actions, the decision is annulled, the applicants in the other actions may be regarded as "parties" to the action . . . subject expressly to the condition that the applicant has cited in his previous application the same ground on which the judgment to be interpreted has annulled the decision or . . . has declared the application well founded. Each of these parties is thus entitled to ask for the interpretation of the judgment which annuls the decision or declares one of the other actions well founded' (Case *5/55 ASSIDER* v. *HA*, above, at pp. 141–2). Nevertheless, in reference proceedings for a preliminary ruling under Art. 177 EEC or Art. 150 Euratom, the parties to the main action pending before the national court are not entitled to request the ECJ to interpret the judgment delivered pursuant to those provisions. The reason is that since Art. 177 EEC and Art. 150 Euratom establish a direct form of co-operation between the ECJ and the national courts by means of a non-contentious procedure, in which the parties to the main action cannot take any initiative, it is 'exclusively for those courts . . . to decide whether they have received adequate clarification by the preliminary ruling given upon their request, or whether they consider it necessary to make a further reference to the Court' (Case 13/67 *Becher* [1968] ECR 187 at p. 197; see also Case 40/70 *Sirena* [1979] ECR 3169 at pp. 3170–1). While it thus seems that the proper procedure for obtaining interpretation of a preliminary ruling is for the national court to make a second reference under Art. 177 EEC or Art. 150 Euratom, the use of the special procedure for the interpretation of judgments is not altogether excluded (see Case 13/67 *Becher*, above, at p. 197); it may be resorted to, for example, by the institutions.

An application for interpretation of a judgment is not subject to time-limit (Case 5/55 *ASSIDER* v. *HA*, above, at p. 140). It must be made against all the parties to the case in which the judgment was given (which is taken to include interveners, see Cases 41, 43, and 44/73—Interpretation *S.A. Générale Sucrière* v. *Commission* [1977] ECR 445 at p. 448), and in the form prescribed for pleadings and applications originating proceedings in general (see Arts. 37 and 38 RP). It must therefore contain the conclusions of the applicant (Case 110/63A *Willame* v. *Commission* [1966] ECR 287 at p. 291) and must moreover indicate the judgment in question as well as the passages whose interpretation is sought (Art. 102(1) RP, see also Case 206/81A *Alverez* v. *Parliament* [1983] ECR 2865 at pp. 2877–8 *per* A.-G. VerLoren van Themaat).

Secondly, the applicant, whether a 'party' or an institution, must establish an interest in the interpretation. An interest will usually exist if the applicant is directly concerned with the interpretation and has no other means of ascertaining the correct meaning of the judgment (Case 5/55 *ASSIDER* v. *HA*, above, at p. 141).

Thirdly, there must exist a 'doubt' as to the 'meaning or scope' of the judgment. According to A.-G. Lagrange, 'this doubt must be specific and of such a nature as to interfere with the enforcement of the judgment . . . The courts are not there to give consultations of an academic nature on the judgments which they have given' (ibid. at p. 147). On the other hand, the term 'doubt' is more general (or less specific) than the term 'contestation' in the French version of the corresponding Art. 60 of the Statute of the International Court of Justice ('dispute' in the English version). Dealing with this question, the ECJ has stated that 'for an application for interpretation to be admissible it is enough that the parties in question give different meanings to the wording of [the] judgment' (ibid. at p. 142) or that 'the applicant alleges the existence of an ambiguity or of obscurity', while 'the question whether the judgment to be interpreted is or is not ambiguous or obscure appertains to the examination of the substance of the application' (Case 110/63A *Willame* v. *Commission*, above, at p. 292. See, however, the opinion of A.-G. VerLoren van Themaat in Case 206/81A *Alvarez* v. *Parliament*, above, at pp. 2876–8, pointing out that the dividing line between the admissibility and the substance of an application for interpretation is not always clear).

It is moreover necessary that the 'doubt' should relate to an issue decided by the judgment, but without reopening what was decided since it is clearly not possible to challenge the authority of *res judicata* under the pretext of interpretation. It follows that 'the Court cannot, for the benefit of an application for interpretation, restrict, extend or amend the rights arising out of its judgment and must limit itself to giving an interpretation where, as a result of some ambiguity in the wording, the judgment has left the extent of the consequences of what it involves in doubt' (Case 5/55 *ASSIDER* v. *HA*, above, at p. 147 *per* A.-G. Lagrange). It also follows that the subject of interpretation can only be those parts of the judgment 'which express the decision of the Court on the matter submitted to it: the operative part and such of the grounds as determine it and are essential for that purpose; those are the parts of the judgment which constitute the actual decision. On the other hand, the Court is not called upon to interpret ancillary matter which supplements or explains those basic grounds' (ibid. at p. 142 *per Curiam*). Moreover, 'in a judgment giving an interpretation the Court can only define the meaning and scope of a previous judgment; it cannot give judgment on matters which have not been decided by that judgment. The parties may not, by means of a request for interpretation, ask for a new decision on new disputes' (ibid. at pp. 143–4). The obscurity or ambiguity must furthermore affect the meaning or scope of the judgment itself in so far as it settles the particular case before the Court as between the parties; the procedure for interpretation may not be used for the purpose of clarifying or defining the possible effect of the judgment on other cases. In other words, the interpretation must concern 'the scope of the judgment as regards the relationship between the parties thereto', and may not deal with the general question of the legal authority of the Court's decisions (Case 70/63A *HA* v. *Collotti and Court of Justice* [1965] ECR 275 at pp. 279–80 *per Curiam*, pp. 282–3 *per* A.-G. Roemer; Case 24/66 *bis Getreidehandel* v. *Commission*, above, at p. 1603 *per Curiam*, pp. 1605–6 *per* A.-G. Reischl; Case 9/81— Interpretation *Court of Auditors* v. *Williams*, above, at p. 2862).

It follows from the foregoing that the Court will dismiss an application for interpretation (either as inadmissible or as unfounded) where the judgment in question is neither ambiguous nor obscure (in which case 'there is in principle nothing to be interpreted', see Case 5/55 *ASSIDER* v. *HA*, above, at p. 143; Case 110/63A *Willame* v. *Commission*, above, at p. 293); where the application concerns a matter with which the judgment did not deal (ibid.); or where the differences of opinion between the parties relate to the 'execution', 'application', or 'implementation', and not to the interpretation, of the judgment concerned (ibid. at p. 291; Case 9/81—Interpretation *Court of Auditors* v. *Williams*, above, at p. 2861; Case 206/81A *Alvarez* v. *Parliament*, above, at p. 2872).

Finally, it may be noted that the Court gives its decision in the form of a judgment the original of which will be annexed to the original of the judgment interpreted (Art. 102(2) RP). Since all the parties to the original case are involved (see above), it is inevitable that the interpreting judgment should have the same force of *res judicata* as the judgment interpreted, of which it must henceforth form part (Case 5/55 *ASSIDER* v. *HA*, above, at p. 149 *per* A.-G. Lagrange). An interpreting judgment is therefore binding not only on the applicant but also on any other party affected by the passage interpreted or by a passage which is exactly similar thereto (Cases 41, 43, and 44/73—Interpretation *S.A. Générale Sucrière* v. *Commission*, above, at p. 464).

See also Judgment, Order, *Res judicata*, Special forms of procedure.

Further reading: Lasok, *The European Court of Justice: Practice and Procedure* (1984), ch. 12, s. VII; Usher, *European Court Practice* (1983), ch. 8, paras. 8–25 *et seq.*

▶ **INTERVENTION** A 'special form of procedure' before the ECJ, the purpose of which is to enable third parties to participate in proceedings pending before the Court in whose result they can establish an interest, provided that they support the conclusions of one of the parties (Arts. 34 ECSC Statute, 37 EEC Statute, 38 Euratom Statute, 93 RP). In Community law, intervention is only possible on a strictly voluntary basis; the Statutes and the Rules of Procedure do not contain any provisions for compulsory intervention, i.e. for the compulsory joinder of third parties (see Case 12/69 *Wonnerth* v. *Commission* [1969] ECR 577 at p. 584; Cases 9 and 12/60—Third party proceedings *Belgium* v. *Vloeberghs and HA* [1962] ECR 171 at p. 187 *per* A.-G. Roemer). Nor do they provide for interpleader proceedings whereby a third party might pursue claims of his own against both parties to the principal action (ibid. at p. 188). The purpose of intervention has been explained by the ECJ as follows:

The efficient administration of justice and the need for certainty in legal relationships demand that persons interested in the result of an action pending before the Court be precluded from asserting their rights once a judgment has been delivered settling the question in dispute. It is precisely in order to meet this requirement that . . . the Protocol[s] on the Statute of the Court make available to third parties whose interests are involved in an action pending before the Court the right of voluntary intervention, provided that the purpose of their conclusions is solely to support . . . the conclusions of a party to the proceedings. (Cases 42 and 49/59—Third party proceedings *Breedband* v. *Aciéries du Temple* [1962] ECR 145 at p. 158; Cases 9 and 12/60—Third party proceedings *Belgium* v. *Vloeberghs and HA*, above, at p. 181.)

The ECSC Statute makes no distinction between the Member States, Community institutions, undertakings, associations, and private individuals but grants the right to intervene in general terms to 'natural or legal persons' establishing an interest in the result of a case. In the interpretation of the ECJ, this enables 'any natural or legal person without any distinction whatever to appear before the Court as an intervener . . .' (Case 25/59 *Netherlands* v. *HA* [1960] ECR 355 at p. 388, where the Court allowed the intervention of a co-operative, a private individual, a firm, a company, and an association), including not only the Member States but even their internal subdivisions having legal personality, such as the *Länder* of West Germany (Cases 3 to 18, 25, and 26/58 *Barbara Erzbergbau* v. *HA* [1960] ECR 173 at p. 187; Case 13/60 *Geitling* v. *HA* [1962] ECR 83 at pp. 143–4).

Under the EEC/Euratom Statutes, Member States and Community institutions enjoy a privileged position in that they may intervene in any case pending before the Court without establishing an interest in the result of that case (Case 15/63 *Lassalle* v. *Parliament* [1964] ECR 31 at p. 54 *per* A.-G. Lagrange). Thus, when in Case 138/79 *Roquette* v. *Council* [1980] ECR 3333 at pp. 3357–8 the Council challenged the power of the Parliament to intervene in an action for annulment brought under Art. 173 EEC, on the grounds that Parliament had not been given a right to bring such an action in its own name and that, furthermore, it could not show a legal interest in the outcome of the proceedings, the Court stated that '. . . all the institutions of the Community have the right to intervene. It is not possible to restrict the exercise of that right by one of them without adversely affecting its institutional position as intended by the Treaty and in particular Article 4(1) ... [Moreover] although ... persons other than States and the institutions may intervene in cases before the Court only if they establish an interest in the result, the right to intervene which institutions, and thus the Parliament, have ... is not subject to that condition.' (See also Case 139/79 *Maizena* v. *Council* [1980] ECR 3393 at pp. 3420–1.)

In addition to the Member States and Community institutions, the right to intervene is open under the EEC/Euratom Statutes to 'any other person' establishing an interest in the result of any case submitted to the Court, save in cases between Member States, between Community institutions, or between Member States and institutions. The Court has interpreted the term 'any other person' in the widest possible sense which includes non-Member States (Cases 91 and 200/82 *Chris International Foods* v. *Commission* [1983] ECR 417 at p. 419, where the Court held that Dominica was 'a person' and therefore allowed to intervene) as well as organizations not having legal personality 'if they display the characteristics which are at the foundation of such personality, in particular, the ability, however circumscribed, to undertake autonomous action and to assume liability' (Cases 41/73 etc. *S.A. Générale Sucrière* v. *Commission* [1973] ECR 1465 at p. 1468).

Thus, consultative bodies as well as associations and unions (including trade unions) formed for the representation and protection of manufacturers, producers, consumers, officials, the professions, etc., and possessing the necessary independence to act as responsible bodies in legal matters, may intervene in cases in whose result they can establish an interest. Since the interest of the intervener need not be distinct from that of the party whom he/it supports, associations concerned with the general and special interests of a trade or profession have a legitimate interest in defending, by way of intervention, the interests of their members. In fact, in the system of the EEC/Euratom Treaties intervention is a procedure particularly well suited to associations which are generally not entitled to institute proceedings in their own name for the protection of the collective interests of their members. Thus, for example, the Court has allowed the following bodies to intervene: the Assemblée permanente des présidents de chambres d'agriculture (Cases 16 and 17/62 *Producteurs de Fruits* v. *Council* [1962] ECR 471 at pp. 488–9; see also ibid. at pp. 479–80 *per Curiam*, p. 486 *per* A.-G. Lagrange); the Unione Nazionale Consumatori (Cases 41/73 etc. *S.A. Générale Sucrière* v. *Commission*, above, at pp. 1468–9); the Federation of European Bearing Manufacturers' Associations (Case 113/77 *Toyo Bearing* v. *Council* [1979] ECR 1185 at p. 1192); the Consultative Committee of the Bars and Law Societies of the European Community (Case 155/79 *AM & S.* v. *Commission* [1982] ECR 1575 at p. 1580), etc. (As regards staff associations and trade unions, see Case 175/73 *Union Syndicale* v. *Council* [1974] ECR 917 at pp. 925–6; Case 18/74 *Syndicat Général du Personnel* v. *Commission* [1974] ECR 933 at p. 945; Case 72/74 *Union Syndicale* v. *Council* [1975] ECR 401 at p. 410.) Nevertheless, entities which lack even the basic aspects of legal personality, i.e. a minimum of independence and responsibility, have no capacity to intervene (Case 15/63 *Lassalle* v. *Parliament*, above, at p. 51, where the Court dismissed as inadmissible an application to intervene made by the Staff Committee of the European Parliament, a body set up as a purely internal agency of an institution).

Under all three Statutes, intervention is subject to two main conditions: first, the intervener (other than Member States and Community institutions under the EEC/Euratom Statutes) must be able to establish an interest in the 'result' of the case, and, secondly, his conclusions must be limited to supporting the conclusions (or, under the ECSC Statute, requesting the rejection of the conclusions) of one of the parties. In the interpretation of the ECJ, these two conditions are very closely interrelated. Thus, the Court has frequently stated that since 'by the expression "result" is to be understood the operative part of the final judgment which [in their conclusions] the parties ask the Court to deliver' (Case 111/63 *Lemmerz-Werke* v. *HA* [1965] ECR 677 at p. 717), the intervener must show a 'direct, existing interest' in the acceptance by the Court of the conclusions of the party whom he supports (ibid. at p. 718). In other words, 'the interest in question must exist in relation to the said conclusions and not in relation to the submissions or arguments put forward' (Cases 116, 124, and 143/77 *Amylum* v. *Council and Commission* [1978] ECR 893 at p. 895; Case 111/63 *Lemmerz-Werke* v. *HA*, above, at p. 718; Case 30/59 *Steenkolenmijnen* v. *HA* [1961] ECR 1 at p. 48; Cases 56 and 58/64 *Consten and Grundig* v. *Commission* [1966] ECR 299 at pp. 383, 386; etc.). An interest in the success of certain abstract legal arguments is therefore not sufficient (ibid.).

Nevertheless, the intervener may advance arguments of his own which are different from, or even conflicting with, those of the party whom he is seeking to support since 'the intervention procedure would be deprived of all meaning if the intervener were to be denied the use of any argument which had not been used by the party which it supported' (Case 30/59 *Steenkolenmijnen* v. *HA*, above, at p. 18). At least under the ECSC Statute, he may also raise objections of inadmissibility which were not put forward by the defendant, since these objections clearly seek the rejection of the applicant's conclusions (Cases 42 and 49/59 *SNUPAT* v. *HA* [1961] ECR 53 at p. 75). Whether he may do so also under the EEC/Euratom Statutes was left open by the Court in Cases 142 and 156/84 *BAT and Reynolds* v. *Commission* [1987] ECR 4487 at p. 4571.

The existence of an interest must further be assessed in relation to the nature and the purpose of the action in question. As the ECJ has stated in the context of the ECSC Statute: 'Although it cannot be denied that it is in the interests of each Member State, as a signatory to the Treaty and responsible for its application, that [its provisions] be observed, it is no less true that the general interest in the observance of the Treaty cannot justify voluntary intervention in any and every action. In fact the interest in intervention in proceedings pending before the Court must be justified as much by reference to the nature of the proceedings in which the intervener asks to be allowed to take part as by reference to the conclusions of one of the parties which the intervener must support or reject' (Cases 9 and 12/60—Third party proceedings *Belgium* v.

331

Vloeberghs and HA, above, at p. 182). Generally, where the purpose of the proceedings is to obtain compensation for loss caused by a wrongful Community act or omission, and not to obtain a declaration with *erga omnes* effect that an act or omission is illegal, it will be more difficult for third parties to establish a 'direct and specific interest' in the outcome of the case, since this (i.e. the payment or non-payment of compensation) will normally only affect the parties themselves (ibid. at pp. 182–3). Thus, for example, in Cases 197 to 200/80 etc. *Ludwigshafener Walzmühle* v. *EEC* [1981] ECR 1041 at p. 1043, involving an action for damages, the Court dismissed an application to intervene made by a trade union since the only purpose of the intervener was to save the jobs of workers employed by the applicant undertakings. The Court held that 'such an interest, which is indirect and remote in its nature, is not sufficiently clearly defined to justify intervention in the proceedings'. Nevertheless, in the same cases the Court did allow two companies to intervene in support of one of the applicants, as well as a Member State (Italy), two trade associations, and a 'legal person' to intervene in support of the defendants (see [1981] ECR 3211 at p. 3219), which shows that intervention is not altogether excluded in actions for damages.

Where the action is directed against a measure adopted by an institution, the system of remedies established by the Treaties requires that the institution concerned itself should defend the validity of its measure and that it alone should decide how to defend its interests. Private persons acting solely in their capacity as members of the defendant institution do not have a sufficiently well-defined interest in such a dispute and hence do not have a right to intervene in support of their institution (Case 358/85 *France* v. *Parliament* [1986] ECR 2149 at p. 2152, dismissing an application to intervene submitted by five Members of the European Parliament. Although the application was brought under Art. 34 ECSC Statute, the principle established by the Court would seem to apply to intervention under the EEC/Euratom Statutes as well).

While under the ECSC Statute natural or legal persons may intervene in cases between Member States and Community institutions, the public law nature of such disputes necessarily imposes limits on the extent of their intervention. Thus, in Case 25/59 *Netherlands* v. *HA*, above, at p. 389, which involved an action under Art. 88 ECSC for the annulment of a High Authority decision recording the failure of the applicant to fulfil its obligations under the Treaty, the Court stated that: 'Although undertakings having an interest can be allowed to intervene in a dispute arising under Article 88, such intervention can, however, be for the sole purpose of obtaining an interpretation of the Treaty, to the exclusion of any consideration of determination of the time-limit which the High Authority can set that State for the fulfilment of its obligations or the detailed rules for the application of any restrictive decision by the Authority against that State since, in these various cases, the very nature of these acts, which take place at the level of the relationship between States, public authorities and the High Authority as the Community agency, precludes the intervention of private persons; and argument on these issues must, therefore, be conducted exclusively between the main parties'.

As regards proceedings other than direct actions, while intervention is not possible in references for a preliminary ruling under Art. 177 EEC or Art. 150 Euratom (Case 6/64 *Costa* [1964] ECR 585 at pp. 614–15; Case 19/68 *De Cicco* [1968] ECR 473 at p. 479. In both cases the Court stated that only those mentioned in Art. 20 EEC Statute might participate in reference proceedings), intervention has been allowed in certain ancillary proceedings, such as proceedings for the suspension of operation of Community acts (see e.g. Cases 71/74R and RR *Fruit- en Groentenimporthandel* v. *Commission* [1974] ECR 1031 at p. 1033) or for the adoption of other interim measures (see e.g. Case 109/75R *National Carbonising Company* v. *Commission* [1975] ECR 1193 at p. 1200) and, perhaps due to the special circumstances of the particular case, in proceedings for the interpretation of a judgment (Case 9/81—Interpretation *Court of Auditors* v. *Williams* [1983] ECR 2859 at p. 2861).

An application to intervene must be made within three months of the publication of the notice of commencement of proceedings in the *Official Journal*, as required by Art. 16(6) RP. It must be in the prescribed form (see Art. 93(2) RP) and must contain, amongst other things, the reasons for the intervener's interest in the result of the case and the conclusions supporting or opposing the conclusions of a party to the original case. The grounds for those conclusions must be stated within the period prescribed by the President of the Court. The parties to the principal action must be given an opportunity to submit their written or oral observations. The right to intervene does not automatically arise with the submission of the application; it arises only from the order whereby the Court allows the intervention (Case 30/59 *Steenkolenmijnen* v. *HA*, above, at p. 48). It follows that until this time the intervener may draw up his application in a language other than that of the case in the main action, but after the intervention has been allowed, he must use the language of the case, subject to the relevant rules (see, in particular, Art. 29(2)(c) RP) (ibid.). If the Court allows the intervention, the intervener must receive a copy of every document served on the parties, but the Court may, at the request of one of the parties, omit secret or confidential documents. The intervener must accept the case as he finds it at the time of his intervention (Art. 93 RP).

See also **Capacity to institute proceedings, Costs, Language of the case, Special forms of procedure, Third party proceedings.**

Further reading: Lasok, *The European Court of Justice: Practice and Procedure* (1984), ch. 5; Usher, *European Court Practice* (1983), ch. 11.

J

▶ **JOINDER OF CASES** Procedural device enabling the ECJ to deal jointly with a number of related cases concerning the same subject-matter. The Court may, at any time, after hearing the parties and the Advocate-General, decide to join cases for the purposes of the written procedure, the oral procedure, the final judgment, or all stages of the procedure (Art. 43 RP). Joinder may be ordered both in direct actions and in references for a preliminary ruling (whether coming from the same or different courts), although in the latter case only after the written observations have been lodged (Art. 103 RP). However, the joinder of a direct action to a reference for a preliminary ruling, although not expressly excluded, would be most unusual owing to the different nature of the proceedings.

Generally, the aim of a joinder is to achieve procedural economy; it serves the interests of a good administration of justice (Cases 27 and 39/59 *Campolongo* v. *HA* [1960] ECR 391 at p. 400). Where it is ordered for the purpose of delivering a single judgment, the objective is 'to avoid the possibility that two different judgments might lead to discordant interpretations' (Cases 36 to 38, and 40/59 *Geitling* v. *HA* [1960] ECR 423 at p. 438). In practice, the Court orders joinder where different applicants challenge the same measure on substantially the same grounds (even if by reason of different interests and for opposite purposes) (ibid.; see also e.g. Cases 19 and 20/74 *Kali-Chemie* v. *Commission* [1975] ECR 499 at p. 517); where different applications or references relate to the same facts, have the same subject-matter, and are supported by the same submissions (see e.g. Cases 112, 144, and 145/73 *Campogrande* v. *Commission* [1974] ECR 957 at p. 974; Cases 10 to 14/75 *Lahaille* [1975] ECR 1053 at p. 1068; Cases 154/78 etc. *Valsabbia* v. *Commission* [1980] ECR 907 at p. 989); or where successive actions are brought by the same applicant against the same defendant relating to the same subject-matter (see e.g. Cases 7 and 9/54 *Industries Sidérurgiques Luxembourgeoises* v. *HA* [1956] ECR 175 at p. 188). While the joinder of several cases does not preclude their separate examination in the same judgment from the point of view of both admissibility and substance (ibid.), in certain circumstances two joined cases may be so closely related that the inadmissibility of one may be covered by the admissibility of the other, and the arguments put forward in the first case may therefore be taken into consideration in deciding them jointly (see e.g. Cases 26 and 86/79 *Forges de Thy-Marcinelle et Monceau* v. *Commission* [1980] ECR 1083 at p. 1092). The joinder of intended future actions, not yet formally brought, with proceedings already pending before the Court, is not possible (Cases 42 and 49/59 *SNUPAT* v. *HA* [1961] ECR 53 at p. 73). The decision to join cases may subsequently be rescinded (Art. 43 RP; for examples of cases which were disjoined, see Cases 19 and 65/63 *Prakash* v. *Commission* [1965] ECR 533 at pp. 574–6; Case 261/78 *Interquell Stärke-Chemie* v. *EEC* [1982] ECR 3271 at pp. 3278–9; Case 262/78 *Diamalt* v. *EEC* [1982] ECR 3293 at pp. 3296–7).

See also Judgment, Oral procedure, Written procedure.

▶ JUDGMENT One of two main forms in which the ECJ makes its decisions (the other being an 'order'; in addition, the Court may give 'opinions', 'rulings', and other decisions). Judgment is normally given when the Court determines the disputed issues between the parties (whether of admissibility or of substance) or gives a preliminary ruling in reference proceedings. The Court also decides in the form of a judgment when it comes to the conclusion that there is no need for it to give a judgment (see e.g. Cases 5, 7, and 8/60 *Meroni* v. *HA* [1961] ECR 107 at p. 112). A judgment may be final, interlocutory (sometimes described as 'interim'), or mixed.

Judgments are adopted as a result of secret deliberations in which only those Judges may participate who were present at the oral proceedings. The number of deliberating Judges must always be uneven since the decision of the Court is determined by a majority vote. Every participating Judge must give his view and the reasons for it. A single judgment is always given and no separate or dissenting opinions are made public (Arts. 18, 29 ECSC Statute; 15, 32 EEC Statute; 15, 33 Euratom Statute; 26, 27 RP).

Apart from the names of the President and the participating Judges, Advocate-General, Registrar, parties, and their representatives, the judgment must contain the 'submissions' (i.e. conclusions) of the parties, a summary of the facts, the grounds (or reasons) for the decision, and the operative part including the decision as to costs (Arts. 30 ECSC Statute, 33 EEC Statute, 34 Euratom Statute, 63 RP). The judgment is divided into two main parts: 'Facts and Issues' (sometimes simply called 'Facts') and 'Decision' (until Mar. 1977, this second part was headed by the word 'Law'). The former contains a summary of the facts, the conclusions, submissions, and arguments of the parties, a brief description of the written and oral procedure, and the date of delivery of the Advocate-General's opinion. This part is based on the Report for the Hearing prepared by the Judge-Rapporteur. The 'Decision' part is further subdivided into the 'operative part' (*dispositif*) which contains the actual ruling of the Court on the issues submitted to it, including the order as to costs (this is printed in heavy type in the official *European Court Reports* at the end of the judgment); and the 'grounds' (*motifs*) which precede it and which contain the reasons for the Court's decision. The conclusions or claims (*petitum*) of the parties are dealt with in the operative part, and the supporting arguments and submissions (*causa petendi*) in the grounds of the judgment. The nature and scope of the operative part is basically determined by the nature and scope of the *petitum* since, on the one hand, the Court is normally required to give a decision on every head of claim (see Art. 67 RP, below) and, on the other hand, in accordance with the *ne ultra petita* rule, the Court cannot go beyond what is requested by the applicant. However, the same considerations do not apply to the grounds of the judgment as there is no rule that the judgment must deal with every argument presented to the Court, whether it is in point or not (Case 8/78 *Milac* [1978] ECR 1721 at p. 1739 *per* A.-G. Warner).

The importance of the distinction made between the different parts of the judgment is explained by the fact that these parts are not all equally binding. It is generally recognized that the binding force of a judgment (i.e. its *res judicata* effect) arises from the operative part which, in the case of doubt, must be interpreted or clarified in the light of the decisive grounds, i.e. those which led to the ruling of the Court and constitute its essential basis (see e.g. Cases 97/86 etc. *Asteris* v. *Commission* [1988] ECR 2181 at p. 2208). As the ECJ has stated, the only parts of a judgment which are legally binding are 'those which express the decision of the Court on the matter submitted to it: the operative part and such of the grounds as determine it and are essential for that purpose' (Case 5/55 *ASSIDER* v. *HA* [1955] ECR 135 at p. 142). Or, as A.-G. Lagrange has put it, 'only the operative part has the authority of *res judicata* although it may be *clarified* by the grounds' (ibid. at p. 148; see also in particular Case 111/63 *Lemmerz-Werke* v. *HA* [1965] ECR 677 at p. 717 *per Curiam*, p. 722 *per* A.-G. Roemer; Case 30/76 *Küster* v. *Parliament* [1976] ECR 1719 at p. 1726 *per Curiam*, p. 1731 *per* A.-G. Reischl; Case 135/77 *Bosch* [1978] ECR 855 at p. 859 *per Curiam*, p. 861 *per* A.-G. Warner). It follows that mere ancillary or subsidiary observations made in the 'Decision' (*obiter dicta*) do not, strictly speaking, produce *res judicata* effects. Nor is the 'Facts and Issues' part legally binding.

The judgment is delivered in open court; the parties must be given notice to attend to hear it. They are served with certified copies of it, the original being deposited at the Registry (Arts. 31 ECSC Statute, 34 EEC Statute, 35 Euratom Statute, 64 RP). The judgment becomes binding from the date of its delivery (Art. 65 RP) and is enforceable in the Member States (Arts. 44 and 92 ECSC, 187 and 192 EEC, 159 and 164 Euratom, 48(4) RP, 22(2) IR). The Registrar is required to arrange for the publication in all the official languages of *Reports of Cases before the Court (European Court Reports)*, which as a rule contain the judgments, interim orders, and opinions of the Court together with the opinions of the Advocates-General (Arts. 68 RP, 24 IR). Since the end of January 1985, the 'Facts and Issues' part of the judgment is not published (except in special cases), its essential contents being incorporated in the 'Decision' part. Since the second half of 1986, reference is made in the judgment to the Report for the Hearing (which since Sept. 1986 is also published) for a more detailed exposition of the facts, the procedure, and the claims and submissions of the parties. The operative part is also published in the *Official Journal of the European Communities* (Art. 25 IR). The only authentic version of a judgment is that drawn up in the language of the case (Arts. 30(2), 31 RP).

Judgments of the Court are final and, apart from applications to set aside a judgment by default, may only be reviewed under the two exceptional review procedures, i.e. third party proceedings and revision. However, without prejudice to the provisions relating to the interpretation of judgments, the Court may, of its own motion or on application by a party made within two weeks after the delivery of a judgment, rectify clerical mistakes, errors in calculation, and obvious slips in it (Art. 66 RP). While rectification may be made to any part of the judgment ('Facts and Issues', 'Decision', and even the operative part), it can only be made to correct purely material errors in cases where no difficulty arises concerning the meaning or scope of the decision. Rectification may therefore not be used to amend, revise, obtain an interpretation of, or in any way alter a legal decision contained in, the judgment (Cases 4 to 13/59 *Mannesmann* v. *HA* [1960] ECR 113 at p. 161; Cases 19/60 etc. *Fives Lille Cail* v. *HA* [1961] ECR 281 at pp. 315–16; Case 27/76 *United Brands* v. *Commission* [1978] ECR 207 at p. 347).

Similarly, if the Court should omit to give a decision on a particular point at issue or on costs, any party may within a month after service of the judgment apply to the Court to supplement its judgment (Art. 67 RP). The term 'party' in this context means a party to a direct action brought before the ECJ; 'parties' to national proceedings in which a reference for a preliminary ruling has been made cannot ask the Court to supplement the judgment given on the reference. The reason for this is that it is exclusively for the national court which has made the reference to decide whether it has received adequate clarification by the preliminary ruling or whether a further reference is necessary (Case 13/67 *Becher* [1968] ECR 187 at p. 197). By contrast, a judgment given in reference proceedings may be rectified by the Court since in this case the Court may act of its own motion (see e.g. Case 158/80 *Rewe OJ* 1981 C219/3). In the case of both rectification and supplementation, the parties may lodge written observations and the Court will make a decision after hearing the Advocate-General.

See also Causa petendi, Costs, Enforcement procedure, European Court of Justice, *European Court Reports, Functus officio,* Interlocutory judgment, Interpretation of judgments, Judgment by default, *Jurisprudence constante,* Language of the case, *Ne ultra petita, Obiter dictum, Official Journal,* Official languages, Opinion, Order, *Petitum, Ratio decidendi, Res judicata,* Retroactive effect, Revision of judgments, *Stare decisis,* Third party proceedings.

Further reading 1. BOOKS: Lasok, *The European Court of Justice: Practice and Procedure* (1984), ch. 12; Usher, *European Court Practice* (1983), ch. 8.

2. ARTICLE: Toth, 'The Authority of Judgments of the European Court of Justice: Binding Force and Legal Effects' (1984) 4 *YEL* 1.

▶ JUDGMENT BY DEFAULT Judgment given by the ECJ in direct actions against a defendant who, after having been duly served with an application orginating proceedings, fails to lodge a defence in the proper form within the time prescribed. Under the ECSC Treaty, judgment by default may only be given in proceedings in which the Court has unlimited jurisdiction (Arts. 35 ECSC Statute, 38 EEC Statute, 39 Euratom Statute, 94 RP).

A judgment by default must be requested by a separate application, which must itself be served on the defendant. This is followed by the oral procedure. Before giving judgment the Court must, after hearing the Advocate-General, consider whether the originating application is admissible, whether the appropriate formalities have been complied with, and whether the application 'appears' well founded. A preparatory inquiry may also be ordered. The judgment is enforceable.

Within one month from the date of service of the judgment, the defendant may apply, in the form prescribed for pleadings and originating applications in general (see Arts. 37 and 38 RP), to have the judgment by default set aside.

337

The other party (the original applicant) may submit written observations within a period fixed by the President of the Court. Pending its decision, the Court may grant a stay of execution of the judgment by default, or it may make execution subject to the provision of security. Following the oral procedure, the Court decides on the application to set aside by way of a judgment which may not itself be set aside. The original of this judgment will be annexed to the original of the judgment by default.

It may be noted that judgments by default constitute a 'special form of procedure', and that the proceedings for setting them aside are one of the only two procedures whereby a party may seek to have a judgment reviewed by the Court (the other being revision).

See also Judgment, Order, Revision of judgments, Special forms of procedure, Unlimited jurisdiction, Written procedure.

Further reading: Lasok, *The European Court of Justice: Practice and Procedure* (1984), ch. 12, s. IV; Usher, *European Court Practice* (1983), ch. 4, paras. 4–60 *et seq.*

▶ JUDICIAL REVIEW Control by the ECJ of the legality of the acts and omissions of the Community institutions, in particular those of the Council, the Commission, and the European Parliament, and also, in a wider sense, of the conformity with Community law of the legislative, executive, and judicial activities of the Member States. In the absence, at the present stage of European integration, of an effective political control by a parliamentary body, judicial review assumes paramount importance in the supranational legal order of the Communities. This is the more so as the Communities are based on the rule of law (Case 294/83 *Les Verts* v. *Parliament* [1986] ECR 1339 at p. 1365. See also *Report on European Union* by the ECJ, Suppl. 9/75—*Bull. EC* p. 17; Case 101/78 *Granaria* [1979] ECR 623 at p. 637). The wide-ranging powers conferred upon the Communities must at all times be exercised by the institutions in strict conformity with the Treaties, and the ECJ is expressly entrusted with the task of ensuring that in the interpretation and application of the Treaties the law is observed (Arts. 31 ECSC, 164 EEC, 136 Euratom; see e.g. Case 22/70 *Commission* v. *Council* [1971] ECR 263 at p. 276; Case 60/81 *IBM* v. *Commission* [1981] ECR 2639 at p. 2651). As the Council and the Commission may act as both legislative and executive organs, the powers of the Court extend to both controlling the constitutionality of legislation and reviewing executive action in the Communities. In the former role the Court normally acts in the public interests as the guardian of legality; in the latter context it is usually required to defend certain defined private interests recognized by the Treaties as worthy of protection.

Judicial review is exercised by the ECJ in two basically different ways, i.e. directly and indirectly. The Court exercises direct judicial control in proceedings specifically designed for that purpose, such as, principally, actions for annulment, actions for failure to act, actions against Member States, and, to a lesser extent, actions against penalties. Indirect judicial review is possible in reference proceedings for preliminary rulings, in actions for damages, and in the context of a plea of illegality. The scope and effect of the Court's power of review may vary according to the nature and purpose of these various proceedings. In some cases, i.e. in actions for annulment and actions against penalties, the Court can annul the illegal act, generally with *erga omnes* and *ex tunc* effects, whereas in others it can only declare an act invalid or inapplicable, such declaration usually (but not necessarily) having *inter partes* and *ex nunc* effects only. Nevertheless, through these various actions and proceedings, taken together, the Treaties established 'a complete system of legal remedies and procedures designed to permit the Court of Justice to review the legality of measures adopted by the institutions' (Case 294/83 *Les Verts* v. *Parliament*, above, at p. 1365).

Judicial control of the institutions by the ECJ is, however, subject to certain important restrictions. These restrictions arise from the fundamental principle of the separation of powers (or institutional balance) within the Communities, according to which each institution is required to act within the limits of the powers conferred upon it by the Treaties (Arts. 3 ECSC, 4 EEC, 3 Euratom). Thus the Court must observe the limits of the sometimes wide discretionary powers conferred upon the Council and the Commission for the purpose of formulating and implementing economic policies. The exercise of these powers involves the evaluation of complex economic facts, tendencies, and market conditions, the definition of the objectives to be pursued, and the choice of the appropriate means of action. In reviewing the legality of the exercise of such wide discretion, the power of the Court is restricted to examining whether an act contains a manifest error or constitutes a misuse of powers or whether the institutions did not clearly exceed the bounds of their discretion. But the Court is not entitled to enter the actual area of the discretion itself, i.e. the sphere of suitability or expediency. It cannot examine whether the measure is good, appropriate, or adequate. Nor can the Court substitute its own evaluation of the economic situation for that of the institutions. By so doing, the Court would replace the legislative discretion of the Council and the Commission by its own views of the economic policies to be pursued by the Communities. This would paralyse the activities of those institutions, causing a total confusion of powers. Under the disguise of judicial review, the Court would in fact assume the role of supreme legislator in the Communities and this is clearly not intended by the Treaties (Art. 33(1) ECSC; see e.g. Case 6/54 *Netherlands* v. *HA* [1955] ECR 103 at pp. 115–16 *per Curiam*, pp. 119, 125–7 *per* A.-G. Roemer; Cases 154/78 etc. *Valsabbia* v. *Commission* [1980] ECR 907 at pp. 991–3, 1002–3, 1005, 1007 *per Curiam*, pp. 1039–41 *per* A.-G. Capotorti; Case 136/77 *Racke* [1978] ECR 1245 at p. 1256; Case 138/79 *Roquette* v. *Council* [1980] ECR 3333 at pp. 3358–9; Cases 197 to 200/80 etc. *Ludwigshafener Walzmühle* v. *Council and Commission* [1981] ECR 3211 at p. 3251).

See also European Court of Justice, Institutional balance, Jurisdiction, Limited jurisdiction, Manifest error, Misuse of powers.

Further reading: Cappelletti, 'The "Mighty Problem" of Judicial Review and the Contribution of Comparative Analysis' (1979/2) *LIEI* 1; Mertens de Wilmars, 'The Case-Law of the Court of Justice in Relation to the Review of the Legality of Economic

339

Policy in Mixed-Economy Systems' (1982/1) *LIEI* 1; Van der Esch, 'Discretionary Powers of the European Executive and Judicial Control' (1968–9) 6 *CML Rev.* 209.

▶ **JURISDICTION (OF THE ECJ)** Power of the ECJ to deal with cases properly brought before it, including the power to decide whether or not it has jurisdiction in any particular case. The jurisdiction of the ECJ does not arise from a single general and all-embracing provision which would enable it to deal with any legal dispute falling within the material scope of application of Community law. The Articles laying down the Court's tasks (Arts. 31 ECSC, 164 EEC, 136 Euratom) do not by themselves confer jurisdiction upon it (Case 23/68 *Klomp* [1969] ECR 43 at p. 53 *per* A.-G. Gand; Case 66/76 *CFDT* v. *Council* [1977] ECR 305 at p. 310 *per Curiam*, p. 314 *per* A.-G. Reischl). Since the Court, like the other Community institutions, can act only within the limits of its powers (Arts. 3 ECSC, 4 EEC, 3 Euratom), it has jurisdiction only where jurisdiction has been expressly conferred upon it by or under a particular provision of the three basic Treaties (i.e. Arts. 32D, 33–43, 47, 63(2), 65(4), 66(5) and (6), 88, 89, 92, 95(4) ECSC; Arts. 93(2)(2), 100A(4), 168A, 169–86, 192, 215(2), 225(2), 228(1) EEC; Arts. 12(4), 18(1) and (2), 21(3) and (4) and (5), 38(3), 81(3) an (4), 82(4), 83(2), 103(3), 104(3), 105(2), 140A, 141–58, 164, 188(2) Euratom), or by or under a subsequent agreement to which all the Member States are parties (see e.g. Arts. 10, 13, 30 of the Merger Treaty of 1965; Art. 1 of the Protocol on the Privileges and Immunities of the European Communities of 1965; Protocols of 3 June 1971 relating to the interpretation of the Convention on Jurisdiction of 1968 and of the Convention on the Mutual Recognition of Companies of 1968; Art. 1(3) of the Treaties of Accession of 1972, 1979, and 1985 and of the accompanying Council Decisions on accession to the ECSC; Art. 31 of the Single European Act of 1986; Art. 25 of the Association Agreement of 1963 between the EEC and Turkey). Since these jurisdictional rules are mandatory in nature, the Court has no authority to depart from them.

Consequently, the Court has no 'residual' or 'inherent' powers, i.e. competence to hear cases not expressly falling within its jurisdiction, for example, to afford judicial protection to private individuals who might otherwise be deprived of all legal redress at both national and Community levels (Case 12/63 *Schlieker* v. *HA* [1963] ECR 85 at pp. 89–90 *per Curiam*, p. 92 *per* A.-G. Roemer; Case 66/76 *CFDT* v. *Council*, above). It follows from the foregoing that every single action brought before the ECJ must have a legal basis in an express jurisdictional clause. In other words, a right of action exists only in so far as the Court has been granted jurisdiction to entertain that particular action. The Court usually examines in the context of admissibility (but occasionally as a separate issue), and *ex officio* if necessary, whether its jurisdiction has been properly invoked. Where it is clear that the Court has no jurisdiction to take cognizance of an application, it may by reasoned order declare the application inadmissible even before it has been served on the opposite party (Art. 92(1) RP; see e.g. Case 46/81 *Benvenuto* [1981] ECR 809 at pp. 810–11; Case 229/81 *CO.DE.MI.* v. *Commission* [1982] ECR 377 at p. 379. See also Art. 92(2) RP and Case 138/80 *Borker*

[1980] ECR 1975 at p. 1977, applying the same rule to a reference for a preliminary ruling).

Since the jurisdictional provisions of the ECSC Treaty differ, in some cases considerably, from those of the EEC/Euratom Treaties (which are almost identical as far as the main forms of action are concerned), the ECJ is in effect subject to three different sets of basic jurisdictional rules (Arts. 3 and 4 of the Convention on Common Institutions 1957). These rules, taken as a whole, encompass a variety of proceedings that do not easily admit of classification. The use of traditional jurisdictional categories, such as international, constitutional, administrative, civil proceedings, can only be of a limited value. While indicating the extreme breadth of the Court's jurisdiction, they necessarily lack any precision of meaning in the context of the supranational legal order of the Communities. On the other hand, most (although not all) of the various proceedings may usefully be grouped into three broad classes according to formal (procedural) criteria. These are: direct actions, references for preliminary rulings, and requests for (advisory) opinions. Direct actions may further be divided into two main types according to the nature and extent of the Court's powers. Thus, in actions involving judicial review of the legality of the institutions' conduct (i.e. actions for annulment and actions for failure to act) the Court's jurisdiction is strictly limited, while in actions involving subjective rights and economic (pecuniary) considerations (i.e. actions for damages, actions against penalties, actions under an arbitration clause, staff cases, and certain other proceedings expressly specified by the Treaties) the Court has what is called unlimited or plenary jurisdiction. In this respect Community law closely follows the classic distinction made in French administrative law between *contentieux de l'annulation* and *contentieux de pleine juridiction* (see Case 3/54 *ASSIDER* v. *HA* [1955] ECR 63 at p. 75 *per* A.-G. Lagrange; Case 1/55 *Kergall* v. *Common Assembly* [1955] ECR 151 at p. 165 *per* A.-G. Roemer; Case 1/56 *Bourgaux* v. *Common Assembly* [1956] ECR 361 at pp. 374–5 *per* A.-G. Roemer).

The jurisdiction of the ECJ is, in principle, carefully separated from that of the courts of the Member States. The ECJ, on the one hand, and the national courts, on the other, are completely independent of one another within their respective spheres of competence. Accordingly, the ECJ has no jurisdiction to interpret (except perhaps in direct enforcement actions against Member States), apply (except where expressly authorized to do so), enforce, repeal, annul, or in any form review the legality of legislative or administrative acts of the Member States (as opposed to their compatibility with Community law) even where such acts have been adopted in implementation of Community provisions. All this is within the competence of the national authorities and courts (see e.g. Case 6/60 *Humblet* v. *Belgium* [1960] ECR 559 at p. 568; Case 10/61 *Commission* v. *Italy* [1962] ECR 1 at p. 9; Case 96/71 *Haegeman* v. *Commission* [1972] ECR 1005 at p. 1015; Case 46/75 *IBC* v. *Commission* [1976] ECR 65 at pp. 79–80; Case 46/81 *Benvenuto*, above).

Nor is the ECJ structurally superimposed upon national courts and proceedings in the sense that decisions taken in those proceedings could be challenged before it: the ECJ is not a Supreme Court of Appeal (see Case

341

276/86 *Belkacem* v. *Germany* [1986] ECR 3975 at p. 3977). Moreover, any overlapping (concurrence) of the respective jurisdictions of the ECJ and the national courts is in principle also excluded. There is thus no possibility of submitting one and the same dispute, either simultaneously or successively, to the decision of them both. To the extent to which the ECJ has been given jurisdiction by or under the Treaties in any given matter, its jurisdiction is exclusive and a prior exhaustion of the domestic judicial or administrative remedies is neither necessary nor possible. Conversely, the fact that a matter properly falls within the competence of the national courts prevents that matter from being submitted to the ECJ in circumvention of the national jurisdiction (see e.g. Case 6/60 *Humblet* v. *Belgium*, above, at pp. 572–3; Case 65/74 *Porrini* [1975] ECR 319 at pp. 333, 334–5 *per* A.-G. Reischl; Case 101/78 *Granaria* [1979] ECR 623 at pp. 638–9; Case 92/78 *Simmenthal* v. *Commission* [1979] ECR 777 at pp. 797–8). Where jurisdiction is not conferred upon the ECJ, disputes to which any of the Communities is a party are not on that ground excluded from the jurisdiction of the courts or tribunals of the Member States (Arts. 40(3) ECSC, 183 EEC, 155 Euratom).

It must be stated, however, that in spite of this clear division of jurisdiction, in principle, between the ECJ and the national courts, difficult problems as to the delimitation of their respective powers do arise in practice. This is so particularly in reference proceedings for preliminary rulings, which are based on a special relationship between the ECJ and the national courts, and in actions for damages involving the question of the legality of and liability for measures taken by national authorities in implementation of Community provisions. In the latter context, exceptionally, prior exhaustion of domestic remedies may become a prerequisite for an action before the ECJ, and the possibility of concurrent jurisdiction may also arise (see e.g. Cases 5, 7, and 13 to 24/66 *Kampffmeyer* v. *Commission* [1967] ECR 245 at pp. 264, 266–7). In general, the ECJ tends to resolve jurisdictional problems in the light of the nature and purpose of the proceedings in which they arise.

The jurisdiction of the ECJ is also delimited towards the International Court of Justice and other courts and tribunals adjudicating on the basis of public international law. The Court has been granted both compulsory (Arts. 89(1) ECSC, 170 EEC, 142 Euratom) and optional jurisdiction (Arts. 89(2) ECSC, 182 EEC, 154 Euratom) in disputes between Member States relating to the application or the subject-matter of the Treaties. Whether compulsory or optional, the jurisdiction of the ECJ is ultimately always exclusive in disputes between Member States falling within the scope of application of Community law, as the States have undertaken not to submit disputes concerning the interpretation or application of the Treaties (which include secondary legislation) to any method of settlement other than those provided for therein (Arts. 87 ECSC, 219 EEC, 193 Euratom). On the other hand, disputes between the Communities or the Member States and third States or international organizations do not normally fall within the jurisdiction of the Court (see Cases 21 to 24/72 *International Fruit Company* [1972] ECR 1219 at p. 1234 *per* A.-G. Mayras), unless such States or organizations have been granted a right of action before the ECJ, e.g. by means of an arbitration clause or an international agreement. Third States may, however, be allowed to intervene in actions pending before the Court (see Cases 91 and 200/82 *Chris International Foods* v. *Commission* [1983] ECR 417 at p. 419, where Dominica was allowed to intervene). Since disputes involving the Communities cannot be brought before the International Court of Justice either (under Art. 34(1) of the ICJ's Statute 'only States may be parties in cases before the Court'), they must be settled according to one of the methods usually available under international law, i.e. by negotiations, conciliation, or arbitration (*see further under* **External relations**, section V).

See also **Arbitration clause, Compulsory jurisdiction, European Court of Justice, External relations, Judicial review, Limited jurisdiction, Optional jurisdiction, Preliminary ruling, Right of action, Unlimited jurisdiction.**

▶ *JURISPRUDENCE CONSTANTE* Established case-law; settled judicial practice arising from a series of similar decisions given in similar cases by the same court. Although, owing to the *res judicata* rule and to the absence of a doctrine of *stare decisis* in Community law, the ECJ is not bound to follow its previous decisions, generally it tends to decide similar cases in a similar way. This is required by the principle of legal certainty and the need for judicial reliability, which is not possible to maintain without a certain degree of stability in the case-law (see the opinion of A.-G. Gand in Case 30/66 *Becher* v. *Commission* [1967] ECR 285 at p. 305). As A.-G. Lagrange has put it: 'Clearly no one will expect that, having given a leading judgment . . . the Court will depart from it in another action without strong reasons' even if it retains the right to do so (Cases 28 to 30/62 *Da Costa* [1963] ECR 31 at p. 42). Or, to cite A.-G. Warner: 'I realize of course that the Court is not strictly bound by its own decisions. But it seldom departs from them, and in this, in my opinion, it is wise, because certainty in the law is of great importance' (Case 62/76 *Strehl* [1977] ECR 211 at p. 220). As a result, over the years the Court has built up a remarkably consistent case-law on both substantive and procedural issues. In its judgments, the Court not only relies upon individual past decisions but, with increasing frequency, it refers to its 'established case-law' (see e.g. Case 284/82 *Busseni* v. *Commission* [1984] ECR 557 at p. 566), 'well-established case-law' (see e.g. Case 8/81 *Becker* [1982] ECR 53 at p. 70), 'consistent' practice (see e.g. Case 199/82 *San Giorgio* [1983] ECR 3595, at p. 3611), 'consistent line of decisions' (see e.g. Case 20/81R *Arbed* v. *Commission* [1981] ECR 721 at p. 730), or 'long line of decisions' (see e.g. Case 152/84 *Marshall* [1986] ECR 723 at p. 748). Clearly, the longer the line of similar past decisions the more 'constant' and 'established' the practice, and the less likely that the Court will depart from it. Thus, while an individual judgment does not in itself have the force of a binding 'precedent', it may generate a series of decisions adopting the same solution and this will ultimately lead to a *jurisprudence constante* which may be relied upon with a great degree of certainty as being followed by the Court in similar future cases.

See also **Res judicata, Stare decisis.**

L

▶ **LACK OF COMPETENCE** One of four grounds of action on which binding acts of the Council, the Commission, and the European Parliament may be challenged before, and declared void by, the ECJ in the framework of annulment proceedings (Arts. 33 and 38 ECSC, 173 EEC, 146 Euratom).

This ground of action gives effect to the general principle that an act is invalid if it originates from a body which does not possess the requisite power for its adoption. The Community institutions possess power (i.e. 'competence') to adopt an act only where such power has been conferred upon them by or under (or may be implied from) a Treaty provision. Each institution is specifically required to act within the limits of the powers so conferred (Arts. 3 ECSC, 4 EEC, 3 Euratom). The ECJ will declare void, for lack of competence, an act which does not have a proper legal basis in a relevant Treaty provision or in another measure itself adopted under the Treaties (see e.g. Cases 228 and 229/82 *Ford* v. *Commission* [1984] ECR 1129 at p. 1162 and the cases cited below).

The institutions' powers are defined by reference to three distinct types of relationship, i.e. those between the Communities and the Member States, those between the various institutions themselves, and those between the Communities and third countries. A lack of competence may therefore occur in three different sets of circumstances. First, where an institution exercises a power not transferred to the Communities from the Member States or acts in an area not placed under Community competence (see e.g. Case 108/83 *Luxembourg* v. *Parliament* [1984] ECR 1945 at pp. 1959–61, where the Court held that the decision to transfer the General Secretariat from Luxembourg to Strasbourg and Brussels was beyond the powers of the European Parliament; Cases 281/85 etc. *Germany and Others* v. *Commission* [1987] ECR 3203 at p. 3255). Secondly, where it exercises a power conferred upon another institution or upon two institutions jointly and not, or not properly, delegated to it or exceeds the limits of delegated powers (see e.g. Case 61/86 *United Kingdom* v. *Commission* [1988] ECR 431 at 464; Case 264/86 *France* v. *Commission* [1988] ECR 973 at p. 998). Thirdly, where it exercises a Community competence in relation to a non-Member State or its subjects (e.g. extraterritorially) in circumstances not authorized by general international law. In each individual case, the limits of the powers conferred on the institutions by a specific Treaty provision must be established by interpreting the wording of that provision in the light of its purpose and its place in the scheme of the Treaty (Cases 188 to 190/80 *France, Italy and United Kingdom* v. *Commission* [1982] ECR 2545 at p. 2573, where the ECJ, after examining the Commission's powers under Art. 90 EEC, rejected the submission of lack of competence). Since lack of competence is a ground of action that concerns public policy, the ECJ will examine this ground of its own motion even if it has not formally been pleaded by the applicant (see e.g. Case 14/59 *Fonderies de Pont-à-Mousson* v. *HA* [1959] ECR 215 at p. 229; Case 19/58 *Germany* v. *HA* [1960] ECR 225 at p. 233).

See also **Grounds of action, Institutional balance.**

► LANGUAGE OF THE CASE Language in which a case is conducted before the ECJ. The language of the case may be one of the nine official languages of the Communities (i.e. Danish, Dutch, English, French, German, Greek, Italian, Portuguese, Spanish) or Irish (Art. 29(1) RP as last amended on 8 May 1987, *OJ* 1987 L165/1).

In direct actions, the language of the case is normally chosen by the applicant. This rule is subject to the following derogations and exceptions:

1. where the application is made against a Member State or a natural or legal person having the nationality of a Member State, the language of the case is the official language of that State. Where that State has more than one official language, the applicant may choose between them;
2. at the joint request of the parties the Court may authorize another of the languages mentioned to be used for all or part of the proceedings;
3. at the request of one of the parties (other than a Community institution), and after hearing the opposite party and the Advocate-General, the Court may likewise authorize another of the languages mentioned to be used for all or part of the proceedings.

In references for a preliminary ruling, the language of the case is the language of the national court or tribunal which refers the matter to the Court (Art. 29(2) RP).

As a general rule, the language of the case must be used at all stages of the procedure, written and oral, in all supporting documents, in the minutes and decisions of the Court and by all parties and other participants (Art. 29(3) RP). This rule is subject to the following derogations and exceptions:

1. an intervener is obliged to use the language of the case only from the time when his intervention is allowed so that he may draw up his application in any other language (Case 30/59 *Steenkolenmijnen* v. *HA* [1961] ECR 1 at p. 48). Where the intervener is a Member State, it is entitled to use its official language both in written statements and in oral addresses (Art. 29(3) RP);
2. a Member State is entitled to use its official language when taking part in reference proceedings for a preliminary ruling; this applies both to written statements and to oral addresses (ibid.);
3. where a witness or expert is unable adequately to express himself in one of the procedural languages, the Court or Chamber may authorize him to give his evidence in another language (Art. 29(4) RP);
4. the President of the Court and the Presidents of Chambers in conducting oral proceedings, the Judge-Rapporteur in his Reports, Judges and Advocates-General in putting questions, and Advocates-General in delivering their opinions may use a procedural language other than the language of the case (Art. 29(5) RP).

Supporting documents drawn up in any other language must be accompanied by a translation into the language of the case (Art. 29(3) RP). Since, however, the ECJ, like the other institutions, is, by virtue of an irrebuttable presumption of law, cognizant of all the official languages, it will take notice not only of the existence but also of the contents of documents produced in any official language, even if not accompanied by a translation (Case 1/60 *FERAM* v. *HA* [1960] ECR 165 at pp. 169–70). It is the duty of the Registrar to arrange for the translation of documents and oral addresses submitted or made in another authorized language into the language of the case (Art. 29(3)–(5) RP). Although the decisions of the Court are published in all the nine official languages, only the version drawn up in the language of the case is authentic (Arts. 30(2) and 31 RP).

See also **Official languages.**

Further reading: Lasok, *The European Court of Justice: Practice and Procedure* (1984), ch. 2; Usher, *European Court Practice* (1983), ch. 3.

▶ **LEGAL AID** Recoverable aid granted by the ECJ for the purpose of assisting a party to a case who is wholly or in part unable to meet the costs of the proceedings (Arts. 76 and 104(3) RP, 4–5 SR). Such a party may at any time apply for legal aid; the application must be accompanied by evidence of his need of assistance, and in particular by a document from the 'competent authority' certifying his lack of means. (It may be noted that the Court's Rules do not specify what is the 'competent authority'.) If the application is made prior to the proceedings which the applicant wishes to commence, it must also state briefly the subject of such proceedings. In this latter case, the application for legal aid need not be made through a lawyer.

The decision whether legal aid should be granted in full or in part, or whether it should be refused, is made by the Chamber to which the Judge-Rapporteur belongs who has been designated by the President to act in the case. After considering the written observations of the opposite party and after hearing the Advocate-General, the Chamber makes an order without giving reasons, from which no appeal lies. (As the order is not reasoned, it is virtually impossible to establish what criteria the Chambers use when deciding whether to grant legal aid and, if so, how much.) Where there is manifestly no cause of action, legal aid is to be refused.

Where the proposed action clearly does not fall within the jurisdiction of the Court, the Chamber may, by reasoned order made under Art. 92(1) RP, declare the application for legal aid inadmissible even without first considering the observations of the opposite party (Case 233/82 *K* v. *Germany and Parliament* [1982] ECR 3637 at p. 3638). Should the circumstances which led to its grant alter during the proceedings, the Chamber may at any time, either of its own motion or on application, withdraw the legal aid.

Where legal aid is granted, the cashier of the Court is required to advance the funds necessary to meet the expenses (Art. 76(5) RP), but if the Registrar is of the opinion that the amount applied for is excessive, he may of his own motion reduce it or order payment by instalments (Art. 21(2) IR). In practice, this seems to be possible only where a Chamber grants legal aid up to a fixed sum (as e.g. in Case 18/63 *Wollast* v. *EEC* [1964] ECR 85 at p. 95, where legal aid was granted up to a limit of 30,000 BF, or in Case 35/67 *Van Eick* v. *Commission* [1968] ECR 329 at p. 332, where the First Chamber granted legal aid up to the amount of 15,000 BF), but not where a Chamber explicitly rules that 'the Cashier of the Court should make the applicant a recoverable advance' of a fixed amount (as in Cases 19 and 65/63 *Prakash* v. *Commission* [1965] ECR 533 at p. 545, or in Case 68/63 *Luhleich* v. *Commission* [1965] ECR 581 at p. 591. In both cases the fixed amount was 25,000 BF). A Chamber may, alternatively, order that legal aid be paid 'when the case is concluded, unless special costs justify an application for an advance payment' (Case 35/67 *Van Eick* v. *Commission*, above, at p. 332).

In its decision as to costs, the Court may order the payment to the cashier of the whole or any part of amounts advanced as legal aid (Art. 76(5) RP). In practice, the sum so advanced is recovered from the party ordered to pay the costs, i.e. in most cases the unsuccessful party. If, therefore, the party who has been granted legal aid fails in his application, he will normally be required to refund any sums received (see e.g. Cases 19 and 65/63 *Prakash* v. *Commission*, above, at p. 561; Case 25/68 *Schertzer* v. *Parliament* [1977] ECR 1729 at pp. 1745–6). If, on the other hand, the legally aided party is successful and is awarded costs, the losing party will be ordered to reimburse to the Court the sum granted by way of legal aid (see e.g. Case 18/63 *Wollast* v. *EEC*, above, at pp. 101–2; Case 68/63 *Luhleich* v. *Commission*, above, at pp. 607–8; Case 175/80 *Tither* v. *Commission* [1981] ECR 2345 at p. 2361). It is for the Registrar to take the necessary steps to obtain the recovery of these sums from the party ordered to pay them (Art. 22 IR).

In references for a preliminary ruling, it is only in 'special circumstances' that the Court may grant legal aid, for the purpose of facilitating the representation or attendance of a party (Art. 104(3) RP; see e.g. Case 152/79 *Lee* [1980] ECR 1495 at p. 1498; Case 240/81 *Einberger* [1982] ECR 3699 at p. 3701. In both cases legal aid was granted to facilitate the representation of one of the parties. By contrast, in Case 96/80 *Jenkins* [1981] ECR 911 at p. 932 *per* A.-G. Warner, legal aid was refused to the respondent, a comparatively small company which, as a result, could not afford to be represented before the Court). Since in reference proceedings it is for the national court to decide as to the costs of the reference (Art. 104(3) RP), it is not clear whether and, if so, how the ECJ may recover sums advanced by it as legal aid in such proceedings.

When granting legal aid, the Court is required to order that a lawyer be appointed to act for the recipient. If the latter does not indicate his choice of lawyer, or if the Court considers that his choice is unacceptable, the Registrar will send a copy of the order and of the application for legal aid to the 'competent authority' of the Member State concerned (which, in the case of the United Kingdom, is either the English, Scottish, or Northern Irish Law Society, depending on the place of residence of the applicant). In the light of the suggestions made by that authority, the Court appoints a lawyer of its own motion. The Court advances the funds necessary to meet expenses, and has the power to adjudicate on the lawyer's disbursements and fees. The President may, on application by the lawyer, order that he should receive an advance (Arts. 4–5 SR).

347

See also Costs, Enforcement procedure.

Further reading 1. BOOKS: Lasok, *The European Court of Justice: Practice and Procedure* (1984), ch. 4, s. v; Usher, *European Court Practice* (1983), ch. 16.

2. ARTICLE: Kennedy, 'Paying the Piper: Legal Aid in Proceedings before the Court of Justice' (1988) 25 *CML Rev.* 559.

▶ **LEGAL CERTAINTY** General principle of law of fundamental importance forming the basis of a stable and reliable Community legal order. In its broadest sense, it means that 'Community legislation must be unequivocal and its application must be predictable for those who are subject to it' (Case 70/83 *Kloppenburg* [1984] ECR 1075 at p. 1086; Cases 212 to 217/80 *Salumi* [1981] ECR 2735 at p. 2751; Case 325/85 *Ireland* v. *Commission* [1987] ECR 5041 at p. 5088). In other words, the rules of Community law, as well as the rules of the Member States in areas covered by Community law, 'must be clear and precise so that [those concerned] may know without ambiguity what are [their] rights and obligations and may take steps accordingly' (Case 169/80 *Gondrand* [1981] ECR 1931 at p. 1942; Case 257/86 *Commission* v. *Italy* [1988] ECR 3249 at p. 3267). It follows that 'any factual situation should normally, in the absence of any contrary provision, be examined in the light of the legal rules existing at the time when that situation obtained' (Case 10/78 *Belbouab* [1978] ECR 1915 at p. 1924).

Owing to its fundamental importance, the principle of legal certainty pervades all aspects of Community law, substantive and procedural alike. It has been applied by the ECJ in a variety of situations in all major areas of Community law, of which the following may be mentioned:

- in *competition law*, the Court formulated the doctrine of 'provisional validity' by reference to the requirement of legal certainty holding that 'it would be contrary to the general principle of legal certainty—a rule of law to be upheld in the application of the Treaty—to render agreements automatically void before it is even possible to tell which are the agreements to which Article 85 [EEC] as a whole applies' (Case 13/61 *Bosch* [1962] ECR 45 at p. 52; Cases 209 to 213/84 *Asjes* [1986] ECR 1425 at p. 1469; see also Case 10/69 *Portelange* [1969] ECR 309 at p. 316 and Case 48/72 *Brasserie de Haecht* [1973] ECR 77 at pp. 86–7, the latter referring to the principle of 'contractual certainty'. See also Case 127/73 *BRT* [1974] ECR 51 at p. 63, where the Court referred to legal certainty in a procedural context);
- in *agricultural law*, the Court interpreted the regulations altering the system and amount of denaturing premiums by reference to the principle of legal certainty (Case 78/74 *Deuka* [1975] ECR 421 at p. 433 *per Curiam*, p. 440 *per* A.-G. Trabucchi; Case 5/75 *Deuka* [1975] ECR 759 at p. 771);
- in *customs law*, the Court relied on the principle of legal certainty in the interpretation of the Common Customs Tariff (Cases 98 and 99/75 *Carstens Keramik* [1976] ECR 241 at p. 250; Case 169/80 *Gondrand*, above, at p. 1942);
- in *social security law*, the Court interpreted the requirement that a

worker must be a national of one of the Member States so as to satisfy the principle of legal certainty (Case 10/78 *Belbouab*, above, at p. 1924); it also ruled that, in the interest of legal certainty, notification of decisions of social security institutions to workers resident in another Member State must be effected without an intermediary, and that 'the national courts of the Member States must . . . take care that legal certainty is not prejudiced by a failure arising from the inability of the worker to understand the language in which a decision is notified to him' (Case 66/74 *Farrauto* [1975] ECR 157 at p. 162);

- in relation to *retroactive effect*, the Court stated that 'in general the principle of legal certainty precludes a Community measure from taking effect from a point in time before its publication' (Case 98/78 *Racke* [1979] ECR 69 at p. 86; Cases 212 to 217/80 *Salumi*, above, at p. 2751; Case 224/82 *Meiko-Konservenfabrik* [1983] ECR 2539 at p. 2548; see also Case 70/83 *Kloppenburg*, above, at p. 1086). On the other hand, the interpretative judgments of the Court itself normally have retroactive effect in that an interpretation given by the Court applies also to legal relationships arising before the date of the judgment. However, the Court may exceptionally, 'in application of the general principle of legal certainty inherent in the Community legal order', restrict the retroactive effect of its interpretative judgments in order not to upset legal relationships established in good faith in the past (Case 61/79 *Denkavit Italiana* [1980] ECR 1205 at p. 1223, citing Case 43/75 *Defrenne* [1976] ECR 455 at p. 481, where the Court, referring to 'important considerations of legal certainty', restricted the application of its judgment establishing the direct effect of Art. 119 EEC to future cases). Likewise, for reasons of legal certainty the Court may restrict the retroactive effect of a judgment declaring a regulation void or invalid, even where this is not expressly provided for by the Treaties (Case 4/79 *Providence Agricole de la Champagne* [1980] ECR 2823 at pp. 2853–4; Case 45/86 *Commission* v. *Council* [1987] ECR 1493 at p. 1522);

- in defining the *legal effects of its judgments* given under Art. 177 EEC, the Court has relied on 'particularly imperative requirements concerning legal certainty'. It has held that national courts may not apply an act of an institution declared to be invalid under Art. 177 without 'creating serious uncertainty as to the Community law applicable', even although they are not, strictly speaking, legally bound by such a ruling (which is binding only on the court which has requested it) (Case 66/80 *International Chemical Corporation* [1981] ECR 1191 at p. 1215);

- in *procedural law*, 'protection of the certainty of legal positions and relationships implies that the existence of decisions of Community authorities governing such positions and relationships cannot for ever be called in question, unless there are new and serious reasons for doing so' (Case 34/65 *Mosthaf* v. *Commission* [1966] ECR 521 at p. 531). It follows that actions challenging the acts and omissions of the institutions must be brought within strict time-limits (ibid.); their admissibility must always be judged 'with due regard to the need for legal certainty,

349

indispensable to the proper functioning of the Community institutions, reflected in the fixing of time-limits' (Cases 15 to 33/73 etc. *Schots-Kortner* v. *Council, Commission and Parliament* [1974] ECR 177 at p. 191; see also Cases 6 and 11/69 *Commission* v. *France* [1969] ECR 523 at p. 539 *per Curiam*, p. 550 *per* A.-G. Roemer; Case 24/69 *Nebe* v. *Commission* [1970] ECR 145 at p. 151; Case 209/83 *Valsabbia* v. *Commission* [1984] ECR 3089 at p. 3096; etc.). Even where Community law lays down no specific periods for certain procedural steps, such as e.g. the 'raising of the matter' (of a failure to act) with the Commission prior to instituting proceedings before the Court under Art. 35 ECSC, legal certainty may require that the necessary steps should 'not be delayed indefinitely' (Case 59/70 *Netherlands* v. *Commission* [1971] ECR 639 at p. 653). The same requirement applies to the institutions also. Thus, although at the relevant time no limitation periods were laid down in competition law in respect of the imposition of penalties, the Court held that 'the fundamental requirement of legal certainty has the effect of preventing the Commission from indefinitely delaying the exercise of its power to impose fines' (Case 48/69 *ICI* v. *Commission* [1972] ECR 619 at p. 653; see also Case 14/61 *Hoogovens* v. *HA* [1962] ECR 253 at p. 273 and Case 111/63 *Lemmerz-Werke* v. *HA* [1965] ECR 677 at p. 690, both cases dealing with the requirement that the retroactive withdrawal of an illegal act granting a benefit must take place within a 'reasonable period of time' and with due regard to legal certainty).

It is apparent from the foregoing that in most cases the principle of legal certainty operates to protect individual rights and interests. In that respect it is very closely related to, and in fact forms the basis of, such other protective principles of Community law as those concerning legitimate expectations and vested rights, and the principle of non-retroactivity. Nevertheless, as the ECJ has pointed out in the context of the retroactive withdrawal of Community measures conferring individual rights and benefits, 'the principle of respect for legal certainty, important as it may be, cannot be applied in an absolute manner, but . . . its application must be combined with that of the principle of legality; the question which of these principles should prevail in each particular case depends upon a comparison of the public interest [represented by the principle of legality] with the private interests in question [safeguarded by the principle of legal certainty] . . .' (Cases 42 and 49/59 *SNUPAT* v. *HA* [1961] ECR 53 at p. 87, commented on by A.-G. Lagrange in Case 14/61 *Hoogovens* v. *HA*, above, esp. at pp. 283, 287). Likewise, the principle of justice must always be harmonized with that of legal certainty: 'these two principles must be so reconciled as to entail the minimum of sacrifice by Community members as a whole' (Cases 17 and 20/61 *Klöckner* v. *HA* [1962] ECR 325 at p. 340; see also Case 5/73 *Balkan-Import-Export* [1973] ECR 1091 at pp. 1111–12).

See also General principles of law, Legitimate expectation, Retroactive effect, Vested rights.

Further reading: See under General principles of law.

► **LEGAL PERSONALITY (OF THE EC)** Fictitious 'personality' which the law confers on or recognizes to a corporate entity for the purpose of endowing it with the requisite capacity to enter into legal relations and thereby acquire rights and assume obligations in its own name and independently of its members. The basic Treaties provide in identical terms that each Community 'shall have legal personality' (Arts. 6 ECSC, 210 EEC, 184 Euratom). Accordingly, each of the three Communities has a separate legal personality which is entirely distinct from that of the others and also from that of the Member States (Case 28/64 *Müller* v. *Council* [1965] ECR 237 at p. 247; Case 43/64 *Müller* v. *Council* [1965] ECR 385 at p. 395). On the other hand, only the Communities as such have legal personality, while their institutions do not. The institutions act, within the limits of the powers conferred upon them by the Treaties, for and on behalf of the Communities, and their acts create rights and obligations or incur liability for the particular Community for which they act in a given case (Cases 7/56 etc. *Algera* v. *Common Assembly* [1957] ECR 39 at p. 58; Cases 43, 45, and 48/59 *Lachmüller* v. *Commission* [1960] ECR 463 at p. 472; Case 15/63 *Lassalle* v. *Parliament* [1964] ECR 31 at pp. 53–5 *per* A.-G. Lagrange). The European Investment Bank established by the EEC Treaty, not being a Community institution, has legal personality of its own (Art. 129 EEC).

The Communities' legal personality raises different problems (1) in international law; (2) in the national laws of the Member States; and (3) in the national laws of non-Member States, which will be considered in turn below.

1. **In international law,** the first question to be examined is whether the Communities possess legal personality at all. Only the ECSC Treaty contains specific provisions in this respect, to the effect that 'in international relations, the Community shall enjoy the legal capacity it requires to perform its functions and attain its objectives' (Art. 6). The EEC and Euratom Treaties do not expressly stipulate whether the legal personality which they confer upon those Communities extends into the international sphere. However, the case-law of the ECJ indicates that in the opinion of the Court it does. Thus, in establishing the *sui generis* (supranational) nature of the Community legal system, the Court considered it as an important factor that the EEC had, amongst other things, 'its own personality, its own legal capacity and capacity of representation on the international plane' (Case 6/64 *Costa* [1964] ECR 585 at p. 593). Also, the Court interpreted the provision that 'The Community shall have legal personality' (Art. 210 EEC) as meaning that 'in its external relations the Community enjoys the capacity to establish contractual links with third countries over the whole field of objectives defined in Part One of the Treaty' and that, in certain circumstances, 'the Community alone is in a position to assume and carry out contractual obligations towards third countries' entirely independently of the Member States (Case 22/70 *Commission* v. *Council* [1971] ECR 263 at p. 274—'ERTA' case; see also Cases 3, 4, and 6/76 *Kramer* [1976] ECR 1279 at p. 1308). Relying on the corresponding provision of the Euratom Treaty (Art. 184), the Court referred to that Community's capacity for 'independent

action in external relations' (Ruling 1/78 *Protection of Nuclear Materials* [1978] ECR 2151 at p. 2179).

Nevertheless, the fact that the Treaties expressly confer legal personality upon the Communities—even if that personality be interpreted so widely as to extend into the international sphere—does not in itself mean that their *international* legal personality can be derived from, or exclusively from, the Treaties. The basis of legal personality in international law is not the constituent instrument of an organization but the international legal order itself, as developed through the practice of States and reflected in the decisions of the International Court of Justice. Under customary international law, States (and only States) enjoy legal personality *ipso facto*, which personality is original in nature and plenary or unlimited in scope. On the other hand, international organizations possess legal personality only to the (limited) extent to which international law recognizes such personality to them. It is this legal order which determines the nature and the scope of that personality, while leaving it to the States which set up an organization to define in its constitution the precise extent to which they wish it to benefit from such personality. Thus, the Member States of an organization are free to decide not to confer legal personality on it at all, or to limit that personality to specific matters only, but the basis is always international law.

That customary international law recognizes (within limits) legal personality to international organizations becomes clear from the Advisory Opinion of the International Court of Justice concerning *Reparation for Injuries Suffered in the Service of the United Nations* (ICJ Reports 1949, p. 174). In that opinion, the Court held that, in order to enable it effectively to discharge its functions, the United Nations had to be regarded as having international legal personality. At the same time, the Court explained that this was not tantamount to saying that the Organization was a State, which it certainly was not, or that its legal personality and rights and duties were the same as those of a State. International legal personality quite simply meant that the entity enjoying it 'is a subject of international law and capable of possessing international rights and duties, and that it has capacity to maintain its rights by bringing international claims' (ibid. at p. 179). The essential difference between a State and an international organization was that 'whereas a State possesses the totality of international rights and duties recognised by international law, the rights and duties of an entity such as [an international organization] must depend upon its purposes and functions as specified or implied in its constituent documents and developed in practice' (ibid. at p. 180).

Although the Court made the above statements in the context of the United Nations, it is widely recognized today that the same principles apply to international organizations generally. Thus, in its Advisory Opinion concerning the *Interpretation of the Agreement of 25 March 1951 between the WHO and Egypt* (ICJ Reports 1980, p. 73), the Court itself said, without any qualifications, that 'international organisations are subjects of international law and, as such, are bound by any obligations incumbent upon them under general rules of international law, under their constitutions or under international agreements to which they are parties' (ibid. at pp. 89–90). Similarly, the Preamble to the Vienna Convention on the Law of Treaties between States and International Organizations or between International Organizations of 1986 refers to international organizations as 'subjects of international law distinct from States' and as possessing the legal capacity 'which is necessary for the exercise of their functions and the fulfilment of their purpose'. In other words, international organizations enjoy international legal personality but, in contrast to States, their personality is derivative in nature and functional (limited) in scope.

It is true that the European Communities represent a *sui generis* type of organization which is more supranational than international, and exhibit more common features with States than any other existing organization. Nevertheless, their legal personality on the international plane must be assimilated to that of international organizations rather than to that of States. Thus, echoing the above advisory opinion, A.-G. Mayras has pointed out that the fact that the EEC has legal personality and powers on the level of international law 'does not turn the Community into a State' because its 'legal personality and capacity are determined in relation to the objectives and functions defined by the Treaty of Rome. Thus it cannot exercise all the powers that a State possesses, but only those powers vested in it which are necessary for it to carry out its tasks'. But, he added, 'when the Community exercises such power[s] it must comply with international law' (Case 48/69 *ICI* v. *Commission* [1972] ECR 619 at pp. 692–3).

In accordance with the principles of international law as stated above, it may be concluded that the Communities possess international legal personality but that this personality is not original and plenary but derived and functional, i.e. strictly related to their objectives and functions as defined in the Treaties or developed in practice. They possess only such of the legal capacities traditionally enjoyed by the subjects of international law as have been transferred to them from the Member States and as are necessary for the attainment of their objectives and for the performance of their functions. These include, in particular, the following capacities:

(*a*) treaty-making power, including the power to set up new international organizations by treaties;
(*b*) participation in existing international organizations;
(*c*) international (diplomatic) representation (active and passive);
(*d*) privileges and immunities;
(*e*) international responsibility (active and passive);
(*f*) capacity to bring an international claim (participation in the international settlement of disputes).

On the other hand, the Communities do not possess the capacity to conduct their own foreign policy, which remains essentially the responsibility of the Member States. The latter co-ordinate their foreign policies and develop a European foreign policy in the framework of European Political Co-operation.

It follows from the foregoing that, for both external and internal reasons, the Communities are not in a position to exercise the above-mentioned capacities in the same way and to the same extent as States. Thus, for example, in the case of international organizations and conferences which admit sovereign States only, Community participation is necessarily restricted to less than full membership, often to observer status. In the case of treaties and agreements concluded in the framework of such organizations and conferences, the participation of the Communities is usually subject to special accession clauses which do not apply to States and which sometimes subordinate their participation to that of some or all of their Member States.

Likewise, the Communities do not always participate on an equal footing with States in bodies set up by and responsible for the implementation and supervision of international agreements to which they are parties. Nor do they enjoy the same level of diplomatic representation as States. Their capacity to bring an international claim does not include the right to appear before the International Court of Justice since only States may be parties in cases before the Court (Art. 34 of the Court's Statute). Owing to an internal division of powers between the Communities and the Member States, the Communities may only exercise such treaty-making competence as has been transferred to them, expressly or by implication, from the Member States ('derivative' as opposed to 'original' competence), although to the extent of the transfer, their treaty-making competence is exclusive. Since the dividing line between the respective competences of the Communities and of the Member States is not precisely and definitively defined, the scope of the Communities' treaty-making power may vary, depending on the current state of integration and on the subject-matter of a particular treaty. Where the Communities do not possess sufficient power to conclude a given agreement, the joint participation of the Member States may become necessary in the form of a 'mixed' agreement (*see further under* **External relations, Mixed agreement, Treaty-making power**).

While the international legal personality of the European Communities cannot be challenged by the Member States, this is not necessarily the case with regard to non-Member States. It is true that in the *Reparation for Injuries* case (above, at p. 185), speaking of the United Nations, the International Court of Justice stated that 'fifty States, representing the vast majority of the members of the international community, had the power, in conformity with international law, to bring into being an entity possessing objective international personality, and not merely personality recognised by them alone . . .' However, it cannot be concluded from this that international law automatically confers 'objective international personality', i.e. personality that may be asserted *erga omnes*, on every and any international organization, whether universal or regional and whether representing a large or a small number of States. It follows that there is no rule of international law requiring third States to accept the European Communities as subjects or 'persons' of international law. Just as in the case of new States, this is a matter of recognition which the existing members of the international community are entirely free to accord to or withhold from the Communities, depending mainly on their own political interests.

While international law has not yet developed a coherent set of rules and principles for the recognition of international organizations, certain analogies may safely be drawn from the rules and principles applicable to the recognition of States. Thus, both recognition and non-recognition may be effected expressly or by implication. So far, no State has expressly recognized the Communities, while prior to June 1988 (see below) the Soviet Union and its East European allies had made explicit declarations of non-recognition or acted in a way which amounted to the same. For example, in several international conferences, the Soviet Union made it clear that its participation in the conference side by side with the EEC in no way signified recognition of the latter, and that the Soviet Union was only willing to enter into binding commitments with the Member States as States, acting in their individual capacity and not as Members of the EEC. On the other hand, establishment of diplomatic relations with the Communities is seen as equivalent to their (implied) recognition as subjects of international law. In practice, this is the most usual form in which recognition is accorded to the Communities (today about 120 States maintain diplomatic relations with the Communities). Thus, the establishment of 'official relations' between the EEC and the Council for Mutual Economic Assistance (CMEA or COMECON) in June 1988 was accompanied, in accordance with the principle of parallelism, by announcements that the Soviet Union and a number of East European countries decided to accredit diplomatic missions to the Community. Diplomatic relations were in fact established in August and September 1988. This is taken as an act of formal recognition of the Community not only by the CMEA as an organization, but also by its Members individually as States (see EEC–CMEA Joint Declaration of 25 June 1988, approved by Council Dec. 88/345 of 22 June 1988, *OJ* 1988 L157/34; see also *Bull. EC* 6–1988, pp. 13–14; 22nd *Gen. Rep. EC* (1988), p. 356. The Res. of the European Parliament of 22 Jan. 1987 on EC–CMEA relations, *OJ* 1987 C46/71, also envisages recognition of the EC by the CMEA and by its Member States as two separate matters. See also EP Res. of 15 Sept. 1988 on EC–Soviet Union relations, point 47, *OJ* 1988 C262/133). While common participation in multilateral treaties does not automatically amount to implied recognition (particularly if it is accompanied with an express declaration of non-recognition), it may do so if there is a clear intention to recognize. There is a stronger presumption of such an intention in the case of bilateral treaties.

Non-recognition may create certain difficulties for the Communities. In itself, it does not prevent the establishment of contacts or even the conclusion of international agreements. In fact, even before June 1988, there had been several contacts between the Soviet Union and the Communities and certain—limited—agreements had also been made with a number of East European countries (see *Bull. EC* 6–1988, p. 13). Nor does it prevent the Communities from exercising their internal legislative, executive, or judicial powers over the subjects of non-recognizing States in respect of acts or matters falling within Community jurisdiction. On the other hand, the most important effect of non-recognition is to deny the transfer of powers from the Member States to the Communities. The non-recognizing State is not willing (and cannot be compelled) to deal with the Communities as such, either in a

355

bilateral or in a multilateral context, either in the framework of conferences or in that of international organizations, even where the matter concerned is clearly within exclusive Community competence. The Member States then have a choice between not entering into treaties and other relations with such a State or derogating from established Community rules and principles. Moreover, non-recognition makes the participation of the Communities in international conferences and organizations and in treaties negotiated within their framework much more difficult.

2. **In the national laws of the Member States,** each Community enjoys the most extensive legal capacity accorded to legal persons; it may, in particular, acquire or dispose of movable and immovable property and may be a party to legal proceedings. To this end, the ECSC is represented by its institutions, each within the limits of its powers (Art. 6 ECSC), while the EEC and Euratom are represented by the Commission (Arts. 211 EEC, 185 Euratom). The ECJ has interpreted the latter provision as meaning that in national legal proceedings the EEC (and Euratom) must always be represented by the Commission, irrespective of which institution is involved in the dispute. On the other hand, in legal proceedings before the ECJ itself the Community should be represented, 'in the interests of a good administration of justice', by the particular institution or institutions against which the matter giving rise to the proceedings is alleged (Cases 63 to 69/72 *Werhahn* v. *Council* [1973] ECR 1229 at p. 1247).

The Communities' legal personality under national law is derived directly from the Treaties; it does not depend upon any special act granting such personality. In Member States which distinguish between legal persons at private and at public law, the Communities' personality is 'one of public law by virtue of the powers and duties appropriate to it' (Cases 43, 45, and 48/59 *Lachmüller* v. *Commission*, above, at p. 472). The reference by the Treaties to the 'most extensive legal capacity accorded to legal persons' under national law may be interpreted in two different ways. It may refer either to the most extensive legal capacity accorded in each Member State, in which case the extent of the Communities' capacities would vary from Member State to Member State. Such an interpretation is certainly tenable under the ECSC Treaty, which refers to the most extensive capacity accorded in each Member State to legal persons 'constituted in that State'. Alternatively, the phrase may describe the most extensive legal capacity accorded to legal persons under *any* of the national laws; in this case the Communities would enjoy the same capacity in all the Member States which would be the one which is the most favourable to them. This interpretation is supported by the slightly different wording of the EEC and Euratom Treaties which refer to the 'laws' of all the Member States. Since the Communities have no nationality of their own, any domestic rules which restrict the legal capacities of foreign nationals (natural or legal persons) cannot be applied to them.

The reference in the Treaties to two particular capacities (the capacity to acquire or dispose of property and procedural capacity) is clearly not exhaustive but is made by way of example only. Thus, amongst the various capacities that legal persons may enjoy under national law, specific mention must be made of one which is perhaps the most important, that is, the capacity to conclude contracts under both public and private law. Such capacity, which is mentioned in several contexts in the Treaties (see e.g. Arts. 42 ECSC; 181 and 215(1) EEC; 10, 29, 52, 101–2, 153, and 188(1) Euratom), is indispensable to the Communities both in the carrying out of their tasks and functions and in their everyday 'civil' life. Thus, the Communities are party to a host of contractual relationships covering such diverse matters as renting and construction of buildings, banking, insurance, administration of funds, supply of goods and services, copyright, public utility services, transportation, research, and employment (see further under **Contractual liability**).

In addition to the various legal capacities, the Communities also enjoy in the territories of the Member States such privileges and immunities as are necessary for the performance of their tasks, under the conditions laid down in a Protocol annexed to the Merger Treaty (Art. 28 MT). Nevertheless, these privileges and immunities do not amount to what is known in international law as 'sovereign immunity', i.e. immunity from the jurisdiction of the national courts. Thus, the Communities may be involved in legal proceedings before the courts or tribunals of the Member States in their own names either as plaintiffs or as defendants, or as interveners on either side. This follows not so much from their capacity to be party to legal proceedings expressly conferred on them (see above), as from those provisions of the Treaties which preserve the jurisdiction of the national courts over disputes to which the Communities are party, unless such disputes fall within the (exclusive) jurisdiction of the ECJ (Arts. 40(3) ECSC, 183 EEC, 155 Euratom).

3. **In the national laws of non-Member States,** the Communities possess legal personality and the corresponding capacities only to the extent to which these laws recognize, in accordance with their own private international law rules, the legal personality of foreign entities. In this respect, therefore, the domestic law of the third State is decisive. In principle, the Communities may be recognized as legal persons under national law (since they are such in the Member States) and may thus be covered by any relevant convention in force between the third State and a Member State providing for the mutual recognition of legal persons. Alternatively, they may be recognized as legal persons under international law (see point 1 above), in which case their status would be similar to that of an international organization. This does not necessarily mean, however, that they would automatically, i.e. in the absence of an agreement with the third State, enjoy the usual privileges and immunities of international organizations (such as e.g. immunity from lawsuit in the domestic courts). These privileges and immunities are always based on agreements concluded between the international organization and a State (Member or non-Member), and it seems doubtful whether, in the absence of an agreement, they could be claimed simply on the basis of customary international law.

See also **Community Treaties, Contractual liability, European Political Co-operation, External relations, Mixed agreement, Privileges and immunities, Treaty-making power, Treaty-making procedure.**

Legitimate expectation (protection of)

Further reading 1. BOOK: Groux and Manin, *The European Communities in the International Order* (1985).

2. ARTICLES: Lachmann, 'International Legal Personality of the EC: Capacity and Competence' (1984/1) *LIEI* 3; Pescatore, 'External Relations in the Case-Law of the Court of Justice of the European Communities' (1979) 16 *CML Rev.* 615.

3. OFFICIAL PUBLICATION: European Parliament, Working Documents 1977–8, 8 Mar. 1978, Doc. 567/77, Report by the Legal Affairs Committee on the Position of the European Communities in Public International Law (Rapporteur: L. Jozeau-Marigné).

▶ **LEGITIMATE EXPECTATION (PROTECTION OF)** General principle of law, recognized by the ECJ as forming part of Community law, based on the concept that 'trust in the Community's legal order must be respected' (Case 5/75 *Deuka* [1975] ECR 759 at p. 776 *per* A.-G. Trabucchi). It requires that 'assurances relied upon in good faith should be honoured' (Case 169/73 *Compagnie Continentale* v. *Council* [1975] ECR 117 at p. 140 *per* A.-G. Trabucchi). This principle is infringed where, without legal justification and without appropriate transitional provisions, the Community institutions bring about abrupt and unforeseeable changes in the law. The legal basis of the principle seems to be that 'a promise made to all and sundry creates a commitment with a corresponding obligation to fulfil it in favour of a promisee who has taken action on the basis of and in relation to the promise' (Case 5/75 *Deuka*, above, at p. 777 *per* A.-G. Trabucchi). The expectation generated by such a promise is not the same as an individual (i.e. vested) right, but it can exist even without a right (ibid.; on this point see further Case 74/74 *CNTA* v. *Commission* [1975] ECR 533 at p. 556 *per* A.-G. Trabucchi). It is an 'expectation', to which all those concerned are entitled, that 'commitments which the institutions have entered into will be met' (Case 164/80 *De Pascale* v. *Commission* [1982] ECR 909 at p. 928). It is 'legitimate' in the sense that it is recognized by the law as worthy of protection and hence enforceable before the ECJ.

The principle of the protection of legitimate expectations, which is applicable to legal provisions and commitments of both an individual and general (i.e. legislative) nature (Case 81/72 *Commission* v. *Council* [1973] ECR 575 at p. 584), has been recognized by the ECJ as constituting a 'superior rule of law' for the protection of the individual. Its infringement may therefore not only entail the invalidity or the annulment of a Community act (see e.g. Case 224/82 *Meiko-Konservenfabrik* [1983] ECR 2539 at pp. 2549–50; Case 81/72 *Commission* v. *Council*, above, at pp. 584, 586; see also Case 112/77 *Töpfer* v. *Commission* [1978] ECR 1019 at p. 1033) but may also establish the non-contractual liability of the Communities in respect of legislative measures involving choices of economic policy (Case 74/74 *CNTA* v. *Commission*, above, at p. 550). Forming part of the Community's legal system, the principle is also binding on the national authorities responsible for applying Community law. However, as the ECJ has pointed out, wrongful conduct on the part of the Community institutions or their officials or a practice by a Member State which is not in conformity with Community legislation cannot give rise to legitimate expectations: a person may not legitimately expect that he will be accorded treatment which is contrary to specific provisions of Community law (Case 316/86 *Krücken* [1988] ECR 2213 at pp. 2339–40).

Like the principle of legal certainty, of which it may be said to be a special application (see Case 1/73 *Westzucker* [1973] ECR 723 at p. 729), the principle of the protection of legitimate expectations is relevant to the whole area of Community law. In practice, it has been applied by the ECJ in staff cases (see e.g. Case 81/72 *Commission* v. *Council*, above, at p. 584; Case 164/80 *De Pascale* v. *Commission*, above, at pp. 928–9), in other disputes (see e.g. Case 84/85 *United Kingdom* v. *Commission* [1987] ECR 3765 at p. 3798), and in cases concerning the financial aspects of the Common Agricultural Policy. It has acquired particular importance in the latter context as a principle protecting the individual against abrupt and unforeseeable alterations in the law caused by constant changes of the economic situation. Thus, in connection with the withdrawal of the monetary compensatory amounts with immediate effect, the ECJ has stated that:

> . . . a trader may legitimately expect that for transactions irrevocably undertaken by him . . . no unforeseeable alteration will occur which could have the effect of causing him inevitable loss . . . The Community is therefore liable if, in the absence of an overriding matter of public interest, the Commission abolished with immediate effect and without warning the application of compensatory amounts in a specific sector without adopting transitional measures which would at least permit traders either to avoid the loss which would have been suffered in the performance of export contracts . . . or to be compensated for such loss. (Case 74/74 *CNTA* v. *Commission*, above, at p. 550; Case 97/76 *Merkur* v. *Commission* [1977] ECR 1063 at p. 1078)

Subsequently, the Court defined both the scope of,. and the limits to, the application of the principle in more general terms, by saying that:

> In the context of economic rules such as those governing the common organisation of agricultural markets, if in order to deal with individual situations the Community institutions have laid down specific rules enabling traders in return for entering into certain obligations with the public authorities to protect themselves—as regards transactions definitively undertaken—from the effects of the necessarily frequent variations in the detailed rules for the application of the common organisation, the principle of respect for legitimate expectations prohibits those institutions from amending those rules without laying down transitional measures unless the adoption of such a measure is contrary to an overriding public interest.
>
> On the other hand, the field of application of this principle cannot be extended to the point of generally preventing new rules from applying to the future effects of situations which arose under the earlier rules in the absence of obligations entered into with the public authorities. This is particularly true in a field such as the common organisation of markets, the purpose of which necessarily involves constant adjustment to the variations of the economic situation in the various agricultural sectors. (Case 84/78 *Tomadini* [1979] ECR 1801 at pp. 1814–15; see also Case 1/73 *Westzucker*, above, at pp. 729–31; Case 90/77 *Stimming* v. *Commission* [1978] ECR 995 at pp. 1005–6)

It follows from the foregoing definitions that an infringement of the principle of the protection of legitimate expectations can only exist if, in abolishing or amending existing rules and arrangements, the Community institutions have acted

- in the absence of any overriding public interest;
- with immediate effect;
- without warning;
- without adopting appropriate transitional measures;
- in a way which was not foreseeable by a prudent trader;
- in the presence of obligations entered into by the trader with the public authorities (e.g. advance fixing).

Applying the above criteria, the Court has established infringements of the principle on the following grounds:

- absence of overriding public interest (Case 81/72 *Commission* v. *Council*, above, at p. 585, where the Court actually refers to the absence of 'circumstances sufficient to justify the abandonment . . . of the [previous] system');
- failure to adopt appropriate transitional measures (Case 74/74 *CNTA* v. *Commission*, above, at p. 550; Case 164/80 *De Pascale* v. *Commission*, above, at p. 929);
- acting in a way which was not reasonably foreseeable (Case 224/82 *Meiko-Konservenfabrik*, above, at p. 2549).

On the other hand, the Court has refused to establish an infringement where the change in the existing legal position

- was justified by the existence of an overriding Community interest (Case 2/75 *Mackprang* [1975] ECR 607 at p. 616; Case 96/77 *Bauche* [1978] ECR 383 at p. 402);
- did not take effect immediately (Case 97/76 *Merkur* v. *Commission*, above, at p. 1078);
- was accompanied by warning (ibid.; Case 90/77 *Stimming* v. *Commission*, above, at p. 1006);
- was accompanied by appropriate transitional measures (ibid.);
- was foreseeable by a 'prudent and discriminating trader' (Cases 95 to 98/74 etc. *Coopératives Agricoles de Céréales* v. *Commission and Council* [1975] ECR 1615 at p. 1640; Case 78/77 *Lührs* [1978] ECR 169 at p. 178; Case 146/77*British Beef Company* [1978] ECR 1347 at p. 1355; Case 127/78 *Spitta* [1979] ECR 171 at p. 180; Case 245/81 *Edeka* [1982] ECR 2745 at p. 2758; etc.);
- affected traders who had not entered into obligations with the public authorities (such as advance fixing, see Case 84/78 *Tomadini*, above, at p. 1815);
- did not, or could not, adversely affect a 'legitimate expectation' worthy of protection (Case 1/73 *Westzucker*, above, at pp. 729–31; Case 100/74 *CAM* v. *Commission* [1975] ECR 1393 at p. 1405; Cases 67 to 85/75 *Lesieur* v. *Commission* [1976] ECR 391 at p. 411; Case 245/81 *Edeka*, above, at p. 2758).

See also General principles of law, Legal certainty, Retroactive effect, Vested rights.

Further reading: Lord Mackenzie Stuart, 'Legitimate Expectations and Estoppel in Community Law and English Administrative Law' (1983/1) *LIEI* 53. *See also under* **General principles of law.**

▶ **LETTERS ROGATORY** Document whereby the ECJ may order that a witness or expert be examined by the judicial authority of his place of permanent residence (Arts. 26 EEC Statute, 27 Euratom Statute, 52 RP, 1–3 SR). Letters rogatory are issued by the Court, either on application by a party or of its own motion, in the form of an order containing the names and addresses of the witness or expert as well as of the parties and their lawyers, setting out the facts on which the witness or expert is to be examined and describing the subject-matter of the dispute. The order is then sent to the 'competent authority' of the Member State in whose territory the witness or expert is to be heard (i.e. the Minister of Justice or, in the case of the United Kingdom, the Secretary of State). This authority will pass on the order to the judicial authority which is competent according to national law, and the latter is required to give effect to the order in accordance with national law. After implementation, the order, together with any documents drawn up in compliance with it and with a statement of costs, is returned to the Court through the 'competent authority'. The expenses occasioned by the letters rogatory are defrayed by the Court which however may, where appropriate, charge them to the parties (as an example for the use of letters rogatory, see Case 160/84 *Oryzomyli Kavallas* v. *Commission* [1985] ECR 675 and [1986] ECR 1633 at pp. 1647–8).

See also **Preparatory inquiries**

▶ *LEX POSTERIOR DEROGAT LEGI PRIORI* Principle according to which in the case of a conflict a later law takes precedence over an earlier law. The application of this principle in Community law is subject to certain important exceptions. Thus, by virtue of the doctrine of the supremacy of Community law, a rule of national law can never override a rule of Community law even if the national law is later in time. Also, an 'implementing' measure adopted by a Community institution can never derogate from a 'basic' measure of the same or another institution even though the implementing measure is, by definition, always later in time. Where, however, two measures of equal rank (e.g. two Council regulations) are in conflict and the later one is not based on the earlier one, it seems that the *lex posterior* principle applies (see e.g. Case 9/73 *Schlüter* [1973] ECR 1135 at pp. 1168–9 *per* A.-G. Roemer, who expressed the opinion that the validity of Council Reg. 974/71, introducing the monetary compensatory amounts, could not be affected by a possible conflict with the earlier Council Reg. 950/68 containing the Common Customs Tariff since it was not based on the latter. The judgment of the Court is, however, somewhat ambiguous since it implies that the validity of Reg. 974/71 was not called in question because it did not contravene the CCT, and not because it was *lex posterior*, which leads to precisely the opposite result, ibid. at pp. 1158–9).

Letters rogatory

Lex posterior derogat legi priori

361

See also *Lex specialis derogat legi generali*, Secondary legislation, Supremacy of Community law.

▶ *LEX SPECIALIS DEROGAT LEGI GENERALI* Principle according to which a special provision takes precedence over a general provision. Thus, for example, the EEC Treaty is said to constitute a *lex generalis* in relation to the ECSC and Euratom Treaties, each of which is a *lex specialis*. Therefore, the EEC Treaty applies also to the coal and steel and the nuclear sectors, but only to the extent to which a matter is not covered by the provisions of the two specialist Treaties or measures adopted under them. Otherwise, the provisions of the ECSC and Euratom Treaties take precedence over those of the EEC Treaty (*see further under* **Community Treaties**, section I). Also, where a measure of an institution can be validly based on a specific provision of the Treaty, such as e.g. Art. 43 (agriculture) or 113 (trade agreements), it may not be based on the general authorization contained in Art. 100 (harmonization) or 235 (Case 131/86 *United Kingdom* v. *Council* [1988] ECR 905 at pp. 917–18 *per* A.-G. Mischo; *see under* **Institutional balance, Supplementary powers**).

Nevertheless, the special and detailed provisions of the founding Treaties cannot, on the basis of the *lex specialis* principle, exclude or override the effects of the introductory Articles to those Treaties (i.e. Arts. 1–5 ECSC, 1–8 EEC, 1–3 Euratom) laying down binding general principles and objectives whose application extends over the whole spectrum of the Treaties. These special and general provisions are complementary and often have to be applied simultaneously and concurrently (Case 2/56 *Geitling* v. *HA* [1957] ECR 3 at p. 20; see also e.g. Case 8/57 *Aciéries Belges* v. *HA* [1958] ECR 245 at p. 253; Cases 7 and 9/54 *Industries Sidérurgiques Luxembourgeoises* v. *HA* [1956] ECR 175 at p. 195). In fact, the special provisions must always be interpreted in the light of those general rules and principles so as to reinforce their effects and further the achievement of their objectives (*see further under* **Interpretation of Community law**).

See also **Community Treaties, Institutional balance, Interpretation of Community law,** *Lex posterior derogat legi priori,* **Supplementary powers.**

▶ **LIMITATION PERIODS** 1. Periods within which the Commission may impose sanctions (i.e. fines, penalties, and periodic penalty payments), and may enforce decisions imposing sanctions, under the ECSC Treaty and under the rules of the EEC relating to transport and competition.

The limitation periods for the imposition of sanctions are as follows:

- three years in the case of infringements of provisions concerning applications, communications, notifications, requests for information, and the carrying out of investigations;
- five years in the case of all other infringements (i.e. infringements of substantive rules).

Time begins to run on the day on which the infringement is committed or, in the case of continuing or repeated infringements, when the infringement ceases (Art. 1 of Reg. 2988/74, *OJ* 1974 L319/1, relating to transport and competition in the EEC; Art. 1 of Dec. 715/78, *OJ* 1978 L94/22, relating to the ECSC Treaty). The limitation period is interrupted by any action taken by the Commission, or by any Member State at the request of the Commission, for the purpose of the preliminary investigation or proceedings in respect of an infringement, such as, in particular, written requests for information, written authorizations or decisions to carry out investigations, commencement of proceedings, and the notification of the statement of objections by the Commission. The limitation period is suspended for as long as the decision of the Commission is the subject of proceedings before the ECJ (Arts. 2 and 3 of Reg. 2988/74; Arts. 2 and 3 of Dec. 715/78).

The limitation period for the enforcement of sanctions is five years from the day on which the decision imposing the sanction becomes final. The period is interrupted by notification of a decision varying or refusing to vary the original amount of the sanction, and by any action of the Commission, or of a Member State at the request of the Commission, for the purpose of enforcing payment. The period is suspended for so long as time to pay is allowed or enforcement of payment is suspended pursuant to a decision of the ECJ (Arts. 4–6 of Reg. 2988/74; Arts. 4–6 of Dec. 715/78).

The above rules also apply in respect of infringements committed before their entry into force (Art. 7 of Reg. 2988/74; entered into force on 1 Jan. 1975; Art. 7 of Dec. 715/78; entered into force on 8 Apr. 1978). Prior to their adoption there was no limitation period under Community law (Case 41/69 *Chemiefarma* v. *Commission* [1970] ECR 661 at p. 683).

2. Limitation periods have also been laid down in respect of the imposition of production levies under Arts. 49 and 50 ECSC (Dec. 5/65 *OJ Sp. Edn.* 1965–6, p. 38) and in respect of the bringing of actions for damages under all three Treaties (Arts. 40 ECSC Statute, 43 EEC Statute, 44 Euratom Statute). On the other hand, Community law at present lays down no limitation periods for the recovery of financial benefits mistakenly granted under Community rules (Cases 119 and 126/79 *Lippische Hauptgenossenschaft* [1980] ECR 1863 at pp. 1879–80); nor for the recovery of charges improperly imposed on the basis of Community provisions (Case 130/79 *Express Dairy Foods* [1980] ECR 1887 at p. 1900). In these respects, therefore, the principles and provisions of national law are applicable, although they must be applied in a non-discriminatory manner (ibid.).

See also **Action for damages, Administrative procedure*, Enforcement procedure, Production levy*, Recovery of undue payments*.**

▶ **LIMITED JURISDICTION** Jurisdiction exercised by the ECJ in actions involving judicial review of the institutions' conduct, i.e. in actions for annulment and actions for failure to act. Following the theory of *recours en annulation* as known in French administrative law, in these proceedings the Court's powers are strictly limited to reviewing the objective legality of the acts or omissions of the institutions, i.e. whether they are in conformity with the Treaties and other mandatory rules and principles of Community law and whether the institutions have not exceeded the limits of their discretionary powers. Subject to certain exceptions, the Court may not review the appropriateness or expediency of the act in question, nor the underlying considerations involving questions of economic policy in the light of which it has been taken. Moreover, the Court has the sole power of declaring an illegal act to be void on one (or more) of the four grounds of action, or declaring an illegal omission to be contrary to the Treaties, while leaving it to the relevant institution to take the measures necessary to comply with its judgment. The Court has no competence to substitute its own decision for the challenged act, nor to vary or correct its terms, nor to award damages or any other form of redress. The Court cannot even indicate, still less prescribe, to the relevant institution what particular measures to take in compliance with its judgment (see in general Case 3/54 *ASSIDER* v. *HA* [1955] ECR 63 at p. 75 *per* A.-G. Lagrange; Case 1/55 *Kergall* v. *Common Assembly* [1955] ECR 151 at p. 165 *per* A.-G. Roemer; Case 1/56 *Bourgaux* v. *Common Assembly* [1956] ECR 361 at pp. 374–5 *per* A.-G. Roemer).

See also **Action for annulment, Action for failure to act, Judicial review, Jurisdiction, Unlimited jurisdiction.**

▶ *LIS PENDENS* A situation which arises when an action is brought before a court which involves the same parties and subject-matter, relates to the same facts, and incorporates essentially the same grounds and conclusions as another action already pending before the same or another court. Should a situation of *lis pendens* arise before the ECJ, the subsequent action will be declared inadmissible by the Court (see e.g. Cases 358/85 and 51/86 *France* v. *Parliament* [1988] ECR para. 12) acting, if necessary, of its own motion. This will be the case, for example, where the later action is directed against an act which is merely a confirmation of an earlier (implied) act which is already being challenged by the same applicant on the same grounds in another action pending before the Court (Cases 45 and 49/70 *Bode* v. *Commission* [1971] ECR 465 at p. 475; Cases 58 and 75/72 *Perinciolo* v. *Council* [1973] ECR 511 at p. 516). Where, however, the subject-matter and the legal basis of the two actions are different (e.g. where one set of proceedings is brought in a national court for the annulment of a decision of a national agency entrusted with the implementation of Community law while another set of proceedings is instituted before the ECJ for obtaining compensation from a Community institution) the objection of *lis pendens* cannot be raised (Cases 64 and 113/76 etc. *Dumortier* v. *Council* [1979] ECR 3091 at p. 3113).

See also **Absolute bar to proceedings.**

▶ **LUXEMBOURG COMPROMISE (1966)** Political agreement reached by the six Member States of the European Communities at the extraordinary Council meeting held in Luxembourg on 28 and 29 January 1966 (also known as the Luxembourg Agreement or Luxembourg Accords). The purpose of the Compromise was to resolve the longest and to date most serious crisis in the history of the Communities. The crisis arose at the Council meeting of 30 June 1965, when France rejected a number of interrelated Commission proposals concerning the financing of the Common Agricultural Policy, the introduction of independent revenue ('own resources') for the Community, and wider budgetary powers for the European Parliament. Coupled with this was the fact that, at the end of the same year, the EEC was scheduled to move into the third stage of the transitional period. According to the Treaty, this was automatically to bring into operation the majority voting procedure in the Council replacing in a number of fields the unanimity rule applied before. The main French argument was that a Member State should not be overruled by the rest whenever one of its vital national interests was at stake. Being unable to agree with the other Member States, France remained absent from all non-technical meetings of the Council for about seven months (see 9th *Gen. Rep. EEC* (1965–6), ch. I; *Bull. EC* 3–1966, p. 5).

The Compromise itself deals with two important issues: the relations between the Commission and the Council and the majority voting procedure (text in 9th *Gen. Rep. EEC* (1965–6), p. 34 and in *Bull. EC* 3–1966, p. 8). Regarding the former, it states that close co-operation between the two institutions is essential for the functioning and development of the Community. In order to improve this co-operation at every level, the document indicates a number of practical methods which the two institutions should adopt jointly. The most important of these are as follows:

- before adopting any important proposal, the Commission should contact the national Governments through the Permanent Representatives, without this procedure compromising its right of initiative;
- proposals of the Commission are not to be made public until the recipients have received them;
- the credentials of Heads of Mission of non-Member States accredited to the Community will be submitted jointly to the President of the Council and to the President of the Commission;
- the Council and the Commission will inform each other of any approaches relating to major issues made to them by non-Member States;
- the two institutions will consult together regarding the establishment of links with international organizations; etc.

As regards the majority voting procedure, the document states that where, in the case of decisions which may be taken by majority vote on a proposal from the Commission, very important interests of one or more Member States are at stake, the Council will endeavour, within a reasonable time, to reach solutions which can be adopted by all of its members. France, however, insisted that where very important interests were at stake the discussion should be continued until unanimous agreement was reached. The members of the Council noted that there was a divergence of views on what should be done in the event of a failure to reach complete agreement. Nevertheless, they considered that this divergence did not prevent the Community's work from

365

being resumed in accordance with the normal procedure. Finally, they agreed that decisions on certain items should be by common consent and drew up a work programme for 1966.

While the first part of the Compromise is based on Art. 162 EEC (since then replaced by Art. 15 MT), which requires the Council and the Commission to consult each other and to settle by common accord their methods of co-operation, the legal nature and validity of the second part are doubtful. In so far as it purports to amend the rules of the Treaty by substituting unanimity for majority voting, it is clearly invalid as the procedure laid down by Art. 236 EEC for Treaty amendment has not been followed. Indeed, the ECJ has stated more than once that 'the Treaty can only be modified by means of the amendment procedure carried out in accordance with Article 236' (Case 43/75 *Defrenne* [1976] ECR 455 at p. 478) and that resolutions and similar measures which express the political will of the Council or of the Member States cannot prevail over the rules contained in the Treaty (ibid.; Case 59/75 *Manghera* [1976] ECR 91 at p. 102). More importantly, the Court has specifically held that 'the rules regarding the manner in which the Community institutions arrive at their decisions [i.e. by a majority vote or by unanimity] are laid down in the Treaty and are not at the disposal of the Member States or of the institutions themselves' (Case 68/86 *United Kingdom* v. *Council* [1988] ECR 855 at p. 900).

For its part, the Commission has never accepted that section of the Compromise dealing with voting. On the contrary, it has on occasions expressly dissociated itself from it saying that it was not a party to the discussions in Luxembourg in 1966 and that, as custodian of the Treaty, it is bound only by the Treaty itself (*Bull. EC* 5–1982, p. 8). Several times, the Commission has urged the Council to return to the use of majority voting (see e.g. 2nd *Gen. Rep. EC* (1968), pp. 15, 18; 3rd *Gen. Rep. EC* (1969), pp. 335, 485; Suppl. to *Bull. EC* 9/10–1969, pp. 33–4; 8th *Gen. Rep. EC* (1974), p. 9; Suppl. 2/78—*Bull. EC*, p. 12; *Bull. EC* 4–1978, p. 10; Suppl. 3/82—*Bull. EC*, p. 7; *Bull. EC* 10–1981, p. 56). The Heads of State or Government have likewise called upon the Council to renounce its decision-making practice based on the Compromise (see the Communiqué issued after the Paris Summit meeting of 9–10 Dec. 1974, 8th *Gen. Rep. EC* (1974), p. 297 at p. 298; *Bull. EC* 12–1974, p. 7 at p. 8. See also the Solemn Declaration on European Union of Stuttgart of 19 June 1983, point 2.2, *Bull. EC* 6–1983, p. 24 at p. 26). Most of the reports dealing with institutional reform have been highly critical of the Luxembourg arrangements, pointing out their detrimental effects on the development of the Communities and on the Council's working methods (see in particular the Vedel, Tindemans, and Three Wise Men's Reports and the Report of the Committee on Institutional Affairs—the Dooge Committee. As to the wider effects of the Luxembourg Agreement, *see further under* **Council**, section III).

In spite of its doubtful legality and negative effects, the Luxembourg Compromise has never been formally renounced or declared invalid by a legally binding measure. Nor has it been challenged before the Court of Justice. Even the Single European Act of 1986, which has extended majority voting in the Council, is silent on it. Yet because it has no firm (or any) basis in law it can be relied on only as long as the Member States are willing to give priority to the vital interests of one State over those of the Community itself. Where this is not the case, there is nothing to prevent the Council from returning to the voting procedure as laid down in the Treaty, which is after all the only lawful method. Thus, at its meeting of 17 and 18 May 1982, the Council, prompted by the Commission, adopted the 1982 agricultural price package by a qualified majority, as required by the Treaty, in spite of the 'veto' of the United Kingdom based on the Luxembourg Compromise (the United Kingdom was against the package mainly for reasons connected with settling the budgetary problem, see *Bull. EC* 5–1982, pp. 7–8). Also, at the Milan meeting of the European Council on 28 and 29 June 1985 the President, noting that the required (simple) majority as laid down in Art. 236 EEC had been obtained, decided to convene an Intergovernmental Conference to draw up amendments to the Treaties (later to become the Single European Act), in spite of the opposition of three Member States, Denmark, Greece, and the United Kingdom (*Bull. EC* 6–1985, pp. 13–14).

At this stage, it would perhaps be early to conclude that the above developments herald the demise of the Luxembourg Compromise. It is, however, certain that the changes in the voting procedures of the Council introduced in July 1987 (*OJ* 1987 L291/27) will make it much more difficult for a single Member State, or a small group of States, to block the decision-making process by invoking vital national interests (*see further under* **Council**, section III).

See also **Commission, Committee on Institutional Affairs, Council, European Union, Institutional balance, Institutions, Single European Act, Solemn Declaration on European Union, Three Wise Men's Report, Tindemans Report, Vedel Report.**

Further reading: Editorial, 'The Vote on the Agricultural Prices: A New Departure?' (1982) 19 *CML Rev.* 371; Pescatore, 'Some Critical Remarks on the "Single European Act" ' (1987) 24 *CML Rev.* 9 (at p. 13); Vasey, 'Decision-Making in the Agriculture Council and the "Luxembourg Compromise" ' (1988) 25 *CML Rev.* 725. *See also under* **Council**.

M

▶ **MANIFEST ERROR** One of only two grounds (the other being misuse of powers) on which the ECJ may review the legality of the exercise by the Council and the Commission of their discretionary powers in formulating and implementing economic policies.

1. **The ECSC Treaty** places an express limitation upon the Court's powers by providing that in reviewing the legality of a Community act, the Court may not examine the evaluation of the situation, resulting from economic facts or circumstances, in the light of which the Commission took its decision, save where the Commission is alleged to have misused its powers or to have manifestly failed to observe the provisions of the Treaty or any rule of law relating to its application (Art. 33(1) ECSC). The ECJ has interpreted the term 'manifest failure to observe the Treaty' as implying a higher than ordinary degree of infringement, a serious misconstruction and misapplication of the provisions of the Treaty resulting from an obvious error in the evaluation of the economic situation in the light of which the challenged measure was taken. Such an obvious (manifest) error exists where the underlying economic situation prima facie reveals no necessity for the contested measure. Unlike misuse of powers, manifest error is not a separate and independent ground for annulment. It is rather a means of enabling the Court to review the Commission's evaluation of the situation arising from the economic facts and circumstances of the case. The objective of this review is precisely to ascertain whether the measure was manifestly unjustified (Case 6/54 *Netherlands* v. *HA* [1955] ECR 103 at pp. 115–16 *per Curiam*, pp. 119, 125–7 *per* A.-G. Roemer. See also Cases 154/78 etc. *Valsabbia* v. *Commission* [1980] ECR 907 at pp. 992, 1005, 1007 *per Curiam*, pp. 1039–41 *per* A.-G. Capotorti).

2. Although **the EEC Treaty** contains no express provision corresponding to Art. 33(1) ECSC, the ECJ has stated in a long line of cases that similar principles apply in the context of the EEC also. Thus, the Court has ruled that where the institutions enjoy a significant freedom of evaluation of complex economic situations in the formulation or implementation of economic policies, 'when examining the lawfulness of the exercise of such freedom, the courts cannot substitute their own evaluation of the matter for that of the competent authority but must restrict themselves to examining whether the evaluation of the competent authority contains a patent error or constitutes a misuse of power' (Case 57/72 *Westzucker* [1973] ECR 321 at p. 340. See also Case 43/72 *Merkur* v. *Commission* [1973] ECR 1055 at pp. 1073–4; Case 98/78 *Racke* [1979] ECR 69 at p. 81 and the cases mentioned under **Judicial review**).

See also **Judicial review, Misuse of powers.**

▶ **MISUSE OF POWERS** 1. One of four grounds of action on which binding acts of the Council, the Commission, and the European Parliament may be challenged before, and declared void by, the ECJ in the framework of annulment proceedings (Arts. 33 ECSC, 173 EEC, 146 Euratom).

2. The sole ground on which undertakings and associations may institute annulment proceedings under the ECSC Treaty against general decisions and general recommendations, and on which a failure of the Commission to exercise a discretionary power under the ECSC Treaty may be challenged (Arts. 33, 35 ECSC).

3. One of only two grounds (the other being manifest error) on which the ECJ may review the legality of the exercise by the Council and the Commission of their discretionary powers in formulating and implementing economic policies (Art. 33(1) ECSC; see e.g. Case 55/75 *Balkan-Import-Export* [1976] ECR 19 at p. 30).

Although the concept of misuse of powers as a ground of illegality is wider in some and narrower in other Member States (see in general Case 3/54 *ASSIDER* v. *HA* [1955] ECR 63 at pp. 74 *et seq. per* A.-G. Lagrange), for the purposes of Community law the ECJ has adopted a narrower definition based entirely on the subjective intentions (motives) of the institutions. Accordingly, misuse of powers occurs where the institutions use their powers for a purpose other than that for which the powers have been conferred (see the cases cited below). Thus, in order for a misuse of powers to exist, two conditions must be fulfilled. First, the institutions must be in the possession of the requisite power and, secondly, that power must be discretionary, at least within certain limits. Where the requisite power is missing, the institutions cannot 'misuse' it, that is, use it for a wrong purpose; and where it is present but can only be used in a certain way strictly specified by the Treaties, leaving the institutions no choice between alternative solutions (so-called 'fettered competence', *compétence liée*), it cannot be 'misused' either: it can only be used illegally or not used at all. The former situation (where the power is missing) constitutes a case of lack of competence; the latter (where the conditions laid down by the Treaties are disregarded) one of infringement of the Treaties, while the situation where the extent of existing powers is exceeded probably both; but none will amount to a misuse of powers (Case 8/55 *Fédération Charbonnière de Belgique* v. *HA* [1956] ECR 245 at p. 303 *per Curiam*, pp. 272–3 *per* A.-G. Lagrange).

In order to establish a misuse of powers in a given case, it is necessary, first, to uncover the real intentions of the institution, that is, the object pursued by it in taking the measure challenged and, secondly, to show that this object is different from the one which it ought to have pursued, or could legitimately have pursued, under the provision under which it has acted (see e.g. Case 92/78 *Simmenthal* v. *Commission* [1979] ECR 777 at pp. 808, 811; and Cases 351 and 360/85 *Fabrique de Fer de Charleroi* v. *Commission* [1987] ECR 3639 at pp. 3674–5, where the Court annulled certain Commission decisions on the ground of misuse of powers). It is not necessary, however, that the institution should pursue a wrong object intentionally. Misuse of powers occurs already if the institution does so through a serious lack of care and circumspection amounting to a misconstruction of, and thus a disregard for, the true purpose of the law. Moreover, it is not necessary that the object pursued should be illegal, i.e. prohibited or not expressly authorized by the Treaties. Misuse of powers can occur if the object, though legitimate in itself,

369

is not the one that could or ought to have been pursued or primarily pursued in the exercise of the power in question.

Where the institution is led by more than one objective, the existence of a misuse of powers must be examined in the light of the most important one. Accordingly, the presence of an unjustified subsidiary motive together with a justified one will not result in a misuse of powers provided that it is the latter that clearly predominates (Case 1/54 *France* v. *HA* [1954] ECR 1 at p. 16). Thus, for example, a measure which is otherwise in conformity with the Treaties will not be invalidated on the ground of misuse of powers just because the additional consideration of administrative convenience also played a certain part in its adoption. By contrast, the ECJ has repeatedly held that the concept of misuse of powers includes a misuse of procedure which occurs when an institution, finding itself faced with a situation which requires the application of a particular provision or procedure laid down in the Treaties, nevertheless proceeds under another provision with the sole, or at least predominant, purpose of evading the guarantees, safeguards, or restrictions of the former (correct) provision or procedure (see e.g. Case 15/57 *Chasse* v. *HA* [1958] ECR 211 at p. 231; Cases 140/82 etc. *Walzstahl* v. *Commission* [1984] ECR 951 at pp. 985–6; Cases 32, 52, and 57/87 *ISA* v. *Commission* [1988] ECR 3305 at pp. 3327, 3330).

To prove misuse of powers in a given case may present difficult problems for two main reasons. First, the institutions enjoy the 'presumption of innocence', i.e. they are presumed to have pursued legitimate objectives in their actions until and unless the opposite is proved. Secondly, what needs to be proved is their intents and motives, which are not easily ascertainable, particularly by private persons who may not have access to the relevant documents. The ECJ normally sets fairly high standards of proof, accepting a misuse of powers only if it appears, on the basis of 'objective, relevant and consistent indications', that a measure has been taken for purposes other than those stated (see e.g. Cases 18 and 35/65 *Gutmann* v. *Commission* [1966] ECR 103 at p. 117; Case 52/86 *Banner* v. *Parliament* [1987] ECR 979 at p. 992). Nevertheless, the Court will admit as evidence any relevant correspondence and declaration of the institution concerned as well as *travaux préparatoires* including deliberations of the consultative bodies (Case 6/54 *Netherlands* v. *HA* [1955] ECR 103 at p. 116). It may also order production by the institution of the minutes of any relevant meetings.

See also **Grounds of action, Judicial review, Manifest error.**

▶ **MIXED AGREEMENT** International agreement to which the European Community (ECSC, Euratom, or EEC, as the case may be) and some or all of its Member States are jointly parties because the subject-matter of the agreement falls in part within the jurisdiction of the Community and in part within the jurisdiction of the Member States and therefore neither the Community nor the Member States, acting alone, have the necessary competence to negotiate and conclude the agreement as a whole. From a legal point of view, a mixed agreement is essentially a device to deal with a situation characterized by a division of powers between the Community and the Member States. It enables them to aggregate or 'pool' their treaty-making powers and thus to enter into treaty relations with third countries or international organizations over and above those which the Community, acting on its own, or the Member States, acting individually or even collectively, would be able to establish. Thus, the adjective 'mixed' in reality signifies mixed competence rather than mixed participation. It follows that an international agreement in which the Community and the Member States jointly participate for reasons other than their shared competence over the subject-matter cannot be described as a 'mixed agreement' in a strict (or substantive) sense of the term (see further below).

1. **The ECSC Treaty** contains no specific provisions expressly conferring treaty-making power on that Community. Most of the agreements which concern matters within the jurisdiction of the ECSC are concluded by the Member States collectively, usually acting through the Representatives of their Governments meeting in Council. Some are concluded by the ECSC itself, and some by the ECSC and the Member States jointly (*see further under* **External relations**).

2. **The Euratom Treaty** expressly envisages the possibility of mixed agreements. Art. 102 refers to agreements concluded with a third State or an international organization to which 'in addition to the Community, one or more Member States are parties'. It provides that such agreements shall not enter into force until the Commission has been notified by all the Member States concerned that those agreements have become applicable in accordance with the provisions of their respective national laws.

The circumstances in which the technique of the mixed agreement may or even must be used, and the legal effects of such an agreement, have been considered by the ECJ in Ruling 1/78 *Protection of Nuclear Materials* [1978] ECR 2151 at pp. 2178–81. In that case, Belgium requested the Court under Art. 103 Euratom to decide whether the participation of the Member States in the Convention on the Physical Protection of Nuclear Materials, Facilities and Transport, then being drawn up within the framework of the International Atomic Energy Agency, was compatible with the Euratom Treaty if the Community did not become a party to the Convention in addition to the Member States. Belgium also raised questions concerning the Community's right to participate and the consequences of such participation.

After analysing the terms of the Draft Convention, the Court came to the conclusion that the measures laid down for the protection of nuclear materials concerned in part the jurisdiction of the Member States and in part that of the Community. Thus, the provisions relating to criminal prosecution and extradition undoubtedly concerned matters falling within the jurisdiction of the Member States. On the other hand, the whole system of physical protection fell within the purview of the Euratom Treaty and it could only function effectively, within the ambit of Community law, if the Community itself was obliged to comply with it in its activities. It followed that the Draft Convention could be implemented, as regards the Community, only by means of a close association between the institutions and the Member States

371

both in the process of negotiation and conclusion and in the fulfilment of the obligations undertaken. This situation came within the scope of Art. 102 of the Treaty, from which it followed that 'where it appears that the subject-matter of an agreement . . . falls in part within the power and jurisdiction of the Community and in part within that of the Member States . . . such obligations may be entered into by the Community in association with the Member States' (ibid. at p. 2179). For the Community's part, agreements of this kind were to be concluded in accordance with the ordinary procedure laid down in Art. 101 in conjunction with Art. 102.

The Court also pointed out that it was not necessary to set out and determine, as regards the other parties to the Convention, the exact nature of the division of powers between the Community and the Member States, particularly as it might change in the course of time. This was a purely 'domestic question in which third parties have no need to intervene' (ibid. at p. 2180). It was sufficient to state only that the matter gave rise to a division of powers within the Community, the important thing being that the implementation of the Convention should not be incomplete. The implementation itself was subject to the same principle of division of powers which governed the negotiation and conclusion of the Convention. It required close co-operation between the Community institutions and the Member States. Thus, the Community was responsible for the implementation of provisions falling within its jurisdiction (i.e. those relating to the supply arrangements, the nuclear Common Market, security, and property ownership), while the Member States were responsible for the implementation of the rest (i.e. intervention of the public authorities, criminal prosecutions, and extradition). Under Art. 115(2) of the Treaty, it was the task of the Council to co-ordinate implementation by the Member States and by the Community.

The final ruling of the Court was that the Member States could only participate in the Draft Convention if, in so far as its own powers and jurisdiction were concerned, the Community as such was also a party on the same lines as the States. Although, strictly speaking, the ruling was given under the Euratom Treaty, the principles established by it are also relevant to the solution of problems arising from the practice of mixed agreements under the EEC Treaty (see below).

3. Although **the EEC Treaty** is silent on mixed agreements, the Community has, since its early days, had frequent and increasing recourse to the mixed agreement formula over a whole range of subject-matters. The great majority of Community treaties are, in fact, concluded in this form (for a list of mixed agreements concluded under all three Treaties up to 1983, see Feenstra, 'A Survey of the Mixed Agreements and their Participation Clauses' in *Mixed Agreements*, listed below under Books, at p. 207. *See further under* **External relations**). The ECJ itself has had opportunity to consider the legal implications of mixed agreements in two important opinions given under Art. 228 of the Treaty. These are discussed below before the present state of Community law is summarized.

Opinion 1/76 *Laying-up Fund* [1977] ECR 741 at p. 756 concerned a Draft Agreement establishing a European Laying-up Fund for Inland Waterway Vessels in which the Community, six of the then nine Member States, and Switzerland were to participate as contracting parties. The Court held that the participation of the six Member States was justified by the fact that they were party to two earlier Conventions (Convention of Mannheim of 1868 and Convention of Luxembourg of 1956) which had to be amended to bring them into line with the Draft Agreement, a task which the six States had undertaken to perform (something which was obviously beyond the Community's competence). The Court expressly stated that 'the participation of these States in the Agreement must be considered as being solely for this purpose and not as necessary for the attainment of other features of the system' (which fell within Community competence). The fact that under its Art. 4 the Agreement was enforceable in the territories of all the Member States including those which were not party to it also showed that, except for the special undertaking mentioned, the legal effects of the Agreement with regard to the Member States resulted exclusively from its conclusion by the Community, and *not* from the participation of the Member States (this followed from Art. 228(2) EEC under which agreements concluded by the Community are binding on the institutions *and* on the Member States). 'In these circumstances', the Court concluded, 'the participation of the six Member States as contracting parties to the Agreement is not such as to encroach on the external power of the Community. There is therefore no occasion to conclude that this aspect of the draft Agreement is incompatible with the Treaty.'

However, in subsequent parts of the opinion the Court found that the participation of the six Member States in the negotiations, although justified for the above purpose, had produced results which were incompatible with Community law. The Court's main objection was that the part played by the Community institutions in the various organs and operations of the Fund set up by the Agreement was extremely limited, with the determinative functions being performed by the Member States. These arrangements, the Court concluded, 'call in question the power of the institutions of the Community and, moreover, alter in a manner inconsistent with the Treaty the relationships between Member States within the context of the Community' (ibid. at p. 757). The Draft Agreement was therefore incompatible with the EEC Treaty.

Opinion 1/78 *Natural Rubber Agreement* [1979] ECR 2871 raised the question whether the negotiation and conclusion of the International Agreement on Natural Rubber in the framework of the United Nations Conference on Trade and Development (UNCTAD) came within the Community's exclusive competence (the Commission's view) or whether it called for a division of powers between the Community and the Member States and therefore had to be concluded by them jointly in the form of a mixed agreement (the Council's view). The Court said that the problem of competence had to be examined from two aspects. The first question was whether the agreement, by reason of its subject-matter and objectives, came as a whole within the sphere of the Common Commercial Policy under Art. 113 of the Treaty. If the answer was affirmative, the second question was whether, 'by reason of certain specific arrangements or special provisions of the agreement concerning matters coming within the powers of the Member States, the participation of the latter in the agreement is *necessary*' (ibid. at p. 2909, emphasis added).

Upon examining the terms of the agreement, the Court concluded that, in spite of a number of special features which distinguished it from classical tariff and trade agreements, it came within the commercial policy as envisaged by Art. 113. In principle, this should give rise to exclusive powers on the part of the Community to negotiate and conclude the agreement. Nevertheless, in this case the exclusive nature of the Community's powers depended on the arrangements for financing the operations of the buffer stock which was to be set up under the agreement, a question which at the time had yet to be settled. The Court held that if the burden of financing the stock was to fall upon the Community budget, the Community would have exclusive powers. On the other hand, if the charges were to be borne directly by the Member States, that would imply the participation of those States in the agreement together with the Community. In that case, the exclusive competence of the Community could not be envisaged (ibid. at pp. 2917–18, 2920).

The Court moreover had to consider the argument that a mixed agreement was also necessary for another reason, i.e. to enable certain 'dependent territories', such as the French Overseas Territories and Hong Kong, which remained outside the sphere of application of the EEC Treaty, to participate in the agreement. However, in dismissing this contention the Court said that the fact that these territories were represented in the agreement by the Member States which were responsible for their international relations had nothing to do with the problem of demarcation of the treaty-making competence between the Community and the Member States. It was in their capacity as international representatives of the territories concerned, and *not* as Member States, that France and the United Kingdom were called upon to participate in the agreement alongside the Community. Legally, therefore, their participation did not give rise to a 'mixed' agreement (ibid. at p. 2919).

Although the ECJ has so far had an opportunity to clarify only some of the many complex issues arising from the practice of mixed agreements, it is clear that it takes a strict view of the circumstances in which such practice may be justified. The present state of Community law on the matter, taking into account the Court's case-law also under the Euratom Treaty, may be summarized as follows.

(*a*) Legally, the conclusion of a mixed agreement is justified only where it is strictly necessary. This is the case only where the subject-matter of the agreement, or certain specific arrangements or special provisions of it, exceed the exclusive treaty-making competence either of the Community or of the Member States. Conversely, a mixed agreement is incompatible with Community law if its subject-matter falls wholly within the exclusive competence of the Community (or of the Member States), or if its effect is to distort the distribution of powers between the institutions and the Member States, or between the Member States, as envisaged by the Treaty.

(*b*) Where the subject-matter of an agreement falls wholly within the non-exclusive or potential treaty-making competence of the Community (i.e. competence which has not been expressly conferred on the Community but flows by implication from the provisions of the Treaty and which has not yet been exercised; *see under* **Treaty-making power**), or where it falls partly within non-exclusive and partly within exclusive competence, resort to a mixed agreement is not legally necessary. Such an agreement can be concluded by the Community alone if the Council is willing to allow the Community to make use of its non-exclusive or implied powers (by deciding that the agreement is 'necessary for the attainment of one of the objectives of the Community'). It may even be argued that the participation of the Member States in such an agreement is contrary to Opinion 1/76 *Laying-up Fund*, above, which dealt with precisely such a situation and in which the Court held that the participation of some of the Member States was only justified by special circumstances (the need to amend certain earlier conventions). It may be added that, on account of the wide extent of the Community's implied treaty-making powers, the vast majority of mixed agreements fall into this category today. It is only exceptionally that the scope of an agreement exceeds the Community's implied powers, like the United Nations Convention on the Law of the Sea of 1982 (UNCLOS III).

(*c*) The fact that in spite of the above considerations there is a frequent and even increasing recourse to mixed (as opposed to exclusive Community) agreements may be explained by a number of circumstances. First, the extreme reluctance of the Member States, for reasons of policy, prestige, or purely national interests, to give up their treaty-making powers entirely. Thus, acting through the Council as the institution which ultimately wields the treaty-making power, the Member States tend to interpret the Community's exclusive competence restrictively, and often refuse to exercise non-exclusive competences, thus creating a 'need' for their own participation. Secondly, although exclusive treaty-making by the Community would have the effect of strengthening its status as an independent actor on the international scene, the Commission tends to accept the practice of mixed agreements as a means of securing the Council's co-operation in the treaty-making process (see further under (*g*) below). Moreover, any attempt to compel the Council, through legal action before the Court of Justice, to use its non-exclusive competence would, on account of the wide discretionary powers which the Council enjoys in the matter, be not only extremely unlikely to succeed but also detrimental to good relations between the institutions. Thirdly, the mixed agreement formula has a great practical advantage. It avoids the need to define precisely which matters fall within Community competence and which within Member States' competence. Such a definition would not only raise controversial issues relating to the distribution of powers, but would also be very difficult to arrive at in practice as the lines dividing the subject-matters in an international agreement do not normally coincide with those dividing the competence between the Community and the Member States. Fourthly, a mixed agreement enables the Community to obtain a larger number of votes (i.e. a number equal to that of the participating

375

Member States) in any decision-making body set up by it than does an exclusive Community agreement (where the Community has normally only one vote). Finally, the mixed formula may enable the Community to participate in agreements made within the framework of international organizations whose constitutions only allow Member States to conclude such agreements.

(*d*) It is doubtful whether the practice of inserting so-called subordination clauses in multilateral agreements is compatible with Community law and justifiable under international law. These are clauses subordinating Community participation to prior participation of one, several, or all of the Member States (see e.g. Arts. 2 and 3 of Annex IX to the Law of the Sea Convention of 1982, whereby an international organization may sign and ratify the Convention only if a majority of its Member States sign and ratify it; Art. 13 of the Ozone Layer Convention of 1985, *OJ* 1988 L297/8, under which at least one Member State is required to become party but only if the organization itself does not undertake all the obligations arising from the Convention). From the point of view of Community law, such clauses are objectionable on several grounds. They tend to weaken the international status of the Community by calling into question its capacity to conclude international agreements independently of its Member States. They interfere in what is essentially an internal matter of Community law, i.e. the division of treaty-making power between the Community and the Member States. They enable the Member States to block Community participation by not ratifying the agreement or at least to determine the date of Community participation (which cannot be earlier than the date of the last required ratification). Where the participation of some, but not all, of the Member States is required, the clause is clearly illogical and can create enormous difficulties for the Community (for example, the Law of the Sea Convention was signed by the EEC in 1984 although two Member States, the United Kingdom and Germany, were not willing to sign it individually).

(*e*) Some agreements require the Community and the Member States to declare their respective competences over the matters covered by the agreement (see e.g. the Convention on the Physical Protection of Nuclear Materials of 1979; Arts. 2, 4, and 5 of Annex IX to the Law of the Sea Convention; Art. 13(3) of the Ozone Layer Convention of 1985 and Annex II containing the Declaration, above). Quite apart from the fact that this is a purely 'domestic question in which third parties have no need to intervene' (Ruling 1/78 *Protection of Nuclear Materials*, above, at p. 2180), such an obligation may give rise to several problems. In the first place, it eliminates one of the obvious advantages of mixed agreements, that of not having to define the internal distribution of powers. Moreover, since the division of powers is subject to continuous development, any such declaration is liable to have limited validity only (see the Declaration of the EEC on signing the Law of the Sea Convention, text in Simmonds (1986) 23 *CML Rev.* 521 at p. 538, listed below under Articles and Papers).

(*f*) In respect of matters falling within Community competence, a mixed agreement produces legal effects for all the Member States, whether or not participating in it, in the same way as an exclusive Community agreement

(Art. 228(2) EEC; Opinion 1/76 *Laying-up Fund*, above, at p. 756. See also the comments and observations of the EEC on the draft articles of the Vienna Convention on the Law of Treaties between States and International Organizations or between International Organizations, *YILC* 1981, Vol. II, Part Two, p. 201 at p. 203). These effects result from the conclusion of the agreement by the Community, and not from the participation of the Member States. For the same reason, a mixed agreement, being an 'act' of one of the institutions, forms an integral part of Community law (Opinion 1/76 *Laying-up Fund*, above, at p. 760; Ruling 1/78 *Protection of Nuclear Materials*, above, at p. 2180). It is subject to the jurisdiction of the ECJ to interpret it by way of a preliminary ruling under Art. 177 EEC (Case 12/86 *Demirel* [1987] ECR 3719 at pp. 3750–1, where the Court left open the question whether it can also interpret those provisions of a mixed agreement which relate to matters falling within the competence of the Member States). It may produce direct effects in the national legal systems, in the sense of creating enforceable individual rights, under the same conditions as an exclusive Community agreement (ibid. at pp. 3752–4, by implication).

A mixed agreement must be implemented by the Community and the Member States, respectively, each side being responsible for matters falling within its own competence (Ruling 1/78 *Protection of Nuclear Materials*, above, at p. 2180). Where the division of competences has been made known to the other contracting parties (see (*e*) above), the same principle seems to govern also the question of international responsibility for breach of treaty obligations which exists under international law towards such contracting parties. Accordingly, the Community is responsible for non-fulfilment of obligations whose implementation falls within its competence, while the Member States are likewise responsible in respect of matters within their own competence. Where a declaration of competence has not been made at the time of the conclusion of the agreement, it is possible to argue that the Community and the Member States are jointly and severally responsible under international law unless either side (Community or Member States) accepts full responsibility (see also Art. 6(2) of Annex IX to the Law of the Sea Convention under which any State party may request an international organization or its Member States participating in the Convention for information as to who has responsibility in respect of any specific matter. Failure to provide such information within a reasonable time or the provision of contradictory information shall result in joint and several responsibility).

(*g*) The negotiation and conclusion of mixed agreements have given rise to certain practical problems, mainly as regards the composition of mixed delegations and the presentation of the Community as one single entity towards the outside world (see Groux, 'Mixed Negotiations' in *Mixed Agreements*, listed below under Books, p. 87 at pp. 92–6). These problems are not so acute in the case of bilateral agreements where the customary formula is always to set up a single delegation of the Community and the Member States, presided over at all levels by a representative of the Member State holding the Presidency of the Council and composed of representatives of the Member States and representatives of the Commission. This formula

377

is also used in the joint organs set up by Association or Co-operation Agreements.

The methods employed in multilateral negotiations, particularly within the framework of international organizations or conferences and in the decision-making bodies of such organizations, are more complex and varied. Somewhat simplified, the following four main formulas may be distinguished:

(i) There is a Community delegation composed solely of representatives of the Commission and of officials from the Council, while each Member State has its own delegation. This formula was used, for example, in the Third United Nations Conference on the Law of the Sea (UNCLOS III).

(ii) There is a Community delegation, distinct from the individual delegations of the Member States, but in addition to the representatives of the Commission and officials from the Council, it also includes representatives of the Member State holding the Presidency of the Council. This formula is used for the representation of the EEC at the General Assembly of the United Nations. It was also used for the negotiation of the Tin and Coffee Agreements.

(iii) The Community delegation, again distinct from the delegations of the Member States, is composed of representatives of the Commission, officials from the Council, representatives of the Member State holding the Presidency of the Council, and, in addition, representatives of each of the other Member States. This formula was used for the negotiation of the Cocoa and Natural Rubber Agreements.

(iv) There is a single delegation for the Community and the Member States. The latter no longer have individual delegations; their representatives are included in the single delegation together with representatives of the Commission and officials from the Council. This is called the Roman formula or the formula of Rome as it was used in Rome in 1967 at the close of the Multilateral Trade Negotiations of the Kennedy Round. It was again used during the Paris Conference on International Economic Co-operation in 1975–7.

By virtue of an arrangement between the Council and the Commission of 30 March 1981, referred to as 'PROBA 20' from the name of the document in which it is contained, the last-mentioned formula should be used in the future for preparatory work and negotiations concerning all agreements on raw materials falling within the Integrated Programme of UNCTAD of 1976, with the exception of agricultural products placed under a common organization of the market.

The arrangement was arrived at at the initiative of the Commission aimed at the improvement of the external image and the strengthening of the internal cohesion and solidarity of the Community. On its part, the Commission undertook not to invoke any legal or institutional considerations in favour of exclusive Community competence to negotiate and conclude these agreements, such as it might be able to derive from the case-law of the Court of Justice (in particular from Opinion 1/78 *Natural Rubber Agreement,* above). Consequently, it was agreed that there should be joint participation of the Commission (representing the Community) and the Member States in all agreements in which both wished to participate. In return for this concession, the Council agreed that this participation should be in the form of a joint delegation expressing the common position through a single spokesman who would normally be the representative of the Commission. The joint delegation, within which the Member States would be individually identifiable but sitting together in the conference room under the nameplate 'EEC', would operate on the basis of a common position previously established by means of the usual procedures. In certain circumstances, the common position might also be presented by the representative of the Member State holding the Council Presidency or by the representative of another Member State. Interventions might be made by Member States but only strictly within the framework of the common position (for the full text of PROBA 20, see *Leading Cases and Materials on the External Relations Law of the EC*, listed below under Books, p. 48).

There is no doubt that it is this formula which best enables the Community to speak 'with one voice' to the outside world. At the same time, it puts an end to interinstitutional disputes as to who and how should negotiate and conclude an important category of international agreements. It is regrettable that such positive results could only be achieved at the price of a political compromise which pays little regard to legal principles established by the Court of Justice.

See also **Common Commercial Policy***, **Community Treaties, Direct effect, External relations, Legal personality, Preliminary ruling, Treaty-making power, Treaty-making procedure.**

Further reading 1. BOOKS: Dolmans, *Problems of Mixed Agreements* (1985); Groux and Manin, *The European Communities in the International Order* (1985); O'Keeffe and Schermers (eds.), *Mixed Agreements* (1983); Timmermans and Völker (eds.), *Division of Powers between the European Communities and their Member States in the Field of External Relations* (1981); Völker and Steenbergen (eds.), *Leading Cases and Materials on the External Relations Law of the EC* (1985).

2. ARTICLES AND PAPERS: Close, 'Subordination Clauses in Mixed Agreements' (1985) 34 *ICLQ* 382; Schermers, 'The Internal Effect of Community Treaty-Making', in O'Keeffe and Schermers (eds.), *Essays in European Law and Integration* (1982), p. 167; Simmonds, 'The Community's Participation in the UN Law of the Sea Convention', ibid. p. 179; id., 'The Community's Declaration upon Signature of the UN Convention on the Law of the Sea' (1986) 23 *CML Rev.* 521; Temple Lang, 'The Ozone Layer Convention: A New Solution to the Question of Community Participation in "Mixed" International Agreements' (1986) 23 *CML Rev.* 157.

3. OFFICIAL PUBLICATION: House of Lords Select Committee on the European Communities, Session 1984–5, 16th Report, 'External Competence of the European Communities' (1985), see esp. the Memorandum by the Commission, p. 104 and pp. 118–21.

See also under **Treaty-making power.**

N

▶ **NATURAL JUSTICE** Concept of English law developed by the courts to control the administrative procedure. Its function is comparable to that of 'due process of law' in the Constitution of the United States. In English law, the concept of natural justice comprises two fundamental rules: *audi alteram partem*, or the right to be heard, and *nemo judex in causa sua*, no one may be a judge in one's own cause (see Case 17/74 *Transocean Marine Paint Association* v. *Commission* [1974] ECR 1063 at p. 1088 *per* A.-G. Warner and H. W. R. Wade, *Administrative Law*, 6th edn. (Oxford, 1988), part v).

In several cases, the ECJ and its various Advocates-General have relied on the concept of 'natural justice', but they seem to have used this term in the sense of 'equity' or 'fairness' rather than according to its original meaning in English law. Thus, dealing with the question whether the Commission and the national authorities may impose a double sanction in one and the same case under competition law, the Court has stated that 'if . . . the possibility of two procedures being conducted separately were to lead to the imposition of consecutive sanctions, a general requirement of natural justice . . . demands that any previous punitive decision must be taken into account in determining any sanction which is to be imposed' (Case 14/68 *Wilhelm* [1969] ECR 1 at p. 15. Dealing with the same question, A.-G. Roemer relied on 'reasons of fairness' rather than on natural justice, ibid. at p. 26. However, in Case 7/72 *Boehringer* v. *Commission* [1972] ECR 1281 at pp. 1294 and 1299 A.-G. Mayras again used the term 'natural justice' in the same context). Sometimes the Court invokes 'the principle of natural justice' to avoid a result which would be unfair (see e.g. Case 140/77 *Verhaaf* v. *Commission* [1978] ECR 2117 at p. 2124; Case 68/79 *Just* [1980] ECR 501 at p. 532 *per* A.-G. Reischl), and sometimes as an aid in interpreting ambiguous texts in a way which is the least onerous for the individual concerned (see e.g. Case 78/77 *Lührs* [1978] ECR 169 at p. 180).

Nevertheless, there are situations where the Court may not be able to satisfy the requirements of natural justice by means of judicial interpretation, namely, where to do so would require legislative action (ibid.). Also, the Court has expressly stated that the concept of natural justice, whether invoked under national law or as a part of Community law, may not be relied on by national customs authorities in order to grant exemption from charges due under Community law, such as e.g. monetary compensatory amounts (Case 118/76 *Balkan-Import-Export* [1977] ECR 1177 at pp. 1189–90). The Court has specifically denied the existence in Community law of a general legal principle, analogous to the German law concept of 'objective unfairness' (*sachliche Unbilligkeit*), according to which a Community provision may not be applied by a national authority if it causes the person concerned hardship which the Community legislature would clearly have sought to avoid if it had envisaged that eventuality when enacting that provision (Case 299/84 *Neumann* [1985] ECR 3663 at pp. 3687–90, where the Court relied on its judgment cited immediately above. It is interesting to note that in the present case the Court referred to 'equitable grounds' while in the previous case it used the term 'natural justice' throughout).

See also Audi alteram partem, Equity, General principles of law, Interpretation of Community law.

▶ *NE ULTRA PETITA* Rule according to which the ECJ may not generally give judgment beyond what is requested in the application originating proceedings; it may not exceed or distort the scope which the applicant intended its action to have (Case 14/59 *Fonderies de Pont-à-Mousson v. HA* [1959] ECR 215 at p. 231; Cases 46 and 47/59 *Meroni v. HA* [1962] ECR 411 at p. 419; Case 33/59 *Chasse* v. *HA* [1962] ECR 381 at p. 394 *per* A.-G. Lagrange). Therefore, the nature and scope of the operative part of a judgment is basically determined by the nature and scope of the *petitum*, i.e. the conclusions contained in the originating application. However, in cases in which the Court has unlimited jurisdiction it may award damages acting of its own motion, i.e. in the absence of any claim to that effect.
See also Application originating proceedings, *Causa petendi*, Judgment, *Petitum*, Unlimited jurisdiction.

▶ *NON BIS IN IDEM* General principle of law which prohibits the institution of criminal, administrative, or disciplinary proceedings and the imposition of the corresponding punishment more than once in respect of the same act. Therefore, once an act has been definitively dealt with by a decision having the force of *res judicata*, it cannot become the subject of further proceedings of the same type and within the same jurisdiction (Cases 18 and 35/65 *Gutmann* v. *Commission* [1966] ECR 103 at p. 119 and [1967] ECR 61 at pp. 65–7, where the Court held that the Commission had infringed the *non bis in idem* principle by initiating two disciplinary proceedings on the basis of the same facts and annulled the second inquiry). It follows that the principle does not exclude the possibility of two sets of proceedings being brought and two sanctions being imposed within different jurisdictions, or if the proceedings and sanctions are of a different nature. Thus, the *non bis in idem* rule does not prevent the institution of parallel competition proceedings before the Community and the national authorities (or those of a third country) in respect of the same conduct, and does not prohibit even a duplication of sanctions. However, in the latter case, a general requirement of 'natural justice' demands that any previous sanction should be taken into account (Case 14/68 *Wilhelm* [1969] ECR 1 at p. 15 *per Curiam*, pp. 24–6 *per* A.-G. Roemer; Case 7/72 *Boehringer* v. *Commission* [1972] ECR 1281 at pp. 1289–90 *per Curiam*, pp. 1293–301 *per* A.-G. Mayras).
See also General principles of law, Natural justice, *Res judicata*.

▶ NON-CONTRACTUAL LIABILITY Liability of the European Communities to make good damage caused by their institutions or by their servants in the performance of their duties, other than damage arising from a breach of contract. Non-contractual liability may be enforced by means of an action for damages brought before the ECJ.

381

Under the ECSC Treaty, the basis for the Community's non-contractual liability is a 'wrongful act or omission on the part of the Community' (*faute de service*) or a 'personal wrong' by a Community servant (*faute personnelle*) (Art. 40 ECSC). Under the EEC/Euratom Treaties, the non-contractual liability of the Communities is to be determined 'in accordance with the general principles common to the laws of the Member States' (Arts. 215(2) EEC, 188(2) Euratom).

Within the meaning of these provisions, the term 'non-contractual liability' refers to 'administrative' or 'governmental' liability, i.e. liability of public authorities for breach of an official duty (*Amtshaftung*), and not to general civil law (i.e. tortious, delictual) liability. 'Non-contractual liability' under the Treaties arises only in respect of damage caused by the Community institutions or servants 'in the performance of their duties'. Injury caused outside the performance of duties gives rise to the civil law liability of the Communities which falls to be determined by the national courts (not by the ECJ) in accordance with the *lex loci delicti*.

The dividing line between the two areas is, however, not clearly defined. Generally speaking, non-contractual liability under the Treaties covers, as regards the conduct of the institutions, first, the damaging consequences of the legal measures whereby the Communities manifest their quasi-sovereign powers; and secondly, damage caused by a malfunctioning of the administration arising from defective departmental organization, negligent administrative action, or lack of adequate supervision. In either case, the wrongful act or omission is 'anonymous', i.e. it cannot be associated with the activities of any specific person. This liability further covers those personal acts of the Community servants which, 'by virtue of an internal and direct relationship, are the necessary extension of the tasks entrusted to the institutions' (Case 9/69 *Sayag* [1969] ECR 329 at p. 336). On the other hand, non-contractual liability under the Treaties does not seem to cover damage arising in the course of the 'civil' life of the Communities, e.g. in connection with the possession and administration of Community assets (buildings, installations, dangerous materials, etc.) or damage arising from purely physical acts connected with the day-to-day running of the departments. Nor does it cover accidents caused by a servant while he is using his private car for transport during the performance of his duties, save in very exceptional circumstances (ibid. at pp. 335–6 *per Curiam*, pp. 340–3, 346 *per* A.-G. Gand. See also Cases 14/60 etc. *Meroni* v. *HA* [1961] ECR 161 at pp. 167–71).

By referring to the 'general principles common to the laws of the Member States', the Treaties deliberately left it to the ECJ to work out the general conditions for the non-contractual liability of the Economic and Euratom Communities. In so doing the Court is justified in drawing upon its own earlier case-law built up under Art. 40 of the ECSC Treaty, where non-contractual liability is based on the concept of 'wrongful act or omission'. Thus, although certain differences still remain (see below), a coherent body of rules is bound ultimately to emerge governing the liability of all three Communities.

In formulating these rules, the ECJ has stated in a series of cases that: 'By virtue of the second paragraph of Article 215 and the general principles to which this provision refers, the liability of the Community presupposes the existence of a set of circumstances comprising actual damage, a causal link between the damage claimed and the conduct alleged against the institution, and the illegality of such conduct' (Case 4/69 *Lütticke* v. *Commission* [1971] ECR 325 at p. 337; Case 153/73 *Holtz & Willemsen* v. *Council and Commission* [1974] ECR 675 at p. 693; Cases 197 to 200/80 etc. *Ludwigshafener Walzmühle* v. *Council and Commission* [1981] ECR 3211 at p. 3246; etc.). In dealing, more specifically, with the last-mentioned requirement the case-law of the Court makes a clear distinction between illegal individual (administrative) acts or omissions and illegal legislative measures. As regards the latter, in a consistent line of decisions the ECJ has held that: '. . . the non-contractual liability of the Community presupposes at the very least the unlawful nature of the act alleged to be the cause of the damage. Where legislative action involving measures of economic policy is concerned, the Community does not incur non-contractual liability for damage suffered by individuals as a consequence of that action, by virtue of the provisions contained in Article 215, second paragraph, of the Treaty, unless a sufficiently flagrant violation of a superior rule of law for the protection of the individual has occurred' (Case 5/71 *Zuckerfabrik Schöppenstedt* v. *Council* [1971] ECR 975 at p. 984; see also the second and third cases cited immediately above and the cases cited below).

So far the ECJ has recognized only a few rules and principles which qualify as 'superior rules of law designed to protect individuals'. It has, moreover, imposed further restrictions on the right of private persons to claim damages on the basis of illegal Community legislative action. Thus, in Cases 83 and 94/76 etc. *HNL* v. *Council and Commission* [1978] ECR 1209 at pp. 1224–5— 'Skimmed-milk powder' cases—the Court recognized that the principle of equality, embodied in particular in Art. 40(3)(2) EEC, which prohibits any discrimination in the common organization of the agricultural markets, was in fact designed for the protection of the individual, and that it was 'impossible to disregard the importance of this prohibition in the system of the Treaty'. Nevertheless, the fact that a legislative measure—an agricultural regulation— had been declared null and void for breach of this principle was insufficient by itself for the Community to incur non-contractual liability for damage caused to individuals by that measure. In accordance with the general principles common to the laws of the Member States, the Court held,

public authorities can only exceptionally and in special circumstances incur liability for legislative measures which are the result of choices of economic policy. This restrictive view is explained by the consideration that the legislative authority, even where the validity of its measures is subject to judicial review, cannot always be hindered in making its decisions by the prospect of applications for damages whenever it has occasion to adopt legislative measures in the public interest which may adversely affect the interests of individuals. It follows from these considerations that individuals may be required, in the sectors coming within the economic policy of the Community, to accept within reasonable limits certain harmful effects on their economic interests as a result of a legislative measure without being able to obtain compensation from public funds even if that

383

measure has been declared null and void. In a legislative field such as the one in question, in which one of the chief features is the exercise of a wide discretion essential for the implementation of the Common Agricultural Policy, the Community does not therefore incur liability unless the institution concerned has *manifestly and gravely disregarded the limits on the exercise of its powers.* [Emphasis added.]

This was not so in the present case since the regulation in question, which provided for the compulsory purchase of skimmed-milk powder at a disproportionately high price, affected very wide categories of traders so that its effects on individual undertakings were considerably lessened. Moreover, the regulation had only a relatively limited effect on the price of feeding-stuffs (made from skimmed-milk powder) as compared with price increases resulting from the variations in the world market prices. Thus, the overall effect of the regulation on the profit-earning capacity of the undertakings 'did not ultimately exceed the bounds of the economic risks inherent in the activities of the agricultural sectors concerned'.

In Cases 116 and 124/77 *Amylum* v. *Council and Commission* [1979] ECR 3497 at p. 3561—'Isoglucose' cases—the Court went even further in dismissing an action for damages based on a Council regulation previously declared illegal. Referring to its above-cited judgment, the Court held that while the fixing of the isoglucose production levy by the regulation in question was vitiated by errors, 'these were not errors of such gravity that it may be said that the conduct of the defendant institutions in this respect was *verging on the arbitrary* and was thus of such a kind as to involve the Community in non-contractual liability' (emphasis added. See also Cases 197 to 200/80 etc. *Ludwigshafener Walzmühle* v. *Council and Commission*, above, esp. at pp. 3246, 3251).

Cases 83 and 94/76 etc. *HNL* v. *Council and Commission*, above, may be contrasted with Case 238/78 *Ireks-Arkady* v. *Council and Commission* [1979] ECR 2955 at p. 2973—'Quellmehl' case—in which the ECJ did recognize that there was on the part of the Council such a 'grave and manifest disregard' of the limits on the exercise of its discretionary powers as to establish the Community's liability. This case was founded on a Council regulation abolishing the production refunds for quellmehl, previously held by the Court to be illegal for infringing the principle of equality by providing for different treatment for quellmehl and starch in respect of production refunds. In the present case the Court held that the principle of equality occupied a 'particularly important place among the rules of Community law intended to protect the interests of the individual'. The disregard of that principle in this case affected a limited and clearly defined group of commercial operators. Further, the damage alleged by the applicants went beyond the bounds of the economic risks inherent in the activities in the sector concerned. Finally, equality of treatment with the producers of maize starch, which had been observed from the beginning of the common organization of the market in cereals, was ended by the Council without sufficient justification. For those reasons the Court arrived at the conclusion that the Community incurred liability for the abolition of the refunds for quellmehl.

A second principle recognized as a 'superior rule of law for the protection of the individual' is that concerning the protection of legitimate expectation or confidence. Thus, the ECJ has stated that:

The Community is . . . liable if, in the absence of an overriding matter of public interest, the Commission abolished with immediate effect and without warning the application of compensatory amounts in a specific sector without adopting transitional measures which would at least permit traders either to avoid the loss which would have been suffered in the performance of export contracts . . . or to be compensated for such loss. In the absence of an overriding matter of public interest, the Commission has violated a superior rule of law, thus rendering the Community liable, by failing to include in Regulation No 189/72 [providing for the withdrawal of the monetary compensatory amounts applicable to colza and rape] transitional measures for the protection of the confidence which a trader might legitimately have had in the Community rules. (Case 74/74 *CNTA* v. *Commission* [1975] ECR 533 at p. 550. For the final judgment in this case, dismissing the application because the applicant could not prove that it had suffered a loss, see [1976] ECR 797 at p. 806.)

Finally, a third principle constituting a superior legal rule is that of proportionality, which can be derived from that provision in Art. 40(3) EEC which stipulates that the common organization of agricultural markets may include only such measures as are 'required to attain the objectives' set out in Art. 39 EEC (see Cases 63 to 69/72 *Werhahn* v. *Council* [1973] ECR 1229 at pp. 1249 *et seq.*; Cases 197 to 200/80 etc. *Ludwigshafener Walzmühle* v. *Council and Commission*, above, at pp. 3247, 3252–3).

As seen above, in defining the conditions of non-contractual liability under Art. 215(2) EEC, the ECJ has laid down three requirements: the existence of actual damage, a causal link between the damage and the institutions' conduct, and the illegality of such conduct. It follows both from the text of the Treaty and from the nature of things that the first and the second condition must always be present since, clearly, in the absence of 'damage' which has been 'caused' by the institutions the question of Community liability and the right to compensation cannot arise. These two requirements therefore form that indispensable minimum which must be shown to exist in every action brought under Art. 215(2) (*see further under* **Causal connection, Damage**). It is, however, far less certain (1) whether the third requirement, that of illegality, also forms an indispensable condition of liability and (2) whether illegality is sufficient, in itself, to establish liability or whether the element of fault (culpability) must be added as a fourth condition. In fact, the mutual relationship of illegality and culpability, which represent, respectively, the objective and the subjective aspects of the concept of liability, is one of the most complex and least clarified areas of the whole law on non-contractual liability.

That fault is, at least under the ECSC Treaty, an essential element of Community liability follows from the very text of Art. 40, which expressly refers to a 'wrongful act or omission' (*faute de service*) on the part of the Community and to a 'personal wrong' (*faute personnelle*) on the part of a servant of the Community. As A.-G. Lagrange has pointed out, 'the basis of liability under Article 40 of the Treaty is the "wrongful act or omission": this is subjective liability and the wrongful act or omission must be established'

385

(Case 33/59 *Chasse* v. *HA* [1962] ECR 381 at p. 395; see also pp. 396, 405). Indeed, the whole case-law of the ECJ under Art. 40 centres upon the concept of 'wrongful act or omission', a concept borrowed originally from national law (mainly French administrative law) but reinterpreted and redefined by the ECJ to suit the particular purposes of Community law. Thus, a wrongful act or omission, which always implies at least an ordinary degree of fault (negligence or carelessness), may consist in errors and defects arising from insufficient, negligent, or defective organization and bad administration (ibid. at p. 389 *per Curiam*; see also Case 23/59 *FERAM* v. *HA* [1959] ECR 245 at p. 251; Cases 14/60 etc. *Meroni* v. *HA*, above, at pp. 168–70) or in a failure to exercise adequate supervision. As the ECJ put it in Cases 19/60 etc. *Fives Lille Cail* v. *HA* [1961] ECR 281 at p. 297, the High Authority (i.e. the Commission) 'gravely neglected the duties of supervision required by a normal standard of care, and it is this shortcoming which gives rise to its liability'. The Commission's duty of supervision exists both over its own departments or agencies set up by it (such as the agencies set up to administer the scrap equalization scheme, see ibid.; see also Cases 29/63 etc. *Usines de la Providence* v. *HA* [1965] ECR 911 at p. 937), and over the Member States by virtue of Art. 88 ECSC, a failure to carry out which may equally establish its liability (Cases 9 and 12/60 *Vloeberghs* v. *HA* [1961] ECR 197 at p. 216 *per Curiam*, p. 240 *per* A.-G. Roemer).

By contrast, Arts. 215(2) EEC and 188(2) Euratom do not mention the concept of 'wrongful act or omission'; nor do they refer to any concept of fault. It may be due to this fact that the case-law of the Court under these provisions has generally paid much less attention to the criterion of culpability than to that of illegality. In theory, four different explanations are possible as to the mutual relationship and relative importance of these two concepts, each of which is supported to some extent by the decisions of the Court and the opinions of the Advocates-General. They are as follows.

1. Illegality of conduct is always a necessary, and at the same time in itself sufficient, prerequisite for the establishment of liability. This seems to be the prevailing view in the case-law today, and is strongly supported by the absence of any reference to fault in the standard definition of the conditions of liability laid down by the Court (see above). Also, the ECJ has stated in the *Schöppenstedt* case, already cited, that 'the non-contractual liability of the Community presupposes at the very least the unlawful nature of the act alleged to be the cause of the damage'. Or, to quote another decision, 'the question of the possible liability of the Community is in the first place linked with that of the legality of [the act] in question' (Case 96/71 *Haegeman* v. *Commission* [1972] ECR 1005 at p. 1015).

Accordingly, the Court normally begins its investigations by examining whether or not the act or omission is illegal. If it comes to the conclusion that it is not, it dismisses the action, there being 'no need to examine the other conditions for non-contractual liability' (Case 43/72 *Merkur* v. *Commission* [1973] ECR 1055 at p. 1074; see also e.g. Case 59/72 *Wünsche* v. *Commission* [1973] ECR 791 at pp. 803–4 and the cases cited under point 4 below). On the other hand, in cases where the Court found that a legislative measure was illegal for breach of a superior rule of law designed to protect individuals, this was in itself sufficient to establish the Community's liability, without any examination of the question of fault (see Case 74/74 *CNTA* v. *Commission*, above; Case 238/78 *Ireks-Arkady* v. *Council and Commission*, above). One possible explanation is that, at least in cases involving legislative measures adopted in violation of such 'superior' (protective) rules and principles of law, in the opinion of the Court illegality automatically implies fault. In other words, culpability is subsumed under the concept of illegality. In the *Wünsche* case, above, at p. 807, A.-G. Mayras indeed referred to 'culpable illegality'. As he put it, 'the absence of any factor likely to affect the legality of the contested Regulations is sufficient proof of the absence of any breach of duty, in the context of Article 215 of the Treaty' (ibid. at p. 812). In other words, 'no illegality, no fault and, therefore, no liability' (ibid. at p. 807).

2. Illegality is in itself not sufficient to create liability; *both* illegality *and* culpability must be established, independently of one another and according to different criteria. Otherwise an action for annulment and an action for damages could be brought on exactly the same grounds despite their different legal consequences, something which could not have been contemplated by the Treaty. Also, where the illegality of an act consists of a formal or procedural defect, this is clearly insufficient to establish liability. This theory is supported by the opinions of various Advocates-General and also by some of the Court's decisions.

Thus, A.-G. Roemer stated that 'a claim founded upon administrative liability can lie only if a *fault* or wrongful conduct in the sense of "faute de service" is proved' (Case 25/62 *Plaumann* v. *Commission* [1963] ECR 95 at p. 120; see also his opinions in the *Werhahn* case, above, at p. 1270, and the *Schöppenstedt* case, above, at pp. 994, 998–9, where he regarded the requirement of fault as a general principle under the legal systems of the Member States). According to A.-G. Trabucchi, in examining the individual conditions of liability, it is necessary to consider 'whether there exists the subjective condition of liability, namely, whether there is any misconduct to be discerned in the action of the Commission arising from its having acted negligently and without due care and circumspection' (Case 26/74 *Roquette* v. *Commission* [1976] ECR 677 at p. 693). In Cases 5, 7, and 13 to 24/66 *Kampffmeyer* v. *Commmission* [1967] ECR 245 at p. 274 A.-G. Gand observed that 'not every illegality or infringement of the rule of law necessarily gives rise to a right to reparation . . . Two conditions must in addition be fulfilled . . . It is necessary [secondly] that the illegality committed should constitute a wrongful act.' It is 'negligence which [gives an] illegal decision a wrongful character' (ibid. at p. 276).

In the last-mentioned cases, the Court itself only considered the question of fault since the illegality of the act causing the damage had already been established in earlier cases. The Court came to the conclusion that the Commission's conduct constituted 'a wrongful act or omission capable of giving rise to liability on the part of the Community'. The wrongful act consisted in the improper application of a regulation. At the same time the Court rejected the Commission's argument that supervisory organizations

387

could not, according to a general principle common to the laws of the Member States, be made liable except in the case of gross negligence (ibid. at p. 262). Also, in Cases 19/69 etc. *Richez-Parise* v. *Commission* [1970] ECR 325 at pp. 338–40, involving Community officials, the Court clearly stated that 'for the application to be well founded it must be established that the defendant is liable for a wrongful act or omission which caused the applicants a still subsisting injury'. In these cases the Commission's departments supplied the applicants with incorrect information concerning their rights. The Court held that while, apart from exceptional situations, 'the adoption of an incorrect interpretation [of legal provisions] does not constitute in itself a wrongful act', a delay in rectifying the error does, and renders the Communities liable. In several cases, the Court examined claims that the failure of the Commission to carry out its supervisory tasks over the Member States under Arts. 155 and 169 EEC constituted a 'wrongful act or omission' giving rise to non-contractual liability (see Case 4/69 *Lütticke* v. *Commission*, above, at pp. 336–8; Case 40/75 *Produits Bertrand* v. *Commission* [1976] ECR 1 at pp. 7–9).

3. A wrongful act or omission, which always implies fault, may in itself establish liability without the existence of illegality. This view seems to gain support from a series of staff cases in which the Court held that a measure which had not been shown to be illegal could still constitute a wrongful act creating liability 'if it contained superfluous criticisms of the person referred to in it' (see e.g. Cases 35/62 and 16/63 *Leroy* v. *HA* [1963] ECR 197 at p. 207; Case 84/63 *De Vos van Steenwijk* v. *Commission* [1964] ECR 321 at p. 334). In Cases 14/60 etc. *Meroni* v. *HA*, above, at pp. 166, 170, brought under Art. 40 ECSC, the Court expressly excluded from its considerations the question whether the measures giving rise to the damage (i.e. the decisions setting up the scrap equalization scheme) were lawful or not, and limited itself to examining the sole question whether there was evidence of a wrongful act or omission during the administration of that scheme. Likewise, in Case 131/81 *Berti* v. *Commission* [1982] ECR 3493 at p. 3504 the Court established the Commission's liability solely on the basis that it committed a wrongful act or omission, without examining the question of legality.

4. In several cases, the applicants put forward the view that the Community might incur non-contractual liability even in the absence of both illegality and fault (the principle of objective or strict liability). This principle is said to form part of the general principles of law common to the Member States, which the Court is required to apply under Art. 215(2) EEC. In particular, the principle is derived either from the German law concept of *Sonderopfer* (special sacrifice) or from the French law concept of *rupture de l'égalité devant les charges publiques* (unequal discharge of public burdens or the principle of the equality of citizens in relation to charges necessitated by the functioning of public services, also known as the theory of created risk), or from a combination of both. According to the former concept, the Community should be held liable to pay compensation even without fault where there is a lawful or unlawful intervention in economic relations comparable to expropriation (see e.g. Cases 5, 7, and 13 to 24/66 *Kampffmeyer* v. *Commission*, above, at

p. 278 *per* A.-G. Gand; Cases 63 to 69/72 *Werhahn* v. *Council*, above, at p. 1253 *per Curiam*, pp. 1273–5 *per* A.-G. Roemer; Cases 56 to 60/74 *Kampffmeyer* v. *Commission and Council* [1976] ECR 711 at p. 747 *per Curiam*, p. 765 *per* A.-G. Reischl). According to the latter concept, the Community should incur liability even in the absence of any illegality and fault where an individual suffers in consequence of general measures a 'direct, special and abnormal' damage or, in other words, where an individual has to bear, in the public interest, a financial burden which would not normally fall upon him and which should be borne by the Community as a whole (see e.g. Case 23/59 *FERAM* v. *HA*, above, at p. 255–6 *per* A.-G. Lagrange; Cases 9 and 11/71 *Compagnie d'Approvisionnement* v. *Commission* [1972] ECR 391 at pp. 407–8 *per Curiam*, pp. 422–3 *per* A.-G. Mayras; interpreted by A.-G. Trabucchi in Case 169/73 *Compagnie Continentale* v. *Council* [1975] ECR 117 at p. 141; Cases 54 to 60/76 *Compagnie Industrielle du Comté de Loheac* v. *Council and Commission* [1977] ECR 645 at pp. 657, 659–60; and the two cases cited below).

While the Court has never rejected these arguments in substance, it always came to the conclusion that in the particular circumstances of the case before it, Community liability could not arise. Thus, for example, in Case 59/83 *Biovilac* v. *EEC* [1984] ECR 4057 at pp. 4080–1 the Court referred to the general principle according to which an action for damages cannot succeed unless the damage arising from legislative action exceeds the limits of the economic risks inherent in operating in the sector concerned. That principle, the Court said, 'would have to be applied *a fortiori* if the concept of liability without fault were accepted in Community law'. Since in the case before it those limits were not exceeded, the Court dismissed the claim without further considering the principle of strict liability (see also Case 267/82 *Développement S.A. and Clemessy* v. *Commission* [1986] ECR 1907 at pp. 1921–2).

It seems that, at the present stage of the development of the law on liability under the EEC and Euratom Treaties, none of the four views discussed may be ruled out as being completely incorrect.

See also **Action for damages, Causal connection, Contractual liability, Damage, Equality, General principles of law, Legitimate expectation, Proportionality.**

Further reading 1. BOOK: Schermers *et al.* (eds.), *The Non-Contractual Liability of the European Communities* (1988).

2. ARTICLES AND REPORTS: Elster, 'Non-Contractual Liability under Two Legal Orders' (1975) 12 *CML Rev.* 91 and 254; Jones, 'The Non-Contractual Liability of the EEC and the Availability of an Alternative Remedy in the National Courts' (1981/1) *LIEI* 1; Lagrange, 'The Non-Contractual Liability of the Community in the E.C.S.C. and in the E.E.C.' (1965–6) 3 *CML Rev.* 10; Lysén, 'Three Questions on the Non-Contractual Liability of the EEC' (1985/2) *LIEI* 86; Lord Mackenzie Stuart, 'The "Non-Contractual" Liability of the European Economic Community' (1975) 12 *CML Rev.* 493; 'The Non-Contractual Liability of the European Communities', Reports for a Colloquium held in The Hague on 5–6 Nov. 1987 (1988) 25 *CML Rev.* 207.

See also under **Action for damages.**

▶ *NON LIQUET* Situation in which a court considers itself unable to give judgment based on law owing to the absence, obscurity, or insufficiency of relevant legal rules. This may lead to a denial of justice which is prohibited in certain national legal systems (see e.g. Art. 4 of Code Napoléon) and which is thought of as being virtually inconceivable in Community law.

See also Denial of justice.

▶ NON-MATERIAL DAMAGE Damage caused by an act or omission of a Community institution which does not involve an economic (i.e. pecuniary) loss and which is, therefore, not quantifiable according to the general rules ('general damage', *préjudice moral*). In a number of staff cases, the ECJ has granted compensation for non-material injury, such as 'shock', 'disturbance', and 'uneasiness' caused by the prospect of an unlawful dismissal (Cases 7/56 etc. *Algera* v. *Common Assembly* [1957] ECR 39 at pp. 66–7); 'uncertain and anxious state of mind' owing to the absence of the compulsory periodic reports (Case 61/76 *Geist* v. *Commission* [1977] ECR 1419 at p. 1436); 'state of uncertainty' arising from an inaction of an institution (Cases 10 and 47/72 *Di Pillo* v. *Commission* [1973] ECR 763 at p. 772; Case 75/77 *Mollet* v. *Commission* [1978] ECR 897 at pp. 908–9); psychological and non-physical consequences of an accident (Cases 169/83 and 136/84 *Leussink* v. *Commission* [1986] ECR 2801 at pp. 2827–8); etc. In these cases the Court assesses the damage *ex aequo et bono* (see e.g. Case 24/79 *Oberthür* v. *Commission* [1980] ECR 1743 at pp. 1759–60; Cases 173/82 etc. *Castille* v. *Commission* [1986] ECR 497 at p. 527) and is even willing to award symbolic damages corresponding to one European monetary unit (Case 18/78 *Mrs V* v. *Commission* [1979] ECR 2093 at p. 2103). Although the Court appears to have so far granted compensation for non-material damage in staff cases only, it is submitted that there is no compelling reason why such compensation should not be awarded, in appropriate cases, even outside the employment relationship.

See also Damage, Non-contractual liability.

▶ NOTIFICATION Procedure whereby ECSC individual decisions/recommendations and EEC/Euratom directives and decisions are brought into force with regard to the addressees. Thus, Art. 15 ECSC provides that 'where decisions and recommendations are individual in character, they shall become binding upon being notified to the party concerned'. Likewise, Arts. 191 EEC and 163 Euratom provide that 'directives and decisions shall be notified to those to whom they are addressed and shall take effect upon such notification'.

Publication of these measures, where not expressly provided for, is not a precondition for their legal validity and has, where it does take place, above all a protective function. Where publication is omitted the measures in question cannot be invoked against third parties affected by, but not notified of, them (Cases 73 and 74/63 *Handelsvereniging Rotterdam* [1964] ECR 1 at p. 14; Case 9/70 *Grad* [1970] ECR 825 at p. 848 *per* A.-G. Roemer; Case

33/70 *SACE* [1970] ECR 1213 at p. 1223 *per Curiam*, p. 1229 *per* A.-G. Roemer). This does not, however, prevent third parties from relying on such measures in defence of their rights, i.e. from deriving benefits from them. Thus, the fact that the publication of EEC/Euratom directives and decisions which are addressed to Member States is not expressly provided for does not mean that such measures can never produce direct effects for individuals. Nevertheless, on account of their importance as (often) quasi-legislative acts, it is desirable that they should be published in the *Official Journal*, which is in fact the usual practice (ibid.). In some cases, e.g. in the field of competition law, even the publication of certain purely 'individual' decisions has been, or may be, made compulsory (see e.g. Art. 21 of Reg. 17, *OJ Sp. Edn.* 1959–62, p. 87; Art. 18 of Reg. 3975/87, *OJ* 1987 L374/1. See also Art. 4(2) of Dec. 22/60, *OJ Sp. Edn.* 2nd Ser. (VIII), p. 13, concerning the publication of ECSC individual decisions/recommendations).

Decisions the publication of which is not compulsory (e.g. those imposing fines under Art. 15 of Reg. 17) may still be published in the *Official Journal* or given publicity in the form of press releases, provided that business secrets are not divulged (Case 41/69 *Chemiefarma* v. *Commission* [1970] ECR 661 at p. 692; Case 54/69 *Francolor* v. *Commission* [1972] ECR 851 at pp. 872–3). Where a measure which is directed to specific named persons or undertakings is also published in the *Official Journal* and there is a discrepancy between the notified and the published texts, only the one which is notified to the addressees is authentic (Cases 56 and 58/64 *Consten and Grundig* v. *Commission* [1966] ECR 299 at p. 337).

Notification and, where expressly so required, publication of individual measures is an essential formal/procedural requirement, the total omission of which will affect the validity of the measure. In the absence of notification, an individual measure cannot become binding upon the addressee(s). Nevertheless, irregularities in the procedure for notification are regarded as being external to the measure itself and therefore incapable of invalidating it. In certain circumstances, such irregularities may prevent the period within which an action for annulment must be lodged with the ECJ from starting to run (Case 48/69 *ICI* v. *Commission* [1972] ECR 619 at p. 652).

The ECJ has held that 'a decision is properly notified within the meaning of the [EEC] Treaty, if it reaches the addressee and puts the latter in a position to take cognizance of it.' Once a decision actually reaches the addressee, the latter 'cannot make use of its own refusal to take cognizance of the decision in order to render this communication ineffective' (Case 6/72 *Continental Can* v. *Commission* [1973] ECR 215 at p. 241; Case 42/85 *Cockerill-Sambre* v. *Commission* [1985] ECR 3749 at p. 3756). The validity of notification is not dependent on effective knowledge actually being acquired of it by the person who, according to the internal rules of the undertaking to which the measure is addressed, is competent to deal with the matter (ibid.; Case 224/83 *Ferriera Vittoria* v. *Commission* [1984] ECR 2349 at p. 2356). Although the precise form of notification is immaterial, the ECJ has accepted that a registered letter with acknowledgment of receipt is a perfectly suitable method as it enables the date from which time begins to run to be determined with certainty (ibid.

391

at p. 2355; Case 42/85 *Cockerill-Sambre* v. *Commission*, above, at p. 3756. See also Art. 4(1) of Dec. 22/60).

In the case of companies established within the Member States, the registered office is the only place which is required by the relevant Community directives to be mentioned in the company's official documents and to be recorded in the public registers. For that reason, notification of a measure to the registered office meets in all cases the requirement of legal certainty and makes it possible for the company to take cognizance of the measure being notified. Consequently, companies have no right to require that the Commission give notice at a place other than the registered office (e.g. the central administration) or to a particular person (ibid. at pp. 3756–7).

In the case of companies having their registered offices outside Community territory, a decision or other document need not be notified through diplomatic channels. It may be sent by post directly to the registered office even though the local law does not recognize as valid this, or any other, method of service of foreign legal documents within the national territory (Case 52/69 *Geigy* v. *Commission* [1972] ECR 787 at pp. 823–4; Case 6/72 *Continental Can* v. *Commission*, above). Alternatively, it may be sent to the registered office of one of the company's subsidiaries established within the Community even though the latter has received no authority from the parent company to accept notification and is not obliged under the local law to forward the documents to the parent company's address. Once it is established that the addressee has full knowledge of the text of the decision and that it has exercised its right to institute proceedings against it before the ECJ within the prescribed period, the question of possible irregularities concerning notification becomes irrelevant (Case 48/69 *ICI* v. *Commission*, above, at p. 652). By contrast, failure to communicate a document in the proper language as required by Community law constitutes a legal defect which is, under given circumstances, capable of affecting the validity of that document (Case 41/69 *Chemiefarma* v. *Commission*, above, at p. 686).

See also **Action for annulment, Decision, Direct effect, Directive, Individual decision, Infringement of an essential procedural requirement, Official languages, Publication, Recommendation.**

▶ *OBITER DICTUM* 1. *In English law*: incidental statement in a judgment; legal proposition which the judge does not consider necessary for reaching his decision and which therefore does not form part of the *ratio decidendi*. According to the doctrine of *stare decisis*, the distinction between *ratio decidendi* and *obiter dictum* is of fundamental importance since the only part of a judicial decision which is legally binding is the *ratio decidendi* (reason for deciding). *Obiter dicta* are never of more than persuasive authority, and although they are frequently followed, there is no question of any judge being bound to apply them (see R. Cross, *Precedent in English Law*, 3rd edn. (Oxford, 1977), pp. 38 *et seq.*, 79 *et seq.*).

2. *In Community law*: ancillary or subsidiary observations in a judgment of the ECJ, which merely supplement and explain the grounds on which the operative part is based, but without themselves being 'decisive'. Since the binding force of a judgment arises from the operative part (*dispositif*) which, in the case of doubt, must be interpreted or clarified in the light of the decisive grounds (*motifs*), *obiter dicta* do not, from a strict procedural point of view, produce the effects of *res judicata*. Statements which are *obiter* are neither definitive nor binding on the Court and on the parties. Issues touched on by them may therefore be raised and judicially considered again in a subsequent case between the same parties (see e.g. Case 14/64 *Gualco* v. *Commission* [1965] ECR 51 at pp. 64–5 *per* A.-G. Roemer). Also, there are certain special forms of procedure, such as interpretation of judgments, intervention, third party proceedings, and revision, which by definition can only concern those parts of a judgment which are legally binding, i.e. the operative part read in the light of the decisive grounds, but not any *obiter dicta* (see e.g. Case 5/55— Interpretation *ASSIDER* v. *HA* [1955] ECR 135 at p. 142 *per Curiam*, pp. 147–8 *per* A.-G. Lagrange; Case 111/63—Intervention *Lemmerz-Werke* v. *HA* [1965] ECR 677 at p. 717 *per Curiam*, p. 722 *per* A.-G. Roemer; Cases 9 and 12/60—Third party proceedings *Belgium* v. *Vloeberghs and HA* [1962] ECR 171 at pp. 183–4 *per Curiam*, pp. 190–1 *per* A.-G. Roemer; Case 116/78—Revision *Bellintani* v. *Commission* [1980] ECR 23 at pp. 26–7).

Nevertheless, from the point of view of substantive law, the distinction between the decisive grounds and any *obiter dicta* has relatively little significance. As A.-G. Roemer has observed, 'The question where, in judgments, the decisive grounds of judgment end and any *obiter dicta* begin seems to me in any case to be of secondary importance. In each case everything that is said in the text of the judgment expresses the will of the Court' (Case 9/61 *Netherlands* v. *HA* [1962] ECR 213 at p. 242). Indeed, when the Court interprets a provision, clarifies a concept, formulates a principle, or defines a rule, from the point of view of the development of Community law it makes very little difference whether it does so in the decisive grounds of the judgment or by way of *obiter dictum*. In fact, some of the most important concepts and principles have first been formulated by the Court as mere *obiter dicta*, but this has not prevented them from becoming as much part of the general corpus of Community law as if they had been cast in the form of legally binding rules (see e.g. the doctrine of the supremacy of Community law, first stated, *obiter*, in Case 6/64 *Costa* [1964] ECR 585 at pp. 593–4; the principle of the protection of fundamental human rights, first enunciated, *obiter*, in Case 29/69 *Stauder* [1969] ECR 419 at p. 425; the principle that the provisions of the EEC Treaty on the free movement of persons and services cannot be applied to situations which are wholly internal to a Member State, first expressed, *obiter*, in Case 115/78 *Knoors* [1979] ECR 399 at p. 410, subsequently restated in the decisive grounds in Case 175/78 *Saunders* [1979] ECR 1129 at p. 1135 and finally in the operative part in Case 180/83 *Moser* [1984] ECR 2539 at pp. 2548–9).

It follows that, in analysing the Court's judgments, possible (and very often dubious) distinctions between decisive grounds and *obiter dicta* must be treated with caution. From the point of view of substantive law, perhaps the only justification for such a distinction is that *obiter dicta* are more readily subject to reconsideration in a subsequent case of which they form the main issues (see e.g. Case 45/75 *Rewe-Zentrale* [1976] ECR 181 at pp. 206–7 *per* A.-G. Reischl; Case 314/85 *Foto-Frost* [1987] ECR 4199 at p. 4217 *per* A.-G. Mancini).

See also **Judgment,** *Ratio decidendi, Res judicata, Stare decisis.*

Further reading: Toth, 'The Authority of Judgments of the European Court of Justice: Binding Force and Legal Effects' (1984) 4 *YEL* 1.

▶ *OFFICIAL JOURNAL (OJ)* Official publication of the three European Communities which, under the full title *Official Journal of the European Communities*, in 1958 replaced the *Official Journal of the ECSC* (see Council Dec. of 15 Sept. 1958, *OJ Sp. Edn.* 1952–8, p. 60).

Since 1 January 1968, the *Official Journal* has been published in two main series as separate issues: the *Legislation* series, known as the 'L' series, and the *Information and Notices* series, known as the 'C' series. The *Legislation* series contains both binding acts whose publication is obligatory, such as ECSC general decisions/recommendations and EEC/Euratom regulations (*see further under* **Publication**), and binding acts whose publication is not obligatory, such as ECSC individual decisions/recommendations and EEC/Euratom directives and decisions (*see further under* **Notification**), as well as decisions etc. of the Representatives of the Governments of the Member States. This series also publishes the texts of international agreements concluded by the Communities and documents concerning the accession of new Member States. The *Information and Notices* series carries a variety of non-binding materials, such as the minutes of the sittings of and texts adopted by the European Parliament including written questions and answers; legislative proposals of the Commission and opinions of the consultative bodies thereon; notices of new cases brought before the ECJ; notices of the removal of cases from the Court's Register; the operative part of every judgment and interim order; the composition of the Chambers and the appointment of certain members of the Court (see Arts. 16(6) RP and 25 IR); statements, communications, and notices concerning Community matters, including the daily value of the European Currency Unit (ECU), etc. In addition to the 'L' and 'C' series, since 1978 there has been a *Supplement* ('S' series) which carries commercial information concerning public contracts, calls for tenders, and project approval arising mainly from the European Development Fund. There is also an *Index* which appears in monthly parts with an annual cumulation. It is issued in two parts, the Alphabetical Index and the Methodological Table.

The *Official Journal* is today published in the nine official languages of the Communities (Art. 5 of Reg. 1, *OJ Sp. Edn.* 1952–8, p. 59 as last amended by the Act of Accession 1985, Annex I, Part XVII). Initially, it was published in the four original languages (i.e. Dutch, French, German, and Italian, see Art. 1 of Reg. 1). Art. 155 of the Act of Accession 1972 provided that the texts of the acts of the institutions adopted before accession and translated into the Danish and English languages shall, from the date of accession, be authentic under the same conditions as the original texts and that they shall be published in the *Official Journal* if the original texts were so published (Arts. 147 and 397 of the Acts of Accession 1979 and 1985, respectively, contain the same rule with regard to the Greek, Spanish, and Portuguese languages). To this end, at the time of the first accession a *Special Edition* of the *Official Journal* was published in Danish and English versions, which reprinted in chronological order 'binding acts of general application throughout the Communities' enacted from 1952 to 1972 and still in force as at 1 January 1973 (see Reg. 857/72, *OJ Sp. Edn.* 1972 (II), p. 351). Subsequently, a *Second Series* of the *Special Edition* was published in ten subject issues containing relevant acts in force whose publication was not obligatory. Publications in these *Special Editions* have the same legal force as publications in the *Official Journal* (Art. 1 of Reg. 857/72).

The *Official Journal* is published by the Office for Official Publications of the European Communities, situated in Luxembourg. The Office has received formal instructions from the Council intended to ensure that the date of publication borne by each issue of the *Official Journal* corresponds to the date on which that issue is in fact available to the public in all the official languages at the Office. The ECJ has held that these provisions give rise to a rebuttable presumption that the date of publication is in fact the date appearing on each issue of the *Official Journal* (Case 98/78 *Racke* [1979] ECR 69 at pp. 84–5 *per Curiam*, pp. 95–6 *per* A.-G. Reischl).

In recent years, all current legal instruments have been stored in facsimile form on large-capacity optical disks. The public now have access to this optical memory, from which they can extract required texts, with all amendments, which are then transmitted in electronic form or by mail. Similarly, the contents pages of new issues of the *Official Journal* are accessible on-line the very morning of their publication. In combination with the optical memory, this service provides virtually instant access to Community legislation (see 22nd *Gen. Rep. EC* (1988), p. 53).

See also European Court Reports, **Notification, Official languages, Publication, Regulation.**

▶ **OFFICIAL LANGUAGES** Languages which must be used by and before the institutions of the European Communities. The official languages are: Danish, Dutch, English, French, German, Greek, Italian, Portuguese, and Spanish (Art. 1 of Reg. 1, *OJ Sp. Edn.* 1952–8, p. 59 as last amended by the Act of Accession 1985, Annex I, Part XVII).

Documents which a Member State or a person subject to the jurisdiction of a Member State sends to the institutions may be drafted in any one of the official languages selected by the sender. The reply must be drafted in the same language (Art. 2 of Reg. 1). Documents which an institution sends to a Member State or to a person subject to the jurisdiction of a Member State must be drafted in the language of that State (Art. 3 of Reg. 1). Where a natural or legal person is subject to the jurisdiction of a non-Member State, the choice of the official language to be used by an institution depends on the relations which may exist within the Community between that person and any one of the Member States. Thus, in Case 6/72 *Continental Can* v. *Commission* [1973] ECR 215 at p. 241 the ECJ held that since one of the applicants, a company having its registered office in the United States, had opened an office in Brussels and set out its written observations in the administrative procedure before the Commission in French, the choice of the French language by the Commission as the official language of its decision sent to the applicant did not offend against Art. 3 of Reg. 1. Failure by an institution to communicate to a person a document in the proper official language selected in accordance with the above rules constitutes an irregularity which is capable of affecting the validity of that document (Case 41/69 *Chemiefarma* v. *Commission* [1970] ECR 661 at pp. 686–7, where however the ECJ held that in the circumstances of the case such an irregularity did not vitiate the document). If a Member State has more than one official language, the language to be used will be governed by the general rules of its law (Art. 8 of Reg. 1).

Regulations and other documents of general application must be drawn up in the nine official languages (Art. 4 of Reg. 1 as amended). The *Official Journal* of the European Communities and the publications of the ECJ including the *European Court Reports* must also be published in the nine official languages (Art. 5 of Reg. 1 as amended; Arts. 30(2) RP, 24 IR). The institutions are free to specify in their Rules of Procedure which of the languages are to be used in specific cases (Art. 6 of Reg. 1). The procedural languages used before the ECJ are laid down in Art. 29(1) RP as last amended on 8 May 1987 (*OJ* 1987 L165/1) and include Irish in addition to the nine official languages.

See also **European Court Reports, Language of the case,** *Official Journal.*

▶ **OPINION** 1. Act of the Council or the Commission falling within the scope of secondary legislation.

(*a*) **Under the ECSC Treaty,** opinions delivered by the Commission 'shall have no binding force' (Art. 14 ECSC). Nevertheless, the ECJ has held that 'although Article 14 of the Treaty makes it clear that an opinion cannot directly involve the person to whom it is addressed in any legal obligation, an opinion is, on the other hand, distinguished from a decision and from a recommendation both by its nature and by its function within the general framework of the Treaty. In addition to the High Authority's [i.e. Commission's] powers of direction, which enable it, by means of its decisions and recommendations, to intervene positively and directly in the organization of the Common Market, the Treaty has invested the High Authority with responsibility for giving guidance, which it discharges by means of, *inter alia*, opinions. These opinions are, therefore, merely advice given to undertakings. The latter thus remain free to pay regard to or ignore it but they must understand that in ignoring an adverse opinion they accept the risks with which they may be faced as the result of a situation which they themselves have helped to create. In other words, the freedom of decision and the responsibility of the undertakings remain, like those of the High Authority, unchanged' (Cases 1 and 14/57 *Usines à Tubes de la Sarre* v. *HA* [1957] ECR 105 at p. 115).

(*b*) **Under the EEC and Euratom Treaties,** opinions delivered by the Council or the Commission 'shall have no binding force' (Arts. 189 EEC, 161 Euratom). 'In order to ensure the proper functioning and development of the Common Market, the Commission shall . . . deliver opinions on matters dealt with in this Treaty, if it expressly so provides or if the Commission considers it necessary' (Art. 155 EEC; see also Art. 124 Euratom). Opinions may be addressed to Member States (see e.g. Art. 72 EEC) or by the Commission to the Council (see e.g. Art. 237(1) EEC). They usually express a point of view or advice, often in reply to a question put to the institution, or form an essential procedural step in the decision-making process.

2. Act whereby the various consultative bodies (e.g. the European Parliament, the ECSC Council and Consultative Committee, the EEC/Euratom Economic and Social Committee, the Court of Auditors, the various Advisory Committees) exercise their advisory powers. Although these opinions are not legally binding, they form an essential part of the decision-making process. Failure to obtain them where consultation is required by the Treaties may render the final measure invalid on the ground of infringement of an essential procedural requirement.

3. Act whereby the ECJ decides whether amendments proposed jointly by the Commission and the Council to the ECSC Treaty (the so-called 'minor revision') are compatible with the provisions of Art. 95(3) ECSC (Art. 95(4) ECSC; see e.g. *Opinion of 17 December 1959* [1959] ECR 260; *Opinion 1/60* [1960] ECR 39; *Opinion 1/61* [1961] ECR 243). Such an opinion must be communicated to the Commission, the Council, and the European Parliament (Art. 109 RP).

4. Act whereby the ECJ states its views, at the request of the Council, the Commission, or a Member State, as to whether an agreement which the EEC intends to conclude with a third State or an international organization is compatible with the provisions of the EEC Treaty. Where the opinion of the Court is adverse, the agreement may enter into force only after the EEC Treaty has been amended (Art. 228(1) EEC). Under Art. 103 Euratom the

ECJ has a similar jurisdiction to decide by means of a 'ruling' on the compatibility with the Euratom Treaty of proposed clauses contained in a draft agreement or contract which a Member State intends to conclude with a third State, an international organization, or a national of a third State. Arts. 104 and 105 Euratom contain comparable provisions on agreements made by persons or undertakings after or before the entry into force of the Treaty. In such an 'opinion' or 'ruling' the ECJ has power to deal with 'all questions capable of submission for judicial consideration . . . in so far as such questions give rise to doubt either as to the substantive or formal validity of the agreement with regard to the Treaty', including the question whether the Community or any Community institution has the power to enter into that agreement (Opinion 1/75 *Local Cost Standard* [1975] ECR 1355 at p. 1361; Art. 107(2) RP. See also Ruling 1/78 *Protection of Nuclear Materials* [1978] ECR 2151 at p. 2167; Opinion 1/78 *Natural Rubber Agreement* [1979] ECR 2871 at p. 2907). The request for and delivery of an 'opinion' or 'ruling' must be made in accordance with Arts. 105–8 RP. The opinion must be reasoned and served on the Council, the Commission, and the Member States (Art. 108 RP).

5. Act which the ECJ must deliver under the ECSC Statute (Art. 13) before the Council may, by unanimous decision, deprive an Advocate-General of his office.

6. Impartial, independent, and reasoned view which the Advocate-General is required to express, orally, in open Court, at the end of the oral procedure, on every case brought before the ECJ, in order to assist the Court in the performance of the task assigned to it by the Treaties (referred to as 'submissions' in the Treaties and the Court's Statutes, and as 'opinions' in the Court's Rules of Procedure and in the official *European Court Reports*: Arts. 32(a) ECSC, 166 EEC, 138 Euratom; 11 and 21 ECSC Statute, 18 EEC and Euratom Statutes; 59 RP). The opinion normally deals with every aspect of the case, substantive and procedural, and after setting out the facts and any relevant legal provisions and authorities and analysing the issues arising, it advises the Court as to the solution it should adopt. However, the opinion is not binding on the Court or on the parties; it is in the nature of a recommendation which the Court is free to follow or not to follow, in whole or in part. In spite of their non-binding nature, the opinions of the Advocates-General carry considerable weight on account of the very high standard of the legal analysis which they contain and are frequently cited in Court as well as in legal writing as (persuasive) authorities.

The opinions of the Advocates-General are not open to comments, observations, or appeal by the parties. The only possibility for a party to challenge any aspect of an opinion is by asking the Court to reopen the oral procedure (under Art. 61 RP)—a device which the Court appears to be most reluctant to allow to be used (see e.g. Case 206/81 *Alvarez* v. *Parliament* [1982] ECR 3369 at pp. 3374–5; Case 51/76 *Nederlandse Ondernemingen* [1977] ECR 113 at p. 123; Cases 36 and 71/80 *Irish Creamery Milk Suppliers Association* [1981] ECR 735 at pp. 745–6). Nevertheless, the Court may order the reopening of the oral procedure of its own motion, in which case the

Advocate-General will deliver a second or supplementary opinion (see e.g. Cases 253/78 etc. *Giry and Guerlain* [1980] ECR 2327 at pp. 2359–60 and p. 2392; Case 155/79 *AM & S.* v. *Commission* [1982] ECR 1575 at pp. 1616–19 and p. 1642). The Court may also order the Advocate-General to deliver a second opinion without formally reopening the whole of the oral procedure (see e.g. Case 127/73 *BRT* [1974] ECR 51 at p. 64 and 313 at p. 320). In addition to giving opinions dealing with the substance of a case, the Advocate-General is required to be heard on purely procedural issues in a number of situations laid down in the Court's Rules of Procedure (see Arts. 29(2)(c), 35(1), 38(7), 42(2), 43, 44(1), 45(1) and (3), 47(1), 60, 61, 66(3), 67, 72(a), 74(1), 76(3), 85, 91(4), 93(3), 94(2), 95(2), 100(1), 102(2), 105(4), 108(2), 109 RP; Art. 6 SR).

See also **Action for annulment, European Court of Justice, Infringement of an essential procedural requirement, Reasoned opinion, Secondary legislation, Statement of reasons, Treaty-making procedure.**

Further reading 1. BOOKS: Lasok, *The European Court of Justice: Practice and Procedure* (1984), ch. 13, ss. III/D, IV/B, and V/E; Usher, *European Court Practice* (1983), ch. 13.

 2. ARTICLE: Gray, 'Advisory Opinions and the European Court of Justice' (1983) 8 *EL Rev.* 24. *See also under* **European Court of Justice.**

▶ **OPTIONAL JURISDICTION** Jurisdiction of a court or tribunal which is subject to a special agreement (*compromis*) between the parties to submit a dispute to it. Although the ECJ has been granted optional jurisdiction in any dispute between Member States which relates to the subject-matter of the Treaties (Arts. 89(2) ECSC, 182 EEC, 154 Euratom), this jurisdiction has not been invoked so far. As most inter-State disputes are likely to arise out of an alleged infringement of a Community obligation, they are likely to be brought before the Court under the provisions conferring compulsory jurisdiction upon the Court.

See also **Action against Member States, Compulsory jurisdiction, Jurisdiction.**

▶ **ORAL PROCEDURE** The final part of the ordinary procedure before the ECJ, following the written procedure and any preparatory inquiries that may have been ordered. The oral procedure consists of the presentation of the Report for the Hearing, the hearing by the Court of the representatives of the parties and, where appropriate, of witnesses and experts, and the delivery of an opinion by the Advocate-General (Arts. 21 ECSC Statute, 18 EEC and Euratom Statutes, 55–62 RP). The oral procedure is basically the same in both direct actions and references for a preliminary ruling (Art. 103(1) RP).

The date for the opening of the oral procedure, which is in fact the date of the hearing, is fixed by the President after the preparatory inquiry has been completed or, in the absence of such inquiry, after the completion of the written procedure (Arts. 44(2) and 54 RP). Subject to the absolute priority of applications for suspension of operation and for other interim measures (Art.

85(3) RP), cases are dealt with in the order in which the preparatory inquiries in them have been completed (or rather in the order in which the Court has decided that such inquiries are not necessary, see Art. 44(2) RP). If several cases were to come up for hearing at the same time, the order is determined by the dates of their respective registration. Nevertheless, the President has power to give priority to certain cases, and the practice is to give priority to references for a preliminary ruling. He may also order, on a joint application by the parties, that a case be deferred (Art. 55 RP). It is also the President's task to establish the cause list (Arts. 28(1) ECSC Statute, 31 EEC Statute, 32 Euratom Statute), although in practice this is delegated to the Registrar (see Art. 7(1) IR).

The proceedings are opened and directed by the President, who is generally responsible for the proper conduct of the hearing. The hearing is public unless the Court, of its own motion or on application by the parties, decides otherwise for 'serious reasons'. In cases which are held in camera the oral proceedings are not published (Arts. 26 ECSC Statute, 28 EEC Statute, 29 Euratom Statute, 56 RP). Since in direct actions legal representation before the ECJ is mandatory at all stages of the proceedings, the parties may address the Court only through their representatives (Arts. 28 ECSC Statute, 29 EEC Statute, 30 Euratom Statute, 58 RP). In references for a preliminary ruling, however, the Court is required to take account of the rules of procedure of the national court which has made the reference (Art. 104(2) RP. *See further under* **Representation before the ECJ**).

Although according to the Court's Statutes the oral hearing is to start with the reading of the Report for the Hearing prepared by the Judge-Rapporteur (see Arts. 21 ECSC Statute, 18 EEC and Euratom Statutes), in practice the Report is not read out but is distributed to the participants and to the members of the Court about three weeks before the hearing, and is also made available to the general public outside the courtroom. The Report contains a summary of the facts of the case and of the conclusions, submissions, and arguments of the parties. Since it normally forms the first part of the Court's judgment (since Sept. 1986 it has been published separately in the *European Court Reports*, before the judgment), Counsel are asked to read it with care and, if they find any inaccuracies, to inform the Registrar before the hearing and suggest appropriate amendments (see 'Notes for the Guidance of Counsel at Oral Hearings', issued by the Court to Counsel before the hearing).

The hearing itself opens with the presentation of oral arguments by the representatives of the parties. Since in direct actions the conclusions, submissions, and arguments of the parties have already been set out in the pleadings exchanged during the course of the written procedure, which will have been read by the members of the Court and summarized in the Report for the Hearing, the object of the hearing is, for the most part, to enable Counsel to present arguments on matters which they were unable to treat in their written pleadings (or observations in the case of references for a preliminary ruling) and to reply to questions put by the Court. Accordingly, Counsel are asked, as a general rule, to limit their address to 30 minutes (15 minutes in cases referred to Chambers consisting of three Judges). Exceptions to this rule may be granted by the Court upon a request sent to the Registrar 14 days before the hearing. Counsel are also expected to simplify their oral presentation so far as possible to make simultaneous interpretation possible (see 'Notes for the Guidance of Counsel', referred to above). Oral arguments must, moreover, remain within the bounds of the dispute as defined in the originating application and the defence as no fresh issues may be raised in the course of the proceedings unless they are based on matters of law or of fact which came to light in the course of the written procedure (Art. 42(2) RP; *see further under* **Written procedure**). This rule, however, does not seem to apply to references for a preliminary ruling (where there is no obligation to submit written observations) even if observations have in fact been submitted (see Art. 103(1) RP). There is also no obligation to attend the hearing, either in direct actions or in reference proceedings, although the normal practice is to present oral arguments at least in direct actions.

In the course of the hearing, the President, the other Judges, and the Advocate-General may put questions to the representatives of the parties (Art. 57 RP). Also, the Court may at any time during the oral procedure, after consulting the Advocate-General, order any measure of inquiry to be taken or that a previous inquiry be repeated or expanded. The Court may itself examine the witnesses, experts, and the parties or may direct the Chamber or the Judge-Rapporteur to carry out the measures of inquiry (Arts. 28 ECSC Statute, 29 EEC Statute, 30 Euratom Statute, 60 RP).

The last step in the oral procedure is the delivery of his opinion by the Advocate-General, usually (although not necessarily) several weeks after the hearing. This must take place orally and in open court, although the parties need not be (and usually are not) present or represented (Arts. 32(a) ECSC; 166 EEC, 138 Euratom, 11 and 21 ECSC Statute, 18 EEC and Euratom Statutes, 59 RP; *see further under* **Opinion**, point 6). After this, the President declares the oral procedure closed.

Nevertheless, the Court has power, after consulting the Advocate-General, to order the reopening of the oral procedure (Art. 61 RP). This may take place both before and after the delivery of the Advocate's-General opinion and may involve not only the hearing of new or additional oral arguments but also the submission of written observations or documents, the undertaking of other measures of inquiry, and the delivery of a second or supplementary opinion by the Advocate-General. Thus, for example, in Case 155/79 *AM & S.* v. *Commission* [1982] ECR 1575 at pp. 1603–5, 1616–19, and 1642 the Court reopened the oral procedure twice, on the second occasion ordered certain measures of inquiry (production of documents), allowed the parties to lodge written memoranda before the second hearing, heard full oral arguments at both hearings, and there were two opinions delivered (by two different Advocates-General), the first twice. In Cases 253/78 etc. *Giry and Guerlain* [1980] ECR 2327 at pp. 2359–60 and 2392 the Court reopened the oral procedure, inviting the parties and other participants to state their views in writing, held a second hearing where oral arguments were presented, and the Advocate-General delivered a supplementary opinion. In Case 127/73 *BRT*

[1974] ECR 51 at p. 64 and 313 at p. 320 the Advocate-General delivered a second opinion without the whole of the oral procedure being repeated.

The Registrar is required to draw up minutes of every hearing, which will constitute an official record and which may be inspected by the parties at the Registry (Arts. 27 ECSC Statute, 30 EEC Statute, 31 Euratom Statute, 62 RP, 7(2) IR).

See also Judgment, Opinion, Preparatory inquiries, Reference proceedings, Representation before the ECJ, Written procedure.

Further reading: Lasok, *The European Court of Justice: Practice and Procedure* (1984), ch. 2; Usher, *European Court Practice* (1983), ch. 7.

▶ **ORDER** One of two main forms in which the ECJ makes its decisions (the other being a 'judgment'; in addition, the Court may give 'opinions', 'rulings', and other decisions). An order is normally made when the Court decides on procedural and ancillary issues (e.g. costs) or adopts interim measures.

According to its Rules of Procedure, the Court makes its decisions in the form of an order concerning the following matters: joinder of cases (Art. 43); preparatory inquiries (Arts. 44(2), 45(1), 60, 84(2), 94(2)); summoning and examination of witnesses and experts (Arts. 47(1) and (2), 49(1), (3), and (5)); reopening of the oral procedure (Art. 61); rectification of judgments (Art. 66(4)); costs (Art. 74(1)); legal aid (Art. 76(3)); removal of a case from the Register (Arts. 77, 78); suspension of operation or enforcement and other interim measures (Arts. 86(1), 89); inspection under Art. 81(3) and (4) Euratom (Art. 90(2)); inadmissibility for lack of jurisdiction (Art. 92); intervention (Art. 93(3)); stay of execution in third party proceedings (Art. 97(2)); letters rogatory (Art. 1 SR); appointment of a lawyer in connection with legal aid (Arts. 4 and 5 SR).

In addition, the Court may decide by way of an order in other cases not specifically mentioned (see e.g. Cases 106 and 107/63 *Toepfer* v. *Commission* [1965] ECR 405 at p. 429—objection of inadmissibility; Case 236/81 *Celanese* v. *Council and Commission* [1982] ECR 1183—confidential treatment of documents), even where the Rules of Procedure expressly provide for a judgment (see e.g. Case 9/81—Interpretation *Court of Auditors* v. *Williams* [1983] ECR 2859 at p. 2861, where the Court ruled on the admissibility of an application for interpretation by way of an order without opening the oral procedure, although Art. 102(2) provides that 'the Court shall give its decision in the form of a judgment'. Presumably the reason was that the Court held the application inadmissible and therefore did not have to interpret the judgment concerned).

While the adoption of orders is subject to the same rules as the adoption of judgments (secrecy of deliberations, uneven number of judges, majority voting, etc.; see Arts. 18, 29 ECSC Statute; 15, 32 EEC Statute; 15, 33 Euratom Statute; 26, 27 RP), the Rules of Procedure lay down no general requirements regarding their form, contents, delivery, publication, and binding effect. There are only a few individual provisions relating to particular types of order. Thus, an order dealing with an application for the suspension of operation or for the adoption of other interim measures must be reasoned (Art. 86(1)), while one dealing with an application for legal aid may not (Art. 76(3)). Orders prescribing measures of inquiry (Art. 45(1)), summoning witnesses (Art. 47(2)), appointing experts (Art. 49(2)), and issuing letters rogatory (Art. 1 SR) require to be served on the parties (and/or witnesses, experts), and the latter must contain certain information as specified. 'Interim orders' must be published in the *European Court Reports* and their operative part also in the *Official Journal* (Arts. 24, 25 IR). Otherwise there are no set requirements, and the form and contents of orders vary greatly, sometimes even of those dealing with the same subject-matter. Thus, some are formally structured like judgments, being divided into the usual 'Facts and Issues' and 'Decision' parts (see e.g. Case 292/84R *Scharf* v. *Commission* [1984] ECR 4349), while others are not (see e.g. Case 258/84R *Nippon Seiko* v. *Council* [1984] ECR 4357—both dealing with interim measures).

Similarly, the Rules of Procedure contain no general provisions on the rectification, supplementation, setting aside, review or revision, interpretation, and enforcement of orders. Some types of order may be withdrawn (legal aid: Art. 76(4)), varied or cancelled (suspension of operation and other interim measures: Arts. 84(2), 87), and enforced (penalties imposed and other measures ordered in respect of witnesses: Art. 48(4); costs: Art. 74(2), see also Case 4/73—Enforcement *Nold* v. *Ruhrkohle* [1977] ECR 1 at p. 3; interim measures: Art. 86(2); inspection under the Euratom Treaty: Art. 90(2); costs payable to the Court: Art. 22(2) IR). It is not clear, however, whether the corresponding provisions relating to these matters laid down in respect of judgments may be applied, *mutatis mutandis*, to orders. It seems that an order may be rectified (see e.g. Case 27/76 *United Brands* v. *Commission* [1978] ECR 207 at pp. 349, 351—rectification of a rectifying order) and perhaps interpreted (see Case 17/68—Costs *Reinarz* v. *Commission* [1970] ECR 1 at p. 2, where the Court did not reject an application for the interpretation of an order on costs as inadmissible, but dismissed it on other grounds).

See also Enforcement procedure, *European Court Reports*, Interpretation of judgments, Judgment, Judgment by default, *Official Journal*, Opinion, Revision of judgments, Third party proceedings.

▶ **OWN RESOURCES** Resources allocated to the European Communities in order to ensure the financing of their budget. The Community budget must, irrespective of other revenue, be financed entirely from the Communities' own resources (Art. 1 of Dec. 88/376 of 24 June 1988, see further below).

Initially, the EEC and Euratom budgets were financed from contributions made by the Member States in accordance with scales laid down in the Treaties (see Arts. 200 EEC, 172 Euratom). However, the Treaties foresaw the possibility that these financial contributions might be replaced by the Communities' own resources (see Arts. 201 EEC, 173 Euratom), and this was in fact achieved by Council Dec. 70/243 of 21 April 1970, *OJ Sp. Edn.*

1970(I), p. 224, which created three types of own resources for the Communities: agricultural levies, customs duties, and up to 1 per cent of national VAT applied to a uniform base. Although the decision provided that the Community budget should be financed entirely from own resources as from 1 January 1975, this did not actually happen until the 1980 financial year, owing to the delay in the adoption and in the subsequent national implementation of the Sixth VAT Directive on the harmonization of the laws of the Member States relating to turnover taxes, which laid down the uniform basis of assessment of the common VAT system (Dir. 77/388, *OJ* 1977 L145/1; see 14th *Gen. Rep. EC* (1980), pp. 42, 56–7).

The decision of 21 April 1970 was replaced by Council Dec. 85/257 of 7 May 1985, *OJ* 1985 L128/15, which raised to 1.4 per cent the limit for each Member State on the rate applied to the uniform VAT base. However, by 1987 the resources available within the limit of 1.4 per cent became insufficient to cover existing Community expenditure and to finance the implementation of the various new policies and objectives laid down in the Single European Act of 1986. Therefore, in response to a comprehensive package of proposals submitted by the Commission early in 1987 (see Suppl. 1/87—*Bull. EC*, esp. at p. 16, and *Bull. EC* 2–1987, p. 7), the Brussels European Councils of 29–30 June 1987 and of 11–13 February 1988 decided to introduce, as part of a wide-ranging budgetary reform, a new system of own resources involving both a substantial increase in the volume and a change in the structure of own resources (see *Bull. EC* 2–1988, p. 8. *See also under* **Community budget**, section IV). The conclusions of the European Council were implemented by Council Dec. 88/376 of 24 June 1988 on the system of the Communities' own resources (*OJ* 1988 L185/24), which entered into force on 1 February 1989 with retroactive effect from 1 January 1988 after being ratified by all the Member States in accordance with Arts. 201 EEC and 173 Euratom (*Bull. EC* 2–1989, p. 55).

According to Art. 2 of the decision of 24 June 1988, own resources comprise revenue accruing from the following four sources:

1. agricultural levies on trade with non-member countries and sugar and isoglucose duties less 10 per cent to be retained by the Member States as collection costs;
2. Common Customs Tariff customs duties and customs duties on products coming under the ECSC Treaty less 10 per cent to be retained by the Member States as collection costs;
3. the application of a uniform rate of (theoretically) 1.4 per cent to the VAT assessment base which is determined in a uniform manner for the Member States according to Community rules but the assessment base may not exceed 55 per cent of the Gross National Product (GNP) at market prices (or, exceptionally, GNP-based financial contributions instead of VAT under Art. 2(7));
4. the application of a rate—to be determined under the budgetary procedure in the light of the total of all other revenue—to each Member State's GNP established in accordance with Community rules to be laid

down in a directive (see Dir. 89/130 of 13 Feb. 1989 on the definition of GNP at market prices, *OJ* 1989 L49/26).

The total amount of own resources assigned to the Communities may not exceed 1.2 per cent of the total GNP of the Community for payment appropriations, and may not exceed a percentage fixed for each year during the 1988 to 1992 period and ranging from 1.15 per cent for 1988 to 1.2 per cent for 1992. The commitment appropriations entered in the Community budget over the 1988–92 period must follow an orderly progression resulting in a total amount which does not exceed 1.3 per cent of the total GNP of the Community in 1992. A precise ratio between commitment and payment appropriations must be maintained to enable the 1.2 per cent ceiling to be observed in subsequent years (Art. 3). Subject to certain exceptions, the revenue accruing from own resources must be used without distinction to finance all expenditure entered in the Community budget (Art. 6). Any surplus revenue over actual expenditure is to be carried over to the following financial year (Art. 7).

The decision makes provisions for the grant of a correction to the United Kingdom in respect of budgetary imbalances. The existence of such imbalances became apparent soon after the accession of the United Kingdom to the European Communities in 1973. They were caused by the fact that, as a substantial importer of food products and raw materials from third countries, the United Kingdom contributed considerably more to the financing of the Communities within the own resources system than the benefit which it was able to derive from the largest item of expenditure in the Community budget, the Common Agricultural Policy (CAP). Already at the Paris Summit Conference of 9–10 December 1974, the Heads of State or Government instructed the institutions to work out a 'correcting mechanism' of general application which, within the framework of the own resources system, could prevent the development of such an 'unacceptable situation' (8th *Gen. Rep. EC* (1974), p. 297, point 37).

The result was the adoption of Reg. 1172/76 on 17 May 1976 (*OJ* 1976 L131/7), which set up a 'financial mechanism' consisting of payments from the Community budget to any Member State in a 'special economic situation' whose economy bore a 'disproportionate burden' in the financing of that budget (Art. 1). The eligibility for and the amount of the payments were to be determined by the Commission in accordance with complex and strict criteria. Although the regulation remained applicable until the end of 1982, the financial mechanism never came into operation as envisaged mainly because the transitional provisions of the Act of Accession 1972 were holding the United Kingdom contribution below the level required to activate it.

By 1978 it became apparent that after the expiry of the transitional arrangements at the end of 1979 the mechanism would not be sufficient to prevent serious difficulties arising. Therefore, at the request of the European Council, in 1979 and 1980 the Commission prepared a series of documents proposing adaptations to the mechanism (see *Bull. EC* 11–1979, p. 121; 1–1980, p. 82; 3–1980, p. 110). On 30 May 1980, the Council reached

405

agreement on the reduction of the United Kingdom's contribution to the Community budget during the next two years (1980–1) and undertook to resolve the problem from 1982 onwards by means of structural changes. At the same time, it gave the Commission a mandate to submit proposals to this end before 30 June 1981 but without calling into question the basic principles of own resources or of the CAP (the so-called 'Mandate of 30 May 1980', *OJ* 1980 C158/1; *Bull. EC* 5–1980, p. 9; for the Commission's proposals for adaptation of the financial mechanism and for supplementary measures, see *Bull. EC* 6–1980, p. 23; for its reports on the Mandate of 30 May 1980, see *Bull. EC* 6–1981, p. 11; Suppls. 1/81 and 4/81—*Bull. EC*. Reg. 1172/76 was amended by Reg. 2743/80, *OJ* 1980 L284/1).

It was, however, not until the meeting of the European Council at Fontainebleau on 25–6 June 1984 that the ten Heads of State or Government were able to reach unanimous agreement on the amount of compensation to be granted to the United Kingdom to reduce its contribution to the Community budget. This agreement was accompanied by a decision on two other aspects of future financing: the raising of the VAT ceiling to 1.4 per cent from 1 January 1986 and budgetary and financial discipline. As regards budgetary imbalances, the European Council decided as follows (see *Bull. EC* 6–1984, p. 10). Any Member State sustaining a budgetary burden which is excessive in relation to its relative prosperity may benefit from a correction at the appropriate time. The basis for the correction is the gap between the share of VAT payments and the share of total allocated expenditure. In the case of the United Kingdom, from 1985 onwards and so long as the 1.4 per cent VAT ceiling is maintained this gap is to be corrected annually at 66 per cent, while for 1984 a lump sum reduction of 1,000 million ECU was granted. The corrections are to be deducted from the United Kingdom's normal VAT share in the budget year following the one in respect of which the correction is granted. The resulting costs will be shared by the other Member States according to their normal VAT share, adjusted to allow Germany's share to move to two-thirds of its VAT share. These arrangements were subsequently incorporated in the decision of 7 May 1985 on the Communities' own resources (see above; see also *Bull. EC* 3–1985, p. 9).

In accordance with the conclusions of the Brussels European Council of 11–13 February 1988, the mechanism decided at Fontainebleau remains applicable for so long as the new own resources decision of 24 June 1988 remains in force, into which the Fontainebleau arrangements were incorporated with the following modifications (see *Bull. EC* 2–1988, p. 13 and Arts. 2, 4, 5, and 9 of the decision of 24 June 1988). The VAT share is replaced by the United Kingdom's share in the sum total of the payments made under the third and fourth resources (i.e. VAT and GNP). The effect on the United Kingdom in respect of a given year of the introduction of the fourth resource, which is not compensated by the above change, is offset by an adjustment to the compensation in respect of that year. This adjustment corrects the 'basic amount' to a 'reference compensation amount'. The compensation remains at 66 per cent. The cost of the compensation to the United Kingdom is borne by the eleven other Member States on the basis of their share of the payments under the fourth resource (GNP). However, the contribution of Germany is reduced by one-third and those of Spain and Portugal are reduced up to 1991 in accordance with the abatement provided for in Arts. 187 and 374 of the Act of Accession 1985. The correction is granted to the United Kingdom by a reduction in its payments made under the third resource (VAT). The costs borne by the other Member States are added to their payments made under the third resource, but only up to a 1.4 per cent VAT rate, and under the fourth resource (GNP). In other words, the 1.4 per cent VAT ceiling includes the United Kingdom abatement. As a result of these arrangements and of the limit on the VAT base (55 per cent of GNP), in 1988 three different VAT rates were actually applied: 1.4 per cent for nine Member States, 1.3649 per cent for Germany, and 0.5851 per cent for the United Kingdom, with the uniform VAT rate being 1.2661 per cent. Portugal paid a financial contribution instead of VAT own resources under Art. 2(7) of the decision of 24 June 1988, determined on the basis of the proportion of its GNP to the total GNP of the Member States (see amending and supplementary budget No. 1 for 1988, OJ 1988 L265/7).

According to Art. 8 of the decision of 24 June 1988, agricultural levies and customs duties are to be collected by the Member States in accordance with their own national provisions imposed by law, regulation, or administrative action, which must be adapted, where appropriate, to meet the requirements of Community rules. Disputes relating to the recovery of sums levied on behalf of the Community therefore come within the jurisdiction of national courts and must be settled by those courts in application of their national law as regards both procedure and substance to the extent to which Community law has not made other provisions in the matter. However, the application of national legislation must be effected in a non-discriminatory manner and may not lead to a restriction of the rights and powers conferred by Community law (Cases 66, 127, and 128/79 *Salumi* [1980] ECR 1237 at pp. 1263–4; Case 130/79 *Express Dairy Foods* [1980] ECR 1887 at pp. 1899–900). It is the responsibility of the Commission to ensure that the national provisions comply with Community law. It is also the Commission's task to administer the system of own resources at Community level in accordance with the budgetary and financial provisions of the Treaties (see in particular Art. 205 EEC).

Member States are required to make the various resources listed in the decision available to the Commission in accordance with detailed provisions laid down for this purpose (see Reg. 2891/77, OJ 1977 L336/1, which repealed the previously applicable Reg. 2/71, OJ Sp. Edn. 1971(I), p. 3, as amended by Reg. 3760/86, OJ 1986 L349/1 and by Reg. 1990/88, OJ 1988 L176/1; and see also Reg. 2892/77, OJ 1977 L336/8 as amended by Reg. 3625/83, OJ 1983 L360/1 and by Reg. 3735/85, OJ 1985 L356/1, which extended its term of validity until 31 Dec. 1988).

Reg. 2891/77 provides, amongst other things, that the amount of own resources established must be credited by each Member State to an account opened for that purpose in the name of the Commission with its Treasury, or with the body appointed to that end, in accordance with the procedure laid down. Different rules apply to VAT and GNP-based resources (Arts. 9 and 10). Any delay in making the entry in the account as required by the above provisions gives rise to the payment of default interest by the Member State concerned, regardless of the reason for the delay (Art. 11 as interpreted and applied by the ECJ in Case 303/84 *Commission* v. *Germany* [1986] ECR 1171 at pp. 1183–4; see also Case 93/85 *Commission* v. *United Kingdom* [1986] ECR 4011 at pp. 4032–6, where the Court interpreted and applied Arts. 10(2), 11, and 12(2) of Reg. 2891/77). The regulation also set up an Advisory Committee on the Communities' Own Resources, consisting of not more than five representatives of each Member State and chaired by a representative of the Commission, to monitor the application of both regulations (Arts. 20–1). The new regulation which replaced Reg. 2891/77 was adopted on 29 May 1989 and applied with effect from 1 January 1989 (Reg. 1552/89, *OJ* 1989 L155/1).

Reg. 2892/77 lays down provisional rules for determining the assessment basis of VAT own resources in the light of the Sixth VAT Directive of 1977. The provisions relating to the definitive uniform system for collecting VAT resources and the relevant procedures were adopted by the Council on 29 May 1989 and applied with effect from 1 January 1989 (Reg. 1553/89, *OJ* 1989 L155/9). They provide for the use of the revenue method as the sole method for determining the VAT resource base. All these regulations contain provisions concerning measures of inspection and control by the Commission (in this respect, see also Case 267/78 *Commission* v. *Italy* [1980] ECR 31 at pp. 54–7).

In summary, it may be observed that, compared to the own resources system created by the 1970 and 1985 decisions, the new system set up in 1988 has introduced new principles into Community financing. Its main innovations are the placing of an overall ceiling on Community resources defined as a percentage of Community GNP, and the introduction of a new, open-ended, GNP-based fourth resource. These innovations have two principal advantages. First, GNP, which includes not only private consumption but also public-sector expenditure, investment, and net exports, reflects more accurately each Member State's ability to pay than VAT, which only reflects private consumption. VAT as an own resource has a degressive effect in that high-consumption, low-income Member States pay relatively more. On the other hand, GNP as a source of finance introduces more proportionality and is able to deal with the problem of black economy caused by tax evasion. Since under the new system VAT is included twice (first as VAT and secondly as a component of GNP), special provisions have been made for high-consumption, low-income Member States by reducing the VAT base to 55 per cent of GNP. The effect is to limit the impact of the VAT resource at Community level and consequently to increase the impact of the GNP resource. (The Commission's original proposal was that the additional—fourth—resource should be equal to the difference between GNP and VAT, which would have meant that when the third and the fourth resources are taxed at the same rate, taken together they would become GNP financing.)

The second advantage of the new system is that the ceiling has been placed on the total amount of own resources instead of the individual sources of finance. Thus, any reduction in revenue from the first and second sources—for example, because of the 10 per cent collection costs retained by the Member States or because of the Community's increasing self-sufficiency in agricultural products and the dismantling of customs tariffs world-wide—or any reduction in revenue from the third source—for example, because of the United Kingdom abatement or because of a slower growth in the harmonized VAT base than expected—will increase the contribution from the fourth source (GNP), which is open-ended, but will have no effect on the total amount of revenue within the overall ceiling. In other words, Community finances have been made dependent only on overall economic growth, as expressed by GNP. This arrangement is expected to provide adequate, stable, and guaranteed resources at least until 1992, enabling the Communities to implement and finance all the major new policies and objectives laid down in the Single European Act.

Nevertheless, the question still remains whether the various sources of finance utilized by the 1970, 1985, and 1988 decisions may be regarded as true 'own resources' or whether they (or some of them) are in fact in the nature of financial contributions from the Member States disguised as own resources. This question has a significance which goes beyond the budgetary and financial spheres and touches upon the very foundations of the Community constitutional order. Own resources signify financial independence, and financial independence of an international organization is the material basis for its political independence of the Member States. The European Communities will have reached full maturity only to the extent to which they are not longer dependent on financial contributions from the Member States.

To answer the question, it is first of all necessary to define the concept of a true 'own resource'. Such a definition has been put forward by the Commission in the document 'Financing the Community Budget: The Way Ahead' in the following terms: '. . . an own resource has a fiscal nature, must be a direct charge on individuals or companies in the Community and be independent of decisions by the Member States; there must also be an automatic link between the Community and the source of revenue, i.e. each economic operation on which the Community tax is levied. Even if the own resource is collected by the Member States this is done on the Communities' account. The revenue is not part of the income of the Member States and ought not to need to be either incorporated into their national budgets or voted by national Parliaments' (Suppl. 8/78—*Bull. EC*, p. 15).

It is clear that, if examined in the light of this definition, the various sources of finance fall into different categories and that, paradoxically—and probably contrary to the intentions of the drafters of the Treaties as expressed in Arts. 201 EEC and 173 Euratom—the more advanced the general state of integration at the time of the introduction of a particular resource the less that resource fulfils the criteria of a true 'own resource'. Undoubtedly, the type of resource that best satisfies the above definition is the one that was first introduced: the levy which the Commission is authorized to impose on the

409

production of coal and steel (see Arts. 49–50 ECSC). However, this is not included in the general concept of the Communities' own resources since the ECSC operating budget does not form part of the general budget of the Communities (*see further under* **Community budget**).

The second category consists of agricultural levies and customs duties, which are commonly referred to as 'traditional own resources'. Customs duties are specifically mentioned in Art. 201 EEC as a possible type of own resource, but—together with agricultural levies—they differ from the kind of own resource envisaged in Art. 173 Euratom. This speaks of 'proceeds of levies collected by the Community in Member States', with the power to assess them and to lay down the method of fixing their rate and the procedure for their collection being vested in the Community institutions, although—as in the case of Art. 201 EEC—subject to ratification by the Member States. While agricultural levies and customs duties represent direct charges on individuals and undoubtedly belong to the Community as of right (although under the new rules only up to 90 per cent) as from the moment they are entered in the account opened in the Commission's name (but not before that date, see Case 93/85 *Commission* v. *United Kingdom*, above, at p. 4033), they are collected by the Member States in accordance with their own national provisions. Although the Member States act under Community supervision, they still retain their exclusive sovereign powers to undertake prosecutions and proceedings for the purpose of the recovery of own resources. In spite of the overwhelming Community interest in the matter, the institutions have no powers of enforcement that are directly exercisable before the national courts (see Cases 178 to 180/73 *Mertens* [1974] ECR 383 at p. 400 *per Curiam*, pp. 404–6 *per* A.-G. Reischl; Case 110/76 *Pretore of Cento* [1977] ECR 851 at p. 856; Case 267/78 *Commission* v. *Italy*, above, at pp. 56–7. As to the separation of powers between the Community and the Member States in respect of the collection of own resources, see also Case 96/71 *Haegeman* v. *Commission* [1972] ECR 1005 at pp. 1014–15). Moreover, by their very nature, agricultural levies and customs duties are not designed as fiscal revenue but as a means to protect the market. Their rate is not fixed by the Community institutions but is determined by international agreements (in the case of customs duties) or by world market prices and other factors (in the case of agricultural levies). It must therefore be concluded that they are not true 'own resources' in the same way as ECSC levies or the levies envisaged by Art. 173 Euratom.

VAT is still further removed from the concept of a genuine own resource. It is basically a national fiscal revenue harmonized at Community level. Its basis is determined in most Member States, at least as a transitional arrangement, according to a statistical method (the revenue method). The rate to which the Community is entitled is not additional to but part of the rate fixed nationally. Each Member State in effect deducts it from its own national VAT revenue and then transfers it to the Community. In practice, Community entitlements are entered in the Commission's account each month in one-twelfths of the total amount resulting from the budget (see Art. 10(3) of Reg. 2891/77). This further underlines the financial contribution character of VAT resources since the monthly payments are not related to the economic transactions from which the tax arises.

Finally, GNP is clearly not a fiscal revenue but a contribution base, necessarily statistical and approximate in nature. GNP rates are not charged on individuals or companies who create wealth but on the Member States as such. There is thus no link between the Community and the source of revenue, i.e. each economic operation on which the tax is levied. Until it is made available to the Commission, the revenue forms part of the income of the Member States. Of all the four sources of finance, the GNP-based resource lies furthest from the concept of a true own resource and resembles financial contributions most.

It may thus be concluded that the four resources provided for by the decision of 24 June 1988 constitute true 'own resources' only in the sense that they are determined independently of the individual Member States in the course of the Community budgetary procedure with binding effect on all the Member States, and that they must be used exclusively to finance Community expenditure which is also determined in the course of the same procedure. Only agricultural levies and customs duties belong to the Communities as of right, but only from the moment they are entered in the Commission's account. The concept of a genuine own resource would imply a tax which is levied by the Community institutions directly on economic operators (and not on the Member States), exclusively for the benefit of the Communities, and collected by the Community institutions or national agencies acting on their behalf in accordance with Community rules (for possible Community taxes that might be introduced, see Suppl. 8/78—*Bull. EC*, p. 19). This would correspond more closely to the idea of a genuine Community which is 'of direct concern' to the private citizen and which includes not only the Member States but also their nationals amongst its subjects (see Case 26/62 *Van Gend en Loos* [1963] ECR 1 at p. 12).

See also **Community budget, Single European Act.**

Further reading 1. BOOK: Strasser, *The Finances of Europe* (1981), ch. VII.

2. ARTICLES: Ehlermann, 'The Financing of the Community: The Distinction between Financial Contributions and Own Resources' (1982) 19 *CML Rev.* 571; Emerson and Scott, 'The Financial Mechanism in the Budget of the European Community: The Hard Core of the British "Renegotiations" of 1974–1975' (1977) 14 *CML Rev.* 209; Jenkins, 'Britain and the Community Budget: The End of a Chapter' (1980) 17 *CML Rev.* 493; Kolte, 'The Community Budget: New Principles for Finance, Expenditure Planning and Budget Discipline' (1988) 25 *CML Rev.* 487; Vanden Abeele, 'The Mandate of 30 May 1980, Budget Financing and the Revitalization of the Community: An Unfinished Journey' (1982) 19 *CML Rev.* 501.

3. OFFICIAL PUBLICATIONS: House of Lords, Select Committee on the European Communities, Session 1983–4, 12th Report, 'Future Financing of the Community' (1984); id., Session 1984–5, 2nd Report, 'Fontainebleau and After' (1985); id., Session 1987–8, 4th Report, 'Financing the Community' (1987).

See also under **Community budget.**

411

P

▶ *PETITUM* The relief or remedy sought by an application brought before the ECJ; the result at which the applicant wishes the Court to arrive in its judgment (see Case 238/78 *Ireks-Arkady* v. *Council and Commission* [1979] ECR 2955 at p. 2979 *per* A.-G. Capotorti). This is referred to as 'the form of order sought by the applicant' in Art. 38(1) RP; as 'submissions' in the English version of the Court's Statutes (Arts. 22 ECSC Statute, 19 EEC and Euratom Statutes); and as 'conclusions' in the English-language *European Court Reports*. The *petitum* must be clearly stated in the application originating proceedings (Art. 38(1) RP). It is dealt with by the Court in the operative part of the judgment (see Case 111/63 *Lemmerz-Werke* v. *HA* [1965] ECR 677 at p. 722 *per* A.-G. Roemer).

See also **Application originating proceedings,** *Causa petendi,* **Judgment,** *Ne ultra petita.*

▶ **PLEA OF ILLEGALITY** Device for indirectly challenging the legality of a general law-making measure in the course of proceedings instituted before the ECJ for a different purpose, which is usually to obtain the annulment of an individual decision based on the measure in question. The plea gives effect to the general principle that an illegal law-making measure ought not to be applied, through implementing decisions, to private individuals or to Member States even though it has not been declared void (or even though the time-limit for declaring it void has expired) and is therefore, formally at least, fully valid.

1. **Under the ECSC Treaty,** the plea of illegality has originally been given only a very limited scope of application. Art. 36(2) and (3) ECSC provide that: 'The Court shall have unlimited jurisdiction in appeals against pecuniary sanctions and periodic penalty payments imposed under this Treaty. In support of its appeal, a party may, under the same conditions as in the first paragraph of Article 33 of this Treaty, contest the legality of the decision or recommendation which that party is alleged not to have observed.'

However, referring to the relevant provisions of the EEC and Euratom Treaties (see below), the ECJ has interpreted this provision widely. It has held that:

That provision of Article 36 should not be regarded as a special rule, applicable only in the case of pecuniary sanctions and periodic penalty payments, but as the application of a general principle, applied by Article 36 to the particular case of an action in which the Court has unlimited jurisdiction. . . . Any other decision would render it difficult, if not impossible, for . . . undertakings and associations . . . to exercise their right to bring actions, because it would oblige them to scrutinize every general decision upon publication thereof for provisions which might later adversely affect them or be considered as involving a misuse of powers affecting them . . . An applicant's right, after the expiration of the period prescribed in the last paragraph of Article 33 [i.e. one month], to take advantage of the irregularity of general decisions or recommendations in support of proceedings against decisions or recommendations which are individual in character cannot lead to the annulment of the general decision, but only to the annulment of the individual decision which is based on it . . . [Such] annulment . . . only affects the effects of the general decision in so far as those effects take concrete shape in the annulled individual decision. To contest an individual decision concerning him, any applicant is entitled to put forward the four grounds of annulment . . . so as to question the legality of the general decisions and recommendations on which the individual decision is based. (Case 9/56 *Meroni* v. *HA* [1958] ECR 133 at pp. 140–1; Case 15/57 *Chasse* v. *HA* [1958] ECR 211 at pp. 224–5; see also Cases 154/78 etc. *Valsabbia* v. *Commission* [1980] ECR 907 at pp. 990–3.)

2. **Under the EEC and Euratom Treaties,** the plea of illegality has been given a more general scope. These Treaties provide that: 'Notwithstanding the expiry of the period laid down in the third paragraph of Article 173 [i.e. two months], any party may, in proceedings in which a regulation of the Council or of the Commission is in issue, plead the grounds specified in the first paragraph of Article 173, in order to invoke before the Court of Justice the inapplicability of that regulation' (Arts. 184 EEC, 156 Euratom).

The ECJ has interpreted this provision thus:

Article 184 of the EEC Treaty gives expression to a general principle conferring upon any party to proceedings the right to challenge, for the purpose of obtaining the annulment of a decision of direct and individual concern to that party, the validity of previous acts of the institutions which form the legal basis of the decision which is being attacked, if that party was not entitled under Article 173 of the Treaty to bring a direct action challenging those acts by which it was thus affected without having been in a position to ask that they be declared void. The field of application of the said article must therefore include acts of the institutions which, although they are not in the form of a regulation, nevertheless produce similar effects and on those grounds may not be challenged under Article 173 by natural or legal persons other than Community institutions and Member States. This wide interpretation of Article 184 derives from the need to provide those persons who are precluded by the second paragraph of Article 173 from instituting proceedings directly in respect of general acts with the benefit of a judicial review of them at the time when they are affected by implementing decisions which are of direct and individual concern to them (Case 92/78 *Simmenthal* v. *Commission* [1979] ECR 777 at p. 800.)

Upon such considerations, the Court in this case found admissible a plea of illegality in respect of certain notices of invitation to tender issued by the Commission. The Court held that, although these notices were not in the strict sense measures laid down by regulation, they were nevertheless 'general acts which determine in advance and objectively the rights and obligations of the traders who wish to participate in the invitations to tender which these notices make public' (ibid. See also Case 294/83 *Les Verts* v. *Parliament* [1986] ECR 1339 at p. 1365).

It follows from the foregoing that under all three Treaties a plea of illegality may be put forward only against general decisions/regulations or measures producing similar effects. It cannot be used to question the legality, out of time, of individual decisions which could have been, but were not, challenged within the proper time-limits. This would contradict the fundamental principle of legal certainty (Case 3/59 *Germany* v. *HA* [1960] ECR 53 at p. 61; Case 156/77 *Commission* v. *Belgium* [1978] ECR 1881 at p. 1896). Where therefore an individual decision is based upon a decision which is also individual, a plea of illegality is not admissible (Case 21/64 *Macchiorlati*

413

Dalmas v. *HA* [1965] ECR 175 at p. 187). It is, moreover, necessary that there should be a direct legal connection between the contested individual decision and the general decision/regulation whose illegality is pleaded (ibid.). This is because 'the intention of [Article 184] is not to allow a party to contest at will the applicability of any regulation in support of an application. The regulation of which the legality is called in question must be applicable, directly or indirectly, to the issue with which the application is concerned' (Case 32/65 *Italy* v. *Council and Commission* [1966] ECR 389 at p. 409). In other words, the individual decision must constitute an implementation of the general measure; legally it must be based on the latter (Cases 275/80 and 24/81 *Krupp* v. *Commission* [1981] ECR 2489 at pp. 2517–18; Case 258/80 *Rumi* v. *Commission* [1982] ECR 487 at p. 502). It may be noted that although a plea of illegality may be raised in respect of a general act without any time-limit, the action in which it is raised must be brought against the contested individual decision within the proper periods as laid down in the Treaties.

The plea of illegality does not constitute a *sui generis* form of action and does not in itself enable parties to institute proceedings before the ECJ. It merely serves to extend the existing remedies by providing an additional ground of action in certain cases; it is a means and not an end in itself. As the ECJ has stated, 'it is clear from the wording and the general scheme of [Article 184] that a declaration of the inapplicability of a regulation is only contemplated in proceedings brought before the Court of Justice itself under some other provision of the Treaty, and then only incidentally and with limited effect . . . The sole object of Article 184 is thus to protect an interested party against the application of an illegal regulation, without thereby in any way calling in issue the regulation itself, which can no longer be challenged because of the expiry of the time-limit laid down in Article 173' (Cases 31 and 33/62 *Wöhrmann* v. *Commission* [1962] ECR 501 at p. 507; Cases 87/77 etc. *Salerno* v. *Commission and Council* [1985] ECR 2523 at p. 2536).

It follows that the effects of a successful plea of illegality are twofold. First, the general decision/regulation will be declared inapplicable and, secondly, the contested individual decision which is the subject-matter of the action will be annulled for lack of a valid legal basis (see e.g. Case 20/71 *Sabbatini* v. *Parliament* [1972] ECR 345 at p. 351; Case 32/71 *Bauduin* v. *Commission* [1972] ECR 363 at p. 370. In both cases the ECJ annulled decisions of the respective institutions withdrawing the applicants'—Community officials—expatriation allowances, on the grounds that Art. 4(3) of Annex VII to the Staff Regulations, on which the contested decisions were based, was illegal because it discriminated between officials on grounds of sex). The declaration of inapplicability of the general measures is made by way of an incidental finding in the grounds of the judgment and has a strictly limited (relative) effect. It applies exclusively in the context of the case in which it is made, with respect to the parties involved (*inter partes*), and for the future only (*ex nunc*). It does not have the effect of annulling (declaring void) the general measure, which could only be done in an action for annulment brought against that measure (Cases 15 to 33/73 etc. *Schots-Kortner* v. *Council, Commission and*

Parliament [1974] ECR 177 at pp. 191–2, where the ECJ interpreted the effects of its own judgments in the two cases cited immediately above). Nevertheless, although the general provision declared illegal formally remains in force, for all intents and purposes it may be regarded as 'dead'. This is because either the institutions will refrain from applying and enforcing it pending its repeal or amendment (this is what happened in the cases cited immediately above) or, if not, the ECJ will find it repeatedly inapplicable in subsequent actions.

Moreover, by applying the principles laid down by the ECJ in Case 66/80 *International Chemical Corporation* [1981] ECR 1191 at p. 1215 in respect of preliminary rulings, it seems permissible to argue that a declaration of inapplicability, although made in the context of a particular case, enables also the national courts to regard the act concerned as inapplicable for the purposes of judgments which they have to give. These considerations explain why a declaration of illegality is sometimes regarded as having a (quasi) *erga omnes* effect (see e.g. Cases 28 to 30/62 *Da Costa* [1963] ECR 31 at p. 41 *per* A.-G. Lagrange).

See also Action for annulment, Grounds of action, Preliminary ruling, Reference proceedings.

Further reading: Barav, 'The Exception of Illegality in Community Law: A Critical Analysis' (1974) 11 *CML Rev.* 366; Bebr, 'Judicial Remedy of Private Parties against Normative Acts of the European Communities: The Role of Exception of Illegality' (1966–7) 4 *CML Rev.* 7. *See also under* **Action for annulment.**

▶ **PRELIMINARY OBJECTION** Objection raised by a party (the defendant in a direct action) against the admissibility of an application pending before the ECJ, usually on the grounds that the applicant lacks *locus standi* or that the application is out of time, or both (see e.g. Case 69/69 *Alcan* v. *Commission* [1970] ECR 385 at p. 393). The objection must be made by means of a separate application stating the grounds of fact and law relied on and the form of order sought (Art. 91 RP). After hearing the parties and the Advocate-General, the Court may either decide on the preliminary objection by a separate judgment, without considering the substance of the case (i.e. where the preliminary issue can be settled on its own without great difficulty or long investigations, see e.g. Case 51/81 *De Franceschi* v. *Council and Commission* [1982] ECR 117 at p. 132), or reserve its decision for the final judgment (i.e. where the question of admissibility is interrelated with the substance of the case, see e.g. Cases 106 and 107/63 *Toepfer* v. *Commission* [1965] ECR 405 at p. 430).

See also **Admissibility of action.**

▶ **PRELIMINARY RULING** Ruling given by the ECJ in the framework of non-contentious proceedings in response to questions referred to it by a national court or tribunal concerning the interpretation of the Treaties and acts of the institutions or the validity of acts of the institutions. Such a ruling is essentially in the nature of an interim step in an action pending before a national court and in which the disputed issues will be determined by the same court in the light of the ECJ's ruling.

In the system of Community law, preliminary rulings fulfil two principal functions. Firstly, as the ECJ has stated in a series of cases, their purpose is 'to ensure that Community law is interpreted and applied in a uniform manner in all the Member States' (see e.g. Case 107/76 *Hoffmann-La Roche* [1977] ECR 957 at p. 973). They are 'essential for the preservation of the Community character of the law established by the Treaty and [have] the object of ensuring that in all circumstances this law is the same in all States of the Community' (Case 166/73 *Rheinmühlen* [1974] ECR 33 at p. 38). Secondly, they complement the system of direct actions created by the Treaties by affording individuals legal protection against Community measures which they have no *locus standi* to challenge before the ECJ and also against national measures which are incompatible with Community law. Thus, in the form of direct actions and preliminary rulings the Treaties established 'a complete system of legal remedies and procedures designed to permit the Court of Justice to review the legality of measures adopted by the institutions' (Case 294/83 *Les Verts* v. *Parliament* [1986] ECR 1339 at p. 1365).

1. **Under the ECSC Treaty** (Art. 41), the ECJ has 'sole jurisdiction to give preliminary rulings on the validity of acts of the High Authority [i.e. Commission] and of the Council where such validity is in issue in proceedings brought before a national court or tribunal'. This jurisdiction has been invoked only in a few cases so far (for the first time in Case 168/82 *Ferriere Sant'Anna* [1983] ECR 1681). Strictly speaking, the preliminary ruling procedure under the ECSC Treaty is available only for the purpose of questioning the 'validity' of the acts of the institutions, but not for the purpose of requesting their 'interpretation' (Case 23/68 *Klomp* [1969] ECR 43 at p. 49). Nevertheless, this cannot prevent the Court from interpreting an act or the ECSC Treaty itself in so far as this is necessary for an appraisal of the validity of the act concerned (Case 36/83 *Mabanaft* [1984] ECR 2497 at p. 2521 *per Curiam*, p. 2530 *per* A.-G. Slynn).

2. **Under the EEC and Euratom Treaties** (Arts. 177 EEC, 150 Euratom), the ECJ has jurisdiction to give preliminary rulings concerning:

- the interpretation of the Treaties;
- the validity and interpretation of acts of the institutions; and
- the interpretation of the statutes of bodies established by an act of the Council, where those statutes so provide.

In view of the different nature and legal effects of preliminary rulings concerning interpretation on the one hand, and of those relating to validity, on the other, they are considered separately below. The discussion is limited to Art. 177 EEC, although everything said is, in principle, applicable to the Euratom Treaty also.

(*a*) The jurisdiction of the ECJ to give *interpretative preliminary rulings* encompasses the whole area of primary and secondary Community law (with the exception of the law of the ECSC, although where an ECSC provision is identical with an EEC/Euratom provision, the Court has the power to interpret it, see Case 101/63 *Wagner* [1964] ECR 195 at pp. 199–200. See also Case 36/86 *Mabanaft*, above, at p. 2521 *per Curiam*, p. 2530 *per* A.-G. Slynn). In particular, it covers the following categories of Community acts:

(i) the 'basic' Community Treaties, i.e. the EEC, Euratom, Merger, Budgetary, and Accession Treaties, the Single European Act (Title II only), together with the various Annexes and Protocols attached to them and forming an integral part thereof, including the Acts of Accession (see e.g. Case 44/84 *Hurd* [1986] ECR 29 at p. 75), although probably not including the various Declarations attached to the Treaties which do not form an 'integral part' thereof;

(ii) such further treaties concluded between the Member States as have been brought within the jurisdiction of the ECJ by means of express provisions. These include the Convention on Jurisdiction and the Enforcement of Judgments in Civil and Commercial Matters of 1968, as amended by the Conventions of Accession of 1978, 1982, and 1989, and the Convention on the Mutual Recognition of Companies and Legal Persons of 1968 (see the two interpretation Protocols of 3 June 1971 as amended); certain provisions of the European Patent Convention of 1973 and the Convention for the European Patent for the Common Market of 1975 ('Community Patent Convention') (see Art. 73 of the latter); the Convention on Contractual Obligations of 1980 (see the interpretation Protocols of 19 Dec. 1988);

(iii) treaties and agreements concluded by the Community with third States and international organizations, with or without the participation of the Member States acting jointly as co-signatories, which agreements form an integral part of the Community legal system (see e.g. Case 181/73 *Haegeman* [1974] ECR 449 at pp. 459–60, interpreting the Association Agreement of 1961 between the EEC and Greece; Case 104/81 *Kupferberg* [1982] ECR 3641 at pp. 3662–3, interpreting the Free Trade Agreement of 1972 between the EEC and Portugal; Cases 267 to 269/81 *SPI and SAMI* [1983] ECR 801 at pp. 828–9, where the Court confirmed its jurisdiction to interpret the GATT since 1 July 1968; Case 12/86 *Demirel* [1987] ECR 3719 at pp. 3750–1, interpreting the Association Agreement of 1963 between the EEC and Turkey, but leaving open the question whether the jurisdiction of the Court also extends to those provisions of a 'mixed agreement' which relate to matters falling within the competence of the Member States);

(iv) all acts of the Community institutions in general, regardless of whether or not they have binding force (see e.g. Case 113/75 *Frecassetti* [1976] ECR 983 at pp. 992–3 *per Curiam*, pp. 996–7 *per* A.-G. Warner, where the Court interpreted a recommendation) and whether or not they produce direct effects (Case 111/75 *Mazzalai* [1976] ECR 657 at p. 665 *per Curiam*, p. 670 *per* A.-G. Reischl. See also Case 32/74 *Haaga* [1974] ECR 1201 at pp. 1205 *et seq.*, where the Court interpreted a directive without first finding that it was directly effective). The Court's jurisdiction thus

417

embraces not only regulations, directives, decisions, recommendations,) and options of the Council and the Commission as listed in Art. 189 EEC, but also acts of the European Parliament, including measures concerning its own internal organization (see e.g. Case 208/80 *Lord Bruce of Donington* [1981] ECR 2205 at pp. 2219–21; Case 149/85 *Wybot* [1986] ECR 2391 at pp. 2408 *et seq.*) and the Rules of Procedure of the ECJ itself (Case 62/72 *Bollmann* [1973] ECR 269 at p. 274), as well as joint acts (e.g. resolutions) of the Council and the Representatives of the Governments of the Member States (Case 9/73 *Schlüter* [1973] ECR 1135 at p. 1161, where the Court interpreted the Resolution of 22 Mar. 1971 adopted jointly by the Council and the Government Representatives of the Member States on the establishment of an Economic and Monetary Union). Whether it also covers measures of the Government Representatives acting on their own is doubtful since these are, strictly speaking, not 'acts of the institutions of the Community'.

On the other hand, the ECJ has no jurisdiction to give preliminary rulings:

(i)   concerning the interpretation of international agreements which bind Member States outside the framework of Community law (Case 130/73 *Vandeweghe* [1973] ECR 1329 at p. 1333; see also Case 28/68 *Torrekens* [1969] ECR 125 at p. 134; Case 44/84 *Hurd*, above, at pp. 76–7);

(ii) concerning the interpretation of private agreements concluded by organizations governed by private law, even if they are provided for by Community acts and published in the *Official Journal* (Case 152/83 *Demouche* [1987] ECR 3833 at pp. 3852–3);

(iii) concerning the interpretation of the national laws of the Member States (see e.g. Case 33/65 *Dekker* [1965] ECR 901 at p. 904; Case 52/76 *Benedetti* [1977] ECR 163 at p. 182);

(vi) involving the application of Community law to the facts of specific cases or deciding upon the compatibility of national law with Community law, since these are matters falling within the jurisdiction of the national court making the reference. Nevertheless, the Court is usually prepared to extract from the wording of the question(s) referred those elements which come within the interpretation of Community law and to give a ruling on them, thus enabling the national court to resolve the legal issues before it (see e.g. Cases 28 to 30/62 *Da Costa* [1963] ECR 31 at p. 38; Case 6/64 *Costa* [1964] ECR 585 at pp. 592–3; Case 82/71 *SAIL* [1972] ECR 119 at p. 135; Case 222/78 *ICAP* [1979] ECR 1163 at p. 1177);

(v)   going outside the scope of the reference or dealing with questions that have not been asked. However, the Court is not rigidly bound by the terms of the reference and may distil from it the questions of Community law that need to be answered (Case 94/74 *IGAV* [1975] ECR 699 at p. 712; Case 51/75 *EMI Records* [1976] ECR 811 at p. 854 *per* A.-G. Warner; Case 119/75 *Terrapin* [1976] ECR 1039 at p. 1060; etc.);

(vi) where the question referred to it concerns neither the interpretation nor the validity of Community provisions (Case 105/79 *Hayange* [1979]

ECR 2257; Case 68/80 *Hayange* [1980] ECR 771; Case 132/81 *Vlaeminck* [1982] ECR 2953 at pp. 2963–4).

As regards the legal effects of interpretative preliminary rulings, the ECJ has stated that 'a judgment in which the Court gives a preliminary ruling on the interpretation or validity of an act of a Community institution conclusively determines a question or questions of Community law and is binding on the national court [which has made the reference] for the purposes of the decision to be given by it in the main proceedings' (Case 69/85 *Wünsche* [1986] ECR 947 at p. 952; Case 52/76 *Benedetti*, above, at p. 183). 'An interpretation given by the Court of Justice binds the national court but it is for the latter to decide whether it is sufficiently enlightened by the preliminary ruling given or whether it is necessary to make a further reference to the Court' (Case 29/68 *Milch-, Fett- und Eier-Kontor* [1969] ECR 165 at p. 180). Such further reference may be justified, for example, when the national court encounters difficulties in understanding or applying the judgment, when it refers a fresh question of law to the Court, or when it submits new considerations which might lead the Court to give a different answer to a question submitted earlier (Case 69/85 *Wünsche*, above, at p. 953).

Although, strictly speaking, it does not follow from the above statements that an interpretative preliminary ruling has an *erga omnes* effect, i.e. that it is also binding upon courts other than those dealing with the specific case in which it has been given, it cannot be denied that a ruling which defines the meaning, scope, and effect of a Community provision is, in practice, authoritative even beyond the individual case. This necessarily follows from the fact that, in formulating its ruling, the ECJ is required to remain at the level of abstraction, giving its interpretation a general scope which makes it applicable to similar future cases. Any national court which is confronted with the same question in a subsequent case will either apply that interpretation or refer the question to the European Court for a further ruling. Such a court may not adopt any different interpretation without misapplying Community law (see the opinion of A.-G. Reischl in Cases 66, 127, and 128/79 *Salumi* [1980] ECR 1237 at pp. 1269–70). If the case is referred to it for a second time, the European Court will give a new judgment, but if the question is identical with that already settled and no new factor or argument is presented, the Court will refer the national court to the previous judgment (see e.g. Cases 28 to 30/62 *Da Costa*, above, at pp. 38–9). Moreover, the ECJ has also held that the authority of an interpretation given under Art. 177 (or in other proceedings) relieves national courts of last instance intending to adopt that interpretation of their obligation to refer under Art. 177(3), whether or not the question of Community law raised before them is strictly identical with a question which has already been interpreted in a previous case (ibid. at p. 38 and Case 283/81 *CILFIT* [1982] ECR 3415 at p. 3429. *See further under* **Reference proceedings**). Thus, interpretative rulings cannot fail to acquire a quasi (or material) *erga omnes* effect, which is in fact essential if the ultimate objectives of the uniform interpretation and application of Community law are to be achieved. This is particularly so where a ruling confirms the direct

419

effect of a Community provision. Since the legal character of such a provision cannot change, the ruling must necessarily have a definitive effect which can no longer be challenged successfully.

As regards the temporal effects of an interpretative ruling, the ECJ has held that 'the interpretation which . . . the Court of Justice gives to a rule of Community law clarifies and defines where necessary the meaning and scope of that rule as it must be or ought to have been understood and applied from the time of its coming into force. It follows that the rule as thus interpreted may, and must, be applied by the courts even to legal relationships arising and established before the judgment ruling on the request for interpretation' (Case 61/79 *Denkavit Italiana* [1980] ECR 1205 at pp. 1223–4; Cases 66, 127, and 128/79 *Salumi*, above, at pp. 1260–1). Nevertheless, the Court has also recognized that exceptionally it may restrict the retroactive effect of an interpretative ruling, i.e. where 'overriding considerations of legal certainty' militate against calling in question, as a result of the ruling, legal relationships established in the past in good faith, which have already run their course. However, such a temporal restriction may only be imposed by the Court of Justice itself, and only in the actual judgment containing the interpretation (ibid. The Court has so far restricted the retroactive effect of its rulings in two cases, namely, in Case 43/75 *Defrenne* [1976] ECR 455 at p. 481 and in Case 24/86 *Blaizot* [1988] ECR 379 at p. 407).

(*b*) The jurisdiction of the ECJ to give *preliminary rulings concerning the validity* of acts of the institutions is not restricted to an examination of the 'formal validity' of such acts, but extends to reviewing their 'substantive legality' also. Thus, in spite of the difference in wording between Art. 177 EEC (which refers to 'validity') and Art. 173 EEC (which uses the word 'legality'), the ECJ can exercise the same degree of judicial control over the acts of the institutions in proceedings for preliminary rulings as in direct actions for annulment (Cases 73 and 74/63 *Handelsvereniging Rotterdam* [1964] ECR 1 at pp. 11 *et seq. per Curiam* (by implication), pp. 19–20 *per* A.-G. Roemer; Case 16/65 *Schwarze* [1965] ECR 877 at pp. 886–7 *per Curiam*, p. 893 *per* A.-G. Gand; Case 294/83 *Les Verts* v. *Parliament*, above).

Unlike Art. 41 ECSC, Art. 177 EEC does not expressly confer upon the ECJ exclusive jurisdiction to decide on the validity of Community acts. Thus, Art. 177 leaves open the question whether national courts themselves may also declare such acts invalid. In an important ruling, the ECJ has held that national courts may consider the validity of a Community act and may conclude that the act is completely valid. On the other hand, national courts do not have the power to declare acts of the Community institutions invalid, except in certain circumstances in proceedings for interim measures. The Court has reached this conclusion partly by reference to the requirements of legal certainty and of the uniform application of Community law in all the Member States, and partly by reference to the 'necessary coherence' of the system of judicial remedies established by the Treaties. Since the Court has exclusive jurisdiction to declare an act void in annulment proceedings, it must also have exclusive power to declare invalid an act which is challenged before a national court (Case 314/85 *Foto-Frost* [1987] ECR 4199 at pp. 4230–2 *per Curiam*, pp. 4214–21 *per* A.-G. Mancini. See also the Court's suggestions to this effect in *Reports on European Union*, Suppl. 9/75—*Bull. EC*, p. 21). It follows from this that if a national court has doubts about the validity of a Community measure, it must refer the matter to the ECJ for a preliminary ruling.

While the validity of the Community Treaties themselves cannot be challenged in court proceedings, the ECJ has jurisdiction under Art. 177 to examine the validity of all acts of the institutions without distinction (Case 9/70 *Grad* [1970] ECR 825 at p. 837; Case 41/74 *Van Duyn* [1974] ECR 1337 at p. 1348; Case 156/77 *Commission* v. *Belgium* [1978] ECR 1881 at p. 1897). However, the ECJ has stated that a preliminary ruling of the Court itself does not rank among the acts of the institutions whose validity is open to review under Art. 177. Therefore, national courts may not use the right to refer further questions to the Court (see above) as a means of contesting the validity of judgments delivered previously (Case 69/85 *Wünsche*, above, at p. 953). Another possible exception is acts adopted by the Representatives of the Governments of the Member States meeting in Council since these acts are, in essence, in the nature of international agreements.

The restrictions which in a direct action for annulment are imposed on the *locus standi* of private individuals in respect of law-making acts and acts addressed to others are not applicable to reference proceedings. Thus, in these proceedings individuals are able to submit to judicial review, through the national courts and without proof of 'direct and individual concern', the validity of regulations (in principle also of directives) and of decisions addressed to Member States (see e.g. Case 216/82 *Universität Hamburg* [1983] ECR 2771 at pp. 2787–8) or to others.

This underlines the importance of preliminary rulings as an additional means of legal protection in the system created by the Treaties (see Cases 73 and 74/63 *Handelsvereniging Rotterdam*, above, and Case 16/65 *Schwarze*, above). As the ECJ has observed, 'If an individual takes the view that he is injured by a Community legislative measure which he regards as illegal he has the opportunity, when the implementation of the measure is entrusted to national authorities, to contest the validity of the measure, at the time of its implementation, before a national court in an action against the national authority. Such a court may, or even must, in pursuance of Article 177, refer to the Court of Justice a question on the validity of the Community measure in question. The existence of such an action is by itself of such a nature as to ensure the efficient protection of the individuals concerned' (Cases 116 and 124/77 *Amylum* v. *Council and Commission* [1979] ECR 3497 at p. 3560; see also Case 294/83 *Les Verts* v. *Parliament*, above). Moreover, a national court may refer questions concerning the validity of an act to the European Court irrespective of whether or not the plaintiff in the main proceedings has *locus standi* to challenge that act directly before the Court. In other words, the possibility of bringing a direct action under Art. 173(2) EEC against an individual decision does not preclude the possibility of questioning the validity of the same decision under Art. 177 (Cases 133 to 136/85 *Rau* [1987] ECR 2289 at p. 2338).

As regards the grounds of invalidity, while under Art. 177 EEC the ECJ may rely on the so-called 'four grounds of action' laid down by Art. 173 EEC for annulment proceedings, it is not restricted to those grounds. As the ECJ has stated, under Art. 177 'the jurisdiction of the Court cannot be limited by the grounds on which the validity of [Community] measures may be contested . . . Such jurisdiction extends to all grounds capable of invalidating those measures . . .' (Cases 21 to 24/72 *International Fruit Company* [1972] ECR 1219 at p. 1226). Nor is the time-limit laid down by Art. 173 applicable to reference proceedings (see Case 216/82 *Universität Hamburg*, above, at p. 2797 *per* A.-G. Slynn), although this fact cannot justify any evasion of that time-limit in the context of a direct action for annulment (Case 156/77 *Commission* v. *Belgium*, above, at p. 1897).

For a long time, authorities have been divided on the question whether a preliminary ruling declaring a Community act invalid under Art. 177 EEC produces *erga omnes* (general) and *ex tunc* (retroactive) effects similar to those of a judgment pronouncing an act null and void under Art. 173 EEC; or whether such a ruling has binding effects *inter partes* (in the particular case) and *ex nunc* (for the future) only (see esp. Case 16/65 *Schwarze*, above, at p. 899 *per* A.-G. Gand; Case 112/76 *Manzoni* [1977] ECR 1647 at pp. 1661–3 *per* A.-G. Warner; Case 238/78 *Ireks-Arkady* v. *Council and Commission* [1979] ECR 2955 at pp. 2989–91 *per* A.-G. Capotorti; Case 66/80 *International Chemical Corporation* [1981] ECR 1191 at pp. 1227–31 *per* A.-G. Reischl, and the authorities cited therein). In the absence of clear provisions in the Treaty on this point, the ECJ has, by analogy, applied and gradually extended the rules determining the legal effects of an annulment under Art. 173 EEC (in particular Arts. 174 and 176 EEC) to preliminary rulings. Thus, in Cases 117/76 and 16/77 *Ruckdeschel* [1977] ECR 1753 at pp. 1771–2, the Court applied the rule in Art. 176(1) (which provides that 'the institution whose act has been declared void . . . shall be required to take the necessary measures to comply with the judgment of the Court of Justice') within the context of a preliminary ruling declaring a regulation incompatible with overriding principles of Community law. In Case 4/79 *Providence Agricole de la Champagne* [1980] ECR 2823 at pp. 2853–4, the Court applied Art. 174(2) (whereby the Court of Justice may 'state which of the effects of the regulation which it has declared void shall be considered as definitive') and ruled that in the particular case before it, for reasons of legal certainty, the invalidity of a regulation pronounced under Art. 177 could not be relied on in respect of the period prior to the date of the judgment. Subsequently, the Court justified the application of Art. 174 to preliminary rulings by reference to the 'necessary consistency' between the preliminary ruling procedure and the action for annulment, and by reference to the requirements of the uniform application of Community law throughout the Community (Case 112/83 *Produits de Maïs* [1985] ECR 719 at pp. 747–8; Case 33/84 *Fragd* [1985] ECR 1605 at p. 1618).

Clearly, imposing a restriction on the temporal effects of a declaration of invalidity (for which the Court claims exclusive jurisdiction, ibid.) implies that, in the opinion of the Court, such a declaration generally has *ex tunc* (retroactive) effects similar to those of an annulment in a direct action (see also the opinion of A.-G. Capotorti in Case 130/79 *Express Dairy Foods* [1980] ECR 1887 at p. 1909). Thus, in Case 238/78 *Ireks-Arkady* v. *Council and Commission*, above, at pp. 2970–4—'Quellmehl' case, following the opinion of A.-G. Capotorti (ibid. at pp. 2990–1), the Court ruled that a declaration of illegality of a regulation made under Art. 177 gave rise to a valid claim for damages with retroactive effect, i.e. with effect from the date of the coming into force of the regulation and not from the date of the judgment declaring it illegal.

As regards the effects of a preliminary ruling upon third parties (*erga omnes*), in Case 66/80 *International Chemical Corporation*, above, at pp. 1215–16, the Court came to the conclusion that 'particularly imperative requirements' concerning legal certainty and the uniform application of Community law prevented national courts from applying an act declared void by the Court, even although the declaration was made in an action brought before other courts and involving other parties. In particular, the Court stated that 'although a judgment of the Court given under Article 177 . . . declaring an act of an institution, in particular a Council or Commission regulation, to be void is directly addressed only to the national court which brought the matter before the Court, it is sufficient reason for any other national court to regard that act as void for the purposes of a judgment which it has to give'. At the same time, the Court confirmed that national courts remained free to refer a case to the Court repeatedly if there was a need to raise once again the question of validity, in particular, 'if questions arise as to the grounds, the scope and possibly the consequences of the invalidity established earlier'. It would seem to follow from this decision that even though a declaration of invalidity does not have exactly the same effects as an annulment made in a direct action, it does produce, like an interpretative preliminary ruling, consequences which go beyond the confines of the particular case and which may be described as quasi (or material) *erga omnes* effects. By contrast, preliminary rulings declaring that an act is not invalid have strictly *inter partes* effects. Such a ruling is not a definitive confirmation of the validity of the act since it is given only in the light of the factors brought to the knowledge of the Court. The validity of the act may therefore be questioned in a subsequent case (see e.g. Case 8/78 *Milac* [1978] ECR 1721 at pp. 1729 *et seq. per Curiam*, p. 1740 *per* A.-G. Warner).

As regards the effects of a declaration of invalidity on the national laws of the Member States, the ECJ has stated that it 'follows from the fact that [a] regulation is invalid that national measures taken on the basis thereof are not in accordance with Community law' (Case 158/80 *Rewe* [1981] ECR 1805 at p. 1838), and that 'it is first of all for the national authorities to draw the consequences in their legal system of the declaration of such invalidity made under Article 177 of the EEC Treaty' (Case 23/75 *Rey Soda* [1975] ECR 1279 at p. 1306). It would seem to follow from this that while implementing domestic measures do not automatically become null and void, they may have to be regarded as at least 'inapplicable' pending their repeal or amendment by the national authorities in accordance with the judgment of the

Court. Thus, the ECJ has pointed out that a declaration that a regulation is invalid 'prevents its application by the national authorities within the limits of the scope of that declaration of invalidity', with the result that criminal proceedings brought pursuant to such a regulation have to be discontinued (Case 162/82 *Cousin* [1983] ECR 1101 at p. 1122).

See also Action for annulment, Direct action, Direct effect, *Erga omnes* effect, *Ex nunc* effect, *Ex tunc* effect, Grounds of action, *Inter partes* effect, Judicial review, Reference proceedings, Right of action.

Further reading 1. BOOKS: Bebr, *Development of Judicial Control of the European Communities* (1981), chs. 9–12; Hartley, *The Foundations of European Community Law*, 2nd edn. (1988), chs. 9 and 14; de Richemont, *Integration of Community Law within the Legal Systems of the Member States: Article 177 of the Treaty of Rome* (1978); Schermers, *Judicial Protection in the European Communities*, 4th edn. (1987), chs. 2 (paras. 469 *et seq.*) and 4 (paras. 684 *et seq.*); Schermers *et al.* (eds.), *Article 177 EEC: Experiences and Problems* (1987); Toth, *Legal Protection of Individuals in the European Communities* (1978) vol. ii, ch. 11. *See also under* **Reference proceedings.**

2. ARTICLES, PAPERS, AND REPORTS: Alexander, 'The Temporal Effects of Preliminary Rulings' (1988) 8 *YEL* 11; Barav, 'Some Aspects of the Preliminary Rulings Procedure in EEC Law' (1977) 2 *EL Rev.* 3; Bebr, 'Preliminary Rulings of the Court of Justice: Their Authority and Temporal Effect' (1981) 18 *CML Rev.* 475; id., 'The Reinforcement of the Constitutional Review of Community Acts under Article 177 EEC Treaty (Cases 314/85 and 133 to 136/85)' (1988) 25 *CML Rev.* 667; Bridge, 'Community Law and English Courts and Tribunals: General Principles and Preliminary Rulings' (1975–6) 1 *EL Rev.* 13; Dashwood and Arnull, 'English Courts and Article 177 of the EEC Treaty' (1984) 4 *YEL* 255; Editorial, 'Preliminary Rulings on Validity' (1988) 13 *EL Rev.* 1; Harding, 'The Impact of Article 177 of the EEC Treaty on the Review of Community Action' (1981) 1 *YEL* 93; Hartley, 'International Agreements and the Community Legal System: Some Recent Developments' (1983) 8 *EL Rev.* 383 at pp. 390–2; Mashaw, 'Ensuring the Observance of Law in the Interpretation and Application of the EEC Treaty: The Role and Functioning of the Renvoi d'Interpretation under Article 177' (1970) 7 *CML Rev.* 258 and 423; Mitchell, 'Sed Quis Custodiet Ipsos Custodes?' (1974) 11 *CML Rev.* 351; Mok, 'Should the "First Paragraph" of Article 177 of the EEC Treaty be Read as a Separate Clause?' (1967–8) 5 *CML Rev.* 458; Pescatore, 'Interpretation of Community Law and the Doctrine of "Acte Clair" ', in Bathurst *et al.* (eds.), *Legal Problems of an Enlarged European Community* (1972), p. 27; Questiaux, 'Interpretation of Community Law', ibid. p. 47; Schermers, 'The Law as it Stands on Preliminary Rulings' (1974/1) *LIEI* 93; Toth, 'The Authority of Judgments of the European Court of Justice: Binding Force and Legal Effects' (1984) 4 *YEL* 1; Usher, 'ECSC Preliminary Ruling on the Validity of an Individual Decision' (1983) 8 *EL Rev.* 326; id., 'Preliminary Rulings on Individual Decisions: The Undecided Question or a Plea of Illegality?' (1984) 9 *EL Rev.* 106; 'Experiences and Problems in Applying the Preliminary Proceedings of Article 177 EEC', Reports for a Colloquium held in The Hague on 5–6 Sept. 1985 (1986) 23 *CML Rev.* 207. *See also under* **Reference proceedings.**

▶ **PREPARATORY INQUIRIES** Measures ordered by the ECJ for the purpose of determining issues of fact where this is necessary to enable it to give judgment (Arts. 24–5 ECSC Statute, 21–7 EEC Statute, 22–8 Euratom

Statute, 45–54 RP). Since the procedure before the Court is basically inquisitorial, it is for the Court to decide, acting either of its own motion or on application by a party, whether to order measures of inquiry (Art. 45(1) RP). The measures that may be adopted are as follows: the personal appearance of the parties; a request for information and production of documents; oral testimony; experts' reports; and an inspection of the place or thing in question (Art. 45(2) RP). The measures of inquiry may be conducted by the Court itself or may be assigned to the Judge-Rapporteur or to a Chamber. In the latter case, the Chamber exercises the powers vested in the Court and its President exercises the powers vested in the President of the Court. The Advocate-General takes part in and the parties are entitled to attend the inquiry (Arts. 44(2), 45(3), 46 RP).

The Court may require the parties to produce all documents and to supply all information which the Court considers desirable (see e.g. Case 155/79 *AM & S.* v. *Commission* [1982] ECR 1575 at p. 1617). However, the Court has no power of enforcement; it can only take 'formal note' of any refusal to comply with its request. The Court may also require the Member States and institutions not being parties to the case to supply all information which the Court considers necessary for the proceedings (Arts. 24 ECSC Statute, 21 EEC Statute, 22 Euratom Statute). Under Art. 23 ECSC Statute, where proceedings are instituted against a decision of an institution, that institution is required to transmit to the Court all the documents relating to the case. When in Case 2/54 *Italy* v. *HA* [1954] ECR 37 at pp. 54–5 the applicant invoked this provision, the Court ordered the High Authority to forward to the Court the minutes and opinions of the Consultative Committee relating to the case and reserved the right to decide subsequently on the possible production of the minutes of the Council and the High Authority. However, the Court expressed its willingness to authorize the omission of the names of the speakers and to examine these documents in camera. Also in proceedings brought under the EEC Treaty, the Court may examine the internal file of the defendant institution relating to the case, e.g. in order to verify whether the challenged decision was influenced by extraneous factors. However, such an examination would constitute an exceptional measure of inquiry which the Court would be willing to order only if it had good reasons to suspect that the decision was adopted for reasons extraneous to Community law and hence amounting to a misuse of powers (Cases 142 and 156/84 *BAT and Reynolds* v. *Commission* [1986] ECR 1899 at pp. 1904–5, where the Commission's decision concerned the application of EEC competition rules).

Generally, the mere fact that a document is confidential, or is described as such, is insufficient to render it privileged from disclosure in the Court (Case 110/75 *Mills* v. *Investment Bank* [1976] ECR 1613 at p. 1635 *per* A.-G. Warner. See also the cases cited immediately above, at p. 1903, where the Court refused to order the Commission to produce certain documents containing business secrets only because the documents were irrelevant to the cases before the Court and not because they were confidential. *See further under* **Confidentiality**, point 3(*d*)). Where a party relies as evidence on a document which is in his possession, he must produce that document himself,

425

and cannot expect the Court to order its production by measures of inquiry (Cases 42 and 49/59 *SNUPAT* v. *HA* [1961] ECR 53 at p. 84). Application by a party for the production of documents by another party must be made during the written stage of the procedure (Case 173/73 *Italy* v. *Commission* [1974] ECR 709 at p. 726 *per* A.-G. Warner). The Court may give a separate decision on such application under Art. 91(4) RP (see e.g. Cases 142 and 156/84 *BAT and Reynolds* v. *Commission*, above, at pp. 1902–3).

The Court may summon witnesses of its own motion or on application by a party or at the instance of the Advocate-General. The witness gives his evidence to the Court, but the parties are invited to attend. The President, the other Judges, the Advocate-General and, subject to the control of the President, the representatives of the parties may put questions to the witness. Witnesses duly summoned are required to attend for examination; defaulting witnesses may be fined (Arts. 28 ECSC Statute, 23–5 EEC Statute, 24–6 Euratom Statute, 47–8 RP).

The Court may at any time entrust any individual, body, authority, committee, or other organization it chooses with the task of giving an expert opinion. The order appointing the expert must define his task and set a time-limit within which he is to make his report. The expert is under the supervision of the Judge-Rapporteur, who may be present during his investigation. The expert may give his opinion only on points which have been expressly referred to him. The Court may examine the expert; the parties may be present and, subject to the control of the President, may put questions to him through their representatives. Both witnesses and experts are required to take an oath or make a solemn affirmation equivalent to an oath. Perjury and breach of duty by a witness or expert is punishable, at the instance of the ECJ, under the criminal law and before the competent courts of his own State. The parties may object to a witness or to an expert; the decision lies with the Court. Witnesses and experts are entitled to reimbursement of their travel and subsistence expenses as well as to compensation for loss of earnings or to fees for their services, respectively. It is the duty of the Registrar to draw up minutes of every hearing which constitute an official record and are open to inspection, together with any expert's report, by the parties (Arts. 25, 28 ECSC Statute; 22, 27 EEC Statute; 23, 28 Euratom Statute; 49–51, 53, 110 RP; 6–7 SR). The Court may, on application by a party or of its own motion, issue letters rogatory for the examination of a witness or expert by the competent judicial authority of his place of permanent residence (Arts. 26 EEC Statute, 27 Euratom Statute, 52 RP, 1–3 SR. *See further under* **Letters rogatory**).

While the rules relating to preparatory inquiries were primarily designed for contentious proceedings, Art. 103(1) RP expressly provides that those rules (i.e. Arts. 43 *et seq.* RP) also apply in reference proceedings for a preliminary ruling. Nevertheless, owing to the fact that in these proceedings it is in principle not for the ECJ to determine issues of fact—apart from special situations—preparatory inquiries are only exceptionally ordered in reference proceedings (*see further under* **Reference proceedings**, point 2(*c*)).

While the Court's Statutes provide that the hearing of witnesses and experts shall form part of the oral procedure (Arts. 21 ECSC Statute, 18 EEC and Euratom Statutes), its Rules of Procedure clearly envisage the preparatory inquiry as a separate stage in the procedure (and this is the arrangement generally followed by the Court in practice). Thus, under Art. 44(2) RP the Court may order a preparatory inquiry after the close of the written procedure or, alternatively, may decide to open the oral procedure without an inquiry. Under Art. 54 RP the President is required to fix the date for the opening of the oral procedure *after* the preparatory inquiry has been completed or, where the Court has prescribed a period within which the parties may lodge written observations concerning the inquiry, after that period has expired. Nevertheless, the Court may order any measure of inquiry to be taken, or that a previous inquiry be repeated or expanded, at any time during the course of the oral procedure (Art. 60 RP; *see further under* Oral procedure).

See also Confidentiality, Letters rogatory, Oral procedure, Reference proceedings, Representation before the ECJ, Written procedure.

Further reading 1. BOOKS: Lasok, *The European Court of Justice: Practice and Procedure* (1984), ch. 10; Usher, *European Court Practice* (1983), ch. 6.

2. ARTICLE: Brealey, 'The Burden of Proof before the European Court' (1985) 10 *EL Rev.* 250.

▶ **PRESUMPTION OF VALIDITY** Legal presumption according to which every Community act (and in particular every regulation) which has been adopted and published in accordance with the essential requirements laid down by the Treaties as to competence, form, and procedure must be presumed to be valid and fully effective, irrespective of its substantive legality or illegality, so long as it has not been properly repealed or withdrawn by the institution which adopted it or declared null and void by the ECJ. In consequence, unlawful or defective Community acts are not as a rule void but voidable (Cases 7/56 etc. *Algera* v. *Common Assembly* [1957] ECR 39 at pp. 60–1; Cases 15 to 33/73 etc. *Schots-Kortner* v. *Council, Commission and Parliament* [1974] ECR 177 at p. 191 *per Curiam*, p. 197 *per* A.-G. Trabucchi; Case 101/78 *Granaria* [1979] ECR 623 at pp. 636–7; Case 15/85 *Consorzio Cooperative d'Abruzzo* v. *Commission* [1987] ECR 1005 at p. 1036).

See also Absolute nullity.

▶ **PRIVILEGES AND IMMUNITIES** Special rights and exemptions enjoyed in the territories of the Member States by the European Communities, the members and officials of their institutions, and certain other bodies and persons. Most of these rights and exemptions are laid down in the Protocol on the Privileges and Immunities of the European Communities of 8 April 1965, annexed to the Merger Treaty (MT) of the same date (hereinafter referred to as the 'Protocol'), which replaced the earlier Protocols on Privileges and Immunities annexed to each of the ECSC, EEC, and Euratom Treaties (Art. 28 MT). The various categories of bodies and persons which/who enjoy privileges and immunities and the privileges and immunities accorded to them are summarized below.

I. The European Communities

1. Inviolability of premises, buildings, and archives. They are exempt from search, requisition, confiscation, or expropriation. The property and assets of the Communities may not be the subject of any administrative or legal measure of constraint without the authorization of the ECJ (Arts. 1–2).

2. Exemption from all direct taxes in respect of assets, revenues, and property. Indirect taxes or sales taxes included in the price of substantial movable or immovable property purchased by the Communities for their official use are to be remitted or refunded wherever possible. No exemption in respect of charges for public utility services (Art. 3).

3. Exemption from all customs duties, prohibitions, and restrictions on imports and exports in respect of articles intended for official use and in respect of publications (Art. 4).

4. Official communications and the transmission of documents enjoy the same treatment as is accorded to diplomatic missions; they may not be subject to censorship (Art. 6).

It may be noted that the above privileges and immunities are by their nature 'functional' privileges in that they are granted only in so far as they are necessary for the performance of the Communities' tasks (Art. 28 MT; Preamble to the Protocol). They do not amount to what is known in international law as 'sovereign immunity', i.e. immunity also from the jurisdiction of the national courts. Thus, the Communities may be involved in legal proceedings before the courts or tribunals of the Member States in their own names either as plaintiffs or as defendants or as interveners on either side, save where jurisdiction in respect of a particular matter is expressly conferred on the ECJ by or under the Treaties (Arts. 6 and 40(3) ECSC, 183 and 211 EEC, 155 and 185 Euratom. *See also under* **Legal personality**, point 2).

II. Members of the European Parliament (MEPs)

1. Exemption from administrative or other restriction on free movement to or from the place of meeting of the EP; privileged treatment in respect of customs and exchange control (Art. 8; see also Rule 2(4) of the EP's Rules of Procedure, 4th edn., 1987).

2. Immunity from any form of inquiry, detention, or legal proceedings in respect of opinions expressed or votes cast in the performance of duties (Art. 9).

3. During the sessions of the EP, its Members enjoy, in the territory of their own State, the immunities accorded to national MPs, and, in the territory of any other Member State, immunity from any measure of detention and from legal proceedings. Immunity also applies to Members while travelling to and from the place of meeting of the EP. However, immunity cannot be claimed when a Member is found in the act of committing an offence. The EP has the right to waive the immunity of its Members (Art. 10; for the procedure to be

followed by the EP in waiving immunity, see Rule 5 of its Rules of Procedure, amended version published in Jan. 1989). The Treaties do not determine the duration of the EP's sessions. They only provide that the EP 'shall hold an annual session. It shall meet, without requiring to be convened, on the second Tuesday in March' (Arts. 22 ECSC, 139 EEC, 109 Euratom as amended by Art. 27 MT). The ECJ has held that the concept of a session must be interpreted in the light of Community law so that it has the same meaning for all the Member States. This follows from the objective of Art. 10 of the Protocol, which is to ensure immunity for the same period for all Members of the EP, whatever their nationality. Since the activities of the EP and of its organs in fact continue throughout the year without interruption (except for August and the Christmas–New Year holiday period), restriction of immunity to the periods when Parliament is actually sitting might prejudice the carrying on of its activities as a whole. Therefore, the EP must be considered to be in session, even if it is not actually sitting, from the moment of its first meeting until the decision is taken closing its annual or extraordinary sessions (Case 149/85 *Wybot* [1986] ECR 2391 at pp. 2407–8, 2409, 2410. For an earlier but similar interpretation of the concept of 'session', see Case 101/63 *Wagner* [1964] ECR 195 at p. 201).

4. No exemption from national taxes is conferred on MEPs since Art. 13 of the Protocol, which accords tax exemption to Community officials, does not apply to them (see below). In the present state of Community law, the remuneration of MEPs is a matter of national law and is not the responsibility of the Community institutions. The Member States are entitled to tax any emoluments derived by MEPs from the exercise of their mandate. However, the ECJ has held that the power of the Member States to impose taxes is subject to certain restrictions. Thus, Community law prohibits the imposition of national tax on lump-sum payments made by the EP to its Members from Community funds by way of reimbursement of travel and subsistence expenses, unless it can be shown in accordance with Community law that such lump-sum reimbursement constitutes in part remuneration (Case 208/80 *Lord Bruce of Donington* [1981] ECR 2205 at pp. 2217–21. *See also under* **European Parliament**).

It may be mentioned that in 1987 the EP approved a Draft Protocol amending the 1965 Protocol in respect of MEPs, the main aim being to ensure that MEPs enjoy the same immunity in all the Member States (see Res. of 10 Mar. 1987, *OJ* 1987 C99/43 and 44).

III. Representatives of Member States taking part in the work of the institutions

These enjoy, in the performance of their duties and during their travel to and from the place of meeting, the 'customary' privileges, immunities, and facilities. The same applies to their advisers, technical experts, and to members of the advisory bodies of the Communities (Art. 11).

IV. Officials and other servants of the Communities

1. Immunity from national legal proceedings in respect of acts performed in an official capacity, including words spoken or written, even after termination of

429

office. This immunity does not affect the liability of officials towards the Communities and the jurisdiction of the ECJ in staff cases (Art. 12(a)). The ECJ has held that the purpose of this immunity is to shield the official activity of the Communities and of their servants from any examination in the light of national law so that such activity may be carried out in full freedom in accordance with the tasks entrusted to the Communities. The immunity from legal proceedings therefore only covers acts which, 'by their nature, represent a participation of the person entitled to the immunity in the performance of the tasks of the institution to which he belongs'. More especially, driving a motor vehicle is not in the nature of an act performed in an 'official capacity', and hence is not covered by immunity from legal proceedings, save in the exceptional cases in which this activity cannot be carried out otherwise than under the authority of the Communities and by their own servants (Case 5/68 *Sayag* [1968] ECR 395 at p. 402).

2. Exemption from immigration restrictions and from formalities for the registration of aliens; this applies also to spouses and dependent members of the family (Art. 12(b)). This exemption prohibits even an indirect constraint to register in the population registers in the Member States in which the places of employment of the Community institutions are situated (Case 85/85 *Commission* v. *Belgium* [1986] ECR 1149 at pp. 1168–9, where the indirect constraint to register was imposed through Belgian municipal tax by-laws).

3. In respect of currency or exchange regulations, enjoyment of the same facilities as are customarily accorded to officials of international organizations (Art. 12(c)).

4. Exemption from import and export duties in respect of personal effects and a motor car for personal use (Art. 12(d) and (e)).

5. Exemption from national taxes on salaries, wages, and emoluments paid by the Communities but liability to a tax for the benefit of the Communities (Art. 13; see also Council Reg. 260/68, *OJ Sp. Edn.* 1968(I), p. 37, laying down the conditions and procedure for applying the tax for the benefit of the Communities). The ECJ has held that this provision is intended, in the interests of the independence of the Communities and equal treatment of their staff, to replace national taxes by a Community tax applicable to the staff of the Communities according to uniform conditions (Case 85/86 *Commission* v. *Board of Governors of the EIB* [1988] ECR 1281 at pp. 1318–19; see further below). Interpreting the similar provisions of the earlier Protocol on Privileges and Immunities annexed to the ECSC Treaty, the ECJ has held that the Protocol prohibits the Member States from imposing on an official any taxation whatsoever which is based in whole or in part on the payment of a salary to him by the Communities. It also prohibits the taking into account of this salary in order to determine the rate of tax applicable to his other income which is not exempted, or to the joint income of the official and of his spouse in respect of tax payable on the spouse's income (Case 6/60 *Humblet* v. *Belgium* [1960] ECR 559 at p. 582). More generally, the ECJ has stated that Art. 13 prohibits any national tax, whatever its nature or method of collection, which has the effect of imposing a burden, directly or indirectly, upon the officials of the Communities by reason of the fact that they are the

beneficiaries of a remuneration paid by the Communities, even if the tax in question is not calculated in proportion to the amount of the remuneration (Case 260/86 *Commission* v. *Belgium* [1988] ECR 955 at pp. 969–70, holding that the refusal by the Belgian authorities to grant reductions in the tax on income from immovable assets, deductible from the rent, where the tenant of the residence or his spouse was an official of the Communities and thus exempt from national taxes, was contrary to Art. 13. See also Case 152/82 *Forcheri* [1983] ECR 2323 at pp. 2336–7).

6. Exemption from death duties on movable property in the country of residence and other tax advantages (Art. 14).

7. Social security benefits under Community law (Art. 15).

8. Entitlement to *laissez-passer* to be recognized as valid travel documents by the Member States and, subject to international agreements to be concluded by the Commission, by third countries (Art. 7).

The above privileges, immunities, and facilities are accorded to officials solely in the interests of the Communities. Each institution is required to waive the immunity wherever it considers that waiver is not contrary to the interests of the Communities (Art. 18). Under Art. 16 of the former ECSC Protocol, it was possible for an official to bring a direct action before the ECJ against a Member State which committed a breach of the privileges and immunities accorded (see Case 6/60 *Humblet* v. *Belgium*, above, at pp. 567 *et seq.*). The ECSC Protocol was, however, repealed by Art. 28 MT and Art. 16 was not reinacted in the sole Protocol of 1965. It is, therefore, no longer possible for an aggrieved official to bring his complaint directly before the ECJ. In the event of a breach, it is primarily for the competent institution to resolve the question by co-operation with the responsible authorities of the Member State concerned (Art. 19; Case 1/82 *D* v. *Luxembourg* [1982] ECR 3709 at p. 3716). The official may also bring his case before the competent national courts which may then refer questions to the ECJ under Art. 177 EEC on the interpretation of the Protocol (ibid.).

V. Missions of third countries accredited to the European Communities

Customary diplomatic privileges and immunities in the Member State in whose territory the Communities have their seat (i.e., provisionally, in Belgium) (Art. 17).

VI. Members of the Commission

The same privileges, immunities, and facilities as are accorded to Community officials and servants, subject to the same conditions (Art. 20).

VII. Members of the Court of Justice, Court of First Instance, and Court of Auditors

The Judges, Advocates-General, Registrar, and Assistant Rapporteurs of the ECJ, the members and the Registrar of the CFI, and the members of the Court of Auditors enjoy the same privileges, immunities, and facilities as are accorded to Community officials and servants, subject to the same conditions (Arts. 21 of the Protocol; 2(5) of Council Dec. 88/591 of 24 Oct. 1988, *OJ*

431

1988 L319/1, establishing the CFI; 78e(10) ECSC; 206(10) EEC; 180(10) Euratom). In addition, the Judges and Advocates-General of the ECJ and the members of the CFI enjoy general immunity from legal proceedings. They continue to enjoy such immunity even after they have ceased to hold office, but only in respect of acts performed by them in their official capacity, including words spoken or written. The ECJ or the CFI, as the case may be, may waive the immunity (Arts. 3, 13, and 44 ECSC Statute; 3, 8, and 44 EEC Statute; 3, 8, and 45 Euratom Statute).

VIII. Agents, advisers, and lawyers appearing before the Court of Justice and the Court of First Instance

Rights and immunities necessary to the independent exercise of their duties, in particular

1. immunity in respect of words spoken or written concerning the case or the parties;
2. exemption from search and seizure in respect of papers and documents relating to the proceedings;
3. entitlement to such allocation of foreign currency as may be necessary for the performance of duties;
4. right to travel in the course of duty without hindrance.

The above privileges, immunities, and facilities are granted exclusively in the interests of the proper conduct of proceedings. The ECJ or the CFI, as the case may be, may waive the immunity where it considers that the proper conduct of proceedings will not be hindered thereby (Arts. 20 and 46 ECSC Statute, 17 and 46 EEC Statute, 17 and 47 Euratom Statute, 32–6 RP).

IX. The European Investment Bank (EIB)

The Protocol applies also to the EIB, to the members of its organs, to its staff, and to the representatives of the Member States taking part in its activities, without prejudice to the Bank's Statute. In addition, the EIB is exempt from turnover tax and from any form of taxation or imposition of a like nature on the occasion of any increase in its capital or on the occasion of its dissolution or liquidation (Arts. 28 MT and 22 of the Protocol). The ECJ has held that the staff of the Bank are in the same legal position as the staff of the Community institutions (Case 110/75 *Mills* v. *Investment Bank* [1976] ECR 955 at p. 968) and that, in particular, Art. 13 of the Protocol providing for the tax treatment of officials and Council Reg. 260/68 adopted for its implementation (see above) are applicable to the Bank and its staff in the same way as they are applicable to the Community institutions and their officials (Case 85/86 *Commission* v. *Board of Governors of the EIB*, above, at pp. 1319–21. *See further under* **European Investment Bank**).

See also **European Investment Bank, European Parliament, Legal personality.**

Further reading 1. ARTICLE: Leopold, 'Privileges and Immunities of MEPs' (1981) 6 *EL Rev.* 275.

2. OFFICIAL PUBLICATION: House of Lords, Select Committee on the European Communities, Session 1985–6, 8th Report, 'Privileges and Immunities of Members of the European Parliament' (1986).

▶ **PROPORTIONALITY** 1. General principle of law, recognized by the ECJ as forming part of Community law, according to which the Community institutions may impose upon Community citizens, for the purposes of the public interest, only such obligations, restrictions, and penalties as are strictly necessary for the attainment of the purposes pursued. This is the principle which guarantees that the individual's freedom of action is not limited beyond the degree necessary in the general (public) interest. There must always exist a 'reasonable relationship' between the measures taken by the institutions and the aim pursued by the Communities: the measures must not exceed what is appropriate and necessary to attain the aim (see e.g. Case 11/70 *Internationale Handelsgesellschaft* [1970] ECR 1125 at p. 1136 *per Curiam*, and especially at pp. 1146–7 *per* A.-G. Dutheillet de Lamothe; Case 44/79 *Hauer* [1979] ECR 3727 at p. 3747). Therefore, in order to ascertain whether a provision of Community law is consonant with the principle of proportionality, it must be established, first, whether the means it employs correspond to the importance of its aim and, secondly, whether they are necessary for its achievement (Case 66/82 *Fromançais* [1983] ECR 395 at p. 404).

In particular, the principle of proportionality requires that in the exercise of their powers the Community institutions should always act with the utmost care and should avoid imposing upon commercial operators burdens and charges which are manifestly out of proportion to the object in view. The aims pursued by the Communities must be attained under the most favourable conditions and with the smallest possible sacrifices by those affected. Nevertheless, the burdens to be imposed need not necessarily be measured in relation to the individual situation of any one particular group of operators. An overall assessment of the advantages and disadvantages of the measures contemplated, a balancing of the often conflicting private and public interests, is sufficient (Case 15/57 *Chasse* v. *HA* [1958] ECR 211 at p. 228; Cases 17 and 20/61 *Klöckner* v. *HA* [1962] ECR 325 at p. 340; Case 5/73 *Balkan-Import-Export* [1973] ECR 1091 at pp. 1110–12; etc.). Where Community legislation makes a distinction between a primary obligation, compliance with which is necessary in order to attain the objective sought, and a secondary obligation, essentially of an administrative nature, it cannot penalize a failure to comply with the secondary obligation as severely as it penalizes a failure to comply with the primary obligation (Case 181/84 *Man (Sugar)* [1985] ECR 2889 at p. 2903; see also Case 21/85 *Maas* [1986] ECR 3537 at pp. 3558–9).

An infringement by the institutions of the principle of proportionality may entail the invalidity or the annulment of the measure in question (see e.g. Case 114/76 *Bela-Mühle* [1977] ECR 1211 at p. 1221; Case 122/78 *Buitoni* [1979] ECR 677 at pp. 684–5; Case 181/84 *Man (Sugar)*, above, at pp. 2905–6; see also Case 240/78 *Atalanta* [1979] ECR 2137 at p. 2151). Moreover,

433

the ECJ has accepted that the principle constitutes a 'superior rule of law' for the protection of the individual and that its infringement may establish the non-contractual liability of the Communities in respect of a legislative measure involving choices of economic policy (Cases 63 to 69/72 *Werhahn* v. *Council*, below, at pp. 1249 *et seq.*; Cases 197 to 200/80 etc. *Ludwigshafener Walzmühle* v. *Council and Commission* [1981] ECR 3211 at pp. 3247, 3252–3).

2. General principle of law according to which the Member States may not impose upon Community citizens, even for the purposes of the public interest, obligations, restrictions, and penalties so onerous as to cause an obstacle to the free movement of goods, persons, services, and capital. Within the area of discretion retained by them, Member States must always select, for a permitted public interest purpose, administrative measures, penalties, and procedures which are proportionate to the aim in view and which are the least restrictive of these basic freedoms (see e.g. Case 16/78 *Choquet* [1978] ECR 2293 at pp. 2302–3; Cases 41, 121, and 796/79 *Testa* [1980] ECR 1979 at pp. 1997–8; Case 203/80 *Casati* [1981] ECR 2595 at p. 2618; Case 261/81 *Rau* [1982] ECR 3961 at p. 3972). Thus, for example, the fact that an importer has failed to comply with the obligation to declare the real origin of imported goods cannot give rise to the application of penalties, such as the seizure of the goods, which are so disproportionate, considering the purely administrative nature of the contravention, as virtually to amount to a measure equivalent to a quantitative restriction (Case 41/76 *Donckerwolcke* [1976] ECR 1921 at p. 1938; Case 52/77 *Cayrol* [1977] ECR 2261 at p. 2281; Case 179/78 *Rivoira* [1979] ECR 1147 at p. 1157). Similarly, a failure to obtain a valid identity card, passport, or residence permit, or to comply with some other administrative provision relating to aliens, cannot be punished by a penalty, such as deportation or imprisonment, which is so disproportionate to the gravity of the infringement that it becomes an obstacle to the free movement of persons (Case 118/75 *Watson and Belmann* [1976] ECR 1185 at p. 1199; Case 8/77 *Sagulo, Brenca and Bakhouche* [1977] ECR 1495 at p. 1506; Case 157/79 *Pieck* [1980] ECR 2171 at p. 2187).

Moreover, the principle of proportionality is also relevant in determining the scope of any permitted derogation by the Member States from an individual right provided for by Community law such as, for example, the right to equal treatment of men and women. Thus, the principle requires that derogations remain within the limits of what is appropriate and necessary for achieving the aim in view, and it is for the national courts to ensure that the principle of proportionality is observed in any given case (Case 222/84 *Johnston* [1986] ECR 1651 at p. 1687).

3. The principle of proportionality is not only a general principle of unwritten law but has also been incorporated in certain provisions of the EEC Treaty itself. Thus, Art. 40(3) EEC applies the principle to the Common Agricultural Policy by providing that the common organization of agricultural markets may include only such measures as are 'required to attain the objectives set out in Article 39' and that it 'shall be limited to pursuit of [these]

objectives' (see e.g. Case 114/76 *Bela-Mühle*, above, at pp. 1220–1; Cases 63 to 69/72 *Werhahn* v. *Council* [1973] ECR 1229 at p. 1251). Similarly, Art. 115 EEC applies the principle to the Common Commercial Policy by providing that the Commission may authorize the Member States to take only the 'necessary protective measures' (see e.g. Case 62/70 *Bock* v. *Commission* [1971] ECR 897 at p. 909; Case 29/75 *Kaufhof* v. *Commission* [1976] ECR 431 at pp. 442–3). In a series of cases the ECJ has held that the last sentence of Art. 36 EEC, which provides that permitted prohibitions or restrictions on the free movement of goods shall not constitute a means of arbitrary discrimination or a disguised restriction on trade between Member States, is based on the principle of proportionality. Consequently, where a prohibition is contrary to that principle, it is not covered by the exception provided for in Art. 36 EEC (see e.g. Case 176/84 *Commission* v. *Greece* [1987] ECR 1193 at pp. 1222–3, 1224, and the cases cited therein).

See also **General principles of law.**

Further reading: Herdegen, 'The Relation between the Principles of Equality and Proportionality' (1985) 22 *CML Rev.* 683; Schmitthoff, 'The Doctrines of Proportionality and Non-Discrimination' (1977) 2 *EL Rev.* 329. *See also under* **General principles of law.**

▶ **PUBLICATION** Procedure whereby ECSC general decisions/recommendations and EEC/Euratom regulations are brought into force. Thus, Art. 15 ECSC provides that general decisions and recommendations 'shall take effect by the mere fact of publication'. Arts. 191 EEC and 163 Euratom provide that 'regulations shall be published in the *Official Journal* of the Community. They shall enter into force on the date specified in them or, in the absence thereof, on the twentieth day following their publication' (similar rules apply to ECSC general decisions and recommendations, see Arts. 5 and 6 of Dec. 22/60, *OJ Sp. Edn.* 2nd Ser. (VIII), p. 13). The ECJ has interpreted this provision as meaning that the institutions are free to specify the date of entry into force of legislative acts. Where justified by the circumstances, this date may even be the date of publication. It is only where a regulation is silent on the matter, and not as a general rule, that it enters into force on the twentieth day following publication (Case 17/67 *Neumann* [1967] ECR 441 at p. 456; Case 57/72 *Westzucker* [1973] ECR 321 at p. 342). However, a regulation may become applicable at a date later than that on which it comes into force (see e.g. Case 100/74 *CAM* v. *Commission* [1975] ECR 1393 at pp. 1403–4; Cases 95 to 98/74 etc. *Coopératives Agricoles de Céréales* v. *Commission and Council* [1975] ECR 1615 at pp. 1638–9).

In the case of legislative measures, publication is thus an essential formal/procedural requirement and has a constitutive effect in the sense that through publication only and exclusively will such measures acquire binding force and become applicable (Case 39/72 *Commission* v. *Italy* [1973] ECR 101 at p. 114; Case 185/73 *König* [1974] ECR 607 at pp. 616–17 *per Curiam*, pp. 623–4 *per* A.-G. Trabucchi). The correct view therefore would seem to be (although this has not so far been definitively decided by the ECJ) that lack of

435

publication entails not merely voidability but absolute nullity of the measure concerned.

The precise date of publication is of importance in two different respects. First, it may determine the date on which the measure enters into force (which may be the date of publication itself). Secondly, it makes time run for the bringing of an action for annulment before the ECJ. The Office for Official Publications of the European Communities, which publishes the *Official Journal*, has received formal instructions from the Council intended to ensure that the date of publication borne by each issue of the *Official Journal* corresponds to the date on which that issue is in fact available to the public in all the official languages at the Office in Luxembourg. The ECJ has held that these provisions give rise to a rebuttable presumption that the date of publication is in fact the date appearing on each issue of the *Official Journal*. However, should evidence be produced that the date on which an issue was in fact available does not correspond to the date which appears on that issue, regard must be had to the date of actual publication. Moreover, it is important that the date of publication should not vary according to the availability of the *Official Journal* in the territory of each Member State. The unity and uniform application of Community law require that, save as otherwise expressly provided, a regulation should enter into force on the same date in all the Member States, regardless of any delays which may occur in spite of efforts to ensure rapid distribution of the *Official Journal* throughout the Community. Therefore, in the absence of evidence to the contrary, a regulation is to be regarded as published throughout the Community on the date borne by the issue of the *Official Journal* containing the text of that regulation (Case 98/78 *Racke* [1979] ECR 69 at pp. 84–5). Where, however, the relevant issue is in fact only published and distributed on the day following the date appearing on it (e.g. because of a strike), a regulation which was to enter into force on the date of publication can only properly be applied from the following day (Case 88/76 *Exportation des Sucres* v. *Commission* [1977] ECR 709 at p. 726).

It may be mentioned that in some cases, e.g. in the field of competition law, even the publication of certain purely individual measures has been, or may be, made compulsory (see e.g. Art. 21 of Reg. 17, *OJ Sp. Edn.* 1959–62, p. 87; Art. 18 of Reg. 3975/87, *OJ* 1987 L374/1. See also Art. 4(2) of Dec. 22/60 concerning the publication of ECSC individual decisions/recommendations). While still an essential formal/procedural requirement, publication in these cases is clearly not meant to have constitutive effect since individual measures enter into force upon their notification to the addressees.

See also **Absolute nullity, Action for annulment, General decision, Infringement of an essential procedural requirement, Notification,** *Official Journal,* **Official languages, Recommendation, Regulation, Retroactive effect.**

▶ *RATIO DECIDENDI* 1. *In English law*: reason for deciding a case; more specifically, 'any rule of law expressly or impliedly treated by the judge as a necessary step in reaching his conclusion, having regard to the line of reasoning adopted by him' (R. Cross, *Precedent in English Law*, 3rd edn. (Oxford, 1977), p. 76). According to the doctrine of *stare decisis*, the only part of a judicial decision which is legally binding is the *ratio decidendi*, and where the judge in a later case is bound by the earlier decision, he must apply the *ratio decidendi* even if he disapproves of it, unless he considers that the two cases are reasonably distinguishable. As a result, the true meaning of the rule *stare decisis* is *stare rationibus decidendi* (keep to the *rationes decidendi* of past cases) (ibid. pp. 38 *et seq.*, p. 105). Although, in theory, there must be a *ratio decidendi* in all cases in which the judgment contains more than factual statements or reasoning on the facts, in practice it is not always that a judge expressly indicates the proposition on which he relies as *ratio decidendi*. Therefore, the search for the *ratio*, which is a peculiar feature of English law, plays an important part in the judicial process; a process in which the distinction between *ratio decidendi* and *obiter dictum* (incidental statement) assumes fundamental significance.

2. *In Community law*: in the absence of a doctrine of *stare decisis* and owing to the different structure of the judgments of the European Court, the concept of *ratio decidendi* has a completely different meaning and significance from that discussed above. According to the *res judicata* rule, the judgments of the ECJ are binding only between the parties and in the particular case. The only part of a judgment which is legally binding is not its *ratio decidendi* but its operative part (*dispositif*), which, in the case of doubt, must be interpreted or clarified in the light of the decisive grounds (*motifs*). The *ratio decidendi* cannot be identified with the operative part since the latter contains the actual ruling or decision of the Court and not the reasons for it. Moreover, in a large number of cases, the operative part consists of one single sentence (apart from the ruling on the costs) to the effect that the Court hereby 'dismisses the application' or 'annuls the decision of the Commission', or the like. Read in themselves, such sentences are clearly meaningless for the purpose of determining the *ratio* of the decision. In Case 112/76 *Manzoni* [1977] ECR 1647 at p. 1662, A.-G. Warner distinguished between the *ratio decidendi* and the operative part on the ground that 'one must allow for cases to which the ruling in the operative part at first sight applies, but which are in reality distinguishable from the case in which that ruling was given'.

Nor can the *ratio decidendi* be identified with the decisive grounds, in spite of the fact that these contain the 'reason for the decision'. The decisive grounds, considered in themselves, never have the finality and the binding force of the operative part, not even in the case in question; how could they then produce binding effects for subsequent cases? (It was precisely for this reason that in Case 111/63 *Lemmerz-Werke* v. *HA* [1965] ECR 677 at p. 723 A.-G. Roemer rejected the argument put forward by the applicant that the grounds of a judgment might establish a binding precedent). The decisive grounds are important in that they may (or must) be resorted to in determining the meaning of the operative part in doubtful cases, but they must always be

R

read in conjunction with the operative part. Read in themselves, they may lead to a result which is different from or even the opposite to that which emerges from the operative part (see e.g. the opinion of A.-G. Roemer in Case 48/72 *Brasserie de Haecht* [1973] ECR 77 at pp. 92–3).

Nor is it correct to say that the *ratio decidendi* can always be established by reading the operative part in conjunction with the relevant decisive grounds. There are a number of cases, including some of the most important decisions ever rendered by the ECJ, in which the *true ratio* is not revealed by the decisive grounds leading up to the ruling of the Court. In these cases, the real *ratio decidendi* can only be found in statements which are, on any analysis, mere *obiter dicta*. Moreover, the European Court often formulates broad principles by way of *obiter dictum*, principles which may prove to be of decisive importance for the whole future development of Community law, while the decision itself is based on a fairly narrow *ratio* of limited significance (see e.g. Case 6/64 *Costa* [1964] ECR 585, first formulating the doctrine of the supremacy of Community law; Case 29/69 *Stauder* [1969] ECR 419, where the Court stated, for the first time, that fundamental human rights formed part of the 'general principles of law' and were protected by the Community legal order; Case 22/70 *Commission* v. *Council* [1971] ECR 263—'ERTA' case, laying down important principles on the treaty-making powers of the EEC; Case 6/72 *Continental Can* v. *Commission* [1973] ECR 215, establishing that, under certain circumstances, the prohibitions of Art. 86 EEC may apply to mergers). Furthermore, in those cases in which a judgment of the European Court may produce legal effects going beyond the confines of the individual dispute, such as a judgment declaring an act of an institution void in a direct action or invalid in reference proceedings, or an interpretative preliminary ruling, it is the actual decision of the Court (i.e. the declaration of nullity or invalidity, or the interpretation) as stated in the operative part that produces the required effects, quite irrespective of the reasons (*ratio*) on which it is based. Thus, it seems that in the majority of cases Community law attaches relatively little importance to the search for the *ratio decidendi* as this concept is understood in English law, and to the distinction made between the *ratio* and any *dicta*. In fact, such a distinction must be treated with caution since it can lead to a mistaken interpretation of both the meaning and the scope of a judgment, as in principle everything said in the judgment expresses the Court's opinion if read in the proper context (see the opinion of A.-G. Roemer in Case 9/61 *Netherlands* v. *HA* [1962] ECR 213 at p. 242).

See also **Judgment,** *Obiter dictum,* **Res judicata, Stare decisis.**

Further reading: Toth, 'The Authority of Judgments of the European Court of Justice: Binding Force and Legal Effects' (1984) 4 *YEL* 1. *See also under* **Stare decisis.**

REASONED DECISION 1. Act whereby the Commission may declare a concentration unlawful under the ECSC Treaty and order appropriate consequential measures. Such a 'reasoned decision' differs from an ordinary 'decision' within the meaning of Art. 14 ECSC in that it may be challenged before the ECJ under Art. 33 ECSC by 'any person directly concerned', including even non-Community undertakings. Moreover, by way of derogation from Art. 33 ECSC, the Court has unlimited jurisdiction in such cases and the institution of proceedings has suspensory effect (Art. 66(5)(2) ECSC; see also Case 12/63 *Schlieker* v. *HA* [1963] ECR 85 at p. 89 *per Curiam*, p. 93 *per* A.-G. Roemer).

2. Act in which the Commission is required to record the failure of a Member State to fulfil a Community obligation under the ECSC Treaty and to set a time limit for remedying the infringement. Although such a 'reasoned decision' may be challenged before the ECJ by the State concerned, it must be clearly distinguished from an ordinary 'decision' within the meaning of Art. 14 ECSC. It has a special procedural significance in the context of the enforcement proceedings instituted by the Commission against a Member State, but it may never have a legislative content of its own (Art. 88 ECSC; Case 20/59 *Italy* v. *HA* [1960] ECR 325 at pp. 338–9; Cases 6 and 11/69 *Commission* v. *France* [1969] ECR 523 at pp. 543–4).

3. Act in which the Commission was required to record an infringement of the competition rules of the EEC prior to the adoption by the Council of measures implementing Arts. 85 and 86 EEC (Art. 89(2) EEC). To the extent to which such implementing measures have been adopted (such as, in particular, Reg. 17, *OJ Sp. Edn.* 1959–62, p. 87), which lay down a more detailed enforcement procedure, this provision has become obsolete. However, in sectors where implementing measures are absent, Art. 89 continues to apply although the Commission appears never to have taken a 'reasoned decision' under it (see Cases 209 to 213/84 *Asjes* [1986] ECR 1425 at pp. 1467–8).

See also Action against Member States, Action for annulment, Administrative procedure*, Concentration*, Decision.

▶ REASONED OPINION 1. Opinion which the Commission may, and in certain circumstances must, deliver on investment programmes under the ECSC Treaty, after giving the undertakings concerned full opportunity to submit their comments (Art. 54(4) ECSC). A 'reasoned opinion' issued under this provision is subject to the general rules relating to 'opinions' as laid down in Arts. 14 and 33 ECSC, and in consequence it has no binding force and is not challengeable for annulment before the ECJ. Such an opinion cannot involve the person to whom it is addressed in any legal obligation. Nor does a favourable opinion constitute an authorization giving the addressee a special right different from the rights of other undertakings (Cases 63 and 147/84 *Finsider* v. *Commission* [1985] ECR 2857 at p. 2881). However, an adverse 'reasoned opinion' delivered by the Commission on certain grounds has the force of a 'decision' within the meaning of Arts. 14 and 33 ECSC and, as such, is binding and may be the subject of annulment proceedings (Art. 54(5) ECSC; Cases 1 and 14/57 *Usines à Tubes de la Sarre* v. *HA* [1957] ECR 105 at p. 114 *per Curiam*, p. 117 *per* A.-G. Lagrange).

2. Essential procedural act which the Commission must adopt under the EEC and Euratom Treaties, if it considers that a Member State has failed to fulfil a Community obligation (or if such a failure has been brought before it by another Member State), before an action may be instituted against the defaulting State before the ECJ (Arts. 169 and 170 EEC, 141 and 142 Euratom). Such a 'reasoned opinion' must be distinguished from an ordinary 'opinion' within the meaning of Arts. 189 and 190 EEC, 161 and 162 Euratom (under which provisions an 'opinion' need not be 'reasoned'), since it has a special procedural significance of its own in the context of actions against Member States (see e.g. Case 48/65 *Lütticke* v. *Commission* [1966] ECR 19 at p. 27; Cases 6 and 11/69 *Commission* v. *France* [1969] ECR 523 at p. 542; Cases 142 and 143/80 *Essevi and Salengo* [1981] ECR 1413 at pp. 1432–3).

See also **Action against Member States, Action for annulment, Opinion.**

▶ **RECOMMENDATION** Act of the Council or the Commission falling within the scope of secondary legislation.

1. **Under the ECSC Treaty,** recommendations made by the Commission 'shall be binding as to the aims to be pursued but shall leave the choice of the appropriate methods for achieving these aims to those to whom the recommendations are addressed . . . In cases where the High Authority [i.e. the Commission] is empowered to take a decision, it may confine itself to making a recommendation' (Art. 14 ECSC).

The ECSC Treaty places two different courses of action at the Commission's disposal to enable it to carry out the tasks assigned to it. Whenever the Commission possesses law-making (regulatory) power under the Treaty, it exercises that power by means of a decision which is binding in its entirety. Where the Commission has not been given power to legislate directly, it can only ensure implementation of obligations arising from the Treaty by way of a recommendation. This is usually the case in those sectors of the economy which have not been placed entirely within Community competence and where the Member States have retained their law-making powers over their nationals. Accordingly, a recommendation usually contains an instruction to Member States defining and clarifying the extent of their obligations under a particular Treaty provision and specifying the aims implied by that provision. It is a 'reminder' for the Member States of their duty to provide for the implementation of a Treaty rule. It cannot impose a new obligation which has no basis in the Treaty; nor can it prescribe specific methods to be followed in the achievement of the aims. The Member States are completely free in their choice of measures provided that such measures conform to the stated aims (see Case 20/59 *Italy* v. *HA* [1960] ECR 325 at p. 338; Case 30/59 *Steenkolenmijnen* v. *HA* [1961] ECR 1 at p. 24; Case 9/61 *Netherlands* v. *HA* [1962] ECR 213 at pp. 232–4).

The Treaty makes a distinction between 'general' recommendations and recommendations which are 'individual in character'. The importance of such a distinction is that it is the general or individual nature of a recommendation which determines whether (*a*) it has to be published in the *Official Journal* or notified to the addressee (Art. 15 ECSC), and whether (*b*) it is challengeable by undertakings before the ECJ (Art. 33 ECSC). In the making of the distinction, the same criteria are used as in the case of general and individual decisions.

2. **Under the EEC and Euratom Treaties,** recommendations made by the Council or the Commission 'shall have no binding force' (Arts. 189 EEC, 161 Euratom). 'In order to ensure the proper functioning and development of the Common Market, the Commission shall . . . formulate recommendations . . . on matters dealt with in this Treaty, if it expressly so provides or if the Commission considers it necessary' (Art. 155 EEC; see also Art. 124 Euratom). Recommendations may be addressed to Member States (see e.g. Art. 102(1) EEC), to individuals (see e.g. Art. 91(1) EEC), or by the Commission to the Council (see e.g. Art. 105(1) EEC). They are usually made for the purpose of obtaining a certain course of action or conduct from the addressee (e.g. harmonization, co-ordination, or approximation of national laws or policies) or of laying down procedures and timetables for the achievement of Community objectives. Although not binding in law, recommendations may carry considerable political and moral weight and in certain cases their non-observance by the addressee may involve legal consequences (see e.g. Art. 102(2) EEC).

See also **Action for annulment, General decision, Individual decision, Notification, Publication, Secondary legislation, Statement of reasons.**

▶ **REFERENCE PROCEEDINGS** Non-contentious proceedings before the ECJ designed to obtain a preliminary ruling in a case pending before a national court. Such proceedings differ from direct actions in two main respects. First, they are commenced by a 'reference' from a court or tribunal of a Member State and not by an 'originating application'. They are characterized by the absence of parties in the proper sense of the word and are based upon a direct judicial co-operation between the ECJ and the national courts. Secondly, in reference proceedings the ECJ is not called upon to decide the disputed issues but merely to give an abstract ruling upon a point of Community law, while the national court before which the case is pending retains its jurisdiction to settle the dispute in the light of the Court's ruling. As the ECJ has stated, reference proceedings are 'non-contentious and are in the nature of a step in the action pending before a national court, as the parties to the main action are merely invited to state their case within the legal limits laid down by the national court' (Case *62/72 Bollmann* [1973] ECR 269 at p. 275. See also Case 13/61 *Bosch* [1962] ECR 45 at p. 56 *per* A.-G. Lagrange; Cases 28 to 30/62 *Da Costa* [1963] ECR 31 at p. 38; Case 6/64 *Costa* [1964] ECR 585 at p. 614; Case 16/65 *Schwarze* [1965] ECR 877 at p. 886; etc.).

1. **Under the ECSC Treaty** (Art. 41), the ECJ has 'sole jurisdiction' to give preliminary rulings on the validity of acts of the Commission and of the Council where such validity is in issue in proceedings brought before a

national court or tribunal. It follows that under the ECSC Treaty the courts and tribunals of the Member States have no jurisdiction to decide upon the validity of Community acts and that, accordingly, whenever such validity is in issue in proceedings pending before them, they are under an obligation to refer the matter to the ECJ for a preliminary ruling. The ECJ has pointed out that, just like Arts. 177 EEC and 150 Euratom (see below), Art. 41 ECSC is based on a 'clearly defined separation of tasks between the national courts and the Court of Justice and does not allow the latter to appraise the facts which are the subject of the main proceedings or to consider whether the request for a preliminary ruling was appropriate in the circumstances. The Court's sole task is to consider the relevant elements of Community law and to provide the national court with a useful answer' (Case 239/84 *Gerlach* [1985] ECR 3507 at p. 3517; see also Case 172/84 *Celestri* [1985] ECR 963 at pp. 969–70). The decision to refer a case to the ECJ must be served on the parties, the Member States, the Commission, and the Council, all of which may, within two months, lodge written statements of case or written observations with the ECJ. Otherwise Arts. 43 *et seq.* of the Court's Rules of Procedure apply (Art. 103(3) RP. See further under point 2(*c*) below).

2. **Under the EEC and Euratom Treaties** (Arts. 177 EEC, 150 Euratom), a distinction is made between optional (or discretionary) and obligatory references, which are considered separately below. The discussion is limited to Art. 177 EEC, although everything said is, in principle, applicable to the Euratom Treaty also.

(*a*) *Optional (or discretionary) references.* 'Any court or tribunal' of a Member State against whose decisions there is judicial remedy under national law (i.e. generally any court of first and second instance) is entitled, but not obliged, to make references to the ECJ provided, first, that a 'question is raised' before it concerning the interpretation of the Treaty or the validity and interpretation of acts of the institutions (including the interpretation of the statutes of bodies set up by the Council) and, secondly, that such a court considers that a decision on the question by the ECJ is 'necessary to enable it to give judgment' (Art. 177(2) EEC).

The power to refer is granted to 'every national court or tribunal without distinction' (Case 166/73 *Rheinmühlen* [1974] ECR 33 at p. 38) and without regard to 'the nature, criminal or otherwise, of the national proceedings within the framework of which the preliminary questions have been formulated' (Case 82/71 *SAIL* [1972] ECR 119 at p. 135). Thus, references may be made in civil, criminal, administrative, fiscal, social, labour law, etc. proceedings, including non-contentious proceedings where the courts merely perform an administrative function in judicial form (e.g. the keeping of the Register of Companies, see Case 32/74 *Haaga* [1974] ECR 1201 at pp. 1205–6 *per Curiam*, p. 1213 *per* A.-G. Mayras) and including proceedings for interlocutory injunctions (see e.g. Case 107/76 *Hoffmann-La Roche* [1977] ECR 957 at pp. 972–3) as well as other special, urgent, or summary forms of procedure (see e.g. Case 162/73 *Birra Dreher* [1974] ECR 201 at p. 211; Case 338/85 *Pardini* [1988] ECR 2041 at pp. 2073–5).

The concept of 'court or tribunal' must be defined according to the criteria of Community rather than national law. Thus, for the purposes of making a reference, a body may have to be recognized as a 'court or tribunal' even though it may not be so considered in its own national legal system, provided that it satisfies at least the following requirements. First, it has been set up and operates with the consent, co-operation, and under the supervision of the public authorities; secondly, it exercises a judicial function, i.e. determines disputes independently and according to rules of law; and thirdly, it follows an adversarial procedure similar to those used in ordinary courts of law, i.e. one which ensures its independence and impartiality as well as the proper hearing of the parties (Case 61/65 *Vaassen* [1966] ECR 261 at pp. 272–3 *per Curiam*, pp. 280–2 *per* A.-G. Gand, where the ECJ accepted a reference from a Dutch Arbitration Tribunal (*Scheidsgerecht*) set up under private law to settle disputes between a Miners' Insurance Fund and its members, although it was not a 'court or tribunal' under Netherlands law; Case 36/73 *Nederlandse Spoorwegen* [1973] ECR 1299 at p. 1308 *per Curiam* (by implication), pp. 1317–20 *per* A.-G. Mayras, where the ECJ accepted a reference from the Litigation Section of the Netherlands Council of State (*Raad van State*), which, in contentious proceedings on an administrative matter, has a strictly advisory competence while the final decision is taken by the Crown; Case 246/80 *Broekmeulen* [1981] ECR 2311 at pp. 2326–8 *per Curiam*, pp. 2335–8 *per* A.-G. Reischl, where the ECJ accepted a reference from the Appeals Committee of the Royal Netherlands Society for the Promotion of Medicine—a private association—set up to hear appeals against the decisions of the General Practitioners Registration Committee of the same Society. The Appeals Committee was not a 'court or tribunal' under Netherlands law. See also Case 14/86 *Pretore di Salò* [1987] ECR 2545 at p. 2567, where the Court admitted a reference from an Italian magistrate combining the functions of both a public prosecutor and an investigating judge. On the other hand, in Case 138/80 *Borker* [1980] ECR 1975 at p. 1977, the ECJ declared that it had no jurisdiction to give a ruling as requested by the Bar Council of the *Cour de Paris* as in the particular case the proceedings before that body were not intended to lead to a 'decision of a judicial nature'. See also Case 318/85 *Greis Unterweger* [1986] ECR 955 at pp. 957–8, where the Court declined jurisdiction for similar reasons, holding that the task of the body making the reference was not to resolve disputes but to submit an opinion within the framework of an administrative procedure).

In the United Kingdom, the concept of a 'court or tribunal' encompasses, in addition to the ordinary civil and criminal courts, various administrative tribunals, such as the National Insurance Commissioner (before 1980) (see e.g. Case 17/76 *Brack* [1976] ECR 1429, esp. at p. 1456 *per* A.-G. Mayras) and the Social Security Commissioner (since 1980) (see e.g. Case 150/82 *Coppola* [1983] ECR 43; Case 149/82 *Robards* [1983] ECR 171), the Special Commissioners of Income Tax (see e.g. Case 208/80 *Lord Bruce of Donington* [1981] ECR 2205; Case 44/84 *Hurd* [1986] ECR 29), the Employment Appeal Tribunal (see e.g. Case 96/80 *Jenkins* [1981] ECR 911), Value Added Tax Tribunals (see e.g. Case 5/84 *Direct Cosmetics* [1985] ECR 617). On the other hand, an arbitration tribunal or sole arbitrator is not considered to be a 'court or tribunal' within the meaning of Art. 177 where there is no sufficiently close link between the arbitration procedure and the organization of legal remedies through the ordinary courts (i.e. where arbitration is resorted to by voluntary agreement between the parties and the public authorities are not in any way involved in the proceedings, see Case 102/81 *Nordsee* [1982] ECR 1095 at pp. 1109–11 *per Curiam*, pp. 1116–23 *per* A.-G. Reischl). Nevertheless, the jurisdiction of the ECJ to give preliminary rulings in arbitration proceedings will, in general, depend on the nature of the arbitration in question (ibid.).

The procedure to obtain a preliminary ruling may be set in motion only by a court or tribunal of a Member State. Thus, the parties to proceedings pending before such a court or tribunal, the Member States themselves, their various internal (legislative, executive, administrative) authorities, the Community institutions, courts of non-Member States, and international courts or tribunals have no standing to refer preliminary questions to the ECJ (Case 246/80 *Broekmeulen*, above, at p. 2336 *per* A.-G. Reischl). The position of the parties to the main action is particularly restricted in reference proceedings. This is because

Article 177 of the EEC Treaty establishes a direct form of cooperation between the Court of Justice and the national courts or tribunals by means of a non-contentious procedure, in which the parties to the main action cannot take any initiative and during the course of which they are only invited to submit their observations within the legal context outlined by the court making the reference. Although within the limits fixed by Article 177 it is thus exclusively for the national courts or tribunals to decide whether to make a reference and what its subject-matter should be, it follows that it is also exclusively for those courts or tribunals to decide whether they have received adequate clarification by the preliminary ruling given upon their request, or whether they consider it necessary to make a further reference to the Court. (Case 13/67 *Becher* [1968] ECR 187 at p. 197.)

It follows from this that the parties to the main action may not:

- make a direct request to the ECJ for a preliminary ruling (Cases 31 and 33/62 *Wöhrmann* v. *Commission* [1962] ECR 501 at p. 507. See also the cases cited below);
- compel the national courts, by the inclusion of an 'arbitration clause' in their contract, to request a preliminary ruling (Case 93/78 *Mattheus* [1978] ECR 2203 at p. 2210);
- alter the wording, scope, or purpose of the questions referred or have them declared without object. In particular, they may not raise the question of validity where the reference relates to interpretation only (Case 44/65 *Hessische Knappschaft* [1965] ECR 965 at pp. 970–1; Case 51/70 *Lütticke* [1971] ECR 121 at pp. 137–8 *per* A.-G. Roemer; Case 5/72 *Grassi* [1972] ECR 443 at pp. 447–8; etc.), although the ECJ may of its own motion consider the validity of a measure 'if it appears that the real purpose of the questions submitted by a national court is concerned rather with the validity of Community measures than with their interpretation' (Case 16/65 *Schwarze*, above, at p. 886; see also

Case 62/76 *Strehl* [1977] ECR 211 at p. 217; Case 20/85 *Roviello* [1988] ECR 2805 at p. 2851; see also the opinion of A.-G. Mancini at pp. 2825–6);

- put forward new questions or supplementary arguments representing an entirely new departure from the order making the reference and seeking to extend its subject-matter (Cases 73 and 74/63 *Handelsvereniging Rotterdam* [1964] ECR 1 at pp. 27–8 *per* A.-G. Roemer; Case 94/74 *IGAV* [1975] ECR 699 at p. 712; Case 119/75 *Terrapin* [1976] ECR 1039 at p. 1060; Case 270/81 *Felicitas* [1982] ECR 2771 at p. 2782; etc.);
- request the ECJ to supplement or interpret judgments delivered by it in previous reference proceedings (Case 13/67 *Becher*, above, at p. 197; Case 40/70 *Sirena* [1979] ECR 3169 at pp. 3170–1).

The power of the national courts to refer is derived directly from, and governed by, the Treaty and not national law. It follows that that power cannot be taken away, fettered, or interfered with in any way by acts of the Community institutions or rules of domestic law. As the ECJ has pointed out, even a rule of precedent, whereby lower courts are bound on points of law by rulings of higher courts, cannot deprive the lower courts of their power to refer questions to the European Court. The free exercise of this power is particularly important where a lower court considers that a ruling made by a superior court misinterprets or misapplies Community provisions and could therefore lead it to give a judgment contrary to Community law (Case 166/73 *Rheinmühlen*, above, at pp. 38–9; see also Case 127/73 *BRT* [1974] ECR 51 at pp. 61–3). Nevertheless, decisions of lower courts to refer questions to the European Court remain subject to the remedies normally available under national law (Case 146/73 *Rheinmühlen* [1974] ECR 139 at p. 147. For a different opinion expressed by A.-G. Warner, see ibid. at pp. 43–7. On the right of appeal against a decision to refer, see also Case 13/61 *Bosch*, above, at pp. 49–50 and Case 31/68 *Chanel* [1970] ECR 403 at pp. 404–6).

It follows from the foregoing that national courts and tribunals against whose decisions there is judicial remedy enjoy wide discretion in referring matters to the ECJ. Subject to a right of appeal under domestic law, mentioned above, and to certain qualifications to be discussed below, they may freely decide whether to refer or not to refer, what legal issues and at what stage in the proceedings to refer, although in certain circumstances it might be convenient to make a reference only after the facts of the case have been established and questions of purely national law have been settled (Cases 36 and 71/80 *Irish Creamery Milk Suppliers Association* [1981] ECR 735 at pp. 747–8). Generally, the choice of the appropriate moment for making a reference in a particular case must be governed by considerations of procedural economy and efficiency whose assessment is a matter for the national court alone (see Case 14/86 *Pretore di Salò*, above, at p. 2568). The ECJ itself is neither required nor authorized to review the decision making the reference, i.e. the facts, grounds, and considerations which may have led the national court to its choice of questions, nor whether the reference is relevant to, or necessary for, the rendering of a judgment in the main action (see e.g. Case 26/62 *Van Gend en Loos* [1963] ECR 1 at p. 11; Case 6/64 *Costa*, above, at p. 593). Nor can the Court investigate whether the reference was made in accordance with national law governing the composition, jurisdiction, and procedure of the court making it (Case 19/68 *De Cicco* [1968] ECR 473 at pp. 478–9; Case 65/81 *Reina* [1982] ECR 33 at pp. 42–3). As the ECJ has stated,

Article 177 is based on a distinct separation of functions between national courts and tribunals on the one hand and the Court of Justice on the other, and it does not give the Court jurisdiction to take cognizance of the facts of the case, or to criticize the reasons for the reference. Therefore, when a national court or tribunal refers a provision of Community law for interpretation, it is to be supposed that the said court or tribunal considers this interpretation necessary to enable it to give judgment in the action. Thus the Court cannot require the national court or tribunal to state expressly that the provision which appears to that court or tribunal to call for an interpretation is applicable. In so far as the quotation of the provision in question is not incorrect on the face of it, there is a valid reference to the Court. The Court of Justice has no jurisdiction to decide whether one or other of the provisions referred for an inter-pretation is applicable to the case at issue; this is a matter for the court making the reference. (Case 13/68 *Salgoil* [1968] ECR 453 at pp. 459–60; Case 10/69 *Portelange* [1969] ECR 309 at p. 315.)

On the basis of the above-cited case-law, the ECJ has for a long time followed the principle that 'a request from a national court may be rejected only if it is quite obvious that the interpretation of Community law or the examination of the validity of a rule of Community law sought by that court bears no relation to the actual nature of the case or to the subject-matter of the main action' (Case 126/80 *Salonia* [1981] ECR 1563 at pp. 1576–7). However, there are cases in which the Court seems to have departed from this practice by actually investigating whether the preliminary ruling requested by the national court was in fact necessary to enable that court to settle a 'genuine dispute'. Thus, in Case 104/79 *Foglia* [1980] ECR 745 at pp. 759–60 the Court held that it had no jurisdiction to give a ruling on the compatibility of a French tax provision with Community law since this issue was raised in proceedings before an Italian court between two private individuals who were in agreement as to the result to be attained (i.e. to obtain a judgment declaring the tax in question to be contrary to Community law) and who inserted a clause in their contract in order to induce the Italian court to give a ruling on the point. The ECJ pointed out the 'artificial nature of this expedient' and held that to give a preliminary ruling in such a situation 'would jeopardize the whole system of legal remedies available to private individuals'. When the same case was referred to it for the second time, the ECJ justified its decision by saying that 'the duty assigned to the Court by Article 177 is not that of delivering advisory opinions on general or hypo-thetical questions but of assisting in the administration of justice in the Member States. It accordingly does not have jurisdiction . . . to give its views on . . . problems of Community law which do not correspond to an objective requirement inherent in the resolution of a dispute.' At the same time the Court reserved to itself the power to examine, where necessary, the conditions in which a case had been referred to it and the reasons which prompted the national court to make the reference (Case 244/80 *Foglia* [1981] ECR 3045 at pp. 3062–4; see also Cases 141 to 143/81 *Holdijk* [1982] ECR 1299 at p. 1311; Case 261/81 *Rau* [1982] ECR 3961 at p. 3971).

It appears, however, that in some of its more recent case-law the Court has returned to its original position by confirming that 'it is, in fact, for the national court, which alone has a direct knowledge of the facts of the case and of the arguments of the parties and which will have to take responsibility for giving judgment in the case, to assess, on the basis of its full knowledge of the case, whether the questions of law raised in the proceedings pending before it are material and whether a preliminary ruling is necessary to enable it to give judgment' (Case 278/82 *Rewe* [1984] ECR 721 at p. 753).

While the discretion of the lower national courts in referring matters to the ECJ is wide, it is not unlimited. There are certain issues which even courts against whose decisions there is a judicial remedy under national law may not decide themselves. Thus, in Case 314/85 *Foto-Frost* [1987] ECR 4199 at pp. 4230–1 the ECJ held that national courts have no power to declare acts of the Community institutions invalid. It follows that whenever the question of the validity of a Community act is raised for the first time and the national court is unable to conclude that the act is valid (a decision which the national court has power to take), it is bound to refer the matter to the European Court (*see further under* **Preliminary ruling**, point 2(*b*)). It is submitted that the same considerations of legal certainty and uniform application of Community law which underlie the Court's decision in the *Foto-Frost* case also prevent national courts from deciding whether or not a Community provision may produce direct effects. The concept of direct effect, like that of validity, is necessarily absolute, uniform, and unchangeable: it cannot vary from case to case and from Member State to Member State. Since only the ECJ has the power to interpret a Community provision authoritatively for the whole Community, national courts must seek such interpretation whenever the question of direct effect of a provision is raised before them for the first time. This seems to follow also from the Court's judgment in Case 104/81 *Kupferberg* [1982] ECR 3641 at pp. 3662–3, which deals with the direct effect of international agreements.

(*b*) *Obligatory references*. Where a question concerning the interpretation or the validity of a Community provision is raised in a case pending before a court or tribunal of a Member State against whose decisions there is no judicial remedy under national law, that court or tribunal is under an obligation to bring the matter before the ECJ (Art. 177(3) EEC). As the ECJ has stated, the particular objectives of this mandatory procedure are 'to prevent a body of national case-law not in accord with the rules of Community law from coming into existence in any Member State' (Case 107/76 *Hoffmann-La Roche*, above, at p. 973; Cases 35 and 36/82 *Morson and Jhanjan* [1982] ECR 3723 at p. 3734) and thus 'to prevent the occurrence within the Community of divergences in judicial decisions on questions of Community law' (Case 283/81 *CILFIT* [1982] ECR 3415 at p. 3428). A

447

failure to comply with the obligation to refer will involve the Member State concerned in a breach of Community law and may make it liable to an action by the Commission (under Art. 169 EEC) or by another Member State (under Art. 170 EEC) before the ECJ and even to pay compensation for any damage caused to private individuals. (For various remedies suggested by the ECJ for infringements of Art. 177 by the national courts, see *Reports on European Union*, Suppl. 9/75—*Bull. EC*, p. 18.)

Legal opinion has been divided on the question which particular courts are subject to the obligation to refer. According to one view, this obligation applies only to those courts whose decisions are, owing to their position in the judicial hierarchy, never subject to appeal, i.e. to courts of last instance alone ('abstract theory'). According to a second view, the duty to refer comprises any court whatever, whether of first, second, or last instance, whose ruling in the particular case in question is not subject to appeal ('concrete theory'). While the ECJ has never conclusively decided this question (although in Case 6/64 *Costa*, above, at p. 592 it seems to have taken the second view), A.-G. Capotorti has suggested that the decisive test should be, not the position of a court in the judicial hierarchy but 'whether the decision to be taken by a court at the conclusion of the proceedings is or is not final . . . in the sense that [it does] not give rise to any review of the case on the request of either of the parties either as regards the facts or even only as regards the law without any fresh facts or exceptional conditions being necessary' (Case 107/76 *Hoffmann-La Roche*, above, at pp. 980–1). Accordingly, he has said, to avoid the risk of an erroneous interpretation becoming final, 'it is reasonable to regard the courts, at every level, as under a duty to seek a preliminary ruling in the course of any proceedings which must of necessity result in a final decision' (ibid. at p. 980).

The opinion of legal writers and national courts has also been divided on the question whether Art. 177(3) EEC imposes a strict obligation on courts of last instance to refer a case to the ECJ whenever a 'question is raised' before them concerning the interpretation or the validity of a Community provision, or whether such courts enjoy at least a margin of discretion to assess if any reasonable doubt exists as to the manner in which the question raised is to be resolved, which would make a preliminary ruling necessary. The ECJ settled this matter, at least with regard to interpretative preliminary rulings, in Case 283/81 *CILFIT*, above, at pp. 3428–30, where it ruled that in certain circumstances courts of last resort are exempted from the obligation to refer. These circumstances are as follows:

(i) where the question of interpretation raised before them is not relevant, that is to say, 'if the answer to that question, regardless of what it may be, can in no way affect the outcome of the case';

(ii) where the question raised is 'materially identical with a question which has already been the subject of a preliminary ruling in a similar case' (this was already held in the earlier Cases 28 to 30/62 *Da Costa*, above, at p. 38) or where 'previous decisions of the Court have already dealt with the point of law in question, irrespective of the nature of the proceedings which led to those decisions, even though the questions at issue are not strictly identical';

(iii) where 'the correct application of Community law [is] so obvious as to leave no scope for any reasonable doubt as to the manner in which the question raised is to be resolved'. However, before a national court comes to that conclusion, it must be convinced that the matter is 'equally obvious to the courts of the other Member States and to the Court of Justice'. In resolving questions of Community law, national courts must bear in mind the 'characteristic features of Community law and the particular difficulties to which its interpretation gives rise'.

In addition, the ECJ has held that a national court or tribunal is exempted from the obligation to refer where a question of interpretation or of validity is raised in interlocutory proceedings for an interim order, even where no judicial remedy is available against the decision to be taken in the context of those proceedings, provided that each of the parties is entitled to institute proceedings on the substance of the case and that during such proceedings the question provisionally decided in the summary proceedings may be re-examined and may be the subject of a reference to the Court under Art. 177 (Case 107/76 *Hoffmann-La Roche*, above, at p. 973; Cases 35 and 36/82 *Morson and Jhanjan*, above, at pp. 3734–5).

It seems, finally, that courts of last resort are also relieved of the obligation to refer where the question raised before them concerns the validity of a Community act which has already been declared invalid by the ECJ in a previous preliminary ruling (or, possibly, declared 'inapplicable' in the context of a plea of illegality under Art. 184 EEC). This follows from the decision of the Court in Case 66/80 *International Chemical Corporation* [1981] ECR 1191 at p. 1215, where the Court held that although a preliminary ruling declaring an act invalid 'is directly addressed only to the national court which brought the matter before the Court, it is sufficient reason for any other national court to regard that act as void for the purposes of a judgment which it has to give'. Since the term 'any other national court' must include courts of last resort also, such courts are obliged to make a reference only if further doubts exist concerning the invalidity of the act in question, relating, in particular, to the grounds, the scope, or the consequences of the invalidity. Otherwise, they may simply treat the act as void.

(*c*) *Form and procedure*. Community law does not prescribe any particular form in which a national court must present its request for a preliminary ruling. It is thus permissible for a reference to be drawn up in a simple and direct way, which must nevertheless enable the ECJ to abstract from it without difficulty the questions of interpretation or of validity on which a ruling is sought (Case 13/61 *Bosch*, above, at p. 50). These questions may be raised and formulated by one of the parties alone, by both parties jointly, or by the court itself of its own motion (Case 166/73 *Rheinmühlen*, above, at p. 38; Case 126/80 *Salonia*, above, at p. 1577; Case 283/81 *CILFIT*, above, at p. 3428). To enable the Court to give a helpful ruling, the national court is

449

generally expected to define precisely the subject-matter of the proceedings (including the main arguments of the parties), indicating the factual and legal context in which the ruling is to be placed. It is also required to explain the grounds (if these are not clearly evident from the file of the case) on which it considers an answer to its questions to be necessary for judgment in the main proceedings (see Cases 141 to 143/81 *Holdijk*, above, at pp. 1311–12 and the cases cited therein).

The decision referring a case to the ECJ must be notified to the Court by the national court or tribunal concerned, which is required to suspend its proceedings (Art. 20 EEC Statute). The reference procedure is automatically set in motion as soon as such a notification is received by the Court (Cases 28 to 30/62 *Da Costa*, above, at p. 38) and continues as long as the decision of the national court has neither been withdrawn nor become devoid of object, even where appellate proceedings have been instituted against it in the higher national courts (Case 13/61 *Bosch*, above, at pp. 49–50; Case 127/73 *BRT*, above, at pp. 61–2; Case 146/73 *Rheinmühlen*, above, at p. 147; Case 65/81 *Reina*, above, at p. 43). The decision to refer is notified by the Registrar of the Court to the parties, to the Member States, to the Commission, and also to the Council if the act in question originates from it. Within two months all those who received such notification are entitled to submit statements of case or written observations to the Court (Art. 20 EEC Statute). Although the European Parliament is not included amongst those entitled to submit observations, it may be invited by the Court to state its opinion on any matter which concerns it (under Art. 21 EEC Statute, see e.g. Case 149/85 *Wybot* [1986] ECR 2391 at p. 2407).

After the lodging of written observations, Arts. 43 *et seq.* of the Court's Rules of Procedure apply (Art. 103(1) RP). These provisions enable the Court to order, if necessary, various measures of preparatory inquiry such as, for example, the submission of evidence. While it is true that in reference proceedings the Court cannot investigate the facts of the case for the purpose of applying the law to them (see e.g. Case 6/64 *Costa*, above, at p. 593), it does have the power to verify the existence of facts in so far as this is necessary to determine the validity of a Community measure (Case 51/75 *EMI Records* [1976] ECR 811 at p. 854 *per* A.-G. Warner; Case 314/85 *Foto-Frost*, above, at p. 4232). Nevertheless, owing to the non-contentious nature of reference proceedings, not all the provisions which follow Art. 43 RP—which were primarily designed for contentious proceedings—can properly be applied in procedures for a preliminary ruling (see Case 62/72 *Bollmann*, above, at p. 275 *per Curiam*, p. 279 *per* A.-G. Roemer; Case 69/85 *Wünsche* [1986] ECR 947 at p. 952). Thus, the following provisions of the Rules of Procedure are not applicable to references for a preliminary ruling: Arts. 55(2) (deferment of a case on a joint application by the parties); 67 (supplementing a judgment, see Case 13/67 *Becher*, above, at p. 197); 69–75 (recovery of costs and expenses, see Case 62/72 *Bollmann*, above, at p. 275); 77 (discontinuance of proceedings by settlement between the parties); 83–90 (suspension of operation and other interim measures); 93 (intervention, see Case 6/64 *Costa*, above, at pp. 614–15; Case 19/68 *De Cicco*, above, at p. 479); 94

(judgment by default, Case 69/85 *Wünsche*, above, at p. 952); 97 (third party proceedings, ibid.); 98–100 (revision of judgments, ibid.); and 102 RP (interpretation of judgments at the request of the parties, ibid.; see also Case 13/67 *Becher*, above, at p. 197; Case 40/70 *Sirena*, above, at pp. 3170–1).

As regards the representation and attendance of the parties to the main proceedings, the ECJ must take account of the rules of procedure of the national court making the reference (Art. 104(2) RP). It will be for this court to decide as to the costs of the reference (see Case 62/72 *Bollmann*, above, at p. 275), but in special circumstances the ECJ may grant, as legal aid, assistance to facilitate the representation or attendance of a party (Art. 104(3) RP). The language of the case before the ECJ is the language of the referring court (Art. 29(2) RP). References are normally assigned by the Court to a Chamber (see Art. 95 RP).

3. **Other treaties.** The provisions of the EEC Treaty, of the EEC Statute, and of the ECJ's Rules of Procedure relating to references for preliminary rulings apply also to the references provided for in the Protocol of 3 June 1971, as amended, concerning the interpretation by the ECJ of the Convention of 29 February 1968 on the Mutual Recognition of Companies and Legal Persons, in the Protocol of 3 June 1971, as amended, concerning the interpretation by the ECJ of the Convention of 27 September 1968 on Jurisdiction and the Enforcement of Judgments in Civil and Commercial Matters as amended by the Conventions of Accession of 1978, 1982, and 1989, and in the Protocols of 19 December 1988 concerning the interpretation by the ECJ of the Convention of 19 June 1980 on Contractual Obligations, except where the Protocols themselves otherwise provide, and to references provided for by other treaties and conventions (Art. 103(2) RP).

See also Acte clair, **Costs, Direct action, Interpretation of Community law, Plea of illegality, Preliminary ruling, Preparatory inquiries.**

Further reading 1. BOOKS: Jacobs and Durand, *References to the European Court: Practice and Procedure* (1975); Lasok, *The European Court of Justice: Practice and Procedure* (1984); Usher, *European Court Practice* (1983). *See also under* **Preliminary ruling.**

2. ARTICLES AND COMMENTS: Alexander and Grabandt, 'National Courts Entitled to Ask Preliminary Rulings under Article 177 of the EEC Treaty: The Case Law of the Court of Justice' (1982) 19 *CML Rev.* 413; Arnull, 'Article 177 and the Retreat from Van Duyn' (1983) 8 *EL Rev.* 365; Barav, 'Preliminary Censorship? The Judgment of the European Court in Foglia v Novello' (1980) 5 *EL Rev.* 443; Bebr, 'Article 177 of the EEC Treaty in the Practice of National Courts' (1977) 26 *ICLQ* 241; id., 'The Existence of a Genuine Dispute: An Indispensable Precondition for the Jurisdiction of the Court under Article 177 EEC Treaty?' (1980) 17 *CML Rev.* 525; id., 'The Possible Implications of Foglia v. Novello II' (1982) 19 *CML Rev.* 421; id., 'Arbitration Tribunals and Article 177 of the EEC Treaty' (1985) 22 *CML Rev.* 489; Collins, 'Article 177 of the EEC Treaty and English Interlocutory Proceedings' (1974) 23 *ICLQ* 840; Crisham and Mortelmans, 'Observations of Member States in the Preliminary Rulings Procedure before the Court of Justice of the European Communities', in O'Keeffe and Schermers (eds.), *Essays in European Law and Integration* (1982), p. 43; Editorial, 'Article 177 EEC and the Obligation to Refer' (1983) 8 *EL Rev.* 81; Everling, 'The Member States of the European Community before their

451

Court of Justice' (1984) 9 *EL Rev.* 215; Gray, 'Advisory Opinions and the European Court of Justice' (1983) 8 *EL Rev.* 24; Jacobs, 'When to Refer to the European Court' (1974) 90 *LQR* 486; id., 'Jurisdiction and Procedure in Preliminary Rulings' (1975–6) 1 *EL Rev.* 391; id., 'Which Courts and Tribunals are Bound to Refer to the European Court?' (1977) 2 *EL Rev.* 119; Mok, 'The Interpretation by the European Court of Justice of Special Conventions Concluded between the Member States' (1971) 8 *CML Rev.* 485; Mortelmans, 'Observations in the Cases Governed by Article 177 of the EEC Treaty: Procedure and Practice' (1979) 16 *CML Rev.* 557; O'Keeffe, 'Appeals against an Order to Refer under Article 177 of the EEC Treaty' (1984) 9 *EL Rev.* 87; Wyatt, 'Following up Foglia: Why the Court is Right to Stick to its Guns' (1981) 6 *EL Rev.* 447. *See also under* **Preliminary ruling.**

▶ **REGULATION** One of the binding acts which the Council and the Commission may adopt under the EEC/Euratom Treaties within the scope of secondary legislation.

In the system of those Treaties, regulations represent the main form of Community legislation and are, therefore, the most important source of secondary Community law. Thus, it is mainly (although not exclusively) regulations which are used to implement the EEC Treaty in the fields, amongst other things, of customs duties and the Common Customs Tariff (Arts. 20, 23(3), 28 EEC), agriculture (Art. 43(2) EEC), free movement of workers (Arts. 48(3) and 49 EEC), social security (Art. 51 EEC), transport (Arts. 75 and 79 EEC), competition (Art. 87(1) EEC), authorization of State aids (Art. 94 EEC), etc. On account of their legislative character, EEC/Euratom regulations largely correspond to general decisions under the ECSC Treaty.

The Treaties define a regulation thus: 'A regulation shall have general application. It shall be binding in its entirety and directly applicable in all Member States' (Arts. 189 EEC, 161 Euratom). It follows from this definition that a regulation has four characteristic features, i.e. it is:

- of general application;
- binding in its entirety;
- directly applicable; and
- applicable in all Member States.

To these two more features must be added which arise from the case-law of the ECJ. Accordingly, a regulation also:

- may produce direct effect; and
- enjoys supremacy over national law.

These characteristics are further considered below.

I. General application

This is what distinguishes a regulation from a decision. According to the ECJ, 'the essential characteristics of a decision arise from the limitation of the persons to whom it is addressed, whereas a regulation, being essentially of a legislative nature, is applicable not to a limited number of persons, defined or identifiable, but to categories of persons viewed abstractly and in their entirety . . . A measure which is applicable to objectively determined situations and which involves immediate legal consequences in all Member States for categories of persons viewed in a general and abstract manner cannot be considered as constituting a decision . . .' (Cases 16 and 17/62 *Producteurs de Fruits* v. *Council* [1962] ECR 471 at pp. 478–9. This definition has been repeated by the Court in a number of subsequent cases, some of which are cited below). 'Moreover, a measure does not lose its character as a regulation simply because it may be possible to ascertain with a greater or lesser degree of accuracy the number or even the identity of the persons to which it applies at any given time as long as there is no doubt that the measure is applicable as the result of an objective situation of law or of fact which it specifies and which is in harmony with its ultimate objective. Furthermore, the fact that a legal provision may have different practical effects on the different persons to whom it applies in no way contradicts its nature as a regulation provided that the situation to which it refers is objectively determined' (Case 6/68 *Zucker-fabrik Watenstedt* v. *Council* [1968] ECR 409 at p. 415; Case 101/76 *Koninklijke Scholten-Honig* v. *Council and Commission* [1977] ECR 797 at p. 808; etc.). 'It is . . . in the nature of a general provision that when uniformly applied it may affect persons concerned in different ways according to their particular situation or activities' (Case 63/69 *Compagnie Française Commerciale* v. *Commission* [1970] ECR 205 at p. 211).

The distinction between regulations and decisions is of primary importance in the context of an action for annulment under Arts. 173 EEC, 146 Euratom. Private individuals may only challenge acts of the institutions which are decisions (or produce similar effects), while they have no *locus standi* to institute annulment proceedings against regulations.

II. Binding in its entirety

This is what distinguishes a regulation from a directive. The ECJ has interpreted the meaning of this term thus: 'Under the terms of Article 189, the Regulation is binding "in its entirety" for Member States. In consequence, it cannot be accepted that a Member State should apply in an incomplete or selective manner provisions of a Community Regulation so as to render abortive certain aspects of Community legislation which it has opposed or which it considers contrary to its national interests. In particular, as regards the putting into effect of a measure of economic policy . . . the Member State which omits to take, within the requisite time limits and simultaneously with the other Member States, the measures which it ought to take, undermines the efficacy of the provision decided upon in common, while at the same time taking an undue advantage to the detriment of its partners . . . The objective scope of rules laid down by the common institutions cannot be modified by reservations or objections which Member States have made at the time the rules were being formulated. In the same way, practical difficulties which appear at the stage when a Community measure has to be put into effect cannot permit a Member State unilaterally to opt out of observing its obligations' (Case 39/72 *Commission* v. *Italy* [1973] ECR 101 at p. 115, concerning grants for slaughtering cows; Case 128/78 *Commission* v. *United*

453

Kingdom [1979] ECR 419 at pp. 428–9, concerning tachographs. In both cases the Court held that by not taking the measures necessary to implement the respective regulations, the two Member States had failed to fulfil their obligations under the Treaty). Similarly, in the absence of a provision of Community law to the contrary, Member States may not have recourse to national measures capable of modifying the application of a regulation (Case 18/72 *Granaria* [1972] ECR 1163 at p. 1171).

III. Direct applicability

This is what distinguishes a regulation from an international agreement made under general international law. Unlike the latter, regulations are automatically, i.e. without national ratification or any other specific act of approval, confirmation, reception, transformation, etc., incorporated into the legal system of each Member State. As the ECJ has stated, 'According to the terms of Article 189 and 191 of the Treaty, Regulations are, as such, directly applicable in all Member States and come into force solely by virtue of their publication in the *Official Journal* of the Communities, as from the date specified in them, or in the absence thereof, as from the date provided in the Treaty. Consequently, all methods of implementation are contrary to the Treaty which would have the result of creating an obstacle to the direct effect of Community Regulations and of jeopardizing their simultaneous and uniform application in the whole of the Community' (Case 39/72 *Commission v. Italy*, above, at p. 114).

In Case 34/73 *Variola* [1973] ECR 981 at pp. 990–1, the ECJ was asked whether the provisions of a regulation could be introduced into the legal order of Member States by internal measures reproducing their contents in such a way that the subject-matter was brought under national law. The Court replied that 'The direct application of a Regulation means that its entry into force and its application in favour of or against those subject to it are independent of any measure of reception into national law. By virtue of the obligations arising from the Treaty and assumed on ratification, Member States are under a duty not to obstruct the direct applicability inherent in Regulations and other rules of Community law. Strict compliance with this obligation is an indispensable condition of simultaneous and uniform application of Community Regulations throughout the Community. More particularly, Member States are under an obligation not to introduce any measure . . . whereby the Community nature of a legal rule is concealed from those subject to it.' (This statement has been repeated by the Court in a number of subsequent cases, see e.g. Case 94/77 *Zerbone* [1978] ECR 99 at pp. 115–16.)

It follows from the concept of direct applicability that, in principle, regulations need no national implementing measures to be fully effective within the Member States. This is particularly so where the provisions of a regulation are drafted in peremptory terms, are clear and capable of direct application without difficulty (see e.g. Case 31/64 *Bertholet* [1965] ECR 81 at p. 86; Case 20/72 *Cobelex* [1972] ECR 1055 at pp. 1061–2). In fact, the Member States are precluded from taking steps, for the purpose of applying the regulation, which are intended to alter its scope or supplement its provisions (see e.g. Case 40/69 *Bollmann* [1970] ECR 69 at p. 79). Nevertheless, as the ECJ has emphasized in a number of cases, 'the fact that a regulation is directly applicable does not prevent the provisions of that regulation from empowering a Community institution or a Member State to take implementing measures. In the latter case the detailed rules for the exercise of that power are governed by the public law of the Member State in question; however, the direct applicability of the measure empowering the Member State to take the national measures in question will mean that the national courts may ascertain whether such national measures are in accordance with the content of the Community regulation . . . There is no incompatibility between the direct applicability of a Community regulation and the exercise of the power conferred on a Member State to take implementing measures on the basis of that regulation' (Case 230/78 *Eridania* [1979] ECR 2749 at pp. 2771–2. See also Case 31/78 *Bussone* [1978] ECR 2429 at pp. 2444–5).

In practice, there are a number of regulations which provide for further implementing measures to be taken by the Member States, particularly in those areas of Community law whose day-to-day operation is entrusted to them, such as the Common Agricultural Policy or the Common Customs Tariff. In these cases, Member States are under an obligation to adopt the necessary provisions (Art. 5 EEC; see e.g. Case 93/71 *Leonesio*, below, at p. 295). Implementation takes place with due respect for the forms and procedures of national law, and the Member States may choose the most appropriate measures. Nevertheless, the uniform application of Community law allows recourse to national rules only to the extent strictly necessary to carry out the regulations (see e.g. Case 39/70 *Fleischkontor* [1971] ECR 49 at p. 58; Cases 89/74, 18 and 19/75 *Arnaud* [1975] ECR 1023 at p. 1035).

IV. Applicable in all Member States

Community law requires the simultaneous and uniform application of regulations in all Member States, i.e. in the entire territory and *vis-à-vis* all the citizens of the Community. As institutional acts adopted on the basis of the Treaty, regulations apply in principle to the same geographical area as the Treaty itself, as that area may be constituted at any given time during their period of validity (Case 61/77 *Commission* v. *Ireland* [1978] ECR 417 at p. 446 concerning sea fisheries). Regulations must be drafted in the nine official languages of the Communities (Art. 4 of Reg. 1, *OJ Sp. Edn.* 1952–8, p. 59 as last amended by the Act of Accession 1985, Annex I, Part XVII). Save as otherwise expressly provided, they enter into force on the same date in all the Member States, which is the date specified in them or, in the absence thereof, the twentieth day following their publication (Arts. 191 EEC, 163 Euratom). By virtue of a rebuttable presumption, a regulation is to be regarded as published throughout the Community on the date borne by the issue of the *Official Journal* containing its text (Case 98/78 *Racke* [1979] ECR 69 at pp. 84–5). Member States are not permitted to vary the date on which a regulation is to enter into force and create rights in favour of individuals in their respective territories (Case 34/73 *Variola*, above, at p. 992). In general, Member States are precluded from adopting any method of implementation that would jeopardize the simultaneous and uniform application of regulations and would result in a different or discriminatory treatment of Community citizens according to national criteria (see e.g. Case 17/67 *Neumann* [1967] ECR 441 at p. 453; Case 39/70 *Fleischkontor*, above, at pp. 58–9; Case 39/72 *Commission* v. *Italy*, above, at p. 114). The national authorities may not, therefore, issue binding rules for the interpretation of regulations (see e.g. Case 40/69 *Bollmann*, above, at p. 80; Case 94/77 *Zerbone*, above, at p. 116).

V. Direct effect

The case-law of the ECJ shows that, in addition to certain provisions of the EEC Treaty, regulations too may produce direct effects within the Member States in the sense of directly creating rights and obligations for individuals enforceable in the national courts, in the legal relationships both between individuals and the Member States and between individuals themselves. The Court's view is, however, somewhat ambiguous on the question what causes a regulation to produce such effects. In a long line of cases the Court has stated that: '... by virtue of Article 189 regulations are directly applicable and therefore by virtue of their nature capable of producing direct effects ...' (Case 9/70 *Grad* [1970] ECR 825 at p. 837; Case 41/74 *Van Duyn* [1974] ECR 1337 at p. 1348; Case 148/78 *Ratti* [1979] ECR 1629 at p. 1641; etc.) or, by using a slightly different wording, that: 'Under the terms ... of Article 189 regulations "shall have general application" and "shall be ... directly applicable in all Member States". Therefore, by reason of their nature and their function in the system of the sources of Community law, regulations have direct effect and are as such, capable of creating individual rights which national courts must protect' (Case 43/71 *Politi* [1971] ECR 1039 at p. 1048; Case 34/73 *Variola*, above, at p. 990; Case 31/78 *Bussone*, above, at p. 2444; etc.). These statements clearly imply that the direct effect of a regulation results, first, from its direct applicability (which in turn results from Art. 189) and, secondly, from its very nature as a legislative measure. It would seem to follow that, since under Art. 189 every regulation is by definition a directly applicable legislative measure, every provision of every regulation must be capable of producing direct effects. This would suggest, at least, that there is a very close connection between direct applicability and direct effect since they must necessarily always go together.

There is, however, a second line of cases which would appear to imply that in the Court's opinion the two concepts are not only closely related but in fact identical. Thus, in Case 93/71 *Leonesio* [1972] ECR 287 at pp. 295–6 the Court stated that 'Community regulations become part of the legal system applicable within the national territory, which must permit the *direct effect provided for in Article 189* to operate in such a way that reliance thereon by individuals may not be frustrated by domestic provisions or practices. Budgetary provisions of a Member State cannot therefore hinder the *direct applicability* of a Community provision and *consequently of the exercise of individual rights created by such a provision*' (emphasis added). And in the operative part of the judgment, the Court made the following categorical statement: 'A Community regulation has direct effect and is, as such, capable of creating individual rights which national courts must protect'. In Case 83/78 *Redmond* [1978] ECR 2347 at p. 2373 the Court held that the provisions of a regulation '*are directly applicable and that as such they confer on individuals rights which the courts of Member States must protect*. This result flows . . . from Article 189 in the terms of which regulations are "directly applicable in all Member States"' (emphasis added). Similarly, in Case 222/82 *Lewis* [1983] ECR 4083 at p. 4125 the Court observed that the *direct effect* of certain agricultural regulations 'derives from the fact that, by virtue of Article 189 of the Treaty, regulations are *directly applicable*' (emphasis added).

As against this, in a third line of cases, the Court established the direct effect of a particular provision in a regulation only after examining it in the light of the usual criteria, i.e. whether it was clear, unconditional, and capable of being applied in the absence of an implementing measure. Thus, in Case 9/73 *Schlüter* [1973] ECR 1135 at p. 1158 the Court said in relation to a bound duty included in the Common Customs Tariff: '. . . this provision, having been incorporated into a Community Regulation, is capable of giving rise to rights of which parties may avail themselves in a court of law. It is itself clear and precise, and does not leave any margin of discretion to the authorities by whom it is to be applied.' In Case 94/77 *Zerbone*, above, at p. 116, the Court stated: 'Article 4(2) of Regulation No. 1013/71 [relating to the application of the monetary compensatory amounts to contracts concluded before 19 December 1971], understood in the light of the fifth recital in the preamble to the regulation, may be interpreted and applied by a court without it being necessary to adopt national legislative provisions for its interpretation. Accordingly the provisions of that article have a direct effect in every Member State and the courts of each Member State have the task . . . of deciding as to their application in all cases of dispute arising in that State.'

These cases would seem to lend support to the view put forward by A.-G. Warner in Case 31/74 *Galli* [1975] ECR 47 at p. 70, where he said that '. . . it does not follow [from Art. 189] that every provision of every Regulation confers rights on the citizens of Member States that they can rely upon in their national Courts. We are all familiar with national Statutes . . . some provisions of which impose obligations on the State or on public authorities without conferring personal rights on citizens. This must be so too in the case of Community Regulations. Their provisions can have direct effect, in the sense of conferring personal rights, capable of being upheld by national Courts, only in so far as they satisfy the familiar tests laid down by the Court, i.e. the tests of being clear and unconditional, and of requiring no further legislative action for their implementation.' (See also A.-G. Warner's opinion in Case 74/76 *Iannelli* [1977] ECR 557 at p. 583, and A.-G. Trabucchi's opinion in Case 2/73 *Geddo* [1973] ECR 865 at pp. 887–8. However, in both the *Galli* (at p. 64) and the *Geddo* (at p. 878) cases the ECJ simply stated,

457

without applying the usual tests, that the regulations in question were directly enforceable by the national courts in accordance with Art. 189.)

It is submitted, however, that there is no irreconcilable conflict between these apparently contradictory views of the relationship between direct applicability and direct effect. The solution seems to lie in regarding them as neither identical nor completely different but mutually complementary concepts, as the two sides of the same coin. Direct applicability concerns the way in which a regulation becomes operative in the Member States; here the regulation is looked at from the angle of the national authorities, including the courts, which have to apply it in practice. Direct effect concerns the way in which a regulation creates rights for individuals; here the regulation is viewed from the standpoint of the individual seeking to enforce his rights. It is clear that an individual will succeed in relying on a regulation only to the extent to which a court is capable of applying that regulation. Here the two concepts meet. By virtue of its direct applicability under Art. 189, a national court will generally be able to enforce the regulation except where the regulation itself, by an express provision or by implication, requires implementation by a Community institution or by a Member State. Whether, in doubtful cases, this is the position must be decided by using the familiar tests of direct effectiveness. Where a regulation or an individual provision of a regulation is not clear, not unconditional, and not capable of judicial application in the form in which it was adopted, an individual cannot derive rights from it until it has been properly implemented. Where the regulation so provides (expressly or by implication), it is a duty incumbent upon the institutions and/or the Member States, as the case may be, to take the requisite implementing measures.

VI. Supremacy

It follows from the fundamental principle of the supremacy of Community law as a whole and from the direct effect of regulations that the latter must enjoy the same primacy over the national laws of the Member States as directly effective provisions of the Treaty itself enjoy. As the ECJ has put it, 'The precedence of Community law is confirmed by Article 189, whereby a regulation "shall be binding" and "directly applicable in all Member States". This provision, which is subject to no reservation, would be quite meaningless if a State could unilaterally nullify its effects by means of a legislative measure which could prevail over Community law' (Case 6/64 *Costa* [1964] ECR 585 at p. 594). Accordingly, 'the effect of a regulation, as provided for in Article 189, is . . . to prevent the implementation of any legislative measure, even if it is enacted subsequently, which is incompatible with its provisions' (Case 43/71 *Politi*, above, at p. 1049; Case 84/71 *Marimex* [1972] ECR 89 at p. 96; Case 31/78 *Bussone*, above, at p. 2444). Or, to put it differently, 'a legislative provision of internal law could not be set up against the direct effect, in the legal order of Member States, of Regulations of the Community . . . without compromising the essential character of Community rules as such and the fundamental principle that the Community legal system is supreme'

(Case 34/73 *Variola*, above, at p. 992; see also Case 93/71 *Leonesio*, above, at pp. 295–6).

See also **Action for annulment, Decision, Direct applicability, Direct effect, Directive, Official languages, Publication, Secondary legislation, Statement of reasons, Supremacy of Community law.**

Further reading: Lauwaars, 'Implementation of Regulations by National Measures' (1983/1) *LIEI* 41. *See also under* **Secondary legislation.**

▶ **REPRESENTATION BEFORE THE ECJ** It is a mandatory requirement of Community law that parties to any action other than a reference for a preliminary ruling must be legally represented or assisted before the Court at all stages of the proceedings, whether written or oral. The same applies to interveners. In the case of individuals, the aim of this requirement is that 'there shall be submitted to the Court only legal opinions and explanations of fact which, having been *examined* by a lawyer are considered by him as fit to be put forward' (Case 108/63 *Merlini* v. *HA* [1965] ECR 1 at p. 16 *per* A.-G. Roemer).

However, different rules of representation apply to Member States and Community institutions, on the one hand, and to all other parties, on the other. The former must be represented by an agent appointed for each case, but the agent may be assisted by a lawyer entitled to practise before a court of a Member State or (under the EEC and Euratom Statutes only) by an adviser (Arts. 20 ECSC Statute, 17 EEC and Euratom Statutes). In this respect, the ECJ has stated that: 'As regards the manner in which the institutions intend to be represented or assisted before the Court the institutions are . . . free to decide whether they will have recourse to the assistance of a lawyer or to appoint as an agent either one of their officials or a person who is not a member of their staff' (Case 126/76—Costs *Dietz* v. *Commission* [1979] ECR 2131 at p. 2134).

Under the ECSC Statute (Art. 20), undertakings and all other natural or legal persons must be 'assisted' by a lawyer entitled to practise before a court of a Member State. In the absence, strictly speaking, of a requirement to be 'represented' (as opposed to 'assisted') by a lawyer, it is possible for natural persons not to be represented at all (see e.g. Case 20/65 *Collotti* v. *Court of Justice* [1965] ECR 847; Cases 19 and 65/63 *Prakash* v. *Commission* [1965] ECR 533), and for legal persons to be represented by whomever may legally represent them under their own national law (see e.g. Case 18/57 *Nold* v. *HA* [1959] ECR 41 at p. 49; Case 3/65 *Espérance-Longdoz* v. *HA* [1965] ECR 1065, where a Belgian *Société Anonyme* was represented by its general manager and secretary-general; Case 75/69 *Hake* v. *Commission* [1970] ECR 901, where a German company was represented by a 'partner having the sole right to represent the company'). However, in either case, there is the mandatory requirement that a private party must be 'assisted' by a lawyer, although it is not quite clear what precise meaning the ECSC Statute intended to assign to each of these two different terms (see the opinion of A.-G. Roemer in Case 18/57 *Nold* v. *HA*, above, at p. 59, who speaks of a general 'principle of the necessity of a lawyer' under the ECSC Statute, and the opinion of A.-G. Capotorti in Cases 220 and 221/78 *ALA and ALFER* v. *Commission* [1979] ECR 1693 at pp. 1701–2, who thought that applications commencing proceedings which were not signed by lawyers but by the legal representatives of the applicant companies—i.e. their managing director—were inadmissible).

Although under the EEC and Euratom Statutes (Art. 17) private parties must be 'represented' by a lawyer entitled to practise before a court of a Member State, and the possibility of their being 'assisted' is not explicitly mentioned, there are cases in which legal persons were represented by non-lawyers and assisted by lawyers (see e.g. Cases 106 and 107/63 *Toepfer* v. *Commission* [1965] ECR 405, where a German limited partnership was represented by its 'agent', and a German limited company by its managers, while they were both assisted by lawyers). Since, as will be seen below, in the case of private parties every procedural step, whether written or oral, must be taken by a lawyer, it seems of little importance whether the lawyer acts under the title of 'representation' or 'assistance'. Under all three Statutes, interveners are subject to the same rules of representation as the parties themselves (Art. 93(2) RP).

The question of who is a lawyer entitled to practise before a court of a Member State is to be determined in accordance with national law. It is also national rather than Community law that governs any question relating to the professional status of the lawyer, i.e. his admission to, or suspension or disbarment from, practice and the effect of these on the power to represent (see Case 18/57 *Nold* v. *HA*, above, at p. 49 *per Curiam*, pp. 59–62 *per* A.-G. Roemer). The lawyer is required to lodge at the Registry a certificate that he is entitled to practise before a court of a Member State (Arts. 38(3) and 40(1) RP). In addition, in the case of legal persons governed by private law, an application or defence must be accompanied by proof that the authority granted to the lawyer has been properly conferred on him by someone authorized for this purpose (Arts. 38(5) and 40(1) RP. In the absence of such proof, the application will be declared inadmissible, see Case 289/83 *GAARM* v. *Commission* [1984] ECR 2789 at pp. 2790–1). However, in the case of natural persons, this is not necessary since 'the lawyer acting for a party is required only to establish his professional status as a lawyer and is not required to produce a duly executed authority to act . . . subject to proof if challenged that he is so authorized' (Case 14/64 *Gualco* v. *Commission* [1965] ECR 51 at p. 57).

Legal representatives must have an address for service in Luxembourg as well as a person who is authorized and willing to accept service (Arts. 38(2) and 40(1) RP). University teachers being nationals of a Member State whose law accords them a right of audience have the same rights before the Court as are accorded to lawyers (Arts. 20 ECSC Statute, 17 EEC and Euratom Statutes). Agents, advisers, and lawyers enjoy before the Court such rights, immunities, privileges, and facilities as are necessary for the independent exercise of their duties and for the proper conduct of the proceedings. Advisers and lawyers are subject to the powers of the Court in respect of their conduct, including the power to exclude them from the proceedings (ibid. and

Arts. 32–6 RP; see e.g. Case 1/60 *FERAM* v. *HA* [1960] ECR 165 at p. 170, where the Court censured the offensive wording used in the application against the defendant. *See further under* **Privileges and immunities**).

As already pointed out, legal representation or assistance is mandatory at all stages of the proceedings. Thus, the original of every pleading must be signed by the party's agent or lawyer (Art. 37(1) RP), the only exception being an application for legal aid submitted prior to the commencement of the proceedings, which need not be made through a lawyer (Art. 76(2) RP). It would seem that the need for a pleading to be signed by an agent or a lawyer is more than merely a formal requirement; a statement which has been drafted by a party and submitted by the lawyer without having been examined by him will be inadmissible even if the lawyer has formally signed and adopted it as his own (Case 108/63 *Merlini* v. *HA*, above, at p. *9 per Curiam*, p. 16 *per* A.-G. Roemer). An application commencing proceedings or requesting the adoption of interim measures which has not been submitted through a lawyer is inadmissible, and this will entail the inadmissibility even of a simultaneous application for legal aid (Case 10/81 *Farrall* v. *Commission* [1981] ECR 717 at p. 718; Case 73/83 *Stavridis* v. *Parliament* [1983] ECR 3803). Although in Cases 220 and 221/78 *ALA and ALFER* v. *Commission*, above, at pp. 1701–2 A.-G. Capotorti expressed the opinion that such a defect could not be cured under Art. 38(7) RP—which in his opinion applied to formal defects only—in the two cases cited immediately above the applications were held inadmissible only after the applicants had been unable or unwilling to resubmit them through a lawyer following a request made to this effect by the Registrar under Art. 38(7) RP. This seems to indicate that an application might be put in order if it is caused to be lodged by a lawyer within the 'reasonable period' prescribed by the Registrar under Art. 38(7) RP. During the course of the oral procedure, a party may address the Court only through his agent, adviser, or lawyer (Arts. 28 ECSC Statute, 29 EEC Statute, 30 Euratom Statute, 58 RP).

So far as private parties are concerned, the rules discussed above do not apply to references for a preliminary ruling. In these proceedings, as regards the representation and attendance of the parties, the ECJ is required to take account of the rules of procedure of the national court or tribunal which made the reference (Art. 104(2) RP). This means that where a party is allowed to appear in person, or to be represented by a non-lawyer, before the national court, he may appear in person or be represented by a non-lawyer before the ECJ also (see e.g. Case 39/75 *Coenen* [1975] ECR 1547 at p. 1554, where Mr Coenen personally presented oral argument at the hearing before the Court). Conversely, where only a special category of lawyers has a right of audience before the referring court (e.g. barristers, *avocats*), only such lawyers may represent the party before the ECJ also.

See also **Costs, Legal aid, Privileges and immunities.**

Further reading: Lasok, *The European Court of Justice: Practice and Procedure* (1984), ch. 4; Usher, *European Court Practice* (1983), chs. 4 and 7.

461

Representatives of ▶
the Governments of
the Member States
meeting in Council

REPRESENTATIVES OF THE GOVERNMENTS OF THE MEMBER STATES MEETING IN COUNCIL Expression used to describe the meetings of the Representatives of the Member States of the European Communities when acting not as a Community institution but as an organ of the collectivity of the Member States. Although composed of the same persons as the Council of the Communities, this body must be legally distinguished from the latter. The Council is a Community institution whose functions, powers, and procedures are laid down in the Treaties. Its acts are the manifestation of the exercise of competences conferred on the Communities and in every respect form an integral part of secondary Community law. By contrast, the meetings of the Representatives are the setting in which the Governments of the Member States concert their activities and decide on principles and methods of co-operation and joint action. Their acts are the product of the exercise by the Member States of competences which remain vested in them. It follows that these acts do not fall within the scope of 'secondary legislation' but form a distinct, *sui generis* source of Community law. They are not designated as 'regulations', 'directives', or 'decisions', but are usually referred to as 'decisions and agreements adopted by the Representatives of the Governments of the Member States meeting in Council'. There is, however, no clear and consistent terminology. Thus, sometimes the terms 'resolution', 'declaration', 'protocol', etc. are used to stress the political and programme-setting rather than the legal nature of the act in question (see in general Case 22/70 *Commission* v. *Council* [1971] ECR 263 at pp. 273, 278 *per Curiam*; pp. 287–8 *per* A.-G. Dutheillet de Lamothe).

There are two main reasons why the Representatives of the Member States should act as an intergovernmental agency rather than as a Community institution. First, there are certain matters which the Treaties have deliberately left within the competence of the Member States and which are therefore beyond the Council's authority (e.g. the appointment of Judges, Advocates-General, the members, President, and Vice-Presidents of the Commission, amendment of the Treaties, designation of the location of the Community institutions; see Arts. 167, 216, and 236 EEC; 11, 14, 37 MT). Dealing with these matters, the Member States will not act 'within the Council' but (theoretically) as a separate body, although their actions are clearly based on the Treaties. The second reason is that, by virtue of the principle of 'conferred powers' (*compétences d'attribution, Enumerationsprinzip*), the Council may only exercise such powers as have been conferred upon it by the Treaties. Even although these include limited implied powers as well as the supplementary (or gap-filling) powers provided in Arts. 95(1) ECSC, 235 EEC, 203 Euratom, there is always a residue of matters, essential to the proper functioning of the Communities, which are beyond the authority of the Council acting under the Treaties. Short of Treaty amendment, which is a complex and exceptional procedure, the Council can deal with these matters only by drawing upon the reserved powers of the Member States. Nevertheless, where a matter falls within the proper authority of the Communities, in principle it should be dealt with by the Council as a Community institution and not as an agency of the Member States (see Case 22/70 *Commission* v. *Council*, above, at pp. 273, 278).

In addition, because of the sweeping frontiers between Community and Member State authority in certain areas, there are situations in which it is difficult to draw a sharp dividing line between the two and consequently there are matters which fall partly within both. In such cases, the two types of authority concentrated in the hands of one body complement one another and the necessary measure will be taken jointly by the Council and the Government Representatives of the Member States (see e.g. the Resolutions adopted by the Council and the Representatives of the Governments of the Member States on 22 Mar. 1971 and 21 Mar. 1972 concerning the establishment of an Economic and Monetary Union, *OJ Sp. Edn.* 2nd Ser. (IX), pp. 40, 65). While thus the Member States, acting through their Representatives meeting within the Council, may adopt measures beyond those authorized or envisaged by the Treaties, and may even bring new matters within the scope of Community law, they may not go so far as virtually to amend rules laid down in the Treaties. This can only be done by means of the amendment procedure carried out in accordance with Arts. 96 ECSC, 236 EEC, 204 Euratom (Case 43/75 *Defrenne* [1976] ECR 455 at p. 478).

The exact legal nature of the acts adopted by the Representatives within the Council is ambiguous. They lie on the borderline between Community law and public international law and may best be described as international agreements dealing with a Community-related subject-matter in a simplified form. Accordingly, they have in fact a dual character. In substance, they belong to Community law and form a source thereof. In form, they constitute international agreements between the Member States even when bearing the title of 'decision'. As such, they may be subject to ratification (in so far as they are intended to create legal effects) and their status is not essentially different from that of the other Community-related treaties concluded between the Member States (*see further under* **Community Treaties**, section II). Since they are not acts of a Community institution but of an intergovernmental agency, they are not subject to judicial review by the ECJ (Case 22/70 *Commission* v. *Council*, above, at pp. 273, 278 *per Curiam*, pp. 288–9, 294 *per* A.-G. Dutheillet de Lamothe). It would seem, however, that where an act is of the mixed type, i.e. jointly adopted by the Council and the Representatives of the Member States, or, to put it another way, where the Council has acted in both of its capacities as a Community institution and as an organ of the collectivity of the Member States, the ECJ will not refuse to give a preliminary ruling as to its interpretation (see e.g. Case 9/73 *Schlüter* [1973] ECR 1135 at p. 1161, where under Art. 177 EEC the Court interpreted the Res. of 22 Mar. 1971 referred to above). Whether the Court could also give a preliminary ruling in respect of the validity of such an act is doubtful as it is difficult to envisage how the Court could separate the Community law and the international law aspects of the act.

It may finally be noted that there does not seem to exist any overriding reason why the acts of the Government Representatives could not produce direct effects within the national legal systems (in the sense of creating

463

enforceable individual rights), provided that they are intended to produce binding legal effects, have been properly ratified where so required, and satisfy the general requirements of direct effect. This question has not, however, been positively decided by the ECJ to date. (In Case 9/73 *Schlüter*, above, at p. 1161 the Court held that the Res. of 22 Mar. 1971 could not create direct effects, not as a matter of principle but 'by reason of its contents', being a policy decision.)

See also **Action for annulment, Community law, Community Treaties, Council, Direct effect, Implied powers, Preliminary ruling, Secondary legislation, Supplementary powers.**

Further reading: Bebr, 'Acts of Representatives of the Governments of the Member States taken within the Council of Ministers of the European Communities' (1966) 14 *Sociaal-economische Wetgeving* 529; Mortelmans, 'The Extramural Meetings of the Ministers of the Member States of the Community' (1974) 11 *CML Rev.* 62. *See also under* **Secondary legislation.**

▶ *RES JUDICATA* Issue definitively decided by a court.

In a general sense, the concept of *res judicata* is used to describe both the finality and the binding force of judicial decisions. Thus, a judgment acquires the force of *res judicata* when it becomes final in a procedural sense, that is, when all ordinary avenues of appeal have been exhausted, exceptional review procedures not included. Since the ECJ is a single instance Court from which no appeal is possible, its judgments become final and therefore binding from the date of their delivery (Art. 65 RP).

A judgment which has thus become *res judicata* is also final in the substantive sense that the issues decided therein cannot be reopened in a subsequent case; they must be regarded as having been definitively settled. As the ECJ has stated, 'the force of *res judicata* prevents rights confirmed by a judgment of the Court from being disputed anew' (Cases 79 and 82/63 *Reynier* v. *Commission* [1964] ECR 259 at p. 266). Or, in the words of A.-G. Roemer, 'all the matters which were in dispute between the same parties in [the previous] proceedings cannot be the subject of a fresh judicial examination before the same court' (Cases 2 to 10/63 *San Michele* v. *HA* [1963] ECR 327 at p. 348; see also his opinion in Case 20/65 *Collotti* v. *Court of Justice* [1965] ECR 847 at p. 854). As a result, the ECJ is barred from entertaining an action or an argument which involves *res judicata*—a question which the Court can raise of its own motion (see Cases 29/63 etc. *Usines de la Providence* v. *HA* [1965] ECR 911 at p. 951 *per* A.-G. Roemer). Such an action or argument is inadmissible. Thus, where an action for the annulment of a Community act is dismissed by the Court, the act in question becomes definitive and the matter becomes *res judicata* as a result of the judgment, so that the legality of the same act can no longer be called in issue by the same party (Case 57/70 *Van Eick* v. *Commission* [1971] ECR 613 at p. 618; Case 263/82 *Klöckner-Werke* v. *Commission* [1983] ECR 4143 at p. 4158). Similarly, where an act is annulled in part only, the remaining parts are to be regarded as confirmed and to be treated as *res judicata*. If they are subsequently re-enacted as part of a new act, they can no longer be challenged for annulment (Case 14/64 *Gualco* v. *Commission* [1965] ECR 51 at p. 58).

In Community law, the finality of judgments and the force of *res judicata* may only be interfered with, and eventually destroyed, by means of two exceptional review procedures, i.e. revision and third party proceedings, and by an application to set aside a judgment by default. Because of the serious consequences involved, these procedures are subject to very strict conditions.

The concept of *res judicata* does not only refer to the finality of judgments, but also determines the scope of their binding force. In accordance with the common civil law traditions of the six original Member States, the binding force of the Court's judgments is strictly relative, and exists only in so far as there is an identity of parties, cause, and subject-matter (*inter easdem personas, ex eadem causa, de eadem re*). In other words, a judgment is binding only as between the parties (*inter partes*) and in respect of that particular case (see in particular the opinion of A.-G. Lagrange in Cases 28 to 30/62 *Da Costa* [1963] ECR 31 at pp. 41–4. In substance, the Court followed his opinion, ibid. at pp. 37–9). The judgment is also binding on the Court itself, but only within those limits. On the other hand, a judgment does not have the authority of *res judicata* where there is a change in any one of those three factors. Thus, a judgment is not binding—either on the Court or on the parties—in a subsequent case where

- although the legal issues (grounds of claim or *causa petendi*) are the same as in the previous case, the subject-matter (claim or *petitum*) and the parties are different (as e.g. in Cases 28 to 30/62 *Da Costa*, above);
- only the parties are different (as e.g. in Case 33/59 *Chasse* v. *HA* [1962] ECR 381 at pp. 392, 395 *per* A.-G. Lagrange; Case 46/64 *Schoffer* v. *Commission* [1965] ECR 811 at p. 820 *per* A.-G. Gand; Case 30/66 *Becher* v. *Commission* [1967] ECR 285 at p. 305 *per* A.-G. Gand; Cases 15 to 33/73 etc. *Schots-Kortner* v. *Council, Commission and Parliament* [1974] ECR 177 at p. 191);
- the parties are the same but the subject-matter is different (as e.g. in Cases 22 and 23/60 *Elz* v. *HA* [1961] ECR 181 at pp. 188–9 *per Curiam*, p. 195 *per* A.-G. Roemer; Cases 2 to 10/63 *San Michele* v. *HA*, above, at pp. 339–40 *per Curiam*, pp. 348–9 *per* A.-G. Roemer; Cases 29/63 etc. *Usines de la Providence* v. *HA*, above, at pp. 951–2 *per* A.-G. Roemer).

It is evident, however, that a judgment dismissing an application will constitute a serious obstacle to a favourable reception of any subsequent application by different parties, having the same subject-matter and based on the same grounds as the one already dismissed, in spite of the absence of *res judicata* in a strict sense (see Case 33/59 *Chasse* v. *HA*, above, at p. 390 *per Curiam*, p. 392 *per* A.-G. Lagrange; Cases 46 and 47/59 *Meroni* v. *HA* [1962] ECR 411 at p. 423; Case 30/66 *Becher* v. *Commission*, above, at p. 305 *per* A.-G. Gand).

There are only three exceptions to the strictly relative effects of *res judicata*. The first is where a judgment declares void an act of an institution in a direct

465

action for annulment (i.e. under Arts. 33, 34 and 37, 38 ECSC; 173, 174 EEC; 146, 147 Euratom). Such a declaration is said to have binding force *erga ommes*. As A.-G. Lagrange has pointed out, while in such an action 'the general principle of the *relative* authority of *res judicata* continues to apply where an application is dismissed, there is an exception in the case of annulments expressed to be "for all purposes" [i.e. *erga omnes*]' (Case 5/55 *ASSIDER* v. *HA* [1955] ECR 135 at p. 146. See also his opinion in Cases 28 to 30/62 *Da Costa*, above, at p. 41).

The second exception is that, although the Communities normally appear in cases before the Court through their institutions which are therefore the 'parties', a judgment given against an institution will be binding on the Community as a whole. As the Court has observed, 'since the Community is a single entity, it is inconceivable that a judgment of the Court which has the force of *res judicata* with regard to an institution ... should not have the same force with regard to the Community as a whole' (Cases 79 and 82/63 *Reynier* v. *Commission*, above, at p. 266).

The third exception is in the case of a judgment interpreting an earlier judgment. Since it is inevitable that the judgment giving the interpretation should have the same force of *res judicata* as the judgment interpreted (of which it must henceforth form part), it follows that 'an interpreting judgment is binding not only on the applicants but also on any other party, in so far as that party is affected by the passage in the judgment which the Court is asked to interpret or by a passage which is exactly similar thereto' (Cases 41, 43, and 44/73—Interpretation *S.A. Générale Sucrière* v. *Commission* [1977] ECR 445 at p. 464. Similar considerations apply, *mutatis mutandis*, to a judgment revising an earlier judgment). This exception is, however, more apparent than real. Since under Art. 102(1) RP an application for interpretation 'must be made against all the parties to the case in which the judgment was given', all these will automatically become parties to the interpretation proceedings and therefore bound by the interpreting judgment.

Finally, it should be stated that the *res judicata* effect of a judgment of the ECJ arises from the operative part (*dispositif*) which, in the case of doubt, must be interpreted or clarified in the light of the decisive grounds (*motifs*) on which it is based (see e.g. Case 5/55 *ASSIDER* v. *HA*, above, at p. 142 *per Curiam*, pp. 147–8 *per* A.-G. Lagrange; Case 14/64 *Gualco* v. *Commission*, above, at p. 64 *per* A.-G. Roemer; Case 111/63 *Lemmerz-Werke* v. *HA* [1965] ECR 677 at p. 717 *per Curiam*, p. 722 *per* A.-G. Roemer; Case 30/76 *Küster* v. *Parliament* [1976] ECR 1719 at p. 1726 *per Curiam*, p. 1731 *per* A.-G. Reischl; Case 135/77 *Bosch* [1978] ECR 855 at p. 859 *per Curiam*, p. 861 *per* A.-G. Warner). It follows that mere ancillary or subsidiary observations (*obiter dicta*) do not, strictly speaking, produce *res judicata* effects.

See also Action for annulment, *Causa petendi, Erga omnes* effect, *Functus officio, Inter partes* effect, Judgment, *Jurisprudence constante,* Obiter dictum, *Petitum,* Preliminary ruling, *Ratio decidendi, Stare decisis.*

Further reading: Toth, 'The Authority of Judgments of the European Court of Justice: Binding Force and Legal Effects' (1984) 4 *YEL* 1. *See also under* **European Court of Justice.**

▶ **RESOLUTION** 1. Act embodying the opinion of the European Parliament on legislative proposals submitted by the Commission to the Council in respect of which the Council is required to consult the Parliament before adopting the final measure (referred to as 'legislative resolution', see Rule 36 of the European Parliament's Rules of Procedure, 4th edn. (1987)). Such a resolution does not have binding effect (see Cases 87/77 etc. *Salerno* v. *Commission and Council* [1985] ECR 2523 at p. 2542).

2. Act which the European Parliament may adopt on its own initiative, by virtue of an 'inherent right', and which may deal with 'any question concerning the Communities' (Case 230/81 *Luxembourg* v. *Parliament* [1983] ECR 255 at p. 287; Rule 63 of Parliament's Rules of Procedure). Depending on its content, such a resolution may be 'of a specific and precise decision-making character, producing legal effect' and, as such, may be challenged for annulment before the ECJ (Case 108/83 *Luxembourg* v. *Parliament* [1984] ECR 1945 at p. 1958).

3. Act of the Council which, not being listed amongst the acts which the Council may adopt under the EEC and Euratom Treaties (see Arts. 189 EEC, 161 Euratom), can produce no binding effects. Such a resolution usually expresses the political will of the Council and, as such, cannot give rise to rights and obligations for individuals. Moreover, such a resolution cannot alter the scope of a provision in the Treaties (Case 59/75 *Manghera* [1976] ECR 91 at p. 102, dealing with Council Res. of 21 Apr. 1970 concerning national monopolies of a commercial character in manufactured tobacco).

4. Act of the Member States relating to a subject-matter falling within the scope of Community law. Such a resolution does not have binding effect in law and cannot modify provisions (e.g. time-limits) laid down in the Treaties (Case 43/75 *Defrenne* [1976] ECR 455 at p. 478 dealing with the Res. of the Member States of 30 Dec. 1961 on the equalization of rates of pay for men and women workers).

5. One of the acts which the Representatives of the Governments of the Member States may adopt either within the Council or acting jointly with the Council. It seems that, in the latter case, a resolution may be the subject of an interpretative preliminary ruling given by the ECJ under Art. 177 EEC. Where such a resolution contains a policy decision it cannot, by reason of its contents, create enforceable individual rights (Case 9/73 *Schlüter* [1973] ECR 1135 at p. 1161 dealing with the Res. of the Council and Government Representatives of 22 Mar. 1971 on the establishment by stages of an Economic and Monetary Union).

6. One of the acts which the European Council may adopt (see e.g. Res. of 5 Dec. 1978 on the establishment of the European Monetary System (EMS) and related matters, *Bull. EC* 12–1978, p. 10). A resolution of the European Council is given legal effect by means of implementing measures adopted by

the Community institutions in the framework of secondary legislation, in accordance with the substantive, procedural, and formal requirements of the Treaties (for the implementation and entry into force of the EMS, see *Bull. EC* 2–1979, p. 7. See also Part A, point 6, and Part B of the Res. of 5 Dec. 1978).

7. Act which the Economic and Social Committee and the ECSC Consultative Committee may adopt in addition to opinions (see e.g. 22nd *Gen. Rep. EC* (1988), pp. 43–4).

See also Council, European Council, European Parliament, Representatives of the Governments of the Member States meeting in Council, Secondary legislation.

▶ *RESTITUTIO IN INTEGRUM* Restoring the original legal position (status quo ante) which has been upset by an illegal act or omission. Thus, where the ECJ declares an act of an institution void, the duty of the institution 'to take the necessary measures to comply with the judgment of the Court' (Arts. 34 ECSC, 176 EEC, 149 Euratom) includes the obligation to bring about full *restitutio in integrum* in order to nullify the effects produced by the annulled act (Case 50/69R *Germany* v. *Commission* [1969] ECR 449 at p. 455 *per* A.-G. Gand; Case 4/69 *Lütticke* v. *Commission* [1971] ECR 325 at p. 343 *per* A.-G. Dutheillet de Lamothe; Case 22/70 *Commission* v. *Council* [1971] ECR 263 at pp. 278–9). A Member State is under a similar duty when the Court finds that it has failed to fulfil an obligation under the Treaties (Arts. 86 ECSC, 171 EEC, 143 Euratom, see Case 6/60 *Humblet* v. *Belgium* [1960] ECR 559 at p. 569).

While *restitutio in integrum* may involve the payment or repayment of sums of money, it must be clearly distinguished from compensation for damage. The former normally automatically follows a successful action for annulment or a judgment otherwise establishing the illegality of an act or omission, whereas the latter may only be claimed by an action for damages. The dividing line between compensation and *restitutio* corresponds to the distinction 'between the payment of a sum of money and the provision of a benefit of another sort, suitable to restore the property of the victim of the damage [restitution in kind] (for example the repair of the damaged object). There is no doubt that every form of compensation for damage serves to restore the property of the victim to the condition in which it would have been if the harmful act had not taken place; but the payment of a sum of money should always be regarded as compensation, even when the damage consisted in the denial of certain monetary amounts . . . [Furthermore] the claim for compensation is normally accompanied by a claim for interest' (Case 238/78 *Ireks-Arkady* v. *Council and Commission* [1979] ECR 2955 at p. 2983 *per* A.-G. Capotorti—'Quellmehl' case). In that case the applicants sought to recover certain production refunds which were wrongly denied them by a Council regulation. The Court, following the opinion of the Advocate-General, classified the claim not as one for *restitutio in integrum* but as one for compensation for damage caused by the absence of the refunds, and ordered the EEC to pay 'the amounts equivalent to the [unpaid] production refunds' with interest (ibid. at p. 2975). By contrast, 'one who seeks repayment of sums paid to national bodies by virtue of Community rules which are subsequently declared invalid is claiming only the right to restitution of undue payment' (and not compensation for damage) (Case 130/79 *Express Dairy Foods* [1980] ECR 1887 at p. 1906 *per* A.-G. Capotorti).

The importance of the above distinction is that individuals claiming payment or repayment of sums which the national authorities, acting under Community law, have improperly collected or withheld will be seeking *restitutio in integrum* and not compensation for damage. The proper remedy will be an action before the competent national courts for the annulment of the national measure ordering or denying the payment (which, if successful, will entail *restitutio in integrum*), and not an action for damages before the ECJ (ibid., see also in particular Case 96/71 *Haegeman* v. *Commission* [1972] ECR 1005 at pp. 1014–15; Case 46/75 *IBC* v. *Commission* [1976] ECR 65 at pp. 79–80; etc.).

In the case of a contractual relationship under private law, when a contract is terminated 'the parties must be restored to the position in which they would have been if they had never entered into the contract. The meaning of the principle of *restitutio ad integrum* is that the parties are under an obligation to return whatever they have received from one another. That obligation extends not only to the asset or sum of money received but also to any yield from that asset or interest generated by the sum received since payment thereof' (Case 426/85 *Commission* v. *Zoubek* [1986] ECR 4057 at p. 4068, dealing with a contract between the Commission and an individual).

See also **Action against Member States, Action for annulment, Action for damages, Damage, Recovery of undue payments*, Unjust enrichment.**

▶ **RETROACTIVE EFFECT** Effect of a legal provision upon acts, events, situations, or legal relationships which occurred or arose before the entry into force of that provision.

In examining the extent to which Community law permits or prohibits retroactivity, a distinction must be made between (1) the provisions of the basic Community Treaties; (2) those of the acts of the institutions; and (3) the judgments of the ECJ.

1. *Community Treaties*. In accordance with a general principle of public international law, incorporated in Art. 28 of the Vienna Convention on the Law of Treaties of 1969, in the absence of an intention or provision to the contrary, treaties do not have retroactive effect. In the words of Art. 28, the provisions of a treaty 'do not bind a party in relation to any act or fact which took place or any situation which ceased to exist before the date of the entry into force of the treaty with respect to that party'. Although, by virtue of its own non-retroactivity, the Vienna Convention itself does not apply to the basic Community Treaties, the principle of non-retroactivity incorporated in it does (see Art. 4 of the Convention). Consequently, in their legal relationships arising under public international law, the Member States are in principle not bound by the basic Community Treaties in respect of

469

pre-existing acts or facts (see also Arts. 234 EEC, 105–6 Euratom. *See further under* **Community Treaties**, section II).

2. *Acts of the institutions.* The Community Treaties contain no provisions expressly permitting or prohibiting the retroactive application of acts of the institutions. While the national laws of the Member States generally prohibit the retroactivity of criminal law, there are no express provisions in their Constitutions limiting the extent to which legislation may be retroactive in the field of civil law. Although, therefore, in all the Member States Parliament is free to legislate retroactively in civil matters, there is a presumption against its doing so. A statute will accordingly be held to have retroactive effect only where its terms so require either expressly or by necessary implication (see the opinion of A.-G. Warner in Case 7/76 *IRCA* [1976] ECR 1213 at pp. 1236–8).

In Community law, the principles developed by the ECJ in relation to retroactivity are complex. This is due to a number of factors, the most important of which is the distinction made between retroactive effect *stricto sensu* (the application of a provision to a 'closed' situation, i.e. one which was completed or ceased to have effects before the entry into force of the provision) and what may be called 'apparent' or 'false' retroactivity (the immediate application of a new provision to a pre-existing situation which continues to produce legal consequences in the future, see the opinions of A.-G. Dutheillet de Lamothe in Case 37/70 *Rewe-Zentrale* [1971] ECR 23 at p. 45 and in Case 62/70 *Bock* v. *Commission* [1971] ECR 897 at pp. 915–16 and the opinion of A.-G. Reischl in Case 108/81 *Amylum* v. *Council* [1982] ECR 3107 at p. 3142). Moreover, different considerations apply depending on the nature of the provision in question (whether it is a legislative or an implementing measure); its contents (whether it lays down substantive rules or relates to procedure and jurisdiction); its relationship to other provisions (whether it is a single provision or one of a series of successive provisions; whether it introduces new legislation or merely amends or interprets an existing one); its objectives, wording, and scheme; the purpose of its authors; etc. The rules and principles developed by the ECJ on retroactivity may be summarized as follows.

(*a*) In principle, the institutions are free to determine the date on which their acts enter into force (Arts. 15 ECSC, 191 EEC, 163 Euratom). However, in the case of regulations, this date may not be earlier than the day of their actual publication in the *Official Journal* so that a regulation cannot normally produce legal effects in respect of events taking place on the day prior to its actual publication (Case 88/76 *Exportation des Sucres* v. *Commission* [1977] ECR 709 at p. 726). In case of doubt, the date of 'actual publication' is the date on which the relevant issue of the *Official Journal* is in fact available to the public in all the official languages at the Office for Official Publications in Luxembourg, since 'a fundamental principle in the Community legal order requires that a measure adopted by the public authorities shall not be applicable to those concerned before they have the opportunity to make themselves acquainted with it' (Case 98/78 *Racke* [1979] ECR 69 at p. 84).

(*b*) While Community law permits regulations to enter into force on the day of their actual publication in the *Official Journal* and thus to produce immediate legal effects, the ECJ has stated that 'an institution cannot, without having an adverse effect on a legitimate regard for legal certainty, resort without reason to the procedure of an immediate entry into force' (Case 17/67 *Neumann* [1967] ECR 441 at p. 456). Such a procedure is justified only where there are 'serious reasons for holding that any interval between the publication and the entry into force of the regulation might . . . have been prejudicial to the Community' (ibid.; Case 57/72 *Westzucker* [1973] ECR 321 at p. 342). A regulation which enters into force immediately does not have retroactive effect *stricto sensu* in so far as 'any transaction which had already taken place and been executed at the moment of its entry into force would be excluded from its application' (Case 17/67 *Neumann*, above, at p. 436; Case 74/74 *CNTA* v. *Commission* [1975] ECR 533 at p. 548).

(*c*) Nor is there, in the opinion of the ECJ, genuine retroactive effect where the provisions of a regulation which take effect immediately upon entry into force 'determine in the present legal consequences of actions in the past' (Case 44/65 *Hessische Knappschaft* [1965] ECR 965 at p. 972). Thus, the Court has confirmed that events occurring before the entry into force of a social security regulation (e.g. an accident) may, once the regulation has entered into force, give rise to the rights and obligations provided for therein (ibid.).

(*d*) The above considerations apply, *a fortiori*, to amending legislation. Thus, in a long line of cases, interpreting the effects of amendments first to social security and later to agricultural regulations, the Court has repeatedly relied on the 'generally accepted principle' that 'amending legislation applies, except where otherwise provided, to the effects in the future of situations which have arisen under the law as it stood before amendment' (Case 68/69 *Bundesknappschaft* [1970] ECR 171 at p. 178; Case 1/73 *Westzucker* [1973] ECR 723 at p. 729; Case 143/73 *SOPAD* [1973] ECR 1433 at p. 1441; etc. In the last two cases the Court held that the amendment of an agricultural regulation applied not only to advance-fixing certificates issued after its entry into force but also to those certificates issued before the amendment inasmuch as the intended transaction—i.e. exportation—had not yet taken place. See also Case 7/76 *IRCA*, above, at p. 1228, where it was held that the fixing of monetary compensatory amounts for periods which had already come to an end at the time when the fixing took place could not be described as retroactive application). However, the application of this principle is subject to the rule that the amendment of a regulation with retroactive effect cannot prejudice entitlement to a right (*in casu*: a social security benefit) acquired before the publication of the amending regulation (Case 100/63 *Kalsbeek* [1964] ECR 565 at p. 575; see also Case 84/81 *Staple Dairy Products* [1982] ECR 1763 at pp. 1778–9). Nor can, in the absence of a valid provision to the contrary, repeal of a regulation entail the abolition of the individual rights which it has created (Case 34/73 *Variola* [1973] ECR 981 at p. 991).

(*e*) As regards retroactive effect *stricto sensu* (i.e. the application of a provision to situations and transactions which were fully completed before its entry into force, and not merely to their future consequences), initially the ECJ stated in categorical terms that a regulation which is 'of a legislative nature . . . cannot have retroactive effect'. Such a regulation cannot be applied, for example, for the purpose of determining the classification of products imported before its entry into force (Case 30/71 *Siemers* [1971] ECR 919 at p. 928; Case 77/71 *Gervais-Danone* [1971] ECR 1127 at p. 1137; Case 158/78 *Biegi* [1979] ECR 1103 at p. 1119; see also Case 104/76 *Jansen* [1977] ECR 829 at p. 840, where it was held that Art. 10(2) of Reg. 1408/71 on the reimbursement of social security contributions 'cannot be extended to facts which occurred outside the period covered by the regulation').

(*f*) Subsequently, however, the Court subjected the above rule to certain exceptions. Thus, in Case 98/78 *Racke*, above, at p. 86 the Court stated, for the first time, that 'although in general the principle of legal certainty precludes a Community measure from taking effect from a point in time before its publication, it may exceptionally be otherwise where the purpose to be achieved so demands and where the legitimate expectations of those concerned are duly respected'. In that case the Court confirmed the applicability of newly fixed monetary compensatory amounts to facts and events which had occurred during a period of two weeks before the actual publication of the relevant regulation in the *Official Journal* (see also Case 99/78 *Decker* [1979] ECR 101 at p. 111). Subsequently, the Court applied the principle laid down in these cases to a variety of situations, accepting retroactivity as lawful only where the two conditions specified were found to have been fulfilled (see e.g. Case 258/80 *Rumi* v. *Commission* [1982] ECR 487 at p. 503; Case 276/80 *Padana* v. *Commission* [1982] ECR 517 at p. 541; Case 84/81 *Staple Dairy Products*, above, at pp. 1777–9; Case 235/82 *Ferriere San Carlo* v. *Commission* [1983] ECR 3949 at pp. 3965–6). Where the conditions were not fulfilled, the measure concerned was declared invalid to the extent to which it produced retroactive effects (see e.g. Case 224/82 *Meiko-Konservenfabrik* [1983] ECR 2539 at pp. 2548–50). Relying on the same principle and applying the same tests, the Court upheld the legality of the retroactive reinstatement by the institutions of measures—whether general or individual—previously annulled by the Court on the grounds of procedural defects (as opposed to substantive illegality), once those defects had been rectified (Case 108/81 *Amylum* v. *Council* [1982] ECR 3107 at pp. 3130–4; Case 110/81 *Roquette* v. *Council* [1982] ECR 3159 at pp. 3178–82; Case 114/81 *Tunnel Refineries* v. *Council* [1982] ECR 3189 at pp. 3206–10—'Isoglucose' cases).

(*g*) In a second line of cases, in determining the effect *ratione temporis* of Community acts, the Court had recourse to 'generally recognised principles of interpretation' and formulated exceptions to the rule of non-retroactivity in the following terms: 'Although procedural rules are generally held to apply to all proceedings pending at the time when they enter into force, this is not the case with substantive rules. On the contrary, the latter are usually interpreted as applying to situations existing before their entry into force only in so far as it clearly follows from their terms, objectives or general scheme that such an effect must be given to them. This interpretation ensures respect for the principles of legal certainty and the protection of legitimate expectation . . . [Where a] regulation contains both procedural and substantive rules which form an indivisible whole and the individual provisions of which may not be considered in isolation, with regard to the time at which they take effect . . . [it] may not be accorded retroactive effect unless sufficiently clear indications lead to such a conclusion . . . [This is not the case where] far from indicating any retroactive effect, both the wording and the general scheme of the regulation lead to the conclusion that the regulation provides only for the future' (Cases 212 to 217/80 *Salumi* [1981] ECR 2735 at pp. 2751–2; see also Case 21/81 *Bout* [1982] ECR 381 at p. 390; Case 113/81 *Reichelt* [1982] ECR 1957 at p. 1965; etc.). These principles apply regardless of whether retroactive application of a regulation might produce favourable or un-favourable effects for the persons concerned (Case 234/83 *Gesamthochschule Duisburg* [1985] ECR 327 at p. 341). It follows from these cases that where a regulation does not expressly provide for its own retroactivity, the question whether it may legitimately have such effects becomes one of its interpretation.

(*h*) Purely interpretative provisions may have retroactive effect in that they may be relevant to the interpretation of other provisions adopted earlier, with regard to facts which arose when the earlier provisions were in force, provided that they have not modified the substance of those earlier provisions (Case 183/73 *Osram* [1974] ECR 477 at p. 485; Cases 36 and 37/76 *Foral* [1976] ECR 2009 at pp. 2018–21; Case 234/83 *Gesamthochschule Duisburg*, above, at pp. 340–1).

(*i*) None of the exceptions to the rule of non-retroactivity may apply in the field of criminal law. Thus, the ECJ has pointed out in clear terms that, quite irrespective of the general legality or otherwise of the retroactive effect of a regulation, 'such retroactivity may not, in any event, have the effect of validating *ex post facto* national measures of a penal nature which impose penalties for an act which, in fact, was not punishable at the time at which it was committed. That would be the case where at the time of the act entailing a criminal penalty, the national measure was invalid because it was in-compatible with Community law. The principle that penal provisions may not have retroactive effect [*nullum crimen, nulla poena, sine lege*] is one which is common to all the legal orders of the Member States and is enshrined in Article 7 of the European Convention for the Protection of Human Rights and Fundamental Freedoms as a fundamental right; it takes its place among the general principles of law whose observance is ensured by the Court of Justice' (Case 63/83 *Kirk* [1984] ECR 2689 at p. 2718).

(*j*) While the above principles have been developed by the ECJ mainly in relation to general—law-making—measures, similar considerations would seem to apply to individual decisions also. Thus, exceptionally, the Court upheld the validity of Commission decisions retroactively authorizing Germany to take certain protective measures with effect from a date earlier than the date of the decisions and their publication in the *Official Journal*. The justification was that the protective measures would not have been capable of attaining their objectives fully if they had not been applicable from the date of the event which had given rise to them (Case 37/70 *Rewe-Zentrale*, above, at

p. 36). Nevertheless, such retroactive authorization is invalid if it is not absolutely necessary in order to attain the end pursued (Case 62/70 *Bock* v. *Commission*, above, at pp. 909–10 *per Curiam*, pp. 915–16 *per* A.-G. Dutheillet de Lamothe; Case 29/75 *Kaufhof* v. *Commission* [1976] ECR 431 at p. 443). The Court has also held that 'the retroactive withdrawal of a legal [i.e. lawful] measure which has conferred individual rights or similar benefits is contrary to the general principles of law' (Cases 42 and 49/59 *SNUPAT* v. *HA* [1961] ECR 53 at p. 78), adding that 'retroactive withdrawal is generally accepted in cases in which the administrative measure in question has been adopted on the basis of false or incomplete information provided by those concerned' (ibid. at p. 87; see also Case 14/61 *Hoogovens* v. *HA* [1962] ECR 253 at pp. 267–75).

On the other hand, there seems to be no valid objection to Community acts which confer rights or benefits on those concerned having retroactive effect. Certain decisions (and even regulations) of the Commission in the field of competition law may lawfully have retroactive effect, e.g. those granting individual or group exemptions from the prohibition laid down in Art. 85(1) EEC (see e.g. Arts. 6 and 7 of Reg. 17; Arts. 3 and 4 of Reg. 19/65; Arts. 3 and 4 of Reg. 2821/71; Arts. 6–8 of Reg. 2349/84; Arts. 7–9 of Reg. 123/85; Art. 11 of Reg. 418/85; Arts. 4(3) and 5(4) of Reg. 3975/87). Such decisions may even be revoked with retroactive effect on certain specified grounds, e.g. where they are based on incorrect information or were induced by deceit (see e.g. Art. 8(3) of Reg. 17; Arts. 5(3) and 6(3) of Reg. 3975/87).

3. *Judgments of the ECJ.* The judgments of the Court are binding from the date of their delivery (Art. 65 RP), and normally produce legal effects for the future only. However, the following three categories of judgment are regarded as having retroactive effect going back in time to the coming into force of the provision to which they relate:

(*a*) judgments given in direct actions for annulment declaring an act of an institution void (under Arts. 33, 34 and 37, 38 ECSC; 173, 174 EEC; 146, 147 Euratom);
(*b*) judgments given in reference proceedings for a preliminary ruling declaring an act of an institution invalid (under Arts. 41 ECSC, 177 EEC, 150 Euratom);
(*c*) interpretative judgments, and in particular interpretative preliminary rulings (under Arts. 177 EEC, 150 Euratom).

See also **Action for annulment, Continuity of the legal system, Exemption*, General principles of law, Legal certainty, Legitimate expectation, Notification, Preliminary ruling, Publication, Vested rights.**

Further reading: Koopmans, 'Retrospectivity Reconsidered' (1980) 39 *Cambridge Law J.* 287; Lamoureux, 'The Retroactivity of Community Acts in the Case Law of the Court of Justice' (1983) 20 *CML Rev.* 269; Waelbroeck, 'May the Court of Justice Limit the Retrospective Operation of its Judgments?' (1981) 1 *YEL* 115. *See also under* **General principles of law.**

▶ **REVISION OF JUDGMENTS** One of two 'exceptional review procedures' available before the ECJ (the other being third party proceedings) and, apart from proceedings for setting aside a judgment by default, the only procedure whereby a party may seek to have a judgment, rendered in a direct action, reviewed by the Court.

An application for revision of a judgment may be made to the Court only on discovery of a fact which is of such a nature as to be a decisive factor and which, when the judgment was given, was unknown to the Court and to the party claiming the revision (Arts. 38 ECSC Statute, 41 EEC Statute, 42 Euratom Statute, 98–100 RP). The ECJ has stated that:

The prerequisite for this is the fulfilment of three conditions. The first of these conditions is the total absence of knowledge on the part of the Court and the applicant of the existence of a fact prior to the delivery of judgment; this requirement is not therefore satisfied if the fact in question has been referred to in any manner, or simply known even if not expressly referred to in the course of the proceedings; prior knowledge of the fact, whether or not fortuitous and, *a fortiori*, the assessment of its importance by the Court, do not therefore constitute a factor making possible an application for revision, which is an exceptional procedure depending on strict requirements and not a means of appeal. The second condition is the requirement of priority in time; at the time of the delivery of judgment the Court must have been unaware of a fact already in existence. Finally, the third condition requires that the unknown fact should have been of such a nature as to be a decisive factor as regards the outcome of the case, in other words, it must be capable of altering the decision of the Court of which revision is sought. The strictness of these conditions . . . may be understood in consideration of the fact that revision defeats the force of *res judicata* . . . (Case 116/78 Rev. *Bellintani* v. *Commission* [1980] ECR 23 at pp. 26–7; see also Case 267/80 Rev. *Riseria Modenese* v. *Council, Commission and Birra Peroni* [1985] ECR 3499 at p. 3504.)

It follows from the foregoing that an application for revision will be dismissed as inadmissible where the fact relied on was known either to the party (see e.g. Case 56/70 *Mandelli* v. *Commission* [1971] ECR 1 at p. 4) or to the Court (see e.g. Case 1/60 *FERAM* v. *HA* [1960] ECR 165 at pp. 169–70) or to both (see e.g. Case 56/75 Rev. *Elz* v. *Commission* [1977] ECR 1617 at p. 1621; Case 285/81 Rev. I and Rev. II *Geist* v. *Commission* [1984] ECR 1789 at pp. 1794–5); where it could not have had a decisive effect on the outcome of the case (ibid. at p. 1794; see also Case 28/64 Rev. *Müller* v. *Council* [1967] ECR 141 at p. 145; Case 40/71 *Richez-Parise* v. *Commission* [1972] ECR 73 at p. 80; Case 37/71 Rev. *Jamet* v. *Commission* [1973] ECR 295 at p. 299; Case 107/79 Rev. *Schuerer* v. *Commission* [1983] ECR 3805 at p. 3808; etc.) or where the applicant, without alleging any new fact, seeks in reality, by the expedient of the procedure for revision, to reopen the previous judgment contrary to the rule of *res judicata* (Case 115/73 Rev. *Serio* v. *Commission* [1974] ECR 671 at p. 673; Case 13/69 *Van Eick* v. *Commission* [1970] ECR 3 at p. 13; as to what may or may not constitute a 'new fact', see also Case 116/78 Rev. *Bellintani* v. *Commission*, above, at pp. 27–8).

An application for revision must be made within three months of the discovery of the fact on which it is based (Art. 98 RP; for a strict application of this time-limit, see Case 40/71 *Richez-Parise* v. *Commission*, above, at p. 80). No application may be made after the lapse of ten years from the date of the judgment. The application must be made against all the parties to the original case (which, by analogy with third party proceedings and interpretation of judgments, must be taken to include interveners) and in the form prescribed for pleadings and applications originating proceedings in general (see Arts. 37 and 38 RP). It must specify the judgment contested as well as the points on which it is contested, together with all supporting facts and evidence (Art. 99 RP).

The Court must first decide on the admissibility of the application by means of a separate preliminary judgment which, if the application is found admissible, will be followed by a further judgment on the merits of the case in accordance with the Rules of Procedure. The original of the revising judgment will be annexed to the original of the judgment revised (Arts. 38 ECSC Statute, 41 EEC Statute, 42 Euratom Statute, 100 RP; see also Case 116/78 Rev. *Bellintani* v. *Commission*, above, at p. 27). Since all the parties to the original case are involved, it is inevitable that the revising judgment should have the same force of *res judicata* as the judgment revised, of which it must henceforth form part. By analogy with an interpreting judgment, a revising judgment is therefore binding not only on the applicant but also on any other party affected by the passage revised (see Cases 41, 43, and 44/73—Interpretation *S.A. Générale Sucrière* v. *Commission* [1977] ECR 445 at p. 464; see also Case 5/55 *ASSIDER* v. *HA* [1955] ECR 135 at p. 149 *per* A.-G. Lagrange. Both cases involved interpretation of judgments).

See also **Interpretation of judgments, Judgment, Judgment by default, Order, Res judicata, Special forms of procedure, Third party proceedings.**

Further reading: Lasok, *The European Court of Justice: Practice and Procedure* (1984), ch. 12, s. VI; Usher, *European Court Practice* (1983), ch. 8, paras. 8–31 *et seq.*

▶ **RIGHT OF ACTION (*LOCUS STANDI*)** The right to institute proceedings before the ECJ.

In the system of Community law, a right of action exists only if it has been specifically granted by an express provision of the Community Treaties or related instruments conferring jurisdiction upon the ECJ. The existence of a right of action in any particular case depends on two circumstances, i.e. on the person of the applicant and on the form of action contemplated. Generally speaking, such a right is granted only to the subjects of Community law, that is, to the Community institutions, the Member States, and natural or legal persons. Third countries and international organizations do not *ipso jure* enjoy a right of action before the ECJ (see Cases 21 to 24/72 *International Fruit Company* [1972] ECR 1219 at p. 1234 *per* A.-G. Mayras), although such right may be extended to them exceptionally, e.g. by virtue of an arbitration clause or an international agreement.

The right of action of Community institutions and Member States is subject to broadly similar conditions, but that of natural or legal persons (i.e. private individuals and corporations) is in general more restricted and the nature and scope of the restriction varies under the three basic Treaties and also as between the different forms of action. Thus, in direct actions involving judicial review of the legality of the institutions' conduct (action for annulment and action for failure to act), Community institutions and Member States have an almost unqualified right of action, while natural or legal persons possess such right only in so far as they can satisfy the strict conditions of admissibility laid down by the relevant Treaty provisions. In direct actions involving the unlimited jurisdiction of the ECJ (action for damages, action against sanctions), any interested (injured or penalized) party has an almost unqualified right of action. On the other hand, in reference proceedings for preliminary rulings neither the Community institutions, nor the Member States, nor private individuals have a right of action; only the courts and tribunals of the Member States may initiate such proceedings. Where the right of action of the applicant is challenged in a case, the ECJ will examine that right in the context of admissibility.

See also **Admissibility of action, Capacity to institute proceedings, Interest to sue, Jurisdiction.**

S

▶ **SCIENTIFIC AND TECHNICAL COMMITTEE** Committee set up by Art. 134 Euratom and attached to the Commission with advisory status. It must be consulted where the Euratom Treaty so provides, but may be consulted in all cases in which the Commission considers this appropriate. The Committee consists of thirty-three members, appointed by the Council after consultation with the Commission (Art. 134(2) Euratom as last amended by Art. 23 of the Act of Accession 1985). The members are appointed in their personal capacity for a renewable term of five years. They are not to be bound by any mandatory instructions. The Committee elects its chairman and officers from among its members each year.

See also Commission.

▶ **SECONDARY LEGISLATION** Term used to describe the acts which the Community institutions may adopt under the ECSC, EEC, and Euratom Treaties.

The term 'secondary legislation' is not mentioned in the Treaties themselves, nor has it been the subject of a precise judicial definition so far. In practice, it is used in two different senses. In a narrower sense, it denotes only those acts which are listed by name in Arts. 14 ECSC, 189 EEC, and 161 Euratom. These include, under the ECSC Treaty, decisions, recommendations, and opinions of the Commission, and under the EEC and Euratom Treaties, regulations, directives, decisions, recommendations, and opinions of the Council and of the Commission. Of these, only ECSC decisions and recommendations and EEC/Euratom regulations, directives, and decisions are legally binding. In a wider sense, the term 'secondary legislation' comprises, in addition, (1) acts of the Council and the Commission not listed in the above provisions, such as resolutions, (general) programmes, and notices, and acts which bear no particular title but which may nevertheless produce legal effects; (2) acts of the European Parliament, such as resolutions, which may or may not be legally binding; (3) acts of the Court of Justice other than judicial acts (i.e. other than judgments, orders, opinions, and rulings), such as its Rules of Procedure; (4) acts of the other bodies or organs not having the full status of a Community institution, such as opinions of the ECSC Consultative Committee, EEC/Euratom Economic and Social Committee, and the Court of Auditors.

Whether understood in a narrower or a wider sense, all the acts falling within the scope of secondary legislation have the following features in common:

1. they are the result or manifestation of the exercise of competences conferred on the Communities by the Treaties;
2. they must be adopted by the institutions, each acting within the limits of its powers, in accordance with the provisions of the Treaties and within the framework of their objectives;
3. they must conform to certain precise formal and procedural requirements.

It follows from the foregoing that, as the term 'secondary' implies, this 'legislation' is derived from, limited by, and hierarchically subordinated to, the primary sources of Community law, i.e. the basic Treaties. This means that, unless the Treaties expressly so provide, a secondary Community law, whatever its title or nature, cannot legally have the aim or the effect of amending, repealing, or altering (widening or restricting) the scope of a primary (Treaty) provision as interpreted by the ECJ. This can only be done by Treaty amendment proper carried out in accordance with the relevant procedures (see e.g. Case 9/69 *Sayag* [1969] ECR 329 at p. 343 *per* A.-G. Gand; Case 37/70 *Rewe-Zentrale* [1971] ECR 23 at p. 34 *per Curiam*, p. 41 *per* A.-G. Dutheillet de Lamothe; Case 36/74 *Walrave* [1974] ECR 1405 at pp. 1424–5 *per* A.-G. Warner; Case 59/75 *Manghera* [1976] ECR 91 at p. 102; Case 43/75 *Defrenne* [1976] ECR 455 at pp. 478–9). Nor can an act falling within secondary legislation conflict with a general principle of law recognized by the ECJ as forming part of Community law. In the case of any incompatibility with the Treaties or with such general principles, the act will be declared null and void, invalid, or inapplicable by the ECJ, depending on the procedure whereby this question came before it. Moreover, an act of secondary law must be interpreted in such a way as to conform to, and further the objectives of, the basic Treaties.

Not only is secondary legislation, as a whole, subordinated to the Treaties, but there is a certain degree of hierarchy amongst the acts falling within secondary legislation itself. Thus, while the acts of the Council and the Commission, adopted directly on the basis of a Treaty provision, are in principle of equal rank, acts of the Commission adopted under powers delegated to it by the Council must conform to the terms of the measure containing the delegation. Implementing measures are subordinated to basic legislation, founded directly on the Treaties, even if they both originate from the same institution (Council or Commission).

Secondary legislation, as a whole, must be distinguished from certain other acts also forming part of Community law in a wider sense, but having an entirely different legal nature. These comprise: (1) decisions of the Representatives of the Governments of the Member States dealing with matters which the Treaties have deliberately left within the competence of the Member States; (2) acts of the same body meeting in the Council; (3) acts of the European Council; and (4) acts of the Foreign Ministers meeting within European Political Co-operation. All these acts are the product of the exercise by the Member States of competences which remain vested in them and not of Community competences. They are therefore not subject to the various rules and restrictions—whether substantive or procedural—which govern secondary legislation.

See also Commission, Community law, Community Treaties, Consultative Committee, Council, Court of Auditors, Decision, Directive, Economic and Social Committee, European Council, European Parliament, European Political Co-operation, General principles of law, Interpretation of Community law, Opinion, Recommendation, Regulation, Representatives of the Governments of the Member States meeting in Council, Resolution.

Self-protection

Settlement

Single European Act (SEA)

Further reading 1. BOOKS: Lauwaars, *Lawfulness and Legal Force of Community Decisions* (1973); Toth, *Legal Protection of Individuals in the European Communities* (1978), vol. i, s. 206. *See also under* **Community law.**

2. ARTICLES AND PAPERS: Brinkhorst, 'Implementation of (Non-Self-Executing) Legislation of the European Economic Community, Including Directives', in Bathurst *et al.* (eds.), *Legal Problems of an Enlarged European Community* (1972), p. 69; Mitchell, 'Community Legislation', ibid. p. 87; van der Esch, 'Legal Policy in an Enlarged European Community' (1973) 10 *CML Rev.* 56.

▶ **SELF-PROTECTION** 'Legitimate self-protection presupposes an action taken by a person which is essential in order to ward off a danger threatening him. The threat must be immediate, the danger imminent, and there must be no other lawful means of avoiding it' (Case 16/61 *Modena* v. *HA* [1962] ECR 289 at p. 303). 'The concept of legitimate self-protection, which implies an act of defence against an unjustified attack, cannot exempt from liability commercial operators who knowingly contravene a general decision the legality of which does not give rise to doubts either taken by itself or in relation to the economic facts and circumstances in the light of which the decision was adopted. In this case, as General Decision No 962/77 [fixing minimum prices for certain concrete reinforcement bars] has been recognised to be lawful as regards the conditions of form and substance laid down by the ECSC Treaty, the applicants have no grounds for relying on legitimate self-protection, since that exonerating factor cannot be pleaded against a public authority acting lawfully within the legal framework of its powers' (Cases 154/78 etc. *Valsabbia* v. *Commission* [1980] ECR 907 at pp. 1021–2).

▶ **SETTLEMENT** Agreement between the parties to proceedings pending before the ECJ, other than annulment, default, and reference proceedings, to terminate their dispute by mutually abandoning their claims against each other before the Court has given its decision. A settlement does not have to be approved by the Court, nor to be incorporated in the judgment, but upon a simple notification thereof the Court will order the case to be removed from the register (Art. 77 RP; see also Case 62/72 *Bollmann* [1973] ECR 269 at p. 279 *per* A.-G. Roemer).

See also **Abandonment of claims, Discontinuance of proceedings.**

▶ **SINGLE EUROPEAN ACT** (**SEA**) Treaty signed by the twelve Member States of the European Communities on 17 and 28 February 1986, amending the ECSC, EEC, and Euratom Treaties and laying down provisions on European co-operation in the sphere of foreign policy (European Political Co-operation or EPC). The Act entered into force on 1 July 1987 (*OJ* 1987 L169/1; Suppl. 2/86—*Bull. EC*).

The adoption of the SEA was prompted by the desire to make 'concrete progress' towards European Union, an objective set at the Paris Summit Conference of 19–21 October 1972 (6th *Gen. Rep. EC* (1972), p. 16).

Following the adoption of the Solemn Declaration on European Union by the Stuttgart European Council on 19 June 1983 and of the Draft Treaty establishing the European Union by the European Parliament on 14 February 1984, the Fontainebleau European Council of 25–6 June 1984 decided to set up two *ad hoc* Committees; one on Institutional Affairs (Dooge Committee) and one on a People's Europe (Adonnino Committee). In its final Report, the Dooge Committee proposed the convening of an Intergovernmental Conference 'to negotiate a draft European Union Treaty'. The Reports of the two Committees, together with the Commission's White Paper on Completing the Internal Market, were considered and endorsed by the Milan European Council on 28–9 June 1985. It was at this meeting that the European Council decided, by a seven to three majority, to convene a conference to draw up (1) a treaty on a common foreign and security policy on the basis of the Franco-German and United Kingdom drafts; and (2) amendments to the EEC Treaty with a view to improving the Council's decision-making procedures, strengthening the Commission's executive power, increasing the powers of the European Parliament, and extending Community policies to include new areas of activity, on the basis of the proposals of the Dooge and Adonnino Committees and of the Commission.

The Intergovernmental Conference was formally convened by the Council on 22–3 July 1985, in accordance with the requirements laid down in Art. 236 EEC. It took place in Luxembourg and Brussels at Foreign Minister level (including Spain and Portugal) from 9 September 1985 to 27 January 1986. Work on the revision of the EEC Treaty was entrusted to a Working Party composed mainly of the Permanent Representatives of the Member States, while the drafting of the treaty concerning EPC was carried out by the Political Committee, consisting of the Political Directors of the Ministries of Foreign Affairs. The Commission was represented on both bodies. Agreement on the proposed changes was reached by the European Council in Luxembourg on 2–3 December 1985, while the Ministerial Conference of 16 and 17 December 1985 finalized all the texts and decided to incorporate both sets of provisions, i.e. those relating to the revision of the EEC Treaty and those dealing with EPC, in a 'Single European Act'. (For general background and legislative history, see *Bull. EC* 6–1985, p. 13; 7/8–1985, p. 7; 11–1985, p. 7; 12–1985, p. 7; 1–1986, p. 8; 2–1986, p. 7; 19th *Gen. Rep. EC* (1985), p. 29; 20th *Gen. Rep. EC* (1986), p. 33; 21st *Gen. Rep. EC* (1987), p. 29. For the opinions of the European Parliament on the SEA, see in particular the following Resolutions: 11 Dec. 1985, *OJ* 1985 C352/60; 16 Jan. 1986, *OJ* 1986 C36/144; 17 Apr. 1986, *OJ* 1986 C120/96; 23 Oct. 1986, *OJ* 1986 C297/119; 11 Dec. 1986, *OJ* 1987 C7/105; 17 June 1988, *OJ* 1988 C187/229.)

The SEA consists of a Preamble and four Titles. Title I contains common provisions; Title II provisions amending and supplementing the Community Treaties; Title III provisions on EPC; and Title IV general and final provisions. The Act is accompanied by a Final Act which contains twenty Declarations. Amongst other things, the common provisions in Title I confer, for the first time, Treaty status on the European Council (Art. 2) and, also for the first

481

time, officially recognize the use of the title 'European Parliament' by that institution (Art. 3(1)). Nearly all the amendments set out in Title II relate to the EEC Treaty; only the provisions concerning the Court of Justice (see below) apply also to the ECSC and Euratom Treaties. Title III on EPC has an autonomous character in that it is not incorporated in the existing Treaties (Art. 32); nor are Titles I and III subject to the jurisdiction of the ECJ (Art. 31). The legal nature of the Declarations is not clear but, in the absence of provisions making them an 'integral part' of the Act and/or requiring their ratification, it seems that they cannot be regarded as possessing binding force either under public international law or under Community law. Since they are explicitly excluded from the jurisdiction of the ECJ (Art. 31), they cannot be interpreted by the Court, nor can they have any effect on the interpretation of the Act by the Court. Since they do not constitute reservations *stricto sensu* under international law, they may in no way restrict, exclude, or modify the legal effects of the Act.

In substance, the SEA deals with the following four matters:

1. *Institutional reform.* Following a number of reports and proposals advocating reform of the Community institutions (see, in addition to the Reports of the two *ad hoc* Committees mentioned above, the Vedel, Tindemans, Spierenburg, and Three Wise Men's Reports), the Act lays down provisions with a view to making the institutional structure more efficient and more democratic. Speeding up of the decision-making process was also necessary in order to enable the internal market to be completed by the target date of 31 December 1992 (see below). The relevant provisions affect all four institutions. The European Parliament has been given increased influence (although not a real power of co-decision) in the legislative process by the introduction of a new co-operation procedure in specified cases, involving two readings both in the Council and in Parliament (Arts. 6 and 7). A real power of co-decision has been conferred on Parliament only with regard to the conclusion of accession treaties and association agreements, where the Council may act in the future only with Parliament's assent (Arts. 8 and 9). To improve the decision-making process within the Council, the Act has amended certain Articles in the EEC Treaty by substituting qualified majority for the previous unanimity requirement (Art. 16). Qualified majority voting has also been extended to measures necessary for the establishment and functioning of the internal market (in particular to measures for the harmonization of laws) and to measures necessary for the implementation of new policies and activities (see below). However, the Act has not abrogated the Luxembourg Compromise of 1966. The executive role of the Commission has been strengthened by the requirement that the Council is to confer on the Commission implementing powers (Art. 10). A new Court of First Instance, to be attached to the ECJ, is to relieve the latter of some of its increased workload (Arts. 4, 11, 26). As mentioned above, only the provisions relating to the ECJ constitute amendments to all three basic Treaties; the other institutional changes affect the EEC Treaty alone.

2. *The internal market.* An internal market, comprising 'an area without

internal frontiers in which the free movement of goods, persons, services and capital is ensured' is to be progressively established by 31 December 1992 (Art. 13). To achieve this objective, a number of provisions have been amended in the EEC Treaty, enabling the Council to act by qualified majority. Certain new provisions have also been inserted, the most important being the new Art. 100A relating to the harmonization of national laws (Arts. 14–19).

3. *New policies and activities.* Five 'new' areas of activity have been formally included in the scope of the EEC Treaty, although most of them already existed in practice in one form or another. These concern the following matters: (*a*) co-operation in economic and monetary policy (Economic and Monetary Union) (Art. 20); (*b*) social policy, with particular reference to the improvement of the working environment (Arts. 21–2); (*c*) economic and social cohesion involving the redressing of regional imbalances in the Community and the reform of the existing structural Funds (i.e. European Agricultural Guidance and Guarantee Fund, Guidance Section, European Social Fund, European Regional Development Fund) to transform them into instruments of economic development (Art. 23); (*d*) a common research and technological development policy (Art. 24); and (*e*) co-ordinated action on the protection of the environment (Art. 25).

4. *European Political Co-operation.* EPC is given, for the first time, a Treaty basis although it is not made an integral part of Community law. The Communities remain governed by the basic Treaties whereas EPC is governed by Title III which is in the nature of an international agreement between the Member States. While it lays down a formal framework for EPC, it leaves the procedures and practices which have been gradually established over the years unaffected (Arts. 1 and 30).

The first three matters above are closely interrelated in that in combination with one another they constitute a comprehensive plan to revitalize the Communities. The SEA has thus succeeded in using the long overdue, but in itself somewhat abstract, institutional reform (or at least partial reform) for the purpose of attaining practical new objectives, i.e. the completion of a large frontier-free market by 1992 and the strengthening of economic and social cohesion. It has thereby given a sense of direction both to the Community and to the Member States. While it is doubtful whether it amounts, in itself, to that 'qualitative leap forward' (as described by the Commission, see *Bull. EC* 2–1987, p. 7) which is necessary to achieve the ultimate goal of establishing a European Union (see the Preamble), the signs are that it has already given new impetus to European integration. Whether it is an adequate instrument to bring about all the major changes contemplated ultimately depends on the political will of the Member States to comply not only with its letter but also with its underlying spirit.

(For a more detailed treatment of the various aspects of the SEA, see the relevant entries listed below.)

See also **Commission, Committee on a People's Europe, Committee on Institutional Affairs, Community budget, Co-operation procedure, Council, Court of First Instance, Economic and monetary policy*, Economic and**

Solemn Declaration on European Union

Monetary Union*, Environmental policy*, European Act, European Agricultural Guidance and Guarantee Fund*, European Council, European Monetary System*, European Parliament, European Political Co-operation, European Regional Development Fund*, European Social Fund*, European Union, Harmonization of laws*, Internal market*, Luxembourg Compromise, Regional policy*, Research and development policy*, Social policy*, Solemn Declaration on European Union, Spierenburg Report, Three Wise Men's Report, Tindemans Report, Treaty-making procedure, Vedel Report.

Further reading 1. ARTICLES: Arnull, 'The Single European Act' (1986) 11 *EL Rev.* 358; Bieber, Pantalis, and Schoo, 'Implications of the Single Act for the European Parliament' (1986) 23 *CML Rev.* 767; Campbell, 'The Single European Act and the Implications' (1986) 35 *ICLQ* 932; Editorial, 'The Single European Act' (1986) 23 *CML Rev.* 249; id., 'The Single European Act Again' (1986) 23 *CML Rev.* 743; id., 'The Delors Plan for Implementing the Single European Act' (1987) 24 *CML Rev.* 139; id., 'The "Grand Rendez-vous"' (1987) 24 *CML Rev.* 357; id., 'The Delors Package: The Result of a Successful Commission Strategy' (1988) 25 *CML Rev.* 479; id., 'Financing the Single Act' (1988) 13 *EL Rev.* 221; Edward, 'The Impact of the Single Act on the Institutions' (1987) 24 *CML Rev.* 19; Ehlermann, 'The Internal Market Following the Single European Act' (1987) 24 *CML Rev.* 361; Flynn, 'How Will Article 100A(4) Work? A Comparison with Article 93' (1987) 24 *CML Rev.* 689; Forwood and Clough, 'The Single European Act and Free Movement: Legal Implications of the Provisions for the Completion of the Internal Market' (1986) 11 *EL Rev.* 383; Freestone and Davidson, 'Community Competence and Part III of the Single European Act' (1986) 23 *CML Rev.* 793; Glaesner, 'The Single European Act' (1986) 6 *YEL* 283; Gulmann, 'The Single European Act: Some Remarks from a Danish Perspective' (1987) 24 *CML Rev.* 31; Krämer, 'The Single European Act and Environment Protection: Reflections on Several New Provisions in Community Law' (1987) 24 *CML Rev.* 659; Lodge, 'The Single European Act: Toward a New European Dynamism' (1986) 24 *JCMS* 203; Louis, '"Monetary Capacity" in the Single European Act' (1988) 25 *CML Rev.* 9; Nuttall, 'European Political Co-operation and the Single European Act' (1985) 5 *YEL* 203; Pescatore, 'Some Critical Remarks on the "Single European Act"' (1987) 24 *CML Rev.* 9; Temple Lang, 'The Irish Court Case which Delayed the Single European Act: Crotty v. An Taoiseach and Others' (1987) 24 *CML Rev.* 709; Toth, 'The Legal Status of the Declarations Annexed to the Single European Act' (1986) 23 *CML Rev.* 803; Williamson, 'The Package, "Making a Success of the Single Act"' (1988) 25 *CML Rev.* 483; de Zwaan, 'The Single European Act: Conclusion of a Unique Document' (1986) 23 *CML Rev.* 747.

2. OFFICIAL PUBLICATIONS: Commission of the European Communities, 'The Single Act: A New Frontier for Europe', Communication from the Commission (COM (87) 100) to the Council. Suppl. 1/87—*Bull. EC*, see also *Bull. EC* 2–1987, p. 7; id., 'Programme of the Commission for 1988', Suppl. 1/88—*Bull. EC*; id., 'Programme of the Commission for 1989', Suppl. 2/89—*Bull. EC*; House of Lords, Select Committee on the European Communities, Session 1985–6, 12th Report, 'Single European Act and Parliamentary Scrutiny' (1986).

▶ **SOLEMN DECLARATION ON EUROPEAN UNION** Declaration signed in Stuttgart on 19 June 1983 by the ten Heads of State or Government of the Member States, acting as the European Council, and their Foreign Ministers

(*Bull. EC* 6–1983, p. 23, text at p. 24). The Declaration originated in the Draft European Act, also known as the 'Genscher–Colombo initiative', which was presented to the Member States in November 1981 by the German and Italian Governments (see *Bull. EC* 11–1981, p. 10, text at p. 87).

With a view to transforming the relations between the Member States into a European Union, the Declaration states a number of objectives and envisages a number of adjustments to the existing institutional structures. It emphasizes the importance of strengthening European Political Co-operation and the need for greater coherence and closer co-ordination between it and the Community structures. It affirms the role of the European Council in the construction of the Union and its ability to act as the Council proper in matters within the scope of the Communities. The Declaration calls upon the Council to use every possible means of facilitating the decision-making process, including, in cases where unanimity is required, the possibility of abstaining from voting. It outlines a number of ways in which the Council and the Commission are to maintain closer relations with the European Parliament, going beyond the requirements of the Treaties. Moreover, the document assigns greater role to the Parliament with respect to the negotiation and conclusion of certain international agreements. It requires the Council to make more frequent use of the possibility of delegating powers to the Commission.

In the field of Community policies, the Solemn Declaration calls for the strengthening of the European Monetary System, which it recognizes as a key element in the progress towards Economic and Monetary Union. It stresses the importance of completing the internal market and of the continued development of the Common Commercial and Agricultural Policies. It proposes closer cultural co-operation between the Member States, including exchanges of teachers and students. An important task is the further approximation of laws, particularly in the field of the protection of industrial and commercial property, consumer protection, and company law, and the strengthening of co-operation among the judicial authorities of the Member States, notably in civil and commercial matters and with regard to the suppression of infringements of Community law.

Finally, the Declaration points out that European Union is being achieved by deepening and broadening the scope of European activities so that they coherently cover, albeit on a variety of legal bases, a growing proportion of the mutual relations of the Member States and of their external relations.

The Declaration was to be reviewed not later than five years from its signature with a view to the possible incorporation of the progress achieved in a Treaty on European Union.

Although the Solemn Declaration is not, and was never intended to be, a legally binding instrument (and in fact failed to obtain the unanimous support of the Member States in some areas), it did play a certain part in the construction of the European Union and the reform of the Community institutions. Together with other documents, it may be regarded as a forerunner of the Single European Act of 1986 which specifically refers to it in its Preamble.

485

See also **Committee on Institutional Affairs, European Act, European Union, Institutions, Single European Act.**

Further reading: Editorial, 'The Solemn Declaration on European Union' (1983) 8 *EL Rev.* 295; Hendry, '. . . of Cabbages and Kings' (1983) 8 *EL Rev.* 394; Neville-Jones, 'The Genscher–Colombo Proposals on European Union' (1983) 20 *CML Rev.* 657.

▶ **SPECIAL FORMS OF PROCEDURE** Procedures before the ECJ which are subject to rules different from, or additional to, those governing ordinary procedures under Title 2 of the Court's Rules of Procedure. Special forms of procedure include those explicitly so qualified under Title 3 of the Rules of Procedure as well as some other procedures provided for elsewhere in the Rules and Statutes of the Court.

The special forms of procedure dealt with under Title 3 RP relate to the following matters:

- suspension of operation or enforcement and other interim measures (Arts. 83–9 RP);
- compulsory inspection under Art. 81 Euratom (Art. 90 RP);
- preliminary objection and other procedural issues (Art. 91 RP);
- lack of jurisdiction and absolute bar to proceedings (Art. 92 RP);
- intervention (Art. 93 RP);
- judgments by default and applications to set them aside (Art. 94 RP);
- assignment of cases to Chambers (Arts. 95–6 RP);
- third party proceedings (Art. 97 RP);
- revision of judgments (Arts. 98–100 RP);
- appeals against decisions of the Euratom Arbitration Committee (Art. 101 RP);
- interpretation of judgments (Art. 102 RP);
- preliminary rulings and other references for interpretation (Arts. 103–4 RP);
- special procedures under Arts. 103–5 Euratom (Arts. 105–6 RP);
- opinions under Art. 228 EEC and Art. 95 ECSC (Arts. 107–9 RP);

In addition, special rules apply to the following matters:

- rectification of judgments (Art. 66 RP);
- supplementing a judgment (Art. 67 RP);
- taxation of costs (Art. 74 RP);
- disputes between Member States under Art. 89 ECSC (Arts. 41–2 ECSC Statute);
- proceedings by third parties under Arts. 63(2) and 66(5) ECSC (Art. 43 ECSC Statute).

It may be noted that the special forms of procedure are governed by the general procedural rules as laid down in Title 2 (Arts. 37–82) RP to the extent to which no special rules are provided for and where the special rules expressly refer back to the provisions of Title 2. Nevertheless, in view of the essential differences between contentious proceedings—for which the rules in Title 2 have been designed—and some of the special forms of procedure—

such as the non-contentious reference proceedings for preliminary rulings—not all the provisions in Title 2 can properly be applied to the latter even where the special rules expressly refer back to them (see e.g. Case 62/72 *Bollmann* [1973] ECR 269 at p. 275 *per Curiam*, p. 279 *per* A.-G. Roemer, holding that the general rules on costs (Arts. 69–75 RP) are not applicable to preliminary rulings in spite of the express provisions in Art. 103(1) RP to the effect that Arts. 43 *et seq.* RP 'shall apply' to preliminary rulings).

See also **Absolute bar to proceedings, Costs, European Court of Justice, Interim measures, Interpretation of judgments, Intervention, Judgment, Judgment by default, Jurisdiction, Opinion, Order, Preliminary objection, Preliminary ruling, Reference proceedings, Revision of judgments, Suspension of operation, Third party proceedings.**

Further reading: Berri, 'The Special Procedures before the Court of Justice of the European Communities' (1971) 8 *CML Rev.* 5.

▶ **SPIERENBURG REPORT** Report submitted to the Commission on 24 September 1979 by a five-member Independent Review Body chaired by Mr Dirk Spierenburg, former Vice-President of the ECSC High Authority and former Dutch Permanent Representative to the EEC and Euratom. The title of the Report is: 'Proposals for Reform of the Commission of the European Communities and its Services' (summary in *Bull. EC* 9–1979, p. 16). The Review Body was set up by the Commission in January 1979 to review the structures and workings of the Commission and to suggest reforms. A separate Report, prepared by the 'Three Wise Men', dealt with the reform of the Community institutions as a whole.

The first part of the Report consists of general observations. While recognizing the achievements of the Commission, it concludes that over the last ten years the Commission's influence, effectiveness, and reputation had declined. This had in part been due to internal weaknesses, such as a certain lack of cohesion in the college of Commissioners; an imbalance between portfolios; insufficient co-ordination among senior officials; a maldistribution of staff between departments; and shortcomings in the career structure of the Commission's civil service.

To remedy these weaknesses, the Report makes the following main recommendations:

- the number of Commissioners should be kept to a strict minimum and should not exceed the number of Member States (i.e. twelve after the accession of Greece, Spain, and Portugal);
- the number of portfolios should be reduced to a maximum of ten; they should be of comparable weight and have a stable content. Leaving aside the President and Vice-President, each Commissioner should be responsible for one 'vertical' portfolio;
- the Presidency should be strengthened; it should consist of a President and a single Vice-President who together should control all 'horizontal' services;

487

- the number of Directorates-General should likewise be reduced from twenty-nine to ten so that after the third enlargement the number of D.-G.s should coincide with that of portfolios and this should constitute the Commission's final structure;
- the position of Director-General should be further strengthened;
- the Members' Offices ('cabinets') should revert to their original function;
- the number of administrative units (specialized Departments and Divisions) should also be reduced;
- there should be more effective departmental co-ordination, improved administrative efficiency, and better career prospects for staff.

While the Commission welcomed the Report and endorsed most of its recommendations, it seems that none of the major proposals has been implemented.

See also **Commission, Committee on Institutional Affairs, Three Wise Men's Report, Tindemans Report.**

▶ **STAFF CASES** Cases involving disputes between the European Communities and their officials or other servants. These cases fall within the exclusive jurisdiction of the ECJ which the Court is to exercise within the limits and under the conditions laid down in the Staff Regulations, in particular Arts. 90 and 91, which provisions also apply by analogy in the context of the Conditions of Employment (Arts. 179 EEC, 152 Euratom; the same applies to the ECSC by virtue of Art. 24 of the Merger Treaty which created a single administration of the three Communities). Staff cases used to be heard and determined by a Chamber of the Court (Art. 95(3) RP), but since the new Court of First Instance became fully operational, they fall, at first instance, within the jurisdiction of that Court (Art. 3(1)(a) of Council Dec. 88/591 establishing a Court of First Instance, *OJ* 1988 L319/1).

Staff cases may be brought by the following:

1. 'officials' of the Communities, i.e. persons who have been appointed under the Staff Regulations to an established post on the staff of one of the institutions of the Communities by an instrument issued by the appointing authority of that institution (Arts. 1, 90–1 of the Staff Regulations, Council Reg. 259/68 *OJ Sp. Edn.* 1968(I), p. 30, as amended. For a consolidated version incorporating all the amendments, see the text published in Apr. 1986);
2. 'servants' engaged under contract by the Communities under the Conditions of Employment and falling into one of the following categories: temporary staff, auxiliary staff, and special advisers. These servants are subject to the same rules as 'officials' as regards appeal to the ECJ (Arts. 1, 46, 73, and 83 of the Conditions of Employment, laid down in the same Reg. as the Staff Regulations, see above. These provisions make Arts. 90–1 of the Staff Regs. applicable by analogy to Community servants);
3. persons claiming the status of officials or of servants as defined above

(Case 65/74 *Porrini* [1975] ECR 319 at p. 329; Cases 87/77 etc. *Salerno v. Commission and Council* [1985] ECR 2523 at p. 2534; etc.);

4. former officials and servants as well as candidates for a post taking part in general competitions, whether or not they are officials or servants. However, former officials and servants must be able to show that they still have a personal interest in the annulment of the contested measure (Cases 81 to 88/74 *Marenco v. Commission* [1975] ECR 1247 at p. 1255; Case 23/64 *Vandevyvere v. Parliament* [1965] ECR 157 at pp. 163–4);

5. since Arts. 179 EEC and 152 Euratom confer on the ECJ jurisdiction in 'any dispute between the Community and its servants', in principle not only the latter but also the Communities themselves, acting through their institutions, may bring staff cases before the Court. This has, however, never happened so far mainly because the Community institutions have the power of enforcing their decisions through binding measures taken as public authorities rather than through Court proceedings.

On the other hand, staff cases may not be brought by the following:

1. local staff, i.e. staff engaged under contract by the Communities under the Conditions of Employment but according to local practice, for manual or service duties. Although they are also 'servants' of the Communities, their employment relationships are governed to a considerable extent by national private (contract) law, and their disputes with the Communities fall within the jurisdiction of the competent national courts (Arts. 4, 79, and 81 of the Conditions of Employment; see also Case 65/74 *Porrini*, above, at p. 328);

2. persons who are not entitled to the status of Community servant within the meaning of the Conditions of Employment, such as a free-lance interpreter engaged under the Commission's internal arrangements regarding free-lance conference interpreters (Case 43/84 *Maag v. Commission* [1985] ECR 2581 at p. 2602);

3. trade unions or staff associations of European officials, since the appeal procedure established by Arts. 90 and 91 of the Staff Regulations is designed to deal exclusively with individual disputes involving officials or servants. Trade unions or staff associations of officials nevertheless have the right to intervene in staff cases subject to the general rules on intervention (Case 175/73 *Union Syndicale v. Council* [1974] ECR 917 at p. 926; Case 18/74 *Syndicat Général du Personnel v. Commission* [1974] ECR 933 at pp. 944–5);

4. members of the institutions as opposed to officials and servants, since they are appointed by the Member States, not by the institutions.

Staff cases may be brought only against one of the institutions of the Communities. These include, for the purposes of the Staff Regulations and the Conditions of Employment, not only the four main institutions, i.e. the European Parliament, the Council, the Commission, and the Court of Justice, but also the Economic and Social Committee and the Court of Auditors (Art.

489

1 of the Staff Regs.; Art. 6 of the Conditions of Employment). Moreover, the ECJ has held that under Art. 179 EEC it also has jurisdiction in any dispute between the European Investment Bank and its officials or servants (Case 110/75 *Mills* v. *Investment Bank* [1976] ECR 955 at pp. 968–9). The Court had exercised jurisdiction based on Art. 179 EEC in disputes between the Community and its officials or servants even before the adoption of the Staff Regulations (see Cases 43, 45, and 48/59 *Lachmüller* v. *Commission* [1960] ECR 463 at pp. 471–2). Although the complaint which must precede the institution of proceedings before the ECJ must be submitted to the 'appointing authority' (see below), the appeal against the rejection of the complaint must be brought against the institution from which the act having an adverse effect on the applicant has emanated (i.e. normally the institution to which he is attached), even if it is a different institution from the appointing authority (Case 28/64 *Müller* v. *Council* [1965] ECR 237 at p. 247; Case 307/85 *Gavanas* v. *Economic and Social Committee and Council* [1987] ECR 2435 at p. 2459, where the Council acted as appointing authority for certain officials of the ESC including the applicant, who had to direct his action against the ESC, not against the Council).

An action before the Court under Art. 91 of the Staff Regulations lies only if the applicant has previously submitted a complaint to the appointing authority in accordance with the procedure laid down in Art. 90(2) against an 'act adversely affecting him', and the complaint has been rejected by express or implied decision. The action must then be brought within three months of the date of notification of the decision or, where the appeal is against an implied decision rejecting the complaint, of the date of expiry of the period prescribed for the reply. However, the applicant may apply for a stay of execution of the contested act or for other interim measures immediately upon submitting his complaint to the appointing authority. The procedures in Arts. 90 and 91 apply not only to those who are officials or other servants but also to those who are or were candidates for a post (Case 130/86 *Du Besset* v. *Council* [1986] ECR 2619 at p. 2621).

As the ECJ has explained, the object of the preliminary complaint procedure is to enable and encourage an amicable settlement of disputes which arise between officials or other servants and the administration. To comply with this requirement, it is essential that the administration be in a position to know the complaints or requests of the person concerned (Case 58/75 *Sergy* v. *Commission* [1976] ECR 1139 at p. 1152; see also the cases cited below). In the absence of a prior complaint, an action will be inadmissible (see e.g. Case 91/76 *De Lacroix* v. *Court of Justice* [1977] ECR 225 at p. 229; Case 174/83 *Amman* v. *Council* [1985] ECR 2133 at p. 2147). It will also be inadmissible if it is brought before a decision is given on the complaint (Cases 259/84 and 259/84R *Strack* v. *Parliament* [1985] ECR 453 at p. 455). A prior complaint is not necessary in the case of appeals against decisions of selection boards, since the appointing authority does not have the power to annul or amend such decisions (see e.g. Case 168/83 *Pasquali-Gherardi* v. *Parliament* [1985] ECR 83 at p. 97) and in the case of appeals against periodic reports, for similar reasons (see e.g. Cases 6 and 97/79 *Grassi* v. *Council* [1980] ECR

2141 at pp. 2157–8). Nevertheless, it is not the function of the complaint to bind strictly and absolutely the judicial stage of the proceedings, provided that the claims submitted at that stage change neither the legal basis nor the subject-matter of the complaint (Case 58/75 *Sergy* v. *Commission*, above, at p. 1153; Case 54/77 *Herpels* v. *Commission* [1978] ECR 585 at pp. 596–7, where the Court admitted a claim for damages although it was not the subject of a complaint; see also e.g. Case 52/85 *Rihoux* v. *Commission* [1986] ECR 1555 at p. 1568 and the cases cited therein. However, in Case 174/83 *Amman* v. *Council*, above, at p. 2147 a claim for compensatory interest was held inadmissible since the complaint only contained a claim for default interest).

The various time-limits laid down in Arts. 90 and 91 of the Staff Regulations are mandatory and are not subject to the discretion of the parties or of the Court, since they are intended to ensure clarity and legal certainty. Therefore, once the time-limits for the commencement of proceedings have expired, a request under Art. 90(1) may be made only in the event of a new circumstance arising which makes it necessary to reconsider the situation (Cases 75 and 117/82 *Razzouk and Beydoun* v. *Commission* [1984] ECR 1509 at p. 1529; Case 191/84 *Barcella* v. *Commission* [1986] ECR 1541 at pp. 1552–3; Case 232/85 *Becker* v. *Commission* [1986] ECR 3401 at pp. 3413–14; etc.).

Moreover, under Art. 91(1) only actions directed against 'an act adversely affecting' the applicant are admissible. According to the established case-law of the Court, only acts which directly and immediately affect the applicant's legal situation can be regarded as adversely affecting him. Thus, an official or servant must have a personal interest in the annulment of the measure in question; he 'is not entitled to act in the interests of the law or of the institutions and may put forward, in support of an action for the annulment of an appointment, only such claims as relate to him personally' (Case 85/82 *Schloh* v. *Council* [1983] ECR 2105 at p. 2123; Cases 81 to 88/74 *Marenco* v. *Commission*, above, at p. 1255; Case 204/85 *Stroghili* v. *Court of Auditors* [1987] ECR 389 at pp. 401–2; etc.).

Under Art. 91(1) of the Staff Regulations, the ECJ has been given jurisdiction to assess 'the legality of an act' adversely affecting the applicant. Therefore, in the first place, actions brought under this provision aim at the judicial review of the acts and omissions of the Community institutions in connection with the employment relationship. However, Art. 91(1) also states that 'in disputes of a financial character the Court of Justice shall have unlimited jurisdiction'. This means, in particular, that in such disputes the 'Court is vested with the power not only to annul the measure in point but also, where appropriate, to order of its own motion that compensation be paid by the defendant for damage caused by maladministration on its part, and this is so even in the absence of any formal claim for such relief. In such a case, the Court may, having regard to all the circumstances of the case, assess the damage *ex aequo et bono*' (Cases 176 and 177/86 *Houyoux* v. *Commission* [1987] ECR 4333 at pp. 4352–3).

The ECJ has held in a long line of cases that, because of its unlimited jurisdiction under Art. 91(1), a dispute between an official and an institution concerning compensation for damage must be pursued, where it originates in the employment relationship, under Arts. 179 EEC and 90–1 of the Staff Regulations and that, as regards in particular the question of admissibility, it lies outside the sphere of application of Arts. 178 and 215 EEC and of Art. 43 of the EEC Statute (Case 9/75 *Meyer-Burckhardt* v. *Commission* [1975] ECR 1171 at p. 1181; Case 48/76 *Reinarz* v. *Commission and Council* [1977] ECR 291 at p. 298; etc.). Accordingly, officials 'have *locus standi* to submit both a claim for annulment and a claim for damages provided that they satisfy the conditions laid down by the Staff Regulations, *which are the same for both means of redress*' (Case 174/83 *Amman* v. *Council*, above, at p. 2147, emphasis added).

It would seem to follow from the foregoing that the Court regards Art. 179 EEC (in conjunction with Arts. 90 and 91 of the Staff Regulations) as a *lex specialis* in relation to Art. 173 EEC (action for annulment) and Arts. 178, 215 EEC (action for damages). As such, Art. 179 must be used in preference to those more general provisions. At least three important consequences follow from this. First, actions are subject to the three-month time-limit laid down in Art. 91(3) and not to the two months specified in Art. 173(3) EEC or to the five-year limitation period mentioned in Art. 43 EEC Statute (in respect of actions for damages). Secondly, 'an official who fails to contest in due time a decision of the appointing authority affecting him is not permitted to rely on the alleged unlawfulness of that decision in an action for damages' (Case 401/85 *Schina* v. *Commission* [1987] ECR 3911 at p. 3929). As the Court explained in a series of earlier cases, although a party may bring an action for damages without being obliged to seek the annulment of the illegal measure which causes him damage, he may not by this means circumvent the inadmissibility (on account of the expiry of the time-limit) of the application which concerns the same illegality and has the same financial end in view (see e.g. Case 59/65 *Schreckenberg* v. *Commission* [1966] ECR 543 at p. 550; Case 799/79 *Bruckner* v. *Commission and Council* [1981] ECR 2697 at p. 2714).

Thirdly, it would also have to follow that an official is not entitled to bring an action for annulment under Art. 173 EEC, just as he may not bring an action for damages under Art. 178 EEC. Indeed, in Case 18/74 *Syndicat Général du Personnel* v. *Commission*, above, at p. 947, A.-G. Trabucchi pointed out that 'the channels of appeal under these legislative provisions [i.e. under Arts. 90–1 of the Staff Regs. and Art. 173 EEC] are not alternative ones but are mutually exclusive, each being for use in widely different circumstances'. Nevertheless, in several cases the Court examined the admissibility of applications for the annulment of certain Council regulations not only under Arts. 90–1 but, alternatively, also under Art. 173. It found that they were inadmissible under both. The regulations challenged were not 'acts adversely affecting the applicants' within the meaning of Art. 91. Nor did they constitute a decision addressed to the applicants or a decision which although in the form of a regulation was of direct and individual concern to them, as required by Art. 173 (see e.g. Case 48/79 *Ooms* v. *Commission* [1979] ECR 3121 at p. 3123; Case 114/77 *Jacquemart* v. *Commission* [1978] ECR 1697 at pp. 1711–12; Case 799/79 *Bruckner* v. *Commission and*

Council, above, at pp. 2713–14). This would appear to indicate that the Court might accept an application for annulment which satisfies the conditions of Art. 173 even although it may not satisfy those of Arts. 90–1. This does not seem compatible with the *lex specialis* nature of the latter provisions.

In addition to the judicial review of the acts and omissions of the institutions and actions for damages brought against them, the jurisdiction of the ECJ in staff cases extends to certain other matters. Thus, under Art. 22 of the Staff Regulations, which has been incorporated in the Conditions of Employment (see Arts. 11, 54, and 83), the Court has unlimited jurisdiction in disputes arising from the obligation of officials and servants to make good any damage suffered by the Communities as a result of serious misconduct on their part in the course of or in connection with the performance of their duties (see also Arts. 40(2) ECSC, 215(3) EEC, 188(3) Euratom). Moreover, the ECJ has recognized that although the Staff Regulations contain no express provisions on the review of elections to the Staff Committees set up within each institution, the Court has jurisdiction in electoral disputes concerning the appointment of those Committees. These disputes may be brought before the Court by voters and candidates subject to the same procedures, formalities, and periods as apply to ordinary staff cases under Arts. 90 and 91. Within this jurisdiction, the Court is required to examine, in accordance with its general task under Arts. 31 ECSC, 164 EEC, 136 Euratom, 'all objections raised against elections having regard to the rules relating to freedom and democracy common to all the Member States in matters of electoral law' (Case 54/75 *De Dapper* v. *Parliament* [1976] ECR 1381 at p. 1389).

See also **Action for annulment, Action for damages, Contractual liability, Court of First Instance, European Investment Bank, Institutions, Unlimited jurisdiction.**

▶ *STARE DECISIS* Follow a previous decision.

1. *In English law*: legal doctrine, also known as the doctrine of precedent, according to which 'every court is bound to follow any case decided by a court above it in the hierarchy, and appellate courts (other than the House of Lords) are bound by their previous decisions' (R. Cross, *Precedent in English Law*, 3rd edn. (Oxford, 1977), p. 7). Until the Practice Statement of 1966, the House of Lords also considered itself bound by its past decisions. The previous decision is called a 'precedent', which may be either of 'persuasive authority' or of 'binding authority'. A precedent is said to be only of persuasive authority if a court is bound to follow it unless there are good reasons for not doing so; it is of binding authority if a court is bound to follow it even if there are good reasons for not doing so (ibid. pp. 4–5). However, the only part of a previous decision which is legally binding is the *ratio decidendi* (reason for deciding), while *obiter dicta* (incidental statements) are never of more than persuasive authority. The distinction between these two concepts is of fundamental importance, as a result of which the rule *stare decisis* in fact means *stare rationibus decidendi* (keep to the *rationes decidendi* of past cases)

493

(ibid. pp. 38 *et seq.*, 76 *et seq.*, 103 *et seq.*). Moreover, a court is bound by a previous decision only in so far as the facts of the case before it and the facts to which the *ratio decidendi* of the previous decision was applied are not reasonably distinguishable. In consequence, distinguishing is an important aspect of the application of the doctrine, and the courts must always pay the most scrupulous attention to the facts of the case before them (ibid.). As a result of the doctrine of *stare decisis*, the *rationes decidendi* of cases decided by the superior courts have the force of law in that they are binding on all inferior courts and on all citizens. Thus, the use of precedent is seen as 'an indispensable foundation upon which to decide what is the law and its application to individual cases' (Practice Statement made in the House of Lords in 1966, ibid. p. 109).

2. *In Community law*: the concept of *stare decisis* or of precedent raises two different questions. The first concerns the extent to which the ECJ itself may be bound to follow its own previous decisions; the second relates to the extent to which the national courts of the Member States may be obliged to follow the decisions of the ECJ.

As regards the first question, in the absence of any provisions in the Treaties or in the Court's Statutes determining the scope of the binding force of its judgments, the Court itself has defined that scope by reference to the rule of *res judicata*. According to that rule, the judgments of the Court are binding only as between the parties (*inter partes*) and binding on the Court as well as on the parties in respect of the particular case only. It follows that the Court is always free in principle when giving its judgments and may depart from its own previous decisions even without giving any reasons for it. As A.-G. Lagrange has explained: 'However important the judgment which [the Court] is led to give on some point may be, whatever may be the *abstract* character which the interpretation of some provision of the Treaty may present . . . the golden rule of *res judicata* should be preserved: it is from the *moral* authority of its decisions, and not from the legal authority of *res judicata*, that [its] jurisdiction . . . should derive its force. Clearly no one will expect that, having given a leading judgment . . . the Court will depart from it in another action without strong reasons, but it should retain the legal right to do so' (Cases 28 to 30/62 *Da Costa* [1963] ECR 31 at p. 42. In substance, the Court followed the A.-G.'s opinion, ibid. at pp. 37–9. See also the opinion of A.-G. Warner in Case 62/76 *Strehl* [1977] ECR 211 at p. 220).

While in its judgments the ECJ frequently refers to and cites from its past decisions, it has never expressly stated, nor can it be inferred from its practice, that it considers itself legally bound by a doctrine of *stare decisis* to follow those decisions. Normally, the Court does not attempt to determine the *ratio decidendi* of the previous case; it does not distinguish between the facts of that case and the facts of the case before it; and it does not apply the *ratio* to the instant case. What the Court does, particularly in preliminary ruling procedures where it cannot apply the law to the facts of the particular case, is to apply a previous abstract ruling (e.g. on the invalidity or interpretation of a provision) to identical legal situations in the absence of new legal factors or arguments. The rule of law applied in the later case is not derived from the previous case but from another source (a Treaty provision, an act of an institution, a general principle of law, etc.) on which that case itself relies. The previous decision will therefore not become the legal basis of the later decision; they are both based on common underlying legal grounds. The former is not a binding 'precedent' from which the latter could derive its validity. It seems therefore that a doctrine of *stare decisis*, comparable to that of English law, does not apply to the Court of Justice.

As regards the question whether the national courts may be obliged to follow the decisions of the European Court, in Case 112/76 *Manzoni* [1977] ECR 1647 at pp. 1661–3 A.-G. Warner distinguished, in the context of preliminary rulings, between the scope of *res judicata* and that of *stare decisis*. While accepting the view that owing to the *res judicata* rule the effect of a ruling is confined to the particular case in which it was given, he thought that there was also scope for the application of the doctrine of *stare decisis*. He explained that in the context of Community law this doctrine means that 'all Courts throughout the Community, with the exception of [the European] Court itself, are bound by the *ratio decidendi* of a Judgment of this Court . . . If one were to reject that conclusion, one would be driven to accept that inferior Courts and Tribunals in the Member States might treat the Court's Judgments as of persuasive authority only, and so ignore them if they thought fit, whereas the superior Courts . . . may not. Acceptance of that conclusion, on the other hand, means that all Courts in the Member States are, in this respect, in the same position' (ibid. at p. 1662). Then, drawing analogy between the European Court and the House of Lords, he pointed out that a 'decision of the House of Lords is, under the doctrine of *stare decisis*, binding upon, the must be followed by, all other Courts throughout the United Kingdom . . . but the House of Lords itself—and it alone—may reconsider and depart from the decision in a subsequent case. If it does so, it is the new decision of the House that becomes binding on other Courts' (ibid. at p. 1663)—implying that similar considerations should apply to the rulings of the European Court also.

A.-G. Warner's opinion was referred to by A.-G. Capotorti and relied on by the Commission in Case 130/79 *Express Dairy Foods* [1980] ECR 1887 at pp. 1891, 1904–5. However, it must be stated that the Community Treaties and the Statutes of the European Court contain no provisions to the effect that a preliminary ruling is binding on all the courts of all the Member States. The ECJ itself has so far only confirmed that an interpretative ruling is binding on the national court which has requested it (Case 29/68 *Milch-, Fett- und Eier-Kontor* [1969] ECR 165 at p. 180; Case 52/76 *Benedetti* [1977] ECR 163 at p. 183). In so far as a preliminary ruling may produce wider effects, going beyond the confines of the individual case, the nature of those effects is to *enable* rather than *oblige* other national courts to follow the ruling. Thus, the ECJ has held that the authority of an interpretation given under Art. 177 (or in other proceedings) relieves national courts of final instance *intending to adopt that interpretation* of their obligation to refer under Art. 177(3) (Cases 28 to 30/62 *Da Costa*, above, at p. 38 and Case 283/81 *CILFIT* [1982] ECR 3415 at p. 3429). Also, a declaration of invalidity

495

of a Community act made under Art. 177 is 'sufficient reason' for any other national court to regard the act concerned as void for the purposes of a judgment which it has to give (Case 66/80 *International Chemical Corporation* [1981] ECR 1191 at p. 1215). In these situations, however, the national courts will apply an abstract interpretation or refrain from applying an act declared invalid, rather than search for and follow the *ratio decidendi* on which that interpretation or declaration of invalidity is based.

Moreover, the ECJ has repeatedly emphasized that Art. 177 was in no way intended to superimpose the European Court upon the national courts; that the reference procedure is in the nature of a 'dialogue between courts'; that it is based on a relationship of co-operation and co-ordination, not on sub-ordination. It implies mutual respect by the courts for each other's jurisdictions (see e.g. Case 16/65 *Schwarze* [1965] ECR 877 at p. 886; Case 44/65 *Hessische Knappschaft* [1965] ECR 965 at p. 971; more recently Case 283/81 *CILFIT*, above, at p. 3428. See also, in general, Case 6/60 *Humblet* v. *Belgium* ECR 559 at p. 572). In the absence of the requisite Treaty provisions, and in the absence of a relationship of hierarchical subordination between the European Court and the national courts—which relationship is one of the foundations of the doctrine of *stare decisis* in English law—it is difficult to see on what precise legal basis a similar doctrine could operate in Community law. Clearly, the drafters of the Treaties aimed to achieve the objective of Art. 177, which is to ensure the uniform interpretation and application of Community law, by means of the system of obligatory references and not by endowing the rulings of the Court with general regulatory (normative) effect.

It follows that, short of Treaty amendment, the doctrine of *stare decisis* can only operate on the basis of a provision of national law, and only in respect of courts which are subject to such a provision. So far, the United Kingdom is the only Member State which has enacted legislation to this effect. Thus, section 3(1) of the European Communities Act 1972 provides in part that: 'For the purposes of all legal proceedings any question as to the meaning or effect of any of the Treaties, or as to the validity, meaning or effect of any Community instrument, shall . . . if not referred to the European Court, be for determination . . . in accordance with the principles laid down by and any relevant decision of the European Court . . .'

It may be noted, however, that upon a strict analysis it seems doubtful whether the effect of section 3(1) is really to extend to relevant decisions of the European Court the rule of strict precedent as applied by United Kingdom courts. While in dealing with domestic cases the courts are bound to follow the *rationes decidendi* of previous decisions, under section 3(1) they are obliged to apply the 'principles' laid down by, and any relevant 'decision' of, the European Court. However, these 'principles' and 'decisions' (i.e. 'rulings') are not (or not necessarily always) identical with the *rationes decidendi* of the Court's judgments. By deliberately avoiding any reference to the *rationes decidendi* of the European Court's decisions, the Act perhaps meant to call the courts' attention to the fact that they cannot approach and analyse those decisions in the same way as they are obliged to approach and analyse judgments of the higher domestic courts. The courts must look for the 'principles' laid down by, and for the 'decisions' (or 'rulings') of, the European Court rather than for the *rationes decidendi* on which they are based.

See also **Judgment,** *Jurisprudence constante, Obiter dictum,* **Preliminary ruling,** *Ratio decidendi, Res judicata.*

Further reading: Koopmans, 'Stare Decisis in European Law', in O'Keeffe and Schermers (eds.), *Essays in European Law and Integration* (1982), p. 11; Lord Mackenzie Stuart and Warner, 'Judicial Decisions as a Source of Community Law', in Grewe, Rupp, and Schneider (eds.), *Festschrift für Hans Kutscher* (1981), p. 273; Toth, 'The Authority of Judgments of the European Court of Justice: Binding Force and Legal Effects' (1984) 4 *YEL* 1. *See also under* **European Court of Justice.**

▶ **STATEMENT OF REASONS** Essential formal requirement for every binding act of the Council and the Commission non-compliance with which entails the invalidity of the act. In particular, under the ECSC Treaty decisions, recommendations, and opinions of the Commission, and under the EEC/Euratom Treaties regulations, directives, and decisions of the Council and of the Commission, are required to 'state the reasons on which they are based' (Arts. 15 ECSC, 190 EEC, 162 Euratom). In addition, under the ECSC Treaty the Community is required to 'publish the reasons for its actions' (Art. 5 ECSC).

The importance of the requirement to give adequate reasons for binding Community acts has been explained by the ECJ thus: 'In imposing upon the Commission the obligation to state reasons for its decisions, Article 190 is not taking mere formal considerations into account but seeks to give an opportunity to the parties of defending their rights, to the Court of exercising its supervisory functions and to Member States and to all interested nationals of ascertaining the circumstances in which the Commission has applied the Treaty. To attain these objectives, it is sufficient for the Decision to set out, in a concise but clear and relevant manner, the principal issues of law and of fact upon which it is based and which are necessary in order that the reasoning which has led the Commission to its Decision may be understood' (Case 24/62 *Germany* v. *Commission* [1963] ECR 63 at p. 69. This statement, which applies equally to all binding acts of the Council and the Commission, has been repeated by the Court, in whole or in part, in a number of subsequent cases some of which are cited below). Upon examining the decision before it, whereby the Commission refused to grant Germany a tariff quota at a reduced rate of duty for the importation of a quantity of wine, the Court concluded that: 'the inadequacy, the vagueness and the inconsistency of the statement of reasons for the Decision . . . do not satisfy the requirements of Article 190' and annulled the decision (ibid. at p. 70).

While the test laid down by the ECJ in the above-cited case applies generally, the sufficiency of a particular statement of reasons must always be determined 'in the context of the circumstances of the case, and in particular the content of the measure in question, the nature of the reasons relied on and the interest which addressees, or other persons to whom the measure is of direct and individual concern, within the meaning of the second paragraph of Article 173 of the Treaty, may have in obtaining explanations' (Case 41/83 *Italy* v. *Commission* [1985] ECR 873 at p. 891). Thus, in a number of cases the Court has stated that: 'The extent of the requirement laid down by Article 190 of the Treaty to state the reasons on which measures are based, depends on the nature of the measure in question. It is a question in the present case of a regulation, that is to say, a measure intended to have general application, the preamble to which may be confined to indicating the general situation which led to its adoption, on the one hand, and the general objectives which it is intended to achieve on the other. Consequently, it is not possible to require that it should set out the various facts, which are often very numerous and complex, on the basis of which the regulation was adopted, or *a fortiori* that it should provide a more or less complete evaluation of those facts' (Case 5/67 *Beus* [1968] ECR 83 at p. 95; Case 87/78 *Welding* [1978] ECR 2457 at pp. 2467–8; Cases 154/78 etc. *Valsabbia* v. *Commission* [1980] ECR 907 at p. 994, applying the same considerations to ECSC general decisions; etc.). Nevertheless, the statement of reasons must provide adequate legal justification for the adoption of the regulation; where this is not the case, the Court will declare the regulation invalid or void (see e.g. Case 158/80 *Rewe* [1981] ECR 1805 at p. 1834; Case 45/86 *Commission* v. *Council* [1987] ECR 1493 at p. 1522, where the statement of reasons contained an insufficiently precise reference to the legal basis of the regulations in question).

The requirement of reasoning is likewise relaxed to some extent in respect of measures addressed to, or concerning solely, the Member States or the Community institutions. These, being closely involved in the Community decision-making process, already enjoy the legal safeguards which the statement of reasons is designed to afford (Case 22/70 *Commission* v. *Council* [1971] ECR 263 at p. 283; Case 13/72 *Netherlands* v. *Commission* [1973] ECR 27 at p. 39). Special considerations apply to price-fixing decisions of the Commission made under agricultural regulations. These need not be reasoned individually; a reference to the reasoning of a previous similar decision is quite sufficient (Case 16/65 *Schwarze* [1965] ECR 877 at pp. 887–9).

By contrast, decisions addressed to private individuals, particularly those imposing pecuniary obligations enforceable within the Member States, must always be supported by precise and detailed reasons. As the ECJ has stated: 'With regard . . . to decisions imposing a fine, the statement of reasons is to be considered sufficient if it indicates clearly and coherently the considerations of fact and of law on the basis of which the fine has been imposed on the parties concerned, in such a way as to acquaint both the latter and the Court with the essential factors of the Commission's reasoning' (Case 41/69 *Chemiefarma* v. *Commission* [1970] ECR 661 at p. 690, dealing with a fine imposed under Reg. 17 for an infringement of EEC competition rules; see also Case 9/56 *Meroni* v. *HA* [1958] ECR 133 at pp. 141–3 and Case 1/63 *Macchiorlati Dalmas* v. *HA* [1963] ECR 303 at pp. 312–13, dealing with enforceable decisions under the ECSC Treaty). Nevertheless, the Commission is not required to discuss all the objections which might be raised against the decision (Case 41/69 *Chemiefarma* v. *Commission*, above; Case 29/67 *De Wendel* v. *Commission* [1968] ECR 263 at p. 280).

Special considerations apply also to measures taken by the institutions in the exercise of a discretionary power. Such measures fall, to some extent, outside the usual scope of judicial review. Their reasoning being the main means through which the ECJ can control their legality, the statement of reasons must always be such as to enable the Court to ascertain whether the institution has acted within the limits of its discretionary powers and whether it has satisfied the various conditions laid down by the Treaties for the exercise of those powers (see e.g. Cases 36 to 38 and 40/59 *Geitling* v. *HA* [1960] ECR 423 at p. 439; Cases 8 to 11/66 *Cimenteries* v. *Commission* [1967] ECR 75 at pp. 93–4; Cases 154/78 etc. *Valsabbia* v. *Commission*, above, at pp. 995–7).

Finally, as the ECJ has pointed out, 'the statement of reasons must in principle be notified to the person concerned at the same time as the decision adversely affecting him and . . . a failure to state the reasons cannot be remedied by the fact that the person concerned learns the reasons for the decision during the proceedings before the Court' (Case 195/80 *Michel* v. *Parliament* [1981] ECR 2861 at p. 2877).

See also **Grounds of action, Infringement of an essential procedural requirement, Institutional balance, Judicial review.**

▶ **SUPPLEMENTARY POWERS** General powers conferred on the Council or the Commission by Arts. 95(1) ECSC, 235 EEC, 203 Euratom, supplementing those which the institutions enjoy under the specific provisions of the Treaties.

Under Art. 95(1) ECSC, the Commission is authorized in a general manner to take a decision or make a recommendation, with the unanimous assent of the Council and after consulting the Consultative Committee, in all cases not otherwise provided for in the Treaty where it becomes apparent that such a measure is necessary to attain, within the Common Market in coal and steel, one of the objectives of the Community set out in Arts. 2, 3, and 4 of the Treaty. According to the ECJ, the object of this provision is to empower the Commission to meet an unforeseen situation. It follows that where a situation has been envisaged by the Treaty and the power to deal with it duly vested in the Commission by a specific provision, there is no need for the Commission to resort to Art. 95(1) (Case 9/61 *Netherlands* v. *HA* [1962] ECR 213 at p. 233).

Art. 235 EEC (to which Art. 203 Euratom is almost identical) likewise contains a general authorization enabling the Council, acting unanimously on a proposal from the Commission and after consulting the European Parliament, to take the 'appropriate measures' if action by the Community should prove necessary to attain, in the course of the operation of the Common Market, one of the objectives of the Community and if the Treaty has not provided the necessary powers. Like Art. 95(1) ECSC, Art. 235 EEC offers a supplementary means of action and may be used as the legal basis for a measure only where no other provision of the Treaty gives the Council the necessary power to adopt that measure. Where, for example, a regulation or a decision falls within the sphere of the Common Commercial Policy and may therefore be properly adopted under Art. 113 EEC, the Council is not justified in adopting it on the basis of Art. 235 (Case 45/86 *Commission* v. *Council* [1987] ECR 1493 at pp. 1520, 1522; Case 165/87 *Commission* v. *Council* [1988] ECR paras. 17–18. See also Cases 73 and 74/63 *Handelsvereniging Rotterdam* [1964] ECR 1 at p. 13; Cases 188 to 190/80 *France, Italy and United Kingdom* v. *Commission* [1982] ECR 2545 at p. 2574; Cases 281/85 etc. *Germany and Others* v. *Commission* [1987] ECR 3203 at p. 3254, confirming the same principle in different contexts). The fact, however, that the Council might adopt a measure under 'implied powers' derived from specific provisions of the Treaty but not clearly and expressly provided for does not prevent it from having recourse to Art. 235. In such a case, the latter procedure is indeed justified in the interest of legal certainty (Case 8/73 *Massey-Ferguson* [1973] ECR 897 at p. 908 *per Curiam*, p. 914 *per* A.-G. Trabucchi. This case must, however, be interpreted in the light of Case 165/87 *Commission* v. *Council*, above. *See further under* **Implied powers, Institutional balance**).

Assessment of the questions, first, whether specific action within the meaning of Art. 235 is necessary to attain a Community objective and, secondly, whether the powers already available under the other provisions of the Treaty are suitable for that purpose, comes within the jurisdiction of the Council, subject to review by the ECJ. Recourse to Art. 235 is therefore justified when the Council, taking into account the nature and overall importance of the matter in question, considers that the specific powers expressly conferred by the Treaty for attaining a particular objective are unsuitable. In other words, the express provision of inadequate powers does not exclude resort to the supplementary powers (see Case 8/73 *Massey-Ferguson*, above, at p. 912 *per* A.-G. Trabucchi). Nevertheless, it must be remembered that Art. 235 does not create an obligation but confers on the Council an option, failure to exercise which cannot affect the validity of measures properly taken under other provisions (Case 22/70 *Commission* v. *Council* [1971] ECR 263 at p. 283—'ERTA' case).

Art. 235 EEC (and Art. 203 Euratom) differs from Art. 95(1) ECSC in two important respects. First, while Art. 95(1) refers specifically to the objectives of the ECSC as set out in Arts. 2, 3, and 4 of the Treaty, Art. 235 aims at the attainment of 'one of the objectives of the Community' irrespective of whether it is a 'general' objective listed in Art. 3 EEC or a 'special' objective mentioned in any other part of the Treaty. It follows that Art. 235 empowers the Council to take appropriate measures in any area of the Treaty including, as the ECJ has indicated, the sphere of external relations (ibid. at p. 283) or the field of social policy (Case 43/75 *Defrenne* [1976] ECR 455 at p. 479). Indeed, the Paris Summit Conference of 19–21 October 1972 invited the institutions to make the widest possible use of Art. 235 in order to accomplish the tasks laid down in the various action programmes in such sectors as social policy, industrial, scientific, and technological policy, and environmental

policy. This clearly indicates that, in the opinion of the Heads of State or
Government of the Member States, these various areas come within the
'objectives of the Community' referred to in Art. 235 (see 6th *Gen. Rep. EC*
(1972), pp. 16, 395). Over the years, a number of important Community
instruments, both internal and external, were adopted on the basis of Art.
235, particularly in the fields of regional, environmental, economic, and
financial policy (see 9th *Gen. Rep. EC* (1975), p. 278). This provision also
served as the legal basis for the creation of new legal persons governed by
Community law, such as the European Centre for the Development of
Vocational Training (Reg. 337/75, *OJ* 1975 L39/1) and the European
Foundation for the Improvement of Living and Working Conditions (Reg.
1365/75, *OJ* 1975 L139/1). It may be noted that where the Single European
Act of 1986 now provides express authorization for the adoption of Community measures in the above-mentioned fields, such measures must in the
future be based on the relevant provisions of the Act rather than on Art. 235.

The second difference is that while Art. 95(1) ECSC authorizes the
Commission specifically to take a decision or to make a recommendation,
Art. 235 EEC enables the Council to take 'the appropriate measures'.
Although the effect of these measures is in some respects to supplement the
Treaty, they are nevertheless adopted by a Community institution proper
(not by the Member States acting together), within the context of the
objectives of the Community and in accordance with Community procedures.
They therefore fall within the scope of 'secondary legislation' and may be
taken in any of the forms laid down by Art. 189 EEC, i.e. in the form of a
regulation, directive, or decision (Case 38/69 *Commission* v. *Italy* [1970]
ECR 47 at pp. 56–7 *per Curiam*, pp. 62–3 *per* A.-G. Gand). In the field of
external relations, the term 'appropriate measures' may include the conclusion
of international agreements, although these, too, are ultimately adopted by
the Council in the form of a regulation or a decision (*see further under* **Treaty-
making power**).

See also **Council, Implied powers, Institutional balance, Treaty-making
power.**

Further reading: Lachmann, 'Some Danish Reflections on the Use of Article 235 of the
Rome Treaty' (1981) 18 *CML Rev.* 447; Schwartz, 'Article 235 and Law-Making
Powers in the European Community' (1978) 27 *ICLQ* 614.

▶ **SUPREMACY OF COMMUNITY LAW** Principle developed by the ECJ
according to which in the case of a conflict between Community law and
national law, Community law should take precedence irrespective of which is
later in time (also referred to as the principle of the primacy or precedence of
Community law).

While already in its earlier case-law the Court had occasionally referred to
the precedence of Community law over national law (see e.g. Case 6/60
Humblet v. *Belgium* [1960] ECR 559 at p. 569, dealing with the ECSC
Treaty), it was in Case 6/64 *Costa* [1964] ECR 585 at pp. 593–4 that the
Court first stated this as a general principle or doctrine which follows

necessarily from the very nature of Community law and forms one of its essential foundations as a supranational legal order. That case involved an alleged conflict between certain provisions of the EEC Treaty and a subsequent Italian nationalization law and in particular a submission by the Italian Government that in such a situation a national court was obliged to apply (the later) national law.

In rejecting that submission, the ECJ has stated:

By contrast with ordinary international treaties, the EEC Treaty has created its own legal system which, on the entry into force of the Treaty, became an integral part of the legal systems of the Member States and which their courts are bound to apply. By creating a Community of unlimited duration, having its own institutions, its own personality, its own legal capacity and capacity of representation on the international plane and, more particularly, real powers stemming from a limitation of sovereignty or a transfer of powers from the States to the Community, the Member States have limited their sovereign rights, albeit within limited fields, and have thus created a body of law which binds both their nationals and themselves.

The integration into the laws of each Member State of provisions which derive from the Community, and more generally the terms and the spirit of the Treaty, make it impossible for the States, as a corollary, to accord precedence to a unilateral and subsequent measure over a legal system accepted by them on a basis of reciprocity. Such a measure cannot therefore be inconsistent with that legal system. The executive force of Community law cannot vary from one State to another in deference to subsequent domestic laws, without jeopardizing the attainment of the objectives of the Treaty set out in Article 5(2) and giving rise to the discrimination prohibited by Article 7. The obligations undertaken under the Treaty establishing the Community would not be unconditional, but merely contingent, if they could be called in question by subsequent legislative acts of the signatories. . . .

It follows from all these observations that the law stemming from the Treaty, an independent source of law, could not, because of its special and original nature, be overridden by domestic legal provisions, however framed, without being deprived of its character as Community law and without the legal basis of the Community itself being called into question. The transfer by the States from their domestic legal system to the Community legal system of the rights and obligations arising under the Treaty carries with it a permanent limitation of their sovereign rights, against which a subsequent unilateral act incompatible with the concept of the Community cannot prevail.

It is thus clear that the Court derives the supremacy of Community law from the following main factors:

- the special and original nature of the EEC Treaty as an independent source of law, and of the whole legal system created by it;
- the acceptance of that legal system by all the Member States on the basis of reciprocity;
- the consequent permanent limitation of national sovereignty or a transfer of powers to the Community;
- the threat which incompatible unilateral national measures would present to the uniform application and integrity, and ultimately to the very survival, of Community law (see also Cases 9 and 58/65 *San Michele* v. *HA* [1967] ECR 1 at pp. 29–30, Order in Case 9/65).

While the *Costa* case remains the corner-stone of the doctrine of supremacy, in subsequent cases the Court had opportunity to define in more detail the practical consequences that follow from that doctrine. Thus, in Case 48/71 *Commission* v. *Italy* [1972] ECR 527 at p. 532—'Art Treasures' case—the Court stated that Community law must be 'fully applicable at the same time and with identical effects over the whole territory of the Community without the Member States being able to place any obstacles in the way'. Therefore, once the Court has declared a national law to be incompatible with Community law (under Arts. 169–71 EEC), all competent national authorities are automatically prohibited from applying that law, without the need to wait for its repeal by a constitutionally appropriate process.

In Case 106/77 *Simmenthal* [1978] ECR 629 at pp. 643–4, the Court was asked to determine the consequences that flow from the direct effect of a provision of Community law in the event of incompatibility with a subsequent legislative measure of a Member State. The Court stated:

. . . in accordance with the principle of the precedence of Community law, the relationship between provisions of the Treaty and directly applicable measures of the institutions on the one hand and the national law of the Member States on the other is such that those provisions and measures not only by their entry into force render automatically inapplicable any conflicting provisions of current national law but—in so far as they are an integral part of, and take precedence in, the legal order applicable in the territory of each of the Member States—also preclude the valid adoption of new national legislative measures to the extent to which they would be incompatible with Community provisions. . . . It follows from the foregoing that every national court must, in a case within its jurisdiction, apply Community law in its entirety and protect rights which the latter confers on individuals and must accordingly set aside any provision of national law which may conflict with it, whether prior or subsequent to the Community rule.

Although it follows from the above cases that any national law which is incompatible with Community law becomes automatically inapplicable, it is still necessary, in the interests of legal certainty, that such law should be repealed or amended by the national legislature. Its maintenance in force may create an ambiguous state of affairs by misleading individuals as to their rights arising from Community law. Purely internal and verbal administrative directions and practices waiving the application of such law on a quasi-discretionary basis are not sufficient (Case 167/73 *Commission* v. *France* [1974] ECR 359 at pp. 372–3; Case 168/85 *Commission* v. *Italy* [1986] ECR 2945 at pp. 2960–1).

The principle of the supremacy of Community law operates in a comprehensive manner. It ensures primacy not only to the provisions of the Treaties, but also to the binding acts of the institutions (i.e. regulations, directives, and decisions addressed to Member States) as well as to agreements concluded by the EEC with third countries. Moreover, it applies to the whole range of Community provisions, whether directly effective or not. One essential difference between these two sets of provisions is, however, that private individuals are able to enforce the primacy of Community law through the national courts only in so far as the provision in question produces direct effects. In that respect, the principle of supremacy forms a logically necessary complement to that of direct effect. The statement that a provision is 'directly effective' is meaningless unless that statement implies that it is also 'superior' in rank, i.e. that no Member State can, by a conflicting national measure, prevent it from having all the effects in the domestic legal system that Community law attributes to it, irrespective of any difficulties, consequences, and repercussions that such effects may entail at the national level. Thus, it is through the combined effects of the two concepts that individuals are able fully to enjoy the rights which they derive from the Community legal order in the face of possible violations on the part of the Member States (see Case 13/68 *Salgoil* [1968] ECR 453 at pp. 462–3; Case 167/73 *Commission* v. *France*, above, at p. 371; Case 118/75 *Watson and Belmann* [1976] ECR 1185 at pp. 1197–8; and in particular Case 106/77 *Simmenthal*, above, at pp. 643–4). While the ECJ has expressly stated that directly effective provisions of regulations, directives, and decisions addressed to Member States enjoy the primacy of Community law in the national courts (*see further under* **Decision, Directive, Regulation**), the same follows by implication with regard to directly effective provisions of agreements concluded by the Community with third countries, from those decisions of the Court in which the Court has held that such agreements (1) are binding upon the Member States; (2) form an 'integral part' of Community law; and (3) may produce direct effects (*see further under* **Direct effect**).

The supremacy of Community law is comprehensive also in the sense that it operates over all branches of the national legal system including, in particular, constitutional law, competition law, and criminal law. Thus, the ECJ has stated in a general fashion that 'no provision whatsoever of national law may be invoked to override [Community law]' (Case 48/71 *Commission* v. *Italy*, above, at p. 532), and that, consequently, 'the validity of Community measures can be judged only in the light of Community law' (Case 249/85 *ALBAKO* [1987] ECR 2345 at p. 2359). It follows that the validity of such a measure or its effect within a Member State 'cannot be affected by allegations that it runs counter to either fundamental rights as formulated by the constitution of that State or the principles of a national constitutional structure' (Case 11/70 *Internationale Handelsgesellschaft* [1970] ECR 1125 at p. 1134).

In the field of competition law, too, the Court has held that conflicts must be resolved by applying the principle that Community law takes precedence. Consequently, application by the national authorities of their own competition laws to an agreement or practice which is also subject to proceedings instituted by the Commission under Community law 'may not prejudice the full and uniform application of Community law or the effects of measures taken or to be taken to implement it' (Case 14/68 *Wilhelm* [1969] ECR 1 at pp. 14–15).

In criminal law, it is an established principle that 'where criminal proceedings are brought by virtue of a national measure which is held to be contrary to Community law, a conviction in those proceedings is also incompatible with that law' and must therefore be avoided (Case 88/77 *Schonenberg* [1978] ECR 473 at p. 491, referring to Case 82/71 *SAIL* [1972] ECR 119; see also

Case 269/80 *Tymen* [1981] ECR 3079 at p. 3094; Case 21/81 *Bout* [1982] ECR 381 at p. 389).

In the United Kingdom, at the time of accession it was thought that the supremacy of Community law would be adequately guaranteed by the combined effects of sections 2(1), 2(4), and 3(1) of the European Communities Act 1972. Section 2(1) gives the force of law in the United Kingdom to all present and future, primary and secondary, Community provisions which under Community law are directly effective. Section 2(4) provides that 'any enactment passed or to be passed . . . shall be construed and have effect subject to the foregoing provisions of this section', i.e. subject to the enforceability of directly effective Community law. Finally, under section 3(1), any question as to the meaning or effect of a Community provision must be determined by the courts 'in accordance with the principles laid down by and any relevant decision of the European Court', i.e. in accordance, amongst other things, with the principle of the supremacy of Community law. It is submitted that these provisions should enable the courts to comply with the ruling of the ECJ in Case 106/77 *Simmenthal*, above.

See also Decision, Direct applicability, Direct effect, Directive, Regulation.

Further reading 1. BOOKS: Bebr, *Development of Judicial Control of the European Communities* (1981), chs. 14–15; Commission of the European Communities, *Thirty Years of Community Law* (1983), part I, ch. 6; Hartley, *The Foundations of European Community Law*, 2nd edn. (1988), chs. 7–8; Schermers, *Judicial Protection in the European Communities*, 4th edn. (1987), ch. 1, part III/C; Toth, *Legal Protection of Individuals in the European Communities* (1978), vol. i, ss. 106–7.

2. ARTICLES: Bebr, 'How Supreme is Community Law in the National Courts?' (1974) 11 *CML Rev.* 3; Hay, 'Supremacy of Community Law in National Courts' (1968) 16 *AJCL* 524; March Hunnings, 'Rival Constitutional Courts: A Comment on Case 106/77' (1978) 15 *CML Rev.* 479 at p. 483; Trindade, 'Parliamentary Sovereignty and the Primacy of European Community Law' (1972) 35 *MLR* 375.

▶ **SUSPENSION OF OPERATION** Provisional stay of execution of an act of a Community institution which is being challenged in proceedings before the ECJ. It is ordered by the President of the Court or—exceptionally—by the full Court by way of summary procedure, pending final judgment by the Court in the main action but without prejudice to the latter (Arts. 39 ECSC, 185 EEC, 157 Euratom, 33 ECSC Statute, 36 EEC Statute, 37 Euratom Statute, 83–90 RP. It may be noted that while the Court's Rules of Procedure use the term 'suspension of operation', the Treaties refer to 'suspension of application', and the Court's Statutes to 'suspension of execution'). As a general rule, actions brought before the ECJ have no suspensory effect (save under Art. 83(2) of the Euratom Treaty which provides for actions against Commission decisions imposing sanctions). Suspension of operation is therefore an exceptional measure the purpose of which is to prevent serious and irreparable damage being caused by a Community act which could not be made good even if the act is subsequently annulled by the Court with retroactive effect (see, in general, the opinion of A.-G. Gand in Case 50/69R *Germany* v. *Commission* [1969] ECR 449 at pp. 454–5).

Suspension of operation must be distinguished from other 'interim measures' which are often applied for simultaneously and the grant of which is subject to basically similar conditions. The main differences are, first, that suspension of operation by definition always implies a negative obligation (an obligation not to execute the act in question) and, secondly, that it may only be ordered against a Community institution, which must moreover be a party (the defendant) to the main action (Case 133/87R *Nashua Corporation* v. *Commission* [1987] ECR 2883 at p. 2887. It is nevertheless conceivable that an order suspending the implementation of a Council regulation or of a binding act of the Parliament—such as the budget—may be addressed to the Commission as the institution responsible for such implementation, even though the main action is brought against the Council or the Parliament, see Case 23/86R *United Kingdom* v. *Parliament* [1986] ECR 1085 at p. 1093). By contrast, other interim measures may require positive action as well as an abstention and may also be granted against third parties not being involved in the main proceedings, whether they be Community institutions, Member States, or even private individuals (natural or legal persons) (*see further under* **Interim measures**).

The conditions for the suspension of the operation of a Community act have been defined by the ECJ in the following terms: 'By virtue [of the Treaties] and Article 83 of the Rules of Procedure, as well as of a consistent line of decisions of the Court, measures of this kind may be adopted by the judge hearing the application for such measures if it is established that their adoption is *prima facie* justified in fact and in law, if they are urgent in the sense that it is necessary, in order to avoid serious and irreparable damage, that they should be laid down, and should take effect, before the decision of the Court on the substance of the action and if they are provisional in the sense that they do not prejudge the decision on the substance of the case, that is to say that they do not at this stage decide disputed points of law or of fact or neutralise in advance the consequences of the decision to be given subsequently on the substance of the action' (Case 20/81R *Arbed* v. *Commission* [1981] ECR 721 at pp. 730–1. For similar definitions, see e.g. Case 220/82R *Moselstahlwerk* v. *Commission* [1982] ECR 2971 at p. 2978; Cases 228 and 229/82R *Ford* v. *Commission* [1982] ECR 3091 at p. 3098; Case 120/83R *Raznoimport* v. *Commission* [1983] ECR 2573 at p. 2577; and the cases cited below).

It appears from the above definition that normally three conditions must be satisfied before suspension of operation may be ordered (although in practice the Court does not always examine if all three conditions are present since the absence of any one of them may in itself entail the rejection of an application). These are as follows: first, there must exist a prima-facie case; secondly, the suspension applied for must be urgent; and thirdly, it must be provisional. These will be considered below in turn.

As regards the first condition, although Art. 83(2) RP requires that an application for the suspension of the operation of an act should state, amongst other things, 'the factual and legal grounds establishing a *prima facie* case for the interim measures applied for', it is clear that what is required is that a prima-facie case be made out showing that the main action itself stands a reasonable chance of succeeding.

However, this requirement has been expressed in different terms over the years. Thus, according to the early case-law, the norm was that 'it should be clearly apparent that there exists a strong presumption that the application in the main action is well-founded (*fumus boni juris*)' or, in other words, that the 'soundness' of the main application had in substance to be 'manifest' (Cases 43, 45, and 48/59 *Lachmüller* v. *Commission* [1960] ECR 463 at p. 492; Case 50/69R *Germany* v. *Commission*, above, at pp. 455, 457 *per* A.-G. Gand). Later it was found sufficient if 'the grounds on which the substantive application is made appear, on first examination, not to be manifestly without foundation' (Case 3/75R *Johnson & Firth Brown* v. *Commission* [1975] ECR 1 at p. 6). Subsequently, it has been accepted that the first condition is fulfilled where 'it appears that the challenge by the applicants to the legality of the Commission's measures . . . is based on serious considerations such as to make the legality of those measures seem doubtful to say the least' (Case 232/81R *Agricola Commerciale Olio* v. *Commission* [1981] ECR 2193 at p. 2199), or where the applicants can show the existence of 'serious doubts', 'doubts', or 'serious problems' concerning the proper application of Community law by the defendant institution (Case 120/83R *Raznoimport* v. *Commission*, above, at pp. 2578–9; Case 1/84R *Ilford* v. *Commission* [1984] ECR 423 at p. 431).

Nevertheless, the first condition must be reconciled with the third condition which requires that the order granting suspension of operation should not prejudge the Court's final decision in the main action (see below). It follows that in examining the existence of a prima-facie case, the Court or its President is normally reluctant to deal in detail with arguments based on the alleged inadmissibility or lack of grounds of the principal case. Thus, the Court has repeatedly stressed that in principle the issue of the admissibility of the main application should not be examined in proceedings relating to the suspension of operation, so as not to prejudge the substance of the case. It is only where an objection is raised that the main application is 'manifestly inadmissible' that the Court will examine whether the main action is prima facie admissible. Such examination is particularly necessary where private parties seek the annulment of a measure of general application (such as an ECSC general decision or an EEC/Euratom regulation) 'in order to prevent a situation where those persons are able, by means of an application for interim measures, to obtain the suspension of the operation of a measure which the Court subsequently refuses to declare void because, on examination of the substance of the case, the application is declared inadmissible' (Case 160/88R *FEDESA* v. *Council* [1988] ECR paras. 22–3; see also Case 82/87R *Autexpo* v. *Commission* [1987] ECR 2131 at p. 2137 and Case 221/86R *Group of the European Right* v. *Parliament* [1986] ECR 2969 at p. 2975 and the cases cited therein. For an earlier statement of the principle, see Case 44/75R *Könecke* v. *Commission* [1975] ECR 637 at p. 640, and for cases brought under the ECSC Treaty, see Case 258/80R *Rumi* v. *Commission* [1980] ECR 3867 at p. 3876; Case 20/81R *Arbed* v. *Commission*, above, at pp. 730–3).

507

Where the Court finds that prima facie the main application is inadmissible, this will entail the inadmissibility of the application for the suspension of operation also (see the first two cases cited immediately above). Where the main application concerns the annulment of an individual decision which is addressed to another person (e.g. a Member State), a prima-facie proof that the applicant is directly and individually concerned by that decision is, under the EEC/Euratom Treaties, necessary to make the application for its suspension admissible. Such proof is without prejudice to the Court's final decision concerning the admissibility of the main action (Case 1/84R *Ilford* v. *Commission*, above, at pp. 427–8). In certain special circumstances, however, suspension of the operation of regulations has been granted in the absence of even a prima-facie examination of direct and individual concern (see e.g. Case 232/81R *Agricola Commerciale Olio* v. *Commission*, above, at pp. 2198–9; Case 120/83R *Raznoimport* v. *Commission*, above, at p. 2578. See also Cases 113/77R and 113/77R-Int. *Toyo Bearing* v. *Council* [1977] ECR 1721 at p. 1725, etc.—'Japanese Ball Bearing' cases).

The second condition for the grant of suspension of operation is that the suspension must be 'urgent'. This means that it must be necessary in order to avoid any 'serious and irreparable damage' that might arise from the immediate execution of the measure. Accordingly, the applicant must be able to show that, if the operation of the contested measure is not suspended, he is liable to suffer imminent damage which is both serious and irreparable (or irreversible). In assessing whether this condition is fulfilled, the Court or its President usually applies very strict criteria. Thus, the anticipated damage must amount to more than mere temporary inconvenience (Case 45/71R *GEMA* v. *Commission* [1971] ECR 791 at p. 795) or alleged financial difficulty (Case 53/65R *Mondini* v. *HA* [1966] ECR 17 at p. 18; Case 27/68R *Renckens* v. *Commission* [1969] ECR 255 at pp. 275–6; Case 20/81R *Arbed* v. *Commission*, above, at p. 732). There must exist 'special difficulties' (Case 234/82R *Ferriere di Roè Volciano* v. *Commission* [1983] ECR 725 at p. 729, where the Court suspended the operation of a Commission decision imposing a fine, without requiring the applicant to provide the usual bank guarantee), an 'extremely difficult situation' (Case 1/84R *Ilford* v. *Commission*, above, at p. 431), or a 'serious disturbance' (Case 45/71R *GEMA* v. *Commission*, above, at p. 794) arising from the special, often exceptional, circumstances of the applicant. The damage must be 'considerably in excess of the inevitable but short-lived disadvantages arising from [the contested] measure' (Cases 228 and 229/82R *Ford* v. *Commission*, above, at p. 3101, where the contested decision itself was an interim, conservatory measure); it must be 'disproportionate' in comparison with the institution's interest in the immediate execution of the contested act (Case 78/83R *Usinor* v. *Commission* [1983] ECR 2183 at p. 2189). Moreover, the risk and the extent of the damage must be assessed in the light of the 'obligation to co-operate which is incumbent upon [the applicant] in order to mitigate the alleged damage' (Case 120/83R *Raznoimport* v. *Commission*, above, at p. 2580). Accordingly, the applicant must take all necessary steps which are reasonable in the circumstances to avoid or mitigate possible damage (ibid.), and his failure to do so cannot be compensated for by a grant of a stay of execution (Case 44/75R *Könecke* v. *Commission*, above, at p. 641).

As well as being 'serious', the damage must also be 'irreparable' or 'irreversible', i.e. such that it 'could not be redressed if [the contested] provision were annulled at the hearing of the main action' (Case 19/59R *Geitling* v. *HA* [1960] ECR 17, 34 at p. 37. For cases where the threat of 'irreparable damage' was established in this sense, see e.g. Case 20/74R *Kali-Chemie* v. *Commission* [1974] ECR 337 at p. 339; Case 260/82R *NSO* v. *Commission* [1982] ECR 4371 at pp. 4376–7; for cases where the threat of such damage was not accepted, see e.g. Case 6/72R *Continental Can* v. *Commission* [1972] ECR 157 at pp. 159–60; Cases 60 and 190/81R *IBM* v. *Commission* [1981] ECR 1857 at pp. 1863–4. All four cases involved the application of EEC competition law by the Commission). The fact that under Community law the possibility always exists, in principle, of obtaining reparation by means of an action for damages does not necessarily mean that the alleged damage cannot be regarded as being irreparable (Case 232/81R *Agricola Commerciale Olio* v. *Commission*, above, at p. 2200; Case 141/84R *De Compte* v. *Parliament* [1984] ECR 2575 at pp. 2581–2; for a contrary ruling see Case 120/83R *Raznoimport* v. *Commission*, above, at p. 2580). Nevertheless, even if the applicant succeeds in proving the threat of a 'serious and irreparable damage', suspension of operation will not be granted if, on balance, it were to cause to interested third parties and/or to the Community damage at least as serious and as irreparable as that with which the applicant is faced (the principle of the 'balance of interests', see e.g. Case 92/78R *Simmenthal* v. *Commission* [1978] ECR 1129 at p. 1137; Case 77/87R *Technointorg* v. *Council* [1987] ECR 1793 at p. 1799; but see also Case 23/86R *United Kingdom* v. *Parliament*, above, at pp. 1097–9).

Finally, the third condition is that suspension of operation must be 'provisional'. This means both that unless the order provides otherwise the suspension lapses upon the delivery of the final judgment, and that the order 'shall have only an interim effect, and shall be without prejudice to the decision of the Court on the substance of the case' (Art. 86(3) and (4) RP). It follows that it is not possible to order by means of this procedure a measure which 'would in reality be irrevocable and would confront the Judges responsible for the substantive decision with an irreversible situation' (Case 44/75R *Könecke* v. *Commission*, above, at p. 641) or which 'would amount not to a suspension of the operation of the contested measure but to a complete reversal, even though only provisional, of such a nature as to denude the main action of its purpose' (Case 91/76R *De Lacroix* v. *Court of Justice* [1976] ECR 1563 at p. 1564; see also e.g. Case 232/81R *Agricola Commerciale Olio* v. *Commission*, above, at p. 2200).

In addition to the three main conditions discussed so far, the case-law of the Court reveals a number of further requirements that must be satisfied before a suspension of operation may be granted. These may be summarized as follows:

- the application for suspension must have a direct link with the subject-matter of the main action (Case 258/80R *Rumi* v. *Commission*, above, at pp. 3878–9);
- the suspension sought must be within 'the scope of an urgent interim measure intended to safeguard temporarily the interest of the applicant' and must therefore not interfere with the rights and legitimate interests of third parties (Case 26/76R *Metro* v. *Commission* [1976] ECR 1353 at p. 1356);
- the contested measure must not have already been applied (implemented) in practice (see Case 121/77R *Nachi Fujikoshi* v. *Council* [1977] ECR 2107 at pp. 2110–11; Case 92/78R *Simmenthal* v. *Commission*, above, at p. 1136);
- the contested measure must not involve a negative decision, i.e. a refusal to grant an authorization or an exemption (e.g. under Art. 65(2) ECSC or under Arts. 85(3), 115, or 226 EEC). In a consistent line of cases it has been stated that, as regards such negative decisions, an application for suspension of operation cannot attain the desired object (i.e. to obtain temporarily the authorization or exemption) and is therefore 'irrelevant', since 'suspension of the operation of a decision of refusal cannot be equivalent to the grant of the authorisation [or exemption] refused by the Commission. The Court has no authority to substitute itself for the Commission in order to take . . . decisions instead and in place of the executive' (Case 50/69R *Germany* v. *Commission*, above, at p. 451; see also e.g. Cases 71/74R and RR *Fruit- en Groentenimporthandel* v. *Commission* [1974] ECR 1031 at p. 1034; Cases 209 to 215 and 218/78R *Van Landewyck* v. *Commission* [1978] ECR 2111 at p. 2114—'FEDETAB' cases).

Owing to its nature as well as to the various conditions and limitations to which its grant is subject, suspension of the operation of an act often cannot, in itself, attain the desired result, i.e. to provide immediate relief. In such cases, suspension of operation is usually combined with other interim measures, which go beyond suspension. In certain situations, the Judge dealing with the application may find it appropriate to impose conditions or to grant partial suspension only, while allowing implementation of the rest of the act subject to specified conditions and reservations (see e.g. Case 3/75R *Johnson & Firth Brown* v. *Commission*, above, at pp. 6–7; Case 232/81R *Agricola Commerciale Olio* v. *Commission*, above, at pp. 2202–3; Cases 228 and 229/82R *Ford* v. *Commission*, above, at pp. 3102–3; Case 1/84R *Ilford* v. *Commission*, above, at p. 432). Suspension of operation may also be made conditional on the lodging by the applicant of security, of an amount and nature to be fixed in the light of the circumstances (Art. 86(2) RP; see e.g. the 'Japanese Ball Bearing' cases, above). Where neither suspension of operation nor any other interim measure is justified, the parties themselves may be invited to co-operate in order to mitigate the risk of damage during the interim period before final judgment (see e.g. Case 20/81R *Arbed* v. *Commission*, above, at p. 1733).

As regards procedure, an application to suspend the operation of a measure is admissible only if the applicant is challenging that measure in proceedings before the Court (Art. 83(1) RP). It must be made by a separate document and in accordance with the provisions relating to pleadings and applications in general (see Arts. 37 and 38 RP). A request for suspension made in the application originating the main proceedings will be dismissed as inadmissible (Case 108/63 *Merlini* v. *HA* [1965] ECR 1 at p. 9; Case 32/64 *Italy* v. *Commission* [1965] ECR 365 at p. 372, referring to the 'essential requirements' of Art. 83(3) RP). So will be one where the main action was clearly brought out of time (Case 50/84R *Bensider* v. *Commission* [1984] ECR 2247 at p. 2252). Although, in the absence of any time-limits, in principle it is for the applicant to decide at what stage of the proceedings to apply for suspension, there are obvious objections to granting such an application where it is made very late in the proceedings, for example after the closing of both the written and the oral procedures and at a time when the Court has already commenced its deliberations upon the substance of the case (see Cases 3 to 18, 25, and 26/58 *Barbara Erzbergbau* v. *HA* [1960] ECR 173 at pp. 223–4). The application must state the subject-matter of the dispute, the circumstances giving rise to urgency, and the factual and legal grounds establishing a prima-facie case for the interim measures applied for (Art. 83(2) RP).

The application is served on the opposite party who may submit written or oral observations. Where the parties are not opposed in law, the President may reach a decision without hearing oral arguments (Case 27/76R *United Brands* v. *Commission* [1976] ECR 425 at p. 429). While the President may order a preparatory inquiry, in extremely urgent cases he also has the power to grant the application even before the observations of the opposite party have been submitted. Such a decision may be varied or cancelled even without any application being made by any party (Art. 84(2) RP. See e.g. Case 107/82R *AEG* v. *Commission* [1982] ECR 1179 at p. 1180; Case 229/82R *Ford* v. *Commission* [1982] ECR 2849 at p. 2851; Case 221/86R *Group of the European Right* v. *Parliament* [1986] ECR 2579 at p. 2583; in all these cases the President temporarily suspended, as a precautionary measure, the operation of the contested acts until the making of the order terminating the interlocutory proceedings).

The President may either decide on the application himself or refer it to the full Court. In the latter case, the Court must give the matter absolute priority and hear the Advocate-General (Art. 85 RP). The decision is made in the form of a reasoned order, from which no appeal lies (Art. 86(1) RP). Nevertheless, on application by a party, the order may at any time be varied or cancelled on account of a change in circumstances (Art. 87 RP). Rejection of an application does not bar the applicant from making a further application on the basis of new facts (Art. 88 RP).

Finally, it may be noted that the rules relating to suspension of operation also apply in a corresponding manner to applications for the suspension of the enforcement of a decision of the Court or of a measure of the other institutions (Art. 89 RP).

See also Costs, Enforcement procedure, Interim measures, Special forms of procedure.

Further reading 1. BOOKS: Lasok, *The European Court of Justice: Practice and Procedure* (1984), ch. 8; Usher, *European Court Practice* (1983), ch. 10.

2. ARTICLES: Borchardt, 'The Award of Interim Measures by the European Court of Justice' (1985) 22 *CML Rev.* 203; Gray, 'Interim Measures of Protection in the European Court' (1979) 4 *EL Rev.* 80.

► **THIRD PARTY PROCEEDINGS** One of two exceptional review procedures available before the ECJ (the other being revision of judgments), and the only procedure whereby third parties may contest a judgment of the Court which has been rendered in a direct action without their being heard and which is prejudicial to their rights (Arts. 36 ECSC Statute, 39 EEC Statute, 40 Euratom Statute, 97 RP).

An application originating third party proceedings may be brought by Member States, Community institutions, and any other natural or legal persons within two months of the publication of the original judgment in the *Official Journal*. The application must be made against all the parties to the original case (which is taken to include interveners, see Cases 42 and 49/59— Third party proceedings *Breedband* v. *Aciéries du Temple* [1962] ECR 145 at p. 147), and in the form prescribed for pleadings and applications originating proceedings in general (see Arts. 37 and 38 RP). In addition to specifying the judgment contested, the application must state, first, how that judgment is prejudicial to the rights of the third party and, secondly, the reasons why the third party was unable to take part in the original case. These two requirements, compliance with which constitutes an essential condition for the admissibility of the application, are further considered below.

The first requirement implies that 'only persons whose rights have been prejudiced by the contested judgment are entitled to bring third party proceedings' (Cases 9 and 12/60—Third party proceedings *Belgium* v. *Vloeberghs and HA* [1962] ECR 171 at p. 183). The ECJ has interpreted this requirement strictly, holding that a 'prejudice to a right' must amount to more than a mere adverse effect on the applicant's legitimate interests. What is required is that the contested judgment should have altered the applicant's legal situation or prevented him from asserting his rights. The prejudice can only arise either from the operative part of that judgment or from its decisive grounds, since only these can produce legally binding effects. Statements made in the grounds of the contested judgment which are not 'decisive', i.e. not necessary to support the operative part, cannot cause prejudice (ibid. at pp. 183–4 *per Curiam*, pp. 190–1 *per* A.-G. Roemer; Case 267/80 TO *Birra Dreher* v. *Riseria Modenese, Council and Commission* [1986] ECR 3901 at p. 3914; Case 292/84 TP *Bolognese* v. *Scharf and Commission* [1987] ECR 3563 at pp. 3567–8). It follows from the foregoing that third party proceedings have a fairly limited scope. Since by virtue of the *res judicata* rule the binding effects of a judgment are restricted to the parties, it is only exceptionally that a judgment can 'prejudice the rights' of third parties.

The second requirement implies that 'any person who was heard or could have taken part in the original case cannot bring third party proceedings' (Cases 9 and 12/60 *Belgium* v. *Vloeberghs and HA*, above, at p. 181). The reason is to prevent persons having an interest in proceedings pending before the Court from asserting their interest after the Court has delivered its judgment and has thus settled the dispute. Such persons may protect their interests by intervening in the case. Third party proceedings are designed to provide a remedy specifically 'for a third party who, having been called upon . . . to take part in the original case, was unable to participate for justifiable reasons and . . . for any person who was not in a position to intervene in the original case' (ibid. at pp. 181–2; see also Cases 42 and 49/59 *Breedband* v. *Aciéries du Temple*, above, at pp. 157–8).

Generally, where the subject-matter of and the conclusions in the original case were duly published in the *Official Journal* as required by Art. 16(6) RP, third parties cannot claim to have been unaware of that case. If they missed the opportunity to intervene owing to their own negligence, they cannot later assert an interest which was put in issue in the original case, especially if their conclusions are identical with those already put forward therein. Third party proceedings will be admissible only if the subject-matter of and the conclusions in the principal action, as published in the *Official Journal*, did not disclose any direct and specific interest establishing a right to intervene voluntarily in that action (this is what happened in Cases 9 and 12/60 *Belgium* v. *Vloeberghs and HA*, above, at pp. 182–3; see also Cases 42 and 49/59 *Breedband* v. *Aciéries du Temple*, above, at pp. 158–9).

The Court may, on application by the third party, order a stay of execution of the contested judgment under the same conditions under which the operation of measures of the institutions may be suspended (see Arts. 83–90 RP). For such an application to succeed the facts and circumstances of the case must be sufficient to warrant an order for a stay of execution (ibid. at p. 169). To the extent that the application for third party proceedings is successful, the contested judgment will be varied. The original of the new judgment will be annexed to the original of the contested judgment (Art. 97(3) RP).

See also Intervention, Judgment, Order, *Res judicata*, Revision of judgments, Special forms of procedure, Suspension of operation.

Further reading: Lasok, *The European Court of Justice: Practice and Procedure* (1984), ch. 12, s. v; Usher, *European Court Practice* (1983), ch. 12.

▶ **THREE WISE MEN'S REPORT** 'Report on European Institutions' submitted to the European Council on 29 and 30 November 1979 by the 'Committee of Wise Men' consisting of Messrs Barend Biesheuvel, Edmund Dell, and Robert Marjolin. Following the initiative of President Giscard d'Estaing of France, the Committee was set up by the European Council in December 1978 to formulate 'specific proposals aimed at ensuring the proper operation of the Community on the basis of and in compliance with the Treaties, including their institutional arrangements, and progress towards European Union' (*Bull. EC* 11–1979, p. 25, containing a summary of the Report). The main proposals of the Report, which should be read in conjunction with the Spierenburg Report, are as follows:

- the European Council should be integrated, so far as possible, within the normal framework of interinstitutional relations; it should adopt a master plan of priorities before 1981;
- the authority of the Presidency of the Council of Ministers should be recognized and strengthened. The Council should concentrate on genuinely political issues while making wider use of delegation to the

Commission of powers of implementation. The Luxembourg Compromise has become a fact of life. However, the Members of the Council (i.e. the Member States) should accept voting as the normal practice in all cases where the Treaty does not impose unanimity and no very important national interests are involved which could bring the Luxembourg Compromise into operation. The Council of Foreign Ministers should continue to play a central role while specialized Councils should hold less frequent meetings;

- the exercise by the Commission of its right of initiative and its role as guardian of the Treaties, together with its management and implementing powers, should be made more effective. The number of Commissioners should be limited to twelve—one per Member State; the number of Directorates-General should likewise be reduced to twelve. The President of the Commission should be chosen by the European Council six months before the renewal of the Commission and he should be consulted by Governments on the selection of Members of the Commission. His authority should generally be strengthened. The Commission should represent the interests of Europe as a whole and not a compromise between different points of view;

- closer contacts should be developed between the European Parliament and the Commission. The President of the European Council should appear once every six months before the Parliament. In general, balanced relations should be maintained between the three political institutions on the basis of the existing Treaties;

- any system of a 'two-speed' Europe which created differences of status between Member States should be rejected;

- a practical solution should be found to the problems created by the use of nine official languages;

- the Community *acquis*, which has been impressive, should be maintained and consolidated;

- in relation to the outside world, the Community and its Member States must act in the most united way possible both on the economic and on the political front.

Some of the above proposals have now been implemented as a result of the adoption of the Single European Act in 1986.

See also Acquis communautaire, **Commission, Committee on Institutional Affairs, Council, European Council, European Parliament, European Union, Institutional balance, Institutions, Luxembourg Compromise, Single European Act, Spierenburg Report, Tindemans Report.**

Further reading: Duff, 'The Report of the Three Wise Men' (1981) 19 *JCMS* 237; Editorial, 'The Report of the "Three Wise Men"' (1980) 17 *CML Rev.* 3.

▶ **TINDEMANS REPORT** 'Report on European Union' submitted to the European Council on 29 December 1975 by Mr Leo Tindemans, Prime Minister of Belgium (*Bull. EC* 12–1975, p. 5; text in Suppl. 1/76—*Bull. EC*). The Report was drawn up at the request of the Paris Summit Conference of 9 and 10 December 1974 (*Bull. EC* 12–1974, p. 9). It was prepared on the basis of the Community institutions' Reports on European Union (see Suppls. 5/75 and 9/75—*Bull. EC*) and of Mr Tindemans's consultations with the Governments of the Member States and representative sectors of public opinion in the Community.

The Report envisages European Union not as a definitive arrangement but as a new phase, a qualitative change, in the history of European unification which can only be achieved by a continuous process. It does not aim at laying down the date of completion of the Union, nor at incorporating in a precise legal text all the constitutional changes which are necessary to achieve it. Instead, the Report makes a number of practical and specific proposals in four closely interrelated areas:

1. *In the field of external relations*, the Member States must present a united front to the outside world. For this purpose, the distinction between political co-operation and matters covered by the Treaties should be brought to an end. The political commitment of the Member States to political co-operation should be changed into a legal obligation.

2. *In the economic and social fields*, European Union requires common economic, monetary, industrial, agricultural, energy, and research policies. The solidarity of the Member States and their peoples must be strengthened; this necessitates fair and just regional and social policies.

3. *With regard to the citizen*, European Union must recognize and protect the rights of the individual, both fundamental rights and economic and social rights. The individual must be able to move freely without frontier controls and to enjoy improved transport, communication, and medical services. There should be student exchanges and collaboration between information media (radio, television). A European Foundation should be set up to promote greater understanding among the peoples of the Union.

4. *In the institutional field*, while European Union can and must be built upon the existing institutional framework, it does require increasing the authority, efficiency, legitimacy, and coherence of that framework. The strengthening of the institutions involves, in particular, the enhancement of the role of the European Council and the Parliament; the extension of the use of majority decision-making (which should become normal practice in the Council); and the co-ordination of the Council's activities. It also implies the increased influence and cohesion of the Commission and the delegation of more implementing power to it. According to the Report, all these are essential measures which should be taken immediately if European Union is to progress.

During the course of 1976, the Tindemans Report was examined by the Foreign Ministers, the Commission, and the European Council which, at its meeting in The Hague on 29 and 30 November 1976, endorsed its main underlying principles. At the same time, it invited the Foreign Ministers and the Commission to report to it once a year on the results achieved in the various sectors of the Union, 'thus translating into reality the common conception of European Union' (*Bull. EC* 11–1976, p. 93; 10th *Gen. Rep.*

EC (1976), p. 25). While the Report did not produce the immediate results which its author had hoped for, it did lay the foundations of future developments leading towards European Union and institutional reform. Its main ideas resurface time and again in virtually all subsequent reports, proposals, and other documents on the subject. The Report may thus be regarded as a distant ancestor of both the Draft Treaty on European Union adopted by the European Parliament in 1984 and of the Single European Act of 1986 which transformed these developments into binding legal obligations.

See also **Committee on a People's Europe, Committee on Institutional Affairs, European Act, European Foundation*, European Union, Institutional balance, Institutions, Single European Act, Solemn Declaration on European Union, Spierenburg Report, Three Wise Men's Report.**

Further reading: Editorial, 'Tindemans, Vedel and the European Parliament' (1975–6) 1 *EL Rev.* 183; id., 'The Tindemans Report' (1976) 13 *CML Rev.* 147; Mitchell, 'The Tindemans Report: Retrospect and Prospect' (1976) 13 *CML Rev.* 455.

▶ **TRANSITIONAL PERIOD** 1. **Under the ECSC Treaty:** Second of two stages in which the implementation of the ECSC Treaty was to be effected. The first stage, referred to as the 'preparatory period', extended from the date of entry into force of the Treaty (25 July 1952) to the date of the establishment of the Common Market for coal, ore, and scrap (10 Feb. 1953, see Case 1/58 *Stork* v. *HA* [1959] ECR 17 at p. 27). During this period the institutions of the Community were to be set up, and the High Authority was to conduct studies and consultations with a view to surveying the situation of the coal and steel industries in the Community and to preparing the way for the measures to be taken during the transitional period itself. In addition, it was required to carry out initial negotiations with third countries. The second stage, described as the 'transitional period', began on the date of the establishment of the Common Market and ended five years later. During this period, the provisions of the ECSC Treaty applied subject to the derogations and supplementary provisions contained in the annexed Convention on the Transitional Provisions. Save where this Convention expressly provided otherwise, these derogations and supplementary provisions ceased to apply at the end of the transitional period (Art. 1 of the Convention on the Transitional Provisions, now spent).

2. **Under the Euratom Treaty:** The Euratom Treaty did not provide for a general 'transitional period' but contained specific provisions for the application of the Treaty during an 'initial period' of undefined length (Arts. 209–23 Euratom, now spent). Also, some of the substantive provisions of the Treaty, particularly those relating to the nuclear Common Market, required action to be taken only some time after the entry into force of the Treaty (see e.g. Arts. 93, 94, 98 Euratom).

3. **Under the EEC Treaty:** A period of twelve years, extending from the date of entry into force of the EEC Treaty (1 Jan. 1958) to 31 December 1969, during which the Common Market was to be progressively established. This transitional period was divided into three stages of four years each (first stage:

517

1 Jan. 1958–31 Dec. 1961; second stage: 1 Jan. 1962–31 Dec. 1965; third stage: 1 Jan. 1966–31 Dec. 1969), to each of which there was assigned a set of actions to be initiated and carried through concurrently. Transition from the first to the second stage was conditional upon a finding that the objectives laid down in the Treaty for the first stage had in fact been attained in substance. Such finding was made by Council Decision of 14 January 1962 (*JO* 1962, p. 164). Although it would have been possible to extend the first, second, and third stages and, up to a maximum of fifteen years, the whole transitional period itself, such extension never took place and the transitional period came to an end automatically on 31 December 1969 in strict conformity with the timetable laid down in Art. 8 EEC (3rd *Gen. Rep. EC* (1969), p. 15). The Acceleration Decision of 26 July 1966 (Dec. 66/532, *JO* 1966, p. 2971) did not have the effect of bringing forward this date of expiry (Case 27/78 *Rasham* [1978] ECR 1761 at p. 1767).

The legal significance of the transitional period was that, save for the exceptions or derogations provided for in the EEC Treaty, the expiry of this period constituted the latest date by which all the rules laid down in the Treaty were to enter into force and all the measures required for establishing the Common Market had to be implemented (Art. 8(7) EEC). Although this provision had not been fully complied with (particularly in the fields of the freedom of establishment and freedom to provide services, free movement of capital, the Common Agricultural and Transport Policies, the adjustment of State monopolies of a commercial character, and commercial relations with Eastern Europe), the expiry of the transitional period and the passage to the definitive stage of the Common Market had important legal consequences in almost every area of Community activity (see the Communication of the Commission to the Council of 19 Feb. 1969, Doc. Sec. (69) 546 def; and 3rd *Gen. Rep. EC* (1969), p. 467). These may be summarized as follows:

(*a*) In a general sense, the expiry of the transitional period meant that, from that time, all the matters and areas explicitly attributed to the Community by the EEC Treaty came definitively under Community jurisdiction. Consequently, any special measures derogating from the Treaty could no longer be determined unilaterally by the Member States concerned, but had to be adopted within the framework of the Community system designed to ensure the protection of the general interest of the Community (Case 231/78 *Commission* v. *United Kingdom* [1979] ECR 1447 at p. 1461; Case 232/78 *Commission* v. *France* [1979] ECR 2729 at p. 2738).

(*b*) All the provisions of the EEC Treaty imposing a clear and unconditional obligation upon the Member States to attain a precise result by the end of the transitional period became directly effective within the Member States, and enforceable in the national courts by individuals, upon the expiry of that period. This was so even in the absence of any implementing measures which the Community institutions were required, but failed, to take during the transitional period. These measures now became legally superfluous, although still useful from a purely practical point of view. Thus, in particular, Art. 8(7) EEC rendered directly effective, as of the end of the transitional period, the provisions of the Treaty requiring Member States to abolish all obstacles to trade between them and all discrimination on grounds of nationality between their nationals with respect to the free movement of goods, persons, services, and the right of establishment (i.e. Arts. 13(2), 30, 37(1), 48, 52, 59(1), and 60(3) EEC, see e.g. Case 2/74 *Reyners* [1974] ECR 631 at pp. 651–2; Case 33/74 *Van Binsbergen* [1974] ECR 1299 at pp. 1311–12; Case 45/75 *Rewe-Zentrale* [1976] ECR 181 at pp. 197–8, although Arts. 59 and 60 did not become directly effective with respect to freedom to provide services in the transport sector, see Case 13/83 *Parliament* v. *Council* [1985] ECR 1513 at p. 1599). Some provisions had been rendered directly effective already by the expiry of the first stage of the transitional period, i.e. from 1 January 1962 (Arts. 16, 95(1) and (2), and 119 EEC, see e.g. Case 43/75 *Defrenne* [1976] ECR 455 at pp. 478–9).

(*c*) The Member States were required to bring the Common Agricultural Policy into force by the end of the transitional period at the latest, but could keep the national market organizations provisionally in existence pending the establishment of a common organization (Arts. 40(1), 43, and 46 EEC). However, this was only permissible until the end of the transitional period with the result that after that date the operation of a national market organization could no longer prevent the full application of the general rules laid down by the Treaty for the establishment of the Common Market, and in particular those prohibiting quantitative restrictions and measures having equivalent effect (Case 48/74 *Charmasson* [1974] ECR 1383 at pp. 1393–5; Cases 231/78 *Commission* v. *United Kingdom* and 232/78 *Commission* v. *France*, see under (*a*) above).

(*d*) In the field of external relations, since the end of the transitional period the Common Commercial Policy and the conclusion of tariff and trade agreements have been based on Art. 113 EEC instead of Art. 111; and the Member States have been required to proceed within the framework of international economic organizations only by common action as opposed to a mere concerted action as before (Art. 116 EEC).

(*e*) In a number of cases, the expiry of the first or second stage or of the transitional period brought about a change in the voting rules of the Council in the sense that the requirement of unanimity in decision-making was replaced by that of a qualified majority (see e.g. Arts. 28, 43(2), 54(2) EEC. But see also the Luxembourg Compromise of 1966).

(*f*) Certain provisions of the EEC Treaty became inapplicable at the end of the transitional period, e.g. Art. 91(1) EEC (dumping); Art. 226 EEC (protective measures).

4. **The Act of Accession 1972** contains no provisions for a 'transitional period' similar to that found in Art. 8 EEC. As the original transitional period laid down in the EEC Treaty had expired before accession and the Treaty had already become fully operative by that time, for the new Member States the Act of Accession 1972 laid down only clearly specified transitional measures ('derogations') in order to facilitate their adjustment to the rules already in force within the Communities. Subject to the dates, time-limits, and special

provisions provided for in the Act, the application of these transitional measures was to terminate at the end of 1977 (Art. 9 of the Act of Accession 1972). Since this is a general rule, any exceptions to it must be narrowly interpreted (Case 231/78 *Commission* v. *United Kingdom*, above, at pp. 1459–62, see under (3a) above, holding that Art. 60(2) of the Act of Accession 1972 constituted a transitional measure—but not a 'special provision'—the application of which terminated at the end of 1977). The Member States have no power to extend the derogations beyond the prescribed time-limits (Case 63/83 *Kirk* [1984] ECR 2689 at pp. 2716–17, interpreting Arts. 100 and 103 of the Act of Accession 1972). Where the Act of Accession 1972 laid down no transitional measures (as e.g. in the case of quantitative restrictions or the right of establishment), the provisions of the original Treaties and Community acts became fully applicable to the new Member States immediately on the date of accession (1 Jan. 1973, see Art. 2 of the Act of Accession 1972; Case 15/74 *Centrafarm* [1974] ECR 1147 at p. 1166; Case 11/77 *Patrick* [1977] ECR 1199 at p. 1205). This date generally had the same effect in the relations between the old and the new Member States as the expiry of the transitional period had for the old Member States.

5. **The Act of Accession 1979,** like the Act of Accession 1972, contains no provisions for a 'transitional period' but lays down transitional measures ('derogations') whose application was to terminate at the end of 1985, subject to any special provisions in the Act prescribing different dates or shorter or longer time-limits (Art. 9 of the Act of Accession 1979). The ECJ has held that the derogations allowed by the Act must be interpreted restrictively and with a view to facilitating the attainment of the aims of the EEC Treaty and to applying its rules in their entirety (Cases 194 and 241/85 *Commission* v. *Greece* [1988] ECR 1037 at p. 1060; see also Case 58/83 *Commission* v. *Greece* [1984] ECR 2027 at p. 2033).

6. **The Act of Accession 1985,** like those of 1972 and 1979, lays down transitional measures ('derogations') without however specifying any date at which their application is to terminate (Art. 9 of the Act of Accession 1985).

See also **Acceleration decisions, Accession Treaties, Direct effect.**

Further reading: Rambow, 'The End of the Transitional Period' (1969) 6 *CML Rev.* 434; Faull, 'The Transitional Period Ends' (1978) 3 *EL Rev.* 33.

▶ *TRAVAUX PRÉPARATOIRES* Preparatory work preceding the conclusion of a treaty or the adoption of a legislative measure, such as minutes of meetings and conferences, successive drafts, preparatory working documents, correspondence. It is generally recognized in international law that such preparatory work may be resorted to as a supplementary means of treaty interpretation, particularly to confirm a meaning already arrived at by other methods of interpretation or, exceptionally, to determine the meaning when the other methods leave it ambiguous or obscure or lead to a result which is manifestly absurd or unreasonable (see Art. 32 of the Vienna Convention on the Law of Treaties of 1969).

In the case of the three basic Community Treaties, no *travaux préparatoires* proper had been made public by the Member States, which had thus deliberately excluded all recourse to them. On the other hand, it is very doubtful whether the positions adopted at the beginning of 1957 by the heads of delegation to the Intergovernmental Conference preparatory to the Treaties of Rome, as well as the unilateral explanations, declarations, and reservations made in some of the Member States on the occasion of the parliamentary ratification of the three basic Treaties, can be regarded as constituting true preparatory work. Even if they could be so considered, they could certainly not be held against the new Member States, which did not participate in the drafting of the original Treaties. The ECJ itself has apparently never resorted to these documents as a means of interpretation, thus adhering to the view that the texts of the Treaties in the form in which they were ratified constitute the final and definitive expression of the intention of the Contracting States (see Case 8/55 *Fédération Charbonnière de Belgique* v. *HA* [1956] ECR 245 at pp. 271–2, 277 *per* A.-G. Lagrange; Case 2/74 *Reyners* [1974] ECR 631 at pp. 665–6 *per* A.-G. Mayras).

The position is, however, different in the case of the acts of the institutions (secondary legislation). While the deliberations of the Council are secret, the legislative process preceding the final adoption of an act is generally not, and where the relevant preparatory documents may throw light on the intentions of the legislator they may be used as a means of interpretation. Thus, the ECJ has occasionally had recourse to preparatory work, such as discussions of Government officials (see e.g. Case 72/69 *Bremer Handelsgesellschaft* [1970] ECR 427 at p. 435), proposed amendments made by Management Committees (see e.g. Case 29/69 *Stauder* [1969] ECR 419 at p. 425), and opinions expressed by the consultative bodies—e.g. the European Parliament—on draft legislation (see e.g. Case 36/77 *Greco* [1977] ECR 2059 at p. 2071. See however the opinion of A.-G. Warner in Case 155/79 *AM & S.* v. *Commission* [1982] ECR 1575 at p. 1621, who entertained 'grave doubt whether it is permissible to interpret a Council Regulation by reference to its "legislative history"'). Nevertheless, the Court's position is that 'in the absence of working documents clearly expressing the intention of the draftsmen of a provision, the Court can base itself only on the scope of the wording as it is and give it a meaning based on a literal and logical interpretation' (Case 15/60 *Simon* v. *Court of Justice* [1961] ECR 115 at p. 125).

See also **Interpretation of Community law.**

▶ **TREATY-MAKING POWER** Capacity to enter into treaties and agreements under public international law. Such capacity is one of the inherent and necessary attributes of international legal personality and is therefore enjoyed by (and only by) the subjects of international law, i.e. States and international organizations. There is, however, an essential difference between the legal capacities of these entities. As the International Court of Justice stated in its Advisory Opinion concerning *Reparation for Injuries Suffered in the Service of the United Nations* (ICJ Reports 1949, p. 174 at p. 180), 'whereas a State possesses the totality of international rights and duties recognised by international law [including treaty-making power], the rights and duties of an entity such as [an international organization] must depend upon its purposes and functions as specified or implied in its constituent documents and developed in practice'. Accordingly, while it is generally recognized that every State possesses capacity to conclude treaties *ipso facto* and (subject to the conditions under which a treaty may be void) without restrictions as to subject-matter, form, or procedure (see Art. 6 of the Vienna Convention on the Law of Treaties of 1969), the capacity of international organizations to enter into treaties is not unlimited but is restricted to what is 'necessary for the exercise of their functions and the fulfilment of their purposes'. In particular, the treaty-making power of an international organization is governed by the rules of that organization, that is to say, by its 'constituent instruments, decisions and resolutions adopted in accordance with them, and established practice' (see the Preamble, Arts. 2(1)(j) and 6 of the Vienna Convention on the Law of Treaties between States and International Organizations or between International Organizations of 1986, and the commentaries of the International Law Commission to the draft of these articles, *YILC* 1982, Vol. II, Part Two, pp. 21, 23–4).

For the purposes of concluding treaties under international law, the European Communities are assimilated to international organizations rather than being treated as *sui generis* supranational entities (see the comments and observations of the EEC on the above-mentioned draft articles of the Vienna Convention of 1986, *YILC* 1981, Vol. II, Part Two, pp. 201–3 esp. at p. 202). Their treaty-making power is therefore derived from the combined effects of public international law and their own constituent instruments, i.e. the founding Treaties, as interpreted and applied in practice by their institutions, in particular by the ECJ. It is international law which provides the legal basis for and determines the nature of that power in so far as it enables the Communities to possess international legal personality, which is the *fons et origo* of the treaty-making capacity. On the other hand, it is Community law which delimits the scope and extent of that capacity, particularly in the relationship between the Communities and their Member States, by conferring, expressly or by implication, treaty-making power upon the Communities. For this reason, a distinction should be made between treaty-making *capacity* in a strict sense, i.e. the ability to enter into treaties, which is ultimately a matter of international law, and treaty-making *competence* or *authority*, i.e. the power to exercise that capacity within more or less precisely defined limits, which is always a question of internal Community law. These two concepts correspond to the external and internal aspects of treaty-making power, respectively. It is the latter which will be considered below (for the external aspects of treaty-making power, *see* **External relations**, section I, **Legal personality**, point 1).

The scope of the Communities' treaty-making power is defined differently under the three basic Treaties, which will therefore be examined separately. It must be remembered, however, that since the capacity to conclude treaties is an attribute of legal personality, in practice it can be exercised only in relation to such States and international organizations as are willing to recognize the Communities as subjects of international law and to enter into treaty relations with them. So far, such recognition has been accorded to the Communities—in varying degrees—by most States and international organizations including, since June 1988, the Soviet Union, its East European allies, and their organization the Council for Mutual Economic Assistance (*see further under* **External relations, Legal personality**).

1. **The ECSC Treaty** contains no specific provisions expressly conferring treaty-making power on that Community. Art. 6 only provides in general terms that 'the Community shall have legal personality' and that 'in international relations, the Community shall enjoy the legal capacity it requires to perform its functions and attain its objectives'. Unlike the EEC Treaty, the ECSC Treaty does not create a Common Commercial Policy which would necessitate the conclusion by the Community itself of tariff and trade agreements with third countries and international organizations. Instead, Art. 71(1) expressly provides that the powers of the Member States in matters of commercial policy shall not be affected by the Treaty, from which it follows that in principle the conclusion of such agreements, in so far as they relate to products subject to the ECSC Treaty (i.e. coal and steel), remains within the competence of the Member States. The latter are only required to keep the Commission informed of proposed commercial agreements to enable it to eliminate, by means of recommendations, any incompatibility between such agreements and the Treaty (Art. 75. See also Arts. 14–22 of the Convention on the Transitional Provisions, annexed to the ECSC Treaty, which lay down detailed rules, mainly of a transitional nature, concerning relations between the Community and third countries).

Nevertheless, the ECJ has pointed out that Art. 71(1) does not enable Member States to pursue a totally independent commercial policy, and that under Art. 3(a) and (f) of the Treaty the Community institutions have certain duties as regards external trade (Case 36/83 *Mabanaft* [1984] ECR 2497 at pp. 2522–3). The Court has also raised the question, but without answering it, whether, in view of the necessity of ensuring that international transactions to which the Communities are party should have as uniform a character as possible, Art. 71(1) retains its former force following the entry into force of the EEC Treaty. In any case, the Court has said, that provision cannot render inoperative Arts. 113 and 114 of the EEC Treaty (see below) and affect the vesting of power in that Community for the negotiation and conclusion of international agreements in the realm of the Common Commercial Policy (Opinion 1/75 *Local Cost Standard* [1975] ECR 1355 at p. 1365). While, in the context of that opinion, it would seem to follow from this that the EEC may include ECSC products in agreements entered into under its own commercial policy, in practice such products are usually the subject of separate international agreements concluded either by the Member States collectively or by the ECSC (sometimes under the general powers granted by Art. 95 of the Treaty, see below) or by the Member States and the ECSC jointly (*see further under* **External relations, Mixed agreement**).

2. It is **the Euratom Treaty** which contains the most comprehensive set of

523

provisions relating to treaty-making (Arts. 101–6). In addition to conferring legal personality upon the Community (Art. 184), it states in general terms that 'the Community may, within the limits of its powers and jurisdiction, enter into obligations by concluding agreements or contracts with a third State, an international organisation or a national of a third State' (Art. 101 (1)).

The ECJ has interpreted the above provisions as creating a division of jurisdiction and powers between the Community and the Member States. Accordingly, in respect of matters for which jurisdiction and powers have been conferred on the Community under the Euratom Treaty the Member States, whether acting individually or even collectively and in a concerted manner, are no longer able to enter into an international agreement without the Community's participation. This would unilaterally impose conditions on the exercise of prerogatives which have been transferred from the field of national sovereignty to the Community. Therefore, to the extent to which the Community is to be bound to comply with an agreement it is necessary that it should assume such obligations by concluding the agreement itself. Thus, the Treaty aims at ensuring the Community's independent action in external relations through its own institutions. In the interpretation of the Court, Art. 101(1) defines the limits of the Community's external (i.e. treaty-making) competence so as to correspond to the limits of its internal competence (the doctrine of 'parallelism', see further below). It follows that in areas in which the Community has been granted exclusive internal powers (e.g. in the fields of nuclear supply, property ownership), it must be able to exercise exclusive external powers as well. On the other hand, where the subject-matter of an agreement falls in part within the jurisdiction of the Community and in part within that of the Member States, the agreement should be entered into by the Community and the Member States jointly in accordance with Art. 102 of the Treaty (the so-called 'mixed agreement') (Ruling 1/78 *Protection of Nuclear Materials* [1978] ECR 2151 at pp. 2171, 2173, 2176, and esp. 2178–81. *See further under* **Mixed agreement**).

It may be noted that in addition to Arts. 101–6, which deal with external relations generally, the Euratom Treaty contains a number of provisions relating to the conclusion of agreements or contracts on specific subject-matters, such as Arts. 10 (research), 29 (exchange of information), 46(2)(e) (Joint Undertaking), 52 (supplies), 206 (association agreements with a third State, a union of States, or an international organization).

3. **The EEC Treaty** expressly confers treaty-making power on the Community with regard to two matters only: the conclusion of tariff and trade agreements within the framework of the Common Commercial Policy (Art. 113) and the conclusion of association agreements with a third State, a union of States, or an international organization (Art. 238). In addition, Arts. 130N and 130R(4) and (5), inserted by Arts. 24 and 25 of the Single European Act of 1986, respectively, provide that the Community may conclude agreements with third countries and international organizations relating to co-operation in research and technological development (Art. 130N) and to the environment (Art. 130R(4) and (5)), but in the latter case only 'to the extent to which

the objectives referred to in paragraph 1 can be attained better at Community level than at the level of the individual Member States'. Since Art. 228, which lays down the treaty-making procedure, expressly refers to the conclusion of agreements 'where this Treaty [so] provides', it was assumed for a long time that the Community's treaty-making power was limited to the two situations expressly specified in the original Treaty (see the opinion of A.-G. Dutheillet de Lamothe in Case 22/70 *Commission* v. *Council*, below, at pp. 293–4). However, in a series of successive judgments and opinions, the ECJ has considerably extended the scope of that power.

In the first major judgment on the matter given in Case 22/70 *Commission* v. *Council* [1971] ECR 263 at pp. 274–6, which concerned the conclusion of the European Road Transport Agreement (*ERTA* case), the Court laid down four important principles which provide the foundation for the EEC's treaty-making power. These may be summarized as follows. First, it follows from the fact that the Community possesses legal personality under Art. 210 EEC that 'in its external relations the Community enjoys the *capacity* to establish contractual links with third countries over the whole field of objectives defined in Part One of the Treaty' (the principle of general powers). Secondly, in individual cases the Community's *authority* to enter into international agreements may arise 'not only from an express conferment by the Treaty . . . but may equally flow [implicitly] from other provisions of the Treaty and from measures adopted, within the framework of those provisions, by the Community institutions' (the principle of implied powers). Thirdly, each time the Community adopts common rules in implementation of a common policy or for the attainment of a Community objective, the Member States 'no longer have the right, acting individually or even collectively, to undertake obligations with third countries which affect those rules' or might alter their scope. As and when such common rules come into being, 'the Community alone is in a position to assume and carry out contractual obligations towards third countries affecting the whole sphere of application of the Community legal system' (the principle of exclusive powers). Therefore, fourthly, 'the system of internal Community measures may not be separated from that of external relations' (*in foro interno, in foro externo*, or the principle of 'parallelism').

Applying these principles to the instant case, the Court held that although the Treaty did not expressly confer on the Community authority to enter into international agreements in the sphere of transport, the bringing into force of a regulation laying down rules for the harmonization of certain social legislation relating to road transport 'necessarily vested in the Community power to enter into any agreements with third countries relating to the subject-matter governed by that regulation', including the ERTA. Those Community powers, the Court concluded, 'exclude the possibility of concurrent powers on the part of Member States, since any steps taken outside the framework of the Community institutions would be incompatible with the unity of the Common Market and the uniform application of Community law'.

In subsequent cases, the Court has restated, clarified, and in certain

525

respects further developed the principles laid down in the *ERTA* decision. Although certain questions still remain to be decided, the law relating to the treaty-making power of the Community, as it stands at present, may be summarized as follows:

(*a*) According to the doctrines of implied powers and parallelism, the 'authority to enter into international commitments may not only arise from an express attribution by the Treaty, but equally may flow implicitly from its provisions . . . Whenever Community law has created for the institutions of the Community powers within its internal system for the purpose of attaining a specific objective, the Community has authority to enter into the international commitments necessary for the attainment of that objective even in the absence of an express provision in that connexion' (Opinion 1/76 *Laying-up Fund* [1977] ECR 741 at p. 755; see also Cases 3, 4, and 6/76 *Kramer* [1976] ECR 1279 at pp. 1308–9).

(*b*) Implied external power exists in all cases in which internal power has already been exercised in order to adopt measures which come within the attainment of common policies (the *ERTA* situation), but is not limited to that eventuality. The prior adoption of internal Community measures is not a prerequisite for the existence of external power since 'the power to bind the Community *vis-à-vis* third countries . . . flows by implication from the provisions of the Treaty creating the internal power and in so far as the participation of the Community in the international agreement is . . . necessary for the attainment of one of the objectives of the Community' (Opinion 1/76 *Laying-up Fund*, above, at p. 755).

(*c*) In the sphere of the Common Commercial Policy, where treaty-making power is based on an express authority granted by the Treaty, the scope of that power is co-extensive with the scope of the policy. The ECJ has stressed that the concept of commercial policy cannot be interpreted restrictively and that, in any case, it cannot have a different or narrower meaning for the Community than for the Member States (Opinion 1/75 *Local Cost Standard*, above, at p. 1362, confirming that export credits fell within the Common Commercial Policy and therefore within the ambit of the Community's treaty-making power). The Common Commercial Policy first of all covers all the matters listed in Art. 113, but that list is not exhaustive. Thus, the Community's treaty-making competence under Art. 113 comprises not only the classical tariff and trade agreements which are based primarily on the operation of customs duties and quantitative restrictions, but also the more structured and elaborate international commodity agreements which aim at a regulation of the world market rather than at a mere liberalization of trade, including any related subsidiary or ancillary matters (Opinion 1/78 *Natural Rubber Agreement* [1979] ECR 2871 at pp. 2909–17).

Moreover, the implementation of the Common Commercial Policy by means of an international agreement does not depend on the prior adoption of internal Community rules, since a commercial policy is made up by the combination and interaction of internal and external measures, without priority being taken by one over the others. As the ECJ has pointed out, 'sometimes agreements are concluded in execution of a policy fixed in advance, sometimes that policy is defined by the agreements themselves' (Opinion 1/75 *Local Cost Standard*, above, at p. 1363). As the Common Commercial Policy itself is the outcome of a progressive development, the precise scope of the Community's treaty-making power under this heading becomes more clearly defined as that policy develops.

(*d*) Where treaty-making power has been expressly conferred on the Community (as under Arts. 113 and 238), that power is exclusive whether or not it has been exercised. In the words of the ECJ, 'it cannot . . . be accepted that, in a field . . . covered . . . by the common commercial policy, the Member States should exercise a power concurrent to that of the Community, in the Community [i.e. internal] sphere and in the international [i.e. external] sphere. The provisions of Articles 113 and 114 . . . show clearly that the exercise of concurrent powers by the Member States and the Community in this matter is impossible' (Opinion 1/75 *Local Cost Standard*, above, at p. 1364). It is submitted that the same principles apply also to the Community's treaty-making power in the field of environmental policy, to the extent to which such power has been conferred upon the Community by the newly inserted Art. 130R(4) and (5). Although Art. 130 R(5)(2) purports to leave intact the Member States' competence to conclude international agreements in this area, a Declaration annexed to the Single European Act makes it clear that this provision does not affect the principles resulting from the case-law of the ECJ, in particular from the *ERTA* decision.

(*e*) Where Community treaty-making power is not expressly provided but exists by implication, it is not a priori exclusive. It becomes exclusive, however, once the internal power on which it is based has been exercised by the adoption of internal rules (Case 22/70 *Commission* v. *Council*, above, at pp. 274–6) or once it has been decided (by the Council) that the conclusion of an international agreement is necessary for the attainment of a specific Community objective (Opinion 1/76 *Laying-up Fund*, above, at p. 755). As long as the institutions have not actually made use of an implied power, the Member States retain residual authority to assume and implement international commitments essential to achieve a Community objective. This is, however, subject to the following three conditions.

First, the Member States' authority is only of a transitional nature and comes to an end when either the Community actually exercises its internal power or the time-limit laid down for its doing so expires. In either case, the Community's power becomes exclusive and definitive. Thus, pending the adoption of Community measures for the conservation of the resources of the sea, or pending the expiry of the six-year period laid down for this purpose by Art. 102 of the Act of Accession of 1972, the Member States themselves were able to enter into fisheries agreements pursuing that objective.

Secondly, during this interim period, the Member States are under a duty not to enter into any international commitment which could hinder the Community in carrying out its tasks in the relevant field, and also under a duty to proceed by common action within the framework of the relevant international organizations as required by Art. 116.

Thirdly, as soon as the Member States' residual authority has come to an

527

end and the Community's competence has become exclusive, the institutions and the Member States are under a duty to use all the political and legal means at their disposal in order to ensure the participation of the Community in any agreements that the Member States may have concluded during t' e interim period (Cases 3, 4, and 6/76 *Kramer*, above, at pp. 1310–11). Once the Community institutions have exercised their power, the provisions adopted by them preclude the adoption or application of any conflicting provisions by the Member States (Case 61/77 *Commission* v. *Ireland* [1978] ECR 417 at p. 448—'Sea fisheries' case).

It may be noted that, in practice, the Member States (acting through the Council) are generally reluctant to allow the Community to make use of its non-exclusive powers. They also tend to interpret exclusive Community powers (particularly Arts. 113 and 238) in a restrictive manner. Moreover, in view of the fact that internal rules may generate exclusive external competences, Member States are frequently reluctant to adopt such rules, at least in certain sensitive areas like sea and air transport where the exercise of the Council's power to legislate is optional rather than mandatory under Art. 84. The purpose and the effect of these practices is for the Member States to retain to themselves as much treaty-making power as possible. (See the Memorandum by the Commission submitted to the House of Lords Select Committee on the European Communities in 1985, in the 16th Report of the Committee, listed below under Official Publications, at pp. 104–6.)

(*f*) So far the ECJ has established the existence of implied treaty-making competence in two areas of Community law: in the spheres of the Common Transport Policy (Case 22/70 *Commission* v. *Council*, above, at pp. 274–5—*ERTA* case, and Opinion 1/76 *Laying-up Fund*, above, at p. 755) and of the Common Fisheries Policy (Cases 3, 4, and 6/76 *Kramer*, above, at pp. 1307–9). In both cases, the implied external powers were derived from provisions of the Treaty conferring *specific* internal powers on the institutions: Arts. 74–5 (transport) and Art. 43(2) (fisheries as part of agriculture). However, the EEC Treaty also confers *general* legislative powers on the Community by Arts. 100 and 235 which do not refer to any particular Community policy but can be applied to attain any of the Community objectives. Thus, under Art. 100 the Council may issue directives for the harmonization (approximation) of the laws of Member States to the extent required for the 'establishment or functioning of the Common Market'. Under Art. 235, the Council may take 'the appropriate measures' if action by the Community should prove necessary 'to attain, in the course of the operation of the Common Market, one of the objectives of the Community and this Treaty has not provided the necessary powers' (see also the comparable Arts. 95 ECSC and 203 Euratom).

The above provisions have been used to introduce new Community policies not specifically provided for in the Treaty, such as the environmental and consumer protection policies. The question arises, however, whether they may also be relied on to establish external treaty-making powers. In the *ERTA* case, above, at p. 283 the Court stated that Art. 235 'empowers the Council to take any "appropriate measures" equally in the sphere of external relations', although it added that the Article did not create an obligation, but conferred on the Council an option. It follows from the doctrine of parallel competence that where internal rules have been enacted in a given area under one of these Articles, the Community acquires a corresponding exclusive external power. Where the internal competence has not yet been used, i.e. no measures have been taken under Art. 100 or 235, the position seems to be (although this has not so far been confirmed by the ECJ) that the Community still has external authority since such authority flows not from any internal measure but 'from the provisions of the Treaty creating the internal power' and in so far as the participation of the Community in the international agreement is necessary 'for the attainment of one of the objectives of the Community' (see Opinion 1/76 *Laying-up Fund*, above, at p. 755). However, until the Council has established in accordance with the procedures laid down in Art. 100 or 235 that the conclusion of an agreement is 'necessary', the Community's external competence remains non-exclusive or potential. It is obvious that this competence is very wide since it is based on the Community's objectives as opposed to common policies. It may encompass any matter covered by the Community's objectives as listed in Art. 3 of the Treaty, even if falling outside the existing common policies, provided that the matter relates to the operation of the Common Market.

In practice, Arts. 100 and 235 have been used, either on their own or in combination with other provisions, as legal bases for international agreements mainly—although not exclusively—relating to environmental matters and consumer protection (although, as A.-G. Mischo pointed out in his opinion in Case 131/86 *United Kingdom* v. *Council* [1988] ECR 905 at p. 915, it is odd that a Council decision—or regulation—which concludes an international agreement should be based on Art. 100 which only provides for the adoption of directives). In the future, agreements relating to the environment must be based on the newly inserted Art. 130R(5), while co-operation agreements concerning research and technological developments on the new Art. 130N.

(*g*) Where the subject-matter of an agreement falls wholly within the exclusive competence of the Community, the Community alone has the power to negotiate and conclude the agreement. On the other hand, where the subject-matter falls in part within Community jurisdiction and in part within that of the Member States, both the Community and the Member States will participate in the negotiation and conclusion of the agreement and become parties to it jointly (the so-called 'mixed agreement') (Opinion 1/76 *Laying-up Fund*, above, at p. 756; Opinion 1/78 *Natural Rubber Agreement*, above, at pp. 2917–18 and 2920. *See further under* **Mixed agreement**).

(*h*) It should be mentioned that, in the context of the Community's treaty-making power, the terms 'treaty' and 'agreement' are used in the broadest possible sense so as to encompass any legally binding instrument governed by public international law. As the ECJ has stated, 'the formal designation of the agreement . . . under international law is not of decisive importance' since the Treaty uses that expression 'in a general sense to indicate any undertaking entered into by entities subject to international law which has binding force, whatever its formal designation' (Opinion 1/75 *Local Cost Standard*, above,

529

at pp. 1359–60). Thus, the Community's treaty-making power enables the Community to participate, in addition to the usual bilateral or multilateral treaties, conventions, agreements, etc. negotiated and concluded directly with States or with international organizations, also in agreements concluded within the framework of international organizations (see Opinion 1/78 *Natural Rubber Agreement*, above, at pp. 2915–16, relating to the conclusion of the International Agreement on Natural Rubber within the framework of the United Nations Conference on Trade and Development (UNCTAD)), and to undertake obligations and commitments arising from binding measures (resolutions, decisions, recommendations, etc.) enacted by the relevant organs of international organizations (see Opinion 1/75 *Local Cost Standard*, above, at pp. 1360 *et seq.*, relating to the Understanding on a Local Cost Standard drawn up in the form of a resolution of the Council of the Organization for Economic Co-operation and Development (OECD); Cases 3, 4, and 6/76 *Kramer*, above, at pp. 1307–9, where the 'international commitments' in question arose from a binding recommendation of the North-East Atlantic Fisheries Commission set up by the North-East Atlantic Fisheries Convention of 1959). Thus, internal Community law enables (and in certain cases requires) the Community to participate in the work of international organizations and in the drafting and adoption of decisions and other binding acts of such organizations and conferences even if such participation is not always possible under existing international law (*see further under* **External relations**, section II).

(*i*) Finally, the ECJ has recognized that the Community is not only able to enter into contractual relations with third countries but also has the competence to co-operate with them in setting up public international institutions with organs having decision-making powers of their own. Nevertheless, this competence does not extend so far as to enable the Community to surrender its independence of action in the field of external relations and to bring about a change in the internal Community structure by altering the prerogatives of the institutions and the position of the Member States *vis-à-vis* one another. Clearly, the institutions may not freely delegate to a non-Community organization powers (other than purely executive powers) granted them by the Treaty and thus create for the Member States the obligation to apply directly in their legal systems rules of law of non-Community origin adopted under conditions not subject to the guarantees of Community law. Such an arrangement would be incompatible with the Treaty. Nor is it advisable to set up, within the framework of such an organization, a judicial body whose jurisdiction might conflict with that of the ECJ (Opinion 1/76 *Laying-up Fund*, above, at pp. 755–62 concerning the Draft Agreement establishing a European laying-up fund for inland waterway vessels in the Rhine and Moselle basins, to which the Community, six Member States, and Switzerland would have been parties. The Court found the Draft Agreement to be incompatible with the EEC Treaty).

See also **Common Commercial Policy***, **Community Treaties, External relations, Legal personality, Mixed agreement, Treaty-making procedure.**

Further reading 1. BOOKS: Groux and Manin, *The European Communities in the International Order* (1985); Hartley, *The Foundations of European Community Law*, 2nd edn. (1988), ch. 6; Timmermans and Völker (eds.), *Division of Powers between the European Communities and their Member States in the Field of External Relations* (1981).

2. ARTICLES AND PAPERS: Close, 'Self Restraint by the EEC in the Exercise of its External Powers' (1981) 1 *YEL* 45; Costonis, 'The Treaty-Making Power of the European Economic Community: The Perspectives of a Decade' (1967–8) 5 *CML Rev.* 421; FIDE, 'The Scope and Nature of the Powers of the European Communities in the Field of External Relations', *Reports for the Tenth FIDE Congress* (1982), vol. iii; Hardy, *for* 'Opinion 1/76 of the Court of Justice: The Rhine Case and the Treaty-Making Powers of the Community' (1977) 14 *CML Rev.* 561; Lachmann, 'International Legal Personality of the EC: Capacity and Competence' (1984/1) *LIEI* 3; Leopold, 'External Relations Power of EEC in Theory and in Practice' (1977) 26 *ICLQ* 54; Maas, 'The External Powers of the EEC with Regard to Commercial Policy: Comment on Opinion 1/75' (1976) 13 *CML Rev.* 379; Malawer, 'Treaty-Making Competence of the European Communities' (1973) 7 *JWTL* 169; Manin, 'The European Communities and the Vienna Convention on the Law of Treaties between States and International Organisations or between International Organisations' (1987) 24 *CML Rev.* 457; Mastellone, 'The External Relations of the EEC in the Field of Environmental Protection' (1981) 30 *ICLQ* 104; Pescatore, 'External Relations in the Case-Law of the Court of Justice of the European Communities' (1979) 16 *CML Rev.* 615; id., 'Treaty-Making by the European Communities', in Jacobs and Roberts (eds.), *The Effect of Treaties in Domestic Law* (1987), p. 171; Schermers, 'The Internal Effect of Community Treaty-Making', in O'Keeffe and Schermers (eds.), *Essays in European Law and Integration* (1982), p. 167; Simmonds, 'External Relations Power of the EEC: A Recent Ruling of the European Court' (1977) 26 *ICLQ* 208; id., 'The Evolution of the External Relations Law of the European Economic Community' (1979) 28 *ICLQ* 644; Swords, 'The External Competence of the European Economic Community in Relation to International Fisheries Agreements' (1979/2) *LIEI* 31; Temple Lang, 'The ERTA Judgment and the Court's Case-Law on Competence and Conflict' (1986) 6 *YEL* 183; Usher, 'The Scope of Community Competence: Its Recognition and Enforcement' (1985) 24 *JCMS* 121.

3. OFFICIAL PUBLICATIONS: European Parliament, Working Documents 1977–8, 8 Mar. 1978, Doc. 567/77, Report by the Legal Affairs Committee on the Position of the European Communities in Public International Law (Rapporteur: L. Jozeau-Marigné); House of Lords Select Committee on the European Communities, Session 1984–5, 16th Report, 'External Competence of the European Communities' (1985).

See also under **Community Treaties, External relations, Mixed agreement.**

▶ **TREATY-MAKING PROCEDURE** Procedure followed by the Community institutions in negotiating and concluding treaties and agreements with third States or international organizations. This procedure is different under the Euratom and EEC Treaties (the ECSC Treaty contains no specific provisions on treaty-making by that Community).

1. **Under the Euratom Treaty**, international agreements are negotiated by the Commission in accordance with the directives of the Council; they are also concluded by the Commission although the approval of the Council, acting by a qualified majority, is necessary. Nevertheless, agreements whose

531

implementation does not require action by the Council and can be effected within the limits of the relevant budget are negotiated and concluded solely by the Commission, while the Council must be kept informed (Art. 101(2) and (3)).

Unlike the EEC Treaty (for which see below), the Euratom Treaty does not lay down a procedure for obtaining the opinion of the ECJ as to the compatibility of proposed Community agreements with the Treaty. It does, however, provide for an analogous procedure to examine the compatibility with the Treaty of agreements which the Member States intend to conclude (Art. 103). Accordingly, Member States are required to communicate to the Commission draft agreements or contracts concerning matters within the purview of the Treaty. If the draft contains clauses which impede the application of the Treaty, the Commission must inform the State concerned accordingly, and the State may not conclude the agreement until it has satisfied the objections of the Commission. It may, however, apply to the ECJ for a 'ruling' on the compatibility of the proposed clauses with the provisions of the Treaty. The application is not subject to any time-limit and must be made in accordance with Art. 105 RP. In examining the compatibility of the draft agreement, the Court must 'take account of all the relevant rules of the Treaty whether they concern questions of substance, of jurisdiction or of procedure' and may thus decide whether the conclusion of the agreement falls within the jurisdiction of the Member States or that of the Community or both (Ruling 1/78 *Protection of Nuclear Materials* [1978] ECR 2151 at p. 2167). The Treaty contains comparable provisions for the scrutinizing by the Commission and the Court of agreements or contracts concluded by persons and undertakings after or before the entry into force of the Treaty (Arts. 104–5; see also Art. 106 RP).

2. **The EEC Treaty** lays down three sets of provisions on treaty-making procedure.

First, *Art. 113* provides that where in implementing the Common Commercial Policy tariff and trade agreements with third countries need to be negotiated, the Commission shall make recommendations to the Council, which then authorizes the Commission to open the necessary negotiations. It is the task of the Commission to conduct these negotiations, acting in consultation with a special committee (consisting of expert representatives from the Member States) appointed by the Council to assist the Commission in this task. The Commission must conduct the negotiations within the framework of such directives as the Council may issue to it. In exercising these powers, the Council acts by a qualified majority. When the negotiations are completed, the agreement is concluded by the Council on behalf of the Community, also acting by a qualified majority (Art. 114) and in accordance with its normal decision-making process.

Secondly, *Art. 228* states in general terms that where the Treaty provides for the conclusion of agreements between the Community and one or more States or an international organization, such agreements are to be negotiated by the Commission and concluded by the Council, after consulting the European Parliament where required by the Treaty. The Council, the Commission, or a Member State may obtain beforehand the opinion of the ECJ as to whether the intended agreement is compatible with the Treaty. Where the opinion of the Court is adverse, the agreement may enter into force only after the Treaty has been amended so as to eliminate the incompatibility.

Thirdly, *Art. 238* makes it clear that association agreements with a third State, a union of States, or an international organization are to be concluded by the Council, acting unanimously after consulting the European Parliament.

It may be mentioned that although under *Art. 237* the accession of new Member States to the Community takes place by means of an agreement to be concluded between the applicant States and the existing Member States (and not the Community as such), the process does involve the Community institutions. The application for admission must be addressed to the Council, which is required to act unanimously after obtaining the opinion of the Commission (*see further under* **Accession Treaties**).

In the first three cases, i.e. under Arts. 113, 228, and 238, the agreement is signed by a member of the Council, usually the President, together with a member of the Commission acting as a Plenipotentiary. After consultation of the European Parliament, where required (see below), the agreement is 'approved' by the Council on behalf of the Community by means of a formal act which may be a regulation or a decision. This act also provides for the deposit of the instrument necessary to bring the agreement into force at the international level (usually an instrument of 'approval' in lieu of ratification). The regulation or decision of the Council is published in the *Official Journal* together with the full text of the agreement. The date of entry into force is also published. These formalities are sufficient to put the agreement into effect, both internationally and internally, without any further act of transformation or implementation being required for the latter purpose. In certain cases, however, further implementing measures (e.g. regulations) have been adopted, depending on the subject-matter of the agreement.

In practice, the treaty-making procedure as envisaged by the original Treaty has been modified in several respects, partly in response to certain institutional developments, and partly as a result of the considerable enlargement of the Community's treaty-making power brought about by the relevant case-law of the ECJ. The most important changes may be summarized as follows.

(*a*) The more detailed provisions of Art. 113 on the initiation and conduct of negotiations of tariff and trade agreements are applied in practice in the case of most other agreements as well. Thus, although this is not expressly required by Arts. 228 and 238, the process normally begins with the Commission recommending the opening of negotiations according to certain directives while the Council takes the necessary decisions constituting the negotiating mandate and defining the terms of the directives within the framework of which the Commission is to negotiate. These directives may be modified in the course of the negotiations by the Council acting upon a recommendation from the Commission, and the Commission also claims a certain degree of flexibility in following them. Likewise, a committee of

533

national experts, as provided for by Art. 113, will usually assist the Commission even where the negotiations are conducted under Arts. 228 or 238 although these Articles do not require the setting up of such a committee.

There is, however, a major difference of view between the Commission and the Council on the majority whereby the Council is required to take these preparatory decisions. In the case of tariff and trade agreements, Art. 113 provides for qualified majority both for the authorization of the negotiations and for the conclusion of the agreement. In the case of association agreements, Art. 238 requires unanimity for the conclusion of the agreement but is silent as regards the commencement of negotiations. From this, the Commission concludes that, in accordance with the general rule laid down in Art. 148(1), a simple majority is sufficient for the latter purpose. On the other hand, the Council holds that the majority for authorizing the initiation of negotiations should be the same as that for adopting the agreement and that therefore unanimity is needed for both purposes. In practice, if the Luxembourg Compromise continues to be observed in this respect (which is doubtful), it remains necessary to seek unanimous approval for all decisions whether concerning the negotiation or the conclusion of agreements (see the Memorandum by the Commission submitted to the House of Lords Select Committee on the European Communities in 1985, in the 16th Report of the Committee, listed below under Official Publications, at pp. 108–10. See also ibid. pp. 20, 123–4, 149–50).

(*b*) The negotiating procedure as provided for in Art. 113—including the setting up of a committee of representatives of Member States—is also followed in the case of treaties made by virtue of implied powers based on the case-law of the ECJ, and in the case of treaties made under Arts. 100 (harmonization) or 235 (general powers). While these treaties are concluded according to the procedure laid down in the relevant Treaty Article for the adoption of the corresponding internal measure (i.e. proposal from the Commission, consultation of the European Parliament, decision by the Council acting by qualified majority in the case of treaties concerned with the Common Agricultural or Transport Policies as required by Arts. 43(2) and 75, respectively, or acting unanimously in the case of treaties based on Arts. 100 or 235), they are negotiated as all other agreements. But here again, the Commission does not share the Council's view that the decision to open negotiations and to define negotiating directives has to be taken in accordance with the voting requirement laid down for the adoption of the internal measure; in the Commission's view, simple majority is sufficient by virtue of Art. 148(1) (see the Memorandum by the Commission, cited above, at pp. 108, 110; see also pp. 114, 143). It may be noted that in the case of 'mixed agreements', i.e. agreements in which the Community participates together with its Member States, the negotiations are conducted in accordance with more complex rules (*see further under* **Mixed agreement**).

(*c*) The role of the European Parliament in the treaty-making process has been considerably enlarged. Under Art. 228, the European Parliament has to be consulted before the conclusion of any agreement 'where [so] required by the Treaty'. However, the Treaty requires consultation only in one case, namely, under Art. 238 in respect of association agreements. Even tariff and trade agreements made under Art. 113 are not subject to consultation. Nevertheless, with the development by the ECJ of the doctrine of implied treaty-making powers, it has been recognized that Parliament needs to be consulted in respect of all those agreements which are based on Treaty Articles requiring consultation on the corresponding internal legislation, such as Arts. 43(2) (agriculture, including fisheries), 75 (transport), 100 (harmonization), and 235 (general powers). According to the practice of the Council, formal consultation takes place before the conclusion (i.e. approval) but after the signature of an agreement, that is to say, at a stage in the process when in the opinion of Parliament it is already too late for it to exert any real influence on the outcome of negotiations. Moreover, Parliament believes that with the transfer of exclusive treaty-making power from the Member States to the Community in respect of tariff and trade agreements, neither the national Parliaments nor the European Parliament can exercise adequate democratic control over the making of such agreements. This is the more serious as these agreements may have substantial budgetary implications for the Community, such as concessions on tariffs and on export subsidies.

In order to remedy the situation, certain interinstitutional arrangements have been set up between the Parliament and the Council, known as the *Luns–Westerterp procedures*. Under the *Luns procedure*, introduced in 1964 in respect of association agreements, debate may take place in the European Parliament even before negotiations begin. During the negotiations, the Commission maintains close contact with the relevant committees of the European Parliament, informing them on the progress of negotiations. After the negotiations have been completed, but before the signing of the agreement, the President of the Council or his representative confidentially and un-officially informs the appropriate committee of the substance of the agreement. The *Westerterp procedure*, instituted in 1973 for trade agreements, is basically similar except that here the final stage consists of the Council informing the European Parliament as a whole (as opposed to its committees) of the contents of the agreement after it has been signed, but before conclusion. This is considered to be equivalent to the consultation of the Parliament on the proposed agreement. These procedures have been extended by the Solemn Declaration on European Union of 19 June 1983 to 'all significant inter-national agreements concluded by the Communities'. At the same time, the European Council also undertook to seek the opinion of the European Parliament before the conclusion of all such 'significant international agree-ments' and accession treaties (Declaration of Stuttgart, *Bull. EC* 6–1983, p. 24, point 2.3.7. See also the Memorandum by the Commission, cited above, pp. 110–11; Memorandum by the Foreign Office, ibid. pp. 2–3; Memorandum by Mme Vayssade MEP, ibid. pp. 91–6; see also ibid. pp. 22, 97–101, 152–3 and the Communication from the Commission of 27 May 1982, listed below under Official Publications).

On several occasions, the European Parliament itself expressed its desire to increase its role in the treaty-making process. Thus, the so-called Blumenfeld Report of 1982 called for a right of ratification of accession treaties (Res. of

18 Feb. 1982, *OJ* 1982 C66/68), while the Draft Treaty on European Union of 1984 provided for a power of co-decision together with the Council (Art. 65(4), *OJ* 1984 C77/33. See also the independent Vedel Report of 1972, Suppl. 4/72—*Bull. EC*, pp. 39–40, 45–6, and the Communication from the Commission of 27 May 1982, listed below under Official Publications). Owing, no doubt, to these various pressures, the Single European Act of 1986 amended Arts. 237 and 238 of the EEC Treaty by requiring the assent of the European Parliament, acting by an absolute majority of its component members, to the conclusion of accession treaties and association agreements, respectively (Arts. 8 and 9 SEA). Under its own Rules of Procedure, as amended in 1986, Parliament may ask the Council to be consulted on the negotiating mandate before the commencement of negotiations on the conclusion, renewal, or amendment of association, trade, co-operation, and other agreements deemed by Parliament to be 'significant' within the terms of the Solemn Declaration on European Union. The Rules also provide that the Commission and the Council shall keep Parliament informed of progress in all treaty negotiations (including accession negotiations) and that the draft of intended association and other 'significant' agreements shall be submitted for its assent before signature (see Rules 32–5 EPRP).

(*d*) In several rulings, the ECJ has given an extensive interpretation to the scope of the procedure laid down in Art. 228(1) to test the compatibility of proposed agreements with the Treaty. In the opinion of the Court, the purpose of this procedure is 'to forestall complications which would result from legal disputes concerning the compatibility with the Treaty of international agreements binding upon the Community. In fact, a possible decision of the Court to the effect that such an agreement is, either by reason of its content or of the procedure adopted for its conclusion, incompatible with the provisions of the Treaty could not fail to provoke, not only in a Community context but also in that of international relations, serious difficulties and might give rise to adverse consequences for all interested parties, including third countries.' In order to avoid such complications, the procedure must be open 'for all questions capable of submission for judicial consideration . . . in so far as such questions give rise to doubt either as to the substantive or formal validity of the agreement with regard to the Treaty' (Opinion 1/75 *Local Cost Standard* [1975] ECR 1355 at pp. 1360–1). Thus, the Court may examine the compatibility of an agreement not only with the substantive provisions of the Treaty but also with those concerning the powers, procedure, or organization of the institutions. Accordingly, questions relating to the scope of the Community's treaty-making power under a given provision (e.g. Art. 113), to the division of powers between the Community and the Member States in the matter of the negotiation and conclusion of international agreements, or to the legitimacy of the practice of 'mixed agreements', may all be submitted to the Court within the framework of the procedure under Art. 228(1) (Opinion 1/78 *Natural Rubber Agreement* [1979] ECR 2871 at pp. 2906–8; see also Opinion 1/75 *Local Cost Standard*, above, at p. 1361; Opinion 1/76 *Laying-up Fund* [1977] ECR 741 at p. 757; and Art. 107(2) RP). By reason of its non-contentious nature, the procedure is not subject to any time-limit; a request for an opinion may be submitted to the Court both at a relatively early stage in the negotiating process, even before the preparation of the final draft (see Opinion 1/78 *Natural Rubber Agreement*, above, at pp. 2908–9), and after the negotiations on the substance of the agreement have been concluded (see Opinion 1/75 *Local Cost Standard*, above, at p. 1361).

See also **Accession Treaties, Community Treaties, External relations, Mixed agreement, Treaty-making power.**

Further reading 1. ARTICLE: Bot, 'Negotiating Community Agreements: Procedure and Practice' (1970) 7 *CML Rev.* 286.

2. OFFICIAL PUBLICATIONS: Communication from the Commission to Parliament and the Council of 27 May 1982, 'The Role of the European Parliament in the Preparation and Conclusion of International Agreements and Accession Treaties' COM (82) 277 final (the Annex contains the texts of the Luns and Westerterp procedures), in Suppl. 3/82—*Bull. EC*, p. 17; see also *Bull. EC* 5–1982, p. 70; House of Lords Select Committee on the European Communities, Session 1984–5, 16th Report, 'External Competence of the European Communities' (1985).

See also under **Treaty-making power.**

U

► **UNJUST ENRICHMENT** General principle of law according to which a person who has been unjustly, i.e. without a valid legal title, enriched at the expense of another person, causing him a corresponding loss, must repay the money or return the object whereby he has been so enriched. As interpreted and applied by the ECJ, three conditions must be fulfilled before an obligation to make restitution on the grounds of an unjust (or, perhaps more properly, unjustified) enrichment may arise. First, there must exist an enrichment, i.e. the party concerned must have received a payment, a service, or any other advantage which has benefited him directly. Secondly, there must be an absence of any justification for this in the dealings between the parties. Thirdly, the other party must have suffered a corresponding loss or impoverishment (see Cases 4 to 13/59 *Mannesmann* v. *HA* [1960] ECR 113 at p. 133 and Case 26/67 *Danvin* v. *Commission* [1968] ECR 315 at p. 322).

While the Court has accepted the principle of unjust enrichment as part of Community law, it has refrained from stating whether it also applies to the relationship between the Community institutions and their officials (ibid. at p. 322. See also the opinion of A.-G. Gand at p. 327). Nevertheless, Art. 85 of the Staff Regulations provides that a sum overpaid by the institutions may be recovered if the recipient was aware, or could not have been unaware, that there was no due reason for the payment, and this provision has been interpreted as a particular application of the principle of unjust enrichment (Case 71/72 *Kuhl* v. *Council* [1973] ECR 705 at p. 718 *per* A.-G. Mayras; see also the Court's decision at pp. 712–13). Also, in ordering the institutions to pay their officials arrears of remuneration on various grounds, in several cases the Court determined the amounts payable in such a way as to avoid any unjustified enrichment of the official (see e.g. Case 18/63 *Wollast* v. *EEC* [1964] ECR 85 at p. 98; Case 110/63 *Willame* v. *Commission* [1965] ECR 649 at pp. 666–7).

Likewise, where charges and taxes are improperly levied by the national authorities, either because they are contrary to Community prohibitions or because they are based on an erroneous interpretation of Community law or imposed in implementation of Community rules subsequently declared to be invalid, the principle of unjust enrichment requires both that they be repaid and that this should not result in an unjust enrichment of traders who have been able to incorporate the undue charges in their prices and thus to pass them on to the purchasers of the products in question (see e.g. Case 68/79 *Just* [1980] ECR 501 at p. 523 *per Curiam*, pp. 529–32 *per* A.-G. Reischl; Case 61/79 *Denkavit Italiana* [1980] ECR 1205 at p. 1226; Case 130/79 *Express* Dairy Foods [1980] ECR 1887 at p. 1900 *per Curiam*, pp. 1906–10 *per* A.-G. Capotorti).

See also **Contractual liability, General principles of law, Recovery of undue payments*.**

Further reading: Smith, 'A European Concept of Condictio Indebiti?' (1982) 19 *CML Rev.* 269. *See also under* **General principles of law.**

▶ UNLIMITED (PLENARY) JURISDICTION Jurisdiction exercised by the ECJ in actions involving subjective rights and economic (pecuniary) considerations as distinct from actions involving judicial review of the institutions' conduct. Thus, the Court exercises unlimited jurisdiction in actions for damages, actions against sanctions, actions under an arbitration clause, in staff cases, and in certain other proceedings expressly specified by the Treaties, e.g. Arts. 66(5)(2), 88, 95(4) ECSC; Art. 12(4) Euratom in conjunction with Art. 144(a) Euratom; also Art. 37 ECSC as interpreted by the ECJ in Cases 2 and 3/60 *Niederrheinische Bergwerks* v. *HA* [1961] ECR 133 at pp. 144 *et seq.* (see also the opinion of A.-G. Lagrange at p. 152). Following the theory of *recours de pleine juridiction* as known in French administrative law, in these proceedings the Court's powers are not limited to reviewing the objective legality of the acts or omissions of the institutions. Rather, the Court is free to deal with all aspects of the case, factual or legal. Thus, it can assess and interpret the facts, it can evaluate the appropriateness or expediency of the act in question in the light of the underlying economic, monetary, etc. considerations, taking into account all relevant circumstances. In annulling the act, the Court is not restricted to the four grounds of action. Moreover, the Court has the power not only to annul but also to vary the challenged act by reducing or even increasing the fine or penalty imposed, and to award any appropriate damages acting, if necessary, of its own motion. In other words, it possesses the full powers of an ordinary civil court that are necessary to enable it to adjudicate as required by the particular form of action before it (see in general Case 3/54 *ASSIDER* v. *HA* [1955] ECR 63 at p. 75 *per* A.-G. Lagrange; Case 1/55 *Kergall* v. *Common Assembly* [1955] ECR 151 at p. 165 *per* A.-G. Roemer; Case 1/56 *Bourgaux* v. *Common Assembly* [1956] ECR 361 at pp. 374–5 *per* A.-G. Roemer; Case 24/79 *Oberthür* v. *Commission* [1980] ECR 1743 at p. 1759; Cases 176 and 177/86 *Houyoux* v. *Commission* [1987] ECR 4333 at pp. 4352–3).

See also **Action against sanctions, Action for damages, Arbitration clause, Jurisdiction, Limited jurisdiction, Staff cases.**

▶ *UT RES MAGIS VALEAT QUAM PEREAT* General principle of interpretation according to which, when a text is open to two interpretations one of which does and the other does not enable it to have full effect (*effet utile*), the former interpretation must be preferred (the principle of effectiveness). While the ECJ has apparently never expressly referred to this phrase, it has consistently used the various methods of interpretation (particularly the teleological method) in such a way as to ensure that the basic provisions of primary and secondary Community law obtain the widest possible scope and the fullest possible effect with a view to achieving the fundamental objectives of the Communities. If there are various possible alternatives, the Court tends to give preference to an interpretation which least undermines the effectiveness or validity of basic Community rules (see e.g. Case 48/69 *ICI* v. *Commission* [1972] ECR 619 at p. 671 *per* A.-G. Mayras; Case 166/73 *Rheinmühlen* [1974] ECR 33 at p. 38, where the Court interpreted Art. 177

EEC in this way; Case 65/76 *Derycke* [1977] ECR 29 at p. 35). Thus, in dealing with the question whether the Community institutions possess certain 'implied powers', the Court has found it appropriate to apply a 'rule of interpretation generally accepted in both international and national law, according to which the rules laid down by an international treaty or a law presuppose [imply] the rules without which that treaty or law would have no meaning or could not be reasonably and usefully [effectively] applied' (Case 8/55 *Fédération Charbonnière de Belgique* v. *HA* [1956] ECR 292 at p. 299; Case 20/59 *Italy* v. *HA* [1960] ECR 325 at p. 336. The bracketed words appear in the latter case).

The principle of effectiveness is of paramount importance especially in the interpretation and application of the provisions laying down the foundations of the EEC, i.e. the free movement of goods, persons, services, and capital, and of the corresponding principle of equality of treatment or non-discrimination. The Court has consistently held that these provisions may not be interpreted restrictively and that, conversely, the various exceptions to and derogations from these basic freedoms permitted by the Treaty must be interpreted strictly in order to avoid the effectiveness of Community law being defeated by unilateral measures of the Member States (see e.g. Cases 2 and 3/62 *Commission* v. *Luxembourg and Belgium* [1962] ECR 425 at pp. 432, 434; Case 29/72 *Marimex* [1972] ECR 1309 at p. 1318; Case 152/73 *Sotgiu* [1974] ECR 153 at pp. 162–4; Case 2/74 *Reyners* [1974] ECR 631 at pp. 654–5; Case 41/74 *Van Duyn* [1974] ECR 1337 at p. 1350; Case 29/75 *Kaufhof* v. *Commission* [1976] ECR 431 at p. 443; Case 53/81 *Levin* [1982] ECR 1035 at p. 1049).

See also **Implied powers, Interpretation of Community law.**

Further reading: See under **Interpretation of Community law.**

VEDEL REPORT Report drawn up by an *ad hoc* Working Party of fourteen independent experts under the chairmanship of Professor Georges Vedel, Honorary Dean of the Faculty of Law and Economic Sciences of the University of Paris. The Working Party was set up by the Commission in July 1971 'to examine the whole corpus of problems connected with the enlargement of the powers of the European Parliament'. The Report was completed on 25 March 1972 (text in Suppl. 4/72—*Bull. EC*).

According to the Report, the need to increase the legislative and budgetary powers of the European Parliament arose from the gradual transfer to the Community institutions of powers which, on the national plane, used to belong wholly or partly to the Parliaments. This was particularly so in the budgetary field owing to the creation in 1970 of the Communities' own resources, and in connection with the then projected introduction of Economic and Monetary Union. Since the growth of the Communities' powers should not result in a reduction of parliamentary powers, the losses of power by the national Parliaments had to be compensated for at the Community level.

The Report recommended that the legislative powers of the European Parliament should be increased in two stages. In the first stage Parliament would be given a real power of co-decision, based on its ability to accept or reject Council decisions, in four matters (referred to as list A), i.e. revision of the Treaties; measures taken under Art. 235 EEC and the corresponding provisions of the other Treaties; admission of new Member States; and ratification of international agreements concluded by the Communities. In addition, also during the first stage, Parliament would be given a greater power of consultation consisting in the right to ask the Council to reconsider a subject, and hence a suspensive veto, in a number of fields (referred to as list B), including the Common Agricultural Policy, special treatment of foreign nationals, mutual recognition of qualifications, the Common Transport Policy, competition, harmonization of taxation and of laws, the Common Commercial Policy, etc. In the second stage, Parliament would be given a power of co-decision in all matters in list B while continuing to exercise its power of co-decision in all matters in list A. This power would mean that a Council decision could not come into force without being approved by Parliament. The matters in list A were selected on the basis that they materially involved either the Communities' constitutive powers or their relations with other subjects of international law. On the other hand, list B concerned either measures for harmonization of legislation which had important effects on national laws or common policies which might also involve harmonization measures. The first stage would begin as soon as the necessary amendments to the original Treaties came into force. The second stage should be introduced in a single step at a date to be fixed in the treaty of amendment and preferably not later than 1978.

The Report further proposed that, in addition to the legislative process, Parliament should be afforded greater participation in the formulation of economic policy plans and programmes of a non-binding nature. In the budgetary field, Parliament's powers should be increased primarily by attributing to it a power of co-decision, as outlined above, with regard to acts

541

with financial implications which are at the basis of Community expenditure. Finally, Parliament should exercise extended powers of control over the other institutions, for example, by having the right to approve the Member States' choice of the President of the Commission. While recognizing that direct elections would considerably contribute to the Communities' democratization and legitimation, the Report concluded that the introduction of the proposed new powers for the Parliament should not be made dependent upon the introduction of election by direct universal suffrage. In the final parts, the Report dealt with the relations between the European Parliament and the national Parliaments and considered certain adjustments to the institutional structure of the Communities which the extension of the Parliament's powers would necessarily entail.

The recommendations of the Vedel Report were not immediately implemented by means of Treaty amendment. Nevertheless, the Report had a profound indirect impact on the institutional development of the Communities. Many of its proposals have been acted upon in practice by the institutions or have been taken up by the various reports and proposals put forward for reforming the institutions, of which it was the first. Some of its ideas were incorporated—albeit in a modified form—in the Single European Act of 1986.

See also **Committee on Institutional Affairs, European Parliament, European Union, Institutional balance, Single European Act, Solemn Declaration on European Union, Three Wise Men's Report, Tindemans Report.**

Further reading: Editorial, 'Tindemans, Vedel and the European Parliament' (1975–6) 1 *EL Rev.* 183.

▶ **VENIRE CONTRA FACTUM PROPRIUM** General principle of law according to which a person, a Community institution, or a Member State may not rely upon an irregular situation brought about by his/its own conduct—act or omission—in order to gain an advantage or a benefit, or as a reason for avoiding an obligation, a penalty, a disciplinary measure, or a legal action. In other words, one may not plead one's own wrong. This principle is akin to, but not identical with, the concept of estoppel in English law, the essence of which is that 'a party is not allowed to deny a state of facts which he has alleged to be true, either expressly in words or impliedly by conduct on some previous occasion' (quoted by A.-G. Roemer in Cases 41 and 50/59 *Hamborner Bergbau* v. *HA* [1960] ECR 493 at p. 520; for a somewhat more complex definition of estoppel, see the opinion of A.-G. Warner in Cases 63 and 64/79 *Boizard* v. *Commission* [1980] ECR 2975 at p. 3002). Or, as A.-G. Mancini has put it, 'estoppel is a characteristic feature of Common Law systems and its purpose is to prohibit a person from performing certain acts where those acts are at variance with the result partly brought about by that person's conduct. That principle, or one similar to it, is employed in international law . . .' However, he added that 'nevertheless the rule of estoppel, the limits to which are already very vague in relations between States, may not be transposed into Community law . . .' (Case 230/81 *Luxembourg* v. *Parliament* [1983] ECR 255 at p. 295).

While in a number of cases the ECJ has applied the broad principle described above, it has never precisely defined it, nor has it been consistent in its use of terminology. Thus, the Court has sometimes referred to the principle by using the phrase *venire contra factum proprium* (see e.g. Case 14/61 *Hoogovens* v. *HA* [1962] ECR 253 at p. 273; Cases 17 and 20/61 *Klöckner* v. *HA* [1962] ECR 325 at p. 342), sometimes by using the term 'estoppel' but without distinguishing it from the English law concept of estoppel (see e.g. Case 18/63 *Wollast* v. *EEC* [1964] ECR 85 at p. 99; Case 108/63 *Merlini* v. *HA* [1965] ECR 1 at p. 10), and sometimes using no name at all (see e.g. Case 12/68 *X* v. *Audit Board* [1969] ECR 109 at p. 115; Case 39/72 *Commission* v. *Italy* [1973] ECR 101 at p. 112); while sometimes the Court has simply relied on the more general concept of good faith from which the principle is ultimately derived (see e.g. Case 36/72 *Meganck* v. *Commission* [1973] ECR 527 at p. 534; Case 156/80 *Morbelli* v. *Commission* [1981] ECR 1357 at p. 1372).

The principle of *venire contra factum proprium* has been invoked and applied against private individuals (mainly, but not exclusively, Community officials), against Community institutions, and against Member States. As regards private individuals, the ECJ has held that:

- an official who has refused to co-operate in an invalidity procedure and to appear before the Invalidity Committee may not later complain about the irregularity of that procedure (which he himself brought about) and about the failure of that Committee to examine him (Case 3/66 *Alfieri* v. *Parliament* [1966] ECR 437 at p. 451). Likewise, an official who has several times and without a valid excuse failed to appear before a disciplinary body may not subsequently complain about the failure of that body to hear him prior to the adoption of a disciplinary measure (Case 12/68 *X* v. *Audit Board*, above, at p. 115);
- an official may not rely on the absence from his file of the periodic report, which constitutes an essential factor for all decisions concerning his career, where he himself has kept that report out of the file (Case 151/80 *De Hoe* v. *Commission* [1981] ECR 3161 at pp. 3175–6);
- an official who has 'placed himself in an irregular situation by his own conduct . . . cannot rely on his good faith to be released from the obligation to return the sums overpaid' him by the institution, as required by Art. 85 of the Staff Regulations (Case 36/72 *Meganck* v. *Commission*, above, at p. 534; Case 71/72 *Kuhl* v. *Council* [1973] ECR 705 at pp. 712–13);
- an undertaking may not make use of its own refusal to take cognizance of a decision of the Commission properly notified to it in order to render this communication ineffective (Case 6/72 *Continental Can* v. *Commission* [1973] ECR 215 at p. 241).

543

As regards Community institutions, the ECJ has stated that:

- where by failing to adopt the necessary measures the institutions bring about an 'equivocal situation' in the law, they may not accuse a Member State of non-fulfilment of its obligations (Case 26/69 *Commission* v. *France* [1970] ECR 565 at p. 578);

- if the Commission adopts a decision with regard to an entity, thereby recognizing it by implication as an 'undertaking' or as an 'association' within the meaning of the ECSC Treaty, it may not later challenge the right of that entity to bring legal proceedings against the decision on the grounds that it is not an 'undertaking' or an 'association' (Case 67/63 *SOREMA* v. *HA* [1964] ECR 151 at pp. 160–1). Likewise, the Commission may not rely on its own failure to reply to a complaint of an official within the prescribed period in order to contest the admissibility of the official's subsequent action before the Court. This would be 'contrary to the good faith which must prevail in relations between the Commission and its employees, including their relations in legal proceedings' (Case 156/80 *Morbelli* v. *Commission*, above, at p. 1372; see also Cases 59 and 129/80 *Turner* v. *Commission* [1981] ECR 1883 at p. 1912);

- nevertheless, a Community institution is 'not always bound by its previous actions in its public activities by virtue of a rule which, in relations between the same parties, forbids them to *venire contra factum proprium*' (Cases 17 and 20/61 *Klöckner* v. *HA*, above, at p. 342).

As regards Member States, the ECJ has held that:

- a Member State 'cannot in any case be allowed to rely upon a *fait accompli* of which it is itself the author so as to escape judicial proceedings' (Case 39/72 *Commission* v. *Italy*, above, at p. 112);

- 'a Member State cannot plead the provisions and practices of its internal order in order to justify failure to observe obligations and time-limits arising from Community regulations' (Case 30/72 *Commission* v. *Italy* [1973] ECR 161 at p. 172);

- 'a Member State which has not adopted substantive measures to implement [a Community] decision cannot claim that traders have failed to fulfil the obligations which it involves' (Case 30/75 *Unil-It* [1975] ECR 1419 at p. 1428);

- 'a Member State which has not adopted the implementing measures required by [a] directive in the prescribed periods may not rely, as against individuals, on its own failure to perform the obligations which the directive entails' (Case 148/78 *Ratti* [1979] ECR 1629 at p. 1642). The ECJ has used this principle to establish a legal basis for the direct effect of directives (ibid.; see also e.g. Case 8/81 *Becker* [1982] ECR 53 at pp. 70–1; Case 152/84 *Marshall* [1986] ECR 723 at pp. 748–9).

See also **Directive, General principles of law, Good faith.**

Further reading: Green, 'Directives, Equity and the Protection of Individual Rights' (1984) 9 *EL Rev.* 295 at p. 302; Lord Mackenzie Stuart, 'Legitimate Expectations and

Estoppel in Community Law and English Administrative Law' (1983/1) *LIEI* 53. *See also under* **General principles of law.**

Vested rights

▶ **VESTED RIGHTS** 1. **In the context of the law relating to Community officials:** rights conferred upon an official by a lawful and valid individual administrative measure, such as, for example, an appointment, a promotion or the grant of a particular benefit. The importance of such rights is that they enjoy special protection by virtue of a general principle of law derived from the administrative laws of the Member States. Thus, the ECJ has stated that 'an administrative measure conferring individual rights on the person concerned cannot in principle be withdrawn, if it is a lawful measure; in that case, since the individual right is vested, the need to safeguard confidence in the stability of the situation thus created prevails over the interests of an administration desirous of reversing its decision. This is true in particular of the appointment of an official. If, on the other hand, the administrative measure is illegal, revocation is possible ... The absence of an objective legal basis for the measure affects the individual right of the person concerned and justifies the revocation of the said measure ... at least within a reasonable period of time' (Cases 7/56 etc. *Algera* v. *Common Assembly* [1957] ECR 39 at pp. 55–6; see also the opinion of A.-G. Lagrange, ibid. at pp. 79–81).

As regards the temporal effects of the termination of a vested right (where permitted), the ECJ has held that 'although the retroactive withdrawal of a wrongful or erroneous decision is generally subject to very strict conditions, on the other hand the revocation of such a decision as regards the future is always possible. In any event, under the law relating to the public service the irregular grant or continued payment of elements of remuneration cannot create vested rights such as to prevent revocation' (Case 54/77 *Herpels* v. *Commission* [1978] ECR 585 at p. 599; see also the opinion of A.-G. Mayras at p. 607. See also Case 15/60 *Simon* v. *Court of Justice* [1961] ECR 115 at p. 123; Case 56/75 *Elz* v. *Commission* [1976] ECR 1097 at p. 1109 *per Curiam*, pp. 1116–17 *per* A.-G. Reischl, where the Court allowed the immediate withdrawal of an irregular benefit previously granted over a period of eight years).

Since vested rights can only be conferred by individual decisions, officials do not possess a vested right to the maintaining in force of regulations, in particular the Staff Regulations. As A.-G. Mayras has pointed out: 'The Community authority is ... entitled at any time to amend the provisions of the [Staff] Regulations in any way which it considers to be in accordance with the interest of the service, on condition that such amendments ... do not have retroactive effect to the detriment of servants ... As to the officials, they cannot take advantage of vested rights except where the event giving rise to such rights took place under the scheme of the Regulations before the amendment adopted by the competent authority' (Case 28/74 *Gillet* v. *Commission* [1975] ECR 463 at p. 477; the Court adopted the same view at p. 473. See also Case 127/80 *Grogan* v. *Commission* [1982] ECR 869 at pp. 880–1 *per Curiam*, p. 898 *per* A.-G. Capotorti).

2. **Under the ECSC Treaty** in general: following the staff cases discussed above, the ECJ has stated in broad terms that 'the retroactive withdrawal of a legal [i.e. lawful] measure which has conferred individual rights or similar benefits is contrary to the general principles of law' (Cases 42 and 49/59 *SNUPAT* v. *HA* [1961] ECR 53 at p. 78), adding that 'retroactive withdrawal is generally accepted in cases in which the administrative measure in question has been adopted on the basis of false or incomplete information provided by those concerned' (ibid. at p. 87). Subsequently, in a series of cases the Court has confirmed that 'the withdrawal of an unlawful measure is permissible, provided that the withdrawal occurs within a reasonable time and provided that the Commission has had sufficient regard to how far the applicant might have been led to rely on the lawfulness of the measure' (Case 14/81 *Alpha Steel* v. *Commission* [1982] ECR 749 at p. 764; Case 15/85 *Consorzio Cooperative d'Abruzzo* v. *Commission* [1987] ECR 1005 at p. 1036, applying the same rule under the EEC Treaty). In the second of these cases, the retroactive withdrawal of a decision, granting a benefit, more than two years after its adoption was held not to be 'reasonable' and to be contrary to the principles of legal certainty and of the protection of legitimate expectations, and conseqently annulled (ibid. at p. 1037. See also Case 14/61 *Hoogovens* v. *HA* [1962] ECR 253 at pp. 272–3 *per Curiam*, pp. 280–3 *per* A.-G. Lagrange; Case 111/63 *Lemmerz-Werke* v. *HA* [1965] ECR 677 at p. 690). In contrast to these cases, which seem to confirm the protection of vested rights (at least within certain limits), when dealing with the right to property the Court stated quite categorically that 'Community law, as it arises under the ECSC Treaty, does not contain any general principle, express or otherwise, guaranteeing the maintenance of vested rights' (Cases 36 to 38 and 40/59 *Geitling* v. *HA* [1960] ECR 423 at p. 439).

3. **Under the EEC Treaty** in general: while the ECJ has frequently referred to the 'general principle of respect for acquired [i.e. vested] rights', usually in conjunction with the principle of respect for legitimate expectations (see e.g. Case 100/74 *CAM* v. *Commission* [1975] ECR 1393 at p. 1405; Case 84/78 *Tomadini* [1979] ECR 1801 at p. 1815), it has been less forthcoming in defining the precise nature of such rights and the precise scope of their protection.

As regards their nature, it appears that the difference between legitimate expectations and vested rights is that while the former are based on strictly subjective considerations (what can a prudent and experienced person legitimately expect in the circumstances?) and can exist even in the absence of a right, the latter are 'the direct result of objective factors inherent in the provisions which in law govern the sector concerned' (Case 74/74 *CNTA* v. *Commission* [1975] ECR 533 at p. 556 *per* A.-G. Trabucchi; see also Case 5/75 *Deuka* [1975] ECR 759 at p. 777 *per* A.-G. Trabucchi). Thus, vested rights can only arise if, and from the time when, all the conditions laid down by law for their creation have actually been fulfilled and the transaction on which they depend performed (Case 74/74 *CNTA* v. *Commission*, above, at p. 548; Cases 95 to 98/74 etc. *Coopératives Agricoles de Céréales* v. *Commission and Council* [1975] ECR 1615 at p. 1636. The Court held that the grant of export certificates with advance fixing of the refund did not create vested rights—as opposed to legitimate expectations—to benefit from a specific monetary compensatory amount; such a right could only arise if and when the export transaction actually took place). Moreover, vested rights can only be conferred by individual measures. Interpreting the term 'individual rights acquired by operators' appearing in an agricultural regulation, the Court stated that that term referred 'only to rights definitively conferred on those operators by individual decisions adopted by the competent . . . authority' (Case 84/81 *Staple Dairy Products* [1982] ECR 1763 at p. 1778; see also the opinion of A.-G. Slynn, ibid. at pp. 1785–6).

As regards the scope of protection, the Court has observed in general terms that 'in the absence of valid provision to the contrary, repeal of a Regulation does not mean abolition of the individual rights which it has created' (Case 34/73 *Variola* [1973] ECR 981 at p. 991). In the case of the annulment of a regulation, the Court has been given power to restrict the *erga omnes* and retroactive effects of its judgment in order to protect acquired rights (Arts. 174(2) EEC, 147(2) Euratom; see Case 92/78 *Simmenthal* v. *Commission* [1979] ECR 777 at p. 811; Case 91/75 *Miritz* [1976] ECR 217 at p. 238 *per* A.-G. Trabucchi). Nor can amendment of a regulation with retroactive effect prejudice entitlement to a (social security) benefit acquired before the publication of the amending regulation (Case 100/63 *Kalsbeek* [1964] ECR 565 at p. 575). Likewise, the Court has held that 'accrued rights are to be recognised and protected under the Community rules on social security for migrant workers if they were acquired by a migrant within the meaning of the [relevant] provisions' (Case 10/78 *Belbouab* [1978] ECR 1915 at p. 1924). Where, however, a sector, such as the common organization of agricultural markets, is governed by variable economic factors which affect its development, an undertaking cannot claim a vested right to the maintenance of an advantage which it obtained and enjoyed at a particular time (Case 230/78 *Eridania* [1979] ECR 2749 at p. 2768, dealing with the alteration of the basic quotas for sugar). In the field of procedural law, since in general provisions amending an administrative procedure and appointing the competent authorities are applicable to pending proceedings, the persons concerned may not claim to have a 'vested right' to have their case dealt with by the authorities who had competence under the previous provisions (Case 312/84 *Continentale Produkten Gesellschaft* v. *Commission* [1987] ECR 841 at p. 865).

See also **General principles of law, Good faith, Legal certainty, Legitimate expectation, Retroactive effect.**

Further reading: See under **General principles of law.**

W

▶ **WRITTEN PROCEDURE** The first, and by far the most important, part of the ordinary procedure before the ECJ. The written procedure, which is not open to the public (Cases 9 and 12/60—Third party proceedings *Belgium* v. *Vloeberghs and HA* [1962] ECR 171 at p. 182), consists of the communication by the Registrar to the parties and to the institutions whose measures are in dispute, of the various written pleadings as well as of all papers and documents submitted in support or of certified copies of them. The pleadings include, in direct actions, the application, defence, reply, and rejoinder, and in references for a preliminary ruling, the statements of case or written observations (Arts. 21 ECSC Statute, 18 and 20 EEC Statute, 18 and 21 Euratom Statute, 37–44 RP. In reference proceedings, only Arts. 43 *et seq.* RP apply, see Art. 103(1) RP. For the procedure in reference proceedings, *see under* **Reference proceedings**, point 2(*c*)).

The procedure commences with the submission of a written application (*see under* **Application originating proceedings**), which must be served by the Registrar on the defendant (Art. 39 RP). Service must be effected at the defendant's address for service either by registered post or by personal delivery (Art. 79 RP). Within a period of one month after service, which may be extended by the President of the Court, the defendant is required to lodge a defence, stating the name and permanent residence of the defendant; the points of fact and law relied on; the form of order sought (i.e. the conclusions); and the nature of any evidence founded upon by him. In other respects, the rules laid down for pleadings in general (Art. 37 RP) and for the application (Art. 38(2)–(5) RP) apply also to the defence in a corresponding manner (Art. 40 RP). If the defendant fails to lodge a defence in the proper form within the time prescribed, the Court may give judgment by default (Arts. 35 ECSC Statute, 38 EEC Statute, 39 Euratom Statute, 94 RP. *See further under* **Judgment by default**).

The application originating the proceedings and the defence may be supplemented within the time-limits fixed by the President by a reply from the applicant and by a rejoinder from the defendant (Art. 41 RP). In the reply or the rejoinder a party may indicate further evidence, giving reasons for the delay in indicating it. However, no fresh issue may be raised in the course of proceedings unless it is based on matters of law or of fact which come to light in the course of the written procedure (Art. 42(2) RP). If in the course of the written procedure one of the parties raises a fresh issue which is so based, the President may allow the other party time to answer on that issue. The decision on the admissibility of the issue is to be reserved for the final judgment (ibid.).

The foregoing provisions, and in particular the rule laid down in Art. 42(2) RP, express an essential procedural principle and underline the vital importance of adequately stating the issues of fact and of law, particularly the grounds and conclusions, in the originating application and in the defence. In practice, these provisions mean that in his reply and rejoinder, respectively, as in the whole course of the subsequent oral procedure, the applicant and the defendant may not as a rule go beyond the scope of the dispute as